Glencoe

WORLD LITERATURE

Glencoe

WORLD LITERATURE

An Anthology of Great
Short Stories, Poetry, and Drama

DONNA ROSENBERG

 **Glencoe**

New York, New York   Columbus, Ohio   Chicago, Illinois   Peoria, Illinois   Woodland Hills, California

This book is dedicated to my husband, Dick, who encouraged me to share my love of literature with others, and to the memory of my parents, Marion and Harold Green, who taught me to love literature.

Acknowledgments

Acknowledgments begin on page 825, which is to be considered an extension of this copyright page.

Cover art: *Femme assise dans un fateuil*, 1920. Pablo Picasso. Oil on canvas, 130 × 89 cm. Private Collection. © 2003 Estate of Pablo Picasso/Artists Rights Society (ARS), New York/Christie's Images Ltd.

Send all inquiries to:
Glencoe/McGraw-Hill
8787 Orion Place
Columbus, OH 43240-4027

ISBN (hardcover) 0-07-860353-6
ISBN (softcover) 0-07-860352-8
ISBN (teacher manual) 0-07-860354-4

Printed in the United States of America.

5 6 7 8 9   MAL   13 12 11 10

CONTENTS

CONTINENTAL EUROPE 105

AFRICA 281

ASIA AND THE SOUTH PACIFIC 387

SOUTH AND CENTRAL AMERICA 513

NORTH AMERICA 585

GREAT BRITAIN AND IRELAND 657

PREFACE

EADING **WORLD LITERATURE** can remove our cultural blinders and thus change our lives. It shows us that all human beings belong to one family—no matter when their time, where their place, and which their culture. We learn this because we see ourselves in the characters that these writers have brought to life upon the printed page. We see ourselves in their joys and in their sorrows; we see ourselves in their challenges and in their conflicts; and we see ourselves in their need for self-respect and in their need for the respect of others. We see ourselves in their attempt to come to terms with the death of a loved one, and we see ourselves in their desire to reconcile their religious faith with the devastation of war and with all that is beyond understanding in human experience. Finally, we see ourselves in their discovery that the wonder and beauty of nature can restore them.

Moreover, the lives of these writers have much to teach us. Read the biographical sketch that precedes each selection and note how difficult the lives of most of these writers have been. Some writers have been too frail to have had an ordinary life. Some have had to cope with the death or divorce of their parents, with dislocations, and with poverty. Others have lived in turbulent times during which writers have been ostracized, imprisoned, and even murdered. Consequently, the writers in *World Literature* can become our models in that they can teach us to face adversity with courage and creativity. Furthermore, their lives and their writing reveal how artistic self-expression can soothe the wounded human soul, and they can inspire us to express our own thoughts and feelings through creative writing.

NEW EDITION

World Literature—in this revised and significantly expanded new edition—continues to be a treasure trove of great short stories, plays, and poems from around the world. I have retained my favorite selections from the first edition while adding many other exciting and provocative works. In my opinion, *Much Ado About Nothing* reigns supreme among the new additions because it contains three of William Shakespeare's most famous characters, provocative issues that we can relate to our own lives, and the celebration of language. Other personal favorites among the new additions include Psalm 8 of David, Emilia Pardo Bazán's "Torn Lace," Shen Congwen's "Life," Rabindranath Tagore's *The Post Office*, Julio Cortázar's "End of the Game," Ernest Hemingway's "Soldier's Home," the anonymous Anglo-Saxon poem

"A Woman's Message," Geoffrey Chaucer's "The Pardoner's Tale," and Matthew Arnold's "Dover Beach."

Like the first edition, *World Literature* is organized geographically into seven sections: The Mediterranean, Continental Europe, Africa, Asia and the South Pacific, South and Central America, North America, and Great Britain and Ireland. While new selections have been added throughout the text, The Mediterranean, Asia and the South Pacific, and Great Britain and Ireland have been significantly revised. Like the first edition, each section includes short stories, poems, and a play. Moreover, with the exception of "The Pardoner's Tale" (which is a part of Chaucer's *Canterbury Tales*), each selection is a complete work.

PEDAGOGY

Every selection in the new edition of *World Literature* invites you to think about what you have read. The classical scholar Gilbert Highet states that books are not "lumps of lifeless paper, but *minds* alive . . . speaking to us, mind to mind, heart to heart." Therefore, I have designed *World Literature* to encourage stimulating class discussions. The group of activities that follows each selection will guide your thinking. The questions listed under Understanding the Selection will help you get the most out of what you have read, whereas those listed under Analyzing Literary Technique will help you appreciate the skill with which the selection was written.

Both essay and creative writing suggestions are listed under Writing About Literature. Your expository essays will often relate to questions that you will have discussed in connection with Understanding the Selection and Analyzing Literary Technique. In contrast, your creative writing will usually involve telling the story from another character's point of view or responding in a personal way to the selection. To encourage you to relate each selection to some aspect of your own life, your instructor may ask you to keep a Personal Literary Journal in which you respond to questions that relate your personal experiences or experiences that you imagine.

ACKNOWLEDGMENTS

You are holding this edition of *World Literature* in your hands because of the invaluable help of my editors. First is my husband, Dick, who always takes the time and summons the energy to be my initial sounding board, reader, and editor. Second is Lisa Stracks, my Glencoe/McGraw-Hill editor. Lisa is the answer to every author's dream—always available, always understanding, and always encouraging. Moreover, she prepared the materials for four of the poets in this new edition—Li Qingzhao, Nguyen Binh Khiem, Sor Juana Inés de la Cruz, and Anne Hébert—as well as the last six section openers. In addition, assistant editor Kathleen Anderson wrote the materials for the poets Rumi and Hafiz. Marisa L'Heureux's excellent editorial skills and Donald Gecewicz's knowledge of world poetry were immensely valuable at the beginning of this revision.

Finally, I am grateful to the reviewers who offered helpful feedback on the first edition as well as on drafts of the table of contents for the new edition. In particular, I thank Janet M. Anderson, Roger Blackwell Bailey, Michael Bielmeier,

Timothy C. Carlisle, Robert W. Chambers Jr., Gary Grieve-Carlson, Robert C. Haight, Robin R. Hass, Martha E. Kendall, Donald N. Mager, Irene Matthews, Inez R. Morris, David Myslewski, Loren Quiring, Joe Rice, Minas Savvas, Thomas Simone, Karen Smith, Henry-York Steiner, Nathaniel Teich, Bettye S. Walsh, and Thomas F. Woods. While no anthology can encompass all of their suggestions, their comments have made this a better book.

Donna Rosenberg

The Mediterranean

The selections from the Mediterranean range from the oldest recorded works of great literature to works of the present day. What is significant is that, whatever their time or place of origin, these literary works reflect timeless human emotions.

The poems "Hymn to the Aton," Psalm 8, and "Two Eclipses" deal with the nature of divinity. For the Akhenaton, writing in ancient Egypt in the fourteenth century B.C., the one god was Aton, the sun, who was the good and beautiful creator of all life. In contrast, the God of both David, writing in ancient Israel in the late tenth and early ninth centuries B.C., and Shmuel HaNagid, writing in medieval Spain in the eleventh century, is still worshiped by Jews and Christians. It is interesting to compare and contrast how these poems express the power and glory of the divinity from different points of view.

Eight Mediterranean writers deal with various aspects of human love. Sappho, writing in ancient Greece in the late seventh and early sixth centuries B.C., expresses someone's love for a soldier's wife far away in the city of Sardis, across the Aegean Sea. Similarly, Nazim Hikmet, writing in Turkey in the twentieth century, writes to his wife from prison to express his love for her. Both Sappho and Hikmet write their love letters in the form of lyric poems.

In contrast, Dante, writing in Italy in the late thirteenth and early fourteenth centuries, uses a lyric poem to express a young man's resentment and anger toward the young woman who has rejected his offer of love. From another point of view, Emilia Pardo Bazán, writing in Spain in the late nineteenth and early twentieth centuries, reveals in the story "Torn Lace" why a bride rejects her groom at the altar.

Sophocles, writing in ancient Athens in the fifth century B.C., expresses in *Antigone* the love of a sister for her deceased brother and the tragic consequences of that love. Similarly, Catullus, writing in ancient Rome in the first century B.C., expresses his love for his deceased brother in a lyric poem that functions as a letter to a friend. In contrast, Luigi Pirandello, writing in Italy in the early twentieth century, reveals in the story "War" how parents may deny their love and take refuge in patriotism as a means of coping with the unbearable loss of their son. Finally, Federico García Lorca, writing in Spain in the twentieth century, expresses his love for a dear friend who was killed in a bullfight. His elegy confers immortality on friend and poet alike.

Strikingly different from all of the above is the "coming of age" story by Naguib Mahfouz. Mahfouz, writing in Egypt in the twentieth century, relates the adventures of a young boy who finds street life in Cairo irresistibly appealing.

The Hymn to the Aton

AKHENATON

*B*etween c. 1379 and c. 1362 B.C., Pharaoh Amenhotep IV attempted a religious revolution in Egypt. Believing the sun to be the source of all life, he proclaimed that it was the one and only god, and he made its worship the national religion. He gave the god of the sun a new name, Aton. He also changed his own name to Akhenaton ("He Who May Serve the Aton"); built a new capital, Akhenaton (modern Tell el-Amarna); and changed traditional practices in literature and art to reflect the beauty of nature and the emotion in human relationships.

As pharaoh, Akhenaton continued the traditional Egyptian practice of interceding between the people and their gods. He was considered the son of the Aton and the only human privileged to know the god. He interpreted the Aton to his subjects, and they worshiped their pharaoh.

Although Akhenaton and his family became monotheists, few other Egyptians adopted his religion. After Akhenaton's death, his son-in-law—the famous King Tutankhamon (c. 1371–1352 B.C.), who ruled from the age of ten to his death at age nineteen—permitted the priests to regain power. Akhenaton's name was permanently removed from the royal records, and traditional religious beliefs and practices were officially reinstated.

Either Akhenaton or a courtier wrote "The Hymn to the Aton" to praise the Aton as ruler of heaven and earth. The hymn also honors Akhenaton, ruler of Upper and Lower Egypt, and Nefertiti, his beloved wife. Two-thirds of the hymn remains intact, engraved in hieroglyphs on the wall of a tomb at Tell el-Amarna. The remainder has been reconstructed from a copy made in 1883 and from shorter versions found on the opposite wall and in other tombs.

Thou appearest beautifully on the horizon of heaven,
Thou living Aton, the beginning of life!
When thou art risen on the eastern horizon,
Thou hast filled every land with thy beauty.
Thou art gracious, great, glistening, and high over every land;   5
Thy rays encompass the lands to the limit of all that thou has made:
As thou art Re,[1] thou reachest to the end of them;
(Thou) subduest them (for) thy beloved son.[2]
Though thou art far away, thy rays are on earth;
Though thou art in *their* faces, *no one knows thy* going.   10

When thou settest in the western horizon,
The land is in darkness, in the manner of death.
They sleep in a room, with heads wrapped up,
Nor sees one eye the other.
All their goods which are under their heads might be stolen,   15
(But) they would not perceive (it).
Every lion is come forth from his den;
All creeping things, they sting.
Darkness *is a shroud,* and the earth is in stillness,
For he who made them rests in his horizon.   20

At daybreak, when thou arisest on the horizon,
When thou shinest as the Aton by day,
Thou drivest away the darkness and givest thy rays.
The Two Lands[3] are in festivity *every day,*
Awake and standing upon (their) feet,   25
For thou hast raised them up.
Washing their bodies, taking (their) clothing,
Their arms are (raised) in praise at thy appearance.
All the world, they do their work.

All beasts are content with their pasturage;   30
Trees and plants are flourishing.
The birds which fly from their nests,
Their wings are (stretched out) in praise to thy *ka.*[4]
All beasts spring upon (their) feet.
Whatever flies and alights,   35
They live when thou hast risen (for) them.

---

[1] *Re:* Originally the sun god and the Egyptians' primary god. Under Akhenaton, Re was considered to be a part of the god Aton and was represented by sunlight.

[2] *thy beloved son:* Akhenaton.

[3] *The Two Lands:* Upper and Lower Egypt, the two kingdoms that were united c. 3100 B.C.

[4] ka: The soul or personality of an individual.

The ships are sailing north and south as well,
For every way is open at thy appearance.
The fish in the river dart before thy face;
Thy rays are in the midst of the great green sea.   40

Creator of seed in women,
Thou who makest fluid into man,
Who maintainest the son in the womb of his mother,
Who soothest him with that which stills his weeping,
Thou nurse (even) in the womb,   45
Who givest breath to sustain all that he has made!
When he descends from the womb to *breathe*
On the day when he is born,
Thou openest his mouth completely,
Thou suppliest his necessities.   50
When the chick in the egg speaks within the shell,
Thou givest him breath within it to maintain him.
When thou has made him his fulfillment within the egg, to break it,
He comes forth from the egg to speak at his completed (time);
He walks upon his legs when he comes forth from it.   55

How manifold it is, what thou hast made!
They are hidden from the face (of man).
O sole god, like whom there is no other!
Thou didst create the world according to thy desire,
Whilst thou wert alone: 60
All men, cattle, and wild beasts,
Whatever is on earth, going upon (its) feet,
And what is on high, flying with its wings.

The countries of Syria and Nubia,[5] the *land* of Egypt,
Thou settest every man in his place,   65
Thou suppliest their necessities:
Everyone has his food, and his time of life is reckoned.
Their tongues are separate in speech,
And their natures as well;
Their skins are distinguished,   70
As thou distinguishest the foreign peoples.
Thou makest a Nile[6] in the underworld,

---

[5] *Syria and Nubia:* Ancient Syria was in Asia; it included modern Syria, Lebanon, Israel, and Jordan. Nubia was an ancient kingdom in northern Africa that included parts of modern Egypt and Sudan.

[6] *Nile:* African river flowing through Egypt into the Mediterranean. Ancient Egyptian culture centered on the annual flood cycle of the Nile.

Thou bringest it forth as thou desirest
To maintain the people (of Egypt)
According as thou madest them for thyself,   75
The lord of all of them, wearying (himself) with them,
The lord of every land, rising for them,
The Aton of the day, great of majesty.

All distant foreign countries, thou makest their life (also),
For thou hast set a Nile in heaven,[7]   80
That it may descend for them and make waves upon the mountains,
Like the great green sea,
To water their fields in their towns.
How effective they are, thy plans, O lord of eternity!
The Nile in heaven, it is for the foreign peoples   85
And for the beasts of every desert that go upon (their) feet;
(While the true) Nile comes from the underworld for Egypt.

Thy rays suckle every meadow.
When thou risest, they live, they grow for thee.
Thou makest the seasons in order to rear all that thou hast made,   90
The winter to cool them,
And the heat that *they* may taste thee.
Thou hast made the distant sky in order to rise therein,
In order to see all that thou dost make.
Whilst thou wert alone,   95
Rising in thy form as the living Aton,
Appearing, shining, *withdrawing or approaching*,
Thou madest millions of forms of thyself alone.
Cities, towns, fields, road, and river—
Every eye beholds thee over against them,   100
For thou art the Aton of the day over the *earth*. . . .

Thou art in my heart,
And there is no other that knows thee
Save thy son Nefer-kheperu-Re Wa-en-Re,[8]
For thou has made him well-versed in thy plans and in thy strength.   105

The world came into being by thy hand,
According as thou hast made them.
When thou hast risen they live,
When thou settest they die.

---

[7] *Nile in heaven:* Rain.

[8] *Nefer-kheperu-Re Wa-en-Re:* Another name for Akhenaton. It means "the son of Re (or Aton)."

Thou art lifetime thy own self,   110
For one lives (only) through thee.
Eyes are (fixed) on beauty until thou settest.
All work is laid aside when thou settest in the west.
(But) when (thou) risest (again),
[*Everything is*] made to flourish for the king, . . .   115
Since thou didst found the earth
And raise them up for thy son,
Who came forth from thy body:
the King of Upper and Lower Egypt, . . . Akh-en-Aton, . . . and the Chief
Wife of the King . . . Nefert-iti, living and youthful forever and ever.   120

UNDERSTANDING THE POEM

1. What is the nature of the Aton?

2. How does all life react to the Aton?

3. What does the poet's view of the Aton reveal about the world in which the poet lived?

ANALYZING LITERARY TECHNIQUE

1. What does the poet achieve by using **apostrophe?**

2. What is the role of **paradox** in the poem?

3. How does the poet use **contrast?** Explain the function of each example.

4. What is the **tone** of the poem? How does the poet achieve it?

5. Why is this a **lyric** poem?

WRITING ABOUT LITERATURE

1. Write an essay in which you analyze the poet's use of detail. Choose three subjects in the poem, such as darkness, nature, and the creator of life, and discuss how each contributes to the total effect of the poem. Use quotations from the poem to support your ideas.

2. Create a hymn to a god of a people who live in an unstable environment, such as an area with unpredictable weather or aggressive neighbors. Consider the following questions: What aspect of nature might this god represent? What characteristics would this god possess? What would be the tone of the hymn?

Psalm 8

DAVID

*D*avid, the shepherd-king of ancient Israel (who ruled from about 1010 until his death in about 970 B.C.), was a great warrior and statesman who created the united kingdom of Israel. A gifted poet, he is reputed to have written many of the psalms in the Bible, including Psalm 8.

David was a young shepherd from the tribe of Judah (one of the twelve tribes of Israel) when Goliath, the gigantic hero of the Philistine people, challenged anyone among the Israelites to fight him in single combat. The Israelite soldiers were too frightened to accept the challenge, but David—armed only with his slingshot and some stones—confronted Goliath and killed him. Thus David became a hero to the people of Israel.

David became an aide in the court of Saul, the first king of Israel. He befriended Saul's son Jonathan and married Saul's daughter Michal. In time, Saul became so jealous of David that David had to flee from Saul's court. After the deaths of Saul and Jonathan, David was proclaimed king of Judah; he became the second king of Israel. When David conquered Jerusalem, he made it the capital of the new united kingdom.

The Book of Psalms in the Bible contains one hundred fifty poems, some of them considered to be among the world's greatest literature. They were written over a period of four hundred years—from the time of King David until the destruction of the Temple (597 B.C.) and the Babylonian exile (587 B.C.). The word *psalm* derives from the Greek word *psalmos* ("to pluck at strings"), indicating that some of the psalms were probably chanted to the musical accompaniment of a small harp-like instrument called a lyre.

Although the psalms have been attributed to King David, it is likely that many of them were written by members of the professional guilds of psalmists who were associated with the Temple in Jerusalem. The psalms reflect the fragile and transitory nature of human existence in a universe in which only God is eternal. They express every human emotion—love and despair, joy and sorrow, hope and fear, faith and doubt. Some psalms express gratitude and praise for God's blessings; others express the need for God's help or forgiveness. Praise of an all-powerful and righteous God is characteristic of all the psalms.

Psalm 8 is one of the most beautiful psalms in the Bible. The beauty and mystery of a clear star-filled sky often lead observers to think about time, space, and the place of human life in the universe. The psalmist wrote the following poem from such an experience. Psalm 8 is both a nature hymn and a hymn of praise. Originally it may have been part of public worship in the Temple, with a chorus singing the refrain at the beginning and the end. Psalm 8 has been a favorite with people throughout the Western world for almost three thousand years.

O Lord, our Lord,
how majestic is your name in all the earth!

You have set your glory
above the heavens.
From the lips of children and infants   5
you have ordained praise
because of your enemies,
to silence the foe and the avenger.

When I consider your heavens,
the work of your fingers,   10
the moon and the stars,
which you have set in place,
what is man that you are mindful of him,
the son of man that you care for him?
You made him a little lower than the heavenly beings   15
and crowned him with glory and honor.

You made him ruler over the works of your hands;
you put everything under his feet:
all flocks and herds,
and the beasts of the field,   20
the birds of the air,
and the fish of the sea,
all that swim the paths of the seas.

O Lord, our Lord,
how majestic is your name in all the earth!   25

UNDERSTANDING THE POEM

1. What is the psalmist's attitude toward God? Why is God's name excellent in all the earth?

2. What is unusual about the psalmist's approach to the praise of God in this psalm?

3. How does the psalmist convey the relative importance of human beings in the universe?

4. What **themes** do you find in this psalm?

5. Compare and contrast Psalm 8 with Sophocles's "Ode to Man" in *Antigone* (lines 376–416).

ANALYZING LITERARY TECHNIQUE

1. How does the psalmist use **irony** to enhance the poem's meaning?

2. Why is this psalm considered to be **lyric** poetry?

3. How does the psalmist use the literary device of **parallelism?** What does it contribute to the poem?

4. Describe the **tone** of Psalm 8. How does the psalmist achieve it?

5. What does the psalmist achieve by using the "envelope" technique of beginning and ending the psalm with a chorus?

6. How does the poet's **voice** in this psalm differ from the poet's voice in the "Ode to Man" in *Antigone* (lines 376–416)? Why is Psalm 8 a lyric poem, while the "Ode to Man" is an **ode?**

WRITING ABOUT LITERATURE

1. Write an essay in which you analyze the tone of Psalm 8. Consider what the poet has chosen to emphasize about God, about human beings, and about the relationship between God and human beings. Use quotations from the poem to support your ideas.

2. Write a psalm that another psalmist might have written to ask God for help. Consider what aspects of life would motive the psalmist to write such a poem.

To an Army
Wife, in Sardis

SAPPHO

$\mathcal{S}$APPHO (c. 630 B.C.–c. 550 B.C.) is among the earliest
known female lyric poets. Famous for her personal, passionate love poems, Sappho's poetic genius was recognized in
ancient Greece as early as c. 600 B.C. The Greek philosopher Plato
(c. 428 B.C.–c. 348 B.C.) stated: "Some say there are nine Muses: How
careless! Look—Sappho of Lesbos is the tenth!" Sappho's poetry later
became the model for the Roman lyric poets Catullus (c. 84 B.C.–
c. 54 B.C.) and Horace (c. 65 B.C.–c. 8 B.C.) and for all who followed
them in writing lyric poetry in the West.

Sappho was born into an aristocratic family in Eresos, on the island
of Lesbos. After her father was killed in a war between Athens and
Lesbos, she lived most of her life among the aristocracy in Mytilene,
her mother's native city on that island. During a period of political
turbulence, Sappho and her daughter took refuge in Syracuse, Sicily
(c. 604 B.C.–c. 595 B.C.). After Sappho's death, the people of Syracuse
honored her memory with a beautiful statue in their town hall. The
great Roman poet Ovid (43 B.C.–c. A.D. 17) relates a story, popular
since the fourth century B.C., in which Sappho is in love with Phaon
and commits suicide. However, it is just a story.

Sappho's lyric poetry is markedly different in its origin and nature
from the great epic poetry of Homer and the oral tradition. Early Greek
poetry was passed from poet to poet with the goal of keeping the work
intact and distinct from the poet who was reciting it. In contrast,
Sappho lived at a time when it was possible to write down personal
poetry and to acknowledge one's identity as its creator. Her poetry
reveals the influence of the folk songs of Lesbos in that it is personal
and direct, as well as without affectation.

Sappho was the leader and teacher of a group of women and girls
from aristocratic families. She wrote most of her poetry for and about
the women in her group, and she recited it during their private meetings. Her poems are about family, friends, and feelings.

Although nine books of Sappho's poetry existed in ancient times, only about five percent of her poetry has survived. What remains is in the form of fragments written on pieces of papyrus that were found in Egypt. Scholars think that the following may be one of only two complete poems that still exist.

Some say a cavalry corps,
some infantry, some, again,
will maintain that the swift oars

of our fleet are the finest
sight on dark earth; but I say   5
that whatever one loves, is.

This is easily proved: did
not Helen—she who had scanned
the flower of the world's manhood—

choose as first among men one   10
who laid Troy's honor in ruin?[1]
warped to his will, forgetting

love due her own blood, her own
child, she wandered far with him.
So Anactoria, although you   15

being far away forget us,
the dear sound of your footstep
and light glancing in your eyes

would move me more than glitter
of Lydian horse or armored   20
tread of mainland infantry.

---

[1] *Helen . . . Troy's honor in ruin:* In Greek mythology, Helen (queen of Sparta and wife of Menelaus) eloped with Paris (son of King Priam of Troy). This event ignited the Trojan War.

UNDERSTANDING THE POEM

1. Reread the introductory material and then consider the following possibilities: (a) Sappho is writing to a friend who is off with her husband in Sardis (a city in the ancient kingdom of Lydia, in what is now Turkey); (b) a soldier, away on a tour of duty, is writing to his wife back home. Who do you think is the speaker of this poem? Is it important to know who the speaker is?

2. Why does the speaker mention the opinions of others ("Some say") as well as his or her own opinions?

3. To what extent, if any, do you think that Anactoria has forgotten the speaker?

ANALYZING LITERARY TECHNIQUE

1. How does Sappho appeal to the senses in this poem? What advantage do you find in her approach?

2. What is the function of **contrast** in this poem?

3. What does Sappho's use of **apostrophe** contribute to the poem?

4. Why does the narrator make an **allusion** to Helen of Troy?

WRITING ABOUT LITERATURE

1. Helen of Troy has inspired Western writers through the ages. She has been treated as a **symbol** of beauty, ambition, and passion. Some authors have portrayed her as vain and thoughtless; others have portrayed her as fearful and helpless. Consult reference books, books of mythology, or other works of literature about Helen of Troy and construct a character sketch of her. Then, in a brief essay, carefully consider Sappho's poem. What is Sappho's attitude toward Helen? On the basis of your character sketch, does Sappho treat Helen fairly? What does Sappho's attitude toward Helen suggest about Sappho's feelings toward Anactoria?

2. Write Anactoria's response to the speaker's poem, either in the form of a poem or in the form of a letter. You may choose to have her discuss her current life or her memories of home. You may want to find out more about this historical period and about life on the island of Lesbos and in Sardis in order to write Anactoria's response.

Antigone

SOPHOCLES

OPHOCLES (496–406 B.C.) was the most prolific and successful of the ancient Greek playwrights. Ninety-six of his 123 plays won first prize at the Athenian festivals held in honor of the god Dionysus. His artistry in depicting the psychology of his characters has influenced playwrights since the fifth century B.C. Unfortunately only seven complete plays by Sophocles have survived. Of these, the best known are the three Theban plays, which are based on the myth of Oedipus: *Oedipus the King*, *Oedipus at Colonus*, and *Antigone*.

Sophocles was born in Colonus (near Athens) into a wealthy family. He was well loved and respected throughout his long life, which encompassed the golden age of Greece (the Age of Pericles) and the rise and fall of the Athenian Empire. This period included the Peloponnesian War and conflicts with the Persian Empire. A friend of both the historian Herodotus and the statesman Pericles, Sophocles participated actively in Athenian affairs. He died two years before the independence and democracy of Athens were destroyed by Sparta's victory in the Peloponnesian War (404 B.C.).

Although Sophocles was highly regarded as an Athenian citizen, his lasting fame is as a dramatist. In his tragedies he deals with timeless religious, social, and political issues that affect relationships within families. He focuses on the reactions of important people to the difficult issues confronting them, and he emphasizes the connection between their personalities and the ensuing tragedy. It is characteristic of Greek myths that their principal characters, who are often heroic figures, share a distinctive type of personality. First, they all possess a particular type of excellence (*aretē*). In addition to this excellence, they often possess an excessive degree of pride (*hubris*). This excessive pride causes them to believe that customary limitations do not apply to them, and they act with imprudence or blind recklessness (*atē*). As a result, their behavior invites disastrous retribution (*nemesis*). In his tragedies, Sophocles combines this traditional heroic personality with another type of heroic personality, one whose rigid and courageous loyalty to a particular principle invites a disastrous fate.

Antigone (441 B.C.) presents both types of Greek heroes in one dramatic situation: Creon is the traditional Greek tragic hero, and Antigone is the Sophoclean tragic hero. The earliest of Sophocles's Theban plays, *Antigone* had become a classic by 346 B.C. The Greek philosopher Aristotle (384–322 B.C.) quoted it repeatedly in his *Politics*, and the great statesman and orator Demosthenes found Creon to be a fine teacher of patriotism. *Antigone* is one of the earliest depictions in Western literature of the competing rights of the state and the individual.

According to Aristotle's *Poetics*, a tragedy is a story of a person's fall from greatness. To be tragic, heroes must be inherently good people who have good intentions. In addition to their changes in fortune, tragic heroes must, in the end, recognize their own responsibility for their behavior and accept their fate with dignity. Aristotle thought the members of the audience should so identify with a tragic hero that they would feel pity for him or her and fear that their own behavior would also lead to suffering. To accomplish this goal, Aristotle advocated that a tragedy's plot be limited to one important action and its consequences. When Aristotle analyzed the nature of tragedy in his *Poetics*, Sophoclean drama was his ideal.

SUMMARY OF THE OEDIPUS MYTH

King Laius of Thebes was warned that if his queen, Jocasta, gave birth to a son, this son would kill him. When a son was born, shepherds were ordered to leave him to die in the mountains, but they disobeyed the order and gave him to the king and queen of Corinth to rear as their own child. They named him Oedipus.

When Oedipus was a young man, the oracle at Delphi told him that he would kill his father and marry his mother. Resolving never to return to Corinth, Oedipus headed toward Thebes. On the road, he inadvertently killed his real father, King Laius, in an argument.

Thebes was plagued by the Sphinx, a monster who asked young men a riddle and ate those who responded incorrectly. Queen Jocasta's brother, Creon, promised Thebes and its queen to anyone who could get rid of the Sphinx by answering her riddle correctly. Oedipus became that man. He thus inadvertently married his real mother and eventually became the father of two daughters (Antigone and Ismene) and two sons (Polynices and Eteocles).

Oedipus reigned successfully for about twenty years. When a new plague infected Thebes, the oracle at Delphi said that Thebes was being punished for harboring Laius's murderer. After a relentless search, Oedipus learned that he himself was to blame. Jocasta hanged herself, Oedipus blinded himself, and Creon exiled Oedipus.

After Eteocles and Polynices agreed to divide the rule of Thebes, Eteocles banished his brother. Later Polynices returned with an army from Argos and tried to regain his kingdom. In the unsuccessful assault, he and the other Argive captains died. Eteocles died as well. Contrary to custom, Creon prohibited the burial of the Argive dead. Years later, in retribution, the sons of these Argive captains attacked and destroyed Thebes.

CHARACTERS

ANTIGONE, *daughter of Oedipus and Jocasta*

ISMENE, *sister of Antigone*

A CHORUS *of old Theban citizens and their* LEADER

CREON, *king of Thebes, uncle of Antigone and Ismene*

A SENTRY

HAEMON, *son of Creon and Eurydice*

TIRESIAS, *a blind prophet*

A MESSENGER

EURYDICE, *wife of Creon*

Guards, attendants, and a boy

Time and Scene: *The royal house of Thebes. It is still night and the invading armies of Argos have just been driven from the city. Fighting on opposite sides, the sons of Oedipus, Eteocles and Polynices, have killed each other in combat. Their uncle,* CREON, *is now king of Thebes.*

Enter ANTIGONE, *slipping through the central doors of the palace. She motions to her sister,* ISMENE, *who follows her cautiously toward an altar at the center of the stage.*

ANTIGONE: My own flesh and blood—dear sister, dear Ismene,
　　how many griefs our father Oedipus handed down!
　　Do you know one, I ask you, one grief
　　that Zeus[1] will not perfect for the two of us
　　while we still live and breathe? There's nothing, 　　　　　　　　　5
　　no pain—our lives are pain—no private shame,
　　no public disgrace, nothing I haven't seen
　　in your griefs and mine. And now this:
　　an emergency decree, they say, the Commander
　　has just declared for all of Thebes. 　　　　　　　　　　　　10
　　What, haven't you heard? Don't you see?
　　The doom reserved for enemies
　　marches on the ones we love the most.

---

[1] *Zeus:* Ruler of the Greek gods.

ISMENE: Not I, I haven't heard a word, Antigone.
   Nothing of loved ones, 15
   no joy or pain has come my way, not since
   the two of us were robbed of our two brothers,
   both gone in a day, a double blow—
   not since the armies of Argos[2] vanished,
   just this very night. I know nothing more, 20
   whether our luck's improved or ruin's still to come.

ANTIGONE: I thought so. That's why I brought you out here,
   past the gates, so you could hear in private.

ISMENE: What's the matter? Trouble, clearly . . .
   you sound so dark, so grim. 25

ANTIGONE: Why not? Our own brothers' burial!
   Hasn't Creon graced one with all the rites,
   disgraced the other? Eteocles, they say,
   has been given full military honors,
   rightly so—Creon's laid him in the earth 30
   and he goes with glory down among the dead.
   But the body of Polynices, who died miserably—
   why, a city-wide proclamation, rumor has it,
   forbids anyone to bury him, even mourn him.
   He's to be left unwept, unburied, a lovely treasure 35
   for birds that scan the field and feast to their heart's content.

   Such, I hear, is the martial law our good Creon
   lays down for you and me—yes, me, I tell you—
   and he's coming here to alert the uninformed
   in no uncertain terms, 40
   and he won't treat the matter lightly. Whoever
   disobeys in the least will die, his doom is sealed:
   stoning to death inside the city walls!

   There you have it. You'll soon show what you are,
   worth your breeding, Ismene, or a coward— 45
   for all your royal blood.

ISMENE: My poor sister, if things have come to this,
   who am I to make or mend them, tell me,
   what good am I to you?

ANTIGONE: Decide.
   Will you share the labor, share the work? 50

ISMENE: What work, what's the risk? What do you mean?

---

   [2] *Argos:* Greek city-state, previously at war with Thebes.

ANTIGONE: *Raising her hands.*
　　Will you lift his body with these bare hands
　　and lower it with me?

ISMENE:　　　　　　　　What? You'd bury him—
　　when a law forbids the city?

ANTIGONE:　　　　　　　Yes!
　　He is my brother and—deny it as you will—   55
　　your brother too.
　　No one will ever convict me for a traitor.

ISMENE: So desperate, and Creon has expressly—

ANTIGONE:　　　　　　　　　　　No,
　　he has no right to keep me from my own.

ISMENE: Oh my sister, think—   60
　　think how our own father died, hated,
　　his reputation in ruins, driven on
　　by the crimes he brought to light himself
　　to gouge out his eyes with his own hands—
　　then mother . . . his mother and wife, both in one,   65
　　mutilating her life in the twisted noose—
　　and last, our two brothers dead in a single day,
　　both shedding their own blood, poor suffering boys,
　　battling out their common destiny hand-to-hand.

　　Now look at the two of us, left so alone . . .   70
　　think what a death we'll die, the worst of all
　　if we violate the laws and override
　　the fixed decree of the throne, its power—
　　we must be sensible. Remember we are women,
　　we're not born to contend with men. Then too,   75
　　we're underlings, ruled by much stronger hands,
　　so we must submit in this, and things still worse.

　　I, for one, I'll beg the dead to forgive me—
　　I'm forced, I have no choice—I must obey
　　the ones who stand in power. Why rush to extremes?   80
　　It's madness, madness.

ANTIGONE:　　　　　　　I won't insist,
　　no, even if you should have a change of heart,
　　I'd never welcome you in the labor, not with me.
　　So, do as you like, whatever suits you best—
　　I'll bury him myself.   85
　　And even if I die in the act, that death will be a glory.
　　I'll lie with the one I love and loved by him—
　　an outrage sacred to the gods! I have longer

to please the dead than please the living here:
in the kingdom down below I'll lie forever.   90
Do as you like, dishonor the laws
the gods hold in honor.

ISMENE: I'd do them no dishonor . . .
but defy the city? I have no strength for that.

ANTIGONE: You have your excuses. I am on my way,
I'll raise a mound for him, for my dear brother.   95

ISMENE: Oh Antigone, you're so rash—I'm so afraid for you!

ANTIGONE: Don't fear for me. Set your own life in order.

ISMENE: Then don't, at least, blurt this out to anyone.
Keep it a secret. I'll join you in that, I promise.

ANTIGONE: Dear god, shout it from the rooftops. I'll hate you   100
all the more for silence—tell the world!

ISMENE: So fiery—and it ought to chill your heart.

ANTIGONE: I know I please where I must please the most.

ISMENE: Yes, if you can, but you're in love with impossibility.

ANTIGONE: Very well, then, once my strength gives out   105
I will be done at last.

ISMENE: You're wrong from the start,
you're off on a hopeless quest.

ANTIGONE: If you say so, you will make me hate you,
and the hatred of the dead, by all rights,
will haunt you night and day.   110
But leave me to my own absurdity, leave me
to suffer this—dreadful thing. I'll suffer
nothing as great as death without glory.

Exit to the side.

ISMENE: Then go if you must, but rest assured,
wild, irrational as you are, my sister,   115
you are truly dear to the ones who love you.

Withdrawing to the palace.

Enter a CHORUS, *the old citizens of Thebes, chanting as the sun begins to rise.*

CHORUS: Glory—great beam of the sun, brightest of all
that ever rose on the seven gates of Thebes,
you burn through night at last!
Great eye of the golden day,   120

mounting the Dirce's banks[3] you throw him back—
the enemy out of Argos, the white shield, the man of bronze—
he's flying headlong now
        the bridle of fate stampeding him with pain!

        And he had driven against our borders,   125
        launched by the warring claims of Polynices—
        like an eagle screaming, winging havoc
        over the land, wings of armor
        shielded white as snow,
        a huge army massing,   130
        crested helmets bristling for assault.

He hovered above our roofs, his vast maw gaping
closing down around our seven gates,
        his spears thirsting for the kill
                but now he's gone, look,   135
before he could glut his jaws with Theban blood
or the god of fire put our crown of towers to the torch.
He grappled the Dragon none can master—Thebes—
        the clang of our arms like thunder at his back!

        Zeus hates with a vengeance all bravado,   140
        the mighty boasts of men. He watched them
        coming on a rising flood, the pride
        of their golden armor ringing shrill—
        and brandishing his lightning
        blasted the fighter just at the goal,   145
        rushing to shout his triumph from our walls.

Down from the heights he crashed, pounding down on the earth!
And a moment ago, blazing torch in hand—
        mad for attack, ecstatic
he breathed his rage, the storm   150
        of his fury hurling at our heads!
But now his high hopes have laid him low
and down the enemy ranks the iron god of war
        deals his rewards, his stunning blows—Ares[4]
        rapture of battle, our right arm in the crisis.   155
        Seven captains marshaled at seven gates
        seven against their equals, gave
        their brazen trophies up to Zeus,
        god of the breaking rout of battle,
        all but two: those blood brothers,   160

---

[3] *Dirce's banks:* A spring named for a former queen of Thebes. Because Dirce was a loyal
    follower of Dionysus, the god caused a spring to burst forth where a bull killed her.
[4] *Ares:* God of war.

one father, one mother—matched in rage,
spears matched for the twin conquest—
clashed and won the common prize of death.

But now for Victory! Glorious in the morning,
joy in her eyes to meet our joy   165
     she is winging down to Thebes,
our fleets of chariots wheeling in her wake—
    Now let us win oblivion from the wars,
thronging the temples of the gods
in singing, dancing choirs through the night!   170
    Lord Dionysus,[5] god of the dance
    that shakes the land of Thebes, now lead the way!

        Enter CREON *from the palace, attended by his guard.*

But look, the king of the realm is coming,
Creon, the new man for the new day,
whatever the gods are sending now . . .   175
what new plan will he launch?
Why this, this special session?
Why this sudden call to the old men
summoned at one command?

CREON: , My countrymen,
the ship of state is safe. The gods who rocked her,   180
after a long, merciless pounding in the storm,
have righted her once more.
                    Out of the whole city
I have called you here alone. Well I know,
first, your undeviating respect
for the throne and royal power of King Laius.   185
Next, while Oedipus steered the land the Thebes,
and even after he died, your loyalty was unshakable,
you still stood by their children. Now then,
since the two sons are dead—two blows of fate
in the same day, cut down by each other's hands,   190
both killers, both brothers stained with blood—
as I am next in kin to the dead,
I now possess the throne and all its powers.

Of course you cannot know a man completely,
his character, his principles, sense of judgment,   195
not till he's shown his colors, ruling the people,
making laws. Experience, there's the test.

---

[5] *Dionysus:* God of wine and celebration; patron god of Thebes, his birthplace; also called
    Bacchus, and sometimes Iacchus.

As I see it, whoever assumes the task,
the awesome task of setting the city's course,
and refuses to adopt the soundest policies   200
but fearing someone, keeps his lips locked tight,
he's utterly worthless. So I rate him now,
I always have. And whoever places a friend
above the good of his own country, he is nothing:
I have no use for him. Zeus my witness,   205
Zeus who sees all things, always—
I could never stand by silent, watching destruction
march against our city, putting safety to rout,
nor could I ever make that man a friend of mine
who menaces our country. Remember this: 210
our country *is* our safety.
Only while she voyages true on course
can we establish friendships, truer than blood itself.
Such are my standards. They make our city great.

Closely akin to them I have proclaimed,   215
just now, the following decree to our people
concerning the two sons of Oedipus.
Eteocles, who died fighting for Thebes,
excelling all in arms: he shall be buried,
crowned with a hero's honors, the cups we pour   220
to soak the earth and reach the famous dead.

But as for his blood brother, Polynices,
who returned from exile, home to his father-city
and the gods of his race, consumed with one desire—
to burn them roof to roots—who thirsted to drink   225
his kinsmen's blood and sell the rest to slavery:
that man—a proclamation has forbidden the city
to dignify him with burial, mourn him at all.
No, he must be left unburied, his corpse
carrion for the birds and dogs to tear,   230
an obscenity for the citizens to behold!

These are my principles. Never at my hands
will the traitor be honored above the patriot,
But whoever proves his loyalty to the state:
I'll prize that man in death as well as life.   235

LEADER: If this is your pleasure, Creon, treating
our city's enemy and our friend this way . . .
The power is yours, I suppose, to enforce it
with the laws, both for the dead and all of us,
the living.

CREON: Follow my orders closely then, 240
be on your guard.

LEADER: We're too old.
Lay that burden on younger shoulders.

CREON: No, no,
I don't mean the body—I've posted guards already.

LEADER: What commands for us then? What other service?

CREON: See that you never side with those who break my orders. 245

LEADER: Never. Only a fool could be in love with death.

CREON: Death is the price—you're right. But all too often
the mere hope of money has ruined many men.

A SENTRY *enters from the side.*

SENTRY: My lord,
I can't say I'm winded from running, or set out
with any spring in my legs either—no sir, 250
I was lost in thought, and it made me stop, often,
dead in my tracks, wheeling, turning back,
and all the time a voice inside me muttering,
"Idiot, why? You're going straight to your death."
Then muttering, "Stopped again, poor fool? 255
If somebody gets the news to Creon first,
what's to save your neck?"

And so,
mulling it over, on I trudged, dragging my feet,
you can make a short road take forever . . .
but at last, look, common sense won out, 260
I'm here, and I'm all yours,
and even though I come up empty-handed
I'll tell my story just the same, because
I've come with a good grip on one hope,
what will come will come, whatever fate— 265

CREON: Come to the point!
What's wrong—why so afraid?

SENTRY: First, myself, I've got to tell you,
I didn't do it, didn't see who did—
Be fair, don't take it out on me. 270

CREON: You're playing it safe, soldier,
barricading yourself from any trouble.
It's obvious, you've something strange to tell.

SENTRY: Dangerous too, and danger makes you delay
for all you're worth. 275

CREON: Out with it—then dismiss!

SENTRY: All right, here it comes. The body—
someone's just buried it, then run off . . .
sprinkled some dry dust on the flesh,
given it proper rites.

CREON: What?
What man alive would dare— 280

SENTRY: I've no idea, I swear it.
There was no mark of a spade, no pickaxe there,
no earth turned up, the ground packed hard and dry,
unbroken, no tracks, no wheelruts, nothing,
the workman left no trace. Just at sunup 285
the first watch of the day points it out—
it was a wonder! We were stunned . . .
a terrific burden too, for all of us, listen:
you can't see the corpse, not that it's buried,
really, just a light cover of road-dust on it, 290
as if someone meant to lay the dead to rest
and keep from getting cursed.
Not a sign in sight that dogs or wild beasts
had worried the body, even torn the skin.

But what came next! Rough talk flew thick and fast, 295
guard grilling guard—we'd have come to blows
at last, nothing to stop it; each man for himself
and each the culprit, no one caught red-handed,
all of us pleading ignorance, dodging the charges,
ready to take up red-hot iron in our fists, 300
go through fire, swear oaths to the gods—
"I didn't do it, I had no hand in it either,
not in the plotting, not the work itself!"

Finally, after all this wrangling came to nothing,
one man spoke out and made us stare at the ground, 305
hanging our heads in fear. No way to counter him,
no way to take his advice and come through
safe and sound. Here's what he said:
"Look, we've got to report the facts to Creon,
we can't keep this hidden." Well, that won out, 310
and the lot fell to me, condemned me,
unlucky as ever, I got the prize. So here I am,
against my will and yours too, well I know—
no one wants the man who brings bad news.

LEADER: My king,
ever since he began I've been debating in my mind,   315
could this possibly be the work of the gods?

CREON: Stop—
before you make me choke with anger—the gods!
You, you're senile, must you be insane?
You say—why it's intolerable—say the gods
could have the slightest concern for that corpse?   320
Tell me, was it for meritorious service
they proceeded to bury him, prized him so? The hero
who came to burn their temples ringed with pillars,
their golden treasures—scorch their hallowed earth
and fling their laws to the winds.   325
Exactly when did you last see the gods
celebrating traitors? Inconceivable!

No, from the first there were certain citizens
who could hardly stand the spirit of my regime,
grumbling against me in the dark, heads together,   330
tossing wildly, never keeping their necks beneath
the yoke, loyally submitting to their king.
These are the instigators, I'm convinced—
they've perverted my own guard, bribed them
to do their work.
                    Money! Nothing worse   335
in our lives, so current, rampant, so corrupting.
Money—you demolish cities, root men from their homes,
you train and twist good minds and set them on
to the most atrocious schemes. No limit,
you make them adept at every kind of outrage,   340
every godless crime—money!
                              Everyone—
the whole crew bribed to commit this crime,
they've made one thing sure at least:
sooner or later they will pay the price.

                              Wheeling on the **SENTRY.**

                    You—
I swear to Zeus as I still believe in Zeus,   345
if you don't find the man who buried that corpse,
the very man, and produce him before my eyes,
simple death won't be enough for you,
not till we string you up alive
and wring the immorality out of you.   350
Then you can steal the rest of your days,

better informed about where to make a killing.
You'll have learned, at last, it doesn't pay
to itch for rewards from every hand that beckons.
Filthy profits wreck most men, you'll see—   355
they'll never save your life.

SENTRY: Please,
    may I say a word or two, or just turn and go?

CREON: Can't you tell? Everything you say offends me.

SENTRY: Where does it hurt you, in the ears or in the heart?

CREON: And who are you to pinpoint my displeasure?   360

SENTRY: The culprit grates on your feelings,
    I just annoy your ears.

CREON: Still talking?
    You talk too much! A born nuisance—

SENTRY: Maybe so,
    but I never did this thing, so help me!

CREON: Yes you did—
    what's more, you squandered your life for silver!   365

SENTRY: Oh it's terrible when the one who does the judging
    judges things all wrong.

CREON: Well now,
    you must be clever about your judgments—
    if you fail to produce the criminals for me,
    you'll swear your dirty money brought you pain.   370

Turning sharply, reentering the palace.

SENTRY: I hope he's found. Best thing by far.
    But caught or not, that's in the lap of fortune;
    I'll never come back, you've seen the last of me.
    I'm saved, even now, and I never thought,
    I never hoped—   375
    dear gods, I owe you all my thanks!

Rushing out.

CHORUS: Numberless wonders
    terrible wonders walk the world but none the match for man—
    that great wonder crossing the heaving gray sea,
            driven on by the blasts of winter
    on through breakers crashing left and right,   380
        holds his steady course
    and the oldest of the gods he wears away—

the Earth, the immortal, the inexhaustible—
as his plows go back and forth, year in, year out
    with the breed of stallions turning up the furrows.   385

And the blithe, lightheaded race of birds he snares,
the tribes of savage beasts, the life that swarms the depths—
            with one fling of his nets
woven and coiled tight, he takes them all,
    man the skilled, the brilliant!   390
He conquers all, taming with his techniques
the prey that roams the cliffs and wild lairs,
training the stallion, clamping the yoke across
    his shaggy neck, and the tireless mountain bull.

And speech and thought, quick as the wind   395
and the mood and mind for law that rules the city—
    all these he has taught himself
and shelter from the arrows of the frost
when there's rough lodging under the cold clear sky
and the shafts of lashing rain—   400
        ready, resourceful man!
           Never without resources
never an impasse as he marches on the future—
only Death, from Death alone he will find no rescue
but from desperate plagues he has plotted his escapes.   405

Man the master, ingenious past all measure
past all dreams, the skills within his grasp—
    he forges on, now to destruction
now again to greatness. When he weaves in
the laws of the land, and the justice of the gods   410
that binds his oaths together
        he and his city rise high—
           but the city casts out
that man who weds himself to inhumanity
thanks to reckless daring. Never share my hearth   415
never think my thoughts, whoever does such things.

    Enter ANTIGONE *from the side, accompanied by the* SENTRY.

    Here is a dark sign from the gods—
    what to make of this? I know her,
    how can I deny it? That young girl's Antigone!
    Wretched, child of a wretched father,   420
    Oedipus. Look, is it possible?
    They bring you in like a prisoner—
    why? did you break the king's laws?
    Did they take you in some act of mad defiance?

SENTRY: She's the one, she did it single-handed—   425
  we caught her burying the body. Where's Creon?

                              Enter CREON *from the palace.*

LEADER: Back again, just in time when you need him.

CREON: In time for what? What is it?

SENTRY: My king,
  there's nothing you can swear you'll never do—
  second thoughts make liars of us all.   430
  I could have sworn I wouldn't hurry back
  (what with your threats, the buffeting I just took),
  but with a stroke of luck beyond our wildest hopes,
  what a joy, there's nothing like it. So,
  back I've come, breaking my oath, who cares?   435
  I'm bringing in our prisoner—this young girl—
  we took her giving the dead the last rites.
  But no casting lots this time; this is *my* luck,
  my prize, no one else's.
                      Now, my lord,
  here she is. Take her, question her,   440
  cross-examine her to your heart's content.
  But set me free, it's only right—
  I'm rid of this dreadful business once for all.

CREON: Prisoner! Her? You took her—where, doing what?

SENTRY: Burying the man. That's the whole story.

CREON: What?   445
  You mean what you say, you're telling me the truth?

SENTRY: She's the one. With my own eyes I saw her
  bury the body, just what you've forbidden.
  There. Is that plain and clear?

CREON: What did you see? Did you catch her in the act?   450

SENTRY: Here's what happened. We went back to our post,
  those threats of yours breathing down our necks—
  we brushed the corpse clean of the dust that covered it,
  stripped it bare . . . it was slimy, going soft,
  and we took to high ground, backs to the wind   455
  so the stink of him couldn't hit us;
  jostling, baiting each other to keep awake,
  shouting back and forth—no napping on the job,
  not this time. And so the hours dragged by
  until the sun stood dead above our heads,   460
  a huge white ball in the noon sky, beating,

blazing down, and then it happened—
suddenly, a whirlwind!
Twisting a great dust-storm up from the earth,
a black plague of the heavens, filling the plain,   465
rippling the leaves off every tree in sight,
choking the air and sky. We squinted hard
and took our whipping from the gods.

And after the storm passed—it seemed endless—
there, we saw the girl!   470
And she cried out a sharp, piercing cry,
like a bird come back to an empty nest,
peering into its bed, and all the babies gone . . .
Just so, when she sees the corpse bare
she bursts into a long, shattering wail   475
and calls down withering curses on the heads
of all who did the work. And she scoops up dry dust,
handfuls, quickly, and lifting a fine bronze urn,
lifting it high and pouring, she crowns the dead
with three full libations.

        Soon as we saw   480
we rushed her, closed on the kill like hunters,
and she, she didn't flinch. We interrogated her,
charging her with offenses past and present—
she stood up to it all, denied nothing. I tell you,
It made me ache and laugh in the same breath.   485
it's pure joy to escape the worst yourself,
it hurts a man to bring down his friends.
But all that, I'm afraid, means less to me
than my own skin. That's the way I'm made.

CREON: *Wheeling on* **ANTIGONE.**
                            You,

with your eyes fixed on the ground—speak up.   490
Do you deny you did this, yes or no?

ANTIGONE: I did it, I don't deny a thing.

CREON: *To the* **SENTRY.**
You, get out, wherever you please—
you're clear of a very heavy charge.
                  He leaves; **CREON** *turns back to* **ANTIGONE.**
You, tell me briefly, no long speeches—   495
were you aware a decree had forbidden this?

ANTIGONE: Well aware. How could I avoid it? It was public.

CREON: And still you had the gall to break this law?

ANTIGONE: Of course I did. It wasn't Zeus, not in the least,
who made this proclamation—not to me.   500
Nor did that Justice, dwelling with the gods
beneath the earth, ordain such laws for men.
Nor did I think your edict had such force
that you, a mere mortal, could override the gods,
the great unwritten, unshakable traditions.   505
They are alive, not just today or yesterday:
they live forever, from the first of time,
and no one knows when they first saw the light.

These laws—I was not about to break them,
not out of fear of some man's wounded pride,   510
and face the retribution of the gods.
Die I must, I've known it all my life—
how could I keep from knowing?—even without
your death-sentence ringing in my ears.
And if I am to die before my time   515
I consider that a gain. Who on earth,
alive in the midst of so much grief as I,
could fail to find his death a rich reward?
So for me, at least, to meet this doom of yours
is precious little pain. But if I had allowed   520
my own mother's son to rot, an unburied corpse—
that would have been an agony! This is nothing.
And if my present actions strike you as foolish,
let's just say I've been accused of folly
by a fool.

LEADER: Like father like daughter,   525
passionate, wild . . .
she hasn't learned to bend before adversity.

CREON: No? Believe me, the stiffest stubborn wills
fall the hardest; the toughest iron,
tempered strong in the white-hot fire,   530
you'll see it crack and shatter first of all.
And I've known spirited horses you can break
with a light bit—proud, rebellious horses.
There's no room for pride, not in a slave,
not with the lord and master standing by.   535

This girl was an old hand at insolence
when she overrode the edicts we made public.
But once she'd done it—the insolence,
twice over—to glory in it, laughing,
mocking us to our face with what she'd done.   540

I'm not the man, not now: she is the man
if this victory goes to her and she goes free.

Never! Sister's child or closer in blood
than all my family clustered at my altar
worshiping Guardian Zeus—she'll never escape, 545
she and her blood sister, the most barbaric death.
Yes, I accuse her sister of an equal part
in scheming this, this burial.

To his attendants.

Bring her here!
I just saw her inside, hysterical, gone to pieces.
It never fails: the mind convicts itself 550
in advance, when scoundrels are up to no good,
plotting in the dark. Oh but I hate it more
when a traitor, caught red-handed,
tries to glorify his crimes.

ANTIGONE: Creon, what more do you want 555
than my arrest and execution?

CREON: Nothing. Then I have it all.

ANTIGONE: Then why delay? Your moralizing repels me,
every word you say—pray god it always will.
So naturally all I say repels you too.

Enough. 560
Give me glory! What greater glory could I win
than to give my own brother decent burial?
These citizens here would all agree,

To the CHORUS.

they'd praise me too
if their lips weren't locked in fear. 565

Pointing to CREON.

Lucky tyrants—the perquisites of power!
Ruthless power to do and say whatever pleases *them.*

CREON: You alone, of all the people in Thebes,
see things that way.

ANTIGONE: They see it just that way
but defer to you and keep their tongues in leash. 570

CREON: And you, aren't you ashamed to differ so from them?
So disloyal!

ANTIGONE: Not ashamed for a moment,
not to honor my brother, my own flesh and blood.

CREON: Wasn't Eteocles a brother too—cut down, facing him?

ANTIGONE: Brother, yes, by the same mother, the same father.   575

CREON: Then how can you render his enemy such honors,
  such impieties in his eyes?

ANTIGONE: He'll never testify to that,
  Eteocles dead and buried.

CREON: He will—
  if you honor the traitor just as much as him.   580

ANTIGONE: But it was his brother, not some slave that died—

CREON: Ravaging our country!—
  but Eteocles died fighting in our behalf.

ANTIGONE: No matter—Death longs for the same rites for all.

CREON: Never the same for the patriot and the traitor.   585

ANTIGONE: Who, Creon, who on earth can say the ones below
  don't find this pure and uncorrupt?

CREON: Never. Once an enemy, never a friend,
  not even after death.

ANTIGONE: I was born to join in love, not hate—   590
  that is my nature.

CREON: Go down below and love,
  if love you must—love the dead! While I'm alive,
  no woman is going to lord it over me.

                    Enter ISMENE *from the palace, under guard.*

CHORUS: Look,
  Ismene's coming, weeping a sister's tears,
  loving sister, under a cloud . . .   595
  her face is flushed, her cheeks streaming.
  Sorrow puts her lovely radiance in the dark.

CREON: You—
  in my own house, you viper, slinking undetected,
  sucking my life-blood! I never knew
  I was breeding twin disasters, the two of you   600
  rising up against my throne. Come, tell me,
  will you confess your part in the crime or not?
  Answer me. Swear to me.

ISMENE: I did it, yes—
  if only she consents—I share the guilt,
  the consequences too.

ANTIGONE: No,   605
  Justice will never suffer that—not you,
  you were unwilling. I never brought you in.

ISMENE: But now you face such dangers . . . I'm not ashamed
　　　to sail through trouble with you,
　　　make your troubles mine.

ANTIGONE: 　　　　　　　　Who did the work? 　　　　　　610
　　　Let the dead and the god of death bear witness!
　　　I've no love for a friend who loves in words alone.

ISMENE: Oh no, my sister, don't reject me, please,
　　　let me die beside you, consecrating
　　　the dead together.

ANTIGONE: 　　　　　　Never share my dying, 　　　　　　615
　　　don't lay claim to what you never touched.
　　　My death will be enough.

ISMENE: What do I care for life, cut off from you?

ANTIGONE: Ask Creon. Your concern is all for him.

ISMENE: Why abuse me so? It doesn't help you now.

ANTIGONE: 　　　　　　　　　　　　You're right— 　　　620
　　　if I mock you, I get no pleasure from it,
　　　only pain.

ISMENE: 　　　Tell me, dear one,
　　　what can I do to help you, even now?

ANTIGONE: Save yourself. I don't grudge you your survival.

ISMENE: Oh no, no, denied my portion in your death? 　　　625

ANTIGONE: You chose to live, I chose to die.

ISMENE: 　　　　　　　　　　　　Not, at least,
　　　without every kind of caution I could voice.

ANTIGONE: Your wisdom appealed to one world—mine, another.

ISMENE: But look, we're both guilty, both condemned to death.

ANTIGONE: Courage! Live your life. I gave myself to death, 　　630
　　　long ago, so I might serve the dead.

CREON: They're both mad, I tell you, the two of them.
　　　One's just shown it, the other's been that way
　　　since she was born.

ISMENE: 　　　　　　True, my king,
　　　the sense we were born with cannot last forever . . . 　　635
　　　commit cruelty on a person long enough
　　　and the mind begins to go.

CREON: 　　　　　　　　Yours did,
　　　when you chose to commit your crimes with her.

ISMENE: How can I live alone, without her?

CREON: Her?
Don't even mention her—she no longer exists.   640

ISMENE: What? You'd kill your own son's bride?

CREON: Absolutely:
there are other fields for him to plow.

ISMENE: Perhaps,
but never as true, as close a bond as theirs.

CREON: A worthless woman for my son? It repels me.

ISMENE: Dearest Haemon, your father wrongs you so!   645

CREON: Enough, enough—you and your talk of marriage!

ISMENE: Creon—you're really going to rob your son of Antigone?

CREON: Death will do it for me—break their marriage off.

LEADER: So, it's settled then? Antigone must die?

CREON: Settled, yes—we both know that.   650

To the guards.

Stop wasting time. Take them in.
From now on they'll act like women.
Tie them up, no more running loose;
even the bravest will cut and run,
once they see Death coming for their lives.   655

The guards escort ANTIGONE *and* ISMENE *into the palace.*
CREON *remains while the old citizens form their chorus.*

CHORUS: Blest, they are the truly blest who all their lives
have never tasted devastation. For others, once
the gods have rocked a house to its foundations
    the ruin will never cease, creating on and on
from one generation on throughout the race—   660
like a great mounting tide
driven on by savage northern gales,
    surging over the dead black depths
roiling up from the bottom dark heaves of sand
and the headlands, taking the storm's onslaught full-force,   665
roar, and the low moaning
                echoes on and on
                      and now
as in ancient times I see the sorrows of the house,
the living heirs of the old ancestral kings,
piling on the sorrows of the dead
    and one generation cannot free the next—   670

some god will bring them crashing down,
the race finds no release.
And now the light, the hope
        springing up from the late last root
in the house of Oedipus, that hope's cut down in turn   675
by the long, bloody knife swung by the gods of death
by a senseless word
                by fury at the heart.
                        Zeús,
yours is the power, Zeus, what man on earth
can override it, who can hold it back?
Power that neither Sleep, the all-ensnaring   680
    no, nor the tireless months of heaven
can ever overmaster—young through all time,
mighty lord of power, you hold fast
        the dazzling crystal mansions of Olympus.[6]
And throughout the future, late and soon   685
as through the past, your law prevails:
no towering form of greatness
        enters into the lives of mortals
                        free and clear of ruin.
                                True,
our dreams, our high hopes voyaging far and wide   690
bring sheer delight to many, to many others
        delusion, blithe, mindless lusts
and the fraud steals on one slowly . . . unaware
till he trips and puts his foot into the fire.
        He was a wise old man who coined   695
the famous saying: "Sooner or later
foul is fair, fair is foul
to the man the gods will ruin"—
        He goes his way for a moment only
                        of blinding ruin.   700

                Enter HAEMON *from the palace.*

    Here's Haemon now, the last of all your sons.
    Does he come in tears for his bride,
    his doomed bride, Antigone—
    bitter at being cheated of their marriage?

CREON: We'll soon know, better than seers could tell us.   705

                        Turning to HAEMON.

_____

[6] *Olympus:* Mount Olympus, the home of the gods.

Son, you've heard the final verdict on your bride?
Are you coming now, raving against your father?
Or do you love me, no matter what I do?

HAEMON: Father, I'm your *son* . . . you in your wisdom
set my bearings for me—I obey you.   710
No marriage could ever mean more to me than you,
whatever good direction you may offer.

CREON: Fine, Haemon.
That's how you ought to feel within your heart,
subordinate to your father's will in every way.
That's what a man prays for: to produce good sons—   715
households full of them, dutiful and attentive,
so they can pay his enemy back with interest
and match the respect their father shows his friend.
But the man who rears a brood of useless children,
what has he brought into the world, I ask you?   720
Nothing but trouble for himself, and mockery
from his enemies laughing in his face.
                                   Oh Haemon,
never lose your sense of judgment over a woman.
The warmth, the rush of pleasure, it all goes cold
in your arms, I warn you . . . a worthless woman   725
in your house, a misery in your bed.
What wound cuts deeper than a loved one
turned against you? Spit her out,
like a mortal enemy—let the girl go.
Let her find a husband down among the dead.   730
Imagine it: I caught her in naked rebellion,
the traitor, the only one in the whole city.
I'm not about to prove myself a liar,
not to my people, no, I'm going to kill her!
That's right—so let her cry for mercy, sing her hymns   735
to Zeus who defends all bonds of kindred blood.
Why, if I bring up my own kind to be rebels,
think what I'd suffer from the world at large.
Show me the man who rules his household well:
I'll show you someone fit to rule the state.   740
That good man, my son,
I have every confidence he and he alone
can give commands and take them too. Staunch
in the storm of spears he'll stand his ground,
a loyal, unflinching comrade at your side.   745

But whoever steps out of line, violates the laws
or presumes to hand out orders to his superiors,

he'll win no praise from me. But that man
the city places in authority, his orders
must be obeyed, large and small,   750
right and wrong.
                    Anarchy—
show me a greater crime in all the earth!
She, she destroys cities, rips up houses,
breaks the ranks of spearmen into headlong rout.
But the ones who last it out, the great mass of them   755
owe their lives to discipline. Therefore
we must defend the men who live by law,
never let some woman triumph over us.
Better to fall from power, if fall we must,
at the hands of a man—never be rated   760
inferior to a woman, never.

LEADER: To us,
    unless old age has robbed us of our wits,
    you seem to say what you have to say with sense.

HAEMON: Father, only the gods endow a man with reason,
    the finest of all their gifts, a treasure.   765
    Far be it from me—I haven't the skill,
    and certainly no desire, to tell you when,
    if ever, you make a slip in speech . . . though
    someone else might have a good suggestion.

    Of course it's not for you,   770
    in the normal run of things, to watch
    whatever men say or do, or find to criticize.
    The man in the street, you know, dreads your glance,
    he'd never say anything displeasing to your face.
    But it's for me to catch the murmurs in the dark,   775
    the way the city mourns for this young girl.
    "No woman," they say, "ever deserved death less,
    and such a brutal death for such a glorious action.
    She, with her own dear brother lying in his blood—
    she couldn't bear to leave him dead, unburied,   780
    food for the wild dogs or wheeling vultures.
    Death? She deserves a glowing crown of gold!"
    So they say, and the rumor spreads in secret,
    darkly . . .
                    I rejoice in your success, father—
    nothing more precious to me in the world.   785
    What medal of honor brighter to his children
    than a father's growing glory? Or a child's
    to his proud father? Now don't, please,

be quite so single-minded, self-involved,
or assume the world is wrong and you are right. 790
Whoever thinks that he alone possesses intelligence,
the gift of eloquence, he and no one else,
and character too . . . such men, I tell you,
spread them open—you will find them empty.

                            No,
it's no disgrace for a man, even a wise man, 795
to learn many things and not to be too rigid.
You've seen trees by a raging winter torrent,
how many sway with the flood and salvage every twig,
but not the stubborn—they're ripped out, roots and all.
Bend or break. The same when a man is sailing: 800
haul your sheets too taut, never give an inch,
you'll capsize, go the rest of the voyage
keel up and the rowing-benches under.

Oh give way. Relax your anger—change!
I'm young, I know, but let me offer this: 805
it would be best by far, I admit,
if a man were born infallible, right by nature.
If not—and things don't often go that way,
it's best to learn from those with good advice.

LEADER: You'd do well, my lord, if he's speaking to the point, 810
to learn from him,

                               Turning to **HAEMON.**
          and you, my boy, from him.
You both are talking sense.

CREON: So,
men our age, we're to be lectured, are we?—
schooled by a boy his age?

HAEMON: Only in what is right. But if I seem young, 815
look less to my years and more to what I do.

CREON: Do? Is admiring rebels an achievement?

HAEMON: I'd never suggest that you admire treason.

CREON: Oh?—
isn't that just the sickness that's attacked her?

HAEMON: The whole city of Thebes denies it, to a man. 820

CREON: And is Thebes about to tell me how to rule?

HAEMON: Now, you see? Who's talking like a child?

CREON: Am I to rule this land for others—or myself?

HAEMON: It's no city at all, owned by one man alone.

CREON: What? The city *is* the king's—that's the law! 825

HAEMON: What a splendid king you'd make of a desert island—
you and you alone.

CREON: *To the* CHORUS.
                    This boy, I do believe,
is fighting on her side, the woman's side.

HAEMON: If you are a woman, yes;
my concern is all for you. 830

CREON: Why, you degenerate—bandying accusations,
threatening me with justice, your own father!

HAEMON: I see my father offending justice—wrong.

CREON: Wrong?
To protect my royal rights?

HAEMON: Protect your rights?
When you trample down the honors of the gods? 835

CREON: You, you soul of corruption, rotten through—
woman's accomplice!

HAEMON: That may be,
but you'll never find me accomplice to a criminal.

CREON: That's what *she* is,
and every word you say is a blatant appeal for her— 840

HAEMON: And you, and me, and the gods beneath the earth.

CREON: You'll never marry her, not while she's alive.

HAEMON: Then she'll die . . . but her death will kill another.

CREON: What, brazen threats? You go too far!

HAEMON: What threat?
Combating your empty, mindless judgments with a word? 845

CREON: You'll suffer for your sermons, you and your empty wisdom!

HAEMON: If you weren't my father, I'd say you were insane.

CREON: Don't flatter me with Father—you woman's slave!

HAEMON: You really expect to fling abuse at me
and not receive the same?

CREON: Is that so! 850
Now, by heaven, I promise you, you'll pay—
taunting, insulting me! Bring her out,
that hateful—she'll die now, here,
in front of his eyes, beside her groom!

HAEMON: No, no, she will never die beside me— 855
don't delude yourself. And you will never

see me, never set eyes on my face again.
Rage your heart out, rage with friends
who can stand the sight of you.

Rushing out.

LEADER: Gone, my king, in a burst of anger.   860
A temper young as his . . . hurt him once,
he may do something violent.

CREON: Let him do—
dream up something desperate, past all human limit!
Good riddance. Rest assured,
he'll never save those two young girls from death.   865

LEADER: Both of them, you really intend to kill them both?

CREON: No, not her, the one whose hands are clean;
you're quite right.

LEADER: But Antigone—
what sort of death do you have in mind for her?

CREON: I'll take her down some wild, desolate path   870
never trod by men, and wall her up alive
in a rocky vault, and set out short rations,
just a gesture of piety
to keep the entire city free of defilement.
There let her pray to the one god she worships: 875
Death—who knows?—may just reprieve her from death.
Or she may learn at last, better late than never,
what a waste of breath it is to worship Death.

Exit to the palace.

CHORUS: Love, never conquered in battle
Love the plunderer laying waste the rich!   880
Love standing the night-watch
                    guarding a girl's soft cheek,
you range the seas, the shepherds' steadings off in the wilds—
not even the deathless gods can flee your onset,
nothing human born for a day—   885
whoever feels your grip is driven mad.
                          Love
you wrench the minds of the righteous into outrage,
swerve them to their ruin—you have ignited this,
this kindred strife, father and son at war
                    and Love alone the victor—   890
warm glance of the bride triumphant, burning with desire!
Throned in power, side-by-side with the mighty laws!

Irresistible Aphrodite,[7] never conquered—
Love, you mock us for your sport.
>   ANTIGONE *is brought from the palace under guard.*
> But now, even I'd rebel against the king,   895
> I'd break all bounds when I see this—
> I fill with tears, can't hold them back,
> not any more. . . . I see Antigone make her way
> to the bridal vault where all are laid to rest.

ANTIGONE: Look at me, men of my fatherland,   900
>   setting out on the last road
> looking into the light of day
> the last I'll ever see . . .
> the god of death who puts us all to bed
> takes me down to the banks of Acheron[8] alive—   905
>   denied my part in the wedding-songs,
> no wedding-song in the dusk has crowned my marriage—
> I go to wed the lord of the dark waters.

CHORUS: Not crowned with glory, crowned with a dirge,
>   you leave for the deep pit of the dead.   910
>   No withering illness laid you low,
>   no strokes of the sword—a law to yourself,
> alone, no mortal like you, ever, you go down
> to the halls of Death alive and breathing.

ANTIGONE: But think of Niobe[9]—well I know her story—   915
>   think what a living death she died,
> Tantalus' daughter, stranger queen from the east:
> there on the mountain heights, growing stone
> binding as ivy, slowly walled her round
> and the rains will never cease, the legends say   920
> the snows will never leave her . . .
>   wasting away, under her brows the tears
> showering down her breasting ridge and slopes—
> a rocky death like hers puts me to sleep.

CHORUS: But she was a god, born of gods,   925
>   and we are only mortals born to die.
>   And yet, of course, it's a great thing

---

[7] *Aphrodite:* Goddess of love.

[8] *banks of Acheron:* River that runs through Hades, the Underworld.

[9] *Niobe:* Daughter of King Tantalus of Lydia and a former queen of Thebes. Niobe had fourteen children. She boasted that she was greater than the goddess Leto, who had only two children (the god and goddess Apollo and Artemis). Apollo and Artemis punished Niobe by killing her children and by transforming Niobe into a mountain in Lydia. The mountain appears to weep when the snow on its slopes melts.

for a dying girl to hear, just hear
she shares a destiny equal to the gods,
during life and later, once she's dead.

ANTIGONE: O you mock me!   930
Why, in the name of all my fathers' gods
why can't you wait till I am gone—
        must you abuse me to my face?
O my city, all your fine rich sons!
And you, you springs of the Dirce,   935
holy grove of Thebes where the chariots gather,
            you at least, you'll bear me witness, look,
unmourned by friends and forced by such crude laws
I go to my rockbound prison, strange new tomb—
        always a stranger, O dear god,   940
    I have no home on earth and none below,
        not with the living, not with the breathless dead.

CHORUS: You went too far, the last limits of daring—
            smashing against the high throne of Justice!
                Your life's in ruins, child—I wonder . . .   945
            do you pay for your father's terrible ordeal?

ANTIGONE: There—at last you've touched it, the worst pain
    the worst anguish! Raking up the grief for father
        three times over, for all the doom
    that's struck us down, the brilliant house of Laius.   950
    O mother, your marriage-bed
    the coiling horrors, the coupling there—
        you with your own son, my father—doomstruck mother!
    Such, such were my parents, and I their wretched child.
    I go to them now, cursed, unwed, to share their home—   955
        I am a stranger! O dear brother, doomed
    in your marriage—your marriage murders mine,
        your dying drags me down to death alive!

                                                      Enter CREON.

CHORUS: Reverence asks some reverence in return—
            but attacks on power never go unchecked,   960
                not by the man who holds the reins of power.
            Your own blind will, your passion has destroyed you.

ANTIGONE: No one to weep for me, my friends,
            no wedding-song—they take me away
            in all my pain . . . the road lies open, waiting.   965
            Never again, the law forbids me to see
            the sacred eye of day. I am agony!
            No tears for the destiny that's mine,
            no loved one mourns my death.

CREON: Can't you see?
If a man could wail his own dirge *before* he dies,   970
he'd never finish.

To the guards.

                    Take her away, quickly!
Wall her up in the tomb, you have your orders.
Abandon her there, alone, and let her choose—
death or a buried life with a good roof for shelter.
As for myself, my hands are clean. This young girl—   975
dead or alive, she will be stripped of her rights,
her stranger's rights, here in the world above.

ANTIGONE: O tomb, my bridal-bed—my house, my prison
cut in the hollow rock, my everlasting watch!
I'll soon be there, soon embrace my own,   980
the great growing family of our dead
Persephone[10] has received among her ghosts.
                                              I,
the last of them all, the most reviled by far,
go down before my destined time's run out.
But still I go, cherishing one good hope: 985
my arrival may be dear to father,
dear to you, my mother,
dear to you, my loving brother, Eteocles—
When you died I washed you with my hands,
I dressed you all, I poured the cups   990
across your tombs. But now, Polynices,
because I laid your body out as well,
this, this is my reward. Nevertheless
I honored you—the decent will admit it—
well and wisely too.
                    Never, I tell you,   995
if I had been the mother of children
or if my husband died, exposed and rotting—
I'd never have taken this ordeal upon myself,
never defied our people's will. What law,
you ask, do I satisfy with what I say?   1000
A husband dead, there might have been another.
A child by another too, if I had lost the first.
But mother and father both lost in the halls of Death,
no brother could ever spring to light again.

For this law alone I held you first in honor.   1005
For this, Creon, the king, judges me a criminal

---

[10] *Persephone:* Goddess of the Underworld.

guilty of dreadful outrage, my dear brother!
And now he leads me off, a captive in his hands,
with no part in the bridal-song, the bridal-bed,
denied all joy of marriage, raising children—   1010
deserted so by loved ones, struck by fate,
I descend alive to the caverns of the dead.
What law of the mighty gods have I transgressed?
Why look to the heavens any more, tormented as I am?
Whom to call, what comrades now? Just think,   1015
my reverence only brands me for irreverence!
Very well: if this is the pleasure of the gods,
once I suffer I will know that I was wrong.
But if these men are wrong, let them suffer
nothing worse than they mete out to me—   1020
these masters of injustice!

LEADER: Still the same rough winds, the wild passion
    raging though the girl.

CREON: *To the guards.*
                Take her away.
    You're wasting time—you'll pay for it too.

ANTIGONE: Oh god, the voice of death. It's come, it's here.   1025

CREON: True. Not a word of hope—your doom is sealed.

ANTIGONE: Land of Thebes, city of all my fathers—
    O you gods, the first gods of the race!
    They drag me away, now, no more delay.
    Look on me, you noble sons of Thebes—   1030
    the last of a great line of kings,
    I alone, see what I suffer now
    at the hands of what breed of men—
    all for reverence, my reverence for the gods!

           She leaves under guard; the CHORUS *gathers.*

CHORUS: Danaë,[11] Danaë—   1035
    even she endured a fate like yours,
      in all her lovely strength she traded
    the light of day for the bolted brazen vault—
    buried within her tomb, her bridal-chamber,
    wed to the yoke and broken.   1040

---

[11] *Danaë:* Danaë was imprisoned underground by her father because of a prophecy that her
    son would kill her father. Zeus transformed himself into a shower of gold to penetrate
    her prison cell and impregnate her.

But she was of glorious birth
             my child, my child
and treasured the seed of Zeus within her womb,
the cloudburst of streaming gold!
      The power of fate is a wonder,
        dark, terrible wonder—   1045
        neither wealth nor armies
        towered walls nor ships
        black bulls lashed by the salt
        can save us from that force.   1050

The yoke tamed him too
      young Lycurgus[12] flaming in anger
king of Edonia, all for his mad taunts
Dionysus clamped him down, encased
in the chain-mail of rock   1055
    and there his rage
               his terrible flowering rage burst—
sobbing, dying away . . . at last that madman
came to know his god—
        the power he mocked, the power   1060
        he taunted in all his frenzy
        trying to stamp out
        the women strong with the god[13]—
        the torch, the raving sacred cries—
        enraging the Muses[14] who adore the flute.   1065

And far north where the Black Rocks
      cut the sea in half
and murderous straits
split the coast of Thrace
      a forbidding city stands   1070
where once, hard by the walls
the savage Ares thrilled to watch
a king's new queen,[15] a Fury[16] rearing in rage

---

[12] *Lycurgus:* King of Edonia or Thrace. Lycurgus attempted to restrict the worship of Dionysus because he disapproved of the wildness of the god's followers. The god punished him by imprisoning him in a cave.

[13] *women strong with the god:* The maenads or bacchantes, followers of Dionysus.

[14] *the Muses:* The nine goddesses of art, music, and poetry.

[15] *a king's new queen:* Cleopatra, daughter of Boreas (the North Wind) and wife of Phineas (king of Salmydessus). She bore Phineas two sons. Later Phineas took a second wife, who hated her stepsons and blinded them. Boreas, who was accompanying the Argonauts on the voyage for the Golden Fleece, helped with their rescue.

[16] *a Fury:* The three Furies avenged crimes against blood relatives by driving the criminals insane.

against his two royal sons—
     her bloody hands, her dagger-shuttle   1075
stabbing out their eyes—cursed, blinding wounds—
their eyes blind sockets screaming for revenge!

They wailed in agony, cries echoing cries
     the princes doomed at birth . . .
and their mother doomed to chains,   1080
walled off in a tomb of stone—
     but she traced her own birth back
to a proud Athenian line and the high gods
and off in caverns half the world away,
born of the wild North Wind   1085
     she sprang on her father's gales,
       racing stallions up the leaping cliffs—
child of the heavens. But even on her the Fates
the gray everlasting Fates rode hard
my child, my child.

               Enter TIRESIAS, *the blind prophet, led by a boy.*

TIRESIAS: Lords of Thebes,   1090
I and the boy have come together,
hand in hand. Two see with the eyes of one . . .
so the blind must go, with a guide to lead the way.

CREON: What is it, old Tiresias? What news now?

TIRESIAS: I will teach you. And you obey the seer.

CREON: I will,   1095
I've never wavered from your advice before.

TIRESIAS: And so you kept the city straight on course.

CREON: I owe you a great deal, I swear to that.

TIRESIAS: Then reflect, my son: you are poised,
once more, on the razor-edge of fate.   1100

CREON: What is it? I shudder to hear you.

TIRESIAS: You will learn
when you listen to the warnings of my craft.
As I sat on the ancient seat of augury,
in the sanctuary where every bird I know
will hover at my hands—suddenly I heard it,   1105
a strange voice in the wingbeats, unintelligible,
barbaric, a mad scream! Talons flashing, ripping,
they were killing each other—that much I knew—
the murderous fury whirring in those wings
made that much clear!

                I was afraid,
I turned quickly, tested the burnt-sacrifice,
ignited the altar at all points—but no fire,
the god in the fire never blazed.
Not from those offerings . . . over the embers
slid a heavy ooze from the long thighbones,
smoking, sputtering out, and the bladder
puffed and burst—spraying gall into the air—
and the fat wrapping the bones slithered off
and left them glistening white. No fire!
The rites failed that might have blazed the future
with a sign. So I learned from the boy here;
he is my guide, as I am guide to others.
                        And it's you—
your high resolve that sets this plague on Thebes.
The public altars and sacred hearths are fouled,
one and all, by the birds and dogs with carrion
torn from the corpse, the doomstruck son of Oedipus!
And so the gods are deaf to our prayers, they spurn
the offerings in our hands, the flame of holy flesh.
No birds cry out an omen clear and true—
they're gorged with the murdered victim's blood and fat.
Take these things to heart, my son, I warn you.
All men make mistakes, it is only human.
But once the wrong is done, a man
can turn his back on folly, misfortune too,
if he tries to make amends, however low he's fallen,
and stops his bullnecked ways. Stubbornness
brands you for stupidity—pride is a crime.
No, yield to the dead!
Never stab the fighter when he's down.
Where's the glory, killing the dead twice over?

I mean you well. I give you sound advice.
It's best to learn from a good adviser
when he speaks for your own good:
it's pure gain.

CREON: Old man—all of you! So,
you shoot your arrows at my head like archers at the target—
I even have *him* loosed on me, this fortune-teller.
Oh his ilk has tried to sell me short
and ship me off for years. Well,
drive your bargains, traffic—much as you like—
in the gold of India, silver-gold of Sardis.[17]

---

[17] *Sardis:* City in the ancient kingdom of Lydia, located in Asia Minor in what is now Turkey.

You'll never bury that body in the grave,
not even if Zeus's eagles rip the corpse
and wing their rotten pickings off to the throne of god!
Never, not even in fear of such defilement
will I tolerate his burial, that traitor.   1155
Well I know, we can't defile the gods—
no mortal has the power.
                    No,
reverend old Tiresias, all men fall,
it's only human, but the wisest fall obscenely
when they glorify obscene advice with rhetoric—   1160
all for their own gain.

TIRESIAS: Oh god, is there a man alive
who knows, who actually believes . . .

CREON: What now?
What earth-shattering truth are you about to utter?

TIRESIAS: . . . just how much a sense of judgment, wisdom   1165
is the greatest gift we have?

CREON: Just as much, I'd say,
as a twisted mind is the worst affliction going.

TIRESIAS: You are the one who's sick, Creon, sick to death.

CREON: I am in no mood to trade insults with a seer.

TIRESIAS: You have already, calling my prophecies a lie.

CREON: Why not?   1170
You and the whole breed of seers are mad for money!

TIRESIAS: And the whole race of tyrants lusts to rake it in.

CREON: This slander of yours—
are you aware you're speaking to the king?

TIRESIAS: Well aware. Who helped you save the city?

CREON: You—   1175
you have your skills, old seer, but you lust for injustice!

TIRESIAS: You will drive me to utter the dreadful secret in my heart.

CREON: Spit it out! Just don't speak it out for profit.

TIRESIAS: Profit? No, not a bit of profit, not for you.

CREON: Know full well, you'll never buy off my resolve.   1180

TIRESIAS: Then know this too, learn this by heart!
The chariot of the sun will not race through
so many circuits more, before you have surrendered
one born of your own loins, your own flesh and blood,

a corpse for corpses given in return, since you have thrust   1185
to the world below a child sprung for the world above,
ruthlessly lodged a living soul within the grave—
then you've robbed the gods below the earth,
keeping a dead body here in the bright air,
unburied, unsung, unhallowed by the rites.   1190

You, you have no business with the dead,
nor do the gods above—this is violence
you have forced upon the heavens.
And so the avengers, the dark destroyers late
but true to the mark, now lie in wait for you,   1195
the Furies sent by the gods and the god of death
to strike you down with the pains that you perfected!

There. Reflect on that, tell me I've been bribed.
The day comes soon, no long test of time, not now,
that wakes the wails for men and women in your halls.   1200
Great hatred rises against you—
cities in tumult, all whose mutilated sons
the dogs have graced with burial, or the wild beasts,
some wheeling crow that wings the ungodly stench of carrion
back to each city, each warrior's hearth and home.   1205
These arrows for your heart! Since you've raked me
I loose them like an archer in my anger,
arrows deadly true. You'll never escape
their burning, searing force.

                                                    Motioning to his escort.

Come, boy, take me home.   1210
So he can vent his rage on younger men,
and learn to keep a gentler tongue in his head
and better sense than what he carries now.

                                                            Exit to the side.

LEADER: The old man's gone, my king—
    terrible prophecies. Well I know,   1215
    since the hair on this old head went gray,
    he's never lied to Thebes.

CREON: I know it myself—I'm shaken, torn.
    It's a dreadful thing to yield . . . but resist now?
    Lay my pride bare to the blows of ruin?   1220
    That's dreadful too.

LEADER: But good advice,
    Creon, take it now, you must.

CREON: What should I do? Tell me . . . I'll obey.

LEADER: Go! Free the girl from the rocky vault
and raise a rocky mound for the body you exposed.   1225

CREON: That's your advice? You think I should give in?

LEADER: Yes, my king, quickly. Disasters sent by the gods
cut short our follies in a flash.

CREON: Oh, it's hard,
giving up the heart's desire . . . but I will do it—
no more fighting a losing battle with necessity.   1230

LEADER: Do it now, go, don't leave it to others.

CREON: Now—I'm on my way! Come, each of you,
take up axes, make for the high ground,
over there, quickly! I and my better judgment
have come round to this—I shackled her,   1235
I'll set her free myself. I am afraid . . .
it's best to keep the established laws
to the very day we die.

Rushing out, followed by his entourage. The CHORUS *clusters around the altar.*

CHORUS: God of a hundred names!
                         Great Dionysus—
              Son and glory of Semele![18] Pride of Thebes—   1240
Child of Zeus whose thunder rocks the clouds—
Lord of the famous lands of evening—
King of the Mysteries!
                    King of Eleusis, Demeter's plain[19]
her breasting hills that welcome in the world—
Great Dionysus!
                    Bacchus, living in Thebes   1245
the mother-city of all your frenzied women—
                                        Bacchus
              living along the Ismenus' rippling waters
              standing over the field sown with the Dragon's teeth![20]

---

[18] *Semele:* Daughter of Cadmus (king of Thebes) and mother of Dionysus. A mortal, Semele
was impregnated by Zeus, who visited her in disguise. When Zeus finally revealed himself to her as a god, she was burned to death by his lightning. Zeus saved Dionysus by
sewing him into his thigh until he was ready to be born.

[19] *Eleusis, Demeter's plain:* Demeter was goddess of grain and the harvest. Eleusis was the
site of the Eleusinian Mysteries, fertility rites centered around Demeter.

[20] *Ismenus' . . . Dragon's teeth:* Cadmus, the first king of Thebes, unknowingly killed the
dragon that guarded the sacred spring of Ares. Athena then told Cadmus to remove the
dragon's teeth and sow half of them. Armed men immediately sprang up and fought each
other. Five of these men survived. Cadmus served Ares for eight years to atone for killing
the dragon. He then was made king of Cadmeia (later called Thebes) by Athena.

You—we have seen you through the flaring smoky fires,
   your torches blazing over the twin peaks   1250
where nymphs of the hallowed cave climb onward
             fired with you, your sacred rage—
we have seen you at Castalia's running spring
and down from the heights of Nysa[21] crowned with ivy
the greening shore rioting vines and grapes   1255
       down you come in your storm of wild women
            ecstatic, mystic cries—
                       Dionysus—
down to watch and warn the roads of Thebes!
First of all cities, Thebes you honor first
you and your mother, bride of the lightning—   1260
come, Dionysus! now your people lie
in the iron grip of plague,
come in your racing, healing stride
          down Parnassus' slopes
or across the moaning straits.
               Lord of the dancing—   1265
dance, dance the constellations breathing fire!
Great master of the voices of the night!
Child of Zeus, God's offspring, come, come forth!
Lord, king, dance with your nymphs, swirling, raving
arm-in-arm in frenzy through the night   1270
     they dance you, Iacchus—
             Dance, Dionysus
giver of all good things!

                    Enter a MESSENGER *from the side.*

MESSENGER: Neighbors,
friends of the house of Cadmus and the kings,
there's not a thing in this life of ours
I'd praise or blame as settled once for all.   1275
Fortune lifts and Fortune fells the lucky
and unlucky every day. No prophet on earth
can tell a man his fate. Take Creon:
there was a man to rouse your envy once,
as I see it. He saved the realm from enemies;   1280
taking power, he alone, the lord of the fatherland,

---

[21] *Castalia's . . . heights of Nysa:* Castalia is a spring near Delphi on Mount Parnassus. Mount Nysa is the mountain on which Dionysus spent his youth. Later he cultivated grapes and invented wine.

he set us true on course—flourished like a tree
with the noble line of sons he bred and reared . . .
and now it's lost, all gone.
                              Believe me,
when a man has squandered his true joys,   1285
he's good as dead, I tell you, a living corpse.
Pile up riches in your house, as much as you like—
live like a king with a huge show of pomp,
but if real delight is missing from the lot,
I wouldn't give you a wisp of smoke for it,   1290
not compared with joy.

LEADER: What now?
What new grief do you bring the house of kings?

MESSENGER: Dead, dead—and the living are guilty of their death!

LEADER: Who's the murderer? Who is dead? Tell us.

MESSENGER: Haemon's gone, his blood spilled by the very hand—   1295

LEADER: His father's or his own?

MESSENGER: His own . . .
raging mad with his father for the death—

LEADER: Oh great seer,
you saw it all, you brought your word to birth!

MESSENGER: Those are the facts. Deal with them as you will.

As he turns to go, **EURYDICE** *enters from the palace.*

LEADER: Look, Eurydice. Poor woman, Creon's wife,   1300
so close at hand. By chance perhaps,
unless she's heard the news about her son.

EURYDICE: My countrymen,
all of you—I caught the sound of your words
as I was leaving to do my part,
to appeal to queen Athena[22] with my prayers.   1305
I was just loosing the bolts, opening the doors,
when a voice filled with sorrow, family sorrow,
struck my ears, and I fell back, terrified,
into the women's arms—everything went black.
Tell me the news, again, whatever it is . . .   1310
sorrow and I are hardly strangers;
I can bear the worst.

---

[22] *Athena:* Goddess of arts, crafts, and defensive war.

MESSENGER: I—dear lady,
    I'll speak as an eye-witness. I was there.
    And I won't pass over one word of the truth.
    Why should I try to soothe you with a story,   1315
    only to prove a liar in a moment?
    Truth is always best.
                        So,
    I escorted your lord, I guided him
    to the edge of the plain where the body lay,
    Polynices, torn by the dogs and still unmourned.   1320
    And saying a prayer to Hecate of the Crossroads,
    Pluto[23] too, to hold their anger and be kind,
    we washed the dead in a bath of holy water
    and plucking some fresh branches, gathering . . .
    what was left of him, we burned them all together   1325
    and raised a high mound of native earth, and then
    we turned and made for that rocky vault of her,
    the hollow, empty bed of the bride of Death.

    And far off, one of us heard a voice,
    a long wail rising, echoing   1330
    out of that unhallowed wedding-chamber;
    he ran to alert the master and Creon pressed on,
    closer—the strange, inscrutable cry came sharper,
    throbbing around him now, and he let loose
    a cry of his own, enough to wrench the heart,   1335
    "Oh god, am I the prophet now? going down
    the darkest road I've ever gone? My son—
    it's *his* dear voice, he greets me! Go, men,
    closer, quickly! Go through the gap,
    the rocks are dragged back—   1340
    right to the tomb's very mouth—and look,
    see if it's Haemon's voice I think I hear,
    or the gods have robbed me of my senses."

    The king was shattered. We took his orders,
    went and searched, and there in the deepest,   1345
    dark recesses of the tomb we found her . . .
    hanged by the neck in a fine linen noose,
    strangled in her veils—and the boy,
    his arms flung around her waist,
    clinging to her, wailing for his bride,   1350
    dead and down below, for his father's crimes

---

[23] *Hecate . . . Pluto:* Hecate was the Underworld goddess of death. Pluto, also called Hades,
    was god of the Underworld.

and the bed of his marriage blighted by misfortune.
When Creon saw him, he gave a deep sob,
he ran in, shouting, crying out to him,
"Oh my child—what have you done? what seized you,   1355
what insanity? what disaster drove you mad?
Come out, my son! I beg you on my knees!"
But the boy gave him a wild burning glance,
spat in his face, not a word in reply,
he drew his sword—his father rushed out,   1360
running as Haemon lunged and missed!—
and then, doomed, desperate with himself,
suddenly leaning his full weight on the blade,
he buried it in his body, halfway to the hilt.

And still in his senses, pouring his arms around her,   1365
he embraced the girl and breathing hard,
released a quick rush of blood,
bright red on her cheek glistening white.
And there he lies, body enfolding body . . .
he has won his bride at last, poor boy,   1370
not here but in the houses of the dead.

Creon shows the world that of all the ills
afflicting men the worst is lack of judgment.

                      EURYDICE *turns and reenters the palace.*

LEADER: What do you make of that? The lady's gone,
    without a word, good or bad.

MESSENGER: I'm alarmed too   1375
    but here's my hope—faced with her son's death,
    she finds it unbecoming to mourn in public.
    Inside, under her roof, she'll set her women
    to the task and wail the sorrow of the house.
    She's too discreet. She won't do something rash.   1380

LEADER: I'm not so sure. To me, at least,
    a long heavy silence promises danger,
    just as much as a lot of empty outcries.

MESSENGER: We'll see if she's holding something back,
    hiding some passion in her heart.   1385
    I'm going in. You may be right—who knows?
    Even too much silence has its dangers.

    Exit to the palace. Enter **CREON** *from the side, escorted by attendants*
                              carrying **HAEMON'S** *body on a bier.*

LEADER: The king himself! Coming toward us,
look holding the boy's head in his hands.
Clear, damning proof, if it's right to say so—   1390
proof of his own madness, no one else's,
no, his own blind wrongs.

CREON: Ohhh,
so senseless, so insane . . . my crimes,
my stubborn, deadly—
Look at us, the killer, the killed,   1395
father and son, the same blood—the misery!
My plans, my mad fanatic heart,
my son, cut off so young!
Ai, dead, lost to the world,
not through your stupidity, no, my own.

LEADER: Too late,   1400
too late, you see what justice means.

CREON: Oh I've learned
through blood and tears! Then, it was then,
when the god came down and struck me—a great weight
shattering, driving me down that wild savage path,
ruining, trampling down my joy. Oh the agony,   1405
the heartbreaking agonies of our lives.

Enter the MESSENGER *from the palace.*

MESSENGER: Master,
what a hoard of grief you have, and you'll have more.
The grief that lies to hand you've brought on yourself—
                          Pointing to HAEMON's *body.*
The rest, in the house, you'll see it all too soon.

CREON: What now? What's worse than this?

MESSENGER: The queen is dead.   1410
The mother of this dead boy . . . mother to the end—
poor thing, her wounds are fresh.

CREON: No, no,
harbor of Death, so choked, so hard to cleanse!—
why me? why are you killing me?
Herald of pain, more words, more grief?   1415
I died once, you kill me again and again!
What's the report, boy . . . some news for me?
My wife dead? O dear god!
Slaughter heaped on slaughter?

The doors open; the body of EURYDICE *is brought out on her bier.*

MESSENGER: See for yourself:
    now they bring her body from the palace.

CREON: Oh no,   1420
    another, a second loss to break the heart.
    What next, what fate still waits for me?
    I just held my son in my arms and now,
    look a new corpse rising before my eyes—
    wretched, helpless mother—O my son!   1425

MESSENGER: She stabbed herself at the altar,
    then her eyes went dark, after she'd raised
    a cry for the noble fate of Megareus, the hero
    killed in the first assault, then for Haemon,
    then with her dying breath she called down   1430
    torments on your head—you killed her sons.

CREON: Oh the dread,
    I shudder with dread! Why not kill me too?—
    run me through with a good sharp sword?
    Oh god, the misery, anguish—
    I, I'm churning with it, going under.   1435

MESSENGER: Yes, and the dead, the woman lying there,
    piles the guilt of all their deaths on you.

CREON: How did she end her life, what bloody stroke?

MESSENGER: She drove home to the heart with her own hand,
    once she learned her son was dead . . . that agony.   1440

CREON: And the guilt is all mine—
    can never be fixed on another man,
    no escape for me. I killed you,
    I, god help me, I admit it all!

                  To his attendants.

    Take me away, quickly, out of sight.   1445
    I don't even exist—I'm no one. Nothing.

LEADER: Good advice, if there's any good in suffering.
    Quickest is best when troubles block the way.

CREON: *Kneeling in prayer.*
    Come, let it come!—that best of fates for me
    that brings the final day, best fate of all.   1450
    Oh quickly, now—
    so I never have to see another sunrise.

LEADER: That will come when it comes;
    we must deal with all that lies before us.
    The future rests with the ones who tend the future.   1455

CREON: That prayer—I poured my heart into that prayer!

LEADER: No more prayers now. For mortal men
there is no escape from the doom we must endure.

CREON: Take me away, I beg you, out of sight.
A rash, indiscriminate fool!   1460
I murdered you, my son, against my will—
you too, my wife . . .
                    Wailing wreck of a man,
whom to look to? where to lean for support?
            Desperately turning from HAEMON *to* EURYDICE *on their biers.*
Whatever I touch goes wrong—once more
a crushing fate's come down upon my head.   1465

The MESSENGER *and attendants lead* CREON *into the palace.*

CHORUS: Wisdom is by far the greatest part of joy,
and reverence toward the gods must be safeguarded.
The mighty words of the proud are paid in full
with mighty blows of fate, and at long last
those blows will teach us wisdom.   1470

The old citizens exit to the side.

UNDERSTANDING THE PLAY

1. Analyze Sophocles's **characterization** of Antigone:
   a) What is Antigone's attitude toward the laws of Thebes? Why doesn't Antigone view herself as a traitor?
   b) Why does Antigone risk death to bury Polynices?
   c) Why won't Antigone let Ismene join her? Why does Antigone want Ismene to publicize her deed?
   d) Would Antigone have fared better if she had treated Creon with respect?
   e) To what extent, if any, is Antigone ambivalent about her sacrifice?
   f) Why is Antigone considered a hero?
   g) To what extent, if any, is behavior like Antigone's dangerous? Consider her devotion to her principles and her attitudes toward advice and death.

2. Analyze Sophocles's characterization of Creon:
   a) To what extent, if any, does it matter that Creon's edict is called an emergency decree? Does Creon have the right to issue such an edict? Explain.

b) Reread the paragraph in the introductory material that discusses the Greek concepts of *aretē*, *hubris*, *atē*, and *nemesis* and explain Creon's actions in terms of these concepts.

c) Could Creon have honored Eteocles and still have buried Polynices? If so, how? Would this have been fair to Eteocles?

d) Why is it important that Haemon is Creon's sole surviving son?

e) What does Creon's attitude toward disobedience reveal about him?

f) Why does Creon change Antigone's sentence from being stoned to death to being buried alive?

g) In what ways do Creon's responses to Tiresias show disrespect for the gods? How do his responses fit into the psychological pattern of *aretē*, *hubris*, and *atē*?

h) Why does Creon bury Polynices before rescuing Antigone?

i) In a statement to Creon, Antigone implies that hatred—not love—motivates his actions. To what extent, if any, does she prove to be correct? To what extent does hatred determine Creon's fate?

j) In what ways is Creon a tragic figure?

k) In 1887, Lord Acton wrote "Power tends to corrupt; absolute power corrupts absolutely." To what extent, if any, does this statement apply to Creon?

3. Examine Sophocles's characterization of Ismene: (a) How is Ismene different from Antigone? (b) Is Ismene a coward? Explain.

4. Examine Sophocles's characterization of Haemon: (a) What aspects of Haemon's speech to Creon are diplomatic? (b) How does Haemon's concept of kingship differ from Creon's?

5. Apply the following statements by the Chorus to the characters in the play:
   a) "For mortal men / there is no escape from the doom we must endure." (lines 1457–58)
   b) "Love / you wrench the minds of the righteous into outrage, / swerve them to their ruin." (lines 886–88)
   c) "No towering form of greatness / enters into the lives of mortals / free and clear of ruin." (lines 687–89)

6. What four **themes** are revealed by the Chorus in the last lines of the play (lines 1466–70)? Are these themes relevant today?

ANALYZING LITERARY TECHNIQUE

1. Sophocles includes several minor characters in *Antigone*. Describe what function the following characters have in driving the **plot** and revealing the meaning of the play: (a) Ismene; (b) Haemon; (c) Tiresias and the Chorus.

2. Why does Sophocles introduce the fact of Antigone's engagement so late in the play?

3. Why is the play called *Antigone* and not *Creon*? Who is more important? Defend your choice.

4. Sophocles is known for his use of **dramatic irony.** Reread the section of the play where Creon first learns that someone has attempted to bury Polynices (beginning with line 277). Where is the dramatic irony in Creon's responses? How does this dramatic irony affect an audience that, like Sophocles's audience, knows the story before seeing the play? What is its dramatic function in the play?

5. What is the role of **paradox** in the play?

6. What incidents mark the **climax,** the **crisis,** and the **discovery** in this play?

7. Beginning with line 915, Antigone and the Chorus allude to a number of mythological characters, including Niobe, Persephone, and Danaë. What is the function of these **allusions?**

WRITING ABOUT LITERATURE

1. Creon states "You cannot know a man completely, / his character, his principles, sense of judgment, / not till he's shown his colors, ruling the people, / making laws" (lines 194–97). Write an essay in which you evaluate Creon's leadership abilities by examining his character, his principles, and his judgment. Provide enough detail about the plot and setting of the play to make the reader understand Creon's situation. Support each of your ideas with at least two quotations from the play. In your conclusion, sum up your evaluation of Creon as a ruler.

2. Analyze and explain how Creon's actions in the play exemplify the Greek concepts of *aretē, hubris, atē,* and *nemesis.* (These terms are explained in the introductory material to *Antigone.*) Explain the meaning of the concepts in terms of human personality. Then analyze how each concept applies to Creon's behavior. Find one or two examples to support each concept. Be sure to explain how the examples you are using are appropriate illustrations of the particular concept. In your conclusion, evaluate Creon's behavior as a human being and as a ruler on the basis of your discussion of these concepts.

3. Analyze the relationship between the paradox expressed in the "Ode to Man" (lines 376–416) and the dramatic irony in the action of the play. Consider the attitudes and behavior of Antigone, Creon, and Haemon and the effect these characters have on one another. Use quotations from the play to support your ideas.

4. Tell the story of *Antigone* from either Ismene's or Haemon's point of view. Consider the following suggestions: For Ismene, relate her feelings about Antigone's rejection of her and reveal what she will do at the end of the play. For Haemon, recount his reasons for wishing to kill his father and then for choosing to die with Antigone. Choose a form for your story: for example, a diary or a conversation with a friend (for Ismene) or a farewell letter or a conversation with a relative in the Underworld (for Haemon).

Though heart's
hurt exhausts me
always now

GAIUS VALERIUS CATULLUS

*G*AIUS VALERIUS CATULLUS (c. 84–c. 54 B.C.) was the greatest lyric poet of ancient Rome. Inspired by the Greek poet Sappho and by later poets of Hellenistic Greece, Catullus wrote as he might speak, expressing his attitudes and feelings with simplicity, clarity, and immediacy. This style, which was unique in Catullus's time, influenced later poets of ancient Rome (such as Virgil, Ovid, and Horace) as well as many later English poets.

Few facts remain about Catullus's life beyond what he reveals through his poetry. Catullus was born into a wealthy Verona family in about 84 B.C. in the northern Roman province of Cisalpine Gaul. Julius Caesar knew Catullus's father well enough to have been a guest.

When Catullus became a young man, he moved to Rome, where he entered fashionable society and associated with such luminaries as Julius Caesar, Cicero, and Pompey. However, Roman politics did not interest Catullus. He became a part of Rome's prestigious literary circles, joining a group of young poets who were interested in the learned and polished writings of the Alexandrian poets of Hellenistic Greece.

Catullus fell in love with Clodia, an aristocratic matron from an important Roman family. Clodia was nearly ten years older than Catullus, and she was the wife of the governor of Cisalpine Gaul. She is reputed to have had many lovers and to have poisoned her husband. Catullus addresses Clodia in his love poems as "Lesbia"—after Sappho of Lesbos, whose poetry he admired for its conversational style and emotional content. Catullus wrote twenty-five poems expressing his intense response to their tumultuous love affair, chronicling his alternating ecstasy when Clodia requited his love and his doubt, jealousy, and anger when she betrayed him. When he decided to end his relationship with Clodia, he wrote about his resignation and self-pity.

After Catullus left Clodia, he traveled to Asia with one of his friends. During these travels, Catullus's brother suddenly died in Troy, and he was buried there. Catullus returned home by way of Troy so he could visit his brother's grave. The loss of both Clodia and his beloved brother caused Catullus to feel alone and abandoned.

Roman poets typically chose historic subjects, such as wars, and expressed their tragic themes in formal verse. Catullus became the first Roman poet to choose subjects from his own experiences. His emotions appear to splash upon the page as spontaneous, direct, and casual expressions of his current state of mind. His poems vary in length, tone, style, and subject. Some of his poems are based on Greek myth; some express friendship and love; others are satires. Some excoriate Roman politicians, while others amuse friends with humorous teasing.

The following poem (number 65) is a poetic letter to his friend "Ortalus"— probably Quintus Hortensius Hortalus (114–50 B.C.), a famous Roman orator. Apparently Hortalus had asked Catullus to translate some of Callimachus's poems into Latin and this poem accompanied the requested translations. Callimachus was a highly esteemed Greek poet and scholar who worked in Alexandria, Egypt, during the Hellenistic Age; Catullus's translation of Callimachus's "The Lock of Berenice" appears as Catallus's poem number 66. "Though heart's hurt exhausts me always now" has a double focus: the sudden death of Catullus's brother at Troy and the belated translations. Catullus expresses himself in the direct conversational style that he made famous.

Though heart's hurt exhausts me always now, and I cannot enjoy
the company of those learned girls, the Muses,
or sweetly bring to birth a verse—
Terrible things have happened, my mind
hovers, incapable, in shock—   5

My brother just crossed the river Lethe, that coldest stream of all's
washed his pale feet. Yanked out of sight
—engulfed by earth,
Trojan soil heaped heavy over him on the shore of Rhoetum.

Brother, I loved you more than life, I'll never see you now. Always I'll   10
    love you,
always sing sadder because of your death,
songs like those the nightingale sings, perched in thickest treeshade, weeping
    her lost love.

Even though I grieve, Ortalus, I send you these poems of Callimachus,
wrung from the Greek into Latin for you,
lest you think your wishes have vanished from my mind   15
like words in the wind, forgotten

like that apple (a lover's secret gift)
the girl in the story hid in a soft fold of clothing—when her mother came in
she stood up, it fell out, shot headlong across the floor
while a guilty blush overspread   20
her sad face.

UNDERSTANDING THE POEM

1. How has the companionship of the Muses enriched Catullus's life? Why is Catullus unable to enjoy the Muses now?

2. How will his brother's death continue to affect Catullus's life?

3. How is Catullus's surprise at his brother's death an issue in this poem?

4. Why does Catullus combine the death of his brother with his need to send his friend translations of Callimachus's poems?

ANALYZING LITERARY TECHNIQUE

1. What does Catullus achieve by using the technique of **apostrophe,** in which he addresses his brother and later Ortalus as if his brother were alive and both men were present?

2. What do Catullus's **allusions** contribute to the poem? Consider the Muses and Lethe.

3. What do **similes** contribute to the poem? Consider "songs like those the nightingale sings" and "your wishes have vanished . . . / like words in the wind."

4. What does Catullus's **Homeric simile** about the girl and the apple contribute to the poem?

5. What do the verbs "bring to birth," "hovers," "yanked," and "wrung" contribute to the poem?

6. What two distinct **themes** are present in this poem?

7. Describe the two distinct **tones** of this poem. How does Catullus achieve these tones? How effective is the use of dual tones?

8. What makes this poem an **elegy?** A **lyric poem?**

WRITING ABOUT LITERATURE

1. Write an essay in which you discuss Catullus's style in this poem. In separate paragraphs, consider the poet's use of conversation, allusion, and **figurative language.** Use quotations from the poem to support your ideas. In a concluding paragraph, evaluate the effect of this poet's style.

2. Write an essay in which you analyze Catullus's tone in this poem. In separate paragraphs, consider the poet's dual themes of sorrow and guilt. Use quotations from the poem to support your ideas. In your concluding paragraph, evaluate the effectiveness of the double focus.

3. Write a piece in prose or in poetry in which you express your feelings about a real or imagined loss. Refer to the past, the present, and the future. Use similes and metaphors so that comparisons will convey the depth of your feelings. Choose your words carefully, making each word express what you want to say.

Two Eclipses

SHMUEL HANAGID

S HMUEL HANAGID (993–1056) lived in medieval Muslim Spain during the Hebrew and Muslim literary renaissance that has become known as Spain's Golden Age. HaNagid was a great Hebrew poet as well as a rabbi and Talmudic scholar. In addition, as vizier (governor) of the Muslim state of Granada, he was one of the foremost political leaders of his time. HaNagid wrote three books of poetry: *Ben Tehillim (Son of Psalms); Ben Mishle (Son of Proverbs);* and *Ben Kohelet (Son of Ecclesiastes).* Written for aristocrats in Andalusia (a region in southern Spain), these books relate the present with the past and the Koranic heritage of the Muslim people to the biblical heritage of the Jewish people.

The man who later became known as Shmuel HaNagid (Samuel the Governor) was born Shmuel ben Yosef HaLevi ibn Nagrela (Samuel, son of Joseph the Levite) in Cordoba, Spain. The son of prosperous Jewish parents, HaLevi was educated in Hebrew, Arabic, and Greek literature and culture. As a young adult he probably became a spice merchant, a career that would have familiarized him with the great trade routes—both over sea and over land—that connected the Far East with western Europe. HaLevi was both a great scholar and an international trader, pursuits that served him well in the economic and political environment in which he lived.

When Berber armies from North Africa conquered Cordoba in 1013, HaLevi took refuge further south, in Malaga, where he continued his spice business. Because of HaLevi's standing in the Jewish community, the vizier of the Berber court at Granada appointed him tax collector of Spain's Jewish population; later he became the vizier's assistant. In 1027 HaLevi became the first Spanish governor (Nagid) of the Jewish community in Spain. Finally, ten years later, the son of the old king made HaLevi chief vizier of the Muslim state of Granada and commander-in-chief of Granada's Muslim army. For sixteen years, HaLevi/HaNagid was active both on and off the battlefield. Under his leadership, Granada became one of the strongest and richest states in Andalusia. Until his death in Granada, HaNagid worked on behalf of the Jewish and the Muslim people in Spain and in the Middle East.

HaNagid uses biblical themes as well as biblical language in his poetry. Proud of his religious and literary heritage, HaNagid referred to himself as the "David of my age." In medieval Muslim Spain, Muslim poets would "light one flame from another" by using phrases from the Koran to express their own thoughts and feelings. The Hebrew poets in Muslim Spain were familiar with the language and style of Arabic literature, and they adopted this technique, kindling their flames from the Bible.

HaNagid's poems are often autobiographical; HaNagid wrote about friendship and love, war and death, God, nature, and old age. Because of his experiences as a warrior, it is not surprising the poems he wrote to his son from the battlefield and those that he wrote to express his thoughts about God are among his best poems.

"Two Eclipses" is found in HaNagid's *Ben Kohelet (Son of Ecclesiastes)*. This collection includes poems inspired by natural phenomena and poems inspired by human mortality. "Two Eclipses" combines both themes. It was probably inspired by the lunar eclipse on the night of November 8, 1044, and the solar eclipse on the morning of November 22, 1044. HaNagid interprets the eclipses as his forefathers interpreted them—as signs of God's divine power. The eclipses made him fear God's judgment. The poem's images, which are based on well-known biblical images, give the poem power.

My friend, are you sleeping?
Rise and wake the dawn,
    look up at the sky
like a leopard skin stippled above us,
and see the moon where it should be full,   5
        go dark like a kettle, or kiln,
    like the face of a girl—
    half of it flushed,
the other darkened in shadow.
    Return and glance at the sun,   10
brought to the end of the month in dimness,
        its halo of light on the darkness,
like a crown on the head of a Libyan princess,
    and the earth whose sun has set,
        reddened—as though with tears.   15

Both of the beacons were stricken
        in the space of a single month
by Him whose dominion is splendor and strength;

He covered the moon with His circle of earth,
           and the sun with His moon: 20
this is the work of the Lord who toys with creation.

    He fashioned patches of dark in the moon,
        and the sun He created clear,
    therefore I liken them now
in their dimness against the dark,   25
        to women bereaved:
             the face of the one is bruised,
        the other both bruised and wounded—
the light of day on a day gone dim,
and the light of night darkened at evening   30
        during the watch.
    Like an angry king who brings trouble
      on his lords in their own domains,
    first He struck the brightness of night,
      and afterwards blotted the daylight,   35
    like a king who prepared a poisonous cup
      for his mistress, and then for his queen.
Behold what happened—look closely in wonder,
    study it well, and read:

        Yours is the greatness,   40
who brought the light in its weight and measure,
    and darkened the moon at its cycle's center,
      like a bird caught in a snare.
    You'll do it again in five months more;
      looking onto the earth,   45
you'll make it reel like a drunkard.
You've ordered the moth and it eats
    the Bear and Orion in great constellation;
you fixed for the living among them
    a place like a shield;   50
and all when you rule will be trodden as one,
    though not with a shout in a winepress.

Yours is the glory, yours entire,
    every horse and chariot houghed.[1]
It's you who brings on heat in winter,   55
    and winter, at summer's height;
      you who upends the abyss,
who brings affliction into the sea

---

[1] *houghed:* Hamstrung.

like a woman in labor;
you who'll cast toward all the living—death,　　　　　　　　60
　　　as the arrow flies to its target;
　　you on the bitter and great
　　and terrible day of judgment
　　who will wake me and judge
all who've forsaken the statues,[2]　　　　　　　　　　　65
　　　　commandments, and Law.

When you place my deeds in judgment's scale,
　　may the side of evil, lighter, rise.
　　On the day you lift me up from my dust
I'll turn and my spirit in fear of your wrath　　　　　　70
　　　will flee, and you'll say:
"Peace be upon you; be still, and do not fear."

If there remains not a trace of my righteousness,
　　may your mercy be near.

UNDERSTANDING THE POEM

1. How does the poet respond to the two eclipses?
2. What are the three examples given of God's beneficial creative power?
3. What are the five examples given of God's negative creative power?
4. Why does the poet fear his day of judgment?
5. What is the poet's ultimate consolation?
6. Compare and contrast "Two Eclipses" with Psalm 8.

ANALYZING LITERARY TECHNIQUE

1. Note how the poet has organized his thoughts. How does he begin and end his poem? How do the middle sections of the poem differ from the opening and closing sections?
2. Why is "Two Eclipses" considered a **lyric poem?**
3. Note the poet's use of **figurative language.**
   a) Why might the poet have chosen "leopard skin stippled" instead of "cloak star-studded" to describe the night sky?
   b) What does the poet's use of "kettle," "kiln," "face of a girl," and "Libyan princess" suggest?

---

[2] *statues:* Probably statutes, or laws.

c) Why might the poet have chosen "reddened—as though with tears" to describe the earth after sunset?

d) What kind of divinity "toys" with creation?

e) What does the poet suggest by describing the eclipsed moon and sun as "women bereaved," the moon with a "bruised" face, and the sun with a face that is "both bruised and wounded"?

f) Why does the poet choose to compare God to "an angry king who brings trouble / on his lords" and to "a king who prepared a poisonous cup / for his mistress, and then for his queen"?

g) Why does the poet choose to describe God in the following ways: (1) as He who darkened the moon "like a bird caught in a snare," (2) as He who will "make it [the earth] reel like a drunkard," and (3) as He who has made the earth into "a place like a shield" upon which all whom He rules "will be trodden"?

h) What does the poet's comparison of a woman in labor with an arrow reveal about the nature of God and the human condition?

4. HaNagid's figurative language is based on biblical sources that were familiar to his readers. How do the following two biblical passages enrich the ideas and attitudes that HaNagid is expressing?

a) (See lines 5–12) "And I will show wonders in the heavens and in the earth, / Blood, and fire, and pillars of smoke. / The sun shall be turned into darkness, / And the moon into blood, / Before the great and terrible day of the Lord come." (Joel 3:4)

b) (See lines 45–46) "The earth reeleth to and fro like a drunken man, / And swayeth to and fro as a lodge; / And the transgression thereof is heavy upon it, / And it shall fall, and not rise again." (Isaiah 24:20)

5. The scale of judgment is a common image in the literature of ancient Egypt and Greece, where the principal divinities used scales to judge the fate of human beings. What does this image reveal about life in ancient times? Why does the poet choose the scale as the closing image in this poem?

6. Why does the poet's figurative language allude to biblical passages that reveal God's power and anger rather than God's love and mercy? For example, compare lines 47–48 of the poem with Isaiah 51:8: "For the moth shall eat them up like a garment, / And the worm shall eat them like wool; / But My favor shall be for ever, / And My salvation unto all generations." Why does the poet ignore the last two lines of the biblical quotation?

7. Describe the **tone** of "Two Eclipses." How does the poet achieve the tone? To what extent, if any, does the tone of "Two Eclipses" differ from the tone of David's Psalm 8? How does David achieve the tone? Why does each poet aim to achieve the tone that he has chosen?

WRITING ABOUT LITERATURE

1. Write an essay in which you analyze the role and importance of three **similes** in this poem. You will need to explain each figure of speech and then relate it to the poem as a whole.

2. Write an essay in which you compare and contrast the tone of "Two Eclipses" with the tone of David's Psalm 8. Consider what each poet chooses to emphasize about God, about human beings, and about the relationship between God and human beings. Use quotations from the two poems to support your ideas.

3. Write an essay in which you analyze the effect of three biblical allusions in HaNagid's poem. (You will find three biblical quotations in **A.L.T.** questions 4 and 6 above.) Write an introductory paragraph in which you explain the poet's ideas and attitudes in this poem. Then analyze each biblical source in a separate paragraph. Conclude your essay with a paragraph in which you explain what these three biblical sources contribute to the poem as a whole.

4. Write a poem or story in which you describe an event in nature and your personal response to it. Consider how you react to the beauty of a sunrise or sunset; the silent shadows of a fog; or (if you have experienced one) a hurricane, a tornado, or a flood. Compare and contrast by using figurative language that expresses your thoughts and feelings.

Because you
know you're young
in beauty yet

DANTE ALIGHIERI

*D*ANTE ALIGHIERI (1265–1321) is best known
for the *Divine Comedy,* a work that many consider to
be the greatest poem, of the Middle Ages, and for
making Italian a literary language. He also wrote a series of love
poems (*The New Life,* 1291) about Beatrice, a young woman he had
seen from afar but never met, who symbolizes goodness, beauty, and
perfection.

Dante was born into a noble family in Florence at a time when
the city was a small thriving Italian republic. He was reared as an aristocrat, receiving a fine education in the classics, theology, philosophy,
and science. He lived in turbulent political times, when his city was
often torn between rival factions.

In 1302, while he was visiting Rome on political business, a change
in power in Florence caused Dante to be wrongly convicted of corruption and graft. His property was confiscated, and he was sentenced to
death. After joining a group of similarly convicted citizens in an
unsuccessful revolution, he was forced to choose between lifelong
exile and death by fire.

Dante was never able to return to Florence. Lacking both powerful
friends and financial resources, and with as yet no literary reputation,
he traveled from city to city, dependent on whatever patronage he
could acquire. By the time he died nineteen years later in Ravenna,
Italy, he had become a famous and honored writer.

An important element in much of Dante's poetry is courtly love,
a tradition that developed and flowered in European poetry of the
twelfth century. Poets writing in this tradition emphasized the joys
and sorrows of love. They wrote about beautiful and virtuous women
of nobility whom knights adored with an idealized love and whom
they served by performing courageous deeds. They also wrote about
heartsick and angry knights whose love for those women was unrequited. Initially, while poets were treating women and love as serious
subjects, contemporary feudal society viewed women as a general

group rather than as individuals, love as irrelevant to marriage, and marriage as an institution that fostered the economic and political ambitions of the nobility. However, the literature of courtly love was so popular that, in time, it became influential in raising women's status in society. Given Dante's stature as a poet, the role of women in his poetry contributed to that development. The following poem, like many of his poems and songs, deals with some aspect of love.

Because you know you're young in beauty yet
And stir the mind to Love you once look toward,
With pride like stone your maiden heart is barred.

You turn a proud and stonelike face to me
Because you feel my death is worth a try: 5
I think that you have done it just to see
Whether by force of Love a man can die.
But though you find none loves you more than I,
For grief I bear, you show me no regard.
Love take you then, and let his rule be hard!   10

UNDERSTANDING THE POEM

1. What attitude does the speaker accuse the woman of having toward him? Is he correct in his analysis of why she has rejected him? What other possible reasons could she have for her actions?

2. Why does the speaker persist in loving someone who does not love him?

3. What is the speaker's state of mind? How do his emotions affect his actions?

4. Should the woman treat the speaker with greater sympathy and understanding? Why or why not?

ANALYZING LITERARY TECHNIQUE

1. What does Dante's use of **apostrophe** achieve in the poem?

2. What is the central image in the poem? How does the image work to convey the speaker's emotions?

3. Examine the structure of this poem. What happens in each **stanza?** How do the two stanzas relate to each other?

WRITING ABOUT LITERATURE

1. Write an essay in which you analyze the relationship between this poem and the tradition of **courtly love** that is described in the introductory material. Consider the nature of the speaker's love for the woman and the extent to which his emotions are characteristic of anyone whose feelings for another are not reciprocated. In your conclusion, evaluate the role that sincerity of emotion plays in this poem.

2. Take the woman's part in this poem and tell the story of the relationship from her **point of view.** You may choose to write in either poetry or prose. Consider the personalities, needs, and interests of both the woman and the man.

Torn Lace

EMILIA PARDO BAZÁN

MILIA PARDO BAZÁN (1851–1921) is one of the most important nineteenth-century Spanish authors. She was a prolific writer—publishing twenty novels, twenty-one novellas, seven plays, almost six hundred short stories, and hundreds of literary essays during her career. She is renowned for her feminist point of view as well as for the quality of her writing.

Pardo Bazán's stories cover a broad spectrum of themes, including folklore, mystery, patriotism, religion, and social issues. Among her favorite themes are the female/male relationship and the nature of love. Her favorite literary techniques include a focus on psychological realism through the use of multiple female narrators and the concept of the epiphany (a spontaneous and superficially trivial event that causes a sudden and profound change in the observer's attitude and behavior). Most of Pardo Bazán's stories appeared first in magazines or in literary journals. However, she later made revisions to the stories and published them in a forty-four volume set entitled *Complete Works*. It was not until 1993 that a collection of Pardo Bazán's short stories, *The White Horse and Other Stories*, first appeared in English translation. *Torn Lace and Other Stories* appeared in 1996.

Pardo Bazán was born in Galicia, a province in northwestern Spain. Although most young women of her social class were taught only French, piano, and embroidery, she was well educated and well read. When she was fifteen, her parents arranged for her to marry a law student. Five years later, in 1871, she won a literary contest with an essay on a feminist eighteenth-century writer. In 1876 she published her first book of poetry, and in 1879 she published her first novel.

In 1883, however, Pardo Bazán aroused public controversy by publishing a provocative essay in which she criticized the philosophical and literary theories of Émile Zola, the French novelist who had founded the literary movement known as naturalism. Her audience chastised her because they thought that a proper woman should not have read an author who, under the banner of naturalism, depicted all that could be found in the gutters of life. Pardo Bazán's husband responded to this public criticism by demanding that she stop writing and content herself with being a housewife and mother. Pardo Bazán refused. Declaring her independence (divorce was not an option), she took their three children and left, choosing to live with her mother and continue her career. In 1891 and 1892, she published a monthly literary journal that contained her essays and a short story.

Pardo Bazán was an ardent feminist. Although she was a professional writer for close to forty years, the short stories she wrote between 1890 and 1914 reveal her attitudes and values at the peak of her career. Her writing focuses on women's issues, such as limited education, problems in the business world, the double standard in sexual issues, and sexual abuse after marriage. With the hope of increasing women's knowledge and self-awareness, she published the multivolume *Woman's Library*, which contained translations of important feminist works. However, the continuing failure of this venture led her to give up on women's rights; in 1913 she concluded the *Library* with the publication of two cookbooks. Finally in 1915 Pardo Bazán's importance as a writer enabled her to become the first female professor (of modern romance literatures) at a Spanish university (the University of Madrid).

The following story, "Torn Lace," is an excellent example of how Pardo Bazán's literary techniques reveal her feminist point of view and includes two of her favorite themes—the female/male relationship and the nature of love. Particularly important are her use of the narrator and the epiphany to convey psychological realism. In human relationships, any incident—no matter how apparently trivial—that enables a person to gain a significant insight into another person's personality and values will inevitably have an important effect upon the observer's attitudes and behavior. At the time the story was written, many of Pardo Bazán's readers considered the feminist values in this story to be ultra modern.

I was invited to the wedding of Micaelita Aránguiz and Bernardo de Meneses, and, being unable to attend, was greatly surprised to learn the following morning—the ceremony had been scheduled for ten o'clock in the evening at the bride's house—that when the bishop of San Juan de Acre asked the bride if she took Bernardo for her husband, she let loose—at the very foot of the altar—with a resounding and energetic "No!" When the question was repeated with astonishment and elicited yet another negative, the groom, after facing for a quarter of an hour the most ridiculous situation in the world, had no choice but to depart, dissolving the gathering and the engagement at the same time.

Such incidents are not unheard-of; we read of them frequently in the newspapers, but they involve people of humble means, in circles where social conventions don't hamper the frank and spontaneous manifestation of sentiment and the will.

What was peculiar about the scene created by Micaelita was the setting in which it occurred. I could picture it in my mind and was very disappointed not to have witnessed it with my own eyes. I imagined the crowded salon; the carefully chosen guests: the ladies dressed in velvet and silk, with necklaces of precious stones, and with white mantillas on their arms, ready to be put over their heads at the proper moment during the ceremony; men resplendent with medals or sporting military insignias on the front of their frock coats; the bride's mother, richly ornamented, solicitous, busily circulating from group to group and accepting congratulations; the bride's sisters filled with emotion and looking very pretty, the eldest in pink and the youngest in blue, displaying the turquoise bracelets that were gifts from their future brother-in-law; the bishop who was to conduct the ceremony, alternately grave and affable, smiling, deigning to recite polite jokes or discreet praise. In the background one would discern the chapel bedecked with flowers, a flood of white roses from the floor to the little cupola, where spokes of snowlike lilacs and roses converged over artistically arranged green boughs; while on the altar stood the statue of the Virgin, protectoress of the aristocratic mansion, partly veiled by a curtain of orange blossoms, a carload of which were sent from Valencia by the very wealthy businessman Aránguiz, uncle and godfather of the bride, who couldn't come in person because of age and infirmity. These details would be circulated by word of mouth, fueling estimates of the magnificent inheritance that would belong to Micaelita—one more source of happiness for the couple, who were to spend their honeymoon in Valencia. In a group of gentlemen, I pictured the groom, somewhat nervous, slightly pale, biting his mustache distractedly, nodding in acknowledgment of the restrained jokes and the words of flattery addressed to him . . .

And, finally, in the doorway leading to the inner rooms of the house, I see a kind of apparition: the bride, whose features are barely distinguishable through a cloud of tulle, her silk gown rustling as she passes, the antique stones of her nuptial jewelry glistening like dewdrops on her hair . . . The ceremony gets under way now: the couple goes forward, led by the best man and the matron of honor, the pure white figure kneels next to the trim and dapper groom . . . the family crowds up front to get the best view of friends and onlookers, and, amidst the silence and the respectful attention of those present, the bishop poses a question, to which a "No" is fired back, sharp as a shot, solid as a bullet. In my imagination, I note the groom's movements as he squirms, wounded; the mother's rush forward as if to defend and protect her daughter; the insistent repetition of the bishop, expressing his astonishment; the shudder of the congregation; the anxious question that spreads in an instant: "What's going on? What is it? Has the bride taken ill? She says no? Impossible! But can it be? What a story!"

All this, in the context of our social life, constitutes a terrible drama. In the case of Micaelita, it was not only drama but also a puzzle. The reason for her refusal never became known.

Micaelita would say only that she had changed her mind and that she was free to turn back, even at the foot of the altar, as long as "I do" hadn't left her lips. Those well acquainted with her family wracked their brains, inventing unlikely explanations. What was certain was that until the fatal moment, the bride and groom had seemed to be happy and very much in love; and the girlfriends who went in to admire the beautifully dressed bride, moments before the scandal, recounted that she was mad with joy and so thrilled and satisfied that she wouldn't have changed places with anybody. These facts served to obscure further the strange enigma that for a long time was a source of gossip for a vexed society ready to offer the most unfavorable explanations for it.

Three years later—when almost no one remembered what happened at Micaelita's wedding—I ran into her in the spa that was currently in fashion, where her mother was taking the mineral baths. Nothing facilitates friendship like resort life, and Miss Aránguiz became such a close friend of mine that one afternoon, on the way to church, she revealed her secret to me, saying that she allowed me to disclose it because she was certain that no one would believe such a simple explanation.

"It was the silliest thing . . . so silly that I refused to speak about it; people always attribute profound and transcendental causes to events, not noticing that our fate is sometimes determined by trifles, the most unimportant little things . . . But they're little things that mean something, and for some people they mean too much. I'll tell you what happened; and I can't imagine why no one realized, because it happened right there, in front of everybody; only they didn't notice because it was really just in the twinkling of an eye.

"You know that my marriage to Bernardo de Meneses seemed to bring every guarantee for happiness. Besides, I confess that I very much liked my fiancé, more than any man I knew or know; I think I was in love with him. The only thing I regretted was not being able to study his character—some people thought him violent, but around me he always was courteous, deferential, soft as a glove. I feared that he was putting up a front to dupe me and conceal a fierce and sour disposition. A thousand times I cursed the helplessness of a single woman, for whom it is impossible to trail her fiancé's every move, thoroughly investigate the truth, and obtain reliable information, frank to the point of harshness—the only kind of information that would put me at ease. I tried to test Bernardo in many ways, and he did well; his behavior was so correct that I came to believe that I could unreservedly entrust my future and my happiness to him.

"The day of the wedding arrived. When I was putting on the white gown, despite my natural excitement, I noticed once again the superb lace that adorned it and that was a gift from my fiancé. That old genuine Alençon[1] was a family heirloom. It was exquisitely designed, a third of a meter wide—a marvel—beautifully preserved and worthy of a museum. Bernardo had given it to me, extolling its worth, which began to exasperate me, for no matter how much the lace was worth, my intended should believe that I deserved more.

"In that solemn moment, when I saw it set off against the dense satin of my gown, it seemed to me that the delicate design of the lace signified a promise of happiness and that its weave, so fragile and yet so strong, captured two hearts in

---

[1] *Alençon:* Lace made in Alençon, France, that is often used for bridal gowns.

its tenuous mesh. I was immersed in these musings as I began to walk toward the parlor, where my fiancé waited at the door. As I was rushing to greet him for the last time before belonging to him body and soul, full of joy, the lace got caught on the wrought iron of the door, so unluckily that when I tried to free myself, I heard the distinctive sound of a rip, and I could see that a length of the magnificent trim lay dangling over my skirt. But I saw something else—Bernardo's face, contorted and disfigured by the most vivid rage; his eyes blazing like coals, his mouth already half open to issue a rebuke and an insult . . . He didn't get that far, because he was surrounded by people; but in that brief moment a curtain was parted, exposing a naked soul behind it.

"I must have turned pale; fortunately, the tulle of my veil covered my face. Something cracked and shattered into pieces inside me, and the joy with which I had crossed the threshold of the salon turned into a profound horror. I still saw Bernardo before me with that expression of rage, cruelty, and contempt that I had just glimpsed in his face; this idea took hold of me, and with it came another one: that I couldn't, that I wouldn't give myself to such a man, not then, not ever . . . Nonetheless I kept walking toward the altar, knelt, listened to the bishop's exhortations . . . But when I was asked, the truth sprang to my lips, impetuous and terrible . . .

"That *no* sprang forth without my meaning it to; I was saying it to myself . . . so that all could hear!"

"But why didn't you reveal the reason when it was talked about so much?"

"I repeat: because of the very simplicity of it . . . They would never have believed me. The natural and commonplace is never accepted. I preferred to let it be thought there were reasons of the sort they call *serious* . . ."

UNDERSTANDING THE STORY

1. Why is it important that the narrator did not attend the wedding?

2. Why does the author have the narrator imagine the wedding scene in such detail?

3. What marred Micaelita's love for Bernardo?

4. What behavior of Bernardo's first motivated Micaelita to question his character?

5. What is the **epiphany** in this story, and what does it reveal to whom?

6. To what extent, if any, did Micaelita have valid reasons for breaking off her wedding?

7. Why is "Torn Lace" an appropriate title for this story?

8. What **themes** does this story contain?

9. What gives this story its power? To what extent would the story have been as powerful if Micaelita had ignored Bernardo's response and married him?

ANALYZING LITERARY TECHNIQUE

1. From whose **point of view** is this story told? What does the point of view contribute to the story?

2. How does the author reveal Bernardo's character in this story?

3. To what extent, if any, is the author's use of an epiphany an effective literary device in this story?

4. Consider the author's use of **figurative language.** Explain what is effective about each of the following:
   a) **simile:** "his eyes blazing like coals."
   b) **metaphor:** "Its weave . . . captured two hearts in its tenuous mesh."
   c) metaphor: "Something cracked and shattered into pieces inside me."
   d) metaphor: "A curtain was parted, exposing a naked soul behind it."
   e) **symbol:** "The delicate design of the lace signified a promise of happiness."

5. How does the author use **foreshadowing** in this story? What is the significance of the foreshadowing?

6. Describe the particular events that create the **crisis,** the **climax,** and the **resolution** of the **plot.**

WRITING ABOUT LITERATURE

1. Write an expository essay in which you analyze the importance of point of view in this story. In your introductory paragraph, define point of view. In each of the next three paragraphs (the body of your essay), explain what the following points of view would have contributed to the story: (a) Micaelita's, (b) Bernardo's (c) an acquaintance's. In your concluding paragraph, explain why the author chose to tell this story from an acquaintance's point of view.

2. Tell this story from Bernardo's point of view. Explain his reaction to the torn lace. Reveal the extent to which he realizes that it was his reaction that provoked Micaelita to leave him standing at the altar. Either have him justify his behavior despite the consequences, or have him learn from this experience and change his ways.

3. Write a story in which one character's response to a particular situation reveals such an important aspect of her or his personality that an epiphany causes a great change in an observer's attitude and behavior.

War

LUIGI PIRANDELLO

*L*UIGI PIRANDELLO (1867–1936), the Italian dramatist, is one of the preeminent writers of the twentieth century. His focus on the social masks that people wear has been a major influence on modern fiction as well as on modern drama. In 1934 he was awarded the Nobel Prize for his "bold and ingenious revival of dramatic and scenic art." He is also the author of approximately three hundred short stories and is considered to be the greatest Italian writer of short stories since Giovanni Boccaccio (1313–1375). Pirandello is best known for the plays *Six Characters in Search of an Author* (1921), *Right You Are if You Think You Are* (1922), and *Henry IV* (1922).

Pirandello was born in Agrigento, Sicily, to wealthy parents. He attended universities in Rome, Italy, and Bonn, Germany. As a young adult, he taught Italian literature and wrote poetry, short stories, and novels. At the age of twenty-seven, he married the daughter of his father's business partner. The family's sulphur mining business supported Pirandello as an author until the business failed, an event that caused his wife to lose her reason. Pirandello chose not to institutionalize her but rather to care for her at home until she died in 1918. In 1913, at the age of forty-six, Pirandello became a playwright and introduced to world theater the symbolic psychological dramas that anticipated French and German existentialism and the theater of the absurd. The international fame that he achieved in the 1920s enabled him to retire from teaching and to travel with a theater group that performed his plays.

Pirandello was fascinated by the contrast between appearance and reality in human behavior. He viewed life as a series of illusions, each concealing a surprising core: comedy in tragedy, sanity in madness, grief in happiness. He saw people as suffering from the necessity of leading insincere public lives, and he watched with compassion as they clung to their delusions. He created literature that he hoped would force people to examine their convictions, acknowledge their inner selves, and lead more authentic lives. "War" is a fine example of Pirandello's work.

The passengers who had left Rome by the night express had had to stop until dawn at the small station of Fabriano[1] in order to continue their journey by the small old-fashioned "local" joining the main line with Sulmona.[2]

At dawn, in a stuffy and smoky second-class carriage in which five people had already spent the night, a bulky woman in deep mourning was hoisted in— almost like a shapeless bundle. Behind her—puffing and moaning, followed her husband—a tiny man, thin and weakly, his face death-white, his eyes small and bright and looking shy and uneasy.

Having at last taken a seat he politely thanked the passengers who had helped his wife and who had made room for her; then he turned round to the woman try-ing to pull down the collar of her coat and politely enquired:

"Are you all right, dear?"

The wife, instead of answering, pulled up her collar again to her eyes, so as to hide her face.

"Nasty world," muttered the husband with a sad smile.

And he felt it his duty to explain to his travelling companions that the poor woman was to be pitied, for the war was taking away from her her only son, a boy of twenty to whom both had devoted their entire life, even breaking up their home at Sulmona to follow him to Rome where he had to go as a student, then allowing him to volunteer for war with an assurance, however, that at least for six months he would not be sent to the front and now, all of a sudden, receiving a wire saying that he was due to leave in three days' time and asking them to go and see him off.

The woman under the big coat was twisting and wriggling, at times growling like a wild animal, feeling certain that all those explanations would not have aroused even a shadow of sympathy from those people who—most likely—were in the same plight as herself. One of them, who had been listening with particular attention, said:

"You should thank God that your son is only leaving now for the front. Mine has been sent there the first day of the war. He has already come back twice wounded and been sent back again to the front."

"What about me? I have two sons and three nephews at the front," said another passenger.

"Maybe, but in our case it is our *only* son," ventured the husband.

---

[1] *Fabriano:* A town to the northeast of Rome.
[2] *Sulmona:* A town east of Rome.

"What difference can it make? You may spoil your only son with excessive attentions, but you cannot love him more than you would all your other children if you had any. Paternal love is not like bread that can be broken into pieces and split amongst the children in equal shares. A father gives *all* his love to each one of his children without discrimination, whether it be one or ten, and if I am suffering now for my two sons, I am not suffering half for each of them but double . . ."

"True . . . true . . ." sighed the embarrassed husband, "but suppose (of course we all hope it will never be your case) a father has two sons at the front and he loses one of them, there is still one left to console him . . . while . . ."

"Yes," answered the other, getting cross, "a son left to console him but also a son left for whom he must survive, while in the case of the father of an only son if the son dies the father can die too and put an end to his distress. Which of the two positions is the worse? Don't you see how my case would be worse than yours?"

"Nonsense," interrupted another traveller, a fat, red-faced man with bloodshot eyes of the palest grey.

He was panting. From his bulging eyes seemed to spurt inner violence of an uncontrolled vitality which his weakened body could hardly contain.

"Nonsense," he repeated, trying to cover his mouth with his hand so as to hide the two missing front teeth. "Nonsense. Do we give life to our children for our own benefit?"

The other travellers stared at him in distress. The one who had had his son at the front since the first day of the war sighed: "You are right. Our children do not belong to us, they belong to the Country. . . ."

"Bosh," retorted the fat traveller. "Do we think of the Country when we give life to our children? Our sons are born because . . . well, because they must be born and when they come to life they take our own life with them. This is the truth. We belong to them but they never belong to us. And when they reach twenty they are exactly what we were at their age. We too had a father and mother, but there were so many other things as well . . . girls, cigarettes, illusions, new ties . . . and the Country, of course, whose call we would have answered—when we were twenty—even if father and mother had said no. Now, at our age, the love of our Country is still great, of course, but stronger than it is the love for our children. Is there any one of us here wouldn't gladly take his son's place at the front if he could?"

There was a silence all around, everybody nodding as to approve.

"Why then," continued the fat man, "shouldn't we consider the feelings of our children when they are twenty? Isn't it *natural* that at their age they should consider the love for their Country (I am speaking of decent boys, of course) even greater than the love for us? Isn't it *natural* that it should be so, as after all they must look upon us as upon old boys who cannot move any more and must stay at home? If Country exists, if Country is a natural necessity like bread, of which each of us must eat in order not to die of hunger, somebody must go to defend it. And our sons go, when they are twenty, and they don't want tears, because if they die, they die inflamed and happy (I am speaking, of course, of decent boys). Now, if one dies young and happy, without having the ugly sides of life, the boredom of it, the pettiness, the bitterness of disillusion . . . what more can we ask for him?

Everyone should stop crying: everyone should laugh, as I do . . . or at least thank God—as I do—because my son, before dying, sent me a message saying that he was dying satisfied at having ended his life in the best way he could have wished. That is why, as you see, I do not even wear mourning. . . ."

He shook his light fawn coat as to show it; his livid lip over his missing teeth was trembling, his eyes were watery and motionless and soon after he ended with a shrill laugh which might well have been a sob.

"Quite so . . . quite so . . ." agreed the others.

The woman who, bundled in a corner under her coat, had been sitting and listening, had—for the last three months—tried to find in the words of her husband and her friends something to console her in her deep sorrow, something that might show her how a mother should resign herself to send her son not even to death but to a probable danger of life. Yet not a word had she found amongst the many which had been said . . . and her grief had been greater in seeing that nobody—as she thought—could share her feelings.

But now the words of the traveller amazed and almost stunned her. She suddenly realized that it wasn't the others who were wrong and could not understand her but herself who could not rise up to the same height of those fathers and mothers willing to resign themselves, without crying, not only to the departure of their sons but even to their death.

She lifted her head, she bent over from her corner trying to listen with great attention to the details which the fat man was giving to his companions about the way his son had fallen as a hero, for his King and his Country, happy and without regrets. It seemed to her that she had stumbled into a world she had never dreamt of, a world so far unknown to her, and she was so pleased to hear everyone joining in congratulating that brave father who could so stoically speak of his child's death.

Then suddenly, just as if she had heard nothing of what had been said and almost as if waking up from a dream, she turned to the old man, asking him:

"Then . . . is your son really dead?"

Everybody stared at her. The old man, too, turned to look at her, fixing his great, bulging, horribly watery light grey eyes, deep in her face. For some little time he tried to answer, but words failed him. He looked and looked at her, almost as if only then—at that silly, incongruous question—he had suddenly realized at last that his son was really dead . . . gone for ever . . . for ever. His face contracted, became horribly distorted, then he snatched in haste a handkerchief from his pocket and, to the amazement of everyone, broke into harrowing, heart-rending, uncontrollable sobs.

UNDERSTANDING THE STORY

1. Why doesn't Pirandello give the characters names?

2. What point does Pirandello make about a parent's love for a child?

3. What does the fat man mean when he says, "We belong to them but they never belong to us"?

4. Why does the woman ask the fat man whether his son has really died?

5. Why is the fat man described as "the old man" at the end of the story?

6. What is Pirandello's attitude toward patriotism in this story? How do you interpret the fat man's expression "decent boys"?

7. What **themes** do you find in this story?

ANALYZING LITERARY TECHNIQUE

1. Both the woman in mourning and the fat man are described as hiding their faces. Why is this an important descriptive detail?

2. How does Pirandello achieve **characterization** when the characters have no names?

3. What is the **conflict** in this story? Is the conflict primarily *external* (a struggle between a character and an outside force) or *internal* (a struggle within the character himself or herself)?

4. What is the **climax** of this story?

5. How does Pirandello use the technique of **reversal?**

6. What is the central **irony** of the story?

WRITING ABOUT LITERATURE

1. "War" is a very short story, yet it has a powerful emotional impact. Write an essay in which you analyze how Pirandello achieves this impact. Consider his use of characterization and irony and the structure of the story. Use quotations from the story to support your ideas.

2. Write a poem in which you examine some aspect of war, such as the call of patriotism, the opportunity for heroism, the destruction and carnage of battle, the toll on loved ones, or the idea of self-sacrifice. Once you have chosen your focus, think about the emotions that it stimulates. Then express your ideas either in prose or as images and phrases. Finally, create a poem from these ideas. Regardless of the method, choose words and images that convey the emotions you wish to communicate.

Lament for Ignacio Sánchez Mejías

FEDERICO GARCÍA LORCA

FEDERICO GARCÍA LORCA (1898–1936) is considered the greatest Spanish writer since Miguel de Cervantes
(1547–1616). He is best known for a collection of his poetry
Gypsy Ballads (1928); for his plays *Blood Wedding* (1933), *Yerma*
(1934), and *The House of Bernada Alba* (1936); and for his elegy,
"Lament for Ignacio Sánchez Mejías" (1935).

García Lorca was born into an affluent family in Granada, a
province in southern Spain. His father was a wealthy farmer, his
mother a fine concert pianist and teacher. The folklore, poetry, and
songs of Granada were an important part of his youth and had a lasting influence on his art. Manuel de Falla (1876–1946), the famous
Spanish composer, was his godfather and music teacher.

After studying law at the University of Granada, García Lorca
attended the University of Madrid. There he became a close friend of
avant-garde writers and artists, including Pablo Neruda and the surrealist painter Salvador Dalí. García Lorca had already begun his career as
a writer, publishing his first prose work in 1918. His first play appeared
in print in 1920, followed by his first book of poetry in 1921. García
Lorca publicly performed his poetry, reciting it while accompanying
himself on his guitar. From 1931 to 1935, the years of the Spanish
Republic, he directed a government-sponsored traveling theater
group called La Barraca, which performed classical and modern drama
(including his own tragedies) throughout Spain.

The Spanish civil war began in 1936. García Lorca felt safe
remaining in Granada because he was an artist, not a political
activist. However, his friendship with leftist intellectuals was well
known, and he was murdered by the Fascists, who dumped his body
into an unmarked grave. The Fascist government of General Francisco
Franco never discussed the matter, and García Lorca's works were
banned in Spain from 1936 until Francisco Franco died in 1975.

García Lorca developed a unique style of writing, one that combines the modern with the ancient and traditional, and lyricism with

drama. He expresses his ideas through images and metaphors. In his poetry and plays, death is part of life, and blood is the link between them.

García Lorca's "Lament for Ignacio Sánchez Mejías" is one of his masterpieces. It is a formal elegy for a fellow poet, good friend, and famous matador who died in a bullfight. In the poem, García Lorca ranges back and forth through time, using allusion to connect his dead friend to the bull-worship of ancient Crete, where the ritual sacrifices of heroic young men and women are thought to have been the original bullfights. Through this poem, García Lorca confers immortality on Sánchez Mejías and on himself as well.

1. Cogida[1] and Death

At five in the afternoon.
It was exactly five in the afternoon.
A boy brought the white sheet
at five in the afternoon.
A frail of lime[2] ready prepared   5
at five in the afternoon.
The rest was death, and death alone
at five in the afternoon.

The wind carried away the cottonwool
at five in the afternoon.   10
And the oxide scattered crystal and nickel
at five in the afternoon.

Now the dove and the leopard wrestle
at five in the afternoon.
And a thigh with a desolate horn   15
at five in the afternoon.
The bass-string struck up
at five in the afternoon.
Arsenic bells and smoke
at five in the afternoon.   20
Groups of silence in the corners
at five in the afternoon.
And the bull alone with a high heart!
At *five in the afternoon.*
When the sweat of snow was coming   25
at five in the afternoon,

---

[1] *Cogida:* Goring or tossing, as by a bull.
[2] *frail of lime:* A basket of quicklime. Quicklime used in burial will speed the decomposition of the body.

when the bull ring was covered in iodine
at five in the afternoon,
death laid eggs in the wound
at five in the afternoon.   30
At five in the afternoon.
Exactly at five o'clock in the afternoon.

A coffin on wheels is his bed
at five in the afternoon.
Bones and flutes resound in his ears   35
at five in the afternoon.
Now the bull was bellowing through his forehead
at five in the afternoon.
The room was iridescent with agony
at five in the afternoon.   40

In distance the gangrene now comes
at five in the afternoon.
Horn of the lily through green groins
at five in the afternoon.
The wounds were burning like suns   45
at five in the afternoon,
and the crowd was breaking the windows
at five in the afternoon.
At five in the afternoon.
Ah, that fatal five in the afternoon!   50
It was five by all the clocks!
It was five in the shade of the afternoon!

2.   *The Spilled Blood*

I will not see it!

Tell the moon to come
for I do not want to see the blood   55
of Ignacio on the sand.

I will not see it!

The moon wide open.
Horse of still clouds,
and the grey bull ring of dreams   60
with willows in the barreras.[3]

---

[3] *barreras:* First row of seats around a bullring.

I will not see it!

Let my memory kindle!
Warn the jasmines
of such minute whiteness!   65

I will not see it!

The cow of the ancient world
passed her sad tongue
over a snout of blood
spilled on the sand,   70
and the bulls of Guisando,[4]
partly death and partly stone,
bellowed like two centuries
sated with treading the earth.
No.   75
I do not want to see it!
I will not see it!

Ignacio goes up the tiers
with all his death on his shoulders.
He sought for the dawn   80
but the dawn was no more.
He seeks for his confident profile
and the dream bewilders him.
He sought for his beautiful body
and encountered his opened blood.   85
I will not see it!
I do not want to hear it spurt
each time with less strength:
that spurt that illuminates
the tiers of seats, and spills   90
over the corduroy and the leather
of a thirsty multitude.
Who shouts that I should come near!
Do not ask me to see it!

His eyes did not close   95
when he saw the horns near,
but the terrible mothers
lifted their heads.
And across the ranches,

---

[4] *Guisando:* Town in central Spain, located in the province of Avila.

an air of secret voices rose,   100
shouting to celestial bulls,
herdsmen of pale mist.
There was no prince in Seville[5]
who could compare with him,
nor sword like his sword   105
nor heart so true.

Like a river of lions
was his marvellous strength,
and like a marble torso
his firm drawn moderation.   110
The air of Andalusian Rome[6]
gilded his head
where his smile was a spikenard[7]
of wit and intelligence.
What a great torero[8] in the ring!   115
What a good peasant in the sierra![9]
How gentle with the sheaves!
How hard with the spurs!
How tender with the dew!
How dazzling in the fiesta![10]   120
How tremendous with the final
banderillas[11] of darkness!

But now he sleeps without end.
Now the moss and the grass
open with sure fingers   125
the flower of his skull.
And now his blood comes out singing;
singing along marshes and meadows,
sliding on frozen horns,
faltering soulless in the mist,   130
stumbling over a thousand hoofs
like a long, dark, sad tongue,
to form a pool of agony
close to the starry Guadalquivir.[12]

---

[5] *Seville:* City in Andalusia, a province in southwest Spain.

[6] *Andalusian Rome:* Seville.

[7] *spikenard:* A sweet-smelling salve.

[8] *torero:* Bullfighter.

[9] *sierra:* Mountain range.

[10] *fiesta:* Celebration or festival.

[11] banderillas: Barbed darts used in a bullfight.

[12] *Guadalquivir:* River that flows through Seville to the Atlantic.

Oh, white wall of Spain! 135
Oh, black bull of sorrow!
Oh, hard blood of Ignacio!
Oh, nightingale of his veins!

No.
I will not see it! 140
No chalice can contain it,
no swallows can drink it,
no frost of light can cool it,
nor song nor deluge of white lilies,
no glass can cover it with silver. 145
No.
I will not see it!

3.   *The Laid Out Body*

Stone is a forehead where dreams grieve
without curving waters and frozen cypresses.
Stone is a shoulder on which to bear Time 150
with trees formed of tears and ribbons and planets.

I have seen grey showers move towards the waves
raising their tender riddled arms,
to avoid being caught by the lying stone
which loosens their limbs without soaking the blood. 155

For stone gathers seed and clouds,
skeleton larks and wolves of penumbra:[13]
but yields not sounds nor crystals nor fire,
only bull rings and bull rings and more bull rings without walls.

Now, Ignacio the well born lies on the stone. 160
All is finished. What is happening? Contemplate his face:
death has covered him with pale sulphur
and has placed on him the head of a dark minotaur.[14]

All is finished. The rain penetrates his mouth.
The air, as if mad, leaves his sunken chest, 165
and Love, soaked through with tears of snow,
warms itself on the peak of the herd.

What are they saying? A stenching silence settles down.
We are here with a body laid out which fades away,

---

[13] *penumbra:* Outer shadowy regions.
[14] *minotaur:* A mythical creature with the head of a bull and the body of a man.

with a pure shape which had nightingales   170
and we see it being filled with depthless holes.

Who creases the shroud? What he says is not true!
Nobody sings here, nobody weeps in the corner,
nobody pricks the spurs, nor terrifies the serpent.
Here I want nothing else but the round eyes   175
to see this body without a chance of rest.

Here I want to see those men of hard voice.
Those that break horses and dominate rivers;
those men of sonorous skeleton who sing
with a mouth full of sun and flint.   180

Here I want to see them. Before the stone.
Before this body with broken reins.
I want to know from them the way out
for this captain strapped down by death.

I want them to show me a lament like a river   185
which will have sweet mists and deep shores,
to take the body of Ignacio where it loses itself
without hearing the double panting of the bulls.

Loses itself in the round bull ring of the moon
which feigns in its youth a sad quiet bull: 190
loses itself in the night without song of fishes
and in the white thicket of frozen smoke.

I don't want them to cover his face with handkerchiefs
that he may get used to the death he carries.
Go, Ignacio; feel not the hot bellowing.   195
Sleep, fly, rest: even the sea dies!

4.   *Absent Soul*

The bull does not know you, nor the fig tree,
nor the horses, nor the ants in your own house.
The child and the afternoon do not know you
because you have died for ever.   200

The back of the stone does not know you,
nor the black satin in which you crumble.
Your silent memory does not know you
because you have died for ever.

The autumn will come with small white snails,   205
misty grapes and with clustered hills,
but no one will look into your eyes
because you have died for ever.

Because you have died for ever,
like all the dead of the Earth,   210
like all the dead who are forgotten
in a heap of lifeless dogs.

Nobody knows you. No. But I sing of you.
For posterity I sing of your profile and grace.
Of the signal maturity of your understanding.   215
Of your appetite for death and the taste of its mouth.
Of the sadness of your once valiant gaiety.

It will be a long time, if ever, before there is born
an Andalusian so true, so rich in adventure.
I sing of his elegance with words that groan,   220
and I remember a sad breeze through the olive trees.

UNDERSTANDING THE POEM

1. Part 1:
   a) What has happened? Where? When?
   b) Why isn't the speaker more specific about what has happened?
   c) Why does the speaker keep repeating "at five in the afternoon"?
   d) What is the relationship between the speaker's attitude and the time in this section of the poem?

2. Part 2:
   a) What is it that the speaker does not want to see?
   b) What is the connection between the speaker's refusal to see and his eulogy of Ignacio?
   c) Why does the speaker keep repeating "I will not see it!"?
   d) What is the relationship between the speaker's attitude and the time in this section of the poem?

3. Part 3:
   a) What problem is the speaker grappling with in this section?
   b) What does the speaker mean by the repeated statement "All is finished"?
   c) Why does the speaker keep repeating "I want . . ."? What does he want?
   d) What is the relationship between the speaker's attitude and the time in this section of the poem?
   e) What does the speaker imply that his role in Ignacio's death is going to be?

4. Part 4:
   a) What problem does the speaker examine in this section?
   b) What does the speaker mean when he says various objects and people "do not know you"?
   c) How does the speaker intend to solve the problem?
   d) What is the relationship between the speaker's attitude and the time in this section of the poem?
   e) What attitude toward life infuses the last two lines?

5. This poem expresses the speaker's reaction to Ignacio's death. To what extent does the writing of the poem seem to function as a **night journey** for the speaker?

ANALYZING LITERARY TECHNIQUE

1. What is the effect of García Lorca's use of **apostrophe** in Parts 3 and 4?

2. In line 163 there is a reference to the Minotaur, the mythical creature killed by the Greek hero Theseus. What does this **allusion** contribute to the poem?

3. What do the references to nature contribute to the poem?

4. How does García Lorca use **contrast** to reinforce the emotional content of the poem?

5. One of the strengths of García Lorca's poetry is his use of language. Choose two or three figures of speech in the poem and explain how each contributes to the poem's meaning and power.

WRITING ABOUT LITERATURE

1. Write an essay in which you analyze García Lorca's use of **repetition** in each of the four parts of the poem. Examine the relationship of the repeated phrases to the meaning of each part of the poem. Consider where each repetition is placed and the effect the repetitive pattern has on that section. Remember to use quotations to support your ideas. In your conclusion, discuss the effect of García Lorca's use of repetition on the poem as a whole.

2. Tell the story of Ignacio Sánchez Mejías's death from the point of view of the bull. The bull will have more to say if you learn about bullfights before beginning to write this story.

3. Write an essay or a poem that eulogizes a person of your choice. First, make a list of that person's qualities that you wish to praise. Next, note situations from the person's life that best support each quality. Then, choose the three most interesting qualities, along with their examples, to include in your essay or poem. After you have written the piece, review it to see where figurative language and better adjectives and verbs will improve the effect of your descriptions.

Letter to My Wife

NAZIM HIKMET

*N*AZIM HIKMET RAN (1902–1963) is one of the great international poets of the twentieth century. Two aspects of his poetry have made him one of the most influential Turkish writers. First, he introduced free verse to Turkish poetry; and second, he made a broad range of contemporary issues legitimate themes for his nation's poetry. Hikmet's goal was to improve the world through his writing; he hoped his writing would help people to love and cooperate with one another. He viewed the artist as "the engineer of the human soul" and art as "an active institution in society."

Although best known for his poetry, Hikmet was also a novelist, short-story writer, dramatist, and journalist. His literary works have been translated into more than fifty languages, and, as a poet, he is often compared with Federico García Lorca and Walt Whitman. *Human Landscapes*, his masterpiece, is one of the great epics of the twentieth century. However, because Hikmet was a communist and communism was banned in Turkey, his epic was not published in his own country until 1966, three years after his death.

Hikmet was born in Thessaloniki, Greece, at a time when that city was part of the Turkish Ottoman Empire and it was called Salonika. In 1917, at the age of fifteen, he published his first poems. From about 1921 until 1924, he studied at the University of the Workers of the East (now known as the University of Moscow), where he became a Marxist. In 1924 he returned to Turkey, joined the Turkish Communist Party, and became a newspaper journalist.

Although Hikmet claimed that the political aspects of communism held no interest for him, he was imprisoned in 1924 for being on the staff of a communist magazine. In 1925 he escaped a second prison sentence by fleeing to Russia; however, he was imprisoned after he returned to Turkey in 1928. In 1938 Hikmet was arrested and convicted on the false charge of instigating a military rebellion among cadets and was sentenced to thirty-five years. However, when he shared the International Peace Prize with Pablo Neruda in 1950, an organized international protest forced the Turkish government to release Hikmet. The following year the Turkish government sent him into exile. He remained in exile—living in Russia and in Poland—until he died in Moscow, Russia, in 1963. His prose, poetry, and plays were banned in Turkey from 1936 until 1966.

In 1938, anticipating that he would be a political prisoner for the duration of his long sentence, he began what became his masterpiece, the epic poem *Human Landscapes*. Hikmet set the action in twentieth-century Turkey and peopled it with a large cast of well-developed characters from many walks of life. This epic reveals three of Hikmet's artistic gifts: He needs only a few lines to breathe life into a character; he finds drama in the life of every human being; and he blends aspects of oral tradition, novels, and motion pictures to create his own innovative style. Hikmet read his epic to his fellow prisoners as he worked on it, soliciting their advice about the details. The project became a five-volume poem of nearly twenty thousand lines. He finished his epic in 1950, the year that he was awarded the peace prize and released from prison.

The following poem, written in prison in 1933, shows the style that made Hikmet famous. The poem conveys Hikmet's love for his wife—one of his favorite subjects. The poem also reveals how Hikmet remained connected with the world despite spending much of his adult life in prison. Through poems such as this, he wrote "letters," "talked" with his wife, and "visited" with friends. Hikmet has been quoted as saying, "Living is no laughing matter; we must live as if one never dies." His poems are his legacy to us, showing us how to live and how to love so that we can face whatever the future brings with courage, self-confidence, and optimism.

11-11-33
Bursa Prison

My one and only!
Your last letter says:
"My head is throbbing,
        my heart is stunned!"
You say: 5
"If they hang you,
    if I lose you,
        I'll die!"
You'll live, my dear—
my memory will vanish like black smoke in the wind.   10
Of course you'll live, red-haired lady of my heart:
in the twentieth century
           grief lasts
               at most a year.

Death—   15
a body swinging from a rope.

My heart
          can't accept such a death.
But
you can bet   20
          if some poor gypsy's hairy black
                    spidery hand
                    slips a noose
                              around my neck,
they'll look in vain for fear   25
                    in Nazim's
                              blue eyes!
In the twilight of my last morning
I
will see my friends and you,   30
and I'll go
to my grave
          regretting nothing but an unfinished song . . .

My wife!
Good-hearted,   35
golden,
eyes sweeter than honey—my bee!
Why did I write you
                    they want to hang me?
The trial has hardly begun,   40
and they don't just pluck a man's head
                              like a turnip.
Look, forget all this.
If you have any money,
          buy me some flannel underwear: 45
my sciatica is acting up again.
And don't forget,
a prisoner's wife
          must always think good thoughts.

UNDERSTANDING THE POEM

1. Why does Hikmet write this letter to his wife?
2. Why does Hikmet write about how his death would affect him?
3. What is significant about Hikmet's two closing requests?
4. How does Hikmet want his wife to respond to his words?
5. What effect does writing this letter have upon the poet?

ANALYZING LITERARY TECHNIQUE

1. Hikmet addresses his wife in **appositives.** What does this use of language contribute to the poem?

2. Hikmet calls Death "a body swinging from a rope." What does this appositive contribute to the poem?

3. Hikmet uses **apostrophe** to address his wife as if she were in his presence. What does the use of apostrophe contribute to the poem?

4. What does the poet's description of the hangman contribute to the poem?

5. What is unusual about the poet's description of his last morning?

6. Hikmet is known for writing in **free verse.** Find four examples of this style and explain what the style contributes to the poem.

7. How does Hikmet use **contrast** in the poem?

8. Where does Hikmet use **satire** and **irony** in the poem? What is his intent? To what extent, if any, is he serious about what he is saying?

9. What **metaphor** does Hikmet use to describe his wife? What does the metaphor reveal about Hikmet? What does it contribute to the poem?

10. Find two **similes** in the poem. What makes these figures of speech effective?

11. What **themes** do you find in this poem?

12. Describe the **tone** of this poem and explain how Hikmet achieves it.

WRITING ABOUT LITERATURE

1. Write an expository essay in which you analyze three aspects of Hikmet's style. Devoting a separate paragraph to each aspect, consider Hikmet's use of appositives, his use of apostrophe, and his use of conversation. Use quotations from the poem as the basis for your analysis. In a concluding paragraph, explain what Hikmet's use of language contributes to the poem.

2. Write an expository essay in which you analyze "Letter to My Wife" as a **dramatic monologue.** These words, written by Hikmet to his wife at this critical moment in his life, reveal what is particularly significant about him. Consider important aspects of Hikmet's past and present, including his attitudes and values, that reveal his true character.

   Write a six-paragraph essay. In your introductory paragraph, state your purpose in writing this essay and define your literary terms. Next, choose four quotations that reveal important aspects of Hikmet's character; analyze each quotation in a separate paragraph. In your concluding paragraph, evaluate this poem as a dramatic monologue.

3. Write a poem or letter in which someone describes a difficult personal situation and attempts to encourage or console the reader. Use language that will make the subject concrete, visible, and immediate.

The Conjurer Made Off with the Dish

NAGUIB MAHFOUZ

AGUIB MAHFOUZ (1911–) is the most important writer of modern Arabic literature. He is viewed as the father of the modern Arabic novel, which continues the Arab tradition of storytelling made world-famous in *The Thousand and One Nights*. In 1988 Mahfouz became the first Arab author to win the Nobel Prize for literature. In the words of the Swedish Academy, "through works rich in nuance—now clear-sightedly realistic, now evocatively ambiguous—[Mahfouz] has formed an Arabian narrative art that applies to all mankind." In English translation, Mahfouz is best known for *The Cairo Trilogy* (*Palace Walk, Palace of Desire*, and *Sugar Street*), the novel *Arabian Nights and Days*, and the short story collection *The Time and the Place*. However, he has published more than forty novels, thirty screenplays, and fourteen volumes of short stories.

Mahfouz was born in the historic district of Gamaliya, in Cairo, Egypt, in 1911. His childhood was often lonely. He attended Islamic elementary schools and a secular high school and then graduated with a degree in philosophy from King Fuad I University (now the University of Cairo) in 1934. He began writing literature at the age of seventeen and published his first work, a short story, in a magazine that year. His writing has been influenced principally by the works of French and Russian authors, including Balzac, Camus, Flaubert, Proust, Zola, Dostoyevski, and Tolstoy.

Mahfouz lives in Agouza, a suburb of Cairo. Between 1934 and his retirement in 1972, he worked for the ministry of culture, where for many years he was in charge of theater and motion-picture censorship. Meanwhile he wrote literature at night. In 1971 he joined the editorial staff of *Al-Ahram*, Egypt's leading daily paper, where he has continued to write a weekly column.

In 1959 the highest Islamic organization in Egypt ruled that Mahfouz's novel *Children of the Alley* (also published as *Children of Gebelaawi*), an allegory about human suffering that was published in serial form in *Al-Ahram*, was heresy. In order to placate the religious authorities, Mahfouz did not publish the novel in Egypt. Despite the risk of offending the authorities, however, from 1975 to 1979 he wrote pro-Israel editorials in *Al-Ahram* and supported Anwar Sadat's peace treaty with Israel. In 1989, not long after he received the Nobel Prize, Mahfouz's support for Salman Rushdie and freedom of speech caused Islamic fundamentalists to condemn him. Consequently many Arab nations banned his works for some time.

Then, on October 14, 1994, Mahfouz almost died from the attempt of an Islamic militant to assassinate him. As a result, the Egyptian government, acting to oppose Islamic militants, lifted its ban on Mahfouz's works; thirty-five years after its initial appearance, *Children of the Alley* was at last published in Egypt.

"The Conjurer Made Off with the Dish" first appeared in the short story collection *Under the Shelter*, published in 1969. In the story, Mahfouz enables his readers to observe one day in the life of an Egyptian boy. Mahfouz always sympathizes with his characters as he explores their personalities and their daily struggles. His writing is enriched by psychologically revealing dialogue and his evocation of the local color of twentieth-century Cairo.

"The time has come for you to be useful," said my mother to me. And she slipped her hand into her pocket, saying, "Take this piaster[1] and go off and buy some beans. Don't play on the way and keep away from the carts."

I took the dish, put on my clogs, and went out, humming a tune. Finding a crowd in front of the bean seller, I waited until I discovered a way through to the marble counter.

"A piaster's worth of beans, mister," I called out in my shrill voice.

He asked me impatiently, "Beans alone? With oil? With cooking butter?"

I did not answer, and he said roughly, "Make way for someone else."

I withdrew, overcome by embarrassment, and returned home defeated.

"Returning with the dish empty?" my mother shouted at me. "What did you do—spill the beans or lose the piaster, you naughty boy?"

"Beans alone? With oil? With cooking butter?—you didn't tell me," I protested.

"Stupid boy! What do you eat every morning?"

"I don't know."

"You good-for-nothing, ask him for beans with oil."

I went off to the man and said, "A piaster's worth of beans with oil, mister."

With a frown of impatience he asked, "Linseed oil? Vegetable oil? Olive oil?"

I was taken aback and again made no answer.

"Make way for someone else," he shouted at me.

---

[1] *piaster:* Coin.

I returned in a rage to my mother, who called out in astonishment, "You've come back empty-handed—no beans and no oil."

"Linseed oil? Vegetable oil? Olive oil? Why didn't you tell me?" I said angrily.

"Beans with oil means beans with linseed oil."

"How should I know?"

"You're a good-for-nothing, and he's a tiresome man—tell him beans with linseed oil."

I went off quickly and called out to the man while still some yards from his shop, "Beans with linseed oil, mister."

"Put the piaster on the counter," he said, plunging the ladle into the pot.

I put my hand into my pocket but did not find the piaster. I searched for it anxiously. I turned my pocket inside out but found no trace of it. The man withdrew the ladle empty, saying with disgust, "You've lost the piaster—you're not a boy to be depended on."

"I haven't lost it," I said, looking under my feet and round about me. "It was in my pocket all the time."

"Make way for someone else and stop bothering me."

I returned to my mother with an empty dish.

"Good grief, are you an idiot, boy?"

"The piaster . . ."

"What of it?"

"It's not in my pocket."

"Did you buy sweets with it?"

"I swear I didn't."

"How did you lose it?"

"I don't know."

"Do you swear by the Koran[2] you didn't buy anything with it?"

"I swear."

"Is there a hole in your pocket?"

"No, there isn't."

"Maybe you gave it to the man the first time or the second."

"Maybe."

"Are you sure of nothing?"

"I'm hungry."

She clapped her hands together in a gesture of resignation.

"Never mind," she said, "I'll give you another piaster but I'll take it out of your money-box, and if you come back with an empty dish, I'll break your head."

I went off at a run, dreaming of a delicious breakfast. At the turning leading to the alleyway where the bean seller was, I saw a crowd of children and heard merry, festive sounds. My feet dragged as my heart was pulled toward them. At least let me have a fleeting glance. I slipped in among them and found the conjurer looking straight at me. A stupefying joy overwhelmed me; I was completely taken out of myself. With the whole of my being I became involved in the tricks

---

[2] *Koran*: Muslim book of sacred writings.

of the rabbits and the eggs, and the snakes and the ropes. When the man came up to collect money, I drew back mumbling, "I haven't got any money."

He rushed at me savagely, and I escaped only with difficulty. I ran off, my back almost broken by his blow, and yet I was utterly happy as I made my way to the seller of beans.

"Beans with linseed oil for a piaster, mister," I said.

He went on looking at me without moving, so I repeated my request.

"Give me the dish," he demanded angrily.

The dish! Where was the dish? Had I dropped it while running? Had the conjurer made off with it?

"Boy, you're out of your mind!"

I retraced my steps, searching along the way for the lost dish. The place where the conjurer had been, I found empty, but the voices of children led me to him in a nearby lane. I moved around the circle. When the conjurer spotted me, he shouted out threateningly, "Pay up or you'd better scram."

"The dish!" I called out despairingly.

"What dish, you little devil?"

"Give me back the dish."

"Scram or I'll make you into food for snakes."

He had stolen the dish, yet fearfully I moved away out of sight and wept in grief. Whenever a passerby asked me why I was crying, I would reply, "The conjurer made off with the dish."

Through my misery I became aware of a voice saying, "Come along and watch!"

I looked behind me and saw a peep show had been set up. I saw dozens of children hurrying toward it and taking it in turns to stand in front of the peepholes, while the man began his tantalizing commentary to the pictures.

"There you've got the gallant knight and the most beautiful of all ladies, Zainat al-Banat."

My tears dried up, and I gazed in fascination at the box, completely forgetting the conjurer and the dish. Unable to overcome the temptation, I paid over the piaster and stood in front of the peephole next to a girl who was standing in front of the other one, and enchanting picture stories flowed across our vision. When I came back to my own world I realized I had lost both the piaster and the dish, and there was no sign of the conjurer. However, I gave no thought to the loss, so taken up was I with the pictures of chivalry, love, and deeds of daring. I forgot my hunger. I forgot even the fear of what threatened me at home. I took a few paces back so as to lean against the ancient wall of what had once been a treasury and the chief cadi's seat of office, and gave myself up wholly to my reveries. For a long while I dreamed of chivalry, of Zainat al-Banat and the ghoul. In my dream I spoke aloud, giving meaning to my words with gestures. Thrusting home the imaginary lance, I said, "Take that, O ghoul, right in the heart!"

"And he raised Zainat al-Banat up behind him on the horse," came back a gentle voice.

I looked to my right and saw the young girl who had been beside me at the performance. She was wearing a dirty dress and colored clogs and was playing with her long plait of hair. In her other hand were the red-and-white sweets called "lady's fleas," which she was leisurely sucking. We exchanged glances, and I lost my heart to her.

"Let's sit down and rest," I said to her.

She appeared to go along with my suggestion, so I took her by the arm and we went through the gateway of the ancient wall and sat down on a step of its stairway that went nowhere, a stairway that rose up until it ended in a platform behind which there could be seen the blue sky and minarets. We sat in silence, side by side. I pressed her hand, and we sat on in silence, not knowing what to say. I experienced feelings that were new, strange, and obscure. Putting my face close to hers, I breathed in the natural smell of her hair mingled with an odor of dust, and the fragrance of breath mixed with the aroma of sweets. I kissed her lips. I swallowed my saliva, which had taken on a sweetness from the dissolved "lady's fleas." I put my arm around her, without her uttering a word, kissing her cheek and lips. Her lips grew still as they received the kiss, then went back to sucking at the sweets. At last she decided to get up. I seized her arm anxiously. "Sit down," I said.

"I'm going," she replied simply.

"Where to?" I asked dejectedly.

"To the midwife Umm Ali," and she pointed to a house on the ground floor of which was a small ironing shop.

"Why?"

"To tell her to come quickly."

"Why?"

"My mother's crying in pain at home. She told me to go to the midwife Umm Ali and tell her to come along quickly."

"And you'll come back after that?"

She nodded her head in assent and went off. Her mentioning her mother reminded me of my own, and my heart missed a beat. Getting up from the ancient stairway, I made my way back home. I wept out loud, a tried method by which I would defend myself. I expected she would come to me, but she did not. I wandered from the kitchen to the bedroom but found no trace of her. Where had my mother gone? When would she return? I was fed up with being in the empty house. A good idea occurred to me. I took a dish from the kitchen and a piaster from my savings and went off immediately to the seller of beans. I found him asleep on a bench outside the shop, his face covered by his arm. The pots of beans had vanished and the long-necked bottles of oil had been put back on the shelf and the marble counter had been washed down.

"Mister," I whispered, approaching.

Hearing nothing but his snoring, I touched his shoulder. He raised his arm in alarm and looked at me through reddened eyes.

"Mister."

"What do you want?" he asked roughly, becoming aware of my presence and recognizing me.

"A piaster's worth of beans with linseed oil."

"Eh?"

"I've got the piaster and I've got the dish."

"You're crazy, boy," he shouted at me. "Get out or I'll bash your brains in."

When I did not move, he pushed me so violently I went sprawling onto my back. I got up painfully, struggling to hold back the crying that was twisting my lips. My hands were clenched, one on the dish and the other on the piaster. I threw him an angry look. I thought about returning home with my hopes dashed, but dreams of heroism and valor altered my plan of action. Resolutely I made a quick decision and with all my strength threw the dish at him. It flew through the air and struck him on the head, while I took to my heels, heedless of everything. I was convinced I had killed him, just as the knight had killed the ghoul. I did not stop running till I was near the ancient wall. Panting, I looked behind me but saw no signs of any pursuit. I stopped to get my breath, then asked myself what I should do now that the second dish was lost? Something warned me not to return home directly, and soon I had given myself over to a wave of indifference that bore me off where it willed. It meant a beating, neither more nor less, on my return, so let me put it off for a time. Here was the piaster in my hand, and I could have some sort of enjoyment with it before being punished. I decided to pretend I had forgotten I had done anything wrong—but where was the conjurer, where was the peep show? I looked everywhere for them to no avail.

Worn out by this fruitless searching, I went off to the ancient stairway to keep my appointment. I sat down to wait, imagining to myself the meeting. I yearned for another kiss redolent with the fragrance of sweets. I admitted to myself that the little girl had given me lovelier sensations than I had ever experienced. As I waited and dreamed, a whispering sound came from behind me. I climbed the stairs cautiously, and at the final landing I lay down flat on my face in order to see what was beyond, without anyone being able to notice me. I saw some ruins surrounded by a high wall, the last of what remained of the treasury and the chief cadi's seat of office. Directly under the stairs sat a man and a woman, and it was from them that the whispering came. The man looked like a tramp; the woman like one of those Gypsies that tend sheep. A suspicious inner voice told me that their meeting was similar to the one I had had. Their lips and the looks they exchanged spoke of this, but they showed astonishing expertise in the unimaginable things they did. My gaze became rooted upon them with curiosity, surprise, pleasure, and a certain amount of disquiet. At last they sat down side by side, neither of them taking any notice of the other. After quite a while the man said, "The money!"

"You're never satisfied," she said irritably.

Spitting on the ground, he said, "You're crazy."

"You're a thief."

He slapped her hard with the back of his hand, and she gathered up a handful of earth and threw it in his face. Then, his face soiled with dirt, he sprang at her, fastening his fingers on her windpipe, and a bitter fight ensued. In vain she gathered all her strength to escape from his grip. Her voice failed her, her eyes bulged out of their sockets, while her feet struck out at the air. In dumb terror, I stared at the scene till I saw a thread of blood trickling down from her nose. A scream escaped from my mouth. Before the man raised his head, I had crawled backward. Descending the stairs at a jump, I raced off like mad to wherever my legs might carry me. I did not stop running till I was breathless. Gasping for breath, I was quite unaware of my surroundings, but when I came to myself I found I was under a raised vault[3] at the middle of a crossroads. I had never set foot there before and had no idea of where I was in relation to our quarter.[4] On both sides sat sightless beggars, and crossing from all directions were people who paid attention to no one. In terror I realized I had lost my way and that countless difficulties lay in wait for me before I found my way home. Should I resort to asking one of the passersby to direct me? What, though, would happen if chance should lead me to a man like the seller of beans or the tramp of the waste plot? Would a miracle come about whereby I would see my mother approaching so that I could eagerly hurry toward her? Should I try to make my own way, wandering about till I came across some familiar landmark that would indicate the direction I should take?

I told myself that I should be resolute and make a quick decision. The day was passing, and soon mysterious darkness would descend.

UNDERSTANDING THE STORY

1. What causes the boy to forget what he should remember?
2. What aspects of this environment attract the boy's interest?
3. Why does the boy tell passersby that the conjurer made off with the dish?
4. What two roles does the young girl play in the story?
5. In what two ways does the peep show affect the boy's actions?
6. What is significant about the boy's observation of the tramp and the gypsy?
7. Why does the boy connect the bean seller with the tramp? What does he learn from their behavior?
8. What choice do you think the boy makes at the end of the story? Why?
9. The boy's errand takes him on a quest that is a journey or odyssey. It is also an initiation rite, in which he must leave his childhood behind and "come of age" by becoming part of the adult world. What is his quest? What does each adventure teach him about the adult world?

---

[3] *vault:* Arch.

[4] *quarter:* Section of a city; neighborhood.

10. How does the boy feel at the end of the story? To what extent, if any, have his experiences changed his attitudes and behavior? Find examples in the text that support your answer.

ANALYZING LITERARY TECHNIQUE

1. The first line of a story is very important because it should lead the reader into the tale that follows. How does the first line of this story relate to what follows? What does it **foreshadow?**

2. How does Mahfouz reveal the **setting** of this story? Find examples of local color that reveal the story's location.

3. How does Mahfouz take the reader into the boy's world? From whose **point of view** is this story told? To what extent, if any, is this technique successful?

4. How does Mahfouz enable the reader to know what the boy is like? What do you learn about the boy from the choices that he makes? What do you learn about him from the way others respond to him?

5. Find examples of Mahfouz's use of **irony** in this story.

6. Describe the **tone** of this story. How does Mahfouz create humor?

7. What is the significance of the story's title?

8. What **themes** does Mahfouz intend to convey in this story? To what extent, if any, does he succeed?

9. To what extent does Mahfouz resolve the issues set forth in this story? To what extent does he leave the story open-ended? Which is more important: the resolution or the question? Why?

WRITING ABOUT LITERATURE

1. Write an essay in which you analyze the thematic content of Mahfouz's story. Choose three themes and show how Mahfouz uses particular aspects of the **plot** to reveal each theme.

2. Write a story in which a character experiences a sense of wonder because of a particular aspect of the world that she or he encounters. Tell the story from that character's point of view.

3. Write a story in which an experience or a series of experiences causes a character to leave childhood behind and "come of age." Be sure to convey the connection between the experience and the character's psychological development.

Continental Europe

*T*HE PLAY, SHORT STORIES, AND POEMS from Continental Europe offer a trove of treasures that evoke feelings of wonder, terror, sorrow, and humor.

The authors of three selections—the poem "Voronezh" and the short stories "The Wall" and "The Guest"—are concerned with human attitudes and behavior in times of political conflict. Anna Akhmatova expresses a poet's courage, hope, and fear in time of political repression. Jean-Paul Sartre deals with the absurd nature of human existence, whereas Albert Camus reveals what happens when a person attempts to remain neutral while living in the presence of two conflicting groups.

The writers of five selections deal with illusion and reality, and four of these selections concern the nature of love. In Ibsen's great play *A Doll's House*, both husband and wife are forced to forego their illusions and confront reality. In Anton Chekhov's amusing story "The Kiss," a young man must also give up his illusions and face reality; however, in Colette's poignant story "The Other Wife," the characters lack the ability to recognize the difference between illusion and reality. In "The Outlaws," Selma Lagerlöf's complex tale of adventure, the distinction between illusion and reality is unclear, and love adds to the ambiguity of the mystery. Leo Tolstoy's short story "How Much Land Does a Man Need?" emphasizes

the critical importance of recognizing the difference between illusion and reality. In contrast, Fyodor Dostoyevsky's story "The Heavenly Christmas Tree" deals with the difficult reality of childhood poverty and the indifference of society to the effects of poverty.

Two poets, Friedrich von Schiller and Rainer Maria Rilke, deal with subjective states of mind. "Human Knowledge" reflects a poet's thoughts about the limitations of human knowledge; "At Sundown" reveals how the mood of nature evokes a mood in the poet.

The stories of both Hans Christian Andersen and Franz Kafka function on multiple levels. On the surface, Andersen's masterpiece "The Shadow" depicts the artist in society. On a deeper level, the tale is a striking dramatization of the divided self and the need to recognize the evil potential in human nature. On the surface, Kafka's story "A Country Doctor" is a "Kafkaesque" nightmare. However, below the surface it is a "night journey" in which the dreamer gains insight into himself and society.

Human Knowledge

FRIEDRICH VON SCHILLER

RIEDRICH VON SCHILLER (1759–1805), a drama-
tist and poet, was a leading figure in Germany's golden age
of literature. Schiller is best known for his "Ode to Joy"
(1786), which Ludwig van Beethoven incorporated into his Ninth
Symphony (*Choral*), and for his historical plays, *Don Carlos* (1787),
The Maid of Orleans (1801), and *William Tell* (1804). Two of these
plays were adapted into operas, *Don Carlos* by Guiseppe Verdi and
William Tell by Gioacchino Rossini.

Schiller was born in Württemberg, Germany, where his father
was an army surgeon. He attended the Stuttgart Military Academy,
where he studied medicine and law. However, it was literature that
excited him, and while at the academy, he began to write his first
play, *The Robbers*. Following graduation, he became a medical officer.
When he left his army post without permission to attend the opening
night of *The Robbers* in Mannheim in 1782, he was dismissed from
military service.

The opening performance of *The Robbers* had another great effect
on Schiller's life. The title page of the play includes the Latin inscrip-
tion "against tyrants," and its theme of freedom was considered so
threatening by the ducal authorities in Mannheim that Schiller was
exiled. To the end of his life, Schiller remained true to his beliefs, and
the themes of his plays reflect his passion for political and religious
freedom.

Schiller's move to Weimar in 1787 finally led to his financial
independence. Within two years, he became a professor of history at
the University of Jena, and later he was granted the title and rights of
a nobleman.

Schiller's poetry ranges from the lyrical to the philosophical and
from subjective romanticism to the more objective classicism.
"Human Knowledge" reflects the philosophical musings of a great
humanitarian.

Since thou readest in her what thou thyself hast there written,
And, to gladden the eye, placest her wonders in groups;—
Since o'er her boundless expanses thy cords to extend thou art able,
Thou dost think that thy mind wonderful Nature can grasp.

Thus the astronomer draws his figures over the heavens,   5
So that he may with more ease traverse the infinite space,
Knitting together e'en suns that by Sirius-distance[1] are parted,
Making them join in the swan and in the horns of the bull.[2]
But because the firmament shows him its glorious surface,
Can he the spheres' mystic dance therefore decipher aright?   10

UNDERSTANDING THE POEM

1. Why do people think that they understand Nature?

2. What leads the astronomer to believe that he understands the universe?

3. How do the two stanzas of the poem relate to each other?

4. What is Schiller criticizing when he discusses the two constellations, the swan and the bull?

5. What **themes** do you find in this poem?

ANALYZING LITERARY TECHNIQUE

1. What does Schiller find **paradoxical** about knowledge?

2. What does the "spheres' mystic dance" (line 10) mean? What effect does this **metaphor** have on the poem?

3. How is this poem more **classical** than **romantic?** More romantic than classical?

4. What is the **tone** of this poem? How does Schiller achieve it?

---

[1] *Sirius-distance:* A great distance, like the distance between the sun and Sirius, the brightest star in the heavens.

[2] *swan . . . the bull:* Two constellations.

WRITING ABOUT LITERATURE

1. Write a short essay in which you examine how Schiller conveys the theme of this poem. Consider how the poet uses examples to support his point of view. Consider also how his use of paradox and tone affect how he conveys the theme of the poem.

2. One characteristic of life in the twenty-first century is that our understanding of the world and how it works is changing rapidly—much more rapidly than in Schiller's time, even though the late eighteenth century was an age of important scientific discovery and development.

   Think about some ways that human understanding of the world has changed in your lifetime, in your parents' lifetime, and in your grandparents' lifetime. For example, what have people in each generation learned about disease control or the effects of pollution? Then think about what people in the next generation might learn about the world. Focus on one particular area. Write a brief sketch or poem about what you think the world will be like in the next generation, basing your ideas on changing knowledge. Will people know everything then?

The Shadow

HANS CHRISTIAN ANDERSEN

Denmark

ANS CHRISTIAN ANDERSEN (1805–1875) is a familiar and beloved name to many families around the world. Since the 1850s, his stories have been translated into over one hundred languages, and generations of children have grown up with "The Emperor's New Clothes," "The Little Match Girl," "The Ugly Duckling," "The Snow Queen," and "The Nightingale."

According to his autobiography, Hans Christian Andersen was born "in a poor little room" in Odense, Denmark. In 1819, at the age of fourteen, Andersen left home for the city of Copenhagen because he was determined to become famous. A love of reading and the theater, great determination, and an unshakable self-confidence were all he had in his favor. For three years, he failed at everything he attempted: acting, singing, dancing, and writing plays. His first published book (1822) sold so poorly that the pages of unsold copies were used as wrapping paper.

Andersen decided to educate himself. In 1828, after five years of public school and a year of private tutoring, he passed his university entrance exams. However, he did not continue his education. Instead he wrote poems, short stories, and plays while earning a living writing opera lyrics and doing translations. Unhappy in love, he left Denmark in 1833 and took up traveling and writing travel books. His autobiographical novel *The Improvisatore, or, Life in Italy* (1835) brought him international fame, and he began writing tales, first for children and soon for their parents as well.

To Andersen, the tale was the ultimate form of poetry. Unlike the Grimm brothers, who collected and recorded folktales and fairy tales from the oral tradition, Andersen created his own tales. Andersen was an astute observer of those around him. He wrote: "Every character is taken from life; I know and have known them all." Andersen was fascinated by people's pretensions, and many of his stories reflect the inability of one character to see another's genuine value. Andersen's focus on the difference between illusion and reality creates ironic situations that are poignant as well as powerful.

Published in 1847, "The Shadow" was inspired by Andersen's feelings and experiences in Naples, Italy, during the summer of 1846. In this tale, he alludes to an earlier well-known German story about a man without a shadow, but "The Shadow" is Andersen's own story, and it is one of his best.

In the hot countries, my word! how the sun scorches you. People become quite brown, like mahogany, and in the very hottest countries they get burnt into negroes. But now we are only going to hear about a learned man who had come straight from a cold climate to a hot one, where he seemed to think he could trot about just as if he were at home. Well, he soon broke himself of that habit. During the day-time he and all sensible people had to stay in their houses with doors and shutters closed. It looked as though the whole house was asleep or nobody at home. To make things worse, the narrow street with the tall houses where he was staying had been built in such a way that from morning till evening it lay in the full blaze of the sun—it was really more than one could stand. The learned man from the cold country—a young, clever man—he felt as if he were in a sweltering oven; it told on him so much that he got quite thin. Even his shadow began to shrink, for the sun affected that as well, and it grew much less than it was at home. These two didn't properly revive until the sun had gone down.

It was really a most amusing sight. As soon as the lamp was brought into the room the shadow stretched itself all along the wall, right up to the ceiling; it was obliged to stretch in order to get its strength back. The learned man went out on to the balcony to have his stretch and, as the stars came out in the clear delicious air, he felt he was coming to life again. On all the balconies in the street—and in the hot countries every window has a balcony—people were coming out, for you must have air, even if you are used to being mahogany. Both above, and below, it grew quite lively. Shoemakers, tailors and all moved out into the street; tables and chairs were brought out, and candles lit—hundreds of them. One gave a speech, and another a song; people strolled about, carriages rolled by, donkeys went tinkling past—ting-a-ling-a-ling—from the bells they were wearing. There were funerals and hymn-singing, street-boys letting off crackers, and bell-ringing from the churches—yes, there was plenty going on down there in the street. Only in the house directly opposite the house of the learned stranger was there no sign or sound of life. And yet someone must be living there because there were flowers on the balcony, growing so beautifully in the hot sun, and they couldn't do that without being watered; so someone must be watering them—there must be people in the house. Besides, towards evening the door over there was opened, but the interior was dark—at any rate, in the front room—though from further inside came the sound of music. The learned stranger thought the music wonderful; but this may have been merely his imagination, because except for the sun itself, he found everything wonderful down there in the hot countries. His landlord said that he didn't know who had taken the house opposite; nobody was ever to be seen and, as for the music, he found it too tiresome for anything. "It's just as though someone were sitting and practising a piece he couldn't get on with—always the same piece. 'I *will* get it right!' he keeps saying; but he won't, however long he practises."

One night the stranger woke up; he was sleeping with his balcony door open. The curtain in front of it was blown a little to one side, and a curious blaze of light seemed to come from the opposite neighbour's balcony. All the flowers shone like flames in the loveliest colours, and there amidst the flowers stood a graceful slender girl; she too seemed to glitter, and the sight of her quite dazzled his eyes. But then he opened them very wide indeed and he had only just woken up. He leapt from his bed, crept behind the curtain . . . but the girl was gone, the glitter was gone, and the flowers had lost their shining splendour, though they stood up as straight as ever. The door was ajar, and from a far corner of the room came the sound of music so soft and enchanting that it could easily make you give way to romantic thoughts. It was, though, a sort of magic—who ever could be living there? Where was the proper way in? The whole ground floor was given up to shops; people couldn't possibly keep on running in and out of these.

The stranger was sitting one evening out on his balcony with a light burning in the room behind him; and so, quite naturally, his shadow appeared over on his neighbour's wall. Yes, there it was, immediately opposite among the flowers on the balcony; and when the stranger moved, then the shadow moved, which is a way that shadows have.

"I believe my shadow is the only living thing to be seen over there," said the learned man. "Look how nicely it sits among the flowers. The door is standing half-open—what a chance for the shadow to pop inside, have a look round and then come and tell me what it has seen! Now then, make yourself useful!" he said in fun. "Kindly step inside . . . Well, aren't you going?" And he gave the shadow a nod, and the shadow nodded back. "That's right, go along—but mind you come back." The stranger stood up, and the shadow over on the neighbour's balcony did the same. And the stranger turned round, and so did the shadow. Anyone watching carefully could have seen quite well that the shadow went in at the half-open balcony door at the very moment that the stranger went into his room and dropped the long curtain behind him.

Next morning the learned man went out to drink his coffee and read the papers. "Hullo!" he exclaimed, as he walked out into the sunshine, "Why, where's my shadow? Then it really did go off last night and never came back. What a fearful nuisance!"

He was very annoyed, not so much because the shadow had disappeared, but because he knew there was a story, well-known to everybody at home in the cold countries, about a man without a shadow;[1] and if he went back now and told them

---

[1] *man without a shadow*: An allusion to a popular German story by Adelbert von Chamisso, entitled *Peter Schlemihl* (1814), in which a man sells his soul to the devil in exchange for a bottomless purse. Another related story is "A Sylvester-Night Tale" by E. T. A. Hoffman.

his own story, they would be sure to say that he was just an imitator, and that was the last thing he wanted. So he made up his mind to say nothing about it, and that was very sensible of him.

When evening came, he went out on to his balcony once more. He had the light put in just the right place behind him, knowing that a shadow always likes to have its master as a screen; but he couldn't get it to come out. He made himself long, he made himself short—there was no shadow, not a sign of it. He coughed. "Ahem! Ahem!" but that was no good.

It was very annoying but after all everything grows so fast in the hot countries, and a week later he noticed to his great delight that he had got a new shadow growing out from his feet whenever he walked in the sun; the roots must still have been there. In another three weeks he found himself with quite a respectable shadow which, as he made his way home to the northern countries, grew more and more on the journey till at last it was twice as big and heavy as he wanted. So the learned man went home and wrote books about what is true and good and beautiful in the world; and days and years went by—yes, many years.

Then one evening he was sitting in his room, and there came a gentle knock at the door. "Come in," he called out; but no one entered. So he went and opened the door, and there in front of him was a—well, really such an astonishingly thin person that he made him feel quite uncomfortable. However, the visitor was very smartly dressed—he was no doubt a man of some distinction.

"Whom have I the honour of addressing?" asked the learned man.

"Yes, I thought you wouldn't recognize me," said the distinguished-looking stranger. "I've now such a body of my own that I've positively got flesh—and clothes too. You never expected to see me as prosperous as this, did you? Don't you know your old shadow? No, of course you never thought I should turn up again. One way and another I am now extremely well off; if I want to purchase my freedom, I can do it." And he rattled a great bunch of valuable seals that were hanging from his watch, and ran his hand along the thick gold chain he was wearing around his neck. Phew! The way his fingers all sparkled with diamond rings—all perfectly genuine too!

"Upon my soul, you take my breath away," said the learned man. "What on earth does it all mean?"

"Well, it *is* rather out of the ordinary," said the Shadow. "But then, you see, you yourself are not ordinary either; and I, ever since I was a little toddler, have trod in your footsteps—you know that well enough. As soon as you felt I was able to make my own way in the world, off I went alone. I've done extremely well for myself; and yet I was seized with a kind of longing to see you just once again before you die—for die you must, one day. I also felt I'd like to revisit this part of the world; for you know, one's always so fond of the country one comes from. I realize that you've got hold of a new shadow—do I owe you, or it, anything? If so, please tell me."

"Well, I never! Is it really you?" cried the learned man. "Now, that *is* extraordinary! I never imagined one's old shadow could turn up again as a human being."

"Tell me what I owe you," said the Shadow. "I don't like the idea of being in any sort of debt to you."

"How can you speak like that?" said the learned man. "What's this debt you're babbling about? You owe me nothing. I am utterly delighted at your good fortune. Sit down, old friend, and do let me hear how it all happened and what you saw at our neighbour's across the street, down there in the middle of the hot countries."

"Very well, I'll tell you," said the Shadow, sitting down. "But, in that case, promise me that, wherever you may meet me here in this town, you will never tell anyone that I have been your shadow. I'm thinking of getting married, for I have ample means to support a family."

"Don't let that worry you," said the learned man. "I shan't tell a soul who you really are. There's my hand on it. I promise you; and a man's as good as his word."

"And so is a shadow," said the Shadow, expressing it the only way possible.

It was, when you come to think of it, quite astonishing how much of a human being the Shadow had become. He was dressed all in black, made of the finest broadcloth, with patent leather boots and a hat that folded up into a matter of crown and brim—to say nothing of the seals, gold chain and diamond rings already mentioned. Yes, there's no doubt about it, the Shadow was got up very smartly, and this it was that made him such a perfect man.

"Well, now you shall hear the whole story," said the Shadow, stamping his patent leather boots down on the sleeve of the learned man's new shadow which lay there at his feet like a poodle. He may have done this out of pride, or possibly because he hoped to make it stick to his own feet. The shadow that was lying there kept perfectly still, not wishing to miss anything; above all, it wanted to find out how one could break away like that and earn the right to be one's own master.

"Whom do you think I found living over there in the neighbour's house?" said the Shadow. "The fairest of the fair—Poetry! I was there for three weeks, and it meant as much as living for three thousand years and reading all that man has imagined and written down. Believe me, that is so. I have seen everything and I know everything."

"Poetry!" cried the learned man. "Yes, yes, in the large towns she often lives like a hermit. Poetry! Yes, I caught a glimpse of her for one short second, but my eyes were full of sleep. She stood on the balcony, glittering as the Northern Lights[2] glitter. Go on, my good fellow; go on! You were on the balcony, you went in at the door, and then—?"

"Then I found myself in the antechamber," said the Shadow. "The room you have always been looking across at is the antechamber. There was no lamp or candle there, but only a sort of twilight. You could see a long row of different-sized rooms, so brightly lit that I should have been quite blinded if I had gone right into Poetry's inner room. But I was careful, I took my time—as indeed one should."

"Yes, you slowcoach, but what did you see after that?" asked the learned man.

---

[2] *Northern Lights:* The aurora borealis, a phenomenon in which streamers of light appear in the night sky.

"I saw everything, and you shall hear all about it; but—mind you, I'm not being in any way stuck up—but, now that I'm independent and so well-informed, to say nothing of my good standing and excellent connections, I should be much obliged if you would address me with rather more respect."

"Oh, I beg your pardon," replied the learned man. "It's sheer force of habit that I can't get rid of. You are perfectly right, sir, and I will bear this in mind. But now please tell me about all that you saw."

"Yes, all," said the Shadow; "for I saw everything and I know everything."

"What did the inner rooms look like?" asked the learned man. "Was it like being in the green forest? Or in some holy church? Were the halls like the starlit sky when one is standing on the mountain heights?"

"Everything was there," said the Shadow. "But I didn't go right inside; I stayed in the twilight of that front room, and it was an especially good place to be, for I saw everything and I know everything. I have been in the antechamber of the court of Poetry."

"Yes, but what did you see, sir? Were all the gods of antiquity striding through those great halls? Were the heroes of old doing battle there? Were the darling children at play, and did they tell you their dreams?"

"I was there, I repeat, and you must understand that I saw everything there was to see. Had you come across, you would not have become a man; but I did. And I also learnt to know my innermost nature, as I received it at birth, my relationship to Poetry. No, when I was with you, I never gave it a thought; but at sunrise and at sunset, you remember, I always grew remarkably large—in the moonlight I stood out almost plainer than yourself. In those days I didn't understand my own nature; in the antechamber it dawned upon me—I was a man. . . . When I came away, I was changed, ripened, but by then you had left the hot countries. As a man, I was ashamed to go about as I did; I was in need of boots, clothes, all that human varnish by which man can be recognized. I took refuge—I can safely tell you this, because you won't put it in a book—I took refuge under the skirt of a woman selling cakes and hid there; the woman had no notion how much she was concealing. Not until nighttime did I venture out. I ran about the streets in the moonlight. I stretched myself right up the wall—that tickles your back so delightfully. Up and down I ran, peeping in at the highest windows, into rooms on the ground floor and rooms under the roof. I peeped where no one else can peep and saw what no others saw—what nobody should see! When all's said and done, it's a low-down world we live in. I would never be a man, if it weren't generally considered to be worth while. I saw the most inconceivable things happening among women, men, parents and their own dear darling children. I saw," added the Shadow, "what none are supposed to know, but what all are dying to know—trouble in the house next door. . . . If I had a newspaper, it would have had plenty of readers! But I used to write direct to the person in question, and there was panic wherever I went. They were terribly afraid of me—and, oh! so fond of me. The professors made me a professor, the tailors gave me new clothes; I was well provided for. The master of the mint made me coins, and the women said I was handsome. And that's how I became the man I am. Well, now I'll say goodbye. Here's my card. I live on the sunny side of the street and am always at home in rainy weather." And the Shadow took his leave.

"How extraordinary!" said the learned man.

Time passed, and the Shadow turned up again.

"How are things going?" he asked.

"Ah, well," sighed the learned man, "I write about the true and the good and the beautiful, but no one bothers his head about that sort of thing. It makes me quite desperate, for it means so much to me."

"It wouldn't worry me," said the Shadow. "I'm getting fat—which is just what one should try to be. I'm afraid you don't understand the world, and you're getting ill. You should travel. I'm going abroad this summer; won't you come with me? I should so like a travelling companion. Come with me, as my shadow! It will be a great pleasure to have you with me, and I'll pay your expenses."

"Surely that's going a bit far," said the learned man.

"It depends how you take it," said the Shadow. "It'll do you a world of good to travel. If you will be my shadow, you shall have everything on the trip for nothing."

"That really is the limit!" said the learned man.

"Well, that's what we have come to nowadays, and there's no going back on it," and with that the Shadow went away.

Things went badly for the learned man. He was dogged by care and sorrow, and his ideas about the true and the good and the beautiful were to most people about as attractive as roses to a cow. He ended by falling quite ill.

"Why, to look at, you're no more than a shadow," they told him; and this made him shudder, for it set him thinking.

"You must go and take the waters somewhere," said the Shadow, who came to see him one day. "That's the only thing. You shall come with me for the sake of old times. I'll pay your expenses, and you can write an account of our travels and kind of keep me amused on the journey. I want to go to a watering-place; my beard isn't growing as it should—that too is an ailment—and one can't do without a beard. Now, be sensible and say you'll come; and of course we'll travel as friends."

And away they went. But now the Shadow was master, and the master shadow; always together, driving, riding, walking; side by side, or one in front and one behind, according to the position of the sun. The Shadow always knew how to hold on to the master's place, whereas the learned man never gave the matter a thought; he was extremely good-natured, gentle and friendly. One day he said to the Shadow: "Seeing that we now travel together as equals like this and that we also grew up from childhood together, oughtn't we to pledge ourselves in a toast of friendship? It would be so much more sociable."

"I dare say," said the Shadow, who was now the real master. "It all sounds very frank, and I'm sure that you mean well; I too mean well and will be just as frank. As a learned man, you know of course how queer nature is. Some people can't bear the feel of grey paper; it upsets them. Others go all goosey if you scrape a nail against a pane of glass. That's just how I feel when you talk to me in the familiar tone of an equal. It's as though I were being thrust back into my first humble position with you. Of course, it's not pride—it's only what I feel. So, although I can't allow you to be familiar with me, I am quite willing to meet you halfway and myself to be familiar with you."

And, from then on the Shadow treated his former master as an inferior.

"It really is a bit steep," thought the learned man, "that I have to call him 'Sir,' while he can call me what he likes." Still, he had to put up with it.

In due course they came to a watering-place, where there were many visitors and among them a beautiful princess, who suffered from the complaint of over-sharp sight, and this was most disturbing.

She noticed at once that the newcomer was utterly different from all the others. "They say he's here to make his beard grow, but I know the real reason; he can't throw a shadow."

Her curiosity was aroused, and so she lost no time in having a stroll and a talk with the foreign gentleman. Being a princess, she didn't need to stand on ceremony, and so she said straight out, "Your trouble is that you can't throw a shadow."

"Your Royal Highness must be very much better," said the Shadow. "I know that the complaint you suffer from is that you see far too clearly, but it must have gone—you are cured. The fact is, I have a most unusual shadow. Haven't you noticed the person who is always with me? Other people have an ordinary shadow, but I am no lover of ordinary. A gentleman gives his lackey for a livery finer cloth than he uses himself; and that's why I have had my shadow tricked out as a human being. Yes, look, I've even given *him* a shadow. It was very expensive, but I like having something that nobody else has got."

"Heavens!" thought the Princess. "Have I really been cured? This spa is the finest in existence. Water nowadays has astonishing properties. But I won't go away; the place is beginning to amuse me. I like this foreigner immensely. I do hope his beard won't grow, because then he would be off at once."

In the great ballroom that evening the Princess danced with the Shadow. She was light enough, but he was still lighter; never had she known a partner like that. She told him the country she came from; he knew it and had been there while she was away; he had peeped in at the windows on every floor and seen all sorts of things through them, so that he was able to answer the Princess and let fall little hints that quite astonished her. He must be the wisest man in the world, she thought, so great was her respect for what he knew. Then they danced together again, and she fell in love—which to the Shadow was obvious enough, for she could very nearly see right through him. And after that they had another dance, and she was on the point of telling him—but she kept her head. She remembered her country and her kingdom and all the people she had to rule over. "He's a wise man," she told herself; "that's a good thing. And he dances beautifully; that's also good. But I wonder how deep his knowledge goes; that is just as important. He must be thoroughly tested." So she gradually began to put to him the most difficult questions, which she herself couldn't have answered; and a curious look came into the Shadow's face.

"You can't answer that!" cried the Princess.

"I learnt that in the nursery," said the Shadow. "I believe even my shadow over there by the door can answer that."

"Your shadow!" said the Princess. "That would be very remarkable."

"Well, I won't say for certain that he can," said the Shadow, "but I should imagine so. He has now been with me so many years, listening to me all the time—I should imagine he can. But may I draw your Royal Highness's attention to one thing: he takes such pride in passing for a human being that, to get him into the right mood (which he has to be, if he is to answer well), he must be treated exactly the same as a human being."

"I do like that," said the Princess.

So then she went up to the learned man by the door and chatted with him about the sun and the moon and about people, both inside and out, and his answers were wonderfully shrewd and sound.

"What a man this must be, when his mere shadow is as wise as that!" she thought. "And what a blessing it would be for my people and my kingdom, if I chose him as a husband! I'll do it."

And they soon came to an understanding, the Princess and the Shadow. But no one must hear of it until she was back in her own kingdom. "No one, not even my shadow," said the Shadow; and he had his own reasons for saying that. At last they reached the country over which the Princess ruled, when she was at home.

"Listen, my friend," said the Shadow to the learned man. "I've now become as happy and powerful as a man can be. Now I should like to do something special for you. You are to live continually with me at the Castle, drive out with me in the royal carriage, and have ten thousand pounds a year. But you must let everybody call you 'Shadow'; you mustn't ever say you have been a man; and once a year, when I sit in the sun on the balcony to show myself to the people, you must lie at my feet in the way that a shadow does. Let me tell you—I am marrying the Princess; the wedding is to take place this evening."

"Goodness gracious!" said the learned man, "what could be worse than that? No, I won't, I won't do it. We'd be swindling the whole country, Princess and all. I'll tell them everything—that I am the man and you are the shadow, and that you are only dressed up."

"Nobody will believe you," said the Shadow. "Be sensible, or I'll call the guard."

"I'm going straight to the Princess," said the learned man. "But I'm going first," said the Shadow, "and you're going to prison." And go he did, for the sentries obeyed the one they knew the Princess wanted to marry.

"You are trembling," said the Princess, as the Shadow came up to her. "Has anything happened? You mustn't get ill to-night, just when we are to have our wedding."

"I have been through the most horrible experience possible," said the Shadow. "Just fancy—of course, a poor shadow-brain like that can't stand much—fancy! my shadow has gone mad. He thinks that he's a man and that I—just imagine— am his shadow!"

"How terrible!" exclaimed the Princess. "He's safely shut up, I hope?"

"Yes, yes. I'm afraid he'll never recover."

"Poor shadow!" said the Princess. "How unfortunate for him! It would be a real kindness to relieve him of the scrap of life that is left him. And now I come to think it over properly, I believe that's what has got to be done—put him quietly out of the way."

"It does seem hard," said the Shadow, "for he was a faithful servant." And he produced a kind of sigh.

"You have a noble character," said the Princess.

At night the whole town was illuminated. Guns went off—boom! Soldiers presented arms. It was no end of a wedding. The Princess and the Shadow came out on to the balcony to show themselves and to get one more round of cheering—hooray!

The learned man heard nothing of all this, for he had already been put to death.

UNDERSTANDING THE STORY

1. What does it mean that the Shadow takes on his own identity while he is inside Poetry's apartment? What do his responses to the learned man's questions reveal about him?

2. Who is more human, the learned man or the Shadow? To what extent, if any, is the learned man correct when he says that the Shadow is a fraud because he is only masquerading as a human being?

3. How does the wisdom of the Shadow differ from the wisdom of the learned man?

4. Why does the Shadow, once he is independent, continue to visit the learned man? Why doesn't the learned man refuse to have anything to do with the Shadow?

5. Should the learned man have accepted the Shadow's terms at the end? Explain your point of view.

6. In what sense do both the learned man and the Shadow triumph at the end?

7. What **themes** do you find in this story?

ANALYZING LITERARY TECHNIQUE

1. At first reading, this story appears very simple, like a fairy tale written for children. How does Andersen achieve this effect? When does it become clear that this is more than a simple tale for children?

2. Describe the relationship between the learned man and the Shadow. To what extent are the learned man and the Shadow **doppelgängers?**

3. How do images of light function in this story?

4. How does Andersen use humor in this story? Pick two elements of the story that you find humorous and describe how they contribute to the total effect of the story.

5. This story includes many examples of **irony.** Find two examples of irony and explain their contribution to the satiric aspects of the story.

WRITING ABOUT LITERATURE

1. Write an essay in which you analyze how Andersen uses humor and irony in "The Shadow" to depict his view of society. Examine the words and actions of the Shadow and the Princess and show how Andersen uses them to depict society. Look closely at the learned man's position in the story. Use quotations to support your ideas.

2. Write a fairy-tale-like story of your own, in prose or in poetry. Choose an incident and characters that will enable you to convey a basic moral. As an alternative, revise a simple fairy tale, either to give it a different moral (if it already seems to have one) or to give it a definite moral (if it doesn't seem to have one).

The Heavenly Christmas Tree

FYODOR DOSTOYEVSKY

*F*YODOR DOSTOYEVSKY (1821–1881), the great Russian novelist, is known for his examination of the human soul through the technique of psychological realism, a narrative perspective that has had a profound influence on writers throughout the world. Dostoyevsky portrays the tragic economic and social conditions of the common people and the moral responsibility of human beings to respond to others' needs by relating his stories through the thoughts and feelings of his characters. He is best known for "Notes from the Underground" (1864), *Crime and Punishment* (1866), "A Gentle Creature" (1876), and *The Brothers Karamazov* (1880), which is considered his greatest novel.

Dostoyevsky was born in Moscow, Russia. He was the son of an army doctor whose temperament was so harsh that he was murdered by the family's serfs. Because Dostoyevsky preferred the career of a writer to his father's choice of army engineer, he resigned his army commission in 1844 in order to write full-time. In 1849, at the age of twenty-eight, he was arrested for participating in a discussion group that criticized the government. After eight months of imprisonment in St. Petersburg, he was sentenced to death. Just as he was about to be shot, he was told that his death sentence had been commuted to imprisonment in Siberia; he was released four years later. During most of his adult life, Dostoyevsky suffered from great poverty. He also suffered from epilepsy. Through it all, he continued to write, and he used his varied experiences to enhance his creativity.

Dostoyevsky was always aware of the plight of the common people in Russian society, and he was gifted in his ability to observe and describe their lives. His first novel, *Poor Folk* (1845), brought him immediate fame. Years later, in 1862, he found conditions in London so disturbing that his visit affected the content and focus of his later writing. He was appalled that industrialization had created a society in which the wealthy few had no interest in the great masses of the poor, who endured so much hardship and suffering.

"The Heavenly Christmas Tree" evolved from Dostoyevsky's observation of a poor child during that London visit. It is characteristic of his writing in that it reflects his compassion for the poor and his interest in portraying the tragic conditions of their lives through the technique of psychological realism. Thus, he tells the story through the thoughts and feelings of a child.

I am a novelist, and I suppose I have made up this story. I write "I suppose," though I know for a fact that I have made it up, but yet I keep fancying that it must have happened on Christmas Eve in some great town in a time of terrible frost.

I have a vision of a boy, a little boy, six years old or even younger. This boy woke up that morning in a cold damp cellar. He was dressed in a sort of little dressing-gown and was shivering with cold. There was a cloud of white steam from his breath, and sitting on a box in the corner, he blew the steam out of his mouth and amused himself in his dullness watching it float away. But he was terribly hungry. Several times that morning he went up to the plank bed where his sick mother was lying on a mattress as thin as a pancake, with some sort of bundle under her head for a pillow. How had she come here? She must have come with her boy from some other town and suddenly fallen ill. The landlady who let the "corners"[1] had been taken two days before to the police station, the lodgers were out and about as the holiday was so near, and the only one left had been lying for the last twenty-four hours dead drunk, not having waited for Christmas. In another corner of the room a wretched old woman of eighty, who had once been a children's nurse but was now left to die friendless, was moaning and groaning with rheumatism, scolding and grumbling at the boy so that he was afraid to go near her corner. He had got a drink of water in the outer room, but could not find a crust anywhere, and had been on the point of waking his mother a dozen times. He felt frightened at last in the darkness: it had long been dusk, but no light was kindled. Touching his mother's face, he was surprised that she did not move at all, and that she was as cold as the wall. "It is very cold here," he thought. He stood a little, unconsciously letting his hands rest on the dead woman's shoulders, then he breathed on his fingers to warm them, and then quietly fumbling for his cap on the bed, he went out of the cellar. He would have gone earlier, but was afraid of the big dog which had been howling all day at the neighbour's door at the top of the stairs. But the dog was not there now, and he went out into the street.

Mercy on us, what a town! He had never seen anything like it before. In the town from which he had come, it was always such black darkness at night. There was one lamp for the whole street, the little, low-pitched, wooden houses were closed up with shutters, there was no one to be seen in the street after dusk, all the people shut themselves up in their houses, and there was nothing but the howling of packs of dogs, hundreds and thousands of them barking and howling

---

[1] "corners": Living space less than a whole room.

all night. But there it was so warm and he was given food, while here—oh, dear, if only he had something to eat! And what a noise and rattle here, what light and what people, horses and carriages, and what a frost! The frozen steam hung in clouds over the horses, over their warmly breathing mouths; their hoofs clanged against the stones through the powdery snow, and everyone pushed so, and—oh, dear, how he longed for some morsel to eat, and how wretched he suddenly felt. A policeman walked by and turned away to avoid seeing the boy.

There was another street—oh, what a wide one, here he would be run over for certain; how everyone was shouting, racing and driving along, and the light, the light! And what was this? A huge glass window, and through the window a tree reaching up to the ceiling; it was a fir tree, and on it were ever so many lights, gold papers and apples and little dolls and horses; and there were children clean and dressed in their best running about the room, laughing and playing and eating and drinking something. And then a little girl began dancing with one of the boys, what a pretty little girl! And he could hear the music through the window. The boy looked and wondered and laughed, though his toes were aching with the cold and his fingers were red and stiff so that it hurt him to move them. And all at once the boy remembered how his toes and fingers hurt him, and began crying, and ran on; and again through another window-pane he saw another Christmas tree, and on a table cakes of all sorts—almond cakes, red cakes and yellow cakes, and three grand young ladies were sitting there, and they gave the cakes to any one who went up to them, and the door kept opening, lots of gentlemen and ladies went in from the street. The boy crept up, suddenly opened the door and went in. Oh, how they shouted at him and waved him back! One lady went up to him hurriedly and slipped a kopeck[2] in his hand, and with her own hands opened the door into the street for him! How frightened he was. And the kopeck rolled away and clinked upon the steps; he could not bend his red fingers to hold it right. The boy ran away and went on, where he did not know. He was ready to cry again but he was afraid, and ran on and on and blew his fingers. And he was miserable because he felt suddenly so lonely and terrified, and all at once, mercy on us! What was this again? People were standing in a crowd admiring. Behind a glass window there were three little dolls, dressed in red and green dresses, and exactly, exactly as though they were alive. One was a little old man sitting and playing a big violin, the two others were standing close by and playing little violins, and nodding in time, and looking at one another, and their lips moved, they were speaking, actually speaking, only one couldn't hear through the glass. And at first the boy thought they were alive, and when he grasped that they were dolls he laughed. He had never seen such dolls before, and had no idea there were such dolls! And he wanted to cry, but he felt amused, amused by the dolls. All at once he fancied that some one caught at his smock behind: a wicked big boy was standing beside him and suddenly hit him on the head, snatched off his cap and tripped him up. The boy fell down on the ground, at once there was a shout, he was numb with fright, he jumped up and ran away. He ran, and not knowing

---

[2] *kopeck:* Russian coin worth $\frac{1}{100}$ of a ruble.

where he was going, ran in at the gate of some one's courtyard, and sat down behind a stack of wood: "They won't find me here, besides it's dark!"

He sat huddled up and was breathless from fright, and all at once, quite suddenly, he felt so happy: his hands and feet suddenly left off aching and grew so warm, as warm as though he were on a stove; then he shivered all over, then he gave a start, why, he must have been asleep. How nice to have a sleep here! "I'll sit here a little and go and look at the dolls again," said the boy, and smiled thinking of them. "Just as though they were alive! . . ." And suddenly he heard his mother singing over him. "Mammy, I am asleep; how nice it is to sleep here!"

"Come to my Christmas tree, little one," a soft voice suddenly whispered over his head.

He thought that this was still his mother, but no, it was not she. Who it was calling him, he could not see, but someone bent over and embraced him in the darkness; and he stretched out his hands to him, and . . . and all at once—oh, what a bright light! Oh, what a Christmas tree! And yet it was not a fir tree, he had never seen a tree like that! Where was he now? Everything was bright and shining, and all round him were dolls; but no, they were not dolls, they were little boys and girls, only so bright and shining. They all came flying round him, they all kissed him, took him and carried him along with them, and he was flying himself, and he saw that his mother was looking at him and laughing joyfully. "Mammy, Mammy; oh, how nice it is here, Mammy!" And again he kissed the children and wanted to tell them at once of those dolls in the shop window.

"Who are you, boys? Who are you, girls?" he asked, laughing and admiring them.

"This is Christ's Christmas tree," they answered. "Christ always has a Christmas tree on this day, for the little children who have no tree of their own . . ." And he found out that all these little boys and girls were children just like himself; that some had been frozen in the baskets in which they had as babies been laid on the doorsteps of well-to-do Petersburg[3] people, others had been boarded out with Finnish women by the Foundling[4] and had been suffocated, others had died at their starved mother's breasts (in the Samara famine[5]), others had died in the third-class railway carriages from the foul air; and yet they were all here, they were all like angels about Christ, and He was in the midst of them and held out His hands to them and blessed them and their sinful mothers. . . . And the mothers of these children stood on one side weeping; each one knew her boy or girl, and the children flew up to them and kissed them and wiped away their tears with their little hands, and begged them not to weep because they were so happy.

And down below in the morning the porter found the little dead body of the frozen child on the woodstack; they sought out his mother too. . . . She had died before him. They met before the Lord God in heaven.

Why have I made up such a story, so out of keeping with an ordinary diary, and a writer's above all? And I promised two stories dealing with real events! But

---

[3] *Petersburg:* Former capital of Russia.

[4] *Foundling:* Organization for the care of abandoned children.

[5] *Samara famine:* Samara was a Russian city, now known as Kuibyshev.

that is just it, I keep fancying that all this may have happened really—that is, what took place in the cellar and on the woodstack; but as for Christ's Christmas tree, I cannot tell you whether that could have happened or not.

UNDERSTANDING THE STORY

1. What is Dostoyevsky's purpose in writing this tale?
2. What does the boy's treatment reveal about society?
3. What effect do the Christmas festivities have on the boy? To what extent would he have been better off without having seen them?
4. How does Dostoyevsky's final comment about Christ's Christmas tree affect the meaning of the story?

ANALYZING LITERARY TECHNIQUE

1. Why does Dostoyevsky make the **protagonist** a six-year-old child?
2. Why does he set the story at Christmastime?
3. How does Dostoyevsky reveal what human traits are important?
4. What elements of Dostoyevsky's style are reminiscent of a **folktale?** What do they contribute to the story? What keeps the story from being a **fairy tale?**
5. Find two examples of **psychological realism.** Explain how Dostoyevsky's use of psychological realism contributes to the total effect of the story.
6. What is the function of **irony** in this story?
7. What is the **tone** of this story, and how does Dostoyevsky achieve it?

WRITING ABOUT LITERATURE

1. **Realism** and **naturalism** were two important movements in nineteenth- and early twentieth-century European fiction. Write an essay explaining whether this story is a realist or a naturalist piece of fiction. Use quotations from the story to support your point of view.
2. Analyze how Dostoyevsky uses psychological realism in this story. Choose at least three examples of psychological realism from the story, and explain what each contributes to the story as a whole. In your conclusion, evaluate what Dostoyevsky achieves by using this technique.
3. Tell this story from the **point of view** of the policeman, or of one of the people at the Christmas party that the boy interrupts. Consider the following questions: How would the policeman or party-goer feel about the boy? How would the other character explain the boy's behavior? To what extent, if any, would the other character feel guilty? Whom would the character hold responsible for the situation?

How Much Land Does a Man Need?

LEO TOLSTOY

OUNT LEO TOLSTOY (1828–1910) was fascinated by both the principles and details of human behavior, and his stories reflect the passion and the philosophical and psychological examination that he brought to his own life. He is best known for his novels *War and Peace* (1863–1869) and *Anna Karenina* (1875–1877) and for his short stories "The Death of Ivan Ilyich" (1886), "The Kreutzer Sonata" (1889), and "Master and Man" (1895).

Tolstoy was born into the Russian nobility on the family estate, Yásnaya Polyána, to the south of Moscow. By the time he was ten years old, both his mother and father had died, and he was reared by his aunt. Tolstoy attended the University of Kazan for three years. After a brief period at home, where he was unsuccessful in his attempts to improve the living conditions of the family's serfs, he joined the army. He spent the years from 1851 to 1855 as an artillery officer. It was during this period that he began his career as a writer. After two autobiographical works, he wrote the war stories that first made him famous. In time, he returned to the family estate, where, in 1859, he established a progressive school for the serfs' children. To him, the good life was the simple life, one that involved the love of his neighbors and of nature.

From the start of his literary career, Tolstoy viewed fiction as a way to examine the nature of life. His first work, *Childhood* (1852), explores life from the point of view of a child, and *Sebastopol Tales* (1855–1856), the work that established his literary reputation, examines life from the perspective of a soldier in the Crimean War. In 1862, at the age of thirty-four, he married and began the happiest and most creative period of his life, which included the writing of *War and Peace* and *Anna Karenina*. However, the writing of *Anna Karenina* caused him to confront the meaning of his own life, and the completion of the novel in 1877 induced what became a severe psychological crisis.

In the early 1880s, Tolstoy emerged a "new" man, with a personal, radically religious view of life that transformed both this private life and the content and style of his writing. He continued to closely examine human behavior in his fiction. However, he now conducted his examinations against a rigid moral and ethical code that demanded love of others, adherence to the truth, and rejection of any type of violence, exploitation, or materialism. In keeping with his new beliefs, Tolstoy tried to live like a simple peasant. One day, in the autumn of 1910, at the age of 82, he disappeared from his estate. He was finally found, dying, in an isolated railroad station. Among his last words was the question: "The serfs—How do serfs die?"

Tolstoy's stories from this period of his life are based on European folktales and Russian medieval legends. He found the clear delineation of character and behavior in folk literature to be the most effective way of artistically conveying the new moral and ethical emphasis in his writing.

I

An elder sister came to visit her younger sister in the country. The elder was married to a tradesman in town, the younger to a peasant in the village. As the sisters sat over their tea talking, the elder began to boast of the advantages of town life: saying how comfortably they lived there, how well they dressed, what fine clothes her children wore, what good things they ate and drank, and how she went to the theatre, promenades, and entertainments.

The younger sister was piqued, and in turn disparaged the life of a tradesman, and stood up for that of a peasant.

"I would not change my way of life for yours," said she. "We may live roughly, but at least we are free from anxiety. You live in better style than we do, but though you often earn more than you need, you are very likely to lose all you have. You know the proverb, 'Loss and gain are brothers twain.' It often happens that people who are wealthy one day are begging their bread the next. Our way is safer. Though a peasant's life is not a fat one, it is a long one. We shall never grow rich, but we shall always have enough to eat."

The elder sister said sneeringly:

"Enough? Yes, if you like to share with the pigs and the calves! What do you know of elegance or manners! However much your goodman may slave, you will die as you are living—on a dung heap—and your children the same."

"Well, what of that?" replied the younger. "Of course our work is rough and coarse. But, on the other hand, it is sure, and we need not bow to any one. But you, in your towns, are surrounded by temptations; to-day all may be right, but tomorrow the Evil One may tempt your husband with cards, wine, or women, and all will go to ruin. Don't such things happen often enough?"

Pahóm, the master of the house, was lying on top of the stove[1] and he listened to the women's chatter.

---

[1] *top of the stove:* Russian stoves often had a shelf above them that served as a place to dry clothes or to sleep.

"It is perfectly true," thought he. "Busy as we are from childhood tilling mother earth, we peasants have no time to let any nonsense settle in our heads. Our only trouble is that we haven't land enough. If I had plenty of land, I shouldn't fear the Devil himself!"

The women finished their tea, chatted a while about dress, and then cleared away the tea-things and lay down to sleep.

But the Devil had been sitting behind the stove, and had heard all that was said. He was pleased that the peasant's wife had led her husband into boasting, and that he had said that if he had plenty of land he would not fear the Devil himself.

"All right," thought the Devil. "We will have a tussle. I'll give you land enough; and by means of that land I will get you into my power."

II

Close to the village there lived a lady, a small land-owner who had an estate of about three hundred acres. She had always lived on good terms with the peasants until she engaged as her steward an old soldier, who took to burdening the people with fines. However careful Pahóm tried to be, it happened again and again that now a horse of his got among the lady's oats, now a cow strayed into her garden, now his calves found their way into her meadows—and he always had to pay a fine.

Pahóm paid up, but grumbled, and going home in a temper, was rough with his family. All through that summer, Pahóm had much trouble because of this steward, and he was even glad when winter came and the cattle had to be stabled. Though he grudged the fodder when they could no longer graze on the pasture-land, at least he was free from anxiety about them.

In the winter the news got about that the lady was going to sell her land and that the keeper of the inn on the high road was bargaining for it. When the peasants heard this they were very much alarmed.

"Well," thought they, "if the innkeeper gets the land, he will worry us with fines worse than the lady's steward. We all depend on that estate."

So the peasants went on behalf of their Commune, and asked the lady not to sell the land to the innkeeper, offering her a better price for it themselves. The lady agreed to let them have it. Then the peasants tried to arrange for the Commune to buy the whole estate, so that it might be held by them all in common. They met twice to discuss it, but could not settle the matter; the Evil One sowed discord among them and they could not agree. So they decided to buy the land individually, each according to his means; and the lady agreed to this plan as she had to the other.

Presently Pahóm heard that a neighbor of his was buying fifty acres, and that the lady had consented to accept one half in cash and to wait a year for the other half. Pahóm felt envious.

"Look at that," thought he, "the land is being sold, and I shall get none of it." So he spoke to his wife.

"Other people are buying," said he, "and we must also buy twenty acres or so. Life is becoming impossible. That steward is simply crushing us with his fines."

So they put their heads together and considered how they could manage to buy it. They had one hundred rúbles[2] laid by. They sold a colt and one half of their bees, hired out one of their sons as a labourer and took his wages in advance; borrowed the rest from a brother-in-law, and so scraped together half the purchase money.

Having done this, Pahóm chose out a farm of forty acres, some of it wooded, and went to the lady to bargain for it. They came to an agreement, and he shook hands with her upon it and paid her a deposit in advance. Then they went to town and signed the deeds; he paying half the price down, and undertaking to pay the remainder within two years.

So now Pahóm had land of his own. He borrowed seed, and sowed it on the land he had bought. The harvest was a good one, and within a year he had managed to pay off his debts both to the lady and to his brother-in-law. So he became a landowner, ploughing and sowing his own land, making hay on his own land, cutting his own trees, and feeding his cattle on his own pasture. When he went out to plough his fields, or to look at his growing corn, or at his grass-meadows, his heart would fill with joy. The grass that grew and the flowers that bloomed there seemed to him unlike any that grew elsewhere. Formerly, when he had passed by that land, it had appeared the same as any other land, but now it seemed quite different.

III

So Pahóm was well-contented, and everything would have been right if the neighbouring peasants would only not have trespassed on his corn-fields and meadows. He appealed to them most civilly, but they still went on: now the Communal herdsman would let the village cows stray into his meadows, then horses from the night pasture would get among his corn. Pahóm turned them out again and again, and forgave their owners, and for a long time he forbore to prosecute any one. But at last he lost patience and complained to the District Court. He knew it was the peasants' want of land, and no evil intent on their part, that caused the trouble, but he thought:

"I cannot go on overlooking it or they will destroy all I have. They must be taught a lesson."

So he had them up, gave them one lesson, and then another, and two or three of the peasants were fined. After a time Pahóm's neighbours began to bear him a grudge for this, and would now and then let their cattle on to his land on purpose. One peasant even got into Pahóm's wood at night and cut down five young lime trees for their bark. Pahóm passing through the wood one day noticed something white. He came nearer and saw the stripped trunks lying on the ground, and close by stood the stumps where the trees had been. Pahóm was furious.

---

[2] *rúbles:* The ruble is a Russian unit of money.

"If he had only cut one here and there it would have been bad enough," thought Pahóm, "but the rascal has actually cut down a whole clump. If I could only find out who did this, I would pay him out."

He racked his brains as to who it could be. Finally he decided: "It must be Simon—no one else could have done it." So he went to Simon's homestead to have a look around, but he found nothing, and only had an angry scene. However, he now felt more certain than ever that Simon had done it, and he lodged a complaint. Simon was summoned. The case was tried, and retried, and at the end of it all Simon was acquitted, there being no evidence against him. Pahóm felt still more aggrieved, and let his anger loose upon the Elder and the Judges.

"You let thieves grease your palms," said he. "If you were honest folk yourselves you would not let a thief go free."

So Pahóm quarrelled with the Judges and with his neighbours. Threats to burn his building began to be uttered. So though Pahóm had more land, his place in the Commune was much worse than before.

About this time a rumour got about that many people were moving to new parts.

"There's no need for me to leave my land," thought Pahóm. "But some of the others might leave our village and then there would be more room for us. I would take over their land myself and make my estate a bit bigger. I could then live more at ease. As it is, I am still too cramped to be comfortable."

One day Pahóm was sitting at home when a peasant, passing through the village, happened to call in. He was allowed to stay the night, and supper was given him. Pahóm had a talk with this peasant and asked him where he came from. The stranger answered that he came from beyond the Vólga,[3] where he had been working. One word led to another, and the man went on to say that many people were settling in those parts. He told how some people from his village had settled there. They had joined the Commune, and had had twenty-five acres per man granted them. The land was so good, he said, that the rye sown on it grew as high as a horse, and so thick that five cuts of a sickle made a sheaf. One peasant, he said, had brought nothing with him but his bare hands, and now he had six horses and two cows of his own.

Pahóm's heart kindled with desire. He thought:

"Why should I suffer in this narrow hole, if one can live so well elsewhere? I will sell my land and my homestead here, and with the money I will start afresh over there and get everything new. In this crowded place one is always having trouble. But I must first go and find out all about it myself."

Towards summer he got ready and started. He went down the Vólga on a steamer to Samára,[4] then walked another three hundred miles on foot, and at last reached the place. It was just as the stranger had said. The peasants had plenty of land: every man had twenty-five acres of Communal land given him for his

---

[3] *Vólga:* River that flows through Russia to the Caspian Sea.
[4] *Samára:* Russian city, now known as Kuibyshev.

use, and any one who had money could buy, besides, at fifty cents an acre as much good freehold land as he wanted.

Having found all he wished to know, Pahóm returned home as autumn came on, and began selling off his belongings. He sold his land at a profit, sold his homestead and all his cattle, and withdrew from membership of the Commune. He only waited till the spring, and then started with his family for the new settlement.

IV

As soon as Pahóm and his family reached their new abode, he applied for admission into the Commune of a large village. He stood treat to the Elders and obtained the necessary documents. Five shares of Communal land were given him for his own and his sons' use: that is to say—125 acres (not all together, but in different fields) besides the use of the Communal pasture. Pahóm put up the buildings he needed, and bought cattle. Of the Communal land alone he had three times as much as at his former home, and the land was good corn-land. He was ten time better off than he had been. He had plenty of arable land and pasturage, and could keep as many head of cattle as he liked.

At first, in the bustle of building and settling down, Pahóm was pleased with it all, but when he got used to it he began to think that even here he had not enough land. The first year, he sowed wheat on his share of the Communal land and had a good crop. He wanted to go on sowing wheat, but had not enough Communal land for the purpose, and what he had already used was not available; for in those parts wheat is only sown on virgin soil or on fallow land. It is sown for one or two years, and then the land lies fallow till it is again overgrown with prairie grass. There were many who wanted such land and there was not enough for all; so that people quarrelled about it. Those who were better off wanted it for growing wheat, and those who were poor wanted to let it to dealers, so that they might raise money to pay their taxes. Pahóm wanted to sow more wheat, so he rented land from a dealer for a year. He sowed much wheat and had a fine crop, but the land was too far from the village—the wheat had to be carted more than ten miles. After a time Pahóm noticed that some peasant-dealers were living on separate farms and were growing wealthy; and he thought:

"If I were to buy some freehold land and have a homestead on it, it would be a different thing altogether. Then it would all be nice and compact."

The question of buying freehold land recurred to him again and again.

He went on in the same way for three years, renting land and sowing wheat. The seasons turned out well and the crops were good, so that he began to lay money by. He might have gone on living contentedly, but he grew tired of having to rent other people's land every year, and having to scramble for it. Wherever there was good land to be had, the peasants would rush for it and it was taken up at once, so that unless you were sharp about it you got none. It happened in the third year that he and a dealer together rented a piece of pasture land from some peasants; and they had already ploughed it up, when there was some dispute and the peasants went to law about it, and things fell out so that the labour was all lost.

"If it were my own land," thought Pahóm, "I should be independent, and there would not be all this unpleasantness."

So Pahóm began looking out for land which he could buy; and he came across a peasant who had bought thirteen hundred acres, but having got into difficulties was willing to sell again cheap. Pahóm bargained and haggled with him, and at last they settled the price at 1,500 rúbles, part in cash and part to be paid later. They had all but clinched the matter when a passing dealer happened to stop at Pahóm's one day to get a feed for his horses. He drank tea with Pahóm and they had a talk. The dealer said that he was just returning from the land of the Bashkírs,[5] far away, where he had bought thirteen thousand acres of land, all for 1,000 rúbles. Pahóm questioned him further, and the tradesman said:

"All one need do is to make friends with the chiefs. I gave away about one hundred rúbles' worth of silk robes and carpets, besides a case of tea, and I gave wine to those who would drink it; and I got the land for less than a penny an acre." And he showed Pahóm the title-deeds, saying:

"The land lies near a river, and the whole prairie is virgin soil."

Pahóm plied him with questions, and the tradesman said:

"There is more land there than you could cover if you walked a year, and it all belongs to the Bashkírs. They are as simple as sheep, and land can be got almost for nothing."

"There now," thought Pahóm, "with my one thousand rúbles, why should I get only thirteen hundred acres, and saddle myself with a debt besides? If I take it out there, I can get more than ten times as much for the money."

V

Pahóm inquired how to get to the place, and as soon as the tradesman had left him, he prepared to go there himself. He left his wife to look after the homestead, and started on his journey taking his man with him. They stopped at a town on their way and bought a case of tea, some wine, and other presents, as the tradesman had advised. On and on they went until they had gone more than three hundred miles, and on the seventh day they came to a place where the Bashkírs had pitched their tents. It was all just as the tradesman had said. The people lived on the steppes, by a river, in felt-covered tents. They neither tilled the ground, nor ate bread. Their cattle and horses grazed in herds on the steppe. The colts were tethered behind the tents, and the mares were driven to them twice a day. The mares were milked, and from the milk kumiss[6] was made. It was the women who prepared kumiss, and they also made cheese. As far as the men were concerned, drinking kumiss and tea, eating mutton, and playing on their pipes was all they cared about. They were all stout and merry, and all the summer long they never thought of doing any work. They were quite ignorant, and knew no Russian, but were good-natured enough.

---

[5] *land of the Bashkírs:* Area in Russia between the Volga River and the Ural Mountains.

[6] *kumiss:* A drink made of fermented mare's milk.

As soon as they saw Pahóm, they came out of their tents and gathered round their visitor. An interpreter was found, and Pahóm told them he had come about some land. The Bashkírs seemed very glad; they took Pahóm and led him into one of the best tents, where they made him sit on some down cushions placed on a carpet, while they sat round him. They gave him some tea and kumiss, and had a sheep killed, and gave him mutton to eat. Pahóm took presents out of his cart and distributed them among the Bashkírs, and divided the tea amongst them. The Bashkírs were delighted. They talked a great deal among themselves, and then told the interpreter to translate.

"They wish to tell you," said the interpreter, "that they like you, and that it is our custom to do all we can to please a guest and to repay him for his gifts. You have given us presents, now tell us which of the things we possess please you best, that we may present them to you."

"What pleases me best here," answered Pahóm, "is your land. Our land is crowded and the soil is exhausted; but you have plenty of land and it is good land. I never saw the like of it."

The interpreter translated. The Bashkírs talked among themselves for a while. Pahóm could not understand what they were saying, but saw that they were much amused and that they shouted and laughed. Then they were silent and looked at Pahóm while the interpreter said:

"They wish me to tell you that in return for your presents they will gladly give you as much land as you want. You have only to point it out with your hand and it is yours."

The Bashkírs talked again for a while and began to dispute. Pahóm asked what they were disputing about, and the interpreter told him that some of them thought they ought to ask their Chief about the land and not act in his absence, while others thought there was no need to wait for his return.

VI

While the Bashkírs were disputing, a man in a large fox-fur cap appeared on the scene. They all became silent and rose to their feet. The interpreter said, "This is our Chief himself."

Pahóm immediately fetched the best dressing-gown and five pounds of tea, and offered these to the Chief. The Chief accepted them, and seated himself in the place of honour. The Bashkírs at once began telling him something. The Chief listened for a while, then made a sign with his head for them to be silent, and addressing himself to Pahóm, said in Russian:

"Well, let it be so. Choose whatever piece of land you like; we have plenty of it."

"How can I take as much as I like?" thought Pahóm. "I must get a deed to make it secure, or else they may say, 'It is yours,' and afterwards may take it away again."

"Thank you for your kind words," he said aloud. "You have much land, and I only want a little. But I should like to be sure which bit is mine. Could it not be measured and made over to me? Life and death are in God's hands. You good people give it to me, but your children might wish to take it away again."

"You are quite right," said the Chief. "We will make it over to you."

"I heard that a dealer had been here," continued Pahóm, "and that you gave him a little land, too, and signed title-deeds to that effect. I should like to have it done in the same way."

The Chief understood.

"Yes," replied he, "that can be done quite easily. We have a scribe, and we will go to town with you and have the deed properly sealed."

"And what will be the price?" asked Pahóm.

"Our price is always the same: one thousand rúbles a day." Pahóm did not understand.

"A day? What measure is that? How many acres would that be?"

"We do not know how to reckon it out," said the Chief. "We sell it by the day. As much as you can go round on your feet in a day is yours, and the price is one thousand rúbles a day."

Pahóm was surprised.

"But in a day you can get round a large tract of land," he said.

The Chief laughed.

"It will all be yours!" said he. "But there is one condition: If you don't return on the same day to the spot whence you started, your money is lost."

"But how am I to mark the way that I have gone?"

"Why, we shall go to any spot you like, and stay there. You must start from that spot and make your round, taking a spade with you. Wherever you think necessary, make a mark. At every turning, dig a hole and pile up the turf; then afterwards we will go round with a plough from hole to hole. You may make as large a circuit as you please, but before the sun sets you must return to the place you started from. All the land you cover will be yours."

Pahóm was delighted. It was decided to start early next morning. They talked a while, and after drinking some more kumiss and eating some more mutton, they had tea again, and then the night came on. They gave Pahóm a feather-bed to sleep on, and the Bashkírs dispersed for the night, promising to assemble the next morning at daybreak and ride out before sunrise to the appointed spot.

VII

Pahóm lay on the feather-bed, but could not sleep. He kept thinking about the land.

"What a large tract I will mark off!" thought he. "I can easily do thirty-five miles in a day. The days are long now, and within a circuit of thirty-five miles what a lot of land there will be! I will sell the poorer land, or let it to peasants, but I'll pick out the best and farm it. I will buy two ox-teams, and hire two more labourers. About a hundred and fifty acres shall be plough-land, and I will pasture cattle on the rest."

Pahóm lay awake all night, and dozed off only just before dawn. Hardly were his eyes closed when he had a dream. He thought he was lying in that same tent and heard somebody chuckling outside. He wondered who it could be, and rose and went out, and he saw the Bashkír Chief sitting in front of the tent holding his sides and rolling about with laughter. Going nearer to the Chief, Pahóm asked: "What are you laughing at?" But he saw that it was no longer the Chief, but the dealer who had recently stopped at his house and had told him about the land. Just as Pahóm was going to ask, "Have you been here long?" he saw that it was not the dealer, but the peasant who had come up from the Vólga, long ago, to Pahóm's old home. Then he saw that it was not the peasant either, but the Devil himself with hoofs and horns, sitting there and chuckling, and before him lay a man barefoot, prostrate on the ground, with only trousers and shirt on. And Pahóm dreamt that he looked more attentively to see what sort of a man it was that was lying there, and he saw that the man was dead, and that it was himself! He awoke horror-struck.

"What things one does dream," thought he.

Looking round he saw through the open door that the dawn was breaking.

"It's time to wake them up," thought he. "We ought to be starting."

He got up, roused his man (who was sleeping in his cart), bade him harness; and went to call the Bashkírs.

"It's time to go to the steppe to measure the land," he said.

The Bashkírs rose and assembled, and the Chief came too. Then they began drinking kumiss again, and offered Pahóm some tea, but he would not wait.

"If we are to go, let us go. It is high time," said he.

VIII

The Bashkírs got ready and they all started: some mounted on horses, and some in carts. Pahóm drove in his own small cart with his servant and took a spade with him. When they reached the steppe, the morning red was beginning to kindle. They ascended a hillock (called by the Bashkírs a *shikhan*) and dismounting from their carts and their horses, gathered in one spot. The Chief came up to Pahóm and stretching out his arm towards the plain:

"See," said he, "all this, as far as your eye can reach, is ours. You may have any part of it you like."

Pahóm's eyes glistened: it was all virgin soil, as flat as the palm of your hand, as black as the seed of a poppy, and in the hollows different kinds of grasses grew breast high.

The Chief took off his fox-fur cap, placed it on the ground and said:

"This will be the mark. Start from here, and return here again. All the land you go round shall be yours."

Pahóm took out his money and put it on the cap. Then he took off his outer coat, remaining in his sleeveless under-coat. He unfastened his girdle and tied it tight below his stomach, put a little bag of bread into the breast of his coat, and tying a flask of water to his girdle, he drew up the tops of his boots, took the spade from his man, and stood ready to start. He considered for some moments which way he had better go—it was tempting everywhere.

"No matter," he concluded, "I will go towards the rising sun."

He turned his face to the east, stretched himself, and waited for the sun to appear above the rim.

"I must lose no time," he thought, "and it is easier walking while it is still cool."

The sun's rays had hardly flashed above the horizon, before Pahóm, carrying the spade over his shoulder, went down into the steppe.

Pahóm started walking neither slowly nor quickly. After having gone a thousand yards he stopped, dug a hole, and placed pieces of turf one on another to make it more visible. Then he went on; and now that he had walked off his stiffness he quickened his pace. After a while he dug another hole.

Pahóm looked back. The hillock could be distinctly seen in the sunlight, with the people on it, and the glittering tyres of the cart-wheels. At a rough guess Pahóm concluded that he had walked three miles. It was growing warmer; he took off his under-coat, flung it across his shoulder, and went on again. It had grown quite warm now; he looked at the sun, it was time to think of breakfast.

"The first shift is done, but there are four in a day, and it is too soon yet to turn. But I will just take off my boots," said he to himself.

He sat down, took off his boots, stuck them into his girdle and went on. It was easy walking now.

"I will go on for another three miles," thought he, "and then turn to the left. This spot is so fine, that it would be a pity to lose it. The further one goes, the better the land seems."

He went straight on for a while, and when he looked round, the hillock was scarcely visible and the people on it looked like black ants, and he could just see something glistening there in the sun.

"Ah," thought Pahóm, "I have gone far enough in this direction, it is time to turn. Besides I am in a regular sweat, and very thirsty."

He stopped, dug a large hole, and heaped up pieces of turf. Next he untied his flask, had a drink, and then turned sharply to the left. He went on and on; the grass was high, and it was very hot.

Pahóm began to grow tired: he looked at the sun and saw that it was noon.

"Well," he thought, "I must have a rest."

He sat down, and ate some bread and drank some water; but he did not lie down, thinking that if he did he might fall asleep. After sitting a little while, he went on again. At first he walked easily: the food had strengthened him; but it had become terribly hot and he felt sleepy, still he went on, thinking: "An hour to suffer, a life-time to live."

He went a long way in this direction also, and was about to turn to the left again, when he perceived a damp hollow: "It would be a pity to leave that out," he thought. "Flax would do well there." So he went on past the hollow, and dug a hole on the other side of it before he turned the corner. Pahóm looked towards the hillock. The heat made the air hazy: it seemed to be quivering, and through the haze the people on the hillock could scarcely be seen.

"Ah!" thought Pahóm, "I have made the sides too long; I must make this one shorter." And he went along the third side, stepping faster. He looked at the sun: it was nearly half-way to the horizon, and he had not yet done two miles of the third side of the square. He was still ten miles from the goal.

"No," he thought, "though it will make my land lopsided, I must hurry back in a straight line now. I might go too far, and as it is I have a great deal of land."

So Pahóm hurriedly dug a hole, and turned straight towards the hillock.

IX

Pahóm went straight towards the hillock, but he now walked with difficulty. He was done up with the heat, his bare feet were cut and bruised, and his legs began to fail. He longed to rest, but it was impossible if he meant to get back before sunset. The sun waits for no man, and it was sinking lower and lower.

"Oh dear," he thought, "if only I have not blundered trying for too much! What if I am too late?"

He looked towards the hillock and at the sun. He was still far from his goal, and the sun was already near the rim.

Pahóm walked on and on; it was very hard walking but he went quicker and quicker. He pressed on, but was still far from the place. He began running, threw away his coat, his boots, his flask, and his cap, and kept only the spade which he used as a support.

"What shall I do," he thought again, "I have grasped too much and ruined the whole affair. I can't get there before the sun sets."

And this fear made him still more breathless. Pahóm went on running, his soaking shirt and trousers stuck to him and his mouth was parched. His breast was working like a blacksmith's bellows, his heart was beating like a hammer, and his legs were giving way as if they did not belong to him. Pahóm was seized with terror lest he should die of the strain.

Though afraid of death, he could not stop. "After having run all that way they will call me a fool if I stop now," thought he. And he ran on and on, and drew near and heard the Bashkírs yelling and shouting to him, and their cries inflamed his heart still more. He gathered his last strength and ran on.

The sun was close to the rim, and cloaked in mist looked large, and red as blood. Now, yes now, it was about to set! The sun was quite low, but he was also quite near his aim. Pahóm could already see the people on the hillock waving their arms to hurry him up. He could see the fox-fur cap on the ground and the money on it, and the Chief sitting on the ground holding his sides. And Pahóm remembered his dream.

"There is plenty of land," thought he, "but will God let me live on it? I have lost my life, I have lost my life! I shall never reach that spot!"

Pahóm looked at the sun, which had reached the earth: one side of it had already disappeared. With all his remaining strength he rushed on, bending his body forward so that his legs could hardly follow fast enough to keep him from falling. Just as he reached the hillock it suddenly grew dark. He looked up—the sun had already set! He gave a cry: "All my labour has been in vain," thought he, and was about to stop, but he heard the Bashkírs still shouting, and remembered that though to him, from below, the sun seemed to have set, they on the hillock could still see it. He took a long breath and ran up the hillock. It was still light there. He reached the top and saw the cap. Before it sat the Chief laughing and holding his sides. Again Pahóm remembered his dream, and he uttered a cry: his legs gave way beneath him, he fell forward and reached the cap with his hands.

"Ah, that's a fine fellow!" exclaimed the Chief. "He has gained much land!"

Pahóm's servant came running up and tried to raise him, but he saw that blood was flowing from his mouth. Pahóm was dead!

The Bashkírs clicked their tongues to show their pity.

His servant picked up the spade and dug a grave long enough for Pahóm to lie in, and buried him in it. Six feet from his head to his heels was all he needed.

UNDERSTANDING THE STORY

1. Why does Tolstoy give this story a rural setting and choose a peasant for the **protagonist?**

2. To what extent, if any, does Tolstoy agree with the younger sister that the peasant is less greedy than the tradesman? Why does the Devil know that he can use land to get Pahóm into his power?

3. Why does Tolstoy include the Devil in the story?

4. How does ownership of land affect Pahóm's personality?

5. What factors does Pahóm ignore in making his choices? Is his behavior wise or foolish? Why?

6. Why is the title of this story appropriate?

7. Why is the Bashkír chief laughing at the end of the story?

8. What is the significance of Pahóm's dream? To what extent, if any, does it represent the role of fate in his life?

9. Does Tolstoy want the reader to believe that it is better to be satisfied with what one has than to strive to improve upon it?

ANALYZING LITERARY TECHNIQUE

1. Why does Tolstoy begin this story with the argument between the two sisters?

2. Tolstoy is known for his skillful **characterization.** How does he achieve this with Pahóm?

3. Find two or three examples of **foreshadowing,** and explain the function of each in the story.

4. Find two or three examples of **irony,** and explain how each example contributes to the total effect of the story.

5. In what way is this tale a **parable?** What lesson does it teach and to whom?

WRITING ABOUT LITERATURE

1. Read the following quotation from Russian author Anton Chekhov's short story "Gooseberries":

   > Man needs not six feet of earth, not a farm, but the whole globe, all nature, where he will have room for the full play of all the capacities and peculiarities of his free spirit.

   How do the ideas expressed in this quotation compare with Tolstoy's view as expressed in "How Much Land Does a Man Need?" Write a brief essay comparing these two points of view. Use quotations from the story to support your argument.

2. Write a letter from Pahóm's wife to her sister in which she reacts positively or negatively to Pahóm's business ventures. Try to make your language characterize Pahóm's wife's personality.

A Doll's House

HENRIK IBSEN

*H*ENRIK IBSEN (1826–1906) profoundly influenced modern
drama with his technique of depicting powerful social and psychological themes through realistic dialogue and uncomplicated
action, a style that was strikingly modern in his time. His twelve major
prose plays reflect his commitment to personal freedom. In the earlier
group, represented by *A Doll's House* (1879), *Ghosts* (1881), and *An
Enemy of the People* (1882), courageous protagonists challenge the
values of the middle-class society in which they live. In the later group,
represented by *The Wild Duck* (1884) and *Hedda Gabler* (1890), Ibsen
reveals his interest and talent in the field of human psychology.

Ibsen was born in Skien, Norway, into a poor family. Finding neither enjoyment nor financial success in assisting a pharmacist, he
decided to pursue his hobby as a poet and playwright. In 1851, at the age
of twenty-three, he accepted an invitation to join the National Theater,
where he performed the functions of playwright, director, costume-
designer, and accountant. He continued to write for the theater
through years of professional failures and financial difficulties until
finally, in 1864, *The Pretenders* became the first of many successes.
That year Ibsen left Norway. He was disappointed in Norway's refusal
to support the concept of a Scandinavian community of nations, and
he felt a need for intellectual and emotional independence. He lived
nearly thirty years in other European countries, during which time he
wrote all of his major plays except *The Master Builder*. By the time he
returned to Norway in 1891, he had achieved his goal of becoming
Norway's great national dramatist.

Between 1871 and 1878, Ibsen was acquainted with a young
Norwegian woman who experienced a situation so disturbing that he
jotted down "Notes for a Modern Tragedy." In his "Notes," Ibsen writes:

> There are two kinds of moral laws, two kinds of conscience, one
> for men and one, quite different, for women. They don't understand
> each other; but in practical life, woman is judged by masculine law,

as though she weren't a woman but a man. . . . A woman cannot be herself in modern society.

Ibsen created the plot of A *Doll's House* from those ideas. Published in December of 1879, A *Doll's House* attacked contemporary social attitudes and conventions. Its production, first in Europe and then throughout the world, brought Ibsen international fame. The plot of A *Doll's House* was so incendiary that in February 1880 the actress who was to play the part of Nora in the German production refused to do so unless the final scene was rewritten with a more conventional ending. (With no copyright laws to protect his work, Ibsen reluctantly chose to rewrite the scene himself. However, the public would tolerate nothing but the original version, so the adaptation was short lived.)

The issues Ibsen raised blazed beyond the theater, into streets and homes. Underlying these issues was a simple but important idea: The principal obligation of each human being is to discover who he or she is and to strive to become that person. In the process one must be free to question existing conditions.

Ibsen was viewed by his contemporaries as a moral and social revolutionary who advocated female emancipation and intellectual freedom. In fact, however, he believed that freedom must come from within individuals rather than from the efforts of social and political organizations. He declared: "I have never written any play to further a social purpose. I have been more of a poet and less of a social philosopher·than most people seem inclined to believe," and "What is really wanted is a revolution of the spirit of man."

Today, a century later, A *Doll's House* continues to raise important issues about relationships between women and men: the right of women to determine and direct the course of their own lives; the role of the wife in a marriage; and, peripherally, the right of women to enjoy equal opportunity and recognition in the business world.

CHARACTERS

TORVALD HELMER

NORA HELMER

DR. RANK

NILS KROGSTAD

MRS. LINDEN

ANNA
ELLEN } *Servants*

IVAR
EMMY } *The Helmers' children*
BOB

Scene: Sitting-room in HELMER'*s House [a flat] in Christiania.*[1]
Time: The present day; Christmastide.
The action takes place on three consecutive days.

ACT I

A room comfortably and tastefully, but not expensively, furnished. In the background, to the right, a door leads to the hall; to the left, another door leads to HELMER'*s study. Between the two doors a pianoforte. In the middle of the left wall, a door, and nearer the front a window. Near the window a round table with armchairs and a small sofa. In the right wall, somewhat to the back, a door; and against the same wall, farther forward, a porcelain stove; in front of it a couple of armchairs and a rocking-chair. Between the stove and the side door a small table. Engravings on the walls. A whatnot with china and bric-à-brac. A small book-case of showily bound books. Carpet. A fire in the stove. A winter day.*

[*A bell rings in the hall outside. Presently the outer door is heard to open. Then* NORA *enters, humming contentedly. She is in out-door dress, and carries several parcels, which she lays on the right-hand table. She leaves the door into the hall open behind her, and a* PORTER *is seen outside carrying a Christmas-tree and a basket, which he gives to the maid-servant who has opened the door.*]

NORA: Hide the Christmas-tree carefully, Ellen; the children mustn't see it before this evening, when it's lighted up. [*To the* PORTER, *taking out her purse.*] How much?

PORTER: Fifty öre.[2]

NORA: There's a crown. No, keep the change. [*The* PORTER *thanks her and goes.* NORA *shuts the door. She continues smiling in quiet glee as she takes off her walking things. Then she takes from her pocket a bag of macaroons, and eats one or two. As she does so, she goes on tip-toe to her husband's door and listens.*]

NORA: Yes; he is at home. [*She begins humming again, going to the table on the right.*]

HELMER [*in his room*]: Is that my lark twittering there?

NORA [*busy opening some of her parcels*]: Yes, it is.

HELMER: Is it the squirrel skipping about?

NORA: Yes!

HELMER: When did the squirrel get home?

NORA: Just this minute. [*Hides the bag of macaroons in her pocket and wipes her mouth.*] Come here, Torvald, and see what I've bought.

---

[1] *Christiana:* Capital of Norway, now known as Oslo.
[2] *öre:* Norwegian coin; 1/100 of a krone or crown.

HELMER: Don't disturb me. [*A little later he opens the door and looks in, pen in hand.*] "Bought," did you say? What! all that? Has my little spendthrift been making the money fly again?

NORA: Why, Torvald, surely we can afford to launch out a little now! It's the first Christmas we haven't had to pinch.

HELMER: Come, come; we can't afford to squander money.

NORA: Oh, yes, Torvald, do let us squander a little—just the least little bit, won't you? You know you'll soon be earning heaps of money.

HELMER: Yes, from New Year's Day. But there's a whole quarter before my first salary is due.

NORA: Never mind; we can borrow in the meantime.

HELMER: Nora! [*He goes up to her and takes her playfully by the ear.*] Thoughtless as ever! Supposing I borrowed a thousand crowns to-day, and you spent it during Christmas week, and that on New Year's Eve a tile blew off the roof and knocked my brains out—

NORA [*laying her hand on his mouth*]: Hush! How can you talk so horridly?

HELMER: But, supposing it were to happen,—what then?

NORA: If anything so dreadful happened, I shouldn't care whether I was in debt or not.

HELMER: But what about the creditors?

NORA: They! Who cares for them? They're only strangers.

HELMER: Nora, Nora! What a woman you are! But seriously, Nora, you know my ideas on these points. No debts! No credit! Home-life ceases to be free and beautiful as soon as it is founded on borrowing and debt. We two have held out bravely till now, and we won't give in at the last.

NORA [*going to the fireplace*]: Very well—as you like, Torvald.

HELMER [*following her*]: Come, come; my little lark mustn't let her wings droop like that. What? Is the squirrel pouting there? [*Takes out his purse.*] Nora, what do you think I've got here?

NORA [*turning around quickly*]: Money!

HELMER: There! [*Gives her some notes.*] Of course I know all sorts of things are wanted at Christmas.

NORA [*counting*]: Ten, twenty, thirty, forty. Oh! thank you, Torvald. This will go a long way.

HELMER: I should hope so.

NORA: Yes, indeed, a long way! But come here, and see all I've been buying. And so cheap! Look here is a new suit for Ivar, and a little sword. Here are a horse and a trumpet for Bob. And here are a doll and a cradle for Emmy. They're only common; but she'll soon pull them all to pieces. And dresses and neckties for the servants; only I should have got something better for dear old Anna.

HELMER: And what's in that other parcel?

NORA [*crying out*]: No; Torvald, you're not to see that until this evening.

HELMER: Oh! ah! But now tell me, you little rogue, what have you got for yourself?

NORA: For myself? Oh, I don't want anything.

HELMER: Nonsense. Just tell me something sensible you would like to have.

NORA: No. Really I want nothing. . . . Well, listen, Torvald—

HELMER: Well?

NORA [*playing with his coat buttons, without looking him in the face*]: If you really want to give me something, you might, you know, you might—

HELMER: Well, well? Out with it!

NORA [*quickly*]: You might give me money, Torvald. Only just what you think you can spare; then I can buy myself something with it later.

HELMER: But Nora—

NORA: Oh, please do, dear Torvald, please do! Then I would hang the money in lovely gilt paper on the Christmas-tree. Wouldn't that be fun?

HELMER: What do they call the birds that are always making the money fly?

NORA: Yes, I know—spendthrifts, of course. But please do as I say, Torvald. Then I shall have time to think what I want most. Isn't that very sensible, now?

HELMER [*smiling*]: Certainly; that is to say, if you really kept the money I gave you, and really bought yourself something with it. But it all goes in house-keeping, and for all sorts of useless things, and then I have to find more.

NORA: But, Torvald—

HELMER: Can you deny it, Nora dear? [*He puts his arm round her.*] It's a sweet little lark; but it gets through a lot of money. No one would believe how much it costs a man to keep such a little bird as you.

NORA: For shame! how can you say so? Why, I save as much as ever I can.

HELMER [*laughing*]: Very true—as much as you can—but you can't.

NORA [*hums and smiles in quiet satisfaction*]: H'm!—you should just know, Torvald, what expenses we larks and squirrels have.

HELMER: You're a strange little being! Just like your father—always eager to get hold of money; but the moment you have it, it seems to slip through your fingers; you never know what becomes of it. Well, one must take you as you are. It's in the blood. Yes, Nora, that sort of thing is inherited.

NORA: I wish I had inherited many of my father's qualities.

HELMER: And I don't wish you anything but just what you are—my own, sweet little song-bird. But, I say—it strikes me—you look so, so—what shall I call it?—so suspicious to-day—

NORA: Do I?

HELMER: You do indeed. Look me full in the face.

NORA [*looking at him*]: Well?

HELMER [*threatening with his finger*]: Hasn't the little sweet-tooth been breaking the rules to-day?

NORA: No; how can you think of such a thing!

HELMER: Didn't she just look in at the confectioner's?

NORA: No, Torvald, really—

HELMER: Not to sip a little jelly?

NORA: No; certainly not.

HELMER: Hasn't she even nibbled a macaroon or two?

NORA: No, Torvald, indeed, indeed!

HELMER: Well, well, well; of course I'm only joking.

NORA [*goes to the table on the right*]: I shouldn't think of doing what you disapprove of.

HELMER: No, I'm sure of that; and, besides, you've given me your word. [*Going toward her.*] Well, keep your little Christmas secrets to yourself, Nora darling. The Christmas-tree will bring them all to light, I daresay.

NORA: Have you remembered to ask Dr. Rank?

HELMER: No. But it's not necessary; he'll come as a matter of course. Besides, I shall invite him when he looks in to-day. I've ordered some capital wine. Nora, you can't think how I look forward to this evening!

NORA: And I too. How the children will enjoy themselves, Torvald!

HELMER: Ah! it's glorious to feel that one has an assured position and ample means. Isn't it delightful to think of?

NORA: Oh, it's wonderful!

HELMER: Do you remember last Christmas? For three whole weeks beforehand you shut yourself up till long past midnight to make flowers for the Christmas-tree, and all sorts of other marvels that were to have astonished us. I was never so bored in my life.

NORA: I did not bore myself at all.

HELMER [*smiling*]: And it came to so little after all, Nora.

NORA: Oh! are you going to tease me about that again? How could I help the cat getting in and spoiling it all?

HELMER: To be sure you couldn't, my poor little Nora. You did your best to amuse us all, and that's the main thing. But, all the same, it's a good thing the hard times are over.

NORA: Oh, isn't it wonderful!

HELMER: Now, I needn't sit here boring myself all alone; and you needn't tire your dear eyes and your delicate little fingers—

NORA [clapping her hands]: No, I needn't, need I, Torvald? Oh! it's wonderful to think of! [Takes his arm.] And now I'll tell you how I think we ought to manage, Torvald. As soon as Christmas is over— [The hall-door bell rings.] Oh, there's a ring! [Arranging the room.] That's somebody come to call. How vexing!

HELMER: I am "not at home" to callers; remember that.

ELLEN [in the doorway]: A lady to see you, ma'am.

NORA: Show her in.

ELLEN [to HELMER]: And the Doctor is just come, sir.

HELMER: Has he gone into my study?

ELLEN: Yes, sir.

[HELMER goes into his study. ELLEN ushers in MRS. LINDEN in traveling costume, and shuts the door behind her.]

MRS. LINDEN [timidly and hesitatingly]: How do you do, Nora?

NORA [doubtfully]: How do you do?

MRS. LINDEN: I daresay you don't recognize me?

NORA: No, I don't think—oh, yes!—I believe— [Effusively]. What! Christina! Is it really you?

MRS. LINDEN: Yes; really I!

NORA: Christina! and to think I didn't know you! But how could I— [More softly.] How changed you are, Christina!

MRS. LINDEN: Yes, no doubt. In nine or ten years—

NORA: Is it really so long since we met? Yes, so it is. Oh! the last eight years have been a happy time, I can tell you. And now you have come to town? All that long journey in mid-winter! How brave of you.

MRS. LINDEN: I arrived by this morning's steamer.

NORA: To keep Christmas, of course. Oh, how delightful! What fun we shall have! Take your things off. Aren't you frozen? [Helping her.] There, now we'll sit down here cosily by the fire. No, you take the arm-chair; I'll sit in this rocking-chair. [Seizes her hand.] Yes, now I can see the dear old face again. It was only at the first glance—But you're a little paler, Christina, and perhaps a little thinner.

MRS. LINDEN: And much, much older, Nora.

NORA: Yes, perhaps a little older—not much—ever so little. [*She suddenly stops; seriously.*] Oh! what a thoughtless wretch I am! Here I sit chattering on, and—Dear, dear Christina, can you forgive me?

MRS. LINDEN: What do you mean, Nora?

NORA [*softly*]: Poor Christina! I forgot, you are a widow?

MRS. LINDEN: Yes; my husband died three years ago.

NORA: I know, I know, I saw it in the papers. Oh! believe me, Christina, I did mean to write to you; but I kept putting it off, and something always came in the way.

MRS. LINDEN: I can quite understand that, Nora dear.

NORA: No, Christina; it was horrid of me. Oh, you poor darling! how much you must have gone through!—and he left you nothing?

MRS. LINDEN: Nothing.

NORA: And no children?

MRS. LINDEN: None.

NORA: Nothing, nothing at all?

MRS. LINDEN: Not even a sorrow or a longing to dwell upon.

NORA [*looking at her incredulously*]: My dear Christina, how is that possible?

MRS. LINDEN [*smiling sadly and stroking her hair*]: Oh, it happens sometimes, Nora.

NORA: So utterly alone. How dreadful that must be! I have three of the loveliest children. I can't show them to you just now; they're out with their nurse. But now you must tell me everything.

MRS. LINDEN: No, no, I want you to tell me—

NORA: No, you must begin; I won't be egotistical to-day. To-day I will think of only you. Oh! I must tell you one thing; but perhaps you've heard of our great stroke of fortune?

MRS. LINDEN: No. What is it?

NORA: Only think! my husband has been made Manager of the Joint Stock Bank.

MRS. LINDEN: Your husband! Oh, how fortunate.

NORA: Yes, isn't it? A lawyer's position is so uncertain, you see, especially when he won't touch any business that's the least bit . . . shady, as of course Torvald won't; and in that I quite agree with him. Oh! you can imagine how glad we are. He is to enter on his new position at the New Year, and then he will have a large salary, and percentages. In future we shall be able to live quite differently—just as we please, in fact. Oh, Christina, I feel so light and happy! It's splendid to have lots of money, and no need to worry about things, isn't it?

MRS. LINDEN: Yes; it must be delightful to have what you need.

NORA: No, not only what you need but heaps of money—heaps!

MRS. LINDEN [*smiling*]: Nora, Nora, haven't you learnt reason yet? In our schooldays you were a shocking little spendthrift!

NORA [*quietly smiling*]: Yes; Torvald says I am still. [*Threatens with her finger.*] But "Nora, Nora," is not so silly as you all think. Oh! I haven't had the chance to be much of a spendthrift. We have both had to work.

MRS. LINDEN: You too?

NORA: Yes, light fancy work; crochet, and embroidery, and things of that sort [*Significantly.*], and other work too. You know, of course, that Torvald left the Government service when we were married. He had little chance of promotion, and of course he required to make more money. But in the first year of our marriage he overworked himself terribly. He had to undertake all sorts of odd jobs, you know, and to work early and late. He couldn't stand it, and fell dangerously ill. Then the doctors declared he must go to the South.

MRS. LINDEN: Yes; you spent a whole year in Italy, didn't you?

NORA: We did. It wasn't easy to manage, I can tell you. It was just after Ivar's birth. But of course we had to go. Oh, it was a delicious journey! And it saved Torvald's life. But it cost a frightful lot of money, Christina.

MRS. LINDEN: So I should think.

NORA: Twelve hundred dollars! Four thousand eight hundred crowns! Isn't that a lot of money?

MRS. LINDEN: How lucky you had the money to spend!

NORA: I must tell you we got it from father.

MRS. LINDEN: Ah, I see. He died just about that time, didn't he?

NORA: Yes, Christina, just then. And only think! I couldn't go and nurse him! I was expecting little Ivar's birth daily. And then I had my Torvald to attend to. Dear, kind old father! I never saw him again, Christina. Oh! that's the hardest thing I've had to bear since my marriage.

MRS. LINDEN: I know how fond you were of him. And then you went to Italy?

NORA: Yes; we had the money, and the doctors insisted. We started a month later.

MRS. LINDEN: And your husband returned completely cured?

NORA: Sound as a bell.

MRS. LINDEN: But—the doctor?

NORA: What about him?

MRS. LINDEN: I thought as I came in your servant announced the Doctor—

NORA: Oh, yes; Doctor Rank. But he doesn't come as a doctor. He's our best friend, and never lets a day pass without looking in. No, Torvald hasn't had an hour's illness since that time. And the children are so healthy and well, and so am I. [*Jumps up and claps her hands.*] Oh, Christina, Christina, it's so lovely to live and to be happy!—Oh! but it's really too horrid of me!—Here am I talking about nothing but my own concerns. [*Sits down upon a footstool close to her and lays her arms on* CHRISTINA's *lap.*] Oh! don't be angry with me!—Now just tell me, is it really true that you didn't love your husband? What made you take him?

MRS. LINDEN: My mother was then alive, bedridden and helpless; and I had my two younger brothers to think of. I thought it my duty to accept him.

NORA: Perhaps it was. I suppose he was rich then?

MRS. LINDEN: Very well off, I believe. But his business was uncertain. It fell to pieces at his death, and there was nothing left.

NORA: And then—?

MRS. LINDEN: Then I had to fight my way by keeping a shop, a little school, anything I could turn my hand to. The last three years have been one long struggle for me. But now it's over, Nora. My poor mother no longer needs me; she is at rest. And the boys are in business, and can look after themselves.

NORA: How free your life must feel!

MRS. LINDEN: No, Nora; only inexpressibly empty. No one to live for. [*Stands up restlessly.*] That is why I couldn't bear to stay any longer in that out-of-the-way corner. Here it must be easier to find something really worth doing—something to occupy one's thoughts. If I could only get some settled employment—some office-work.

NORA: But, Christina, that's so tiring, and you look worn out already. You should rather go to some watering-place and rest.

MRS. LINDEN [*going to the window*]: I have no father to give me the money, Nora.

NORA [*rising*]: Oh! don't be vexed with me.

MRS. LINDEN [*going toward her*]: My dear Nora, don't you be vexed with me. The worst of a position like mine is that it makes one bitter. You have no one to work for, yet you have to be always on the strain. You must live; and so you become selfish. When I heard of the happy change in your circumstances—can you believe it?—I rejoiced more on my own account than on yours.

NORA: How do you mean? Ah! I see. You mean Torvald could perhaps do something for you.

MRS. LINDEN: Yes; I thought so.

NORA: And so he shall, Christina. Just you leave it all to me. I shall lead up to it beautifully, and think of something pleasant to put him in a good humor! Oh! I should so love to do something for you.

MRS. LINDEN: How good of you, Nora! And doubly good in you, who know so little of the troubles of life.

NORA: I? I know so little of—?

MRS. LINDEN [*smiling*]: Ah, well! a little fancy-work, and so forth. You're a mere child, Nora.

NORA [*tosses her head and paces the room*]: Oh, come, you mustn't be so patronizing!

MRS. LINDEN: No?

NORA: You're like the rest. You all think I'm fit for nothing really serious—

MRS. LINDEN: Well—

NORA: You think I've had no troubles in this weary world.

MRS. LINDEN: My dear Nora, you've just told me all your troubles.

NORA: Pooh—these trifles. [*Softly.*] I haven't told you the great thing.

MRS. LINDEN: The great thing? What do you mean?

NORA: I know you look down upon me, Christina; but you've no right to. You're proud of having worked so hard and so long for your mother?

MRS. LINDEN: I'm sure I don't look down upon anyone; but it's true I'm both proud and glad when I remember that I was able to make my mother's last days free from care.

NORA: And you're proud to think of what you have done for your brothers?

MRS. LINDEN: Have I not the right to be?

NORA: Yes, surely. But now let me tell you, Christina—I too, have something to be proud and glad of.

MRS. LINDEN: I don't doubt it. But what do you mean?

NORA: Hush! Not so loud. Only think, if Torvald were to hear! He mustn't—not for worlds! No one must know about it, Christina—no one but you.

MRS. LINDEN: What can it be?

NORA: Come over here. [*Draws her beside her on the sofa.*] Yes—I, too, have something to be proud of and glad of. I saved Torvald's life.

MRS. LINDEN: Saved his life? How?

NORA: I told you about our going to Italy. Torvald would have died but for that.

MRS. LINDEN: Yes—and your father gave you the money.

NORA [*smiling*]: Yes, so Torvald and everyone believes; but—

MRS. LINDEN: But—

NORA: Father didn't give us one penny. *I* found the money.

MRS. LINDEN: You? All that money?

NORA: Twelve hundred dollars. Four thousand eight hundred crowns. What do you say to that?

MRS. LINDEN: My dear Nora, how did you manage it? Did you win it in the lottery?

NORA [*contemptuously*]: In the lottery? Pooh! Any fool could have done that!

MRS. LINDEN: Then wherever did you get it from?

NORA [*hums and smiles mysteriously*]: H'm; tra-la-la-la!

MRS. LINDEN: Of course you couldn't borrow it.

NORA: No? Why not?

MRS. LINDEN: Why, a wife can't borrow without her husband's consent.

NORA [*tossing her head*]: Oh! when the wife knows a little of business, and how to set about things, then—

MRS. LINDEN: But, Nora, I don't understand—

NORA: Well you needn't. I never said I borrowed the money. Perhaps I got it another way. [*Throws herself back on the sofa.*] I may have got it from some admirer. When one is so—attractive as I am—

MRS. LINDEN: You're too silly, Nora.

NORA: Now I'm sure you're dying of curiosity, Christina—

MRS. LINDEN: Listen to me, Nora dear. Haven't you been a little rash?

NORA [*sitting upright again*]: Is it rash to save one's husband's life?

MRS. LINDEN: I think it was rash of you, without his knowledge—

NORA: But it would have been fatal for him to know! Can't you understand that? He was never to suspect how ill he was. The doctors came to me privately and told me that his life was in danger—that nothing could save him but a trip to the South. Do you think I didn't try diplomacy first? I told him how I longed to have a trip abroad, like other young wives; I wept and prayed; I said he ought to think of my condition, and not thwart me; and then I hinted that he could borrow the money. But then, Christina, he got almost angry. He said I was frivolous, and that it was his duty as a husband not to yield to my whims and fancies—so he called them. Very well, thought I, but saved you must be; and then I found the way to do it.

MRS. LINDEN: And did your husband never learn from your father that the money was not from him?

NORA: No; never. Father died at that very time. I meant to have told him all about it, and begged him to say nothing. But he was so ill—unhappily, it was not necessary.

MRS. LINDEN: And you have never confessed to your husband?

NORA: Good Heavens! What can you be thinking of? Tell him, when he has such a loathing of debt? And besides—how painful and humiliating it would be for Torvald, with his manly self-reliance, to know that he owed anything to me! It would utterly upset the relation between us; our beautiful, happy home would never again be what it is.

MRS. LINDEN: Will you never tell him?

NORA [*thoughtfully, half-smiling*]: Yes, some time perhaps—after many years, when I'm—not so pretty. You mustn't laugh at me. Of course I mean when Torvald is not so much in love with me as he is now; when it doesn't amuse him any longer to see me skipping about, and dressing up and acting. Then it might be well to have something in reserve. [*Breaking off.*] Nonsense! nonsense! That time will never come. Now, what do you say to my grand secret, Christina? Am I fit for nothing now? You may believe it has cost me a lot of anxiety. It has been no joke to meet my engagements punctually. You must know, Christina, that in business there are things called instalments and quarterly interest, that are terribly hard to meet. So I had to pinch a little here and there, wherever I could. I could not save anything out of house-keeping, for of course Torvald had to live well. And I couldn't let the children go about badly dressed; all I got for them, I spent on them, the darlings.

MRS. LINDEN: Poor Nora! So it had to come out of your own pocket-money.

NORA: Yes, of course. After all, the whole thing was my doing. When Torvald gave me money for clothes and so on, I never used more than half of it; I always bought the simplest things. It's a mercy everything suits me so well; Torvald never noticed anything. But it was often very hard, Christina dear. For it's nice to be beautifully dressed. Now, isn't it?

MRS. LINDEN: Indeed it is.

NORA: Well, and besides that, I made money in other ways. Last winter I was so lucky—I got a heap of copying to do. I shut myself up every evening and wrote far on into the night. Oh, sometimes I was so tired, so tired. And yet it was splendid to work in that way and earn money. I almost felt as if I was a man.

MRS. LINDEN: Then how much have you been able to pay off?

NORA: Well, I can't precisely say. It's difficult to keep that sort of business clear. I only know that I paid off everything I could scrape together. Sometimes I really didn't know where to turn. [*Smile.*] Then I used to imagine that a rich old gentleman was in love with me—

MRS. LINDEN: What! What gentleman?

NORA: Oh! nobody—that he was now dead, and that when his will was opened, there stood in large letters: Pay over at once everything of which I die possessed to that charming person, Mrs. Nora Helmer.

MRS. LINDEN: But, dear Nora, what gentleman do you mean?

NORA: Dear, dear, can't you understand? There wasn't any old gentleman: it was only what I used to dream, and dream when I was at my wit's end for money. But it's all over now—the tiresome old creature may stay where he is for me; I care nothing for him or his will; for now my troubles are over. [*Springing up.*] Oh, Christina, how glorious it is to think of? Free from cares! Free, quite free. To be able to play and romp about with the children; to have things tasteful and pretty in the house, exactly as Torvald likes it! And then the spring is coming, with the great blue sky. Perhaps then we shall have a short holiday. Perhaps I shall see the sea again. Oh, what a wonderful thing it is to live and to be happy!

[*The hall door-bell rings.*]

MRS. LINDEN [*rising*]: There is a ring. Perhaps I had better go.

NORA: No; do stay. It's sure to be some one for Torvald.

ELLEN [*in the doorway*]: If you please, ma'am, there's a gentleman to speak to Mr. Helmer.

NORA: Who is the gentleman?

KROGSTAD [*in the doorway to the hall*]: It is I, Mrs. Helmer.

[ELLEN *goes.* MRS. LINDEN *starts and turns away to the window.*]

NORA [*goes a step toward him, anxiously, half aloud*]: You? What is it? What do you want with my husband?

KROGSTAD: Bank business—in a way. I hold a small post in the Joint Stock Bank, and your husband is to be our new chief, I hear.

NORA: Then it is—?

KROGSTAD: Only tiresome business, Mrs. Helmer; nothing more.

NORA: Then will you please go to his study.

[KROGSTAD *goes. She bows indifferently while she closes the door into the hall. Then she goes to the fireplace and looks to the fire.*]

MRS. LINDEN: Nora—who was that man?

NORA: A Mr. Krogstad. Do you know him?

MRS. LINDEN: I used to know him—many years ago. He was in a lawyer's office in our town.

NORA: Yes, so he was.

MRS. LINDEN: How he has changed!

NORA: I believe his marriage was unhappy.

MRS. LINDEN: And he is now a widower?

NORA: With a lot of children. There! now it'll burn up. [*She closes the stove and pushes the rocking-chair a little aside.*]

MRS. LINDEN: His business is not of the most creditable, they say.

NORA: Isn't it? I daresay not. I don't know—But don't let us think of business—it's so tiresome.

[DR. RANK *comes out of* HELMER's *room.*]

RANK [*still in the doorway*]: No, no; I won't keep you. I'll just go and have a chat with your wife. [*Shuts the door and sees* MRS. LINDEN.] Oh, I beg your pardon. I am *de trop*[3] here too.

---

[3] de trop: Superfluous; in the way.

NORA: No, not in the least. [*Introduces them.*] Doctor Rank—Mrs. Linden.

RANK: Oh, indeed; I've often heard Mrs. Linden's name. I think I passed you on the stairs as we came up.

MRS. LINDEN: Yes; I go so very slowly. Stairs try me so much.

RANK: You're not very strong?

MRS. LINDEN: Only overworked.

RANK: Ah! Then you have come to town to find rest in a round of dissipation.

MRS. LINDEN: I have come to look for employment.

RANK: Is that an approved remedy for over-work?

MRS. LINDEN: One must live, Doctor Rank.

RANK: Yes, that seems to be the general opinion.

NORA: Come, Doctor Rank, you yourself want to live.

RANK: To be sure I do. However wretched I may be, I want to drag on as long as possible. And my patients have all the same mania. It's just the same with people whose complaint is moral. At this very moment Helmer is talking to such a wreck as I mean.

MRS. LINDEN [*softly*]: Ah!

NORA: Whom do you mean?

RANK: Oh, a fellow named Krogstad, a man you know nothing about—corrupt to the very core of his character. But even he began by announcing solemnly that he must live.

NORA: Indeed? Then what did he want with Torvald?

RANK: I really don't know; I only gathered that it was some Bank business.

NORA: I didn't know that Krog—that this Mr. Krogstad had anything to do with the Bank?

RANK: He has some sort of place there. [*To* MRS. LINDEN.] I don't know whether, in your part of the country, you have people who go wriggling and snuffing around in search of moral rottenness—whose policy it is to fill good places with men of tainted character whom they can keep under their eye and in their power? The honest men they leave out in the cold.

MRS. LINDEN: Well, I suppose the—delicate characters require most care.

RANK [*shrugs his shoulders*]: There we have it! It's that notion that makes society a hospital. [NORA, *deep in her own thoughts, breaks into half-stifled laughter and claps her hands.*] What are you laughing at? Have you any idea what society is?

NORA: What do I care for your tiresome society. I was laughing at something else—something awfully amusing. Tell me, Doctor Rank, are all the employees at the Bank dependent on Torvald now?

RANK: Is that what strikes you as awfully amusing?

NORA [smiles and hums]: Never mind, never mind! [Walks about the room.] Yes, it is amusing to think that we—that Torvald has such power over so many people. [Takes the box from her pocket.] Doctor Rank, will you have a macaroon?

RANK: Oh, dear, dear—macaroons! I thought they were contraband here.

NORA: Yes; but Christina brought me these.

MRS. LINDEN: What! I?

NORA: Oh, well! Don't be frightened. You couldn't possibly know that Torvald had forbidden them. The fact is, he is afraid of me spoiling my teeth. But, oh bother, just for once. That's for you, Doctor Rank! [Puts a macaroon into his mouth.] And you too, Christina. And I will have one at the same time— only a tiny one, or at the most two. [Walks about again.] Oh, dear, I am happy! There is only one thing in the world that I really want.

RANK: Well; what's that?

NORA: There's something I should so like to say—in Torvald's hearing.

RANK: Then why don't you say it?

NORA: Because I daren't, it's so ugly.

MRS. LINDEN: Ugly?

RANK: In that case you'd better not. But to us you might. What is it you would so like to say in Helmer's hearing?

NORA: I should love to say—"Damn!"

RANK: Are you out of your mind?

MRS. LINDEN: Good gracious, Nora!

RANK: Say it. There he is!

NORA [hides the macaroons]: Hush-sh-sh.

[HELMER comes out of his room, hat in hand, with his overcoat on his arm.]

[Going toward him.] Well, Torvald, dear, have you got rid of him?

HELMER: Yes; he's just gone.

NORA: May I introduce you?—This is Christina, who has come to town—

HELMER: Christina? Pardon me, but I don't know—?

NORA: Mrs. Linden, Torvald dear—Christina Linden.

HELMER [to MRS. LINDEN]: A schoolfriend of my wife's, no doubt?

MRS. LINDEN: Yes; we knew each other as girls.

NORA: And only think! She has taken this long journey on purpose to speak to you.

HELMER: To speak to me!

MRS. LINDEN: Well, not quite—

NORA: You see Christina is tremendously clever at accounts, and she is so anxious to work under a first-rate man of business in order to learn still more—

HELMER: Very sensible indeed.

NORA: And when she heard you were appointed Manager—it was telegraphed, you know—she started off at once, and—Torvald dear, for my sake, you must do something for Christina. Now can't you?

HELMER: It's not impossible. I presume you are a widow?

MRS. LINDEN: Yes.

HELMER: And have already had some experience in office-work?

MRS. LINDEN: A good deal.

HELMER: Well then, it is very likely I may find a place for you.

NORA [clapping her hands]: There now! there now!

HELMER: You have come at a lucky moment, Mrs. Linden.

MRS. LINDEN: Oh! how can I thank you—?

HELMER [smiling]: There's no occasion. [Puts his overcoat on.] But for the present you must excuse me.

RANK: Wait; I'll go with you. [Fetches his fur coat from the hall and warms it at the fire.]

NORA: Don't be long, dear Torvald.

HELMER: Only an hour; not more.

NORA: Are you going too, Christina?

MRS. LINDEN [putting on her walking things]: Yes; I must set about looking for lodgings.

HELMER: Then perhaps we can go together?

NORA [helping her]: What a pity we haven't a spare room for you; but I'm afraid—

MRS. LINDEN: I shouldn't think of troubling you. Good-by, dear Nora, and thank you for all your kindness.

NORA: Good-by for a little while. Of course you'll come back this evening. And you too, Doctor Rank. What! if you're well enough? Of course you'll be well enough. Only wrap up warmly. [They go out into the hall, talking. Outside on the stairs are heard children's voices.] There they are! there they are! [She runs to the door and opens it. The nurse ANNA enters with the children.] Come in! come in! [Bends down and kisses the children.] Oh! my sweet darlings! Do you see them, Christina? Aren't they lovely?

RANK: Don't let us stand here chattering in the draught.

HELMER: Come, Mrs. Linden; only mothers can stand such a temperature.

[DR. RANK, HELMER *and* MRS. LINDEN *go down the stairs;* ANNA *enters the room with the children;* NORA *also, shutting the door.*]

NORA: How fresh and bright you look! And what red cheeks you have!—like apples and roses. [*The children talk low to her during the following.*] Have you had great fun? That's splendid. Oh, really! you've been giving Emmy and Bob a ride on your sledge!—Both at once, only think! Why you're quite a man, Ivar. Oh, give her to me a little, Anna. My sweet little dolly! [*Takes the smallest from the nurse and dances with her.*] Yes, yes; mother will dance with Bob too. What! did you have a game of snow-balls? Oh! I wish I'd been there. No; leave them, Anna; I'll take their things off. Oh yes, let me do it; it's such fun. Go to the nursery; you look frozen. You'll find some hot coffee on the stove. [*The nurse goes into the room on the left.* NORA *takes off the children's things and throws them down anywhere, while the children talk to each other and to her.*] Really! A big dog ran after you all the way home? But he didn't bite you? No; dogs don't bite dear little dolly children. Don't peep into those parcels, Ivar. What is it? Wouldn't you like to know? Oh, take care—it'll bite! What! shall we have a game? What shall we play at? Hide-and-seek? Yes, let's play hide-and-seek. Bob shall hide first. Am I to? Yes, let me hide first.

[*She and the children play, with laughter and shouting, in the room and the adjacent one to the right. At last* NORA *hides under the table; the children come rushing in, look for her but cannot find her, hear her half-choked laughter, rush to the table, lift up the cover, and see her. Loud shouts. She creeps out, as though to frighten them. Fresh shouts. Meanwhile there has been a knock at the door leading into the hall. No one has heard it. Now the door is half opened and* KROGSTAD *is seen. He waits a little; the game is renewed.*]

KROGSTAD: I beg your pardon, Mrs. Helmer—

NORA [*with a suppressed cry, turns round and half jumps up*]: Ah! What do you want?

KROGSTAD: Excuse me; the outer door was ajar—somebody must have forgotten to shut it—

NORA [*standing up*]: My husband is not at home, Mr. Krogstad.

KROGSTAD: I know it.

NORA: Then—what do want here?

KROGSTAD: To say a few words to you.

NORA: To me? [*To the children, softly.*] Go in to Anna. What? No, the strange man won't hurt mamma. When he's gone we'll go on playing. [*She leads the children into the left-hand room, and shuts the door behind them. Uneasy, with suspense.*] It's with me you wish to speak?

KROGSTAD: Yes.

NORA: To-day? But it's not the first yet—

KROGSTAD: No; to-day is Christmas Eve. It will depend upon yourself whether you have a merry Christmas.

NORA: What do you want? I certainly can't to-day—

KROGSTAD: Never mind that just now. It's about another matter. You have a minute to spare?

NORA: Oh, yes, I suppose so; although—

KROGSTAD: Good, I was sitting in the restaurant opposite, and I saw your husband go down the street.

NORA: Well!

KROGSTAD: With a lady.

NORA: What then?

KROGSTAD: May I ask if the lady was a Mrs. Linden?

NORA: Yes.

KROGSTAD: Who has just come to town?

NORA: Yes. To-day.

KROGSTAD: I believe she's an intimate friend of yours?

NORA: Certainly. But I don't understand—

KROGSTAD: I used to know her too.

NORA: I know you did.

KROGSTAD: Ah! you know all about it. I thought as much. Now, frankly, is Mrs. Linden to have a place in the bank?

NORA: How dare you catechise me in this way, Mr. Krogstad, you, a subordinate of my husband's? But since you ask you shall know. Yes, Mrs. Linden is to be employed. And it's I who recommended her, Mr. Krogstad. Now you know.

KROGSTAD: Then my guess was right.

NORA [*walking up and down*]: You see one has a little wee bit of influence. It doesn't follow because one's only a woman that—When one is in a subordinate position, Mr. Krogstad, one ought really to take care not to offend anybody who—h'm—

KROGSTAD: Who has influence?

NORA: Exactly!

KROGSTAD [*taking another tone*]: Mrs. Helmer, will you have the kindness to employ your influence on my behalf?

NORA: What? How do you mean?

KROGSTAD: Will you be so good as to see that I retain my subordinate position in the bank?

NORA: What do you mean? Who wants to take it from you?

KROGSTAD: Oh, you needn't pretend ignorance. I can very well understand that it cannot be pleasant for your friend to meet me; and I can also understand now for whose sake I am to be hounded out.

NORA: But I assure you—

KROGSTAD: Come now, once for all: there is time yet, and I advise you to use your influence to prevent it.

NORA: But Mr. Krogstad, I have absolutely no influence.

KROGSTAD: None? I thought you just said—

NORA: Of course not in that sense—I! How should I have such influence over my husband?

KROGSTAD: Oh! I know your husband from our college days. I don't think he's firmer than other husbands.

NORA: If you talk disrespectfully of my husband, I must request you to go.

KROGSTAD: You are bold, madam.

NORA: I am afraid of you no longer. When New Year's Day is over, I shall soon be out of the whole business.

KROGSTAD [controlling himself]: Listen to me, Mrs. Helmer. If need be, I shall fight as though for my life to keep my little place in the bank.

NORA: Yes, so it seems.

KROGSTAD: It's not only for the money: that matters least to me. It's something else. Well, I'd better make a clean breast of it. Of course you know, like every one else, that some years ago I—got into trouble.

NORA: I think I've heard something of the sort.

KROGSTAD: The matter never came into court; but from that moment all paths were barred to me. Then I took up the business you know about. I was obliged to grasp at something; and I don't think I've been one of the worst. But now I must clear out of it all. My sons are growing up; for their sake I must try to win back as much respectability as I can. This place in the bank was the first step, and now your husband wants to kick me off the ladder, back into the mire.

NORA: But I assure you, Mr. Krogstad, I haven't the power to help you.

KROGSTAD: You have not the will; but I can compel you.

NORA: You won't tell my husband that I owe you money!

KROGSTAD: H'm; suppose I were to?

NORA: It would be shameful of you! [With tears in her voice.] This secret which is my joy and my pride—that he should learn it in such an ugly, coarse way—and from you! It would involve me in all sorts of unpleasantness.

KROGSTAD: Only unpleasantness?

NORA [*hotly*]: But just do it. It will be the worst for you, for then my husband will see what a bad man you are, and then you certainly won't keep your place.

KROGSTAD: I asked if it was only domestic unpleasantness you feared?

NORA: If my husband gets to know about it, he will of course pay you off at once, and then we'll have nothing more to do with you.

KROGSTAD [*stepping a pace nearer*]: Listen, Mrs. Helmer. Either you have a weak memory, or you don't know much about business. I must make your position clearer to you.

NORA: How so?

KROGSTAD: When your husband was ill, you came to me to borrow twelve hundred dollars.

NORA: I knew nobody else.

KROGSTAD: I promised to find you the money—

NORA: And you did find it.

KROGSTAD: I promised to find you the money under certain conditions. You were then so much taken up about your husband's illness, and so eager to have the money for your journey, that you probably did not give much thought to the details. Let me remind you of them. I promised to find you the amount in exchange for a note of hand which I drew up.

NORA: Yes, and I signed it.

KROGSTAD: Quite right. But then I added a few lines, making your father a security for the debt. Your father was to sign this.

NORA: Was to? He did sign it!

KROGSTAD: I had left the date blank. That is to say, your father was himself to date his signature. Do you recollect that?

NORA: Yes, I believe—

KROGSTAD: Then I gave you the paper to send to your father. Is not that so?

NORA: Yes.

KROGSTAD: And of course you did so at once? For within five or six days you brought me back the paper, signed by your father, and I gave you the money.

NORA: Well! Haven't I made my payments punctually?

KROGSTAD: Fairly—yes. But to return to the point. You were in great trouble at the time, Mrs. Helmer.

NORA: I was indeed.

KROGSTAD: Your father was very ill, I believe?

NORA: He was on his deathbed.

KROGSTAD: And died soon after?

NORA: Yes.

KROGSTAD: Tell me, Mrs. Helmer: do you happen to recollect the day of his death? The day of the month, I mean?

NORA: Father died on the 29th of September.

KROGSTAD: Quite correct. I have made inquiries, and here comes in the remarkable point—[*Produces a paper.*] which I cannot explain.

NORA: What remarkable point? I don't know—

KROGSTAD: The remarkable point, madam, that your father signed this paper three days after his death!

NORA: What! I don't understand—

KROGSTAD: Your father died on the 29th of September. But look here, he has dated his signature October 2d! Is not that remarkable, Mrs. Helmer? [NORA *is silent.*] Can you explain it? [NORA *continues silent.*] It is noteworthy too that the words "October 2d" and the year are not in your father's handwriting, but in one which I believe I know. Well, this may be explained; your father may have forgotten to date his signature, and somebody may have added the date at random before the fact of his death was known. There is nothing wrong in that. Everything depends on the signature. Of course it is genuine, Mrs. Helmer? It was really your father who with his own hand wrote his name here?

NORA [*after a short silence throws her head back and looks defiantly at him*]: No; I wrote father's name there.

KROGSTAD: Ah! Are you aware, madam, that that is a dangerous admission?

NORA: Why? You'll soon get your money.

KROGSTAD: May I ask you one more question? Why did you not send the paper to your father?

NORA: It was impossible. Father was ill. If I had asked him for his signature I should have had to tell him why I wanted the money; but he was so ill I really could not tell him that my husband's life was in danger. It was impossible.

KROGSTAD: Then it would have been better to have given up your tour.

NORA: No, I couldn't do that; my husband's life depended on that journey. I couldn't give it up.

KROGSTAD: And did you not consider that you were playing me false?

NORA: That was nothing to me. I didn't care in the least about you. I couldn't endure you for all the cruel difficulties you made, although you knew how ill my husband was.

KROGSTAD: Mrs. Helmer, you have evidently no clear idea what you have really done. But I can assure you it was nothing more and nothing worse that made me an outcast from society.

NORA: You! You want me to believe that you did a brave thing to save your wife's life?

KROGSTAD: The law takes no account of motives.

NORA: Then it must be a very bad law.

KROGSTAD: Bad or not, if I lay this document before a court of law you will be condemned according to law.

NORA: I don't believe that. Do you mean to tell me that a daughter has no right to spare her dying father anxiety?—that a wife has no right to save her husband's life? I don't know much about the law, but I'm sure that, somewhere or another, you will find that *that* is allowed. And you don't know that—you, a lawyer! You must be a bad one, Mr. Krogstad.

KROGSTAD: Possibly. But business—such business as ours—I do understand. You believe that? Very well; now do as you please. But this I may tell you, that if I'm flung into the gutter a second time, you shall keep me company.

[*Bows and goes out through hall.*]

NORA [*stands awhile thinking, then throws her head back*]: Never! He wants to frighten me. I'm not so foolish as that. [*Begins folding the children's clothes. Pauses.*] But—? No, it's impossible. I did it for love!

CHILDREN [*at the door, left*]: Mamma, the strange man is gone now.

NORA: Yes, yes, I know. But don't tell anyone about the strange man. Do you hear? Not even papa!

CHILDREN: No, mamma; and now will you play with us again?

NORA: No, no, not now.

CHILDREN: Oh, do, mamma; you know you promised.

NORA: Yes, but I can't just now. Run to the nursery; I've so much to do. Run along, run along, and be good, my darlings! [*She pushes them gently into the inner room, and closes the door behind them. Sits on the sofa, embroiders a few stitches, but soon pauses.*] No! [*Throws down work, rises, goes to the hall-door and calls out.*] Ellen, bring in the Christmas-tree! [*Goes to table, left, and opens the drawer; again pauses.*] No, it's quite impossible!

ELLEN [*with the Christmas-tree*]: Where shall I stand it, ma'am?

NORA: There, in the middle of the room.

ELLEN: Shall I bring in anything else?

NORA: No, thank you, I have all I want.

[ELLEN, *having put down the tree, goes out.*]

NORA [*busy dressing the tree*]: There must be a candle here, and flowers there.— The horrid man! Nonsense, nonsense! there's nothing in it. The Christmas-tree shall be beautiful. I will do everything to please you, Torvald; I'll sing and dance, and—

[*Enter* HELMER *by the hall-door, with bundle of documents.*]

NORA: Oh! you're back already?

HELMER: Yes. Has anybody been here?

NORA: Here? No.

HELMER: Curious! I saw Krogstad come out of the house.

NORA: Did you? Oh, yes, by the bye, he was here for a minute.

HELMER: Nora, I can see by your manner that he has been asking you to put in a good word for him.

NORA: Yes.

HELMER: And you were to do it as if of your own accord? You were to say nothing to me of his having been here! Didn't he suggest that too?

NORA: Yes, Torvald; but—

HELMER: Nora, Nora! and you could condescend to that! To speak to such a man, to make him a promise! And then to tell me an untruth about it!

NORA: An untruth!

HELMER: Didn't you say nobody had been here? [*Threatens with his finger.*] My little bird must never do that again. A song-bird must never sing false notes. [*Puts his arm round her.*] That's so, isn't it? Yes, I was sure of it. [*Lets her go.*] And now we'll say no more about it. [*Sits down before the fire.*] Oh, how cosy and quiet it is here. [*Glances into his documents.*]

NORA [*busy with the tree, after a short silence*]: Torvald.

HELMER: Yes.

NORA: I'm looking forward so much to the Stenborgs' fancy ball[4] the day after to-morrow.

HELMER: And I'm on tenterhooks to see what surprise you have in store for me.

NORA: Oh, it's too tiresome!

HELMER: What is?

NORA: I can't think of anything good. Everything seems so foolish and meaningless.

HELMER: Has little Nora made that discovery?

NORA [*behind his chair, with her arms on the back*]: Are you very busy, Torvald?

HELMER: Well—

NORA: What sort of papers are those?

HELMER: Bank business.

NORA: Already?

---

[4] *fancy ball:* Costume party.

HELMER: I got the retiring manager to let me make some changes in the staff, and so forth. This will occupy Christmas week. Everything will be straight by the New Year.

NORA: Then that's why that poor Krogstad—

HELMER: H'm.

NORA [still leaning over the chair-back, and slowly stroking his hair]: If you hadn't been so very busy I should have asked you a great, great favor, Torvald.

HELMER: What can it be? Let's hear it.

NORA: Nobody has such exquisite taste as you. Now I should so love to look well at the fancy ball. Torvald dear, couldn't you take me in hand, and settle what I'm to be, and arrange my costume for me?

HELMER: Aha! so my wilful little woman's at a loss, and making signals of distress.

NORA: Yes, please, Torvald. I can't get on without you.

HELMER: Well, well, I'll think it over, and we'll soon hit upon something.

NORA: Oh, how good that is of you! [Goes to the tree again; pause.] How well the red flowers show. Tell me, was it anything so very dreadful this Krogstad got into trouble about?

HELMER: Forgery, that's all. Don't you know what that means?

NORA: Mayn't he have been driven to it by need?

HELMER: Yes, or like so many others, done it out of heedlessness. I'm not so hard-hearted as to condemn a man absolutely for a single fault.

NORA: No, surely not, Torvald.

HELMER: Many a man can retrieve his character if he owns his crime and takes the punishment.

NORA: Crime?

HELMER: But Krogstad didn't do that; he resorted to tricks and dodges, and it's that that has corrupted him.

NORA: Do you think that—?

HELMER: Just think how a man with that on his conscience must be always lying and canting and shamming. Think of the mask he must wear even toward his own wife and children. It's worst for the children, Nora!

NORA: Why?

HELMER: Because such a dust-cloud of lies poisons and contaminates the whole air of home. Every breath the children draw contains some germ of evil.

NORA [closer behind him]: Are you sure of that!

HELMER: As a lawyer, my dear, I've seen it often enough. Nearly all cases of early corruption may be traced to lying mothers.

NORA: Why—mothers?

HELMER: It generally comes from the mother's side, but of course the father's influence may act in the same way. And this Krogstad has been poisoning his own children for years past by a life of lies and hypocrisy—that's why I call him morally ruined. [*Stretches out his hands toward her.*] So my sweet little Nora must promise not to plead his cause. Shake hands upon it. Come, come, what's this? Give me your hand. That's right. Then it's a bargain. I assure you it would have been impossible for me to work with him. It gives me a positive sense of physical discomfort to come in contact with such people.

[NORA *snatches her hand away, and moves to the other side of the Christmas-tree.*]

NORA: How warm is it here; and I have so much to do.

HELMER: Yes, and I must try to get some of these papers looked through before dinner; and I'll think over your costume too. And perhaps I may even find something to hang in gilt paper on the Christmas-tree! [*Lays his hand on her head.*] My precious little song-bird.

[*He goes into his room and shuts the door behind him.*]

NORA [*softly, after a pause*]: It can't be—It's impossible. It must be impossible!

ANNA [*at the door, left*]: The little ones are begging so prettily to come to mamma.

NORA: No, no, don't let them come to me! Keep them with you, Anna.

ANNA: Very well, ma'am.

[*Shuts the door.*]

NORA [*pale with terror*]: Corrupt my children!—Poison my home! [*Short pause. She raises her head.*] It's not true. It can never, never be true.

ACT II

The same room. In the corner, beside the piano, stands the Christmas-tree, stripped, and the candles burnt out. NORA's walking things lie on the sofa. NORA discovered walking about restlessly. She stops by sofa, takes up cloak, then lays it down again.

NORA: There's somebody coming. [*Goes to hall door; listens.*] Nobody, nobody is likely to come to-day, Christmas Day; nor to-morrow either. But perhaps— [*Opens the door and looks out.*] No, nothing in the letter box; quite empty. [*Comes forward.*] Stuff and nonsense! Of course he only meant to frighten me. There's no fear of any such thing. It's impossible! Why I have three little children.

[*Enter ANNA, from the left, with a large cardboard box.*]

ANNA: At last I've found the box with the fancy dress.[5]

---

[5] *fancy dress:* Costume.

NORA: Thanks; put it down on the table.

ANNA [*does so*]: But it is very much out of order.

NORA: Oh, I wish I could tear it into a hundred thousand pieces.

ANNA: Oh, no. It can easily be put to rights—just a little patience.

NORA: I'll go and get Mrs. Linden to help me.

ANNA: Going out again! In such weather as this! You'll catch cold, ma'am, and be ill.

NORA: Worse things might happen—What are the children doing?

ANNA: They're playing with their Christmas presents, poor little dears; but—

NORA: Do they often ask for me?

ANNA: You see they've been so used to having their mamma with them.

NORA: Yes; but, Anna, in the future I can't have them so much with me.

ANNA: Well, little children get used to anything.

NORA: Do you think they do? Do you believe they would forget their mother if she went away?

ANNA: Gracious me! Quite away?

NORA. Tell me, Anna—I've so often wondered about it—how could you bring yourself to give your child up to strangers?

ANNA: I had to when I came as nurse to my little Miss Nora.

NORA: But how could you make up your mind to it?

ANNA: When I had the chance of such a good place? A poor girl who's been in trouble must take what comes. That wicked man did nothing for me.

NORA: But your daughter must have forgotten you.

ANNA: Oh, no, ma'am, that she hasn't. She wrote to me both when she was confirmed and when she was married.

NORA [*embracing her*]: Dear old Anna—you were a good mother to me when I was little.

ANNA: My poor little Nora had no mother but me.

NORA: And if my little ones had nobody else, I'm sure you would—nonsense, nonsense! [*Opens the box.*] Go in to the children. Now I must—. To-morrow you shall see how beautiful I'll be.

ANNA: I'm sure there will be no one at the ball so beautiful as my Miss Nora.

[*She goes into room on left.*]

NORA [*takes the costume out of the box, but soon throws it down again*]: Oh, if I dared go out. If only nobody would come. If only nothing would happen here in the meantime. Rubbish; nobody will come. Only not to think. What a delicious muff! Beautiful gloves, beautiful gloves! Away with it all—away with it all! One, two, three, four, five, six— [*With a scream.*] Ah, there they come— [*Goes toward the door, then stands undecidedly.*]

[MRS. LINDEN *enters from hall where she has taken off her things.*]

NORA: Oh, it's you, Christina. Is nobody else there? How delightful of you to come.

MRS. LINDEN: I hear you called at my lodgings.

NORA: Yes, I was just passing. I do so want you to help me. Let us sit here on the sofa—so. To-morrow evening there's to be a fancy ball at Consul Stenborg's overhead, and Torvald wants me to appear as a Neapolitan fisher girl, and dance the tarantella; I learnt it at Capri.[6]

MRS. LINDEN: I see—quite a performance!

NORA: Yes, Torvald wishes me to. Look, this is the costume. Torvald had it made for me in Italy; but now it is all so torn, I don't know—

MRS. LINDEN: Oh! we'll soon set that to rights. It's only the trimming that's got loose here and there. Have you a needle and thread? Ah! here's the very thing.

NORA: Oh, how kind of you.

MRS. LINDEN: So you're to be in costume, to-morrow, Nora? I'll tell you what—I shall come in for a moment to see you in all your glory. But I've quite forgotten to thank you for the pleasant evening yesterday.

NORA [*rises and walks across room*]: Oh! yesterday, it didn't seem so pleasant as usual. You should have come a little sooner, Christina. Torvald has certainly the art of making home bright and beautiful.

MRS. LINDEN: You, too, I should think, or you wouldn't be your father's daughter. But tell me—is Doctor Rank always so depressed as he was yesterday?

NORA: No; yesterday it was particularly striking. You see he has a terrible illness. He has spinal consumption, poor fellow. They say his father led a terrible life—kept mistresses and all sorts of things—so the son has been sickly from his childhood, you understand.

MRS. LINDEN [*lets her sewing fall into her lap*]: Why, my darling Nora, how do you learn such things?

NORA [*walking*]: Oh! when one has three children one has visits from women who know something of medicine—and they talk of this and that.

MRS. LINDEN [*goes on sewing—a short pause*]: Does Doctor Rank come here every day?

NORA: Every day. He's been Torvald's friend from boyhood, and he's a good friend of mine too. Doctor Rank is quite one of the family.

---

[6] *tarantella . . . Capri:* The tarantella is an Italian folk dance. Capri is an Italian island in the Bay of Naples.

MRS. LINDEN: But tell me—is he quite sincere? I mean, doesn't he like to say flattering things to people?

NORA: On the contrary. Why should you think so?

MRS. LINDEN: When you introduced us yesterday he declared he had often heard my name; but I noticed your husband had no notion who I was. How could Doctor Rank—?

NORA: Yes, he was quite right, Christina. You see Torvald loves me so indescribably he wants to have me all to himself, as he says. When we were first married he was almost jealous if I even mentioned one of the people at home; so I naturally let it alone. But I often talk to Doctor Rank about the old times, for he likes to hear about them.

MRS. LINDEN: Listen to me, Nora! You're still a child in many ways. I am older than you, and have more experience. I'll tell you something: you ought to get clear of the whole affair with Doctor Rank.

NORA: What affair?

MRS. LINDEN: You were talking yesterday of a rich admirer who was to find you money—

NORA: Yes, one who never existed, worse luck. What then?

MRS. LINDEN: Has Doctor Rank money?

NORA: Yes, he has.

MRS. LINDEN: And nobody to provide for?

NORA: Nobody. But—?

MRS. LINDEN: And he comes here every day?

NORA: Yes, every day.

MRS. LINDEN: I should have thought he'd have had better taste.

NORA: I don't understand you.

MRS. LINDEN: Don't pretend, Nora. Do you suppose I don't guess who lent you the twelve hundred dollars?

NORA: Are you out of your senses? You think *that!* A friend who comes here every day! How painful that would be!

MRS. LINDEN: Then it really is not he?

NORA: No, I assure you. It never for a moment occurred to me. Besides, at that time he had nothing to lend; he came into his property afterward.

MRS. LINDEN: Well, I believe that was lucky for you, Nora dear.

NORA: No, really, it would never have struck me to ask Doctor Rank. But I'm certain that if I did—

MRS. LINDEN: But of course you never would?

NORA: Of course not. It's inconceivable that it should ever be necessary. But I'm quite sure that if I spoke to Doctor Rank—

MRS. LINDEN: Behind your husband's back?

NORA: I must get out of the other thing; that's behind his back too. I must get out of that.

MRS. LINDEN: Yes, yes, I told you so yesterday; but—

NORA [*walking up and down*]: A man can manage these things much better than a woman.

MRS. LINDEN: One's own husband, yes.

NORA: Nonsense. [*Stands still.*] When everything is paid, one gets back the paper?

MRS. LINDEN: Of course.

NORA: And can tear it into a hundred thousand pieces, and burn it, the nasty, filthy thing!

MRS. LINDEN [*looks at her fixedly, lays down her work, and rises slowly*]: Nora, you're hiding something from me.

NORA: Can you see that in my face?

MRS. LINDEN: Something has happened since yesterday morning. Nora, what is it?

NORA [*going toward her*]: Christina [*Listens.*] —Hush! There's Torvald coming home. Here, go into the nursery. Torvald cannot bear to see dressmaking. Let Anna help you.

MRS. LINDEN [*gathers some of the things together*]: Very well, but I shan't go away until you've told me all about it.

[*She goes out to the left as* HELMER *enters from hall.*]

NORA [*runs to meet him*]: Oh! how I've been longing for you to come, Torvald dear.

HELMER: Was the dressmaker here?

NORA: No, Christina. She is helping me with my costume. You'll see how well I shall look.

HELMER: Yes, wasn't that a lucky thought of mine?

NORA: Splendid. But isn't it good of me, too, to have given in to you?

HELMER [*takes her under the chin*]: Good of you! To give in to your own husband? Well, well, you little madcap, I know you don't mean it. But I won't disturb you. I dare say you want to be "trying on."

NORA: And you're going to work, I suppose?

HELMER: Yes. [*Shows her bundle of papers.*] Look here. [*Goes toward his room.*] I've just come from the Bank.

NORA: Torvald.

HELMER [*stopping*]: Yes?

NORA: If your little squirrel were to beg you for something so prettily—

HELMER: Well?

NORA: Would you do it?

HELMER: I must know first what it is.

NORA: The squirrel would jump about and play all sorts of tricks if you would only be nice and kind.

HELMER: Come, then, out with it.

NORA: Your lark would twitter from morning till night—

HELMER: Oh, that she does in any case.

NORA: I'll be an elf and dance in the moonlight for you, Torvald.

HELMER: Nora—you can't mean what you were hinting at this morning?

NORA [coming nearer]: Yes, Torvald, I beg and implore you.

HELMER: Have you really the courage to begin that again?

NORA: Yes, yes; for my sake, you must let Krogstad keep his place in the bank.

HELMER: My dear Nora, it's his place I intend for Mrs. Linden.

NORA: Yes, that's so good of you. But instead of Krogstad, you could dismiss some other clerk.

HELMER: Why, this is incredible obstinacy! Because you thoughtlessly promised to put in a word for him, I am to—

NORA: It's not that, Torvald. It's for your own sake. This man writes for the most scurrilous newspapers; you said so yourself. He can do you such a lot of harm. I'm terribly afraid of him.

HELMER: Oh, I understand; it's old recollections that are frightening you.

NORA: What do you mean?

HELMER: Of course you're thinking of your father.

NORA: Yes, of course. Only think of the shameful things wicked people used to write about father. I believe they'd have got him dismissed if you hadn't been sent to look into the thing and been kind to him and helped him.

HELMER: My dear Nora, between your father and me there is all the difference in the world. Your father was not altogether unimpeachable. I am; and I hope to remain so.

NORA: Oh, no one knows what wicked men can hit upon. We could live so happily now, in our cosy, quiet home, you and I and the children, Torvald! That's why I beg and implore you—

HELMER: And it's just by pleading his cause that you make it impossible for me to keep him. It's already known at the bank that I intend to dismiss Krogstad. If it were now reported that the new manager let himself be turned round his wife's little finger—

NORA: What then?

HELMER: Oh, nothing! So long as a wilful woman can have her way I am to make myself the laughing-stock of everyone, and set people saying I am under petticoat government? Take my word for it, I should soon feel the consequences. And besides, there's one thing that makes Krogstad impossible for me to work with.

NORA: What thing?

HELMER: I could perhaps have overlooked his shady character at a pinch—

NORA: Yes, couldn't you, Torvald?

HELMER: And I hear he is good at his work. But the fact is, he was a college chum of mine—there was one of those rash friendships between us that one so often repents of later. I don't mind confessing it—he calls me by my Christian name; and he insists on doing it even when others are present. He delights in putting on airs of familiarity—Torvald here, Torvald there! I assure you it's most painful to me. He would make my position at the Bank perfectly unendurable.

NORA: Torvald, you're not serious?

HELMER: No? Why not?

NORA: That's such a petty reason.

HELMER: What! Petty! Do you consider me petty?

NORA: No, on the contrary, Torvald dear; and that's just why—

HELMER: Never mind, you call my motives petty; then I must be petty too. Petty! Very well. Now we'll put an end to this once for all. [Goes to the door into the hall and calls.] Ellen!

NORA: What do you want?

HELMER [searching among his papers]: To settle the thing. [ELLEN enters.] There, take this letter, give it to a messenger. See that he takes it at once. The address is on it. Here is the money.

ELLEN: Very well. [Goes with the letter.]

HELMER [arranging papers]: There, Madame Obstinacy!

NORA [breathless]: Torvald—what was in that letter?

HELMER: Krogstad's dismissal.

NORA: Call it back again, Torvald! There is still time. Oh, Torvald, get it back again! For my sake, for your own, for the children's sake! Do you hear, Torvald? Do it. You don't know what that letter may bring upon us all.

HELMER: Too late.

NORA: Yes, too late.

HELMER: My dear Nora, I forgive your anxiety, though it's anything but flattering to me. Why should I be afraid of a blackguard scribbler's spite? But I forgive you all the same, for it's a proof of your great love for me. [*Takes her in his arms*.] That's how it should be, my own dear Nora. Let what will happen—when the time comes, I shall have strength and courage enough. You shall see, my shoulders are broad enough to bear the whole burden.

NORA [*terror-struck*]: What do you mean by that?

HELMER: The whole burden, I say.

NORA [*firmly*]: That you shall never, never do.

HELMER: Very well; then we'll share it, Nora, as man and wife. [*Petting her.*] Are you satisfied now? Come, come, come, don't look like a scared dove. It is all nothing—fancy. Now you must play the tarantella through, and practice the tambourine. I shall sit in my inner room and shut both doors, so that I shall hear nothing. You can make as much noise as you please. [*Turns round in doorway.*] And when Rank comes, just tell him where I'm to be found. [*He nods to her and goes with his papers into his room, closing the door.*]

NORA [*bewildered with terror, stands as though rooted to the ground and whispers*]: He would do it. Yes, he would do it. He would do it, it spite of all the world. No, never that, never, never! Anything rather than that! Oh, for some way of escape! What to do! [*Hall bell rings.*] Anything rather than that—anything, anything!

[NORA *draws her hands over her face, pulls herself together, goes to the door and opens it.* RANK *stands outside, hanging up his greatcoat. During the following, it grows dark.*]

NORA: Good afternoon, Doctor Rank. I knew you by your ring. But you mustn't go to Torvald now. I believe he's busy.

RANK: And you?

NORA: Oh, you know very well I've always time for you.

RANK: Thank you. I shall avail myself of your kindness as long as I can!

NORA: What do you mean? As long as you can?

RANK: Yes. Does that frighten you?

NORA: I think it's an odd expression. Do you expect anything to happen?

RANK: Something I've long been prepared for; but I didn't think it would come so soon.

NORA [*seizing his arm*]: What is it, Doctor Rank? You must tell me.

RANK [*sitting down by the stove*]: I am running down hill. There's no help for it.

NORA [*draws a long breath of relief*]: It's *you*?

RANK: Who else should it be? Why lie to one's self? I'm the most wretched of all my patients, Mrs. Helmer. I have been auditing my life-account—bankrupt! Before a month is over I shall lie rotting in the churchyard.

NORA: Oh! What an ugly way to talk!

RANK: The thing itself is so confoundedly ugly, you see. But the worst of it is, so many other ugly things have to be gone through first. There is one last investigation to be made, and when that is over I shall know exactly when the break-up will begin. There's one thing I want to say to you. Helmer's delicate nature shrinks so from all that is horrible; I will not have him in my sick room.

NORA: But, Doctor Rank—

RANK: I won't have him, I say—not on any account! I shall lock my door against him. As soon as I have ascertained the worst, I shall send you my visiting card with a black cross on it; and then you will know that the horror has begun.

NORA: Why you're perfectly unreasonable to-day. And I did so want you to be in a really good humor.

RANK: With death staring me in the face? And to suffer thus for another's sin! Where's the justice of it? And in every family you can see some such inexorable retribution—

NORA [stopping her ears]: Nonsense, nonsense; now cheer up.

RANK: Well, after all, the whole thing's only worth laughing at. My poor innocent spine must do penance for my father's wild oats.

NORA [at table, left]: I suppose he was too fond of asparagus and Strasbourg paté, wasn't he?

RANK: Yes; and truffles.

NORA: Yes, truffles, to be sure. And oysters, I believe?

RANK: Yes, oysters; oysters of course.

NORA: And then all the port and champagne. It's sad all these good things should attack the spine.

RANK: Especially when the spine attacked never had the good of them.

NORA: Yes, that's the worst of it.

RANK [looks at her searchingly]: H'm—

NORA [a moment later]: Why did you smile?

RANK: No; it was you that laughed.

NORA: No; it was you that smiled, Doctor Rank.

RANK [standing up]: You're deeper than I thought.

NORA: I'm in such a crazy mood to-day.

RANK: So it seems.

NORA [with her hands on his shoulders]: Dear, dear Doctor Rank, death shall not take you away from Torvald and me.

RANK: Oh, you'll easily get over the loss. The absent are soon forgotten.

NORA [looks at him anxiously]: Do you think so?

RANK: People make fresh ties, and then—

NORA: Who make fresh ties?

RANK: You and Helmer will, when I'm gone. You yourself are taking time by the forelock, it seems to me. What was that Mrs. Linden doing here yesterday?

NORA: Oh! You're surely not jealous of Christina?

RANK: Yes, I am. She will be my successor in this house. When I'm gone, this woman will perhaps—

NORA: Hush! Not so loud; she is in there.

RANK: To-day as well? You see!

NORA: Only to put my costume in order—how unreasonable you are! [*Sits on sofa.*] Now do be good, Doctor Rank. To-morrow you shall see how beautifully I dance; and then you may fancy that I am doing it all to please you— and of course Torvald as well. [*Takes various things out of box.*] Doctor Rank, sit here, and I'll show you something.

RANK [*sitting*]: What is it?

NORA: Look here. Look!

RANK: Silk stockings.

NORA: Flesh-colored. Aren't they lovely? Oh, it's so dark here now; but to-morrow—No, no, no, you must only look at the feet. Oh, well, I suppose you may look at the rest too.

RANK: H'm—

NORA: What are you looking so critical about? Do you think they won't fit me?

RANK: I can't possibly have any valid opinion on that point.

NORA [*looking at him a moment*]: For shame! [*Hits him lightly on the ear with the stockings.*] Take that. [*Rolls them up again.*]

RANK: And what other wonders am I to see?

NORA: You shan't see any more, for you don't behave nicely. [*She hums a little and searches among the things.*]

RANK [*after a short silence*]: When I sit here gossiping with you, I simply can't imagine what would have become of me if I had never entered this house.

NORA [*smiling*]: Yes, I think you do feel at home with us.

RANK [*more softly—looking straight before him*]: And now to have to leave it all—

NORA: Nonsense. You sha'n't leave us.

RANK [*in the same tone*]: And not to be able to leave behind the slightest token of gratitude; scarcely even a passing regret—nothing but an empty place, that can be filled by the first comer.

NORA: And if I were to ask for—? No—

RANK: For what?

NORA: For a great proof of your friendship.

RANK: Yes?—Yes?

NORA: No, I mean—for a very, very great service.

RANK: Would you really for once make me so happy?

NORA: Oh! you don't know what it is.

RANK: Then tell me.

NORA: No, I really can't; it's far, far too much—not only a service, but help and advice besides—

RANK: So much the better. I can't think what you can mean. But go on. Don't you trust me?

NORA: As I trust no one else. I know you are my best and truest friend. So I will tell you. Well, then, Doctor Rank, you must help me to prevent something. You know how deeply, how wonderfully Torvald loves me; he would not hesitate a moment to give his very life for my sake.

RANK [*bending toward her*]: Nora, do you think he is the only one who—

NORA [*with a slight start*]: Who?

RANK: Who would gladly give his life for you?

NORA [*sadly*]: Oh!

RANK: I have sworn that you shall know it before I—go. I should never find a better opportunity—Yes, Nora, now you know it, and now you know too that you can trust me as you can no one else.

NORA [*standing up, simply and calmly*]: Let me pass, please.

RANK [*makes way for her, but remains sitting*]: Nora—

NORA [*in the doorway*]: Ellen, bring the lamp. [*Crosses to the stove.*] Oh, dear, Doctor Rank, that was too bad of you.

RANK [*rising*]: That I have loved you as deeply as—anyone else? Was that too bad of me?

NORA: No, but that you should tell me so. It was so unnecessary—

RANK: What do you mean? Did you know—?

[ELLEN *enters with the lamp; sets it on table and goes out again.*]

RANK: Nora—Mrs. Helmer—I ask you, did you know?

NORA: Oh, how can I tell what I knew or didn't know. I really can't say—How could you be so clumsy, Doctor Rank? It was all so nice!

RANK: Well at any rate, you know now that I am yours, soul and body. And now, go on.

NORA [*looking at him*]: Go on—now?

RANK: I beg you to tell what you want.

NORA: I can tell you nothing now.

RANK: Yes, yes! You mustn't punish me in that way. Let me do for you whatever a man can.

NORA: You can really do nothing for me now. Besides, I really want no help. You'll see it was only my fancy. Yes, it must be so. Of course! [Sits in the rocking-chair smiling at him.] You're a nice one, Doctor Rank. Aren't you ashamed of yourself now the lamp's on the table?

RANK: No, not exactly. But perhaps I ought to go—for ever.

NORA: No, indeed you mustn't. Of course you must come and go as you've always done. You know very well that Torvald can't do without you.

RANK: Yes, but you?

NORA: Oh, you know I always like to have you here.

RANK: That's just what led me astray. You're a riddle to me. It has often seemed to me as if you liked being with me almost as much as being with Helmer.

NORA: Yes, don't you see?—there are some people one loves, and others one likes to talk to.

RANK: Yes—there's something in that.

NORA: When I was a girl I naturally loved papa best. But it always delighted me to steal into the servants' room. In the first place they never lectured me, and in the second it was such fun to hear them talk.

RANK: Oh, I see; then it's their place I have taken?

NORA [jumps up and hurries toward him]: Oh, my dear Doctor Rank, I don't mean that. But you understand, with Torvald it's the same as with papa—

[ELLEN enters from the hall.]

ELLEN: Please, ma'am— [Whispers to NORA and gives her a card.]

NORA [glances at the card]: Ah! [Puts it in her pocket.]

RANK: Anything wrong?

NORA: No, not in the least. It's only—it's my new costume—

RANK: Why, it's there.

NORA: Oh, that one, yes. But it's another that—I ordered it—Torvald mustn't know—

RANK: Aha! so that's the great secret.

NORA: Yes, of course. Do just go to him; he's in the inner room; do keep him as long as you can.

RANK: Make yourself easy; he sha'n't escape. [Goes into HELMER's room.]

NORA [to ELLEN]: Is he waiting in the kitchen?

ELLEN: Yes, he came up the back stair—

NORA: Didn't you tell him I was engaged?

ELLEN: Yes, but it was no use.

NORA: He won't go away?

ELLEN: No, ma'am, not until he has spoken with you.

NORA: Then let him come in; but quietly. And, Ellen—say nothing about it; it's a surprise for my husband.

ELLEN: Oh, yes, ma'am, I understand— [*She goes out.*]

NORA: It's coming. It's coming after all. No, no, no, it can never be; it shall not!

[*She goes to* HELMER's *door and slips the bolt.* ELLEN *opens the hall-door for* KROGSTAD *and shuts it after him. He wears a travelling coat, high boots, and a fur cap.*]

NORA: Speak quietly; my husband is at home.

KROGSTAD: All right. I don't care.

NORA: What do you want?

KROGSTAD: A little information.

NORA: Be quick, then. What is it?

KROGSTAD: You know I've got my dismissal.

NORA: I could not prevent it, Mr. Krogstad. I fought for you to the last, but it was no good.

KROGSTAD: Does your husband care for you so little? He knows what I can bring upon you, and yet he dares—

NORA: How can you think I should tell him?

KROGSTAD: I knew very well you hadn't. It wasn't like my friend Torvald Helmer to show so much courage—

NORA: Mr. Krogstad, be good enough to speak respectfully of my husband.

KROGSTAD: Certainly, with all due respect. But since you're so anxious to keep the matter secret, I suppose you're a little clearer than yesterday as to what you have done.

NORA: Clearer than you could ever make me.

KROGSTAD: Yes, such a bad lawyer as I—

NORA: What is it you want?

KROGSTAD: Only to see how you're getting on, Mrs. Helmer. I've been thinking about you all day. A mere money-lender, a penny-a-liner, a—in short, a creature like me—has a little bit of what people call "heart."

NORA: Then show it; think of my little children.

KROGSTAD: Did you and your husband think of mine? But enough of that. I only wanted to tell you that you needn't take this matter too seriously. I sha'n't lodge any information for the present.

NORA: No, surely not. I knew you would not.

KROGSTAD: The whole thing can be settled quite quietly. Nobody need know. It can remain among us three.

NORA: My husband must never know.

KROGSTAD: How can you prevent it? Can you pay off the debt?

NORA: No, not at once.

KROGSTAD: Or have you any means of raising the money in the next few days?

NORA: None that I will make use of.

KROGSTAD: And if you had it would be no good to you now. If you offered me ever so much ready money you should not get back your IOU.

NORA: Tell me what you want to do with it.

KROGSTAD: I only want to keep it, to have it in my possession. No outsider shall hear anything of it. So, if you've got any desperate scheme in your head—

NORA: What if I have?

KROGSTAD: If you should think of leaving your husband and children—

NORA: What if I do?

KROGSTAD: Or if you should think of—something—worse—

NORA: How do you know that?

KROGSTAD: Put all that out of your head.

NORA: How did you know what I had in my mind?

KROGSTAD: Most of us think of *that* at first. I thought of it, too; but I had not the courage—

NORA [*voicelessly*]: Nor I.

KROGSTAD [*relieved*]: No one hasn't. You haven't the courage either, have you?

NORA: I haven't, I haven't.

KROGSTAD: Besides, it would be very silly—when the first storm is over—I have a letter in my pocket for your husband—

NORA: Telling him everything?

KROGSTAD: Sparing you as much as possible.

NORA [*quickly*]: He must never have that letter. Tear it up. I will get the money somehow.

KROGSTAD: Pardon me, Mrs. Helmer, but I believe I told you—

NORA: Oh, I'm not talking about the money I owe you. Tell me how much you demand from my husband—I'll get it.

KROGSTAD: I demand no money from your husband.

NORA: What *do* you demand then?

KROGSTAD: I'll tell you. I want to regain my footing in the world. I want to rise; and your husband shall help me to do it. For the last eighteen months my record has been spotless; I've been in bitter need all the time; but I was content to fight my way up, step by step. Now, I've been thrust down, and I won't be satisfied with merely being allowed to sneak back again. I want to rise, I tell you. I must get into the bank again, in a higher position than before. Your husband shall create a place on purpose for me—

NORA: He will never do that!

KROGSTAD: He will do it! I know him—he won't dare to refuse! And when I'm in, you'll soon see! I shall be the manager's right hand. It won't be Torvald Helmer, but Nils Krogstad, that manages the Joint Stock Bank.

NORA: That will never be.

KROGSTAD: Perhaps you'll—?

NORA: *Now* I have the courage for it.

KROGSTAD: Oh, you don't frighten me. A sensitive, petted creature like you—

NORA: You shall see, you shall see.

KROGSTAD: Under the ice, perhaps? Down in the cold, black, water? And next spring to come up again, ugly, hairless, unrecognizable—

NORA: You can't terrify me.

KROGSTAD: Nor you me. People don't do that sort of thing, Mrs. Helmer. And, after all, what good would it be? I have your husband in my pocket all the same.

NORA: Afterward? When I am no longer—

KROGSTAD: You forget, your reputation remains in my hands! [NORA *stands speechless and looks at him.*] Well, now you are prepared. Do nothing foolish. So soon as Helmer has received my letter I shall expect to hear from him. And remember that it is your husband himself who has forced me back again into such paths. That I will never forgive him. Good-by Mrs. Helmer. [*Goes through hall.* NORA *hurries to the door, opens it a little, and listens.*]

NORA: He's going. He is not putting the letter into the box. No, no, it would be impossible. [*Opens the door farther and farther.*] What's that? He's standing still; not going downstairs. Is he changing his mind? Is he—? [*A letter falls into the box.* KROGSTAD's *footsteps are heard gradually receding down the stair.* NORA *utters suppressed shriek; pause.*] In the letter-box. [*Slips shrinkingly up to the door.*] There it lies—Torvald, Torvald—now we are lost!

[MRS. LINDEN *enters from the left with the costume.*]

MRS. LINDEN: There, I think it's all right now. Shall we just try it on?

NORA [*hoarsely and softly*]: Christina, come here.

MRS. LINDEN [*throws dress on sofa*]: What's the matter? You look quite aghast.

NORA: Come here. Do you see that letter? There, see—through the glass of the letter-box.

MRS. LINDEN: Yes, yes, I see it.

NORA: That letter is from Krogstad—

MRS. LINDEN: Nora—it was Krogstad who lent you the money!

NORA: Yes, and now Torvald will know everything.

MRS. LINDEN: Believe me, Nora it's the best thing for you both.

NORA: You don't know all yet. I have forged a name—

MRS. LINDEN: Good heavens!

NORA: Now listen to me, Christina, you shall bear me witness.

MRS. LINDEN: How "witness"? What am I to—

NORA: If I should go out of my mind—it might easily happen—

MRS. LINDEN: Nora!

NORA: Or if anything else should happen to me—so I couldn't be here myself—

MRS. LINDEN: Now Nora, you're quite beside yourself!

NORA: In case any one wanted to take it all upon himself—the whole blame, you understand—

MRS. LINDEN: Yes, but how can you think—

NORA: You shall bear witness that it's not true, Christina. I'm not out of my mind at all; I know quite well what I'm saying; and I tell you nobody else knew anything about it; I did the whole thing, I myself. Don't forget that.

MRS. LINDEN: I won't forget. But I don't understand what you mean—

NORA: Oh, how should you? It's the miracle coming to pass.

MRS. LINDEN: The miracle?

NORA: Yes, the miracle. But it's so terrible, Christina;—it mustn't happen for anything in the world.

MRS. LINDEN: I will go straight to Krogstad and talk to him.

NORA: Don't; he will do you some harm.

MRS. LINDEN: Once he would have done anything for me.

NORA: He?

MRS. LINDEN: Where does he live?

NORA: Oh, how can I tell—? Yes [*Feels in her pocket.*]; Here's his card. But the letter, the letter—!

HELMER [*knocking outside*]: Nora.

NORA [*shrieks in terror*]: What is it? What do you want?

HELMER: Don't be frightened, we're not coming in; you've bolted the door. Are you trying on your dress?

NORA: Yes, yes, I'm trying it on. It suits me so well, Torvald.

MRS. LINDEN [*who has read the card*]: Then he lives close by here?

NORA: Yes, but it's no use now. The letter is actually in the box.

MRS. LINDEN: And your husband has the key?

NORA: Always.

MRS. LINDEN: Krogstad must demand his letter back, unread. He must make some excuse—

NORA: But this is the very time when Torvald generally—

MRS. LINDEN: Prevent him. Keep him occupied. I'll come back as quickly as I can.

[*She goes out quickly through the hall door.*]

NORA [*opens* HELMER'*s door and peeps in*]: Torvald!

HELMER: Well, now may one come back into one's own room? Come, Rank, we'll have a look— [*In the doorway.*] But how's this?

NORA: What, Torvald dear?

HELMER: Rank led me to expect a grand dressing-up.

RANK [*in the doorway*]: So I understood. I suppose I was mistaken.

NORA: No, no one shall see me in my glory till to-morrow evening.

HELMER: Why, Nora dear, you look so tired. Have you been practising too hard?

NORA: No, I haven't practised at all yet.

HELMER: But you'll have to—

NORA: Yes, it's absolutely necessary. But, Torvald, I can't get on without your help. I've forgotten everything.

HELMER: Oh, we'll soon freshen it up again.

NORA: Yes, do help me, Torvald. You must promise me.—Oh, I'm so nervous about it. Before so many people—this evening you must give yourself up entirely to me. You mustn't do a stroke of work! Now promise, Torvald dear!

HELMER: I promise. All this evening I will be your slave. Little helpless thing!—But, by the by, I must first— [*Going to hall door.*]

NORA: What do you want there?

HELMER: Only to see if there are any letters.

NORA: No, no, don't do that, Torvald.

HELMER: Why not?

NORA: Torvald, I beg you not to. There are none there.

HELMER: Let me just see. [*Is going.* NORA, *at the piano, plays the first bars of the tarantella.*]

HELMER [*at the door, stops*]: Aha!

NORA: I can't dance to-morrow if I don't rehearse with you first.

HELMER [*going to her*]: Are you really so nervous, dear Nora?

NORA: Yes, dreadfully! Let me rehearse at once. We have time before dinner. Oh! do sit down and accompany me, Torvald dear; direct me as you used to do.

HELMER: With all the pleasure in life, if you wish it.

[*Sits at piano.* NORA *snatches the tambourine out of the box, and hurriedly drapes herself in a long parti-colored shawl; then, with a bound, stands in the middle of the floor.*]

NORA: Now play for me! Now I'll dance!

[HELMER *plays and* NORA *dances.* RANK *stands at the piano behind* HELMER *and looks on.*]

HELMER [*playing*]: Slower! Slower!

NORA: Can't do it slower.

HELMER: Not so violently, Nora.

NORA: I must! I must!

HELMER [*stops*]: Nora—That'll never do.

NORA [*laughs and swings her tambourine*]: Didn't I tell you so?

RANK: Let me accompany her.

HELMER [*rising*]: Yes, do—then I can direct her better.

[RANK *sits down to the piano and plays.* NORA *dances more and more wildly.* HELMER *stands by the stove and addresses frequent corrections to her. She seems not to hear. Her hair breaks loose and falls over her shoulders. She does not notice it, but goes on dancing.* MRS. LINDEN *enters and stands spellbound in the doorway.*]

MRS. LINDEN: Ah!

NORA [*dancing*]: We're having such fun here, Christina!

HELMER: Why, Nora dear, you're dancing as if it were a matter of life and death.

NORA: So it is.

HELMER: Rank, stop! this is the merest madness. Stop I say! [RANK *stops playing and* NORA *comes to a sudden standstill.* HELMER *going toward her.*] I couldn't have believed it. You've positively forgotten all I taught you.

NORA [*throws tambourine away*]: You see for yourself.

HELMER: You really do want teaching.

NORA: Yes, you see how much I need it. You must practise with me up to the last moment. Will you promise me, Torvald?

HELMER: Certainly, certainly.

NORA: Neither to-day nor to-morrow must you think of anything but me. You mustn't open a single letter—mustn't look at the letter-box!

HELMER: Ah! you're still afraid of that man—

NORA: Oh, yes, yes, I am.

HELMER: Nora, I can see it in your face—there's a letter from him in the box.

NORA: I don't know, I believe so. But you're not to read anything now; nothing must come between us until all is over.

RANK [*softly to* HELMER]: You mustn't contradict her.

HELMER [*putting his arm around her*]: The child shall have her own way. But to-morrow night, when the dance is over—

NORA: Then you will be free.

[ELLEN *appears in doorway, right.*]

ELLEN: Dinner is ready, ma'am.

NORA: We'll have some champagne, Ellen!

ELLEN: Yes, ma'am. [*Goes out.*]

HELMER: Dear me! Quite a feast.

NORA: Yes, and we'll keep it up till morning. [*Calling out.*] And macaroons, Ellen—plenty—just this once.

HELMER [*seizing her hands*]: Come, come, don't let's have this wild excitement! Be my own little lark again.

NORA: Oh, yes I will. But now go into the dining-room; and you too, Doctor Rank. Christina, you must help me to do up my hair.

RANK [*softly as they go*]: There is nothing in the wind? Nothing—I mean—

HELMER: Oh, no, nothing of the kind. It's merely this babyish anxiety I was telling you about. [*They go out right.*]

NORA: Well?

MRS. LINDEN: He's gone out of town.

NORA: I saw it in your face.

MRS. LINDEN: He comes back to-morrow evening. I left a note for him.

NORA: You shouldn't have done that. Things must take their course. After all, there's something glorious in waiting for the miracle.

MRS. LINDEN: What are you waiting for?

NORA: Oh, you can't understand. Go to them in the dining-room; I'll come in a moment. [MRS. LINDEN *goes into dining-room;* NORA *stands for a moment as though collecting her thoughts; then looks at her watch.*] Five. Seven hours till midnight. Then twenty-four hours till the next midnight. Then the tarantella will be over. Twenty-four and seven? Still thirty-one hours to live.

[HELMER *appears at door, right.*]

HELMER: What's become of my little lark?

NORA [*runs to him with open arms*]: Here she is!

ACT III

The same room. The table with the chairs around it is in the middle. A lamp lit on the table. The door to the hall stands open. Dance music is heard from the floor above. MRS. LINDEN *sits by the table, and turns the pages of a book absently. She tries to read, but seems unable to fix her attention; she frequently listens and looks anxiously toward the hall door.*

MRS. LINDEN [*looks at her watch*]: Still not here; and the time's nearly up. If only he hasn't—[*Listens again.*] Ah! there he is— [*She goes into the hall and opens the outer door; soft footsteps are heard on the stairs; she whispers:*] Come in; there's no one here.

KROGSTAD [*in the doorway*]: I found a note from you at my house. What does it mean?

MRS. LINDEN: I must speak with you.

KROGSTAD: Indeed? And in this house?

MRS. LINDEN: I could not see you at my rooms. They have no separate entrance. Come in; we are quite alone. The servants are asleep and the Helmers are at the ball upstairs.

KROGSTAD [*coming into room*]: Ah! So the Helmers are dancing this evening. Really?

MRS. LINDEN: Yes, why not?

KROGSTAD: Quite right. Why not?

MRS. LINDEN: And now let us talk a little.

KROGSTAD: Have we anything to say to each other?

MRS. LINDEN: A great deal.

KROGSTAD: I should not have thought so.

MRS. LINDEN: Because you have never really understood me.

KROGSTAD: What was there to understand? The most natural thing in the world—a heartless woman throws a man over when a better match offers.

MRS. LINDEN: Do you really think me so heartless? Do you think I broke with you lightly?

KROGSTAD: Did you not?

MRS. LINDEN: Do you really think so?

KROGSTAD: If not, why did you write me that letter?

MRS. LINDEN: Was it not best? Since I had to break with you, was it not right that I should try to put an end to your love for me?

KROGSTAD [*pressing his hands together*]: So that was it? And all this—for the sake of money.

MRS. LINDEN: You ought not to forget that I had a helpless mother and two little brothers. We could not wait for you, as your prospects then stood.

KROGSTAD: Did that give you the right to discard me for another?

MRS. LINDEN: I don't know. I've often asked myself whether I did right.

KROGSTAD [*more softly*]: When I had lost you the very ground seemed to sink from under my feet. Look at me now. I am a shipwrecked man clinging to a spar.

MRS. LINDEN: Rescue may be at hand.

KROGSTAD: It was at hand; but then you stood in the way.

MRS. LINDEN: Without my knowledge, Nils. I did not know till to-day that it was you I was to replace in the bank.

KROGSTAD: Well, I take your word for it. But now you do know, do you mean to give way?

MRS. LINDEN: No, for that would not help you.

KROGSTAD: Oh, help, help—! I should do it whether or no.

MRS. LINDEN: I have learnt prudence. Life and bitter necessity have schooled me.

KROGSTAD: And life has taught me not to trust fine speeches.

MRS. LINDEN: Then life has taught you a very sensible thing. But deeds you will trust?

KROGSTAD: What do you mean?

MRS. LINDEN: You said you were a shipwrecked man, clinging to a spar.

KROGSTAD: I have good reason to say so.

MRS. LINDEN: I am a shipwrecked woman clinging to a spar. I have no one to care for.

KROGSTAD: You made your own choice.

MRS. LINDEN: I had no choice.

KROGSTAD: Well, what then?

MRS. LINDEN: How if we two shipwrecked people could join hands?

KROGSTAD: What!

MRS. LINDEN: Suppose we lashed the spars together?

KROGSTAD: Christina!

MRS. LINDEN: What do you think brought me to town?

KROGSTAD: Had you any thought of me?

MRS. LINDEN: I must have work, or I can't live. All my life, as long as I can remember, I have worked; work has been my one great joy. Now I stand quite alone in the world, so terribly aimless and forsaken. There is no happiness in working for one's self. Nils, give me somebody and something to work for.

KROGSTAD: No, no, that can never be. It's simply a woman's romantic notion of self-sacrifice.

MRS. LINDEN: Have you ever found me romantic?

KROGSTAD: Would you really—? Tell me, do you know my past?

MRS. LINDEN: Yes.

KROGSTAD: And do you know what people say of me?

MRS. LINDEN: Did not you say just now that with me you would have been another man?

KROGSTAD: I am sure of it.

MRS. LINDEN: Is it too late?

KROGSTAD: Christina, do you know what you are doing? Yes, you do; I see it in your face. Have you the courage?

MRS. LINDEN: I need some one to tend, and your children need a mother. You need me, and I—I need you. Nils, I believe in your better self. With you I fear nothing.

KROGSTAD [seizing her hands]: Thank you—thank you, Christina. Now I shall make others see me as you do. Ah, I forgot—

MRS. LINDEN [listening]: Hush! The tarantella! Go, go!

KROGSTAD: Why? What is it?

MRS. LINDEN: Don't you hear the dancing overhead? As soon as that is over they will be here.

KROGSTAD: Oh, yes, I'll go. But it's too late now. Of course you don't know the step I have taken against the Helmers?

MRS. LINDEN: Yes, Nils, I do know.

KROGSTAD: And yet you have the courage to—

MRS. LINDEN: I know what lengths despair can drive a man to.

KROGSTAD: Oh, if I could only undo it!

MRS. LINDEN: You can—. Your letter is still in the box.

KROGSTAD: Are you sure?

MRS. LINDEN: Yes, but—

KROGSTAD [*looking at her searchingly*]: Ah, now I understand. You want to save your friend at any price. Say it out—is that your idea?

MRS. LINDEN: Nils, a woman who has once sold herself for the sake of others does not do so again.

KROGSTAD: I will demand my letter back again.

MRS. LINDEN: No, no.

KROGSTAD: Yes, of course; I'll wait till Helmer comes; I'll tell him to give it back to me—that it's only about my dismissal—that I don't want it read.

MRS. LINDEN: No, Nils, you must not recall the letter.

KROGSTAD: But tell me, wasn't that just why you got me to come here?

MRS. LINDEN: Yes, in my first terror. But a day has passed since then, and in that day I have seen incredible things in this house. Helmer must know everything; there must be an end to this unhappy secret. These two must come to a full understanding. They can't possibly go on with all these shifts and concealments.

KROGSTAD: Very well, if you like to risk it. But one thing I can do, and at once—

MRS. LINDEN [*listening*]: Make haste. Go, go! The dance is over; we are not safe another moment.

KROGSTAD: I'll wait for you in the street.

MRS. LINDEN: Yes, do; you must take me home.

KROGSTAD: I never was so happy in all my life! [KROGSTAD *goes, by the outer door. The door between the room and hall remains open.*]

MRS. LINDEN [*setting furniture straight and getting her out-door things together*]: What a change! To have some one to work for; a home to make happy. I shall have to set to work in earnest. I wish they would come. [*Listens.*] Ah, here they are! I must get my things on.

[*Takes bonnet and cloak.* HELMER's *and* NORA's *voices are heard outside; a key is turned in the lock, and* HELMER *drags* NORA *almost by force into the hall. She wears the Italian costume with a large black shawl over it. He is in evening dress and wears a black domino.*[7]]

NORA [*still struggling with him in the doorway*]: No, no, no, I won't go in! I want to go up-stairs again; I don't want to leave so early!

HELMER: But my dearest girl!

NORA: Oh, please, please, Torvald, only one hour more.

---

[7] *domino*: A long cape.

HELMER: Not one minute more, Nora dear; you know what we agreed! Come, come in; you are catching cold here! [*He leads her gently into the room in spite of her resistance.*]

MRS. LINDEN: Good evening.

NORA: Christina!

HELMER: What, Mrs. Linden, you here so late!

MRS. LINDEN: Yes, pardon me! I did so want to see Nora in her costume!

NORA: Have you been sitting here waiting for me?

MRS. LINDEN: Yes, unfortunately I came too late. You had already gone upstairs, and I couldn't go away without seeing you.

HELMER [*taking* NORA's *shawl off*]: Well then, just look at her! I think she's worth looking at. Isn't she lovely, Mrs. Linden?

MRS. LINDEN: Yes, I must say—

HELMER: Isn't she exquisite? Everyone said so. But she is dreadfully obstinate, dear little creature. What's to be done with her? Just think, I had almost to force her away.

NORA: Oh, Torvald, you'll be sorry some day you didn't let me stop, if only for one half hour.

HELMER: There! You hear her, Mrs. Linden? She dances her tarantella with wild applause, and well she deserved it, I must say—though there was, per-haps, a little too much nature in her rendering of the idea—more than was, strictly speaking, artistic. But never mind—she made a great success, and that's the main thing. Ought I to let her stop after that—to weaken the impression? Not if I know it. I took my sweet little Capri girl—my capricious little Capri girl, I might say—under my arm; a rapid turn round the room, a courtesy to all sides, and—as they say in novels—the lovely apparition vanished! An exit should always be effective, Mrs. Linden; but I can't get Nora to see it. By Jove, it's warm here. [*Throws his domino on a chair, and opens the door to his room.*] What! No light here? Oh, of course! Excuse me—

[*Goes in and lights candles.*]

NORA [*whispers breathlessly*]: Well?

MRS. LINDEN: I have spoken to him.

NORA: And?

MRS. LINDEN: Nora—you must tell your husband everything—

NORA [*almost voiceless*]: I knew it!

MRS. LINDEN: You have nothing to fear from Krogstad; but you must speak out.

NORA: I shall not speak!

MRS. LINDEN: Then the letter will.

NORA: Thank you, Christina. Now I know what I have to do. Hush!

HELMER [*coming back*]: Well, Mrs. Linden, have you admired her?

MRS. LINDEN: Yes; and now I'll say good-night.

HELMER: What! already? Does this knitting belong to you?

MRS. LINDEN [*takes it*]: Yes, thanks; I was nearly forgetting it.

HELMER: Then you do knit?

MRS. LINDEN: Yes.

HELMER: Do you know, you ought to embroider instead?

MRS. LINDEN: Indeed! Why?

HELMER: Because it's so much prettier. Look now! You hold the embroidery in the left hand so, and then work the needle with the right hand, in a long, easy curve, don't you?

MRS. LINDEN: Yes, I suppose so.

HELMER: But knitting is always ugly. Look now, your arms close to your sides, and the needles going up and down—there's something Chinese about it.—They really gave us splendid champagne to-night.

MRS. LINDEN: Well, good-night, Nora, and don't be obstinate any more.

HELMER: Well said, Mrs. Linden!

MRS. LINDEN: Good-night, Mr. Helmer.

HELMER [*going with her to the door*]: Good-night, good-night; I hope you'll get safely home. I should be glad to—but really you haven't far to go. Good-night, good-night! [*She goes;* HELMER *shuts the door after her and comes down again.*] At last we've got rid of her; she's an awful bore.

NORA: Aren't you very tired, Torvald?

HELMER: No, not in the least.

NORA: Nor sleepy?

HELMER: Not a bit. I feel particularly lively. But you? You do look tired and sleepy.

NORA: Yes, very tired. I shall soon sleep now.

HELMER: There, you see. I was right after all not to let you stop longer.

NORA: Oh, everything you do is right.

HELMER [*kissing her forehead*]: Now my lark is speaking like a reasonable being. Did you notice how jolly Rank was this evening?

NORA: Was he? I had no chance of speaking to him.

HELMER: Nor I, much; but I haven't seen him in such good spirits for a long time. [*Looks at* NORA *a little, then comes nearer her.*] It's splendid to be back in our own home, to be quite alone together! Oh, you enchanting creature!

NORA: Don't look at me in that way, Torvald.

HELMER: I am not to look at my dearest treasure?—at the loveliness that is mine, mine only, wholly and entirely mine?

NORA [goes to the other side of the table]: You mustn't say these things to me this evening.

HELMER [following]: I see you have the tarantella still in your blood—and that makes you all the more enticing. Listen! the other people are going now. [More softly.] Nora—soon the whole house will be still.

NORA: I hope so.

HELMER: Yes, don't you, Nora darling? When we're among strangers do you know why I speak so little to you, and keep so far away, and only steal a glance at you now and then—do you know why I do it? Because I am fancying that we love each other in secret, that I am secretly betrothed to you, and that no one guesses there is anything between us.

NORA: Yes, yes, yes. I know all your thoughts are with me.

HELMER: And then, when we have to go, and I put the shawl about your smooth, soft shoulders, and this glorious neck of yours, I imagine you are my bride, that our marriage is just over, that I am bringing you for the first time to my home, and that I am alone with you for the first time, quite alone with you, in your quivering loveliness. All this evening I was longing for you, and you only. When I watched you swaying and whirling in the tarantella—my blood boiled—I could endure it no longer; and that's why I made you come home with me so early.

NORA: Go now, Torvald. Go away from me. I won't have all this.

HELMER: What do you mean? Ah! I see you're teasing me! Won't! won't! Am I not your husband?

[A knock at the outer door.]

NORA [starts]: Did you hear?

HELMER [going toward the hall]: Who's there?

RANK [outside]: It's I; may I come in a moment?

HELMER [in a low tone, annoyed]: Oh! what can he want? [Aloud.] Wait a moment. [Opens door.] Come, it's nice of you to give us a look in.

RANK: I thought I heard your voice, and that put it into my head. [Looks round] Ah! this dear old place! How cosy you two are here!

HELMER: You seemed to find it pleasant enough upstairs, too.

RANK: Exceedingly. Why not? Why shouldn't one get all one can out of the world? All one can for as long as one can. The wine was splendid—

HELMER: Especially the champagne.

RANK: Did you notice it? It's incredible the quantity I contrived to get down.

NORA: Torvald drank plenty of champagne too.

RANK: Did he?

NORA: Yes, and it always puts him in such spirits.

RANK: Well, why shouldn't one have a jolly evening after a well-spent day?

HELMER: Well spent! Well, I haven't much to boast of.

RANK [*slapping him on the shoulder*]: But I have, don't you see?

NORA: I suppose you've been engaged in a scientific investigation, Doctor Rank?

RANK: Quite right.

HELMER: Bless me! Little Nora talking about scientific investigations!

NORA: Am I to congratulate you on the result?

RANK: By all means.

NORA: It was good then?

RANK: The best possible, both for doctor and patient—certainty.

NORA [*quickly and searchingly*]: Certainty?

RANK: Absolute certainty. Wasn't I right to enjoy myself after it?

NORA: Yes, quite right, Doctor Rank.

HELMER: And so say I, provided you don't have to pay for it to-morrow.

RANK: Well, in this life nothing's to be had for nothing.

NORA: Doctor Rank, aren't you very fond of masquerades?

RANK: Yes, when there are plenty of comical disguises.

NORA: Tell me, what shall we two be at our next masquerade?

HELMER: Little insatiable! Thinking of your next already!

RANK: We two? I'll tell you. You must go as a good fairy.

HELMER: Oh, but what costume would indicate that?

RANK: She has simply to wear her every-day dress.

HELMER: Capital! But don't you know what you yourself will be?

RANK: Yes, my dear friend, I'm perfectly clear upon that point.

HELMER: Well?

RANK: At the next masquerade I shall be invisible.

HELMER: What a comical idea!

RANK: There's a big, black hat—haven't you heard of the invisible hat? It comes down all over you, and then no one can see you.

HELMER [*with a suppressed smile*]: No, you're right there.

RANK: But I'm quite forgetting what I came for. Helmer, give me a cigar, one of the dark Havanas.

HELMER: With the greatest pleasure.

[*Hands case.*]

RANK [*takes one and cuts the end off*]: Thanks.

NORA [*striking a wax match*]: Let me give you a light.

RANK: A thousand thanks. [*She holds match. He lights his cigar at it.*] And now, good-by.

HELMER: Good-by, good-by, my dear fellow.

NORA: Sleep well, Doctor Rank.

RANK: Thanks for the wish.

NORA: Wish me the same.

RANK: You? Very well, since you ask me—sleep well. And thanks for the light. [*He nods to them both and goes out.*]

HELMER [*in an undertone*]: He's been drinking a good deal.

NORA [*absently*]: I dare say. [HELMER *takes his bunch of keys from his pocket and goes into the hall.*] Torvald, what are you doing there?

HELMER: I must empty the letter-box, it's quite full; there will be no room for the newspapers to-morrow morning.

NORA: Are you going to work to-night?

HELMER: Not very likely! Why, what's this? Some one's been at the lock.

NORA: The lock?

HELMER: I'm sure of it. What does it mean? I can't think that the servants—? Here's a broken hairpin. Nora, it's one of yours.

NORA [*quickly*]: It must have been the children.

HELMER: Then you must break them of such tricks. H'm, h'm! There! at last I've got it open. [*Takes contents out and calls into the kitchen.*] Ellen, Ellen, just put the hall-door lamp out. [*He returns with letters in his hand and shuts the inner door.*] Just see how they've accumulated. [*Turning them over.*] Why, what's this?

NORA [*at the window*]: The letter! Oh, no, no, Torvald!

HELMER: Two visiting cards—from Rank.

NORA: From Doctor Rank?

HELMER [*looking at them*]: Doctor Rank. They were on the top. He must have put them in.

NORA: Is there anything on them?

HELMER: There's a black cross over the name. Look at it. What a horrid idea! It looks just as if he were announcing his own death.

NORA: So he is.

HELMER: What! Do you know anything? Has he told you anything?

NORA: Yes. These cards mean that he has taken his last leave of us. He intends to shut himself up and die.

HELMER: Poor fellow! Of course I knew we couldn't hope to keep him long. But so soon—and then to go and creep into his lair like a wounded animal—

NORA: What must be, must be, and the fewer words the better. Don't you think so, Torvald?

HELMER [*walking up and down*]: He had so grown into our lives. I can't realize that he's gone. He and his sufferings and his loneliness formed a sort of cloudy background to the sunshine of our happiness. Well, perhaps it's best so—at any rate for him. [*Stands still.*] And perhaps for us too, Nora. Now we two are thrown entirely upon each other. [*Puts his arm round her.*] My darling wife! I feel as if I could never hold you close enough. Do you know, Nora, I often wish some danger might threaten you, that I might risk body and soul, and everything, for your dear sake.

NORA [*tears herself from him and says firmly*]: Now you shall read your letters, Torvald.

HELMER: No, no; not to-night. I want to be with you, sweet wife.

NORA: With the thought of your dying friend?

HELMER: You are right. This has shaken us both. Unloveliness has come between us—thoughts of death and decay. We must seek to cast them off. Till then we will remain apart.

NORA [*her arms round his neck*]: Torvald! good-night, good-night.

HELMER [*kissing her forehead*]: Good-night, little bird. Sleep well, Nora. Now I'll go and read my letters. [*He goes into his room and shuts the door.*]

NORA [*with wild eyes, gropes about her, seizes* HELMER'*s domino, throws it round her and whispers quickly, hoarsely, and brokenly*]: Never to see him again. Never, never, never. [*Throws her shawl over her head.*] Never to see the children again. Never, never. Oh, that black icy water! Oh, that bottomless— If it were only over! Now he has it; he's reading it. Oh, no, no, no, not yet. Torvald, good-by. Good-by my little ones—!

[*She is rushing out by the hall; at the same moment* HELMER *tears his door open and stands with an open letter in his hand.*]

HELMER: Nora!

NORA [*shrieking*]: Ah—!

HELMER: What is this? Do you know what is in this letter?

NORA: Yes, I know. Let me go! Let me pass!

HELMER [*holds her back*]: Where do you want to go?

NORA [*tries to get free*]: You sha'n't save me, Torvald.

HELMER [*falling back*]: True! Is it true what he writes? No, no, it cannot be true.

NORA: It is true. I have loved you beyond all else in the world.

HELMER: Pshaw—no silly evasions.

NORA [*a step nearer him*]: Torvald—!

HELMER: Wretched woman! what have you done?

NORA: Let me go—you shall not save me. You shall not take my guilt upon yourself.

HELMER: I don't want any melodramatic airs. [*Locks the door.*] Here you shall stay and give an account of yourself. Do you understand what you have done? Answer. Do you understand it?

NORA [*looks at him fixedly, and says with a stiffening expression*]: Yes; now I begin fully to understand it.

HELMER [*walking up and down*]: Oh, what an awful awakening! During all these eight years—she who was my pride and my joy—a hypocrite, a liar—worse, worse—a criminal. Oh! the hideousness of it! Ugh! Ugh! [NORA *is silent, and continues to look fixedly at him.*] I ought to have foreseen something of the kind. All your father's dishonesty—be silent! I say all your father's dishonesty you have inherited—no religion, no morality, no sense of duty. How I am punished for shielding him! I did it for your sake, and you reward me like this.

NORA: Yes—like this!

HELMER: You have destroyed my whole happiness. You have ruined my future. Oh! it's frightful to think of! I am in the power of a scoundrel; he can do whatever he pleases with me, demand whatever he chooses, and I must submit. And all this disaster is brought upon me by an unprincipled woman.

NORA: When I'm gone, you will be free.

HELMER: Oh, no fine phrases. Your father, too, was always ready with them. What good would it do to me if you were "gone," as you say? No good in the world! He can publish the story all the same; I might even be suspected of collusion. People will think I was at the bottom of it all and egged you on. And for all this I have you to thank—you whom I have done nothing but pet and spoil during our whole married life. Do you understand now what you have done to me?

NORA [*with cold calmness*]: Yes.

HELMER: It's incredible. I can't grasp it. But we must come to an understanding. Take that shawl off. Take it off, I say. I must try to pacify him in one way or other—the secret must be kept, cost what it may. As for ourselves, we must live as we have always done; but of course only in the eyes of the world. Of course you will continue to live here. But the children cannot be left to your care. I dare not trust them to you—Oh, to have to say this to one I have loved so tenderly—whom I still—but that must be a thing of the past. Henceforward there can be no question of happiness, but merely of saving the ruins, the shreds, the show of it! [*A ring;* HELMER *starts.*] What's that? So late! Can it be the worst? Can he—? Hide yourself, Nora; say you are ill.

[NORA *stands motionless.* HELMER *goes to the door and opens it.*]

ELLEN [*half dressed, in the hall*]: Here is a letter for you, ma'am.

HELMER: Give it to me. [*Seizes letter and shuts the door.*] Yes, from him. You shall not have it. I shall read it.

NORA: Read it!

HELMER [*by the lamp*]: I have hardly courage to. We may be lost, both you and I. Ah! I must know. [*Tears the letter hastily open; reads a few lines, looks at an enclosure; a cry of joy.*] Nora. [NORA *looks interrogatively at him.*] Nora! Oh! I must read it again. Yes, yes, it is so. I am saved! Nora, I am saved!

NORA: And I?

HELMER: You too, of course; we are both saved, both of us. Look here, he sends you back your promissory note. He writes that he regrets and apologizes— that a happy turn in his life—Oh', what matter what he writes. We are saved, Nora! No one can harm you. Oh! Nora, Nora—; no, first to get rid of this hateful thing. I'll just see— [*Glances at the IOU.*] No, I won't look at it; the whole thing shall be nothing but a dream to me. [*Tears the IOU and both letters in pieces, throws them into the fire and watches them burn.*] There, it's gone. He wrote that ever since Christmas Eve—Oh, Nora, they must have been three awful days for you.

NORA: I have fought a hard fight for the last three days.

HELMER: And in your agony you saw no other outlet but—no; we won't think of that horror. We will only rejoice and repeat—it's over, all over. Don't you hear, Nora? You don't seem to be able to grasp it. Yes, it's over. What is the set look on your face? Oh, my poor Nora, I understand; you can't believe that I have forgiven you. But I have Nora, I swear it. I have forgiven everything. I know that what you did was all for love of me.

NORA: That's true.

HELMER: You loved me as a wife should love her husband. It was only the means you misjudged. But do you think I love you the less for your helplessness? No, no, only lean on me. I will counsel and guide you. I should be no true man if this very womanly helplessness did not make you doubly dear in my eyes. You mustn't think of the hard things I said in my first moment of terror, when the world seemed to be tumbling about my ears. I have forgiven you, Nora—I swear I have forgiven you.

NORA: I thank you for your forgiveness. [*Goes out, right.*]

HELMER: No, stay. [*Looks in.*] What are you going to do?

NORA [*inside*]: To take off my doll's dress.

HELMER [*in doorway*]: Yes, do, dear. Try to calm down, and recover your balance, my scared little song-bird. You may rest secure, I have broad wings to shield you. [*Walking up and down near the door.*] Oh, how lovely—how cosy our home is, Nora. Here you are safe; here I can shelter you like a hunted dove, whom I have saved from the claws of the hawk. I shall soon bring your poor beating heart to rest, believe me, Nora, I will. To-morrow all this will seem quite different—everything will be as before; I shall not need to tell you again that I forgive you; you will feel for yourself that it is true. How could I find it in my heart to drive you away, or even so much as to reproach you? Oh, you don't know a true man's heart, Nora. There is something indescribably sweet and soothing to a man in having forgiven his wife—honestly forgiven her from the bottom of his heart. She becomes his property in a double sense. She is as though born again; she has become, so to speak, at once his wife and child. That is what you shall henceforth be to me, my bewildered, helpless darling. Don't worry about anything, Nora; only open your heart to me, and I will be both will and conscience to you. [NORA *enters, crossing to table in everyday dress.*] Why, what's this? Not gone to bed? You have changed your dress.

NORA: Yes, Torvald; now I have changed my dress.

HELMER: But why now so late?

NORA: I shall not sleep to-night.

HELMER: But Nora dear—

NORA [*looking at her watch*]: It's not so late yet. Sit down, Torvald, you and I have much to say to each other.

[*She sits on one side of the table.*]

HELMER: Nora, what does this mean; your cold set face—

NORA: Sit down. It will take some time; I have much to talk over with you.

[HELMER *sits at the other side of the table.*]

HELMER: You alarm me; I don't understand you.

NORA: No, that's just it. You don't understand me; and I have never understood you—till to-night. No, don't interrupt. Only listen to what I say. We must come to a final settlement, Torvald!

HELMER: How do you mean?

NORA [*after a short silence*]: Does not one thing strike you as we sit here?

HELMER: What should strike me?

NORA: We have been married eight years. Does it not strike you that this is the first time we two, you and I, man and wife, have talked together seriously?

HELMER: Seriously! Well, what do you call seriously?

NORA: During eight whole years and more—ever since the day we first met—we have never exchanged one serious word about serious things.

HELMER: Was I always to trouble you with the cares you could not help me to bear?

NORA: I am not talking of cares. I say that we have never yet set ourselves seriously to get to the bottom of anything.

HELMER: Why, my dear Nora, what have you to do with serious things?

NORA: There we have it! You have never understood me. I have had great injustice done me, Torvald, first by my father and then by you.

HELMER: What! by your father and me?—by us who have loved you more than all the world?

NORA [shaking her head]: You have never loved me. You only thought it amusing to be in love with me.

HELMER: Why, Nora, what a thing to say!

NORA: Yes, it is so, Torvald. While I was at home with father he used to tell me all his opinions and I held the same opinions. If I had others I concealed them, because he would not have liked it. He used to call me his doll child, and play with me as I played with my dolls. Then I came to live in your house—

HELMER: What an expression to use about our marriage.

NORA [undisturbed]: I mean I passed from father's hands into yours. You settled everything according to your taste; and I got the same tastes as you; or I pretended to—I don't know which—both ways perhaps. When I look back on it now, I seem to have been living here like a beggar, from hand to mouth. I lived by performing tricks for you, Torvald. But you would have it so. You and father have done me a great wrong. It's your fault that my life has been wasted.

HELMER: Why, Nora, how unreasonable and ungrateful you are. Haven't you been happy here?

NORA: No, never; I thought I was, but I never was.

HELMER: Not—not happy?

NORA: No, only merry. And you have always been so kind to me. But our house has been nothing but a play-room. Here I have been your doll-wife, just as at home I used to be papa's doll-child. And the children in their turn have been my dolls. I thought it fun when you played with me, just as the children did when I played with them. That has been our marriage, Torvald.

HELMER: There is some truth in what you say, exaggerated and over-strained though it be. But henceforth it shall be different. Playtime is over; now comes the time for education.

NORA: Whose education? Mine or the children's?

HELMER: Both, my dear Nora.

NORA: Oh, Torvald, you can't teach me to be a fit wife for you.

HELMER: And you say that?

NORA: And I—am I fit to educate the children?

HELMER: Nora!

NORA: Did you not say yourself a few minutes ago you dared not trust them to me?

HELMER: In the excitement of the moment! Why should you dwell upon that?

NORA: No—you are perfectly right. That problem is beyond me. There's another to be solved first—I must try to educate myself. You are not the man to help me in that. I must set about it alone. And that is why I am now leaving you!

HELMER [jumping up]: What—do you mean to say—

NORA: I must stand quite alone to know myself and my surroundings; so I cannot stay with you.

HELMER: Nora! Nora!

NORA: I am going at once. Christina will take me in for to-night—

HELMER: You are mad. I shall not allow it. I forbid it.

NORA: It's no use your forbidding me anything now. I shall take with me what belongs to me. From you I will accept nothing, either now or afterward.

HELMER: What madness!

NORA: To-morrow I shall go home.

HELMER: Home!

NORA: I mean to what was my home. It will be easier for me to find some opening there.

HELMER: Oh, in your blind experience—

NORA: I must try to gain experience, Torvald.

HELMER: To forsake your home, your husband, and your children! You don't consider what the world will say.

NORA: I can pay no heed to that! I only know that I must do it.

HELMER: It's exasperating! Can you forsake your holiest duties in this way?

NORA: What do you call my holiest duties?

HELMER: Do you ask me that? Your duties to your husband and your children.

NORA: I have other duties equally sacred.

HELMER: Impossible! What duties do you mean?

NORA: My duties toward myself.

HELMER: Before all else you are a wife and a mother.

NORA: That I no longer believe. I think that before all else I am a human being, just as much as you are—or, at least, I will try to become one. I know that most people agree with you, Torvald, and that they say so in books. But henceforth I can't be satisfied with what most people say, and what is in books. I must think things out for myself and try to get clear about them.

HELMER: Are you not clear about your place in your home? Have you not an infallible guide in questions like these? Have you not religion?

NORA: Oh, Torvald, I don't know properly what religion is.

HELMER: What do you mean?

NORA: I know nothing but what our clergyman told me when I was confirmed. He explained that religion was this and that. When I get away from here and stand alone I will look into that matter too. I will see whether what he taught me is true, or, at any rate, whether it is true for me.

HELMER: Oh, this is unheard of! But if religion cannot keep you right, let me appeal to your conscience— I suppose you have some moral feeling? Or, answer me, perhaps you have none?

NORA: Well, Torvald, it's not easy to say. I really don't know—I am all at sea about these things. I only know that I think quite differently from you about them. I hear, too, that the laws are different from what I thought; but I can't believe that they are right. It appears that a woman has no right to spare her dying father, or to save her husband's life. I don't believe that.

HELMER: You talk like a child. You don't understand the society in which you live.

NORA: No, I don't. But I shall try to. I must make up my mind which is right— society or I.

HELMER: Nora, you are ill, you are feverish. I almost think you are out of your senses.

NORA: I never felt so much clearness and certainty as to-night.

HELMER: You are clear and certain enough to forsake husband and children?

NORA: Yes, I am.

HELMER: Then there is only one explanation possible.

NORA: What is that?

HELMER: You no longer love me.

NORA: No, that is just it.

HELMER: Nora! Can you say so?

NORA: Oh, I'm so sorry, Torvald; for you've always been so kind to me. But I can't help it. I do not love you any longer.

HELMER [keeping his composure with difficulty]: Are you clear and certain on this point too?

NORA: Yes, quite. That is why I won't stay here any longer.

HELMER: And can you also make clear to me, how I have forfeited your love?

NORA: Yes, I can. It was this evening, when the miracle did not happen. For then I saw you were not the man I had taken you for.

HELMER: Explain yourself more clearly; I don't understand.

NORA: I have waited so patiently all these eight years; for, of course, I saw clearly enough that miracles do not happen every day. When this crushing blow threatened me, I said to myself, confidently, "Now comes the miracle!" When Krogstad's letter lay in the box, it never occurred to me that you would think of submitting to that man's conditions. I was convinced that you would say to him, "Make it known to all the world," and that then—

HELMER: Well? When I had given my own wife's name up to disgrace and shame—

NORA: Then I firmly believed that you would come forward, take everything upon yourself, and say, "I am the guilty one."

HELMER: Nora!

NORA: You mean I would never have accepted such a sacrifice? No, certainly not. But what would my assertions have been worth in opposition to yours? That was the miracle that I hoped for and dreaded. And it was to hinder that that I wanted to die.

HELMER: I would gladly work for you day and night, Nora—bear sorrow and want for your sake—but no man sacrifices his honor, even for one he loves.

NORA: Millions of women have done so.

HELMER: Oh, you think and talk like a silly child.

NORA: Very likely. But you neither think nor talk like the man I can share my life with. When your terror was over—not for me, but for yourself—when there was nothing more to fear,—then it was to you as though nothing had happened. I was your lark again, your doll—whom you would take twice as much care of in the future, because she was so weak and fragile. [*Stands up.*] Torvald, in that moment it burst upon me, that I had been living here these eight years with a strange man, and had borne him three children— Oh! I can't bear to think of it—I could tear myself to pieces!

HELMER [*sadly*]: I see it, I see it; an abyss has opened between us—But, Nora, can it never be filled up?

NORA: As I now am, I am no wife for you.

HELMER: I have strength to become another man.

NORA: Perhaps—when your doll is taken away from you.

HELMER: To part—to part from you! No, Nora, no; I can't grasp the thought.

NORA [*going into room, right*]: The more reason for the thing to happen. [*She comes back with out-door things and a small travelling bag, which she puts on a chair.*]

HELMER: Nora, Nora, not now! Wait till to-morrow.

NORA [*putting on cloak*]: I can't spend the night in a strange man's house.

HELMER: But can't we live here as brother and sister?

NORA [*fastening her hat*]: You know very well that would not last long. Good-by, Torvald. No, I won't go to the children. I know they are in better hands than mine. As I now am, I can be nothing to them.

HELMER: But some time, Nora—some time—

NORA: How can I tell? I have no idea what will become of me.

HELMER: But you are my wife, now and always?

NORA: Listen, Torvald—when a wife leaves her husband's house, as I am doing, I have heard that in the eyes of the law he is free from all the duties toward her. At any rate I release you from all duties. You must not feel yourself bound any more than I shall. There must be perfect freedom on both sides. There, there is your ring back. Give me mine.

HELMER: That too?

NORA: That too.

HELMER: Here it is.

NORA: Very well. Now it is all over. Here are the keys. The servants know about everything in the house, better than I do. To-morrow, when I have started, Christina will come to pack up my things. I will have them sent after me.

HELMER: All over! All over! Nora, will you never think of me again?

NORA: Oh, I shall often think of you, and the children—and this house.

HELMER: May I write to you, Nora?

NORA: No, never. You must not.

HELMER: But I must send you—

NORA: Nothing, nothing.

HELMER: I must help you if you need it.

NORA: No, I say. I take nothing from strangers.

HELMER: Nora, can I never be more than a stranger to you?

NORA [*taking her travelling bag*]: Oh, Torvald, then the miracle of miracles would have to happen.

HELMER: What is the miracle of miracles?

NORA: Both of us would have to change so that—Oh, Torvald, I no longer believe in miracles.

HELMER: But I will believe. We must so change that—?

NORA: That communion between us shall be a marriage. Good-by.

[*She goes out.*]

HELMER [*sinks in a chair by the door with his face in his hands*]: Nora! Nora! [*He looks around and stands up.*] Empty. She's gone! [*A hope inspires him.*] Ah! The miracle of miracles—?!

[*From below is heard the reverberation of a heavy door closing.*]

UNDERSTANDING THE PLAY

1. (I) At the beginning of Act I, what does Nora's lie about eating the macaroons reveal about her husband and their relationship?

2. (I) What does Torvald's comment "No one would believe how much it costs a man to keep such a little bird as you" reveal about his attitudes toward himself, Nora, and marriage?

3. (I) Several times in Act I, Nora protests to Mrs. Linden that she is serious, not silly. She states that she will tell Torvald of her secret life only when he is no longer amused by her "skipping about, and dressing up and acting." What does Nora's description of her own behavior reveal about her?

4. (I) What is ironic about Nora's situation at the end of Act I?

5. (II) When talking about her costume for the dance, Nora says to Torvald, "Isn't it good of me, too, to have given in to you?" What does this comment reveal about her?

6. (II) What would happen to Torvald's image at the bank if he allowed his wife or others to influence him?

7. (II) At the end of Act II, Nora says to Mrs. Linden, "Things must take their course. After all, there's something glorious in waiting for the miracle." What is the significance of these lines? What miracle is Nora waiting for?

8. (III) Near the beginning of Act III, Mrs. Linden tells Krogstad, "I have seen incredible things in this house. Helmer [Torvald] must know everything; there must be an end to this unhappy secret." What "incredible things" is Mrs. Linden referring to? Why does she urge Krogstad to leave his letter for Torvald to read?

9. (III) Why isn't Nora flattered and pleased after the dance when Torvald says to her, "I am not to look at my dearest treasure?—at the loveliness that is mine, mine only, wholly and entirely mine?"

10. (III) What do Torvald's reactions to Dr. Rank's suffering, loneliness, and imminent death reveal about Torvald?

11. (III) Nora tells Torvald, "I have never understood you—till to-night." Why has she been so blind to the kind of man Torvald is?

12. (III) What concerns Torvald most about Nora's decision to leave him and their children? Is his attitude surprising?

13. To what extent is Nora's problem due to her own and Torvald's personalities, and to what extent is it due to the values of the society in which they lived? To what extent has Nora solved her problems at the end of the play?

14. Does Nora have a greater responsibility to herself or to her family?

15. Who is the more important character, Nora or Torvald? Defend your choice.

16. What **themes** do you find in this play?

ANALYZING LITERARY TECHNIQUE

1. **Foreshadowing:**
   a) (I) What is the opening conflict between Nora and Torvald? What does Nora consider the best Christmas gift? Why? How does this become a major issue in the play?
   b) (I) What is significant about Torvald's reaction to Krogstad's crime?
   c) (II) What information is revealed during the opening scene of Act II, between Nora and Anna, her nurse?
   d) (II) Near the end of Act II, Krogstad tells Nora, "A mere money-lender, a penny-a-liner, a—in short, a creature like me—has a little bit of what people call 'heart.'" Why are these lines important?
   e) (II) Dr. Rank tells Nora that he will not have Torvald in his sickroom because "Helmer's delicate nature shrinks so from all that is horrible." How are these words proved true?

2. Much of the powerful impact of this play depends on Ibsen's use of **irony,** both **dramatic irony** and **verbal irony.**
   a) Find three examples in the play of dramatic irony and explain how they contribute to the total effect of the play.
   b) Find three examples of verbal irony and explain how they contribute to the impact of the scene or to the audience's understanding of the events and meaning of the whole play.

3. Function of minor characters:
   a) Compare and contrast Mrs. Linden and Nora. How does Mrs. Linden contribute to Nora's psychological growth?
   b) What is Krogstad's significance in the play?
   c) What is Dr. Rank's relationship to Nora?

WRITING ABOUT LITERATURE

1. Write an essay in which you trace Nora's transition from dependence to independence. Choose at least three major factors (attitudes and experiences) that influenced Nora's decisions and discuss them in detail. You also may wish to consider Mrs. Linden's, Dr. Rank's, and Torvald's influence on Nora. Evaluate Nora's final situation: What are her gains and her losses, and which outweighs the other?

2. Write a character sketch of Torvald. Trace Torvald's attitudes throughout the play to show consistency of character. In the process, evaluate Torvald's response to Krogstad's letter. Explain why Nora should not have been surprised by his attitudes. Use quotations to support your ideas.

3. At the end of the play, Torvald tells Nora, "No man sacrifices his honor, even for one he loves," and Nora responds, "Millions of women have done so." Is Torvald correct? What does Nora's response suggest? Is honor a clearly defined concept? Evaluate Torvald's and Nora's conceptions of what honor is. Choose which concept you find preferable and explain why. Use quotes from the play to support your ideas.

4. Write a letter from a friend to Nora in which she responds to Nora's remarks at the end of the play. Explain the friend's opinion of one or more of the following statements: (a) "It's your [you and my father's] fault that my life has been wasted." (b) "[I'm not] fit to educate the children." (c) "I must stand quite alone to know myself and my surroundings; so I cannot stay with you." (d) "I no longer believe [that before all I am a wife and mother]. I think that before all else I am a human being."

5. Create a conversation between Anna (the nurse) and Ellen (the maid) in which they discuss the effect of Nora's departure on Torvald. Consider the following questions: Do Torvald's attitudes change as he told Nora they would? What is life without Nora like? Is Dr. Rank correct that out of sight is out of mind?

The Outlaws

SELMA LAGERLÖF

IN 1909 THE SWEDISH NOVELIST SELMA LAGERLÖF **(1858–1940)** became the first woman to win the Nobel Prize for literature, awarded "in appreciation of the lofty idealism, vivid imagination, and spiritual perception that characterize her writings." She is best known for her first novel, *Gosta Berling's Saga* (1891), which is based on folktales from the Swedish oral tradition, and for her internationally famous children's book *The Wonderful Adventures of Nils* (1906–1907).

Lagerlöf grew up in southern Sweden on a small comfortable family estate. After polio made her a semi-invalid in her youth, she turned for enjoyment to reading and writing fiction and poetry. In 1883, at the age of twenty-five, she became a teacher in a country school. In 1895 she gave up teaching and became a professional writer.

Contemporaries considered both the subject matter and the style of Lagerlöf's fiction to be unusual. At a time when traditional European subjects and the works of Henrik Ibsen and August Strindberg were popular, she preferred to depict the life of the peasants in rural Sweden. Her work is characterized by her love of Swedish legends and folktales, her personal Christian morality, her psychological insight, and her interest in literary style. The conflict between ancient rural traditions and modern religion inspired Lagerlöf to write tales such as "The Outlaws," in which elements from legends and folktales add extraordinary vitality and universal appeal.

A peasant who had murdered a monk took to the woods and was made an outlaw. He found there before him in the wilderness another outlaw, a fisherman from the outermost islands, who had been accused of stealing a herring net. They joined together, lived in a cave, set snares, sharpened darts, baked bread on a granite rock and guarded one another's lives. The peasant never left the woods, but the fisherman, who had not committed such an abominable crime, sometimes loaded game on his shoulders and stole down among men. There he got in exchange for black-cocks, for long-eared hares and fine-limbed red deer, milk and butter, arrowheads and clothes. These helped the outlaws to sustain life.

The cave where they lived was dug in the side of a hill. Broad stones and thorny sloe-bushes hid the entrance. Above it stood a thick growing pine-tree. At its roots was the vent-hole of the cave. The rising smoke filtered through the tree's thick branches and vanished into space. The men used to go to and from their dwelling-place, wading in the mountain stream, which ran down the hill. No one looked for their tracks under the merry, bubbling water.

At first they were hunted like wild beasts. The peasants gathered as if for a chase of bear or wolf. The wood was surrounded by men with bows and arrows. Men with spears went through it and left no dark crevice, no bushy thicket unexplored. While the noisy battue[1] hunted through the wood, the outlaws lay in their dark hold, listening breathlessly, panting with terror. The fisherman held out for a whole day, but he who had murdered was driven by unbearable fear out into the open, where he could see his enemy. He was seen and hunted, but it seemed to him seven times better than to lie still in helpless inactivity. He fled from his pursuers, slid down precipices, sprang over streams, climbed up perpendicular mountain walls. All latent strength and dexterity in him was called forth by the excitement of danger. His body became elastic like steel spring, his foot made no false step, his hand never lost its hold, eye and ear were twice as sharp as usual. He understood what the leaves whispered and the rocks warned. When he had climbed up a precipice, he turned toward his pursuers, sending them gibes in biting rhyme. When the whistling darts whizzed by him, he caught them, swift as lightning, and hurled them down on his enemies. As he forced his way through whipping branches, something within him sang a song of triumph.

The bald mountain ridge ran through the wood and alone on its summit stood a lofty fir. The red-brown trunk was bare, but in the branching top rocked an eagle's nest. The fugitive was now so audaciously bold that he climbed up there, while his pursuers looked for him on the wooded slopes. There he sat twisting the young eaglets' necks, while the hunt passed by far below him. The male and female eagle, longing for revenge, swooped down on the ravisher. They fluttered before his face, they struck with their beaks at his eyes, they beat him with their wings and tore with their claws bleeding weals in his weather-beaten skin. Laughing, he fought with them. Standing upright in the shaking nest, he cut at them with his sharp knife and forgot in the pleasure of the play his danger and his pursuers. When he found time to look for them, they had gone by to some other part of the forest. No one had thought to look for their prey on the bald mountain-ridge. No one had raised his eyes to the clouds to see him practicing boyish tricks and sleep-walking feats while his life was in the greatest danger.

The man trembled when he found that he was saved. With shaking hands he caught at a support, giddy he measured the height to which he had climbed.

---

[1] *battue:* A forest hunt in which people beat the bushes and underbrush to flush out game.

And moaning with the fear of falling, afraid of the birds, afraid of being seen, afraid of everything, he slid down the trunk. He laid himself down on the ground, so as not to be seen, and dragged himself forward over the rocks until the under-brush covered him. There he hid himself under the young pine-tree's tangled branches. Weak and powerless, he sank down on the moss. A single man could have captured him.

Tord was the fisherman's name. He was not more than sixteen years old, but strong and bold. He had already lived a year in the woods.

The peasant's name was Berg, with the surname Rese. He was the tallest and the strongest man in the whole district, and moreover handsome and well-built. He was broad in the shoulders and slender in the waist. His hands were as well shaped as if he had never done any hard work. His hair was brown and his skin fair. After he had been some time in the woods he acquired in all ways a more formidable appearance. His eyes became piercing, his eyebrows grew bushy, and the muscles which knitted them lay finger thick above his nose. It showed now more plainly than before how the upper part of his athlete's brow projected over the lower. His lips closed more firmly than of old, his whole face was thinner, the hollows at the temples grew very deep, and his powerful jaw was much more prominent. His body was less well filled out but his muscles were as hard as steel. His hair grew suddenly gray.

Young Tord could never weary of looking at this man. He had never before seen anything so beautiful and powerful. In his imagination he stood high as the forest, strong as the sea. He served him as a master and worshiped him as a god. It was a matter of course that Tord should carry the hunting spears, drag home the game, fetch the water and build the fire. Berg Rese accepted all his services, but almost never gave him a friendly word. He despised him because he was a thief.

The outlaws did not lead a robber's or brigand's life; they supported them-selves by hunting and fishing. If Berg Rese had not murdered a holy man, the peasants would soon have ceased to pursue him and have left him in peace in the mountains. But they feared great disaster to the district, because he who had raised his hand against the servant of God was still unpunished. When Tord came down to the valley with game, they offered him riches and pardon for his own crime if he would show them the way to Berg Rese's hole, so that they might take him while he slept. But the boy always refused; and if anyone tried to sneak after him up to the wood, he led him so cleverly astray that he gave up the pursuit.

Once Berg asked him if the peasants had not tried to tempt him to betray him, and when he heard what they had offered him as a reward, he said scorn-fully that Tord had been foolish not to accept such a proposal.

Then Tord looked at him with a glance, the like of which Berg Rese had never before seen. Never had any beautiful woman in his youth, never had his wife or child looked so at him. "You are my lord, my elected master," said the glance. "Know that you may strike me and abuse me as you will, I am faithful notwithstanding."

After that Berg Rese paid more attention to the boy and noticed that he was bold to act but timid to speak. He had no fear of death. When the ponds were first frozen, or when the bogs were most dangerous in the spring, when the quagmires were hidden under richly flowering grasses and cloudberry, he took his way over them by choice. He seemed to feel the need of exposing himself to danger as a compensation for the storms and terrors of the ocean, which he had no longer to meet. At night he was afraid in the woods, and even in the middle of the day the darkest thickets or the wide-stretching roots of a fallen pine could frighten him. But when Berg Rese asked him about it, he was too shy to even answer.

Tord did not sleep near the fire, far in in the cave, on the bed which was made so fat with moss and warm with skins, but every night, when Berg had fallen asleep, he crept out to the entrance and lay there on a rock. Berg discovered this, and although he well understood the reason, he asked what it meant. Tord would not explain. To escape any more questions, he did not lie at the door for two nights, but then he returned to his post.

One night, when the drifting snow whirled about the forest tops and drove into the thickest underbrush, the driving snowflakes found their way into the outlaws' cave. Tord, who lay just inside the entrance, was, when he waked in the morning, covered by a melting snowdrift. A few days later he fell ill. His lungs wheezed, and when they were expanded to take in air, he felt excruciating pain. He kept up as long as his strength held out, but when one evening he leaned down to blow the fire, he fell over and remained lying.

Berg Rese came to him and told him to go to bed. Tord moaned with pain and could not raise himself. Berg then thrust his arms under him and carried him there. But he felt as if he had got hold of a slimy snake; he had a taste in the mouth as if he had eaten the unholy horseflesh, it was so odious to him to touch the miserable thief.

He laid his own big bearskin over him and gave him water, more he could not do. Nor was it anything dangerous. Tord was soon well again. But through Berg's being obliged to do his tasks and to be his servant, they had come nearer to one another. Tord dared to talk to him when he sat in the cave in the evening and cut arrow shafts.

"You are of a good race, Berg," said Tord. "Your kinsmen are the richest in the valley. Your ancestors have served with kings and fought in their castles."

"They have oftener fought with bands of rebels and done the kings great injury," replied Berg Rese.

"Your ancestors gave great feasts at Christmas, and so did you, when you were at home. Hundreds of men and women could find a place to sit in your big house, which was already built before Saint Olof[2] first gave the baptism here in Viken. You owned old silver vessels and great drinking-horns, which passed from man to man, filled with mead."

---

[2] *Saint Olof:* King of Norway from 1016 to 1028, Olof (or Olaf) was responsible for spreading Christianity throughout Scandinavia; he became the patron saint of Norway.

Again Berg Rese had to look at the boy. He sat up with his legs hanging out of the bed and his head resting on his hands, with which he at the same time held back the wild masses of hair which would fall over his eyes. His face had become pale and delicate from the ravages of sickness. In his eyes fever still burned. He smiled at the pictures he conjured up: at the adorned house, at the silver vessels, at the guests in gala array and at Berg Rese, sitting in the seat of honor in the hall of his ancestors. The peasant thought that no one had ever looked at him with such shining, admiring eyes, or thought him so magnificent, arrayed in his festival clothes, as that boy thought him in the torn skin dress.

He was both touched and provoked. That miserable thief had no right to admire him.

"Were there no feasts in your house?" he asked.

Tord laughed. "Out there on the rocks with father and mother! Father is a wrecker and mother is a witch. No one will come to us."

"Is your mother a witch?"

"She is," answered Tord, quite untroubled. "In stormy weather she rides out on a seal to meet the ships over which the waves are washing, and those who are carried overboard are hers."

"What does she do with them?" asked Berg.

"Oh, a witch always needs corpses. She makes ointments out of them, or perhaps she eats them. On moonlight nights she sits in the surf, where it is whitest, and the spray dashes over her. They say that she sits and searches for shipwrecked children's fingers and eyes."

"That is awful," said Berg.

The boy answered with infinite assurance: "That would be awful in others, but not in witches. They have to do so."

Berg Rese found that he had here come upon a new way of regarding the world and things.

"Do thieves have to steal, as witches have to use witchcraft?" he asked sharply.

"Yes, of course," answered the boy; "everyone has to do what he is destined to do." But then he added, with a cautious smile: "There are thieves also who have never stolen."

"Say out what you mean," said Berg.

The boy continued with his mysterious smile, proud at being an unsolvable riddle: "It is like speaking of birds who do not fly, to talk of thieves who do not steal."

Berg Rese pretended to be stupid in order to find out what he wanted. "No one can be called a thief without having stolen," he said.

"No; but," said the boy, and pressed his lips together as if to keep in the words, "but if someone had a father who stole," he hinted after a while.

"One inherits money and lands," replied Berg Rese, "but no one bears the name of thief if he has not himself earned it."

Tord laughed quietly. "But if somebody has a mother who begs and prays him to take his father's crime on him. But if such a one cheats the hangman and escapes to the woods. But if someone is made an outlaw for a fish-net which he has never seen."

Berg Rese struck the stone table with his clenched fist. He was angry. This fair young man had thrown away his whole life. He could never win love, nor riches, nor esteem after that. The wretched striving for food and clothes was all which was left him. And the fool had let him, Berg Rese, go on despising one who was innocent. He rebuked him with stern words, but Tord was not even as afraid as a sick child is of its mother, when she chides it because it has caught cold by wading in the spring brooks.

On one of the broad, wooded mountains lay a dark tarn. It was square, with as straight shores and as sharp corners as if it had been cut by the hand of man. On three sides it was surrounded by steep cliffs, on which pines clung with roots as thick as a man's arm. Down by the pool, where the earth had been gradually washed away, their roots stood up out of the water, bare and crooked and wonderfully twisted about one another. It was like an infinite number of serpents which had wanted all at the same time to crawl up out of the pool but had got entangled in one another and been held fast. Or it was like a mass of blackened skeletons of drowned giants which the pool wanted to throw up on the land. Arms and legs writhed about one another, the long fingers dug deep into the very cliff to get a hold, the mighty ribs formed arches, which held up primeval trees. It had happened, however, that the iron arms, the steel-like fingers with which the pines held themselves fast, had given way, and a pine had been borne by a mighty north wind from the top of the cliff down into the pool. It had burrowed deep down into the muddy bottom with its top and now stood there. The smaller fish had a good place of refuge among its branches, but the roots stuck up above the water like a many-armed monster and contributed to make the pool awful and terrifying.

On the tarn's fourth side the cliff sank down. There a little foaming stream carried away its waters. Before this stream could find the only possible way, it had tried to get out between stones and tufts, and had by so doing made a little world of islands, some no bigger than a little hillock, others covered with trees.

Here where the encircling cliffs did not shut out all the sun, leafy trees flourished. Here stood thirsty, gray-green alders and smooth-leaved willows. The birch-tree grew there as it does everywhere where it is trying to crowd out the pine woods, and the wild cherry and the mountain ash, those two which edge the forest pastures, filling them with fragrance and adorning them with beauty.

Here at the outlet there was a forest of reeds as high as a man, which made the sunlight fall green on the water just as it falls on the moss in the real forest. Among the reeds there were open places; small, round pools, and water-lilies were floating there. The tall stalks looked down with mild seriousness on those sensitive beauties, who discontentedly shut their white petals and yellow stamens in a hard, leather-like sheath as soon as the sun ceased to show itself.

One sunshiny day the outlaws came to this tarn to fish. They waded out to a couple of big stones in the midst of the reed forest and sat there and threw out bait for the big, green-striped pickerel that lay and slept near the surface of the water.

These men, who were always wandering in the woods and the mountains, had, without their knowing it themselves, come under nature's rule as much as the plants and the animals. When the sun shone, they were open-hearted and brave, but in the evening, as soon as the sun had disappeared, they became silent; and the night, which seemed to them much greater and more powerful than the day, made them anxious and helpless. Now the green light, which slanted in between the rushes and colored the water with brown and dark-green streaked with gold, affected their mood until they were ready for any miracle. Every outlook was shut off. Sometimes the reeds rocked in an imperceptible wind, their stalks rustled, and the long, ribbon-like leaves fluttered against their faces. They sat in gray skins on the gray stones. The shadows in the skins repeated the shadows of the weather-beaten, mossy stone. Each saw his companion in his silence and immovability change into a stone image. But in among the rushes swam mighty fishes with rainbow-colored backs. When the men threw out their hooks and saw the circles spreading among the reeds, it seemed as if the motion grew stronger and stronger, until they perceived that it was not caused only by their cast. A sea-nymph, half human, half a shining fish, lay and slept on the surface of the water. She lay on her back with her whole body under water. The waves so nearly covered her that they had not noticed her before. It was her breathing that caused the motion of the waves. But there was nothing strange in her lying there, and when the next instant she was gone, they were not sure that she had not been only an illusion.

The green light entered through the eyes into the brain like a gentle intoxication. The men sat and stared with dulled thoughts, seeing visions among the reeds, of which they did not dare to tell one another. Their catch was poor. The day was devoted to dreams and apparitions.

The stroke of oars was heard among the rushes, and they started up as from sleep. The next moment, a flat-bottomed boat appeared, heavy, hollowed out with no skill and with oars as small as sticks. A young girl, who had been picking water-lilies, rowed it. She had dark-brown hair, gathered in great braids, and big dark eyes; otherwise she was strangely pale. But her paleness toned to pink and not to gray. Her cheeks had no higher color than the rest of her face, the lips had hardly enough. She wore a white linen shirt and a leather belt with a gold buckle. Her skirt was blue with a red hem. She rowed by the outlaws without seeing them. They kept breathlessly still, but not for fear of being seen, but only to be able to really see her. As soon as she had gone they were as if changed from stone images to living beings. Smiling, they looked at one another.

"She was white like the water-lilies," said one. "Her eyes were as dark as the water there under the pine-roots."

They were so excited that they wanted to laugh, really laugh as no one had ever laughed by that pool, till the cliffs thundered with echoes and the roots of the pines loosened with fright.

"Did you think she was pretty?" asked Berg Rese.

"Oh, I do not know, I saw her for such a short time. Perhaps she was."

"I do not believe you dared to look at her. You thought that it was a mermaid."

And they were again shaken by the same extravagant merriment.

Tord had once as a child seen a drowned man. He had found the body on the shore on a summer day and had not been at all afraid, but at night he had dreamed terrible dreams. He saw a sea, where every wave rolled a dead man to his feet. He saw, too, that all the islands were covered with drowned men who were dead and belonged to the sea, but who still could speak and move and threaten him with withered white hands.

It was so with him now. The girl whom he had seen among the rushes came back in his dreams. He met her out in the open pool, where the sunlight fell even greener than among the rushes, and he had time to see that she was beautiful. He dreamed that he had crept up on the big pine-root in the middle of the dark tarn, but the pine swayed and rocked so that sometimes he was quite under water. Then she came forward on the little islands. She stood under the red mountain ashes and laughed at him. In the last dream-vision he had come so far that she kissed him. It was already morning, and he heard that Berg Rese had got up, but he obstinately shut his eyes to be able to go on with his dream. When he awoke, he was as though dizzy and stunned by what had happened to him in the night. He thought much more now of the girl than he had done the day before.

Toward night he happened to ask Berg Rese if he knew her name.

Berg looked at him inquiringly. "Perhaps it is best for you to hear it," he said. "She is Unn. We are cousins."

Tord then knew that it was for that pale girl's sake Berg Rese wandered an outlaw in forest and mountain. Tord tried to remember what he knew of her. Unn was the daughter of a rich peasant. Her mother was dead, so that she managed her father's house. This she liked, for she was fond of her own way and she had no wish to be married.

Unn and Berg Rese were the children of brothers, and it had long been said that Berg preferred to sit with Unn and her maids and jest with them than to work on his own lands. When the great Christmas feast was celebrated at his house, his wife had invited a monk from Draksmark, for she wanted him to remonstrate with Berg, because he was forgetting her for another woman. This monk was hateful to Berg and to many on account of his appearance. He was very fat and quite white. The ring of hair about his bald head, the eyebrows above his watery eyes, his face, his hands and his whole cloak, everything was white. Many found it hard to endure his looks.

At the banquet table, in the hearing of all the guests, this monk now said, for he was fearless and thought that his words would have more effect if they were heard by many, "People are in the habit of saying that the cuckoo is the worst of birds because he does not rear his young in his own nest, but here sits a man who does not provide for his home and his children, but seeks his pleasure with a strange woman. Him will I call the worst of men."—Unn then rose up. "That, Berg, is said to you and me," she said. "Never have I been so insulted, and my father is not here either." She had wished to go, but Berg sprang after her. "Do not move!" she said. "I will never see you again." He caught up with her in the hall and asked her what he should do to make her stay. She had answered with flashing eyes that he must know that best himself. Then Berg went in and killed the monk.

Berg and Tord were busy with the same thoughts, for after a while Berg said: "You should have seen her, Unn, when the white monk fell. The mistress of the house gathered the small children about her and cursed her. She turned their faces toward her, that they might forever remember her who had made their father a murderer. But Unn stood calm and so beautiful that the men trembled. She thanked me for the deed and told me to fly to the woods. She bade me not to be robber, and not to use the knife until I could do it for an equally just cause."

"Your deed had been to her honor," said Tord.

Berg Rese noticed again what had astonished him before in the boy. He was like a heathen, worse than a heathen; he never condemned what was wrong. He felt no responsibility. That which must be, was. He knew of God and Christ and the saints, but only by name, as one knows the gods of foreign lands. The ghosts of the rocks were his gods. His mother, wise in witchcraft, had taught him to believe in the spirits of the dead.

Then Berg Rese undertook a task which was as foolish as to twist a rope about his own neck. He set before those ignorant eyes the great God, the Lord of justice, the Avenger of misdeeds, who casts the wicked into places of everlasting torment. And he taught him to love Christ and His mother and the holy men and women, who with lifted hands kneeled before God's throne to avert the wrath of the great Avenger from the hosts of sinners. He taught him all that men do to appease God's wrath. He showed him the crowds of pilgrims making pilgrimages to holy places, the flight of self-torturing penitents and monks from a worldly life.

As he spoke, the boy became more eager and more pale, his eyes grew large as if for terrible visions. Berg Rese wished to stop, but thoughts streamed to him, and he went on speaking. The night sank down over them, the black forest night, when the owls hoot. God came so near to them that they saw his throne darken the stars, and the chastising angels sank down to the tops of the trees. And under them the fires of Hell flamed up to the earth's crust, eagerly licking that shaking place of refuge for the sorrowing races of men.

The autumn had come with a heavy storm. Tord went alone in the woods to see after the snares and traps. Berg Rese sat at home to mend his clothes. Tord's way led in a broad path up a wooded height.

Every gust carried the dry leaves in a rustling whirl up the path. Time after time, Tord thought that someone went behind him. He often looked round. Sometimes he stopped to listen, but he understood that it was the leaves and the wind, and went on. As soon as he started on again, he heard someone come dancing on silken foot up the slope. Small feet came tripping. Elves and fairies played behind him. When he turned round, there was no one, always no one. He shook his fists at the rustling leaves and went on.

They did not grow silent for that, but they took another tone. They began to hiss and to pant behind him. A big viper came gliding. Its tongue dripping venom hung far out of its mouth, and its bright body shone against the withered leaves. Beside the snake pattered a wolf, a big, gaunt monster, who was ready to seize fast in his throat when the snake had twisted about his feet and bitten him in the heel. Sometimes they were both silent, as if to approach him unperceived, but they soon betrayed themselves by hissing and panting, and sometimes the wolf's claws rung against a stone. Involuntarily Tord walked quicker and quicker, but the creatures hastened after him. When he felt that they were only two steps distant and were preparing to strike, he turned. There was nothing there, and he had known it the whole time.

He sat down on a stone to rest. Then the dry leaves played about his feet as if to amuse him. All the leaves of the forest were there: small, light yellow birch leaves, red speckled mountain ash, the elm's dry, dark-brown leaves, the aspen's tough light red, and the willow's yellow green. Transformed and withered, scarred and torn were they, and much unlike the downy, light green, delicately shaped leaves, which a few months ago had rolled out of their buds.

"Sinners," said the boy, "sinners, nothing is pure in God's eyes. The flame of his wrath has already reached you."

When he resumed his wandering, he saw the forest under him bend before the storm like a heaving sea, but in the path it was calm. But he heard what he did not feel. The woods were full of voices.

He heard whisperings, wailing songs, coarse threats, thundering oaths. There was laughter and laments, there was the noise of many people. That which hounded and pursued, which rustled and hissed, which seemed to be something and still was nothing, gave him wild thoughts. He felt again the anguish of death, as when he lay on the floor in his den and the peasants hunted him through the wood. He heard again the crashing of branches, the people's heavy tread, the ring of weapons, the resounding cries, the wild, bloodthirsty noise, which followed the crowd.

But it was not only that which he heard in the storm. There was something else, something still more terrible, voices which he could not interpret, a confusion of voices, which seemed to him to speak in foreign tongues. He had heard mightier storms than this whistle through the rigging, but never before had he heard the wind play on such a many-voiced harp. Each tree had its own voice; the pine did not murmur like the aspen nor the poplar like the mountain ash. Every hole had its note, every cliff's sounding echo its own ring. And the noise of the brooks and the cry of the foxes mingled with the marvelous forest storm. But all that he could interpret; there were other strange sounds. It was those which made him begin to scream and scoff and groan in emulation with the storm.

He had always been afraid when he was alone in the darkness of the forest. He liked the open sea and the bare rocks. Spirits and phantoms crept about among the trees.

Suddenly he heard who it was who spoke in the storm. It was God, the great Avenger, the God of justice. He was hunting him for the sake of his comrade. He demanded that he should deliver up the murderer to His vengeance.

Then Tord began to speak in the midst of the storm. He told God what he had wished to do, but had not been able. He had wished to speak to Berg Rese and to beg him to make his peace with God, but he had been too shy. Bashfulness had made him dumb. "When I heard that the earth was ruled by a just God," he cried, "I understood that he was a lost man. I have lain and wept for my friend many long nights. I knew that God would find him out, wherever he might hide. But I could not speak, nor teach him to understand. I was speechless, because I loved him so much. Ask not that I shall speak to him, ask not that the sea shall rise up against the mountain."

He was silent, and in the storm the deep voice, which had been the voice of God for him, ceased. It was suddenly calm, with a sharp sun and a splashing as of oars and a gentle rustle as of stiff rushes. These sounds brought Unn's image before him.—The outlaw cannot have anything, not riches, nor women, nor the esteem of men.—If he should betray Berg, he would be taken under the protection of the law.—But Unn must love Berg, after what he had done for her. There was no way out of it all.

When the storm increased, he heard again steps behind him and sometimes a breathless panting. Now he did not dare to look back, for he knew that the white monk went behind him. He came from the feast at Berg Rese's house, drenched with blood, with a gaping axewound in his forehead. And he whispered: "Denounce him, betray him, save his soul. Leave his body to the pyre, that his soul may be spared. Leave him to the slow torture of the rack, that his soul may have time to repent."

Tord ran. All this fright of what was nothing in itself grew, when it so continually played on the soul, to an unspeakable terror. He wished to escape from it all. As he began to run, again thundered that deep, terrible voice, which was God's. God himself hunted him with alarms, that he should give up the murderer. Berg Rese's crime seemed more detestable than ever to him. An unarmed man had been murdered, a man of God pierced with shining steel. It was like a defiance of the Lord of the world. And the murderer dared to live! He rejoiced in the sun's light and in the fruits of the earth as if the Almighty's arm were too short to reach him.

He stopped, clenched his fists and howled out a threat. Then he ran like a madman from the wood down to the valley.

Tord hardly needed to tell his errand; instantly ten peasants were ready to follow him. It was decided that Tord should go alone up to the cave, so that Berg's suspicions should not be aroused. But where he went he should scatter peas, so that the peasants could find the way.

When Tord came to the cave, the outlaw sat on the stone bench and sewed. The fire gave hardly any light, and the work seemed to go badly. The boy's heart swelled with pity. The splendid Berg Rese seemed to him poor and unhappy. And the only thing he possessed, his life, should be taken from him. Tord began to weep.

"What is it?" asked Berg. "Are you ill? Have you been frightened?"

Then for the first time Tord spoke of his fear. "It was terrible in the wood. I heard ghosts and saw specters. I saw white monks."

" 'Sdeath, boy!"

"They crowded round me all the way up Broad mountain. I ran, but they followed after and sang. Can I never be rid of the sound? What have I to do with them? I think that they could go to one who needed it more."

"Are you mad tonight, Tord?"

Tord talked, hardly knowing what words he used. He was free from all shyness. The words streamed from his lips.

"They are all white monks, white, pale as death. They all have blood on their cloaks. They drag their hoods down over their brows, but still the wound shines from under; the big, red, gaping wound from the blow of the axe."

"The big, red, gaping wound from the blow of the axe?"

"Is it I who perhaps have struck it? Why shall I see it?"

"The saints only know, Tord," said Berg Rese, pale and with terrible earnestness, "what it means that you see a wound from an axe. I killed the monk with a couple of knife-thrusts."

Tord stood trembling before Berg and wrung his hands. "They demand you of me! They want to force me to betray you!"

"Who? The monks?"

"They, yes, the monks. They show me visions. They show me her, Unn. They show me the shining, sunny sea. They show me the fishermen's camping-ground, where there is dancing and merry-making. I close my eyes, but still I see. 'Leave me in peace,' I say. 'My friend has murdered, but he is not bad. Let me be, and I will talk to him, so that he repents and atones. He shall confess his sin and go to Christ's grave. We will both go together to the places which are so holy that all sin is taken away from him who draws near them.'"

"What do the monks answer?" asked Berg. "They want to have me saved. They want to have me on the rack and wheel."

"Shall I betray my dearest friend, I ask them," continued Tord. "He is my world. He has saved me from the bear that had his paw on my throat. We have been cold together and suffered every want together. He has spread his bear-skin over me when I was sick. I have carried wood and water for him; I have watched over him while he slept; I have fooled his enemies. Why do they think that I am one who will betray a friend? My friend will soon of his own accord go to the priest and confess, then we will go together to the land of atonement."

Berg listened earnestly, his eyes sharply searching Tord's face. "You shall go to the priest and tell him the truth," he said. "You need to be among people."

"Does that help me if I go alone? For your sin, Death and all his specters follow me. Do you not see how I shudder at you? You have lifted your hand against God himself. No crime is like yours. I think that I must rejoice when I see you on rack and wheel. It is well for him who can receive his punishment in this world and escapes the wrath to come. Why did you tell me of the just God? You compel me to betray you. Save me from that sin. Go to the priest." And he fell on his knees before Berg.

The murderer laid his hand on his head and looked at him. He was measuring his sin against his friend's anguish, and it grew big and terrible before his soul. He saw himself at variance with the Will which rules the world. Repentance entered his heart.

"Woe to me that I have done what I have done," he said. "That which awaits me is too hard to meet voluntarily. If I give myself up to the priests, they will torture me for hours; they will roast me with slow fires. And is not this life of misery, which we lead in fear and want, penance enough? Have I not lost lands and home? Do I not live parted from friends and everything which makes a man's happiness? What more is required?"

When he spoke so, Tord sprang up wild with terror. "Can you repent?" he cried. "Can my words move your heart? Then come instantly! How could I believe that! Let us escape! There is still time."

Berg Rese sprang up, he too. "You have done it, then—"

"Yes, yes, yes! I have betrayed you! But come quickly! Come, as you can repent! They will let us go. We shall escape them!"

The murderer bent down to the floor, where the battle-axe of his ancestors lay at his feet. "You son of a thief!" he said, hissing out the words, "I have trusted you and loved you."

But when Tord saw him bend for the axe, he knew that it was now a question of his own life. He snatched his own axe from his belt and struck at Berg before he had time to raise himself. The edge cut through the whistling air and sank in the bent head. Berg Rese fell head foremost to the floor, his body rolled after. Blood and brains spouted out, the axe fell from the wound. In the matted hair, Tord saw a big, red, gaping hole from the blow of the axe.

The peasants came rushing in. They rejoiced and praised the deed.

"You will win by this," they said to Tord.

Tord looked down at his hands as if he saw there the fetters with which he had been dragged forward to kill him he loved. They were forged from nothing. Of the rushes' green light, of the play of the shadows, of the song of the storm, of the rustling of the leaves, of dreams were they created. And he said aloud: "God is great."

But again the old thought came to him. He fell on his knees beside the body and put his arm under his head.

"Do him no harm," he said. "He repents; he is going to the Holy Sepulcher.[3] He is not dead, he is not a prisoner. We were just ready to go when he fell. The white monk did not want him to repent, but God, the God of justice, loves repentance."

He lay beside the body, talked to it, wept and begged the dead man to awake. The peasants arranged a bier. They wished to carry the peasant's body down to

---

[3] *going to the Holy Sepulcher:* Going to be with Christ in heaven.

his house. They had respect for the dead and spoke softly in his presence. When they lifted him up on the bier, Tord rose, shook the hair back from his face, and said with a voice which shook with sobs—

"Say to Unn, who made Berg Rese a murderer, that he was killed by Tord the fisherman, whose father is a wrecker and whose mother is a witch, because he taught him that the foundation of the world is justice."

UNDERSTANDING THE STORY

1. Does Lagerlöf want the reader to believe that Tord is destined to kill Berg?

2. How is Tord's family background important in the story?

3. Consider Tord's relationships with his parents, with Berg, and with God. What do all of these relationships have in common? What does this tell you about Tord's character?

4. Why does Berg give Tord a sermon about "the Lord of justice"?

5. Why does Tord betray Berg? Consider to what extent he is motivated by (a) his love of Unn, (b) his desire for wealth and acceptance, (c) his desire for freedom, (d) his belief in religious principles, and (e) his particular personality.

6. Is Berg a villain or a victim? Explain.

7. Why does Berg at first consider Tord foolish for not betraying him but then later try to kill Tord for doing so?

8. Why doesn't Tord's tale of the white monk lead Berg to think that Tord will kill him?

9. Why does Tord become obsessed with a God of justice rather than with a God of forgiveness?

10. To what extent, if any, has Tord understood Berg's sermon? Is Tord better off before or after the sermon? Explain.

11. How does Tord's killing of Berg in self-defense justify his action?

12. Why does Tord praise God's greatness after killing Berg?

ANALYZING LITERARY TECHNIQUE

1. Find two examples of **foreshadowing** in the story. What is the function of each?

2. The interplay of light and darkness contributes to the **tone** of the story. Find two examples of the contrast of light and dark and explain what light and dark symbolize in the story.

3. This story turns on many instances of **situational irony.** Find two examples of situational irony and explain how each contributes to the total effect of the story.

4. What role do women play in this story? Consider Tord's mother and Unn.

5. Gothic literature is known for containing mystery, horror, and supernatural occurrences. What elements in this story are Gothic? What is the effect of the Gothic elements on the story?

WRITING ABOUT LITERATURE

1. Examine "The Outlaws" from the standpoint of justice. Do you think that Tord kills Berg because the world is founded on justice or because justice exists in the eye of the beholder, leaving people to behave as they choose? Use quotations from the story to support your point of view.

2. Continue the story of "The Outlaws" after Berg's death. Consider the following questions: What happens to Tord? Does he return to his parents? Does he have any contact with Unn? What is his new position in society?

The Kiss

ANTON CHEKHOV

NTON CHEKHOV (1860–1904), the Russian writer and
playwright, is considered by many to be the greatest short-story
writer of all time. His focus on the ordinary person's feelings and
his impersonal, unobtrusive style have left their mark on all subsequent
writers in this genre. Chekhov's short stories have been published in
fourteen volumes. He is also known for his plays, the most famous of
which are *Uncle Vanya* (1899), *The Three Sisters* (1901), and *The Cherry
Orchard* (1904).

Chekhov was born in Taganrog, a small town by the Sea of Azov,
in southern Russia. His grandfather, who was born a serf, bought the
family's freedom. His father was a poor grocer by vocation; he was a
musician and an artist by avocation. When Chekhov's father found
himself in debt, he secretly moved to Moscow. Chekhov was left to
finish his remaining three years of high school and to support himself
by tutoring. Chekhov later entered the Moscow University Medical
School, where he supported himself by writing humorous stories. His
background enabled him to write from personal knowledge about
shopkeepers and peasants. Once he became a doctor, Chekhov stated:
"Medicine is my lawful wife, and literature is my mistress." In spite of
his continuous battle against tuberculosis, Chekhov selflessly devoted
himself to both loves.

Maksim Gorky wrote that in Chekhov's stories, one can "hear the
quiet, deep sigh of a pure and human heart, the hopeless sigh of sympathy for men who do not know how to respect human dignity." Chekhov
advised other writers to "remember that no honest man can be called
insignificant," and he practiced what he preached. Each of his short
stories focuses on the experience of an ordinary person leading an ordinary life; the story is a realistic slice from that person's life. The principal character feels lonely or deprived or confused or trapped by the
absurdity of life. The character wrestles with frustrated hopes, fragile
self-esteem, and deep need to make connections in a world where others, equally isolated, are preoccupied with their own interests. Under

Chekhov's objective yet humane microscope, the human condition reveals itself to be humorous, sad, and ironic. "The Kiss" is a fine example of Chekhov's writing.

On the evening of the twentieth of May, at eight o'clock, all six batteries of the N Artillery Brigade on their way to camp arrived at the village of Miestechky with the intention of spending the night.

The confusion was at its worst—some officers fussed about the guns, others in the church square arranged with the quartermaster—when from behind the church rode a civilian upon a most remarkable mount. The small, short-tailed bay with a well-shaped neck progressed with a wobbly motion, all the time making dance-like movements with its legs as if some one were switching its hoofs. When he had drawn rein level with the officers the rider doffed his cap and said ceremoniously—

"His Excellency, General von Rabbek, whose house is close by, requests the honour of the officers' company at tea. . . ."

The horse shook its head, danced, and wobbled to the rear; its rider again took off his cap, and, turning his strange steed, disappeared behind the church.

"The devil take it!" was the general exclamation as the officers dispersed to their quarters. "We can hardly keep our eyes open, yet along comes this von Rabbek with his tea! I know that tea!"

The officers of the six batteries had lively memories of a past invitation. During recent manoeuvres they had been asked, together with their Cossack comrades, to tea at the house of a local country gentleman, an officer in retirement, by title a Count; and this hearty, hospitable Count overwhelmed them with attentions, fed them to satiety, poured vodka down their throats, and made them stay the night. All this, of course, they enjoyed. The trouble was that the old soldier entertained his guests too well. He kept them up till daybreak while he poured forth tales of past adventures; he dragged them from room to room to point out valuable paintings, old engravings, and rare arms; he read them holograph letters from celebrated men. And the weary officers, bored to death, listened, gaped, yearned for their beds, and yawned cautiously in their sleeves, until at last when their host released them it was too late for sleep.

Was von Rabbek another old Count? It might easily be. But there was no neglecting his invitation. The officers washed and dressed, and set out for von Rabbek's house. At the church square they learnt that they must descend the hill to the river, and follow the bank till they reached the general's gardens, where they would find a path direct to the house. Or, if they chose to go up hill, they would reach the general's barns half a verst[1] from Miestechky. It was this route they chose.

---

[1] *verst:* Russian unit of distance; slightly more than one kilometer.

"But who is this von Rabbek?" asked one. "The man who commanded the N Cavalry Division at Plevna?"

"No, that was not von Rabbek, but simply Rabbe—without the von."

"What glorious weather!"

At the first barn they came to, two roads diverged; one ran straight forward and faded in the dusk; the other turning to the right led to the general's house. As the officers drew near they talked less loudly. To right and left stretched rows of red-roofed brick barns, in aspect heavy and morose as the barracks of provincial towns. In front gleamed the lighted windows of von Rabbek's house.

"A good omen, gentlemen!" cried a young officer. "Our setter runs in advance. There is game ahead!"

On the face of Lieutenant Lobytko, the tall stout officer referred to, there was not one trace of hair though he was twenty-five years old. He was famed among comrades for the instinct which told him of the presence of women in the neighbourhood. On hearing his comrade's remark, he turned his head and said—

"Yes. There are women there. My instinct tells me."

A handsome, well-preserved man of sixty, in mufti, came to the hall door to greet his guests. It was von Rabbek. As he pressed their hands, he explained that though he was delighted to see them, he must beg pardon for not asking them to spend the night; as guests he already had his two sisters, their children, his brother, and several neighbours—in fact, he had not one spare room. And though he shook their hands and apologised and smiled, it was plain that he was not half as glad to see them as was last year's Count, and that he had invited them merely because good manners demanded it. The officers climbing the soft-carpeted steps and listening to their host understood this perfectly well; and realised that they carried into the house an atmosphere of intrusion and alarm. Would any man— they asked themselves—who had gathered his two sisters and their children, his brother and his neighbours, to celebrate, no doubt, some family festival, find pleasure in the invasion of nineteen officers whom he had never seen before?

A tall, elderly lady, with a good figure, and a long face with black eyebrows, who resembled closely the ex-Empress Eugenie,[2] greeted them at the drawing-room door. Smiling courteously and with dignity, she affirmed that she was delighted to see the officers, and only regretted that she could not ask them to stay the night. But the courteous, dignified smile disappeared when she turned away, and it was quite plain that she had seen many officers in her day, that they caused not the slightest interest, and that she had invited them merely because an invitation was dictated by good breeding and by her position in the world.

In a big dining-room seated at a big table sat ten men and women, drinking tea. Behind them, veiled in cigar-smoke, stood several young men, among them one, red-whiskered and extremely thin, who spoke English loudly with a lisp. Through an open door the officers saw into a brightly lighted room with blue wall-paper.

---

[2] *ex-Empress Eugenie:* Wife of Napoleon III and empress of France from 1853 to 1871.

"You are too many to introduce singly, gentlemen!" said the general loudly, with affected joviality. "Make one another's acquaintance, please—without formalities!"

The visitors, some with serious, even severe faces, some smiling constrainedly, all with a feeling of awkwardness, bowed, and took their seats at the table. Most awkward of all felt Staff-Captain Riabovich, a short, round-shouldered, spectacled officer, whiskered like a lynx. While his brother officers looked serious or smiled constrainedly, his face, his lynx whiskers, and his spectacles seemed to explain: "I am the most timid, modest, undistinguished officer in the whole brigade." For some time after he took his seat at the table he could not fix his attention on any single thing. Faces, dresses, the cut-glass cognac bottles, the steaming tumblers, the moulded cornices—all merged in a single, overwhelming sentiment which caused him intense fright and made him wish to hide his head. Like an inexperienced lecturer he saw everything before him, but could distinguish nothing, and was in fact the victim of what men of science diagnose as "psychical blindness."

But slowly conquering his diffidence, Riabovich began to distinguish and observe. As became a man both timid and unsocial, he remarked first of all the amazing temerity of his new friends. Von Rabbek, his wife, two elderly ladies, a girl in lilac, and the red-whiskered youth who, it appeared, was a young von Rabbek, sat down among the officers as unconcernedly as if they had held rehearsals, and at once plunged into various heated arguments in which they soon involved their guests. That artillerists have a much better time than cavalrymen or infantrymen was proved conclusively by the lilac girl, while von Rabbek and the elderly ladies affirmed the converse. The conversation became desultory. Riabovich listened to the lilac girl fiercely debating themes she knew nothing about and took no interest in, and watched the insincere smiles which appeared on and disappeared from her face.

While the von Rabbek family with amazing strategy inveigled their guests into the dispute, they kept their eyes on every glass and mouth. Had every one tea, was it sweet enough, why didn't one eat biscuits, was another fond of cognac? And the longer Riabovich listened and looked, the more pleased he was with this disingenuous, disciplined family.

After tea the guests repaired to the drawing-room. Instinct had not cheated Lobytko. The room was packed with young women and girls, and ere a minute had passed the setter-lieutenant stood beside a very young, fair-haired girl in black, and, bending down as if resting on an invisible sword, shrugged his shoulders coquettishly. He was uttering, no doubt, most unentertaining nonsense, for the fair girl looked indulgently at his sated face, and exclaimed indifferently, "Indeed!" And this indifferent "Indeed!" might have quickly convinced the setter that he was on a wrong scent.

Music began. As the notes of a mournful valse[3] throbbed out of the open window, through the heads of all flashed the feeling that outside that window it

---

[3] *valse:* Waltz.

was spring-time, a night of May. The air was odorous of young poplar leaves, of roses and lilacs—and the valse and the spring were sincere. Riabovich, with valse and cognac mingling tipsily in his head, gazed at the window with a smile; then began to follow the movements of the women; and it seemed that the smell of roses, poplars, and lilacs came not from the gardens outside, but from the women's faces and dresses.

They began to dance. Young von Rabbek valsed twice round the room with a very thin girl; and Lobytko, slipping on the parqueted floor, went up to the girl in lilac, and was granted a dance. But Riabovich stood near the door with the wall-flowers, and looked silently on. Amazed at the daring of men who in sight of a crowd could take unknown women by the waist, he tried in vain to picture himself doing the same. A time had been when he envied his comrades their courage and dash, suffered from painful heart-searchings, and was hurt by the knowledge that he was timid, round-shouldered, and undistinguished, that he had lynx whiskers, and that his waist was much too long. But with years he had grown reconciled to his own insignificance, and now looking at the dancers and loud talkers, he felt no envy, but only mournful emotions.

At the first quadrille[4] von Rabbek junior approached and invited two non-dancing officers to a game of billiards. The three left the room; and Riabovich who stood idle, and felt impelled to join in the general movement, followed. They passed the dining-room, traversed a narrow glazed corridor, and a room where three sleepy footmen jumped from a sofa with a start; and after walking, it seemed, through a whole houseful of rooms, entered a small billiard-room.

Von Rabbek and the two officers began their game. Riabovich, whose only game was cards, stood near the table and looked indifferently on, as the players, with unbuttoned coats, wielded their cues, moved about, joked, and shouted obscure technical terms. Riabovich was ignored, save when one of the players jostled him or caught his cue, and turning towards him said briefly, "Pardon!" so that before the game was over he was thoroughly bored, and impressed by a sense of his superfluity, resolved to return to the drawing-room, and turned away.

It was on the way back that his adventure took place. Before he had gone far he saw that he had missed the way. He remembered distinctly the room with the three sleepy footmen; and after passing through five or six rooms entirely vacant, he saw his mistake. Retracing his steps, he turned to the left, and found himself in an almost dark room which he had not seen before; and after hesitating a minute, he boldly opened the first door he saw, and found himself in complete darkness. Through a chink of the door in front peered a bright light; from afar throbbed the dulled music of a mournful mazurka.[5] Here, as in the drawing-room, the windows were open wide, and the smell of poplars, lilacs, and roses flooded the air.

Riabovich paused in irresolution. For a moment all was still. Then came the sound of hasty footsteps; then, without any warning of what was to come, a dress rustled, a woman's breathless voice whispered "At last!" and two soft, scented,

---

[4] *quadrille:* A square dance.
[5] *mazurka:* A Polish folk dance.

unmistakably womanly arms met round his neck, a warm cheek impinged on his, and he received a sounding kiss. But hardly had the kiss echoed through the silence when the unknown shrieked loudly, and fled away—as it seemed to Riabovich— in disgust. Riabovich himself nearly screamed, and rushed headlong towards the bright beam in the doorchink.

As he entered the drawing-room his heart beat violently, and his hands trembled so perceptibly that he clasped them behind his back. His first emotion was shame, as if every one in the room already knew that he had just been embraced and kissed. He retired into his shell, and looked fearfully around. But finding that hosts and guests were calmly dancing or talking, he regained courage, and surrendered himself to sensations experienced for the first time in life. The unexampled had happened. His neck, fresh from the embrace of two soft, scented arms, seemed anointed with oil; near his left moustache, where the kiss had fallen, trembled a slight, delightful chill, as from peppermint drops; and from head to foot he was soaked in new and extraordinary sensations, which continued to grow and grow.

He felt that he must dance, talk, run into the garden, laugh unrestrainedly. He forgot altogether that he was round-shouldered, undistinguished, lynx-whiskered, that he had an "indefinite exterior"—a description from the lips of a woman he had happened to overhear. As Madame von Rabbek passed him he smiled so broadly and graciously that she came up and looked at him questioningly.

"What a charming house you have!" he said, straightening his spectacles.

And Madame von Rabbek smiled back, said that the house still belonged to her father, and asked were his parents alive, how long he had been in the Army, and why he was so thin. After hearing his answers she departed. But though the conversation was over, he continued to smile benevolently, and think what charming people were his new acquaintances.

At supper Riabovich ate and drank mechanically what was put before him, heard not a word of the conversation, and devoted all his powers to the unraveling of his mysterious, romantic adventure. What was the explanation? It was plain that one of the girls, he reasoned, had arranged a meeting in the dark room, and after waiting some time in vain had, in her nervous tension, mistaken Riabovich for her hero. The mistake was likely enough, for on entering the dark room Riabovich had stopped irresolutely as if he, too, were waiting for some one. So far the mystery was explained.

"But which of them was it?" he asked, searching the women's faces. She certainly was young, for old women do not indulge in such romances. Secondly, she was not a servant. That was proved unmistakably by the rustle of her dress, the scent, the voice . . .

When at first he looked at the girl in lilac she pleased him; she had pretty shoulders and arms, a clever face, a charming voice. Riabovich piously prayed that it was she. But, smiling insincerely, she wrinkled her long nose, and that at once gave her an elderly air. So Riabovich turned his eyes on the blonde in black. The blonde was younger, simpler, sincerer; she had charming kiss-curls, and drank from her tumbler with inexpressible grace. Riabovich hoped it was she—but soon he noticed that her face was flat, and bent his eyes on her neighbour.

"It is a hopeless puzzle," he reflected. "If you take the arms and shoulders of the lilac girl, add the blonde's curls, and the eyes of the girl on Lobytko's left, then—"

He composed a portrait of all these charms, and had a clear vision of the girl who had kissed him. But she was nowhere to be seen.

Supper over, the visitors, sated and tipsy, bade their entertainers goodbye. Both host and hostess again apologised for not asking them to spend the night.

"I am very glad, very glad, gentlemen!" said the general, and this time seemed to speak sincerely, no doubt because speeding the parting guest is a kindlier office than welcoming him unwelcomed. "I am very glad indeed! I hope you will visit me on your way back. Without ceremony, please! Which way will you go? Up the hill? No, go down the hill and through the garden. That way is shorter."

The officers took his advice. After the noise and glaring illumination within doors, the garden seemed dark and still. Until they reached the wicket-gate all kept silence. Merry, half tipsy, and content, as they were, the night's obscurity and stillness inspired pensive thoughts. Through their brains, as through Riabovich's, sped probably the same question: "Will the time ever come when I, like von Rabbek, shall have a big house, a family, a garden, the chance of being gracious—even insincerely—to others, of making them sated, tipsy, and content?"

But once the garden lay behind them, all spoke at once, and burst into causeless laughter. The path they followed led straight to the river, and then ran beside it, winding around bushes, ravines, and over-hanging willow-trees. The track was barely visible; the other bank was lost entirely in gloom. Sometimes the black water imaged stars, and this was the only indication of the river's speed. From beyond it sighed a drowsy snipe, and beside them in a bush, heedless of the crowd, a nightingale chanted loudly. The officers gathered in a group, and swayed the bush, but the nightingale continued his song.

"I like his cheek!" they echoed admiringly. "He doesn't care a kopeck![6] The old rogue!"

Near their journey's end the path turned up the hill, and joined the road not far from the church enclosure; and there the officers, breathless from climbing, sat on the grass and smoked. Across the river gleamed a dull red light, and for want of a subject they argued the problem, whether it was a bonfire, a window-light, or something else. Riabovich looked also at the light, and felt that it smiled and winked at him as if it knew about the kiss.

On reaching home, he undressed without delay, and lay upon his bed. He shared the cabin with Lobytko and a Lieutenant Merzliakov, a staid, silent little man, by repute highly cultivated, who took with him everywhere *The Messenger of Europe*,[7] and read it eternally. Lobytko undressed, tramped impatiently from corner to corner, and sent his servant for beer. Merzliakov lay down, balanced the candle on his pillow, and hid his head behind *The Messenger of Europe*.

---

[6] *kopeck:* Russian coin; 1/100 of a ruble.

[7] The Messenger of Europe: A Russian magazine.

"Where is she now?" muttered Riabovich, looking at the soot-blacked ceiling.

His neck still seemed anointed with oil, near his mouth still trembling the speck of peppermint chill. Through his brain twinkled successively the shoulders and arms of the lilac girl, the kiss-curls and honest eyes of the girl in black, the waists, dresses, brooches. But though he tried his best to fix these vagrant images, they glimmered, winked, and dissolved; and as they faded finally into the vast black curtain which hangs before the closed eyes of all men, he began to hear hurried footsteps, the rustle of petticoats, the sound of a kiss. A strong, causeless joy possessed him. But as he surrendered himself to this joy, Lobytko's servant returned with the news that no beer was obtainable. The lieutenant resumed his impatient march up and down the room.

"The fellow's an idiot," he exclaimed, stopping first near Riabovich and then near Merzliakov. "Only the worst numbskull and blockhead can't get beer! *Canaille!*"[8]

"Every one knows there's no beer here," said Merzliakov, without lifting his eyes from *The Messenger of Europe*.

"You believe that!" exclaimed Lobytko. "Lord in heaven, drop me on the moon, and in five minutes I'll find both beer and women! I will find them myself! Call me a rascal if I don't!"

He dressed slowly, silently lighted a cigarette, and went out.

"Rabbek, Grabbek, Labbek," he muttered, stopping in the hall. "I won't go alone, devil take me! Riabovich, come for a walk! What?"

As he got no answer, he returned, undressed slowly, and lay down. Merzliakov sighed, dropped *The Messenger of Europe*, and put out the light. "Well?" muttered Lobytko, puffing his cigarette in the dark.

Riabovich pulled the bed-clothes up to his chin, curled himself into a roll and strained his imagination to join the twinkling images into one coherent whole. But the vision fled him. He soon fell asleep, and his last impression was that he had been caressed and gladdened, that into his life had crept something strange, and indeed ridiculous, but uncommonly good and radiant. And this thought did not forsake him even in his dreams.

When he awoke the feeling of anointment and peppermint chill were gone. But joy, as on the night before, filled every vein. He looked entranced at the window-panes gilded by the rising sun, and listened to the noises outside. Some one spoke loudly under the very window. It was Lebedetzky, commander of his battery, who had just overtaken the brigade. He was talking to the sergeant-major, loudly, owing to lack of practice in soft speech.

"And what next?" he roared.

"During yesterday's shoeing, your honour, *Golubtchik*[9] was pricked. The *Feldscher*[10] ordered clay and vinegar. And last night, your honour, mechanic

---

[8] Canaille: Riffraff; rabble.

[9] Golubtchik: Nickname meaning "little pigeon."

[10] Feldscher: Army surgeon.

Artemieff was drunk, and the lieutenant ordered him to be put on the limber of the reserve gun-carriage."

The sergeant-major added that Karpov had forgotten the tent-pegs and the new lanyards for the friction-tubes, and that the officers had spent the evening at General von Rabbek's. But here at the window appeared Lebedetzky's red-bearded face. He blinked his short-sighted eyes at the drowsy men in bed, and greeted them.

"Is everything all right?"

"The saddle wheeler galled his withers with the new yoke," answered Lobytko.

The commander sighed, mused a moment, and shouted—

"I am thinking of calling on Alexandra Yegorovna. I want to see her. Good-bye! I will catch you up before night."

Fifteen minutes later the brigade resumed its march. As he passed von Rabbek's barns Riabovich turned his head and looked at the house. The Venetian blinds were down; evidently all still slept. And among them slept she— she who had kissed him but a few hours before. He tried to visualize her asleep. He projected the bedroom window opened wide with green branches peering in, the freshness of the morning air, the smell of poplars, lilacs, and roses, the bed, a chair, the dress which rustled last night, a pair of tiny slippers, a ticking watch in the table—all these came to him clearly with every detail. But the features, the kind, sleepy smile—all, in short, that was essential and characteristic—fled his imagination as quicksilver flees the hand. When he had covered half a verst he again turned back. The yellow church, the house, gardens, and river were bathed in light. Imagining an azure sky, the green-banked river specked with silver sunshine flakes was inexpressibly fair; and, looking at Miestechky for the last time, Riabovich felt sad, as if parting forever with something very near and dear.

By the road before him stretched familiar, uninteresting scenes; to the right and left, fields of young rye and buckwheat with hopping rooks; in front, dust and the napes of human necks; behind, the same dust and faces. Ahead of the column marched four soldiers with swords—that was the advance guard. Next came the bandsmen. Advance guard and bandsmen, like mutes in a funeral procession, ignored the regulation intervals and marched too far ahead. Riabovich, with the first gun of Battery No. 5, could see four batteries ahead.

To a layman, the long, lumbering march of an artillery brigade is novel, interesting, inexplicable. It is hard to understand why a single gun needs so many men; why so many, such strangely harnessed horses are needed to drag it. But to Riabovich, a master of all these things, it was profoundly dull. He had learned years ago why a solid sergeant-major rides beside the officer in front of each battery, why the sergeant-major is called the *unosi*, and why the drivers of leaders and wheelers ride behind him. Riabovich knew why the near horses are called saddle-horses, and why the off horses are called led-horses—and all of this was interesting beyond words. On one of the wheelers rode a soldier still covered with yesterday's dust, and with a cumbersome ridiculous guard on his right leg. But Riabovich, knowing the use of this leg-guard, found it in no way ridiculous. The drivers, mechanically and with occasional cries, flourished their whips. The guns themselves were impressive. The limbers were packed with tarpaulin-covered sacks of oats; and the guns themselves, hung around with tea-pots and satchels, looked like harmless animals, guarded for some obscure reasonable men and horses. In the lee of the gun tramped six gunners, swinging their arms; and behind each gun came more *unosniye*, leaders, wheelers; and yet more guns, each as ugly and uninspiring as the one in front. And as every one of the six batteries in the brigade had four guns, the procession stretched along the road at least half a verst. It ended with a wagon train, with which, its head bent in thought, walked the donkey Magar, brought from Turkey by a battery commander.

Dead to his surroundings, Riabovich marched onward, looking at the napes ahead or at the faces behind. Had it not been for last night's event, he would have been half asleep. But now he was absorbed in novel, entrancing thoughts. When the brigade set out that morning he had tried to argue that the kiss had no significance save as a trivial though mysterious adventure; that it was without real import; and that to think of it seriously was to behave himself absurdly. But logic soon flew away and surrendered him to his vivid imaginings. At times he saw himself in von Rabbek's dining-room, *tête-à-tête*[11] with a composite being, formed of the girl in lilac and the blonde in black. At times he closed his eyes, and pictured himself with a different, this time quite unknown, girl of cloudy feature; he spoke to her, caressed her, bent over her shoulder; he imagined war and parting . . . the reunion, the first supper together, children. . . .

"To the brakes!" rang the command as they topped the brow of each hill.

Riabovich also cried "To the brakes!" and each time dreaded that the cry would break the magic spell, and recall him to realities.

They passed a big country house. Riabovich looked across the fence into the garden, and saw a long path, straight as a ruler, carpeted with yellow sand, and shaded by young birches. In an ecstacy of enchantment, he pictured little feminine feet treading the yellow sand; and, in a flash, imagination restored the woman who had kissed him, the woman he had visualised after supper the night before. The image settled in his brain and never afterwards forsook him.

The spell reigned until midday, when a loud command came from the rear of the column.

"Attention! Eyes right! Officers!"

In a *calèche*[12] drawn by a pair of white horses appeared the general of the brigade. He stopped at the second battery, and called out something which no one understood. Up galloped several officers, among them Riabovich.

"Well, how goes it?" The general blinked his red eyes, and continued, "Are there any sick?"

Hearing the answer, the little skinny general mused a moment, turned to an officer, and said—

"The driver of your third-gun wheeler has taken off his leg-guard and hung it on the limber. *Canaille!* Punish him!"

---

[11] tête-à-tête: In private conversation with.

[12] calèche: Two-wheeled carriage.

Then raising his eyes to Riabovich, he added—

"And in your battery, I think, the harness is too loose."

Having made several other equally tiresome remarks, he looked at Lobytko, and laughed.

"Why do you look so downcast, Lieutenant Lobytko? You are sighing for Madame Lopukhov, eh? Gentleman, he is pining for Madame Lopukhov."

Madame Lopukhov was tall, stout lady, long past forty. Being partial to big women, regardless of age, the general ascribed the same taste to his subordinates. The officers smiled respectfully; and the general, pleased that he had said something caustic and laughable, touched the coachman's back and saluted. The *calèche* whirled away.

"All this, though it seems to me impossible and unearthly, is in reality very commonplace," thought Riabovich, watching the clouds of dust raised by the general's carriage. "It is an everyday event, and within every one's experience. . . . This old general, for instance, must have loved in his day; he is married now, and has children. Captain Wachter is also married, and his wife loves him, though he has an ugly red neck and no waist. . . . Salmanoff is coarse, and a typical Tartar,[13] but he has had a romance ending in marriage. . . . I, like the rest, must go through it all sooner or later."

And the thought that he was an ordinary man, and that his life was ordinary, rejoiced and consoled him. He boldly visualized *her* and his happiness, and let his imagination run mad.

Towards evening the brigade ended its march. While the other officers sprawled in their tents, Riabovich, Merzliakov, and Lobytko sat around a packing-case and supped. Merzliakov ate slowly, and, resting *The Messenger of Europe* on his knees, read on steadily. Lobytko, chattering without cease, poured beer into his glass. But Riabovich, whose head was dizzy from uninterrupted day-dreams, ate in silence. When he had drunk three glasses he felt tipsy and weak; and an overmastering impulse forced him to relate his adventure to his comrades.

"A most extraordinary thing happened to me at von Rabbek's," he began, doing his best to speak in an indifferent, ironical tone. "I was on my way, you understand, from the billiard-room . . ."

And he attempted to give a very detailed history of the kiss. But in a minute he had told the whole story. In that minute he had exhausted every detail; and it seemed to him terrible that the story required such a short time. It ought, he felt, to have lasted all the night. As he finished, Lobytko, who as a liar himself believed in no one, laughed incredulously. Merzliakov frowned, and, with his eyes still glued to *The Messenger of Europe*, said indifferently—

"God know who it was! She threw herself on your neck, you say, and didn't cry out! Some lunatic, I expect!"

"I, too, have had adventures of that kind," began Lobytko, making a frightful face. "I was on my way to Kovno.[14] I travelled second class. The carriage was

---

[13] *Tartar:* Person from the Tatary region of Russia. Tartars were reputed to have bad tempers.

[14] *Kovno:* City in Lithuania, now known as Kaunas.

packed, and I couldn't sleep. So I gave the guard a ruble, and he took my bag, and put me in a *coupé*.[15] I lay down, and pulled my rug over me. It was pitch dark, you understand. Suddenly, I felt some one tapping my shoulder and breathing in my face. I stretched out my hand and felt an elbow. Then I opened my eyes. Imagine! A woman! Coal-black eyes, lips red as good coral, nostrils breathing passion, breasts—buffers!"

"Draw it mild!" interrupted Merzliakov in his quiet voice. "I can believe about the breasts, but if it was pitch dark how could you see the lips?"

By laughing at Merzliakov's lack of understanding, Lobytko tried to shuffle out of the dilemma. The story annoyed Riabovich. He rose from the box, lay on his bed, and swore that he would never again take any one into his confidence.

Life in camp passed without event. The days flew by, each like the one before. But on every one of these days Riabovich felt, thought, and acted as a man in love. When at daybreak his servant brought him cold water, and poured it over his head, it flashed at once into his half-awakened brain that something good and warm and caressing had crept into his life.

At night when his comrades talked of love and of women, he drew in his chair, and his face was the face of an old soldier who talks of battles in which he has taken part. And when the rowdy officers, led by setter Lobytko, made Don Juanesque[16] raids upon the neighbouring "suburb," Riabovich, though he accompanied them, was morose and conscience-struck, and mentally asked *her* forgiveness. In free hours and sleepless nights, when his brain was obsessed by memories of childhood, of his father, his mother, of everything akin and dear, he remembered always Miestechky, the dancing horse, von Rabbek, von Rabbek's wife, so like the ex-Empress Eugenie, the dark room, the chink in the door.

On the thirty-first of August he left camp, this time not with the whole brigade but with only two batteries. As an exile returning to his native land, he was agitated and enthralled by day-dreams. He longed passionately for the queer-looking horse, the church, the insincere von Rabbeks, the dark room; and that internal voice which cheats so often the love-lorn whispered an assurance that he should see her again. But doubt tortured him. How should he meet her? What must he say? Would she have forgotten the kiss? If it came to the worst— he consoled himself—if he never saw her again, he might walk once more through the dark room and remember. . . .

Towards evening the white barns and well-known church rose on the horizon. Riabovich's heart beat wildly. He ignored the remark of an officer who rode by, he forgot the whole world, and he gazed greedily at the river glimmering afar, at the green roofs, at the dove-cote, over which fluttered birds, dyed golden by the setting sun.

As he rode towards the church, and heard again the quartermaster's raucous voice, he expected every second a horseman to appear from behind the fence and

---

[15] coupé: A small train compartment.

[16] *Don Juanesque:* Don Juan was a legendary seducer of women.

invite the officers to tea. . . . But the quartermaster ended his harangue, the officers hastened to the village, and no horseman appeared.

"When Rabbek hears from the peasants that we are back he will send for us," thought Riabovich. And so assured was he of this, that when he entered the hut he failed to understand why his comrades had lighted a candle, and why the servants were preparing the samovar.

A painful agitation oppressed him. He lay on his bed. A moment later he rose to look for the horseman. But no horseman was in sight. Again he lay down; again he rose; and this time, impelled by restlessness, went into the street, and walked towards the church. The square was dark and deserted. On the hill stood three silent soldiers. When they saw Riabovich they started and saluted, and he, returning their salute, began to descend the well-remembered path.

Beyond the stream, in a sky stained with purple, the moon slowly rose. Two chattering peasant women walked in a kitchen garden and pulled cabbage leaves; behind them their log cabins stood out black against the sky. The river bank was as it had been in May; the bushes were the same; things differed only in that the nightingale no longer sang, that it smelt no longer of poplars and young grass.

When he reached von Rabbek's garden Riabovich peered through the wicket-gate. Silence and darkness reigned. Save only the white birch trunks and patches of pathway, the whole garden merged in a black, impenetrable shade. Riabovich listened greedily, and gazed intent. For a quarter of an hour he loitered; then hearing no sound, and seeing no light, he walked wearily towards home.

He went down to the river. In front rose the general's bathing box; and white towels hung on the rail of the bridge. He climbed on to the bridge and stood still; then, for no reason whatever, touched a towel. It was clammy and cold. He looked down at the river which sped past swiftly, murmuring almost inaudibly against the bathing-box piles. Near the left bank glowed the moon's ruddy reflection, overrun by ripples which stretched it, tore it in two, and, it seemed, would sweep it away as twigs and shavings are swept.

"How stupid! How stupid!" thought Riabovich, watching the hurrying ripples. "How stupid everything is!"

Now that hope was dead, the history of the kiss, his impatience, his ardour, his vague aspirations and disillusion appeared in a clear light. It no longer seemed strange that the general's horseman had not come, and that he would never again see *her* who had kissed him by accident instead of another. On the contrary, he felt, it would be strange if he did ever see her again. . . .

The water flew past him, whither and why no one knew. It had flown past in May; it had sped a stream into a great river; a river, into the sea; it had floated on high in mist and fallen again in rain; it might be, the water of May was again speeding past under Riabovich's eyes. For what purpose? Why?

And the whole world—life itself seemed to Riabovich an inscrutable, aimless mystification. . . . Raising his eyes from the stream and gazing at the sky, he recalled how Fate in the shape of an unknown woman had once caressed him; he recalled his summer fantasies and images—and his whole life seemed to him unnaturally thin and colourless and wretched. . . .

When he reached the cabin his comrades had disappeared. His servant informed him that all had set out to visit "General Fonrabbkin," who had sent a horseman to bring them. . . . For a moment, Riabovich's heart thrilled with joy. But that joy he extinguished. He cast himself upon his bed, and wroth with his evil fate, as if he wished to spite it, ignored the invitation.

UNDERSTANDING THE STORY

1. Why is Riabovich so profoundly affected by the kiss?
2. What does Riabovich's behavior once he has been kissed reveal about him?
3. How does the woman's reaction to the kiss affect the reader's response to Riabovich's reactions?
4. Why does Riabovich spend so much emotional energy imagining the woman's appearance?
5. Why is Riabovich sorry that he told Merzliakov and Lobytko about the kiss?
6. Why does Riabovich ignore von Rabbek's second invitation?
7. How does the experience of the kiss change Riabovich? Would he have been better off if the experience had never happened? What does Chekhov seem to be saying about the role of illusion in life?

ANALYZING LITERARY TECHNIQUE

1. What is Chekhov's primary focus in the story? How does the **narrative perspective** help accomplish the goal of the story?
2. This story contains several **leitmotifs** that help unify the story. Examine Chekhov's use of leitmotif in "The Kiss." Identify one or two examples of leitmotif and explain how the examples function in the story.
3. Why does Chekhov describe the artillery brigade in such detail? How does the world of the story relate to Riabovich's fantasy world?
4. Examine the **contrast** between Riabovich and Lobytko.
5. What is suggested by the servant's mispronunciation of von Rabbek's name at the end of the story?
6. What is the **tone** of this story, and how does Chekhov achieve the tone?
7. Locate two examples of **irony** in the story. How does irony contribute to the story's tone and meaning?
8. Examine Chekhov's use of **satire** in "The Kiss." What is being satirized?
9. **Realism** was an important movement in nineteenth- and early-twentieth-century European fiction. Realist writers attempted to present characters and situations as if they were reporting from real life. What characteristics of realism does this story possess?

WRITING ABOUT LITERATURE

1. Consider the effect that the realistic details of "the Kiss" have on your understanding and appreciation of the story. Do the details—such as the descriptions of von Rabbek's guests or of the life of artillery soldiers—add to or detract from the story's effectiveness? Does the realism of the story help you to sympathize with Riabovich, or does it distract you? Write a brief essay in which you defend or criticize Chekhov's use of realistic details in this story. Use quotations from the story to support your argument.

2. Choose an incident from the story (such as the moment of the kiss) and rewrite it from Riabovich's point of view. What information do you need to provide? Try to convey Riabovich's emotions as directly as possible. How does he interpret the event as it happens?

The Other Wife

COLETTE

IDONIE-GABRIELLE COLETTE (1873–1954), called "Colette," is considered the outstanding female French writer of the first half of the twentieth century. Known both as a novelist and a writer of short stories, she is famous for her ability to write about love with sophisticated feminine wisdom. Her short stories are models of the genre.

Colette was reared in a small village in Burgundy. In 1893 she married a Parisian music critic, who urged her to write novels that he published under his own pen name. After they divorced in 1906, Colette became a music-hall dancer. Following her second marriage and divorce, she achieved fame as a journalist, novelist, and author of short stories. She received many honors and, upon her death, a state funeral.

Colette's writing often focuses on the interaction between men and women in situations where women are strong and independent. "The Other Wife" displays Colette at her best, skillfully depicting a present moment in time that encompasses the past and the future as well. Sensitive to the paradoxes and nuances of human nature, she achieves psychological realism through subtle details of speech and action that culminate effortlessly and inevitably in a striking climax.

"Table for two? This way, Monsieur, Madame, there is still a table next to the window, if Madame and Monsieur would like a view of the bay."

Alice followed the maître d'.[1]

---

[1] *maître d'*: Headwaiter.

"Oh, yes. Come on, Marc, it'll be like having lunch on a boat on the water . . ."

Her husband caught her by passing his arm under hers. "We'll be more comfortable over there."

"There? In the middle of all those people? I'd much rather . . ."

"Alice, please."

He tightened his grip in such a meaningful way that she turned around. "What's the matter?"

"Shh . . ." he said softly, looking at her intently, and led her toward the table in the middle.

"What is it, Marc?"

"I'll tell you, darling. Let me order lunch first. Would you like the shrimp? Or the eggs in aspic?"

"Whatever you like, you know that."

They smiled at one another, wasting the precious time of an overworked maître d', stricken with a kind of nervous dance, who was standing next to them, perspiring.

"The shrimp," said Marc. "Then the eggs and bacon. And the cold chicken with a romaine salad. *Fromage blanc?*[2] The house specialty? We'll go with the specialty. Two strong coffees. My chauffeur will be having lunch also, we'll be leaving again at two o'clock. Some cider? No, I don't trust it . . . Dry champagne."

He sighed as if he had just moved an armoire, gazed at the colorless midday sea, at the pearly white sky, then at his wife, whom he found lovely in her little Mercury hat[3] with its large, hanging veil.

"You're looking well, darling. And all this blue water makes your eyes look green, imagine that! And you've put on weight since you've been traveling . . . It's nice up to a point, but only up to a point!"

Her firm, round breasts rose proudly as she leaned over the table.

"Why did you keep me from taking that place next to the window?"

Marc Seguy never considered lying. "Because you were about to sit next to someone I know."

"Someone I don't know?"

"My ex-wife."

She couldn't think of anything to say and opened her blue eyes wider.

"So what, darling? It'll happen again. It's not important."

The words came back to Alice and she asked, in order, the inevitable questions. "Did she see you? Could she see that you saw her? Will you point her out to me?"

"Don't look now, please, she must be watching us. . . . The lady with brown hair, no hat, she must be staying in this hotel. By herself, behind those children in red . . ."

"Yes, I see."

Hidden behind some broad-brimmed beach hats, Alice was able to look at the woman who, fifteen months ago, had still been her husband's wife.

---

[2] fromage blanc: A mild white cheese, something like cottage cheese.

[3] *Mercury hat:* Hat with a feather.

"Incompatibility," Marc said. "Oh, I mean . . . total incompatibility! We divorced like well-bred people, almost like friends, quietly, quickly. And then I fell in love with you, and you really wanted to be happy with me. How lucky we are that our happiness doesn't involve any guilty parties or victims!"

The woman in white, whose smooth, lustrous hair reflected the light from the sea in azure patches, was smoking a cigarette with her eyes half closed. Alice turned back toward her husband, took some shrimp and butter, and ate calmly. After a moment's silence she asked: "Why didn't you ever tell me that she had blue eyes, too?"

"Well, I never thought about it!"

He kissed the hand she was extending toward the bread basket and she blushed with pleasure. Dusky and ample, she might have seemed somewhat coarse, but the changeable blue of her eyes and her wavy, golden hair made her look like a frail and sentimental blonde. She vowed overwhelming gratitude to her husband. Immodest without knowing it, everything about her bore the overly conspicuous marks of extreme happiness.

They ate and drank heartily, and each thought the other had forgotten the woman in white. Now and then, however, Alice laughed too loudly, and Marc was careful about his posture, holding his shoulders back, his head up. They waited quite a long time for their coffee, in silence. An incandescent river, the straggled reflection of the invisible sun overhead, shifted slowly across the sea and shone with a blinding brilliance.

"She's still there, you know," Alice whispered.

"Is she making you uncomfortable? Would you like to have coffee somewhere else?"

"No, not at all! She's the one who must be uncomfortable! Besides, she doesn't exactly seem to be having a wild time, if you could see her . . ."

"I don't have to. I know that look of hers."

"Oh, was she like that?"

He exhaled his cigarette smoke through his nostrils and knitted his eyebrows. "Like that? No. To tell you honestly, she wasn't happy with me."

"Oh, really now!"

"The way you indulge me is so charming, darling . . . It's crazy . . . You're an angel . . . You love me . . . I'm so proud when I see those eyes of yours. Yes, those eyes . . . She . . . I just didn't know how to make her happy, that's all. I didn't know how."

"She's just difficult!"

Alice fanned herself irritably, and cast brief glances at the woman in white, who was smoking, her head resting against the back of the cane chair, her eyes closed with an air of satisfied lassitude.

Marc shrugged his shoulders modestly.

"That's the right word," he admitted. "What can you do? You have to feel sorry for people who are never satisfied. But we're satisfied . . . Aren't we, darling?"

She did not answer. She was looking furtively, and closely, at her husband's face, ruddy and regular; at his thick hair, threaded here and there with white silk;

at his short, well-cared-for hands; and doubtful for the first time, she asked herself, "What more did she want from him?"

And as they were leaving, while Marc was paying the bill and asking for the chauffeur and about the route, she kept looking, with envy and curiosity, at the woman in white, this dissatisfied, this difficult, this superior . . .

UNDERSTANDING THE STORY

1. Why does Marc refuse to sit near his ex-wife?
2. Why does Alice laugh too loudly?
3. Why does Marc improve his posture?
4. Was Marc wise to tell Alice why his previous marriage failed? Explain.
5. What **themes** do you find in this story?

ANALYZING LITERARY TECHNIQUE

1. Explain the **irony** in Marc's statement "But we're satisfied . . . Aren't we, darling?" Consider both Marc and Alice.
2. What is the function of **contrast** in this story?
3. How does the **narrative perspective** affect your understanding of the characters and the **conflict** in the story?
4. What **paradox** does Colette employ in this story?

WRITING ABOUT LITERATURE

1. Analyze how Marc's and Alice's attitudes toward the ex-wife affect the actions and outcome of the story. For example, consider how the luncheon would have been different if Marc had criticized his ex-wife for being insensitive and unpleasant. Write an essay in which you discuss how the characterization of Marc and Alice, as revealed through the dialogue and through the narrator's descriptions, shapes the conflict of this story. Predict the future of Marc and Alice's marriage, basing your ideas on your analysis of their characters.

2. Consider how this story would have been different if Marc and Alice had seen Alice's ex-husband instead of Marc's ex-wife. Using the characterization of Alice and Marc that is presented in "The Other Wife," rewrite the story so that it centers on seeing "the other husband." You may use both dialogue and narrative, as in the original story, or just narrative in your revision.

At Sundown

RAINER MARIA RILKE

*R*AINER MARIA RILKE (1875–1926), the German lyric
poet, is one of the major poets of the late nineteenth and
early twentieth centuries. A prominent critic calls him "the
first great poet of the unconscious." He is well known for *New Poems*
(1907–1908) and for his two last collections of poetry, *Duino Elegies*
(1923) and *Sonnets to Orpheus* (1923).

Rilke was born in Prague, Czech Republic (then a provincial capital of the Austro-Hungarian empire), into a middle-class German family. His mother called him Sophie and treated him as a little girl until he
was five. He was a sickly, sensitive child who hated the military acade-
mies he was forced to attend from 1886 to 1891. He rejected a military
career to study in Prague and Munich. From 1899 to the end of his life,
he traveled throughout Europe, never permanently settling in one place.

Rilke published his first collection of poetry, *Life and Songs*, in 1894.
Between 1895 and 1901, he wrote drama and fiction and then devoted
the remainder of his life to poetry; various wealthy women served as
his patrons. He wrote in German, Russian, Italian, and French.

Rilke was preoccupied with reconciling himself to the human
condition: the transitory nature of life, the existence of human suffering, and the inevitability of mortality. His search for the meaning and
purpose of life bypassed Christianity in favor of poetry; he reached a
low point during World War I, when he questioned the value of poetry
and its role in his life. Finally, while enjoying the solitude of the castle
of Duino, on the Adriatic Sea, he completed the *Duino Elegies*, in
which he concludes that the artist—through literature and poetry—
can transform what is ephemeral into what will endure.

In his poetry, Rilke aimed for a child's view of the world, admiring
"the child's wise incapacity to understand." He was particularly interested in the poetry of the French Symbolists, and he sought to express
the essence of emotion by using concrete images. The following lyric,
"At Sundown," reveals Rilke's ability to convey the transitory nature
of an experience in this way.

Slowly the evening starts to change her raiments
for veils held up by rows of distant trees
You watch how gradually the landscape's contours change,
some rising heavenward as others downward fall;

leaving you alone, to neither quite belonging,   5
nor quite as dark as houses silent keep,
nor quite so sure beseeching the eternal
as that which nightly turns to star and rises—

and leaving you (impossible to disentangle)
your life, fearful, gigantic and still ripening,   10
which, now limited, now comprehending,
alternatingly becomes stone in you and star.

UNDERSTANDING THE POEM

1. What is evening compared to? What are the "raiments" and "veils"?

2. What makes the speaker feel alone?

3. What division does the speaker feel within himself?

ANALYZING LITERARY TECHNIQUE

1. What is the function of **apostrophe** in this poem?

2. What effect does **personification** achieve in the poem?

3. What is the function of **contrast** in the poem?

4. What do the **images** of "stone" and "star" contribute to the poem?

5. The stages of human life are often compared with seasons or with times of the day. What stage in life is suggested by the poem? How do you know?

WRITING ABOUT LITERATURE

1. Consider this poem as an essay on the mood of twilight. How much of the poem's tone depends on the natural events that the poet describes—the sun's setting and the star's coming out—and how much depends on the poet's interpretation of these events? Write a brief essay in which you analyze how Rilke achieves the tone of this poem. Use quotations from the poem to support your ideas.

2. Choose your favorite time of day and write a short poem or paragraph about the various moods or emotions that time of day suggests. Try to use **figurative language (metaphors, similes,** personification) and descriptive words to convey a mood appropriate to that time of day.

A Country Doctor

FRANZ KAFKA

*F*RANZ KAFKA (1883–1924) is considered by many to be the literary voice of the twentieth century. He was the first major writer to reveal in fiction certain nightmarish aspects of modern life. In his short stories and novels, his protagonists often must confront an indifferent power with whom they cannot communicate. Kafka created such lasting images of inadequacy, frustration, failure, anxiety, guilt, and despair that the feelings and the situations that produce them have come to be called "Kafkaesque." During his lifetime, he published only a few short stories, but when the remainder of his work was published after his death, his novels quickly brought him international fame. Kafka is best known for "The Metamorphosis" (1915), *The Trial* (1925), and *The Castle* (1926).

Kafka was born in Prague, Czechoslovakia (then a provincial capital of the Austro-Hungarian Empire), into a prosperous Jewish family. His father was an authoritarian self-made merchant. His mother was a devoted wife, taking an active role in the operation of the family business. Kafka was the oldest of six children and the only surviving son. Like many other middle-class Jewish children, he was educated in German schools; in 1906 he received a degree in law from the German University in Prague.

Until tuberculosis made it necessary for him to enter a sanitarium in 1922, Kafka led two vastly different lives. During the day he was a successful insurance company executive. Then late at night he immersed himself in "this fearful world which I venture to take on only during my nights of writing." Working into the early morning hours, he delved into his inner emotional life by keeping a diary and writing letters, short stories, and novels. His need as an author for independence and solitude was so great that he never permitted himself to marry. In a diary entry of 1914, he writes: "My talent for portraying my dreamlike inner life has thrust all other matters into the background. . . . Nothing else will ever satisfy me."

In his fiction, Kafka traps the reader in the consciousness of a narrator who clearly and objectively reports bizarre occurrences. His works mean different things to different readers. Whatever the interpretation, "A Country Doctor" illuminates three of Kafka's favorite themes: the nature of human beings, their relationship to the society in which they live, and the responsibility that they owe to themselves and to others.

I was in great perplexity; I had to start on an urgent journey; a seriously ill patient was waiting for me in a village ten miles off; a thick blizzard of snow filled all the wide spaces between him and me; I had a gig, a light gig with big wheels, exactly right for our country roads; muffled in furs, my bag of instruments in my hand, I was in the courtyard all ready for the journey; but there was no horse to be had, no horse. My own horse had died in the night, worn out by the fatigues of this icy winter; my servant girl was now running round the village trying to borrow a horse; but it was hopeless, I knew it, and I stood there forlornly, with the snow gathering more and more thickly upon me, more and more unable to move. In the gateway the girl appeared, alone, and waved the lantern; of course, who would lend a horse at this time for such a journey? I strode through the courtway once more; I could see no way out; in my confused distress I kicked at the dilapidated door of the year-long uninhabited pigsty. It flew open and flapped to and fro on its hinges. A steam and smell as of horses came out of it. A dim stable lantern was swinging inside from a rope. A man, crouching on his hams in that low space, showed an open blue-eyed face. "Shall I yoke up?" he asked, crawling out on all fours. I did not know what to say and merely stooped down to see what else was in the sty. The servant girl was standing beside me. "You never know what you're going to find in your own house," she said, and we both laughed. "Hey there, Brother, hey there, Sister!" called the groom and two horses, enormous creatures with powerful flanks, one after the other, their legs tucked close to their bodies, each well-shaped head lowered like a camel's, by sheer strength of buttocking squeezed out through the door hole which they filled entirely. But at once they were standing up, with their long legs and their bodies steaming thickly. "Give him a hand," I said, and the willing girl hurried to help the groom with the harnessing. Yet hardly was she beside him when the groom clapped hold of her and pushed his face against hers. She screamed and fled back to me; on her cheek stood out in red the marks of two rows of teeth. "You brute," I yelled in fury, "do you want a whipping?" but in the same moment reflected that the man was a stranger; that I did not know where he came from, and that of his own free will he was helping me out when everyone else had failed me. As if he knew my thoughts he took no offense at my threat but, still busied with the horses, only turned round once towards me. "Get in," he said then, and indeed: everything was ready. A magnificent pair of horses, I observed, such as I had never sat behind, and I climbed in happily. "But I'll drive, you don't know the way," I said. "Of course," said he, "I'm not coming with you anyway, I'm staying with Rose." "No," shrieked Rose, fleeing into the house with a justified presentiment that her fate was inescapable; I heard the door chain rattle as she put it up; I heard the key turn in the lock; I could see, moreover, how she put out the lights in the entrance hall and in further flight all through the rooms to keep herself from being discovered. "You're coming with me," I said to the groom, "or I won't go, urgent as my journey is. I'm not thinking of paying for it by handing the girl over to you." "Gee up!" he said; clapped his hands; the gig whirled off like a log in a freshet; I could just hear the door of my house splitting and bursting as the groom charged at it and then I was deafened and blinded by a storming rush that steadily buffeted all my senses. But this only for a moment, since, as if my patient's farmyard had opened out just before my courtyard gate, I was already there; the horses had come quietly to a standstill; the blizzard had stopped; the moonlight all around; my patient's parents hurried out of the house, his sister behind them; I was almost lifted out of the gig; from their confused ejaculations I gathered not a word; in the sick room the air was almost unbreathable; the neglected stove was smoking; I wanted to push open a window; but first I had to look at my patient. Gaunt, without any fever, not cold, not warm, with vacant eyes, without a shirt, the youngster heaved himself up from under the feather bedding, threw his arms around my neck, and whispered in my ear: "Doctor, let me die." I glanced round the room; no one had heard it; the parents were leaning forward in silence waiting for my verdict; the sister had set a chair for my handbag; I opened the bag and hunted among my instruments; the boy kept clutching at me from his bed to remind me of his entreaty; I picked up a pair of tweezers, examined them in the candlelight and laid them down again. "Yes," I thought blasphemously, "in cases like this the gods are helpful, send the missing horse, add to it a second because of the urgency, and to crown everything bestow even a groom—" And only now did I remember Rose again; what was I to do, how could I rescue her, how could I pull her away from under that groom at ten miles' distance, with a team of horses I couldn't control. These horses, now, they had somehow slipped the reins loose, pushed the window open from the outside, I did not know how; each of them had stuck a head in at the window, and quite unmoved by the startled cries of the family, stood eyeing the patient. "Better go back at once," I thought, as if the horses were summoning me to the return journey, yet I permitted the patient's sister, who fancied that I was dazed by the heat, to take my fur coat from me. A glass of rum was poured out for me, the old man clapped me on the shoulder, a familiarity justified by this offer of his treasure. I shook my head; in the narrow confines of the old man's thoughts I felt ill; that was my only reason for refusing the drink. The mother stood by the bedside and cajoled me towards it; I yielded, and, while one of the horses whinnied loudly to the ceiling, laid my head to the boy's breast, which shivered under my wet beard. I confirmed what I already knew, the boy was quite sound, something a little wrong with his circulation, saturated with coffee by his solicitous mother, but sound and best turned out of bed with one shove. I am no world reformer and so I let him lie. I was the district doctor and I did my duty to the uttermost, to the point where it became almost too much. I was badly paid and yet generous and helpful to the poor. I had still to see that Rose was alright, and then the boy might have his way and I wanted to die too. What was I doing there in that endless winter! My horse was dead, and not a single person in the village would lend me another. I had to get my team out of the pigsty; if they hadn't chanced to be horses I should have had to travel with swine. That was how it was. And I nodded to the family. They knew nothing about it, and, had they known, would not have believed it. To write prescriptions is easy, but to come to an understanding with people is hard. Well, this should be the end of my visit, I had once more been called out needlessly, I was used to that, the whole district made my life a torment with my night bell, but that I should have to sacrifice Rose this time as well, the pretty girl who had lived in my house for years almost without my noticing her—that sacrifice was too much to ask, and I had somehow to get it reasoned out in my head with the help of what craft I could muster, in order not to let fly at this family, which with the best will in the world could not restore Rose to me. But as I shut my bag and put an arm out for my fur coat, the family meanwhile standing together, the father sniffing at the glass of rum in his hand, the mother, apparently disappointed in me—why, what do people expect?—biting her lips with tears in her eyes, the sister fluttering a blood-soaked towel, I was somehow ready to admit conditionally that the boy might be ill after all. I went towards him, he welcomed me smiling as if I were bringing him the most nourishing invalid broth—ah, now both horses were whinnying together; the noise, I suppose, was ordained by heaven to assist my examination of the patient—and this time I discovered that the boy was indeed ill. In his right side, near the hip, was an open wound as big as the palm of my hand. Rose-red, in many variations of shade, dark in the hollows, lighter at the edges, softly granulated, with irregular clots of blood, open as a surface mine to the daylight. That was how it looked from a distance. But on a closer inspection there was another complication. I could not help a low whistle of surprise. Worms, as thick and as long as my little finger, themselves rose-red and blood-spotted as well, were wriggling from their fastness in the interior of the wound towards the light, with small white heads and many little legs. Poor boy, you were past helping. I had discovered your great wound; this blossom in your side was destroying you. The family was pleased; they saw me busying myself; the sister told the mother, the mother the father, the father told several guests who were coming in, through the moonlight at the open door, walking on tiptoe, keeping their balance with outstretched arms. "Will you save me?" whispered the boy with a sob, quite blinded by the life within his wound. That is what people are like in my district. Always expecting the impossible from the doctor. They have lost their ancient beliefs; the parson sits at home and unravels his vestments, one after another; but the doctor is supposed to be omnipotent with his merciful surgeon's hand. Well, as it pleases them; I have not thrust my services on them; if they misuse me for sacred ends, I let that happen to me too; what better do I want, old country doctor that I am, bereft of my servant girl! And so they came, the family and the village elders, and stripped my clothes off me; a school choir with the teacher at the head of it stood before the house and sang these words to an utterly simple tune:

> Strip his clothes off, then he'll heal us,
> If he doesn't, kill him dead!
> Only a doctor, only a doctor.

Then my clothes were off and I looked at the people quietly, my fingers in my beard and my head cocked to one side. I was altogether composed and equal to the situation and remained so, although it was no help to me, since they now took me by the head and feet and carried me to the bed. They laid me down in it next to the wall, on the side of the wound. Then they all left the room; the door was shut; the singing stopped; clouds covered the moon; the bedding was warm around me; the horses' heads in the opened windows wavered like shadows. "Do you know," said a voice in my ear, "I have very little confidence in you. Why, you were only blown in here, you didn't come on your own feet. Instead of helping me, you're cramping me on my death bed. What I'd like best is to scratch your eyes out." "Right," I said, "it's a shame. And yet I am a doctor. What am I to do? Believe me, it is not too easy for me either." "Am I supposed to be content with this apology? Oh, I must be, I can't help it. I always have to put up with things. A fine wound is all I brought into the world; that was my sole endowment." "My young friend," said I, "your mistake is: you have not a wide enough view. I have been in all the sickrooms, far and wide, and I tell you: your wound is not so bad. Done in a tight corner with two strokes of the ax. Many a one proffers his side and can hardly hear the ax in the forest, far less that it is coming nearer to him." "Is that really so, or are you deluding me in my fever?" "It is really so, take the word of honor of an official doctor." And he took it and lay still. But now it was time for me to think of escaping. The horses were still standing faithfully in their places. My clothes, my fur coat, my bag were quickly collected; I didn't want to waste time dressing; if the horses raced home as they had come, I should only be springing, as it were, out of this bed into my own. Obediently a horse backed away from the window; I threw my bundle into the gig; the fur coat missed its mark and was caught on a hook only by the sleeve. Good enough. I swung myself on to the horse. With the reins loosely trailing, one horse barely fastened to the other, the gig swaying behind, my fur coat last of all in the snow. "Geeup!" I said, but there was no galloping; slowly, like old men, we crawled through the snowy wastes; a long time echoed behind us the new but faulty song of the children:

> O be joyful, all you patients,
> The doctor's laid in bed beside you!

Never shall I reach home at this rate; my flourishing practice is done for; my successor is robbing me, but in vain, for he cannot take my place; in my house the disgusting groom is raging; Rose is the victim; I do not want to think about it any more. Naked, exposed to the frost of this most unhappy of ages, with an earthly vehicle, unearthly horses, old man that I am, I wander astray. My fur coat is hanging from the back of the gig, but I cannot reach it, and none of my limber pack of patients lifts a finger. Betrayed! Betrayed! A false alarm on the night bell once answered—it cannot be made good, not ever.

UNDERSTANDING THE STORY

1. Identify four challenges that confront the doctor.
2. What frustration accompanies each challenge?
3. Why might this story be called a nightmare?
4. What **themes** do you find in this story?

ANALYZING LITERARY TECHNIQUE

1. How does Kafka's use of **setting** function in the story?
2. What effect does Kafka's choice of **narrative perspective** have on this story?
3. The author of an **allegory** expects readers to look for a meaning below the surface of the story. To what extent can this story be considered an allegory?
4. What is the **irony** of the main character's profession?
5. How does the simple style of this story relate to the story's meaning? What does Kafka achieve by writing the entire story in one paragraph?
6. Is **plot** or character more important in this story? Explain.
7. How does the concept of the **night journey** relate to this story?
8. How does Kafka achieve **psychological realism** in this story? What effect does this technique have?

WRITING ABOUT LITERATURE

1. Write an essay in which you analyze the elements in "A Country Doctor" that make the story a nightmare. Consider the setting, the characters, and the plot. In your introduction, explain the criteria for judging an experience to be a nightmare. Then set forth your analysis and summarize how the story meets the criteria. Use quotations from the story to support each of your points.
2. Create a nightmare version of a real event. For example, you could write about the nightmare a new doctor might have arising from the insecurity over joining an older doctor's practice. Consider how secure the new doctor would feel about his or her medical knowledge and the prospect of success with the older doctor's patients. Remember that the individual you write about does not have to play his or her everyday role in the nightmare.

Voronezh

ANNA AKHMATOVA

ANNA AKHMATOVA (1888–1966) is considered to be one of Russia's greatest modern poets. She is known for *Forty-Seven Love Poems* (1927), various editions of *Selected Poems* (published from 1969 to 1989), and *The Complete Poems of Anna Akhmatova* (1992). Her longest and most famous poem, "Poem Without a Hero" (composed from 1940 to 1965 and published in 1973), is a reflection of her life in St. Petersburg from 1913 to 1962, a period that includes World War II and its aftermath. The poem is viewed as one of the greatest poems of the twentieth century.

Akhmatova was born Anna Andreyevna Gorenko, in a suburb of Odessa, in Russia. Her father was an officer in the merchant marine. After her parents separated in 1905, she moved with her mother and her four siblings to Kiev and later to St. Petersburg (which was renamed Leningrad from 1924 to 1991). Akhmatova, who was particularly influenced by the poems of French and Russian Symbolists, began to write poems in 1907. She was married to Nikolai Gumilyov, an important prerevolutionary poet, from 1910 until 1918. He published *Evening* (1912), her first collection of poetry. *Rosary* (1914), which reflects her unhappy marriage and expresses the variety of her moods, became popular and brought her fame.

Given the circumstances of her life, it is easy to understand why Akhmatova's happiest years were in the St. Petersburg of her youth. In 1921 Gumilyov participated in an anti-Bolshevik plot. Gumilyov's "treachery," which led to his execution, left an indelible blot upon Akhmatova and their son, Lev. In 1935 Lev was arrested during a reign of terror in which those who were thought to be enemies of the government were imprisoned and killed. Released but rearrested in 1938, Lev was condemned to spend more than fifteen years in a Soviet concentration camp. However, with Hitler's invasion of Russia, he was released from prison and sent to serve in the war. Between 1935 and 1940, Akhmatova wrote "Requiem," a cycle of lyrical poems that expresses her grief over her son's arrest and imprisonment; the poems were never published unabridged in Soviet Russia. In 1949 Lev was arrested for the third time and sent into exile in Siberia. Fearing that the authorities would search her home, Akhmatova burned many of her poems and refused to put others into written form. The following year, in the hope of saving her son's life, Akhmatova wrote fifteen poems in which she praised Stalin and Soviet communism. Lev was finally freed in 1956.

Akhmatova had an enduring love for St. Petersburg, where she spent most of her life and where she chose to remain throughout Stalin's years of terror. She believed that her role in life was to endure Soviet tyranny and, through her poetry, to bear witness to that tyranny. From 1922 until 1940 and from 1946 until the death of Stalin in 1953, the Central Committee of the Communist Party banned Akhmatova's poetry on the grounds that it was too personal, too religious, and too apolitical, which made it both subversive and dangerous. Akhmatova earned a meager living translating the works of other poets, including Rabindranath Tagore.

In 1964 Akhmatova's membership in the Union of Soviet Writers was finally restored. The next year her poetry was finally published in its original form, and the Soviet government permitted her to travel outside of the Soviet Union for the first time in fifty years. When Akhmatova died at the age of seventy-eight, she felt that she had met the goals that she had set for herself. In her poem "This Cruel Age Has Deflected Me . . ." (written in Leningrad in 1944), she declares, "But if I could step outside myself / and contemplate the person that I am, / I should know at last what envy is."

Akhmatova's poetry covers fifty-nine years of her life. Her poems include early love lyrics; religious poems; war poems that express courage, pity, and compassion; and poems that reflect the serenity of her old age after she was finally accepted and recognized by the Soviet government. Akhmatova's favorite theme was love—the happy love of her youth as well as her memory of love. Her best poems combine the lyricism of her early work with the despair and compassion that she developed in response to government persecution and her own great personal suffering. Her poems are valued for the clear, concrete imagery with which she expresses her thoughts and feelings.

As her poem "Voronezh" reveals so clearly, Akhmatova's poetry fuses the external world associated with a particular place and time with her own internal world. She dedicated "Voronezh," written in 1936, to Osip Mandelstam, one of the greatest Russian poets of the twentieth century. In 1934 she was staying in Moscow with the Mandelstams when the Soviet secret police arrested the poet because he had written a poem in which he criticized Stalin. He was condemned to live in exile in Voronezh, a city located three hundred miles to the south of Moscow; Akhmatova visited him in Voronezh. The site of the battle of Kulikovo, which took place in 1380, is located nearby.

As Akhmatova predicts in this poem, "the night" did come "with quickened pace." In 1937 and 1938, Stalin empowered his commissar of internal affairs to imprison and murder as he chose. This period became known as "the years of terror" or "Stalin's Great Terror." Mandelstam, who returned to Moscow in 1937, was arrested in 1938 and imprisoned in a concentration camp near Vladivostok, where he died at the end that year. When "Voronezh" was first published, in 1940, the last four lines were deleted. It was not until 1965 that the complete poem was published in the Soviet Union in *The Flight of Time*.

(*To Osip Mandelstam*[1])
The city is caught in the grip of ice—
Trees, walls, snow, are as under glass.
Over crystals, I and the patterned sleighs
Go our separate, unsteady ways.
And above St. Peter's steeple—crows,
And poplars—a light-green vault that glows—
Blurred, lackluster, in the sunny dust.
The triumphant landscape blows into thought
This is where Kulikovo[2] was fought.
And the poplars like wineglasses raised in a toast
Suddenly ring out more clearly above us.
As though at a wedding the assembled host
Were drinking our union to show how they love us.
But Fear and the Muse in turn guard the place
Where the banished poet has gone.
And the night that comes with quickened pace
Is ignorant of dawn.

UNDERSTANDING THE POEM

1. Why do the poet and "the patterned sleighs / go [their] separate, unsteady ways"?

2. What is triumphant about the landscape that the poet observes?

3. Why does the poet make an **allusion** to Kulikovo?

4. What is the similarity between poplars and wineglasses raised in a toast?

5. Who is being united in the wedding **simile?**

6. Who is "the assembled host" in the wedding simile? Whom does "the assembled host" love, and why?

---

[1] *Osip Mandelstam:* (1891–1939) noted Russian poet who was arrested twice and died in prison.
[2] *Kulikovo:* great battle against the Tartars, 1378.

7. Why do "Fear and the Muse . . . guard the place / Where the banished poet has gone"?

8. Why does the poet choose not to name "the banished poet" or "the assembled host"?

9. What do "the night" and "dawn" refer to?

10. What **comparison** does the poet make in this poem?

11. What **tone** does the poet express in this poem? Another translation concludes with the words "and the night is coming on, / which has no hope of dawn." How does this translation affect the tone of the poem? Which translation appears to be more consistent with the rest of the poem?

12. Why was the poem first published in Soviet Russia without the last four lines?

ANALYZING LITERARY TECHNIQUE

1. What do ice, glass, and crystals contribute to this poem?

2. What is the significance of the wedding simile?

3. What does the poet achieve by **personifying** Fear and the Muse?

4. What does the poet achieve by making **metaphors** of night and dawn?

WRITING ABOUT LITERATURE

1. Write an expository essay in which you compare the following two translations of the last two lines of the poem and analyze which translation is more consistent with the tone of the rest of the poem: (a) "and the night is coming on, / which has no hope of dawn"; (b) "And the night that comes with quickened pace / Is ignorant of dawn" (the translation in this text).

   Consider the significance of the church steeple and the poplar trees, the poet's reference to the battle of Kulikovo, and the extended simile of the wedding.

2. Write an expository essay in which you analyze what the poet's use of **figurative language** contributes to this poem. In your opening paragraph, explain what your essay will discuss. Then define simile, metaphor, and personification. In the body of your essay, quote three examples of the poet's figurative language and explain why she uses each example. In your concluding paragraph, explain what the poet's use of figurative language contributes to this poem.

3. Write a story in which a person sees something that calls to mind an earlier event. Compare the observer's attitude and feelings toward the present scene and the past event.

The Wall

JEAN-PAUL SARTRE

France

J EAN-PAUL SARTRE (1905–1980), an important French writer, is known as the leading existential author. He was a gifted, philosophically oriented playwright, novelist, short-story writer, essayist, and critic. In 1964 he was awarded the Nobel Prize for literature, but he refused to accept it. His most famous works are *The Flies* (1942), his adaptation of a play by Sophocles applied to the German occupation of France; *Being and Nothingness*, his philosophical treatise on existentialism (1943); *Nausea* (1938), a novel; and *The Wall and Other Stories* (1939), a collection of short stories.

Sartre was born in Paris. From the age of two, after the death of his father, he was reared in the household of his maternal grandfather. Sartre felt that this environment stifled his independence, and he escaped into his own world by writing adventure stories. For many years, he was a high-school teacher, teaching in Laon, Le Havre, and Paris. In 1939 he entered World War II as a medical orderly, and in 1940 he was imprisoned by the Germans for nine months. Upon his return to Paris in 1941, he resumed his teaching and became active in the French resistance movement. At the end of the war, he left the teaching profession and founded the periodical *Modern Times*.

Existentialism flourished in the years between 1940 and 1965 because its philosophy met the needs of people who were disillusioned by World War II. Existentialism denies that one's beliefs and actions are determined by a divine providence, human nature, heredity, or environment. Instead, it asserts that all human beings define themselves by their actions. In his famous lecture "Existentialism Is a Humanism," Sartre states, "Man is nothing else but that which he makes of himself."

Sartre was considered to be the leader of the existential movement, although he did not create its principles. It was he who made them comprehensible by embodying them in the attitudes and behavior of the protagonists of his stories and dramas. "The Wall" is one of the classic existentialist writings. Set in Spain in the late 1930s, it deals with a group of men who are condemned to die by General Franco's Fascist government.

They pushed us into a large white room and my eyes began to blink because the light hurt them. Then I saw a table and four fellows seated at the table, civilians, looking at some papers. The other prisoners were herded together at one end and we were obliged to cross the entire room to join them. There were several I knew, and others who must have been foreigners. The two in front of me were blond with round heads. They looked alike. I imagine they were French. The smaller one kept pulling at his trousers, out of nervousness.

This lasted about three hours. I was dog-tired and my head was empty. But the room was well-heated, which struck me as rather agreeable; we had not stopped shivering for twenty-four hours. The guards led the prisoners in one after the other in front of the table. Then the four fellows asked them their names and what they did. Most of the time that was all—or perhaps from time to time they would ask such questions as: "Did you help sabotage the munitions?" or, "Where were you on the morning of the ninth and what were you doing?" They didn't even listen to the replies, or at least they didn't seem to. They just remained silent for a moment and looked straight ahead, then they began to write. They asked Tom if it was true he had served in the International Brigade.[1] Tom couldn't say he hadn't because of the papers they had found in his jacket. They didn't ask Juan anything, but after he told them his name, they wrote for a long while.

"It's my brother José who's the anarchist," Juan said. "You know perfectly well he's not here now. I don't belong to any party. I never did take part in politics." They didn't answer.

Then Juan said, "I didn't do anything. And I'm not going to pay for what the others did."

His lips were trembling. A guard told him to stop talking and led him away. It was my turn.

"Your name is Pablo Ibbieta?"

I said yes.

The fellow looked at his papers and said, "Where is Ramon Gris?"

"I don't know."

"You hid him in your house from the sixth to the nineteenth."

"I did not."

They continued to write for a moment and the guards led me away. In the hall, Tom and Juan were waiting between two guards. We started walking. Tom asked one of the guards, "What's the idea?" "How do you mean?" the guard asked. "Was that just the preliminary questioning, or was that the trial?" "That was the

---

[1] *International Brigade:* Fighting forces made up of Spanish Loyalists and volunteer sympathizers from many other countries during the Spanish civil war (1936–1939). The International Brigades fought in defense of the Spanish Republic.

trial," the guard said. "So now what? What are they going to do with us?" The guard answered drily, "The verdict will be told you in your cell."

In reality, our cell was one of the cellars of the hospital. It was terribly cold there because it was very drafty. We had been shivering all night long and it had hardly been any better during the day. I had spent the preceding five days in a cellar in the archbishop's palace, a sort of dungeon that must have dated back to the Middle Ages. There were lots of prisoners and not much room, so they housed them just anywhere. But I was not homesick for my dungeon. I hadn't been cold there, but I had been alone, and that gets to be irritating. In the cellar I had company. Juan didn't say a word; he was afraid, and besides, he was too young to have anything to say. But Tom was a good talker and knew Spanish well.

In the cellar there were a bench and four straw mattresses. When they led us back we sat down and waited in silence. After a while Tom said, "Our goose is cooked."

"I think so too," I said. "But I don't believe they'll do anything to the kid."

Tom said, "They haven't got anything on him. He's the brother of a fellow who's fighting, and that's all."

I looked at Juan. He didn't seem to have heard.

Tom continued, "You know what they do in Saragossa?[2] They lay the guys across the road and then they drive over them with trucks. It was a Moroccan deserter who told us that. They say it's just to save ammunition."

I said, "Well, it doesn't save gasoline."

I was irritated with Tom; he shouldn't have said that.

He went on, "There are officers walking up and down the roads with their hands in their pockets, smoking, and they see that it's done right. Do you think they'd put 'em out of their misery? Like hell they do. They just let 'em holler. Sometimes as long as an hour. The Moroccan said the first time he almost puked."

"I don't believe they do that here," I said, "unless they really are short of ammunition."

The daylight came in through four air vents and a round opening that had been cut in the ceiling, to the left, and which opened directly onto the sky. It was through this hole, which was ordinarily closed by means of a trapdoor, that they unloaded coal into the cellar. Directly under the hole, there was a big pile of coal dust; it had been intended for heating the hospital, but at the beginning of the war they had evacuated the patients and the coal had stayed there unused; it even got rained on from time to time, when they forgot to close the trapdoor.

Tom started to shiver. "God damn it," he said, "I'm shivering. There, it is starting again."

He rose and began to do gymnastic exercises. At each movement, his shirt opened and showed his white, hairy chest. He lay down on his back, lifted his legs in the air and began to do the scissors movement. I watched his big buttocks tremble. Tom was tough, but he had too much fat on him. I kept thinking that

---

[2] *Saragossa:* Zaragoza, a city in northwest Spain.

soon bullets and bayonet points would sink into that mass of tender flesh as though it were a pat of butter.

I wasn't exactly cold, but I couldn't feel my shoulders or my arms. From time to time, I had the impression that something was missing and I began to look around for my jacket. Then I would suddenly remember they hadn't given me a jacket. It was rather awkward. They had taken our clothes to give them to their own soldiers and had left us only our shirts and these cotton trousers the hospital patients wore in mid-summer. After a moment, Tom got up and sat down beside me, breathless.

"Did you get warmed up?"

"Damn it, no. But I'm all out of breath."

Around eight o'clock in the evening, a Major came in with two falangists.[3]

"What are the names of those three over there?" he asked the guard.

"Steinbock, Ibbieta, and Mirbal," said the guard.

The Major put on his glasses and examined his list.

"Steinbock—Steinbock . . . Here it is. You are condemned to death. You'll be shot tomorrow morning."

He looked at his list again.

"The other two, also," he said.

"That's not possible," said Juan. "Not me."

The Major looked at him with surprise. "What's your name?"

"Juan Mirbal."

"Well, your name is here," said the Major, "and you're condemned to death."

"I didn't do anything," said Juan.

The Major shrugged his shoulders and turned toward Tom and me.

"You are both Basque."[4]

"No, nobody's Basque."

He appeared exasperated.

"I was told there were three Basques. I'm not going to waste my time running after them. I suppose you don't want a priest?"

We didn't even answer.

Then he said, "A Belgian doctor will be around in a little while. He has permission to stay with you all night."

He gave a military salute and left.

"What did I tell you?" Tom said. "We're in for something swell."

"Yes," I said. "It's a damned shame for the kid."

I said that to be fair, but I really didn't like the kid. His face was too refined and it was disfigured by fear and suffering, which had twisted all his features. Three days ago, he was just a kid with a kind of affected manner some people like. But now he looked like an aging fairy, and I thought to myself he would never be young again, even if they let him go. It wouldn't have been a bad thing

---

[3] *falangists:* Members of the Fascist political party that ruled Spain after the civil war, under the dictatorship of Francisco Franco (1892–1975).

[4] *Basque:* An inhabitant of the western Pyranees in Spain.

to show him a little pity, but pity makes me sick, and besides, I couldn't stand him. He hadn't said anything more, but he had turned gray. His face and hands were gray. He sat down again and stared, round-eyed at the ground. Tom was good-hearted and tried to take him by the arm, but the kid drew himself away violently and made an ugly face. "Leave him alone," I said quietly. "Can't you see he's going to start to bawl?" Tom obeyed regretfully. He would have liked to console the kid; that would have kept him occupied and he wouldn't have been tempted to think about himself. But it got on my nerves. I had never thought about death, for the reason that the question had never come up. But now it had come up, and there was nothing else to do but think about it.

Tom started talking. "Say, did you ever bump anybody off?" he asked me. I didn't answer. He started to explain to me that he had bumped off six fellows since August. He hadn't yet realized what we were in for, and I saw clearly he didn't *want* to realize it. I myself hadn't quite taken it in. I wondered if it hurt very much. I thought about the bullets; I imagined their fiery hail going through my body. All that was beside the real question; but I was calm, we had all night in which to realize it. After a while Tom stopped talking and I looked at him out of the corner of my eye. I saw that he, too, had turned gray and that he looked pretty miserable. I said to myself, "It's starting." It was almost dark, a dull light filtered through the air vents across the coal pile and made a big spot under the sky. Through the hole in the ceiling I could already see a star. The night was going to be clear and cold.

The door opened and two guards entered. They were followed by a blond man in a tan uniform. He greeted us.

"I'm the doctor," he said. "I've been authorized to give you any assistance you may require in these painful circumstances."

He had an agreeable, cultivated voice.

I said to him, "What are you going to do here?"

"Whatever you want me to do. I shall do everything in my power to lighten these few hours."

"Why did you come to us? There are lots of others: the hospital's full of them."

"I was sent here," he answered vaguely. "You'd probably like to smoke, wouldn't you?" he added suddenly. "I've got some cigarettes and even some cigars."

He passed around some English cigarettes and some *puros*,[5] but we refused them. I looked him straight in the eye and he appeared uncomfortable.

"You didn't come here out of compassion," I said to him. "In fact, I know who you are. I saw you with some fascists in the barracks yard the day I was arrested."

I was about to continue, when all at once something happened to me which surprised me: the presence of this doctor had suddenly ceased to interest me. Usually, when I've got hold of a man I don't let go. But somehow the desire to speak had left me. I shrugged my shoulders and turned away. A little later, I looked up and saw he was watching me with an air of curiosity. The guards had sat down

---

[5] puros: Cigars.

on one of the mattresses. Pedro, the tall thin one, was twiddling his thumbs, while the other shook his head occasionally to keep from falling asleep.

"Do you want some light?" Pedro suddenly asked the doctor. The other fellow nodded, "Yes." I think he was not over-intelligent, but doubtless he was not malicious. As I looked at his big, cold, blue eyes, it seemed to me the worst thing about him was his lack of imagination. Pedro went out and came back with an oil lamp which he set on the corner of the bench. It gave a poor light, but it was better than nothing; the night before we had been left in the dark. For a long while I stared at the circle of light the lamp threw on the ceiling. I was fascinated. Then, suddenly, I came to, the light circle paled, and I felt as if I were being crushed under an enormous weight. It wasn't the thought of death, and it wasn't fear; it was something anonymous. My cheeks were burning hot and my head ached.

I roused myself and looked at my two companions. Tom had his head in his hands and only the fat, white nape of his neck was visible. Juan was by far the worst off; his mouth was wide open and his nostrils were trembling. The doctor came over to him and touched him on the shoulder, as though to comfort him; but his eyes remained cold. Then I saw the Belgian slide his hand furtively down Juan's arm to his wrist. Indifferent, Juan let himself be handled. Then, as though absent-mindedly, the Belgian laid three fingers over his wrist; at the same time, he drew away somewhat and managed to turn his back to me. But I leaned over backward and saw him take out his watch and look at it a moment before relinquishing the boy's wrist. After a moment, he let the inert hand fall and went and leaned against the wall. Then, as if he had suddenly remembered something very important that had to be noted down immediately, he took a notebook from his pocket and wrote a few lines in it. "The son-of-a-bitch," I thought angrily. "He better not come and feel my pulse; I'll give him a punch in his dirty jaw."

He didn't come near me, but I felt he was looking at me. I raised my head and looked back at him. In an impersonal voice, he said, "Don't you think it's frightfully cold here?"

He looked purple with cold.

"I'm not cold," I answered him.

He kept looking at me with a hard expression. Suddenly I understood, and I lifted my hands to my face. I was covered with sweat. Here, in this cellar, in mid-winter, right in a draft, I was sweating. I ran my fingers through my hair, which was stiff with sweat; at the same time, I realized my shirt was damp and sticking to my skin. I had been streaming with perspiration for an hour, at least, and had felt nothing. But this fact hadn't escaped that Belgian swine. He had seen the drops rolling down my face and had said to himself that it showed an almost pathological terror; and he himself had felt normal and proud of it because he was cold. I wanted to get up and go punch his face in, but I had hardly started to make a move before my shame and anger had disappeared. I dropped back onto the bench with indifference.

I was content to rub my neck with my handkerchief because now I felt the sweat dripping from my hair onto the nape of my neck and that was disagreeable. I soon gave up rubbing myself, however, for it didn't do any good; my handkerchief was already wringing wet and I was still sweating. My buttocks, too, were sweating, and my damp trousers stuck to the bench.

Suddenly, Juan said, "You're a doctor, aren't you?"

"Yes," said the Belgian.

"Do people suffer—very long?"

"Oh! When . . . ? No, no," said the Belgian, in a paternal voice, "it's quickly over."

His manner was as reassuring as if he had been answering a paying patient.

"But I . . . Somebody told me—they often have to fire two volleys."

"Sometimes," said the Belgian, raising his head, "it just happens that the first volley doesn't hit any of the vital organs."

"So then they have to reload their guns and aim all over again?" Juan thought for a moment, then added hoarsely, "But that takes time!"

He was terribly afraid of suffering. He couldn't think about anything else, but that went with his age. As for me, I hardly thought about it any more and it certainly was not fear of suffering that made me perspire.

I rose and walked toward the pile of coal dust. Tom gave a start and looked at me with a look of hate. I irritated him because my shoes squeaked. I wondered if my face was as putty-colored as his. Then I noticed that he, too, was sweating. The sky was magnificent; no light at all came into our dark corner and I had only to lift my head to see the Big Bear.[6] But it didn't look the way it had before. Two days ago, from my cell in the archbishop's palace, I could see a big patch of sky and each time of day brought back a different memory. In the morning, when the sky was a deep blue, and light, I thought of beaches along the Atlantic; at noon, I could see the sun, and I remembered a bar in Seville where I used to drink manzanilla[7] and eat anchovies and olives; in the afternoon, I was in the shade, and I thought of the deep shadow which covers half of the arena while the other half gleams in the sunlight: it really gave me a pang to see the whole earth reflected in the sky like that. Now, however, no matter how much I looked up in the air, the sky no longer recalled anything. I liked it better that way. I came back and sat down next to Tom. There was a long silence.

Then Tom began to talk in a low voice. He had to keep talking, otherwise he lost his way in his own thoughts. I believe he was talking to me, but he didn't look at me. No doubt he was afraid to look to me, because I was gray and sweating. We were both alike and worse than mirrors for each other. He looked at the Belgian, the only one who was alive.

"Say, do you understand? I don't."

Then I, too, began to talk in a low voice. I was watching the Belgian.

"Understand what? What's the matter?"

"Something's going to happen to us that I don't understand."

---

[6] *Big Bear:* A constellation.

[7] *Seville . . . manzanilla:* Seville is a city in southwest Spain. Manzanilla is a dry sherry-like wine.

There was a strange odor about Tom. It seemed to me that I was more sensitive to odors than ordinarily. With a sneer, I said, "You'll understand, later."

"That's not so sure," he said stubbornly. "I'm willing to be courageous, but at least I ought to know . . . Listen, they're going to take us out into the courtyard. All right. The fellows will be standing in line in front of us. How many of them will there be?"

"Oh, I don't know. Five, or eight. Not more."

"That's enough. Let's say there'll be eight of them. Somebody will shout 'Shoulder arms!' and I'll see all eight rifles aimed at me. I'm sure I'm going to feel like going through the wall. I'll push against the wall as hard as I can with my back, and the wall won't give in. The way it is in a nightmare. . . . I can imagine all that. Ah, if you only knew how well I can imagine it!"

"Skip it!" I said. "I can imagine it too."

"It must hurt like the devil. You know they aim at your eyes and mouth so as to disfigure you," he added maliciously. "I can feel the wounds already. For the last hour I've been having pains in my head and neck. Not real pains—it's worse still. They're the pains I'll feel tomorrow morning. And after that, then what?"

I understood perfectly well what he meant, but I didn't want to seem to understand. As for the pains, I, too, felt them all through my body, like a lot of little gashes. I couldn't get used to them, but I was like him, I didn't think they were very important.

"After that," I said roughly, "you'll be eating daisies."

He started talking to himself, not taking his eyes off the Belgian, who didn't seem to be listening to him. I knew what he had come for, and that what we were thinking didn't interest him. He had come to look at our bodies, our bodies which were dying alive.

"It's like in a nightmare," said Tom. "You want to think of something, you keep having the impression you've got it, that you're going to understand, and then it slips away from you, it eludes you and it's gone again. I say to myself, afterwards, there won't be anything. But I don't really understand what that means. There are moments when I almost do—and then it's gone again. I start to think of the pains, the bullets, the noise of the shooting. I am a materialist, I swear it; and I'm not going crazy, either. But there's something wrong. I see my own corpse. That's not hard, but it's *I* who see it, with *my* eyes. I'll have to get to the point where I think—where I think I won't see anything more. I won't hear anything more, and the world will go on for the others. We're not made to think that way, Pablo. Believe me, I've already stayed awake all night waiting for something. But this is not the same thing. This will grab us from behind, Pablo, and we won't be ready for it."

"Shut up," I said. "Do you want me to call a father confessor?"[8]

He didn't answer. I had already noticed that he had a tendency to prophesy and call me "Pablo" in a kind of pale voice. I didn't like that very much, but it seems all the Irish are like that. I had a vague impression that he smelled of urine.

---

[8] *father confessor:* A priest.

Actually, I didn't like Tom very much, and I didn't see why, just because we were going to die together, I should like him any better. There are certain fellows with whom it would be different—with Ramon Gris, for instance. But between Tom and Juan, I felt alone. In fact, I liked it better that way. With Ramon I might have grown soft. But I felt terribly hard at that moment, and I wanted to stay hard.

Tom kept on muttering, in a kind of absent-minded way. He was certainly talking to keep from thinking. Naturally, I agreed with him, and I could have said everything he was saying. It's not *natural* to die. And since I was going to die, nothing seemed natural any more: neither the coal pile, nor the bench, nor Pedro's dirty old face. Only it was disagreeable for me to think the same things Tom thought. And I knew perfectly well that all night long, within five minutes of each other, we would keep on thinking things at the same times, sweating or shivering at the same time. I looked at him sideways and, for the first time, he seemed strange to me. He had death written on his face. My pride was wounded. For twenty-four hours I had lived side by side with Tom, I had listened to him, I had talked to him, and I knew we had nothing in common. And now we were as alike as twin brothers, simply because we were going to die together. Tom took my hand without looking at me.

"Pablo, I wonder . . . I wonder if it's true that we just cease to exist."

I drew my hand away.

"Look between your feet, you dirty dog."

There was a puddle between his feet and water was dripping from his trousers.

"What's the matter?" he said, frightened.

"You're wetting your pants," I said to him.

"It's not true," he said furiously. "I can't be . . . I don't feel anything."

The Belgian had come closer to him. With an air of false concern, he asked, "Aren't you feeling well?"

Tom didn't answer. The Belgian looked at the puddle without comment.

"I don't know what that is," Tom said savagely, "but I'm not afraid. I swear to you, I'm not afraid."

The Belgian made no answer. Tom rose and went to the corner. He came back, buttoning his fly, and sat down, without a word. The Belgian was taking notes.

We were watching the doctor. Juan was watching him too. All three of us were watching him because he was alive. He had the gestures of a living person, the interests of a living person; he was shivering in this cellar the way living people shiver; he had an obedient, well-fed body. We, on the other hand, didn't feel our bodies any more—not the same way, in any case. I felt like touching my trousers, but I didn't dare to. I looked at the Belgian, well-planted on his two legs, master of his muscles—and able to plan for tomorrow. We were like three shadows deprived of blood; we were watching him and sucking his life like vampires.

Finally he came over to Juan. Was he going to lay his hand on the nape of Juan's neck for some professional reason, or had he obeyed a charitable impulse? If he had acted out of charity, it was the one and only time during the whole night. He fondled Juan's head and the nape of his neck. The kid let him do it, without taking his eyes off him. Then, suddenly, he took hold of the doctor's hand and looked at it in a funny way. He held the Belgian's hand between his own two hands and there was nothing pleasing about them, those two gray paws squeezing that fat red hand. I sensed what was going to happen and Tom must have sensed it, too. But all the Belgian saw was emotion, and he smiled paternally. After a moment, the kid lifted the big red paw to his mouth and started to bite it. The Belgian drew back quickly and stumbled toward the wall. For a second, he looked at us with horror. He must have suddenly understood that we were not men like himself. I began to laugh, and one of the guards started up. The other had fallen asleep with his eyes wide open, showing only the whites.

I felt tired and over-excited at the same time. I didn't want to think any more about what was going to happen at dawn—about death. It didn't make sense, and I never got beyond just words, or emptiness. But whenever I tried to think about something else I saw the barrels of rifles aimed at me. I must have lived through my execution twenty times in succession; one time I thought it was the real thing; I must have dozed off for a moment. They were dragging me toward the wall and I was resisting; I was imploring their pardon. I woke with a start and looked at the Belgian. I was afraid I had cried out in my sleep. But he was smoothing his mustache; he hadn't noticed anything. If I had wanted to, I believe I could have slept for a while. I had been awake for the last forty-eight hours, and I was worn out. But I didn't want to lose two hours of life. They would have had to come and wake me at dawn. I would have followed them, drunk with sleep, and I would have gone off without so much as "Gosh!" I didn't want it that way, I didn't want to die like an animal. I wanted to understand. Besides, I was afraid of having nightmares. I got up and began to walk up and down and, so as to think about something else, I began to think about my past life. Memories crowded in on me, helter-skelter. Some were good and some were bad—at least that was how I had thought of them before. There were faces and happenings. I saw the face of a little *novilero* who had gotten himself horned during the *Feria*, in Valencia.[9] I saw the face of one of my uncles, of Ramon Gris. I remembered all kinds of things that had happened: how I had been on strike for three months in 1926, and had almost died of hunger. I recalled a night I had spent on a bench in Granada;[10] I hadn't eaten for three days, I was nearly wild, I didn't want to give up the sponge. I had to smile. With what eagerness I had run after happiness, and women, and liberty! And to what end? I had wanted to liberate Spain, I admired Py Margall,[11] I had belonged to the anarchist movement, I had spoken at public meetings. I took everything as seriously as if I had been immortal.

At that time I had the impression that I had my whole life before me, and I thought to myself, "It's all a damn lie." Now it wasn't worth anything because it was finished. I wondered how I had ever been able to go out and have a good time

---

[9] novilero . . . Feria, in Valencia: A *novilero* is a novice bullfighter. A *feria* is a fair or carnival. Valencia is a city on the east coast of Spain.

[10] *Granada:* A city in the south of Spain.

[11] *Py Margall:* Francisco Pi y Margall (1824–1901) was a Spanish journalist and statesman who was president of the first Spanish republic and a hero among anarchists.

with girls. I wouldn't have lifted my little finger if I had ever imagined that I would die like this. I saw my life before me, finished, closed, like a bag, and yet what was inside was not finished. For a moment I tried to appraise it. I would have liked to say to myself, "It's been a good life." But it couldn't be appraised, it was only an outline. I had spent my time writing checks on eternity, and had understood nothing. Now, I didn't miss anything. There were a lot of things I might have missed: the taste of manzanilla, for instance, or the swims I used to take in summer in a little creek near Cadiz.[12] But death had taken the charm out of everything.

Suddenly the Belgian had a wonderful idea.

"My friends," he said to us, "if you want me to—and providing the military authorities give their consent—I could undertake to deliver a word or some token from you to your loved ones. . . ."

Tom growled, "I haven't got anybody."

I didn't answer. Tom waited for a moment, then he looked at me with curiosity. "Aren't you going to send any message to Concha?"

"No."

I hated that sort of sentimental conspiracy. Of course, it was my fault, since I had mentioned Concha the night before, and I should have kept my mouth shut. I had been with her for a year. Even as late as last night, I would have cut my arm off with a hatchet just to see her again for five minutes. That was why I had mentioned her. I couldn't help it. Now I didn't care any more about seeing her. I hadn't anything more to say to her. I didn't even want to hold her in my arms. I loathed my body because it had turned gray and was sweating—and I wasn't even sure that I didn't loathe hers too. Concha would cry when she heard about my death; for months she would have no more interest in life. But still it was I who was going to die. I thought of her beautiful, loving eyes. When she looked at me something went from her to me. But I thought to myself that it was all over; if she looked at me *now* her gaze would not leave her eyes, it would not reach out to me. I was alone.

Tom, too, was alone, but not the same way. He was seated astride his chair and had begun to look at the bench with a sort of smile, with surprise, even. He reached out his hand and touched the wood cautiously, as though he were afraid of breaking something, then he drew his hand back hurriedly, and shivered. I wouldn't have amused myself touching that bench, if I had been Tom, that was just some more Irish playacting. But somehow it seemed to me too that the different objects had something funny about them. They seemed to have grown paler, less massive than before. I had only to look at the bench, the lamp or the pile of coal dust to feel I was going to die. Naturally, I couldn't think clearly about my death, but I saw it everywhere, even on the different objects, the way they had withdrawn and kept their distance, tactfully. It was *his own death* Tom had just touched on the bench.

In the state I was in, if they had come and told me I could go home quietly, that my life would be saved, it would have left me cold. A few hours, or a few

---

[12] *Cadiz:* Town on the southwest coast of Spain, on the Gulf of Cadiz.

years of waiting are all the same, when you've lost the illusion of being eternal. Nothing mattered to me any more. In a way, I was calm. But it was a horrible kind of calm—because of my body. My body—I saw with its eyes and I heard with its ears, but it was no longer I. It sweat and trembled independently, and I didn't recognize it any longer. I was obliged to touch it and look at it to know what was happening to it, just as if it had been someone else's body. At times I still felt it, I felt a slipping, a sort of headlong plunging, as in a falling airplane, or else I heard my heart beating. But this didn't give me confidence. In fact, everything that came from my body had something damned dubious about it. Most of the time it was silent, it stayed put and I didn't feel anything other than a sort of heaviness, a loathsome presence against me. I had the impression of being bound to an enormous vermin.

The Belgian took out his watch and looked at it.

"It's half-past three," he said.

The son-of-a-bitch! He must have done it on purpose. Tom jumped up. We hadn't yet realized the time was passing. The night surrounded us like a formless, dark mass; I didn't even remember it had started.

Juan started to shout. Wringing his hand, he implored, "I don't want to die! I don't want to die!"

He ran the whole length of the cellar with his arms in the air, then he dropped down onto one of the mattresses, sobbing. Tom looked at him with dismal eyes and didn't even try to console him any more. The fact was, it was no use; the kid made more noise than we did, but he was less affected, really. He was like a sick person who defends himself against his malady with a high fever. When there's not even any fever left, it's much more serious.

He was crying. I could tell he felt sorry for himself; he was thinking about death. For one second, one single second, I too felt like crying, crying out of pity for myself. But just the contrary happened. I took one look at the kid, saw his thin, sobbing shoulders, and I felt I was inhuman. I couldn't feel pity either for these others or for myself. I said to myself, "I want to die decently."

Tom had gotten up and was standing just under the round opening looking out for the first signs of daylight. I was determined, I wanted to die decently, and I only thought about that. But underneath, ever since that doctor had told us the time, I felt time slipping, flowing by, one drop at a time.

It was still dark when I heard Tom's voice.

"Do you hear them?"

"Yes."

People were walking in the courtyard.

"What the hell are they doing? After all, they can't shoot in the dark."

After a moment, we didn't hear anything more. I said to Tom, "There's the daylight."

Pedro got up yawning, and came and blew out the lamp. He turned to the man beside him. "It's hellish cold."

The cellar had grown gray. We could hear shots at a distance.

"It's about to start," I said to Tom. "That must be in the back courtyard."

Tom asked the doctor to give him a cigarette. I didn't want any; I didn't want either cigarettes or alcohol. From that moment on, the shooting didn't stop.

"Can you take it in?" Tom said.

He started to add something, then he stopped and began to watch the door. The door opened and a lieutenant came in with four soldiers. Tom dropped his cigarette.

"Steinbock?"

Tom didn't answer. Pedro pointed him out.

"Juan Mirbal?"

"He's the one on the mattress."

"Stand up," said the Lieutenant.

Juan didn't move. Two soldiers took hold of him by the armpits and stood him up on his feet. But as soon as they let go of him he fell down.

The soldiers hesitated a moment.

"He's not the first one to get sick," said the Lieutenant. "You'll have to carry him, the two of you. We'll arrange things when we get there." He turned to Tom. "All right, come along."

Tom left between two soldiers. Two other soldiers followed, carrying the kid by his arms and legs. He was not unconscious; his eyes were wide open and tears were rolling down his cheeks. When I turned to go out, the Lieutenant stopped me.

"Are you Ibbieta?"

"Yes."

"You wait here. They'll come and get you later on."

They left. The Belgian and the two jailers left too, and I was alone. I didn't understand what had happened to me, but I would have liked it better if they had ended it all right away. I heard the volleys at almost regular intervals; at each one, I shuddered. I felt like howling and tearing my hair. But instead, I gritted my teeth and pushed my hands deep into my pockets, because I wanted to stay decent.

An hour later, they came to fetch me and took me up to the first floor in a little room which smelt of cigar smoke and was so hot it seemed to me suffocating. Here there were two officers sitting in comfortable chairs, smoking, with papers spread out on their knees.

"Your name is Ibbieta?"

"Yes."

"Where is Ramon Gris?"

"I don't know."

The man who questioned me was small and stocky. He had hard eyes behind his glasses.

"Come nearer," he said to me.

I went nearer. He rose and took me by the arms, looking at me in a way calculated to make me go through the floor. At the same time he pinched my arms with all his might. He didn't mean to hurt me; it was quite a game; he wanted to dominate me. He also seemed to think it was necessary to blow his fetid breath right into my face. We stood like that for a moment, only I felt more like laughing than anything else. It takes a lot more than that to intimidate a man who's about to die; it didn't work. He pushed me away violently and sat down again.

"It's your life or his." he said "You'll be allowed to go free if you tell us where he is."

After all, these two bedizened fellows with their riding crops and boots were just men who were going to die one day. A little later than I, perhaps, but not a great deal. And there they were, looking for names among their papers, running after other men in order to put them in prison or do away with them entirely. They had their opinions on the future of Spain and on other subjects. Their petty activities seemed to me to be offensive and ludicrous. I could no longer put myself in their place. I had the impression they were crazy.

The little fat fellow kept looking at me, tapping his boots with his riding crop. All his gestures were calculated to make him appear like a spirited, ferocious animal.

"Well? Do you understand?"

"I don't know where Gris is," I said. "I thought he was in Madrid."[13]

The other officer lifted his pale hand indolently. This indolence was also calculated. I saw through all their little tricks, and I was dumbfounded that men should still exist who took pleasure in that kind of thing.

"You have fifteen minutes to think it over," he said slowly. "Take him to the linen-room, and bring him back here in fifteen minutes. If he continues to refuse, he'll be executed at once."

They knew what they were doing. I had spent the night waiting. After that, they had made me wait another hour in the cellar, while they shot Tom and Juan, and now they locked me in the linen-room. They must have arranged the whole thing the night before. They figured that sooner or later people's nerves wear out and they hoped to get me that way.

They made a big mistake. In the linen-room I sat down on a ladder because I felt very weak, and I began to think things over. Not their proposition, however. Naturally I knew where Gris was. He was hiding in his cousins' house, about two miles outside of the city. I knew, too, that I would not reveal his hiding place, unless they tortured me (but they didn't seem to be considering that). All that was definitely settled and didn't interest me in the least. Only I would have liked to understand the reasons for my own conduct. I would rather die than betray Gris. Why? I no longer liked Ramon Gris. My friendship for him had died shortly before dawn along with my love for Concha, along with my own desire to live. Of course I still admired him—he was hard. But it was not for that reason that I was willing to die in his place; his life was no more valuable than mine. No life was of any value. A man was going to be stood up against a wall and fired at till he dropped dead. It didn't make any difference whether it was I or Gris or somebody else. I knew perfectly well he was more useful to the Spanish cause than I was, but I didn't give a damn about Spain or anarchy, either; nothing had any importance now. And yet, there I was. I could save my skin by betraying Gris and I refused to do it. It seemed more ludicrous to me than anything else; it was stubbornness.

---

[13] *Madrid:* The capital of Spain.

I thought to myself, "Am I hard-headed!" And I was seized with a strange sort of cheerfulness.

They came to fetch me and took me back to the two officers. A rat darted out under our feet and that amused me. I turned to one of the falangists and said to him, "Did you see that rat?"

He made no reply. He was gloomy, and took himself very seriously. As for me, I felt like laughing, but I restrained myself because I was afraid that if I started, I wouldn't be able to stop. The falangist wore mustaches. I kept after him. "You ought to cut off those mustaches, you fool."

I was amused by the fact that he let hair grow all over his face while he was still alive. He gave me a kind of half-hearted kick, and I shut up.

"Well," said the fat officer, "have you thought things over?"

I looked at them with curiosity, like insects of a very rare species.

"I know where he is," I said. "He's hiding in the cemetery. Either in one of the vaults, or in the gravediggers' shack."

I said that just to make fools of them. I wanted to see them get up and fasten their belts and bustle about giving orders.

They jumped to their feet.

"Fine. Moles, go ask Lieutenant Lopez for fifteen men. And as for you," the little fat fellow said to me, "if you've told the truth, I don't go back on my word. But you'll pay for this, if you're pulling our leg."

They left noisily and I waited in peace, still guarded by the falangists. From time to time I smiled at the thought of the face they were going to make. I felt dull and malicious. I could see them lifting up the gravestones, or opening the doors of the vaults one by one. I saw the whole situation as though I were another person: the prisoner determined to play the hero, the solemn falangists with their mustaches and the men in uniform running around among the graves. It was irresistibly funny.

After half an hour, the little fat fellow came back alone. I thought he had come to give the order to execute me. The others must have stayed in the cemetery.

The officer looked at me. He didn't look at all foolish.

"Take him out in the big courtyard with the others," he said. "When military operations are over, a regular tribunal will decide his case."

I thought I must have misunderstood.

"So they're not—they're not going to shoot me?" I asked.

"Not now, in any case. Afterwards, that doesn't concern me."

I still didn't understand.

"But why?" I said to him.

He shrugged his shoulders without replying, and the soldiers led me away. In the big courtyard there were a hundred or so prisoners, women, children and a few old men. I started to walk around the grass plot in the middle. I felt absolutely idiotic. At noon we were fed in the dining hall. Two or three fellows spoke to me. I must have known them, but I didn't answer. I didn't even know where I was.

Toward evening, about ten new prisoners were pushed into the courtyard. I recognized Garcia, the baker.

He said to me, "Lucky dog! I didn't expect to find you alive."

"They condemned me to death," I said, "and then they changed their minds. I don't know why."

"I was arrested at two o'clock," Garcia said.

"What for?"

Garcia took no part in politics.

"I don't know," he said. "They arrest everybody who doesn't think the way they do."

He lowered his voice.

"They got Gris."

I began to tremble.

"When?"

"This morning. He acted like a damned fool. He left his cousins' house Tuesday because of a disagreement. There were any number of fellows who would have hidden him, but he didn't want to be indebted to anybody any more. He said, 'I would have hidden at Ibbieta's, but since they've got him, I'll go hide in the cemetery.'"

"In the cemetery?"

"Yes. It was the damnedest thing. Naturally they passed by there this morning; that had to happen. They found him in the gravediggers' shack. They opened fire at him and they finished him off."

"In the cemetery!"

Everything went around in circles, and when I came to I was sitting on the ground. I laughed so hard the tears came to my eyes.

UNDERSTANDING THE STORY

1. Why does Pablo criticize Tom's comment about Saragossa?

2. Pablo says of Juan, "It wouldn't have been a bad thing to show him a little pity, but pity makes me sick." What does this comment reveal about Pablo?

3. Why does Pablo enjoy feeling alone and hard?

4. What does Pablo mean when he says to himself, "I want to die decently"?

5. What changes does Pablo's imminent death make in his attitude toward life?

6. What does Pablo gain from his approach to death?

7. Why does Pablo refuse to turn in Ramon Gris?

8. What **themes** do you find in this story?

ANALYZING LITERARY TECHNIQUE

1. What are Tom's and Juan's functions in the story? Note their relationship to Pablo and consider to what extent, if any, each is an **alter ego** or a **doppelgänger** of Pablo.

2. What does Pablo's humor reveal about Pablo? Why does he laugh at the end? What kind of laughter is it?

3. To what extent is "The Wall" a **symbol?** Discuss the ways in which the title is an appropriate title for this story.

4. Why is the **narrative perspective** appropriate to the story's theme?

5. Find two or three examples of **irony** and examine how they relate to the **theme** of the story.

WRITING ABOUT LITERATURE

1. One of the central ideas of **existentialism** is the following **paradox:** People believe that they live in a comprehensible, connected, and predictable universe, but the universe is actually irrational, disconnected, and unpredictable. Existentialism claims that, in such an irrational world, each individual must attempt to make sense of the world—to give meaning to life—in his or her own way. The process of striving to give meaning to life is a valid end in itself.

   "The Wall" is often used to teach existential philosophy. Analyze the following statement by Pablo. Then write a brief essay showing how Pablo's statement relates to the central ideas of existentialism and explaining why you think "The Wall" is or is not a good story for illustrating existential ideas.

   > I was alone. I didn't understand what had happened to me, but I would have liked it better if they had ended it all right away. I heard the volleys at almost regular intervals; at each one, I shuddered. I felt like howling and tearing my hair. But instead, I gritted my teeth and pushed my hands deep into my pockets, because I wanted to stay decent.

2. Create a diary (one or two entries) in which Pablo describes his feelings and actions once he finds that he has been released. Consider the following questions: Does Pablo regain his lust for life? Does he again care about others? Comment on the validity of the following statement by Pablo:

   > In the state I was in, if they had come and told me I could go home quietly, that my life would be saved, it would have left me cold. A few hours, or a few years of waiting are all the same, when you've lost the illusion of being eternal. Nothing mattered to me any more.

The Guest

ALBERT CAMUS

*A*LBERT CAMUS (1913–1960), the French author, was awarded the Nobel Prize for literature in 1957 "for his important literary production which with clear-sighted earnestness illuminates the problems of the human conscience in our times." He was a novelist, playwright, essayist, journalist, and critic. He is best known for his essay "The Myth of Sisyphus" (1942) and his novels *The Stranger* (1942) and *The Plague* (1948).

Camus was born in Mondovi, Algeria, to immigrant parents. After his father's death in 1914 in the Battle of the Marne in World War I, Camus was reared by his deaf, illiterate mother, who lived in a poor suburb of Algiers and worked as a cleaning woman. He worked his way through school, finally specializing in the study of philosophy at the University of Algiers. In 1935 and 1936, he was a communist, but he left the party because he disapproved of the Soviet government's harsh treatment of many of its citizens. He became a reporter and also founded an amateur theater group in which he was director, actor, and playwright. He moved to Paris in 1940, left during the German occupation in World War II, and in 1942 joined the French resistance movement in nonoccupied France. He became one of the three editors of the underground newspaper *Combat*, a position that brought him wide recognition. With the end of the war, his writing brought him international fame. He died in an automobile accident at the age of forty-six.

Camus's attitudes and beliefs emerged from his life experiences. Life with his mother fostered a love and compassion for others and a hatred of injustice and cruelty. Life in Algeria impressed him with the beauty of the universe, the pleasure of being alive, and the suffering of poor and innocent people. The horrors of World War II caused Camus to consider the problem of living in a world that is "absurd," a world that is indifferent to basic human needs for logic and justice, a world where being human involves suffering and, inevitably, dying. In response to the world's absurdity, Camus focused on the responsibility of human beings to treat one another with respect and concern. He found dignity in the experience of being alive, in active commitment to moral values, and in each individual's stubborn struggle to improve the human condition by opposing evil and relieving human suffering in spite of obstacles.

Camus's stories depict human beings in situations where personal involvement is necessary and where the important values of independence, tolerance, compassion, and justice are difficult to preserve. "The Guest," from his collection of short stories *Exile and the Kingdom* (1957), is set on a high plateau near the Atlas Mountains in Algeria at the beginning of the rebellion that resulted in Algeria's independence from France.

The schoolmaster was watching the two men climb toward him. One was on horseback, the other on foot. They had not yet tackled the abrupt rise leading to the schoolhouse built on the hillside. They were toiling onward, making slow progress in the snow, among the stones, on the vast expanse of the high, deserted plateau. From time to time the horse stumbled. Without hearing anything yet, he could see the breath issuing from the horse's nostrils. One of the men, at least, knew the region. They were following the trail although it had disappeared days ago under a layer of dirty white snow. The schoolmaster calculated that it would take them half an hour to get onto the hill. It was cold; he went back into the school to get a sweater.

He crossed the empty, frigid classroom. On the blackboard the four rivers of France, drawn with four different colored chalks, had been flowing toward their estuaries for the past three days. Snow had suddenly fallen in mid-October after eight months of drought without the transition of rain, and the twenty pupils, more or less, who lived in the villages scattered over the plateau had stopped coming. With fair weather they would return. Daru now heated only the single room that was his lodging, adjoining the classroom and giving also onto the plateau to the east. Like the class windows, his window looked to the south too. On that side the school was a few kilometers from the point where the plateau began to slope toward the south. In clear weather could be seen the purple mass of the mountain range where the gap opened onto the desert.

Somewhat warmed, Daru returned to the window from which he had first seen the two men. They were no longer visible. Hence they must have tackled the rise. The sky was not so dark, for the snow had stopped falling during the night. The morning had opened with a dirty light which had scarcely become brighter as the ceiling of clouds lifted. At two in the afternoon it seemed as if the day were merely beginning. But still this was better than those three days when the thick snow was falling amidst unbroken darkness with little gusts of wind that rattled the double door of the classroom. Then Daru had spent long hours in his room, leaving it only to go to the shed and feed the chickens or get some coal. Fortunately the delivery truck from Tadjid,[1] the nearest village to the north, had brought his supplies two days before the blizzard. It would return in forty-eight hours.

Besides, he had enough to resist a siege, for the little room was cluttered with bags of wheat that the administration left as a stock to distribute to those of his pupils whose families had suffered from the drought. Actually they had all been victims because they were all poor. Every day Daru would distribute a ration to the children. They had missed it, he knew, during these bad days. Possibly one of the fathers or big brothers would come this afternoon and he could supply them with grain. It was just a matter of carrying them over to the next harvest. Now shiploads of wheat were arriving from France and the worst was over. But it would be hard to forget that poverty, that army of ragged ghosts wandering in the sunlight, the plateaus burned to a cinder month after month, the earth shriveled up little by little, literally scorched, every stone bursting into dust under one's foot. The sheep had died then by thousands and even a few men, here and there, sometimes without anyone's knowing.

In contrast with such poverty, he who lived almost like a monk in his remote schoolhouse, nonetheless satisfied with the little he had and with the rough life, had felt like a lord with his whitewashed walls, his narrow couch, his unpainted shelves, his well, and his weekly provision of water and food. And suddenly this snow, without warning, without the foretaste of rain. This is the way the region was, cruel to live in, even without men—who didn't help matters either. But Daru had been born here. Everywhere else, he felt exiled.

He stepped out onto the terrace in front of the schoolhouse. The two men were now halfway up the slope. He recognized the horseman as Balducci, the old gendarme[2] he had known for a long time. Balducci was holding on the end of a rope an Arab who was walking behind him with hands bound and head lowered. The gendarme waved a greeting to which Daru did not reply, lost as he was in contemplation of the Arab dressed in a faded blue jellaba,[3] his feet in sandals but covered with socks of heavy raw wool, his head surmounted by a narrow, short chèche.[4] They were approaching. Balducci was holding back his horse in order not to hurt the Arab, and the group was advancing slowly.

Within earshot, Balducci shouted: "One hour to do the three kilometers from El Ameur!" Daru did not answer. Short and square in his thick sweater, he watched them climb. Not once had the Arab raised his head. "Hello," said Daru when they got up onto the terrace. "Come in and warm up." Balducci painfully got down from his horse without letting go the rope. From under his bristling mustache he smiled at the schoolmaster. His little dark eyes, deep-set under a tanned forehead, and his mouth surrounded with wrinkles made him look attentive and studious.

---

[1] *Tadjid:* A city on the Algerian plateau, south of the Mediterranean Sea and north of the Sahara.

[2] *gendarme:* Police officer.

[3] *jellaba:* Loose cloak with a hood.

[4] chèche: A cap with a tassel.

Daru took the bridle, led the horse to the shed, and came back to the two men, who were now waiting for him in the school. He led them into his room. "I am going to heat up the classroom," he said. "We'll be more comfortable there." When he entered the room again, Balducci was on the couch. He had undone the rope tying him to the Arab, who had squatted near the stove. His hands still bound, the *chèche* pushed back on his head, he was looking toward the window. At first Daru noticed only his huge lips, fat, smooth, almost Negroid; yet his nose was straight, his eyes were dark and full of fever. The *chèche* revealed an obstinate forehead and, under the weathered skin now rather discolored by the cold, the whole face had a restless and rebellious look that struck Daru when the Arab, turning his face toward him, looked him straight in the eyes. "Go into the other room," said the schoolmaster, "and I'll make you some mint tea." "Thanks," Balducci said. "What a chore! How I long for retirement." And addressing his prisoner in Arabic: "Come on, you." The Arab got up and, slowly, holding his bound wrists in front of him, went into the classroom.

With the tea, Daru brought a chair. But Balducci was already enthroned on the nearest pupil's desk and the Arab had squatted against the teacher's platform facing the stove, which stood between the desk and the window. When he held out the glass of tea to the prisoner, Daru hesitated at the sight of his bound hands. "He might perhaps be untied." "Sure," said Balducci. "That was for the trip." He started to get to his feet. But Daru, setting the glass on the floor, had knelt beside the Arab. Without saying anything, the Arab watched him with his feverish eyes. Once his hands were free, he rubbed his swollen wrists against each other, took the glass of tea, and sucked up the burning liquid in swift little sips.

"Good," said Daru. "And where are you headed?"

Balducci withdrew his mustache from the tea. "Here, son."

"Odd pupils! And you're spending the night?"

"No. I'm going back to El Ameur. And you will deliver this fellow to Tinguit. He is expected at police headquarters."

Balducci was looking at Daru with a friendly little smile.

"What's this story?" asked the schoolmaster. "Are you pulling my leg?"

"No, son. Those are the orders."

"The orders? I'm not . . ." Daru hesitated, not wanting to hurt the old Corsican. "I mean, that's not my job."

"What! What's the meaning of that? In wartime people do all kinds of jobs."

"Then I'll wait for the declaration of war!"

Balducci nodded.

"O.K. But the orders exist and they concern you too. Things are brewing, it appears. There is talk of a forthcoming revolt. We are mobilized, in a way."

Daru still had his obstinate look.

"Listen, son," Balducci said. "I like you and you must understand. There's only a dozen of us at El Ameur to patrol throughout the whole territory of a small department and I must get back in a hurry. I was told to hand this guy over to you and return without delay. He couldn't be kept there. His village was beginning to stir; they wanted to take him back. You must take him to Tinguit tomorrow before the day is over. Twenty kilometers shouldn't faze a husky fellow like you. After that, all will be over. You'll come back to your pupils and your comfortable life."

Behind the wall the horse could be heard snorting and pawing the earth. Daru was looking out the window. Decidedly, the weather was clearing and the light was increasing over the snowy plateau. When all the snow was melted, the sun would take over again and once more would burn the fields of stone. For days, still, the unchanging sky would shed its dry light on the solitary expanse where nothing had any connection with man.

"After all," he said, turning around toward Balducci, "what did he do?" And, before the gendarme had opened his mouth, he asked: "Does he speak French?"

"No, not a word. We had been looking for him for a month, but they were hiding him. He killed his cousin."

"Is he against us?"

"I don't think so. But you can never be sure."

"Why did he kill?"

"A family squabble, I think. One owed the other grain, it seems. It's not at all clear. In short, he killed his cousin with a billhook. You know, like a sheep, *kreezk!*"

Balducci made the gesture of drawing a blade across his throat and the Arab, his attention attracted, watched him with a sort of anxiety. Daru felt a sudden wrath against the man, against all men with their rotten spite, their tireless hates, their blood lust.

But the kettle was singing on the stove. He served Balducci more tea, hesitated, then served the Arab again, who, a second time, drank avidly. His raised arms made the jellaba fall open and the schoolmaster saw his thin muscular chest.

"Thanks, kid," Balducci said. "And now, I'm off."

He got up and went toward the Arab, taking a small rope from his pocket.

"What are you doing?" Daru asked dryly.

Balducci, disconcerted, showed him the rope.

"Don't bother."

The old gendarme hesitated. "It's up to you. Of course, you are armed?"

"I have my shotgun."

"Where?"

"In the trunk."

"You ought to have it near your bed."

"Why? I have nothing to fear."

"You're crazy, son. If there's an uprising, no one is safe, we're all in the same boat."

"I'll defend myself. I'll have time to see them coming."

Balducci began to laugh, then suddenly the mustache covered the white teeth.

"You'll have time? O.K. That's just what I was saying. You have always been a little cracked. That's why I like you, my son was like that."

At the same time he took out his revolver and put it on the desk.

"Keep it; I don't need two weapons from here to El Ameur."

The revolver shone against the black paint of the table. When the gendarme turned toward him, the schoolmaster caught the smell of leather and horseflesh.

"Listen, Balducci," Daru said suddenly, "every bit of this disgusts me, and first of all your fellow here. But I won't hand him over. Fight, yes, if I have to. But not that."

The old gendarme stood in front of him and looked at him severely.

"You're being a fool," he said slowly. "I don't like it either. You don't get used to putting a rope on a man even after years of it, and you're even ashamed—yes, ashamed. But you can't let them have their way."

"I won't hand him over," Daru said again.

"It's an order, son, and I repeat it."

"That's right. Repeat to them what I've said to you: I won't hand him over."

Balducci made a visible effort to reflect. He looked at the Arab and Daru. At last he decided.

"No, I won't tell them anything. If you want to drop us, go ahead; I'll not denounce you. I have an order to deliver the prisoner and I'm doing so. And now you'll just sign this paper for me."

"There's no need. I'll not deny that you left him with me."

"Don't be mean with me. I know you'll tell the truth. You're from hereabouts and you are a man. But you must sign, that's the rule."

Daru opened his drawer, took out a little square bottle of purple ink, the red wooden penholder with the "sergeant-major" pen he used for making models of penmanship, and signed. The gendarme carefully folded the paper and put it into his wallet. Then he moved toward the door.

"I'll see you off," Daru said.

"No," said Balducci. "There's no use being polite. You insulted me."

He looked at the Arab, motionless in the same spot, sniffed peevishly, and turned away toward the door. "Good-by, son," he said. The door shut behind him. Balducci appeared suddenly outside the window and then disappeared. His footsteps were muffled by the snow. The horse stirred on the other side of the wall and several chickens fluttered in fright. A moment later Balducci reappeared outside the window leading the horse by the bridle. He walked toward the little rise without turning around and disappeared from sight with the horse following him. A big stone could be heard bouncing down. Daru walked back toward the prisoner, who, without stirring, never took his eyes off him. "Wait," the schoolmaster said in Arabic and went toward the bedroom. As he was going through the door, he had a second thought, went to the desk, took the revolver, and stuck it in his pocket. Then, without looking back, he went into his room.

For some time he lay on his couch watching the sky gradually close over, listening to the silence. It was this silence that had seemed painful to him during the first days here, after the war. He had requested a post in the little town at the base of the foothills separating the upper plateaus from the desert. There, rocky walls, green and black to the north, pink and lavender to the south, marked the frontier of eternal summer. He had been named to a post farther north, on the plateau itself. In the beginning, the solitude and the silence had been hard for him on these wastelands peopled only by stones. Occasionally, furrows suggested cultivation, but they had been dug to uncover a certain kind of stone good for building. The only plowing here was to harvest rocks. Elsewhere a thin layer of soil accumulated in the hollows would be scraped out to enrich paltry village gardens. This is the way it was: bare rock covered three quarters of the region. Towns sprang up, flourished, then disappeared; men came by, loved one another or fought bitterly, then died. No one in this desert, neither he nor his guest, mattered. And yet, outside this desert neither of them, Daru knew, could have really lived.

When he got up, no noise came from the classroom. He was amazed at the unmixed joy he derived from the mere thought that the Arab might have fled and that he would be alone with no decision to make. But the prisoner was there. He had merely stretched out between the stove and the desk. With eyes open, he was staring at the ceiling. In that position, his thick lips were particularly noticeable, giving him a pouting look. "Come," said Daru. The Arab got up and followed him. In the bedroom, the schoolmaster pointed to a chair near the table under the window. The Arab sat down without taking his eyes off Daru.

"Are you hungry?"

"Yes," the prisoner said.

Daru set the table for two. He took flour and oil, shaped a cake in a frying pan, and lighted the little stove that functioned on bottled gas. While the cake was cooking, he went out to the shed to get cheese, eggs, dates, and condensed milk. When the cake was done he set it on the window sill to cool, heated some condensed milk diluted with water, and beat up the eggs into an omelette. In one of his motions he knocked against the revolver stuck in his right pocket. He set the bowl down, went into the classroom, and put the revolver in his desk drawer. When he came back to the room, night was falling. He put on the light and served the Arab. "Eat," he said. The Arab took a piece of the cake, lifted it eagerly to his mouth, and stopped short.

"And you?" he asked.

"After you. I'll eat too."

The thick lips opened slightly. The Arab hesitated, then bit into the cake determinedly.

The meal over, the Arab looked at the schoolmaster. "Are you the judge?"

"No, I'm simply keeping you until tomorrow."

"Why do you eat with me?"

"I'm hungry."

The Arab fell silent. Daru got up and went out. He brought back a folding bed from the shed, set it up between the table and the stove, perpendicular to his own bed. From a large suitcase which, upright in a corner, served as a shelf for paper, he took two blankets and arranged them on the camp bed. Then he stopped, felt useless, and sat down on his bed. There was nothing more to do or to get ready. He had to look at this man. He looked at him, therefore, trying to imagine his face bursting with rage. He couldn't do so. He could see nothing but the dark yet shining eyes and the animal mouth.

"Why did you kill him?" he asked in a voice whose hostile tone surprised him.

The Arab looked away.

"He ran away. I ran after him."

He raised his eyes to Daru again and they were full of a sort of woeful inter-rogation. "Now what will they do to me?"

"Are you afraid?"

He stiffened, turning his eyes away.

"Are you sorry?"

The Arab stared at him openmouthed. Obviously he did not understand. Daru's annoyance was growing. At the same time he felt awkward and self-conscious with his big body wedged between the two beds.

"Lie down there," he said impatiently. "That's your bed."

The Arab didn't move. He called to Daru:

"Tell me!"

The schoolmaster looked at him.

"Is the gendarme coming back tomorrow?"

"I don't know."

"Are you coming with us?"

"I don't know. Why?"

The prisoner got up and stretched out on top of the blankets, his feet toward the window. The light from the electric bulb shone straight into his eyes and he closed them at once.

"Why?" Daru repeated, standing beside the bed.

The Arab opened his eyes under the blinding light and looked at him, try-ing not to blink.

"Come with us," he said.

In the middle of the night, Daru was still not asleep. He had gone to bed after undressing completely; he generally slept naked. But when he suddenly realized that he had nothing on, he hesitated. He felt vulnerable and the temp-tation came to him to put his clothes back on. Then he shrugged his shoulders; after all, he wasn't a child and, if need be, he could break his adversary in two. From his bed he could observe him, lying on his back, still motionless with his eyes closed under the harsh light. When Daru turned out the light, the darkness seemed to coagulate all of a sudden. Little by little, the night came back to life in the window where the starless sky was stirring gently. The schoolmaster soon made out the body lying at his feet. The Arab still did not move, but his eyes seemed open. A faint wind was prowling around the schoolhouse. Perhaps it would drive away the clouds and the sun would reappear.

During the night the wind increased. The hens fluttered a little and then were silent. The Arab turned over on his side with his back to Daru, who thought he heard him moan. Then he listened for his guest's breathing, become heavier and more regular. He listened to that breath so close to him and mused without being able to go to sleep. In this room where he had been sleeping alone for a year, this presence bothered him. But it bothered him also by imposing on him a sort of brotherhood he knew well but refused to accept in the present circumstances. Men who share the same rooms, soldiers or prisoners, develop a strange alliance as if, having cast off their armor with their clothing, they fraternized every evening, over and above their differences, in the ancient community of dream and fatigue. But Daru shook himself; he didn't like such musings, and it was essential to sleep.

A little later, however, when the Arab stirred slightly, the schoolmaster was still not asleep. When the prisoner made a second move, he stiffened, on the alert. The Arab was lifting himself slowly on his arms with almost the motion of a sleepwalker. Seated upright in bed, he waited motionless without turning his head toward Daru, as if he were listening attentively. Daru did not stir; it had just occurred to him that the revolver was still in the drawer of his desk. It was better to act at once. Yet he continued to observe the prisoner, who, with the same slithery motion, put his feet on the ground, waited again, then began to stand up slowly. Daru was about to call out to him when the Arab began to walk, in a quite natural but extraordinarily silent way. He was heading toward the door at the end of the room that opened into the shed. He lifted the latch with precaution and went out, pushing the door behind him but without shutting it. Daru had not stirred. "He is running away," he merely thought. "Good riddance!" Yet he listened attentively. The hens were not fluttering; the guest must be on the plateau. A faint sound of water reached him, and he didn't know what it was until the Arab again stood framed in the doorway, closed the door carefully, and came back to bed without a sound. Then Daru turned his back on him and fell asleep. Still later he seemed, from the depths of his sleep, to hear furtive steps around the schoolhouse. "I'm dreaming! I'm dreaming!" he repeated to himself. And he went on sleeping.

When he awoke, the sky was clear; the loose window let in a cold, pure air. The Arab was asleep, hunched up under the blankets now, his mouth open, utterly relaxed. But when Daru shook him, he started dreadfully, staring at Daru with wild eyes as if he had never seen him and such a frightened expression that the schoolmaster stepped back. "Don't be afraid. It's me. You must eat." The Arab nodded his head and said yes. Calm had returned to his face, but his expression was vacant and listless.

The coffee was ready. They drank it seated together on the folding bed as they munched their pieces of the cake. Then Daru led the Arab under the shed and showed him the faucet where he washed. He went back into the room, folded the blankets and the bed, made his own bed and put the room in order. Then he went through the classroom and out onto the terrace. The sun was already rising in the blue sky; a soft, bright light was bathing the deserted plateau. On the ride the snow was melting in spots. The stones were about to reappear. Crouched on the edge of the plateau, the schoolmaster looked at the deserted expanse. He thought of Balducci. He had hurt him, for he had sent him off in a way as if he didn't want to be associated with him. He could still hear the gendarme's farewell and, without knowing why, he felt strangely empty and vulnerable. At that moment, from the other side of the schoolhouse, the prisoner coughed. Daru listened to him almost despite himself and then, furious, threw a pebble that whistled through the air before sinking into the snow. That man's stupid crime revolted him, but to hand him over was contrary to honor. Merely thinking of it made him smart with humiliation. And he cursed at one and the same time his own people who had sent him this Arab and the Arab too who had dared to kill and not managed to get away. Daru got up, walked in a circle on the terrace, waited motionless, and then went back into the schoolhouse.

The Arab, leaning over the cement floor of the shed, was washing his teeth with two fingers. Daru looked at him and said: "Come." He went back into the room ahead of the prisoner. He slipped a hunting-jacket on over his sweater and put on walking-shoes. Standing he waited until the Arab had put on his *chèche* and sandals. They went into the classroom and the schoolmaster pointed to the exit, saying: "Go ahead." The fellow didn't budge. "I'm coming," said Daru. The Arab went out. Daru went back into the room and made a package of pieces of rusk, dates, and sugar. In the classroom, before going out, he hesitated a second in front of his desk, then crossed the threshold and locked the door. "That's the way," he said. He started toward the east, followed by the prisoner. But, a short distance from the schoolhouse, he thought he heard a slight sound behind them. He retraced his steps and examined the surroundings of the house; there was no one there. The Arab watched him without seeming to understand. "Come on," said Daru.

They walked for an hour and rested beside a sharp peak of limestone. The snow was melting faster and faster and the sun was drinking up the puddles at once, rapidly cleaning the plateau, which gradually dried and vibrated like the air itself. When they resumed walking, the ground rang under their feet. From time to time a bird rent the space in front of them with a joyful cry. Daru breathed in deeply the fresh morning light. He felt a sort of rapture before the vast familiar expanse, now almost entirely yellow under its dome of blue sky. They walked an hour more, descending toward the south. They reached a level height made up of crumbly rocks. From there on, the plateau sloped down, east-ward, toward a low plain where there were a few spindly trees and, to the south, toward outcroppings of rock that gave the landscape a chaotic look.

Daru surveyed the two directions. There was nothing but the sky on the horizon. Not a man could be seen. He turned toward the Arab, who was looking at him blankly. Daru held out the package to him. "Take it," he said. "There are dates, bread, and sugar. You can hold out for two days. Here are a thousand francs too." The Arab took the package and the money but kept his full hands at chest level as if he didn't know what do to with what was being given him. "Now look," the schoolmaster said as he pointed in the direction of the east, "there's the way to Tinguit. You have a two-hour walk. At Tinguit you'll find the administration and the police. They are expecting you." The Arab looked toward the east, still holding the package and the money against his chest. Daru took his elbow and turned him rather roughly toward the south. At the foot of the height on which they stood could be seen a faint path. "That's the trail across the plateau. In a day's walk from here you'll find pasturelands and the first nomads. They'll take you in and shelter you according to their law." The Arab had now turned toward Daru and a sort of panic was visible in his expression. "Listen," he said. Daru shook his head; "No, be quiet. Now I'm leaving you." He turned his back on him, took two long steps in the direction of the school, looked hesitantly at the motionless Arab, and started off again. For a few minutes he heard nothing but his own step resounding on the cold ground and did not turn his head. A moment later, however, he turned around. The Arab was still there on the edge of the hill, his arms hanging now, and he was looking at the schoolmaster. Daru felt something rise in his throat. But he swore with impatience, waved vaguely, and started off again. He had already gone some distance when he again stopped and looked. There was no longer anyone on the hill.

Daru hesitated. The sun was now rather high in the sky and was beginning to beat down on his head. The schoolmaster retraced his steps, at first somewhat uncertainly, then with decision. When he reached the little hill, he was bathed in sweat. He climbed it as fast as he could and stopped, out of breath, at the top. The rock-fields to the south stood out sharply against the blue sky, but on the plain to the east a steamy heat was already rising. And in that slight haze, Daru, with heavy heart, made out the Arab walking slowly on the road to prison.

A little later, standing before the window of the classroom, the schoolmaster was watching the clear light bathing the whole surface of the plateau, but he hardly saw it. Behind him on the blackboard, among the winding French rivers, sprawled the clumsily chalked-up words he had just read: "You handed over our brother. You will pay for this." Daru looked at the sky, the plateau, and beyond, the invisible lands stretching all the way to the sea. In this vast landscape he had loved so much, he was alone.

UNDERSTANDING THE STORY

1. Explain the relationship between Daru's surroundings and his personality. What is most important to Daru? Why does he feel exiled from the rest of the world?

2. What is the principal **conflict** in the story, and how is it resolved?

3. Why does Balducci think that Daru has "always been a little cracked"? Why does Balducci give Daru freedom of choice?

4. Why does the Arab's crime revolt Daru? Why then does he treat the Arab as his guest?

5. Why does Daru find the idea of taking the Arab to the government officials in Tinguit to be contrary to his sense of honor and humiliating?

6. What difference does it make that despite all the suspense, fear, and allusion to violence, Camus omits violence from the story?

7. To what extent, if any, is the end tragic? Why does Camus use the words "had loved" instead of "loved" in describing the landscape?

8. Camus liked the fact that, in French, the same word means both "guest" and "host." Why might the translator have chosen to call the story "The Guest"? To what extent, if any, would "The Host" be a better title?

ANALYZING LITERARY TECHNIQUE

1. What is Balducci's function in this story?
2. How does Camus create an environment of suspense and fear in the story?
3. How does the political setting of the story affect the plot?
4. What does the **point of view** contribute to the story?
5. Choose two or three examples of **irony** and explain their function in the story.
6. The author of an **allegory** expects readers to look for meaning below the surface of the story. To what extent can this story be considered an allegory? Consider Daru's physical environment as symbolic of Camus's universe and Daru himself as symbolic of the human condition.

WRITING ABOUT LITERATURE

1. Write a brief essay in which you apply the following statement from "Meditation XVII" by the English poet John Donne (1571?–1631) to Daru's experience in "The Guest." Consider Daru's attitudes and goals, his behavior, and his fate.

   > No man is an island, entire of itself; every man is a piece of the Continent, a part of the main; if a clod be washed away by the sea, Europe is the less, as well as if a promontory were, as well as if a manor of thy friends or of thine own were; any man's death diminishes me, because I am involved in Mankind; And therefore never send to know for whom the bell tolls; It tolls for thee.

2. Write an essay explaining whether you think Daru was right to act as he did. Consider whether he would have acted differently if he had foreseen the note on his blackboard. Use quotations from the story to support your arguments.
3. Tell the story of "The Guest" from the Arab's point of view. Consider such questions as the following: How does the Arab view Daru? Why does the Arab reject the option of freedom? What relationship is there between his crime and his decision to turn himself in to the authorities?

Africa

THE LITERATURE OF AFRICA addresses a range of emotional issues, such as the conflict between races or between traditional culture and new ideas, in gripping and poignant ways.

The division between black and white has long been an issue in African culture. Two noted writers use different approaches to touch on this difficult subject. Alan Paton, in his short story "A Drink in the Passage," simultaneously convinces us of the humanity of both sides of the racial barrier and of the difficulty—even for the best-intentioned people—in overcoming that barrier. In "Good Climate, Friendly Inhabitants," Nadine Gordimer demonstrates how some people cannot see past the color line to find the true value and character of others.

A second theme that comes through in African literature is the tension between traditional and contemporary behavior. In "Mista Courifer," Adelaide Casely-Hayford uses humor and irony to depict the generation gap as a young man decides to stand up for his convictions. In Chinua Achebe's "Marriage Is a Private Affair," the conflict between tradition and contemporary behavior is poignantly drawn as a father and son struggle with handling the conflict that arises between them when the son chooses his own bride instead of accepting the bride his father has chosen for him. The characters in Grace Ogot's "The Rain Came" struggle with the needs of the individual versus the good of society as they question traditional patterns of behavior. Bessie Head's short story "The Lovers" operates on two levels. On one level, it is a romantic story of a young man and a young woman who choose to love each other in spite of the objections of their tribe; on a deeper level, it is the story of a society crippled by its devotion to traditions that control human behavior.

In contrast to writers who focus on the struggles that Africans face are writers who celebrate the heritage and accomplishments of the people of Africa. This is particularly true of the authors belonging to the Négritude movement. In the poem "Dry Your Tears, Africa!" Bernard Dadié personifies Africa as a loving mother and Africans who have left their homeland as her children. Léopold Sédar Senghor calls on Africans in his poem "Prayer to Masks" to have pride in their heritage and to recognize that they have a unique contribution to make in the world.

The place of human beings in the universe is another theme in African literature. In Doris Lessing's coming-of-age story "A Sunrise on the Veld," a boy's feelings of control and power in a benign universe give way to his awareness of nature as a separate entity as he comes to an understanding that both animals and humans are part of the totality of the universe. The "Song for the Dead" from the Dahomean culture, on the other hand, celebrates life; the poem, recognizing that all people share an inevitable mortality, expresses the importance of enjoying life.

Finally, in *The Trials of Brother Jero*, the farcical play by Wole Soyinka, the weaknesses of all humans are exposed as every character tries to cope with the ordinary problems of life.

Song for the Dead

DAHOMEY (Traditional)

Now known as the country of Benin, the ancient kingdom of Dahomey was formed in 1625, when Dako, the chief of the Fon nation, conquered the two city-states Calmina and Abomey. Dako began his conquests by disregarding the sacred laws of hospitality and murdering his guest, the chief of the Calmina nation. Dako then conquered Calmina and attacked Abomey. He killed Da, the chief of the Abomey, by slashing his stomach. Dako then built a palace for himself in Abomey, placed Da's corpse beneath its foundation, and called the structure Dahomey (*Da* refers to the Abomey chief, and *homey* means "belly.")

The Dahomeans were viewed by their Yoruba and Mahi neighbors as a formidable military power because of their great courage and skill in battle. European visitors who arrived early in the eighteenth century were impressed by the existence of a newly established women's army. This army was still flourishing a century later.

Melville and Frances Herskovits gathered a large collection of Dahomean myths, histories, tales, songs, and riddles, which Northwestern University Press published as *Dahomean Narrative* in 1958 (republished in 1981). The following "Song for the Dead" comes from this collection. The song has no author because it is part of the oral tradition of Dahomey.

I see it,
There is no enjoying beyond Death,
And I say to all of you say,
That which your senses taste of Life
Goes with you.   5

I say to you say
The wives you have,
The passion you know of them
Goes with you.

I say to you say   10
The drinks you drink,
The pleasure of them
Goes with you.

I say to you say
The meats you eat,   15
The relish you have of them
Goes with you.

I say to you say
The pipes you smoke,
The quiet they bring   20
Goes with you.

Come, then
Dance all the colors of Life
For a lover of pleasure
Now dead.   25

UNDERSTANDING THE POEM

1. Why do the Dahomeans dance for the dead?

2. What attitude toward life or what theme does the song express?

ANALYZING LITERARY TECHNIQUE

1. What is appropriate about the metaphor "all the colors of Life"?

2. What is the effect of repetition in the song?

3. Why are the stanzas arranged in this order?

WRITING ABOUT LITERATURE

1. Analyze the organization of the poem. In what way is the poem's structure like the structure of an expository essay?

2. Write an essay or a poem that expresses the Dahomean philosophy of life or another philosophy of life. Make sure that you state your central idea and provide supporting details. What **metaphors** or images are appropriate to the philosophy you wish to express?

Mista Courifer

ADELAIDE CASELY-HAYFORD

ADELAIDE CASELY-HAYFORD (1868–1959) was a member of an educated and well-known literary family in Ghana. She was one of the first Africans to write literary works in English. Her stories reveal her talent for observing and evaluating the life around her. She was interested in the various ways her people reacted to the fact that their country, with a heritage of its own, was a British colony. She herself found admirable customs among both the English and the Africans, and she was comfortable blending the best of both worlds. With her lively prose style, she deftly and sympathetically examines attitudes and behaviors prevalent among her people and captures the multifaceted nature of human experience.

The story "Mista Courifer" is set in the country of Sierra Leone, which, like Ghana, was a British colony. Sierra Leone gained its independence in 1961, after the time of this story.

Not a sound was heard in the coffin-maker's workshop, that is to say no human sound. Mista Courifer, a solid citizen of Sierra Leone, was not given to much speech. His apprentices, knowing this, never dared address him unless he spoke first. Then they only carried on their conversation in whispers. Not that Mista Courifer did not know how to use his tongue. It was incessantly wagging to and fro in his mouth at every blow of the hammer. But his shop in the heart of Freetown[1] was a part of his house. And, as he had once confided to a friend, he was a silent member of his own household from necessity. His wife, given to much speaking, could out-talk him.

---

[1] *Freetown:* Capital of Sierra Leone.

"It's no use for argue wid woman," he said cautiously. "Just like 'e no use for teach woman carpentering; she nebba sabi[2] for hit de nail on de head. If 'e argue, she'll hit eberything but de nail; and so wid de carpentering."

So, around his wife, with the exception of his tongue's continual wagging like a pendulum, his mouth was kept more or less shut. But whatever self-control he exercised in this respect at home was completely sent to the wind in his official capacity as the local preacher at chapel, for Mista Courifer was one of the pillars of the church, being equally at home in conducting a prayer meeting, superintending the Sunday school or occupying the pulpit.

His voice was remarkable for its wonderful gradations of pitch. He would insist on starting most of his tunes himself; consequently they nearly always ended in a solo. If he happened to pitch in the bass, he descended into such a de profundis[3] that his congregations were left to flounder in a higher key; if he started in the treble, he soared so high that the children stared at him open-mouthed and their elders were lost in wonder and amazement. As for his prayers, he roared and volleyed and thundered to such an extent that poor little mites were quickly reduced to a state of collapse and started to whimper from sheer fright.

But he was most at home in the pulpit. It is true, his labours were altogether confined to the outlying village districts of Regent, Gloucester and Leicester, an arrangement with which he was by no means satisfied. Still, a village congregation is better than none at all.

His favourite themes were Jonah and Noah[4] and he was for ever pointing out the great similarity between the two, generally finishing his discourse after this manner: "You see my beloved Brebren,[5] den two man berry much alike. All two lived in a sinful and adulterous generation. One get inside an ark; de odder one get inside a whale. Day bof seek a refuge from de swelling waves.

"And so it is today my beloved Brebren. No matter if we get inside a whale or get inside an ark, as long as we get inside some place of safety—as long as we can find some refuge, some hiding-place from de wiles ob de debil."

But his congregation was by no means convinced.

Mr. Courifer always wore black. He was one of the Sierra Leone gentlemen who consider everything European to be not only the right thing, but the *only* thing for the African, and having read somewhere that English undertakers generally appeared in sombre attire, he immediately followed suit.

He even went so far as to build a European house. During his short stay in England, he had noticed how the houses were built and furnished and had forthwith erected himself one after the approved pattern—a house with stuffy little

---

[2] *sabi:* Savvy; understand.

[3] de profundis: Out of the depths.

[4] *Jonah and Noah:* Two characters from the Bible. Jonah, an Israelite prophet who resisted a call to preach, was swallowed by a great fish. When he repented, he was vomited up, and then he fulfilled his mission. Noah was warned by God that there would be a great flood. He built an ark (ship) to save his family and one pair of every living creature.

[5] *Brebren:* Brethren.

passages, narrow little staircases and poky rooms, all crammed with saddlebags and carpeted with Axminsters. No wonder his wife had to talk. It was so hopelessly uncomfortable, stuffy and insanitary.

So Mr. Courifer wore black. It never struck him for a single moment that red would have been more appropriate, far more becoming, far less expensive and far more national. No! It must be black. He would have liked blue-black, but he wore rusty black for economy.

There was one subject upon which Mr. Courifer could talk even at home, so no one ever mentioned it: his son, Tomas. Mista Courifer had great expectations of his son; indeed in the back of his mind he had hopes of seeing him reach the high-water mark of red-tape officialism, for Tomas was in the government service. Not very high up, it is true, but still he was in it. It was an honour that impressed his father deeply, but Tomas unfortunately did not seem to think quite so much of it. The youth in question, however, was altogether neutral in his opinions in his father's presence. Although somewhat feminine as to attire, he was distinctly masculine in his speech. His neutrality was not a matter of choice, since no one was allowed to choose anything in the Courifer family but the paterfamilias[6] himself.

From start to finish, Tomas's career had been cut out, and in spite of the fact that nature had endowed him with a black skin and an African temperament, Tomas was to be an Englishman. He was even to be an Englishman in appearance.

Consequently, once a year mysterious bundles arrived by parcel post. When opened, they revealed marvellous checks and plaids in vivid greens and blues after the fashion of a Liverpool counterjumper,[7] waistcoats decorative in the extreme with their bold designs and rows of brass buttons, socks vying with the rainbow in glory and pumps very patent in appearance and very fragile as to texture.

Now, Tomas was no longer a minor and he keenly resented having his clothes chosen for him like a boy going to school for the first time. Indeed on one occasion, had it not been for his sister's timely interference, he would have chucked the whole collection into the fire.

Dear little Keren-happuch, eight years his junior and not at all attractive, with a very diminutive body and a very large heart. Such a mistake! People's hearts ought always to be in proportion to their size, otherwise it upsets the dimensions of the whole structure and often ends in its total collapse.

Keren was that type of little individual whom nobody worshipped, consequently she understood the art of worshipping others to the full. Tomas was the object of her adoration. Upon him she lavished the whole store of her boundless wealth and whatever hurt Tomas became positive torture as far as Keren-happuch was concerned.

"Tomas!" she said, clinging to him with the tenacity of a bear, as she saw the faggots piled up high, ready for the conflagration, "Do yah! No burn am oh! Ole

---

[6] *paterfamilias:* Male head of a household.

[7] *Liverpool counterjumper:* A salesclerk in Liverpool, a northern industrial city in England; in other words, not a very fashionable person.

man go flog you oh! Den clos berry fine! I like am myself too much. I wish"—she added wistfully—"me na boy; I wish I could use am."

This was quite a new feature which had never struck Tomas before. Keren-happuch had never received a bundle of English clothes in her life, hence her great appreciation of them.

At first Tomas only laughed—the superior, dare-devil, don't-care-a-damn-about-consequences laugh of the brave before the dead. But after hearing that wistful little sentence, he forgot his own annoyance and awoke to his responsibilities as an elder brother.

A few Sundays later, Tomas Courifer, Jr., marched up the aisle of the little Wesleyan chapel[8] in all his Liverpool magnificence accompanied by a very elated little Keren-happuch whose natural unattractiveness had been further accentuated by a vivid cerise costume—a heterogeneous mass of frill and furbelows. But the glory of her array by no means outshone the brightness of her smile. Indeed that smile seemed to illuminate the whole church and to dispel the usual melancholy preceding the recital of Jonah and his woes.

Unfortunately, Tomas had a very poor opinion of the government service and in a burst of confidence he had told Keren that he meant to chuck it at the very first opportunity. In vain his sister expostulated and pointed out the advantages connected with it—the honour, the pension—and the awful nemesis upon the head of anyone incurring the head-of-the-family's ire.

"Why you want to leave am, Tomas?" she asked desperately.

"Because I never get a proper holiday. I have been in the office four and a half years and have never had a whole week off yet. And," he went on vehemently, "these white chaps come and go, and a fresh one upsets what the old one has done and a newcomer upsets what he does and they all only stay for a year and a half and go away for four months, drawing big fat pay all the time, not to speak of passages, whereas a poor African like me has to work year in and year out with never a chance of a decent break. But you needn't be afraid, Keren dear," he added consolingly, "I shan't resign, I shall just behave so badly that they'll chuck me and then my ole man can't say very much."

Accordingly, when Tomas, puffing a cigarette, sauntered into the office at 9 A.M. instead of 8 A.M. for the fourth time that week, Mr. Buckmaster, who had hitherto maintained a discreet silence and kept his eyes shut, opened them wide and administered a sharp rebuke. Tomas's conscience was profoundly stirred. Mr. Buckmaster was one of the few white men for whom he had a deep respect, aye, in the depth of his heart, he really had a sneaking regard. It was for fear of offending him that he had remained so long at his post.

But he had only lately heard that his chief was due for leave so he decided there and then to say a long good-bye to a service which had treated him so shabbily. He was a vociferous reader of half penny newspapers and he knew that the humblest shop assistant in England was entitled to a fortnight's holiday every year. Therefore it was ridiculous to argue that because he was an African working in Africa there

[8] *Wesleyan chapel:* Methodist church.

was no need for a holiday. All his applications for leave were quietly pigeon-holed for a more convenient season.

"Courifer!" Mr. Buckmaster said sternly. "Walk into my private office, please." And Courifer knew that this was the beginning of the end.

"I suppose you know that the office hours are from 8 A.M. till 4 P.M. daily?" commenced Mr. Buckmaster, in a freezing tone.

"Yes, er-sir!" stammered Courifer with his heart in his mouth and his mouth twisted up into a hard sailor's knot.

"And I suppose you also know that smoking is strictly forbidden in the office?"

"Yes, er-er-sir!" stammered the youth.

"Now hitherto," the even tones went on, "I have always looked upon you as an exemplary clerk, strictly obliging, punctual, accurate and honest, but for the last two or three weeks I have had nothing but complaints about you. And from what I myself have seen, I am afraid they are not altogether unmerited."

Mr. Buckmaster rose as he spoke, took a bunch of keys out of his pocket and, unlocking his roll-top desk, drew out a sheaf of papers. "This is your awful work, is it not?" he said to the youth.

"Yes, er-er-sir!" he stuttered, looking shamefacedly at the dirty ink-stained blotched sheets of closely typewritten matter.

"Then what in heaven's name is the matter with you to produce such work?"

Tomas remained silent for a moment or two. He summoned up courage to look boldly at the stern countenance of his chief. And as he looked, the sternness seemed to melt and he could see genuine concern there.

"Please, er-sir!" he stammered, "may-I-er-just tell you everything?"

Half an hour later, a very quiet, subdued, penitent Tomas Courifer walked out of the office by a side door. Mr. Buckmaster followed later, taking with him an increased respect for the powers of endurance exercised by the growing West African youth.

Six weeks later, Mista Courifer was busily occupied wagging his tongue when he looked up from his work to see a European man standing in his doorway.

The undertaker found speech and a chair simultaneously. "Good afternoon, sah!" he said, dusting the chair before offering it to his visitor. "I hope you don't want a coffin, sah!" which was a deep-sea lie for nothing pleased him more than the opportunity of making a coffin for a European. He was always so sure of the money. Such handsome money—paid it is true with a few ejaculations, but paid on the nail and without any deductions whatsoever. Now with his own people things were different. They demurred, they haggled, they bartered, they gave him detailed accounts of all their other expenses and then, after keeping him waiting for weeks, they would end by sending him half the amount with a stern exhortation to be thankful for that.

Mr. Buckmaster took the proffered chair and answered pleasantly: "No thank you, I don't intend dying just yet. I happened to be passing so I thought I should just like a word with you about your son."

Mr. Courifer bristled all over with exultation and expectation. Perhaps they were going to make his son a kind of under-secretary of state. What an unexpected honour for the Courifer family. What a rise in their social status; what a rise out of their neighbours. How good God was!

"Of course you know he is in my office?"

"Oh yes, sah. He often speaks about you."

"Well, I am going home soon and as I may not be returning to Sierra Leone I just wanted to tell you how pleased I should be at any time to give him a decent testimonial."

Mr. Courifer's countenance fell. What a come-down!

"Yes, sah," he answered somewhat dubiously.

"I can recommend him highly as being steady, persevering, reliable and trustworthy. And you can always apply to me if ever such a thing be necessary."

Was that all! What a disappointment! Still it was something worth having. Mr. Buckmaster was an Englishman and a testimonial from him would certainly be a very valuable possession. He rubbed his hands together as he said: "Well, I am berry much obliged to you, sah, berry much obliged. And as time is short and we nebba know what a day may bring forth, would you mind writing one down now, sah?"

"Certainly. If you will give me a sheet of paper, I shall do so at once."

Before Tomas returned home from his evening work, the testimonial was already framed and hanging up amidst the moth-eaten velvet of the drawing-room.

On the following Monday morning, Courifer Jr. bounced into his father's workshop, upsetting the equilibrium of the carpenter's bench and also of the voiceless apprentices hard at work.

"Well, sah?" ejaculated his father, surveying him in disgust. "You berry late. Why you no go office dis morning?"

"Because I've got a whole two month's holiday, sir! Just think of it—two whole months—with nothing to do but just enjoy myself!"

"Tomas," his father said solemnly, peering at him over his glasses, "you must larn for make coffins. You get fine chance now."

Sotto voce:[9] "I'll be damned if I will!" Aloud: "No thank you, sir. I am going to learn how to make love, after which I am going to learn how to build myself a nice mud hut."

"And who dis gal you want married?" thundered his father, ignoring the latter part of the sentence altogether.

A broad smile illuminated Tomas's countenance. "She is a very nice girl, sir, a very nice girl. Very quiet and gentle and sweet, and she doesn't talk too much."

"I see. Is dat all?"

"Oh, no. She can sew and clean and make a nice home. And she has plenty sense; she will make a good mother."

"Yes, notting pass dat!"

"She has been to school for a long time. She reads nice books and she writes, oh, such a nice letter," said Tomas, patting his breast-pocket affectionately.

"I see. I suppose she sabi cook good fashion?"

---

[9] sotto voce: In an undertone.

"I don't know, I don't think so, and it doesn't matter very much."

"What!" roared the old man, "you mean tell me you want married woman who no sabi cook?"

"I want to marry her because I love her, sir!"

"Dat's all right, but for we country, de heart and de stomach always go to-gedder. For we country, black man no want married woman who no sabi cook! Dat de berry first requisitional. You own mudder sabi cook."

That's the reason why she has been nothing but your miserable drudge all these years, thought the young man. His face was very grave as he rejoined: "The style in our country is not at all nice, sir. I don't like to see a wife slaving away in the kitchen all times to make good chop for her husband who sits down alone and eats the best of everything himself, and she and the children only get the leavings. No thank you! And besides, sir, you are always telling me that you want me to be an Englishman. That is why I always try to talk good English to you."

"Yes, dat's all right. Dat's berry good. But I want make you *look* like Englishman. I don't say you must copy all der different way!"

"Well, sir, if I try till I die, I shall never look like an Englishman, and I don't know that I want to. But there are some English customs that I like very much indeed. I like the way white men treat their wives; I like their home life; I like to see mother and father and the little family all sitting down eating their meals together."

"I see," retorted his father sarcastically. "And who go cook den meal. You tink say wid your four pound[10] a month, you go able hire a perfessional cook?"

"Oh, I don't say so, sir. And I am sure if Accastasua does not know how to cook now, she will before we are married. But what I want you to understand is just this, that whether she is able to cook or not, I shall marry her just the same."

"Berry well," shouted his father, wrath delineated in every feature, "but instead of building one mud hut you better go one time build one madhouse."

"Sir, thank you. But I know what I am about and a mud hut will suit us perfectly for the present."

"A mud hut!" ejaculated his father in horror. "You done use fine England house wid staircase and balustrade and tick carpet and handsome furnitures. You want to go live in mud hut? You ungrateful boy, you shame me, oh!"

"Dear me, no sir! I won't shame you. It's going to be a nice clean spacious mud hut. And what is more, it is going to be a sweet little home, just big enough for two. I am going to distemper the walls pale green, like at the principal's rooms at Keren's school."

"How you sabi den woman's rooms?"

"Because you have sent me two or three times to pay her school fees, so I have looked at those walls and I like them too much."

"I see. And what else you go do?" asked his father ironically.

"I am going to order some nice wicker chairs from the Islands and a few good pieces of linoleum for the floors and then. . . ."

---

[10] *pound:* Unit of money in the United Kingdom.

"And den what?"

"I shall bring home my bride."

Mr. Courifer's dejection grew deeper with each moment. A mud hut! This son of his—the hope of his life! A government officer! A would-be Englishman! To live in a mud hut! His disgust knew no bounds. "You ungrateful wretch!" he bellowed. "You go disgrace me. You go lower your pore father. You go lower your position for de office."

"I am sorry, sir," retorted the young man. "I don't wish to offend you. I'm grateful for all you have done for me. But I have had a raise in salary and I want a home of my own which, after all, is only natural, and"—he went on steadily, staring his father straight in the face—"I am as well tell you at once, you need not order any more Liverpool suits for me."

"Why not?" thundered his irate parent, removing his specs lest any harm should befall them.

"Well, I am sorry to grieve you, sir, but I have been trying to live up to your European standards all this time. Now I am going to chuck it once and for all. I am going back to the native costume of my mother's people, and the next time I appear in chapel it will be as a Wolof."[11]

The very next Sunday the awful shock of seeing his son walk up the aisle of the church in pantaloons and the bright loose over-jacket of a Wolof from Gambia, escorting a pretty young bride the colour of chocolate, also in native dress, so unnerved Mista Courifer that his mind suddenly became a complete blank. He could not even remember Jonah and the whale, nor could his tongue possess one word to let fly, not one. The service had to be turned into a prayer meeting.

Mista Courifer is the local preacher no longer. Now he only makes coffins.

UNDERSTANDING THE STORY

1. Why does Mista Courifer value certain English styles more than African styles? What does this reveal about him?

2. What factors lead Tomas to oppose his father's values? What does this reveal about Tomas?

3. What kind of a father has Mista Courifer been?

4. Compare and contrast the characters of Tomas and his father.

5. What factors lead Tomas to change his mind about his job?

6. If preaching is the occupation Mista Courifer prefers, why does he give it up?

7. What is the author's attitude toward Mista Courifer?

8. What is the author's attitude toward Tomas?

---

[11] *Wolof:* A people in the country of Gambia.

9. Why is the story named for the father rather than for the son?

10. What **themes** do you find in this story?

ANALYZING LITERARY TECHNIQUE

1. What is the symbolic connection between Mista Courifer's favorite sermons and his life experience?

2. How does the author's attitude toward Mista Courifer's values affect the tone of the story?

3. What is Keren-happuch's function in the story?

4. Find two examples of **humor** and explain what each contributes to the story.

5. Find two or three examples of **irony** and explain their function in the story.

WRITING ABOUT LITERATURE

1. Write an essay in which you analyze Casely-Hayford's use of irony or humor in "Mista Courifer." How does irony or humor enable her to treat the story's serious themes? In your essay, examine three examples of irony or humor, using quotations and explaining what each contributes to the story. In your conclusion, evaluate what irony or humor contributes to the story as a whole.

2. Imagine life in the Courifer family after Tomas's marriage. Write a letter from Keren-happuch to a cousin in which she relates what has happened between Tomas and his father and how the matter ends. Do father and son come to a mutual understanding? If so, how does this occur? If not, why not?

A Drink in
the Passage

ALAN PATON

LAN PATON (1903–1988), the important South African novelist, brought worldwide attention to the tragedy of apartheid with his poignant and lyrical novel *Cry, the Beloved Country* (1948). It became an international classic and was made into the stage musical *Lost in the Stars* (1949) and a motion picture (1952). Paton is also known for another fine novel, *Too Late the Phalarope* (1953).

Paton was born in Pietermaritzburg, in the Republic of South Africa. After attending the University of Natal, he became a school-teacher. In the 1930s, he became interested in delinquent youths, and in 1935 he became the principal of a model reformatory for black delinquents near Johannesburg. After World War II, while Paton was visiting reformatories in Europe and studying prison reform, he became homesick and wrote *Cry, the Beloved Country*. Its success led him to become a professional writer. Meanwhile, he became actively involved in politics. Paton was president of the South African Liberal Party, which advocated the establishment of a multiracial democracy through constitutional nonviolent procedures, from the party's inception in 1953 until it was outlawed by the government in 1968.

In his writing, Paton explores the relationship between whites and blacks in his country. He is concerned about "the tragic plight of black-skinned people in a white man's world." Paton's stories are poignant reminders that many able and sensitive people of goodwill do their best to improve the society in which they live, but they find their efforts frustrated by the wall that divides the two races. His works ask for mutual understanding and cooperative effort to achieve justice for all. "A Drink in the Passage," from his collection of short stories *Tales from a Troubled Land* (1961), is an excellent example of his work.

In the year 1960 the Union of South Africa celebrated its Golden Jubilee,[1] and there was a nation-wide sensation when the one-thousand pound[2] prize for the finest piece of sculpture was won by a black man, Edward Simelane. His work, *African Mother and Child,* not only excited the admiration, but touched the conscience or heart or whatever it is, of white South Africa, and was likely to make him famous in other countries.

It was by an oversight that his work was accepted, for it was the policy of the Government that all the celebrations and competitions should be strictly segregated. The committee of the sculpture section received a private reprimand for having been so careless as to omit the words "for whites only" from the conditions, but was told, by a very high personage it is said, that if Simelane's work "was indisputably the best," it should receive the award. The committee then decided that this prize must be given along with the others, at the public ceremony which would bring this particular part of the celebrations to a close.

For this decision it received a surprising amount of support from the white public, but in certain powerful quarters, there was an outcry against any departure from the "traditional policies" of the country, and a threat that many white prize-winners would renounce their prizes. However a crisis was averted, because the sculptor was "unfortunately unable to attend the ceremony."

> *"I wasn't feeling up to it," Simelane said mischievously to me. "My parents, and my wife's parents, and our priest, decided that I wasn't feeling up to it. And finally I decided so too. Of course Majosi and Sola and the others wanted me to go and get my prize personally, but I said, 'boys I'm a sculptor, not a demonstrator.'*
>
> *"This cognac is wonderful," he said, "especially in these big glasses. It's the first time I've had such a glass. It's also the first time I've drunk a brandy so slowly. In Orlando you develop a throat of iron, and you just put back your head and pour it down, in case the police should arrive."*
>
> *He said to me, "This is the second cognac I've had in my life. Would you like to hear the story of how I had my first?"*

*****

You know the Alabaster Bookshop in von Brandis Street? Well, after the competition they asked me if they could exhibit my *African Mother and Child.* They gave a whole window to it, with a white velvet backdrop, if there is anything in the world called white velvet, and some complimentary words, *black man conquers white world.*

---

[1] *Golden Jubilee:* Fiftieth anniversary.

[2] *pound:* Unit of money in the United Kingdom.

Well somehow I could never go and look in that window. On my way from the station to the *Herald* office, I sometimes went past there, and I felt good when I saw all the people standing there, but I would only squint at it out of the corner of my eye.

Then one night I was working late at the *Herald*, and when I came out there was hardly anyone in the streets, so I thought I'd go and see the window, and indulge certain pleasurable human feelings. I must have got a little lost in the contemplation of my own genius, because suddenly there was a young white man standing next to me.

He said to me, "What do you think of that, mate?" And you know, one doesn't get called "mate" every day.

"I'm looking at it," I said.

"I live near here," he said, "and I come and look at it nearly every night. You know it's by one of your own boys, don't you? See, Edward Simelane."

"Yes, I know."

"It's beautiful," he said. "Look at that mother's head. She's loving that child, but she's somehow watching too. Do you see that? Like someone guarding. She knows it won't be an easy life."

He cocked his head on one side, to see the thing better.

"He got a thousand pounds for it," he said. "That's a lot of money for one of your boys. But good luck to him. You don't get much luck, do you?"

Then he said confidentially, "Mate, would you like a drink?"

Well honestly I didn't feel like a drink at that time of night, with a white stranger and all, and me still with a train to catch to Orlando.

"You know we black people must be out of the city by eleven," I said.

"It won't take long. My flat's just around the corner. Do you speak Afrikaans?"[3]

"Since I was a child," I said in Afrikaans.

"We'll speak Afrikaans then. My English isn't too wonderful. I'm van Rensburg. And you?"

I couldn't have told him my name. I said I was Vakalisa, living in Orlando. "Vakalisa, eh? I haven't heard that name before."

By this time he had started off, and I was following, but not willingly. That's my trouble, as you'll soon see. I can't break off an encounter. We didn't exactly walk abreast, but he didn't exactly walk in front of me. He didn't look constrained. He wasn't looking around to see if anyone might be watching.

He said to me, "Do you know what I wanted to do?"

"No," I said.

---

[3] *Afrikaans:* Language related to Dutch that is one of the official languages of South Africa.

"I wanted a bookshop, like that one there. I always wanted that, ever since I can remember. When I was small, I had a little shop of my own." He laughed at himself. "Some were real books, of course, but some of them I wrote myself. But I had bad luck. My parents died before I could finish school."

Then he said to me, "Are you educated?"

I said unwillingly, "Yes." Then I thought to myself, how stupid, for leaving the question open.

And sure enough he said, "Far?"

And again unwillingly, I said, "Far."

He took a big leap and said, "Degree?"

"Yes."

"Literature?"

"Yes."

He expelled his breath, and gave a long "ah." We had reached his building, Majorca Mansions, not one of those luxurious places. I was glad to see that the entrance lobby was deserted. I wasn't at my ease. I don't feel at my ease in such places, not unless I am protected by friends, and this man was a stranger. The lift was at ground level, marked "Whites only. Slegs vir Blankes."[4] van Rensburg opened the door and waved me in. Was he constrained? To this day I don't know. While I was waiting for him to press the button, so that we could get moving and away from that ground floor, he stood with his finger suspended over it, and looked at me with a kind of honest, unselfish envy.

"You were lucky," he said. "Literature, that's what I wanted to do."

He shook his head and pressed the button, and he didn't speak again until we stopped high up. But before we got out he said suddenly, "If I had had a bookshop, I'd have given that boy a window too."

We got out and walked along one of those polished concrete passageways, I suppose you could call it a stoep[5] if it weren't so high up, let's call it a passage. On the one side was a wall, and plenty of fresh air, and far down below von Brandis Street. On the other side were the doors, impersonal doors; you could hear radio and people talking, but there wasn't a soul in sight. I wouldn't like living so high; we Africans like being close to the earth. van Rensburg stopped at one of the doors, and said to me, "I won't be a minute." Then he went in, leaving the door open, and inside I could hear voices. I thought to myself, he's telling them who's here. Then after a minute or so, he came back to the door, holding two glasses of red wine. He was warm and smiling.

"Sorry there's no brandy," he said. "Only wine. Here's happiness."

Now I certainly had not expected that I would have my drink in the passage. I wasn't only feeling what you may be thinking. I was thinking that one of the

---

[4] *Slegs vir Blankes:* For whites only.

[5] *stoep:* Porch or stoop.

impersonal doors might open at any moment, and someone might see me in a "white" building, and see me and van Rensburg breaking the liquor laws of the country. Anger could have saved me from the whole embarrassing situation, but you know I can't easily be angry. Even if I could have been, I might have found it hard to be angry with this particular man. But I wanted to get away from there, and I couldn't. My mother used to say to me, when I had said something anti-white, "Son, don't talk like that, talk as you are." She would have understood at once why I took a drink from a man who gave it to me in the passage.

van Rensburg said to me, "Don't you know this fellow Simelane?"

"I've heard of him," I said.

"I'd like to meet him," he said. "I'd like to talk to him." He added in explanation, "you know, talk out my heart to him."

A woman of about fifty years of age came from the room beyond, bringing a plate of biscuits. She smiled and bowed to me. I took one of the biscuits, but not for all the money in the world could I have said to her *"dankie, my nooi,"*[6] or that disgusting *"dankie, missus,"* nor did I want to speak to her in English because her language was Afrikaans, so I took the risk of it and used the word *"mevrou"*[7] for the politeness of which some Afrikaners would knock a black man down, and I said, in high Afrikaans, with a smile and a bow too, *"Ek is u dankbaar, Mevrou."*[8]

But nobody knocked me down. The woman smiled and bowed, and van Rensburg, in a strained voice that suddenly came out of nowhere, said, "Our land is beautiful. But it breaks my heart."

The woman put her hand on his arm, and said "Jannie, Jannie."

Then another woman and a man, all about the same age, came up and stood behind van Rensburg.

"He's a B.A.," van Rensburg told them. "What do you think of that?"

The first woman smiled and bowed to me again, and van Rensburg said, as though it were a matter for grief, "I wanted to give him brandy, but there's only wine."

The second woman said, "I remember, Jannie. Come with me."

She went back into the room, and he followed her. The first woman said to me, "Jannie's a good man. Strange, but good."

And I thought the whole thing was mad, and getting beyond me, with me a black stranger being shown a testimonial for the son of the house, with these white strangers standing and looking at me in the passage, as though they wanted for God's sake to touch me somewhere and didn't know how, but I saw the earnestness of the woman who had smiled and bowed to me, and I said to her "I can see that, *Mevrou.*"

---

[6] dankie, my nooi: Thank you, missus. This is a relatively informal form of address.

[7] mevrou: Madam, a title of respect.

[8] Ek is u dankbaar, Mevrou: Thank you very much, madam. This is a very formal form of address.

"He goes down every night to look at the statue," she said. "He says only God could make something so beautiful, therefore God must be in the man who made it, and he wants to meet him and talk out his heart to him."

She looked back at the room, and then she dropped her voice a little, and said to me, "Can't you see, it's somehow because it's a black woman and a black child?" And I said to her, "I can see that, *Mevrou*."

She turned to the man and said of me, "He's a good boy."

Then the other woman returned with van Rensburg, and van Rensburg had a bottle of brandy. He was smiling and pleased, and he said to me, "This isn't ordinary brandy, it's French."

He showed me the bottle, and I, wanting to get the hell out of that place, looked at it and saw it was cognac. He turned to the man and said, "Uncle, you remember? When you were ill? The doctor said you must have good brandy. And the man at the bottle-store said this was the best brandy in the world."

"I must go," I said. "I must catch the train."

"I'll take you to the station," he said. "Don't you worry about that."

He poured me a drink and one for himself.

"Uncle," he said, "what about one for yourself?"

The older man said, "I don't mind if I do," and he went inside to get himself a glass.

van Rensburg said, "Happiness," and lifted his glass to me. It was good brandy, the best I've ever tasted. But I wanted to get the hell out of there. I stood in the passage and drank van Rensburg's brandy. Then Uncle came back with his glass, and van Rensburg poured him a brandy, and Uncle raised his glass to me too. All of us were full of goodwill, but I was waiting for the opening of one of those impersonal doors. Perhaps they were too, I don't know. Perhaps when you want so badly to touch someone you don't care. I was drinking my brandy almost as fast as I would have drunk it in Orlando.

"I must go," I said.

van Rensburg said, "I'll take you to the station." He finished his brandy, and I finished mine too. We handed the glasses to Uncle, who said to me, "Good night my boy." The first woman said "May God bless you," and the other woman bowed and smiled. Then van Rensburg and I went down in the lift to the basement, and got into his car.

"I told you I'd take you to the station," he said, "I'd take you home, but I'm frightened of Orlando at night."

We drove up Eloff Street and he said, "Did you know what I meant?" I knew that he wanted an answer to something, and I wanted to answer him, but I couldn't because I didn't know what that something was. He couldn't be talking about being frightened of Orlando at night, because what more could one mean than just that?

"By what?" I asked.

"You know," he said, "about our land being beautiful?"

Yes, I knew what he meant, and I knew that for God's sake he wanted to touch me too and he couldn't; for his eyes had been blinded by years in the dark. And I thought it was a pity, for if men never touch each other, they'll hurt each other one day. And it was a pity he was blind, and couldn't touch me, for black men don't touch white men any more; only by accident, when they make something like *Mother and Child*.

He said to me, "What are you thinking?"

I said, "Many things," and my inarticulateness distressed me, for I knew he wanted something from me. I felt him fall back, angry, hurt, despairing, I didn't know. He stopped at the main entrance to the station, but I didn't tell him I couldn't go in there. I got out and said to him, "Thank you for the sociable evening."

"They liked having you," he said. "Did you see that they did?"

I said, "Yes, I saw that they did."

He sat slumped in his seat, like a man with a burden of incomprehensible, insoluble grief. I wanted to touch him, but I was thinking about the train. He said "Goodnight" and I said it too. We each saluted the other. What he was thinking, God knows, but I was thinking he was like a man trying to run a race in iron shoes, and not understanding why he cannot move.

When I got back to Orlando, I told my wife the story, and she wept.

*****

We didn't speak for a long time.

Then I said, "Even the angels would weep."

"Don't weep," he said, "write it."

"Write it," he said eagerly. "Perhaps that way I could make amends."

Then after a time he said to me, "Do you think we'll ever touch each other? Your people and mine? Or is it too late?"

But I didn't give him any answer. For though I may hope, and though I may fear, I don't really know.

UNDERSTANDING THE STORY

1. What about Simelane's sculpture appeals to van Rensburg? Why does he feel that "God must be in the man who made it"?

2. What do the issues of the sculpture competition and Simelane's visit to van Rensburg's apartment reveal about the structure of society in South Africa at the time?

3. When Simelane says "I'm a sculptor, not a demonstrator," what does he mean? How would the story have been different if he were a demonstrator?

4. Why doesn't Simelane tell van Rensburg who he really is?

5. Why is van Rensburg's background important?

6. Why does van Rensburg offer Simelane a drink in the passage?

7. Why does Simelane consider how to thank the woman who serves him? Given his reactions to his choices, what seems to be wrong with each choice?

8. What does van Rensburg mean when he says that their country breaks his heart? Why does he want to be sure that Simelane understands him?

9. How does van Rensburg feel at the end of the story? Why?

10. Why does Simelane's wife weep over the story?

11. Why does Simelane ask Paton to write his story?

ANALYZING LITERARY TECHNIQUE

1. What does telling a story within a story achieve?

2. To what extent, if any, does Paton use **foreshadowing** in this story?

3. What is the **climax** of the story? Relate it to the theme.

4. Consider the sculpture's caption in the window: "Black man conquers white world." To what extent is it a good caption, and to what extent is it ironic?

5. Examine the role of liquor in the story and discuss its function as a **symbol.**

6. Near the beginning of the story, van Rensburg calls Simelane "mate." In what way is this label symbolic? In what way is it ironic?

7. What are some of the common **metaphors,** or images, in the story? How do they contribute to the story's meaning and effect?

WRITING ABOUT LITERATURE

1. Write an essay in which you explain why Paton chooses to have a sculpture of an African mother and child create a bridge between Simelane and van Rensburg. Consider the function of the sculpture (and its caption) as a symbol in the story. Use quotations from the story to support your ideas.

2. If van Rensburg had known that he was conversing with Simelane, he would have "talk[ed] out his heart to him." Write the conversation between the two men that would then have occurred. Consider van Rensburg's feelings about Simelane's sculpture and about their country. Imagine why van Rensburg wants the conversation to occur. Consider also Simelane's feelings about the social, economic, and political aspects of apartheid.

Prayer to Masks

LÉOPOLD SÉDAR SENGHOR

ÉOPOLD SÉDAR SENGHOR (1906–2001) was a
major West African poet and essayist who inspired many
younger African writers. He was one of the founders of
Négritude, an anti-assimilationist African literary movement begun
in 1934 to promote a return to Africa's distinctive values and culture.
He was also the founder of the nation of Senegal and was its president
for twenty years (1960–1980). He is best known as the editor of the
Anthology of the New Black and Malagasy Poetry in French (1948), a
major collection of African poetry, and for *Ethiopics* (1956), a collection of his own poetry.

Senghor was born in Joal, an old Portuguese settlement south of
Dakar, Senegal. His father was a prosperous groundnut trader in the
Serere tribe, so Senghor grew up listening to fishermen and farmers
relate tales about the African peoples who lived before the French
conquered Senegal in 1850. Senghor received an intensive French
education. He attended an assimilationist high school in Dakar and
in 1928 entered university in Paris, France. He was the first African
graduate of the Sorbonne (1933), and he became the first African to
teach in a French university.

Senghor served in the French army during World War II and was
a prisoner of war in Germany from 1940 to 1942. After the liberation
of France, he became actively involved in politics. He returned to
Senegal and became his country's deputy in the French National
Assembly. There he played a major role in winning the independence
of the French African colonies. As president of Senegal, he promoted
human rights in such areas as marriage, religion, and education. He
died in 2001, twenty years after he retired from public office.

Senghor's poems and essays are written in French. His poetry often
expresses the values of Négritude, yet having been reared within two
cultures, he felt a deep love for both French and African customs. His
poems speak of the beauty of Africa and its women, the protective
guidance of the dead in the lives of the living, the destructive effect of

European colonization on African culture, the need for cultural interdependence, and the world's need for Africa's special qualities of passion and spontaneity.

"Prayer to Masks" appears in *Songs of Shadow* (1945), the first of Senghor's five published collections of poetry. In addition to reflecting Négritude values, the poem reflects the role of ancestors in traditional African life. The spirits of those who have died remain a vital part of life. Ancestor shrines occupy a special room in the house to facilitate communication between the living and the dead. On special occasions, people display and wear their ancestral masks, each designed to convey the essential qualities of a particular ancestor.

Mask! Masks!
Black mask red mask, you white-and-black masks
Mask of the four points from which the Spirit blows
In silence I salute you!
Nor you the least, the Lion-headed Ancestor[1]   5
You guard this place forbidden to all laughter of women, to all smiles that fade
You distil this air of eternity in which I breathe the air of my Fathers.
Masks of unmasked faces, stripped of the marks of illness and the lines of age
You who have fashioned this portrait, this my face bent over the altar of white
        paper
In your own image, hear me!   10
The Africa of the empires is dying, see, the agony of a pitiful princess[2]
And Europe too where we are joined by the navel.
Fix your unchanging eyes upon your children, who are given orders
Who give away their lives like the poor their last clothes.
Let us report present at the rebirth of the World   15
Like the yeast which white flour needs.
For who would teach rhythm to a dead world of machines and guns?
Who would give the cry of joy to wake the dead and the bereaved at dawn?
Say, who would give back the memory of life to the man whose hopes are
        smashed?
They call us men of coffee cotton oil   20
They call us men of death.
We are the men of the dance, whose feet draw new strength pounding the hardened
        earth.

---

[1] *Lion-headed Ancestor:* Mask in the shape of a lion's head. The lion may be the family's totem or emblem.

[2] *The Africa . . . princess:* The poet is remembering the great empires of Africa that existed before contact with European culture. The princess is the old Africa.

UNDERSTANDING THE POEM

1. Why is the speaker calling upon the masks?

2. What does the poem indicate about the traditional relationship between the living and the dead?

3. When the West Africans fought alongside the French in World War II, they were treated as inferior beings. What does the simile "Who give away their lives like the poor their last clothes" (line 14) imply?

4. What **themes** do you find in the poem?

ANALYZING LITERARY TECHNIQUE

1. What are "masks of unmasked faces" (line 8)?

2. What does the technique of personifying Africa as "a pitiful princess" (line 11) achieve?

3. In what ways would Africa and Europe metaphorically have been "joined by the navel" (line 12)?

4. Examine the **simile** in line 16, "Like the yeast which white flour needs." What does this simile mean? What components in the "yeast" enable it to help "white flour" become bread?

5. Why are Africans called "men of coffee cotton oil" (line 20)?

6. What is the effect of Senghor's use of repetition?

7. What is the function of **irony** in the poem?

8. How does Senghor use **paradox?**

WRITING ABOUT LITERATURE

1. Analyze how Senghor instills pride in one's African heritage in this poem. Examine his use of **figurative language** and paradox. Use quotations to support your ideas.

2. Write a poem in which you express the aspects of your own cultural heritage that are a source of pride for you. Consider the contributions of people of your cultural heritage to the arts, science, sports, and public life.

Dry Your Tears, Africa!

BERNARD DADIÉ

BERNARD DADIÉ (1916–) is an important West African poet, short-story writer, novelist, and dramatist. Writing in French, he became known as a poet with his publication of *Africa on Its Feet* (1950). He is also known for two collections of stories, *African Legends* (1953) and *The Black Loincloth* (1955); a second collection of poetry, *The Circle of Days* (1956); and the plays *Mr. Thôgô-gnini* (1970) and *Stormy Islands* (1973).

Dadié was born in Assinie, Ivory Coast. His mother, who had only one good eye, decided that she had put a curse on her first three children because all of them had died. She therefore sent Dadié, her fourth child, to live with his uncle, from whom he acquired his love of African folktales. Dadié was educated in Dakar, Senegal; he has spent his adult life working in Senegal and the Ivory Coast. He worked at the French Institute of Black Africa in Dakar, becoming its director of fine arts in 1969. There he established an important center for dramatic arts. Later he returned to the Ivory Coast, where he became the director of fine arts and research in Abidjan and then the minister of culture.

"Dry Your Tears, Africa!" is written in the spirit of Négritude, an anti-assimilationist literary movement with the goal of inspiring pride in one's heritage by emphasizing Africa's natural beauty and traditions.

Dry your tears, Africa!
Your children come back to you
Out of the storm and squalls of fruitless journeys.

Through the crest of the wave and the babbling of the breeze,
Over the gold of the east   5
and the purple of the setting sun,

the peaks of the proud mountains
and the grasslands drenched with light
They return to you
out of the storm and squalls of fruitless journeys.   10

Dry your tears, Africa!
We have drunk
From all the springs
   of ill fortune
   and of glory.   15

And our senses are now opened
   to the splendour of your beauty
   to the smell of your forests
   to the charm of your waters
   to the clearness of your skies   20
   to the caress of your sun
And to the charm of your foliage pearled by the dew.

Dry your tears, Africa!
Your children come back to you
their hands full of playthings   25
and their hearts full of love.
They return to clothe you
in their dreams and their hopes.

UNDERSTANDING THE POEM

1. Given their "fruitless journeys," would Africa's children have been better off if they had never left Africa?

2. With what "playthings" do Africa's children return? Why does Dadié call them "playthings"?

ANALYZING LITERARY TECHNIQUE

1. Examine Dadié's use of water imagery in this poem. How do the images contribute to the poem's total effect?

2. How does Dadié use **personification?** Why is it an effective choice?

3. How does Dadié's use of **contrast** contribute to the poem?

4. What is the effect of Dadié's use of repetition, and how does it reinforce his theme?

WRITING ABOUT LITERATURE

1. Dadié describes Africa's children as returning "Out of the storm and squalls of fruitless journeys." What kind of journey do you think the Africans made? Where have they been? Has the journey been a literal journey away from the continent of Africa, or has it been a psychological separation from Africa? Write a brief essay describing the journey. Use lines from the poem to support your argument that it was a literal journey or a figurative journey.

2. If you were to travel away from your hometown or native country for a time, what would you miss? What would you bring with you on your return? Write a poem or a brief prose description of your thoughts about being away from home and returning to it.

A Sunrise
on the Veld

DORIS LESSING

*D*ORIS LESSING (1919–), an important Rhodesian and English writer, is a noted humanitarian and a master of literary realism. Most of her work reflects her interest in equal political, economic, and social opportunities for black Africans and for women. Her first novel, *The Grass Is Singing* (1950), and her first collection of short stories, *This Was the Old Chief's Country* (1951), are both set in Africa; they remain among her finest work. She has published numerous novels, essays, poems, and autobiographical works; she is best known for her feminist novel *The Golden Notebook* (1962).

Lessing was born in Persia (Iran) to a British banker and his wife. When she was five years old, her family moved to Southern Rhodesia (now Zimbabwe), where her father became a farmer. At the age of fifteen, Lessing quit school and began a string of jobs, working as nursemaid, secretary, and telephone operator. A political liberal, she was active for a time in the Communist Party because, in her words, to live in Africa is "to be reminded twenty times a day of injustice, and always the same brand of it." In 1949, at the age of thirty, she moved to London as a political exile and became a professional writer. She was finally allowed to enter South Africa in 1995 to visit her grandchildren.

Lessing chose "A Sunrise on the Veld,"[1] from *This Was the Old Chief's Country*, to be reprinted in *African Stories* (1963 and 1981). The story reflects her attitude that "atrophy of the imagination prevents us from seeing ourselves in every creature that breathes under the sun." In the Preface to *African Stories*, she says:

> I believe that the chief gift from Africa to writers, white and black, is the continent itself, its presence which for some people is like an old fever, latent always in their blood; or like an old wound throbbing in the bones as the air changes. That is not a place to visit unless one chooses to be an exile

---

[1] *Veld:* Grassland in eastern and southern Africa.

ever afterwards from an inexplicable majestic silence lying just over the border of memory or of thought. Africa gives you the knowledge that man is a small creature, among other creatures, in a large landscape.

Revealing Lessing's great narrative gifts, "A Sunrise on the Veld" is both the story of a rite of passage and a tribute to Africa as a primal landscape that imprints its power on one's soul.

E very night that winter he said aloud into the dark of the pillow: Half-past four! Half-past four! till he felt his brain had gripped the words and held them fast. Then he fell asleep at once, as if a shutter had fallen; and lay with his face turned to the clock so that he could see it first thing when he woke.

It was half-past four to the minute, every morning. Triumphantly pressing down the alarm-knob of the clock, which the dark half of his mind had outwitted, remaining vigilant all night and counting the hours as he lay relaxed in sleep, he huddled down for a last warm moment under the clothes, playing with the idea of lying abed for this once only. But he played with it for the fun of knowing that it was a weakness he could defeat without effort; just as he set the alarm each night for the delight of the moment when he woke and stretched his limbs, feeling the muscles tighten, and thought: Even my brain—even that! I can control every part of myself.

Luxury of warm rested body, with the arms and legs and fingers waiting like soldiers for a word of command! Joy of knowing that the precious hours were given to sleep voluntarily!—for he had once stayed awake three nights running, to prove that he could, and then worked all day, refusing even to admit that he was tired; and now sleep seemed to him a servant to be commanded and refused.

The boy stretched his frame full-length, touching the wall at his head with his hands, and the bedfoot with his toes; then he sprung out, like a fish leaping from water. And it was cold, cold.

He always dressed rapidly, so as to try and conserve his night-warmth till the sun rose two hours later; but by the time he had on his clothes his hands were numbed and he could scarcely hold his shoes. These he could not put on for fear of waking his parents, who never came to know how early he rose.

As soon as he stepped over the lintel, the flesh of his soles contracted on the chilled earth, and his legs began to ache with cold. It was night: the stars were glittering, the trees standing black and still. He looked for signs of day, for the greying of the edge of a stone, or a lightening in the sky where the sun would rise, but there was nothing yet. Alert as an animal he crept past the dangerous window, standing poised with his hand on the sill for one proudly fastidious moment, looking in at the stuffy blackness of the room where his parents lay.

Feeling for the grass-edge of the path with his toes, he reached inside another window further along the wall, where his gun had been set in readiness the night before. The steel was icy, and numbed fingers slipped along it, so that he had to hold it in the crook of his arm for safety. Then he tiptoed to the room where the dogs slept, and was fearful that they might have been tempted to go before him; but they were waiting, their haunches crouched in reluctance at the cold, but ears and swinging tails greeting the gun ecstatically. His warning under-tone kept them secret and silent till the house was a hundred yards back: then they bolted off into the bush,[2] yelping excitedly. The boy imagined his parents turning in their beds and muttering: Those dogs again! before they were dragged back in sleep; and he smiled scornfully. He always looked back over his shoulder at the house before he passed a wall of trees that shut it from sight. It looked so low and small, crouching there under a tall and brilliant sky. Then he turned his back on it, and on the frowsting[3] sleepers, and forgot them.

He would have to hurry. Before the light grew strong he must be four miles away; and already a tint of green stood in the hollow of a leaf, and the air smelled of morning and the stars were dimming.

He slung the shoes over his shoulder, veld skoen[4] that were crinkled and hard with the dews of a hundred mornings. They would be necessary when the ground became too hot to bear. Now he felt the chilled dust push up between his toes, and he let the muscles of his feet spread and settle into the shapes of the earth; and he thought: I could walk a hundred miles on feet like these! I could walk all day, and never tire!

He was walking swiftly through the dark tunnel of foliage that in day-time was a road. The dogs were invisibly ranging the lower travelways of the bush, and he heard them panting. Sometimes he felt a cold muzzle on his leg before they were off again, scouting for a trail to follow. They were not trained, but free-running com-panions of the hunt, who often tired of the long stalk before the final shots, and went off on their own pleasure. Soon he could see them, small and wild-looking in a wild strange light, now that the bush stood trembling on the verge of colour, waiting for the sun to paint earth and grass afresh.

The grass stood to his shoulders; and the trees were showering a faint silvery rain. He was soaked; his whole body was clenched in a steady shiver.

Once he bent to the road that was newly scored with animal trails, and regret-fully straightened, reminding himself that the pleasure of tracking must wait till another day.

He began to run along the edge of a field, noting jerkily how it was filmed over with fresh spiderweb, so that the long reaches of great black clods seemed netted in glistening grey. He was using the steady lope he had learned by watching the natives, the run that is a dropping of the weight of the body from one foot to the next in a slow balancing movement that never tires, nor shortens the breath; and he felt the blood pulsing down his legs and along his arms, and the exultation

---

[2] *bush:* Wilderness of thick undergrowth.

[3] *frowsting:* Lounging or lolling.

[4] *veld skoen:* Shoes used for walking the veld.

and pride of body mounted in him till he was shutting his teeth hard against a violent desire to shout his triumph.

Soon he had left the cultivated part of the farm. Behind him the bush was low and black. In front was a long vlei,[5] acres of long pale grass that sent back a hollowing gleam of light to a satiny sky. Near him thick swathes of grass were bent with the weight of water, and diamond drops sparkled on each frond.

The first bird woke at his feet and at once a flock of them sprang into the air calling shrilly that day had come; and suddenly, behind him, the bush woke into song, and he could hear the guinea fowl calling far ahead of him. That meant they would now be sailing down from their trees into thick grass, and it was for them he had come: he was too late. But he did not mind. He forgot he had come to shoot. He set his legs wide, and balanced from foot to foot, and swung his gun up and down in both hands horizontally, in a kind of improvised exercise, and let his head sink back till it was pillowed in his neck muscles, and watched how above him small rosy clouds floated in a lake of gold.

Suddenly it all rose in him: it was unbearable. He leapt up into the air, shouting and yelling wild, unrecognisable noises. Then he began to run, not carefully, as he had before, but madly, like a wild thing. He was clean crazy, yelling mad with the joy of living and a superfluity of youth. He rushed down the vlei under a tumult of crimson and gold, while all the birds of the world sang about him. He ran in great leaping strides, and shouted as he ran, feeling his body rise into the crisp rushing air and fall back surely on to sure feet; and thought briefly, not believing that such a thing could happen to him, that he could break his ankle any moment, in this thick tangled grass. He cleared bushes like a duiker,[6] leapt over rocks; and finally came to a dead stop at a place where the ground fell abruptly away below him to the river. It had been a two-mile-long dash through waist-high growth, and he was breathing hoarsely and could no longer sing. But he poised on a rock and looked down at stretches of water that gleamed through stooping trees, and thought suddenly, I am fifteen! Fifteen! The word came new to him; so that he kept repeating them wonderingly, with swelling excitement; and he felt the years of his life with his hands, as if he were counting marbles, each one hard and separate and compact, each one a wonderful shining thing. That was what he was: fifteen years of this rich soil, and this slow-moving water, and air that smelt like a challenge whether it was warm and sultry at noon, or as brisk as cold water, like it was now.

There was nothing he couldn't do, nothing! A vision came to him, as he stood there, like when a child hears the word "eternity" and tries to understand it, and time takes possession of the mind. He felt his life ahead of him as a great and wonderful thing, something that was his; and he said aloud, with the blood rushing to his head: all the great men of the world have been as I am now, and there is nothing I can't become, nothing I can't do; there is no country in the world I cannot make part of myself, if I choose. I contain the world. I can make

---

[5] *vlei:* Lowland.
[6] *duiker:* Small antelope.

of it what I want. If I choose, I can change everything that is going to happen: it depends on me, and what I decide now.

The urgency and the truth and the courage of what his voice was saying exulted him so that he began to sing again, at the top of his voice, and the sound went echoing down the river gorge. He stopped for the echo, and sang again: stopped and shouted. That was what he was!—he sang, if he chose; and the world had to answer him.

And for minutes he stood there, shouting and singing and waiting for the lovely eddying sound of the echo; so that his own new strong thoughts came back and washed round his head, as if someone were answering him and encouraging him; till the gorge was full of soft voices clashing back and forth from rock to rock over the river. And then it seemed as if there was a new voice. He listened, puzzled, for it was not his own. Soon he was leaning forward, all his nerves alert, quite still: somewhere close to him there was a noise that was no joyful bird, nor tinkle of falling water, nor ponderous movement of cattle.

There it was again. In the deep morning hush that held his future and his past, was a sound of pain, and repeated over and over: it was a kind of shortened scream, as if someone, something, had no breath to scream. He came to himself, looked about him, and called for the dogs. They did not appear; they had gone off on their own business, and he was alone. Now he was clean sober, all the madness gone. His heart beating fast, because of that frightened screaming, he stepped carefully off the rock and went towards a belt of trees. He was moving cautiously, for not so long ago he had seen a leopard in just this spot.

At the edge of the trees he stopped and peered, holding his gun ready; he advanced, looking steadily about him, his eyes narrowed. Then all at once, in the middle of a step, he faltered, and his face was puzzled. He shook his head impatiently, as if he doubted his own sight.

There, between two trees, against a background of gaunt black rocks, was a figure from a dream, a strange beast that was horned and drunken-legged, but like something he had never even imagined. It seemed to be ragged. It look like a small buck that had black ragged tufts of fur standing up irregularly all over it, with patches of raw flesh beneath . . . but the patches of rawness were disappearing under moving black and came again elsewhere; and all the time the creature screamed, in small gasping screams, and leaped drunkenly from side to side, as if it were blind.

Then the boy understood: it *was* a buck. He ran closer, and again stood still, stopped by a new fear. Around him the grass was whispering and alive. He looked wildly about, and then down. The ground was black with ants, great energetic ants that took no notice of him, but hurried and scurried towards the fighting shape, like glistening black water flowing through the grass.

And, as he drew in his breath and pity and terror seized him, the beast fell and the screaming stopped. Now he could hear nothing but one bird singing, and the sound of the rustling, whispering ants.

He peered over at the writhing blackness that jerked convulsively with the jerking nerves. It grew quieter. There were small twitches from the mass that still looked vaguely like the shape of a small animal.

It came into his mind that he should shoot it and end its pain; and he raised the gun. Then he lowered it again. The buck could no longer feel; its fighting was a mechanical protest of the nerves. But it was not that which made him put down the gun. It was a swelling feeling of rage and misery and protest that expressed itself in the thought: if I had not come it would have died like this: so why should I interfere? All over the bush things like this happen; they happen all the time; this is how life goes on, by living things dying in anguish. He gripped the gun between his knees and felt in his own limbs the myriad swarming pain of the twitching animal that could no longer feel, and set his teeth, and said over and over again under his breath: I can't stop it. I can't stop it. There is nothing I can do.

He was glad that the buck was unconscious and had gone past suffering so that he did not have to make decision to kill it even when he was feeling with his whole body: this is what happens, this is how things work.

It was right—that was what he was feeling. *It was right and nothing could alter it.*

The knowledge of fatality, of what had to be, had gripped him and for the first time in his life; and he was left unable to make any movement of brain or body, except to say: "Yes, yes. That is what living is." It had entered his flesh and his bones and grown in to the furthest corners of his brain and would never leave him. And at that moment he could not have performed the smallest action of mercy, knowing as he did, having lived on it all his life, the vast unalterable, cruel veld, where at any moment one might stumble over a skull or crush the skeleton of some small creature.

Suffering, sick, and angry, but also grimly satisfied with his new stoicism, he stood there leaning on his rifle, and watched the seething black mound grow smaller. At his feet, now, were ants trickling back with pink fragments in their mouths, and there was a fresh acid smell in his nostrils. He sternly controlled the uselessly convulsing muscles of his empty stomach, and reminded himself: the ants must eat too! At the same time he found that the tears were streaming down his face, and his clothes were soaked with the sweat of that other creature's pain.

The shape had grown small. Now it looked like nothing recognisable. He did not know how long it was before he saw the blackness thin, and bits of white showed through, shining in the sun—yes, there was the sun, just up, glowing over the rocks. Why, the whole thing could not have taken longer than a few minutes.

He began to swear, as if the shortness of the time was in itself unbearable, using the words he had heard his father say. He strode forward, crushing ants with each step, and brushing them off his clothes, till he stood above the skeleton, which lay sprawled under a small bush. It was clean-picked. It might have been lying there years, save that on the white bone were pink fragments of gristle. About the bones ants were ebbing away, their pincers full of meat.

The boy looked at them, big black ugly insects. A few were standing and gazing up at him with small glittering eyes.

"Go away!" he said to the ants, very coldly. "I am not for you—not just yet, at any rate. Go away." And he fancied that the ants turned and went away.

He bent over the bones and touched the sockets in the skull, that was where the eyes were, he thought incredulously, remembering the liquid dark eyes of a buck. And then he bent the slim foreleg bone, swinging it horizontally in his palm.

That morning, perhaps an hour ago, this small creature had been stepping proud and free through the bush, feeling the chill on its hide even as he himself had done, exhilarated by it. Proudly stepping the earth, tossing its horns, frisking a pretty white tail, it had sniffed the cold morning air. Walking like kings and conquerors it had moved through this free-held bush, where each blade of grass grew for it alone, and where the river ran pure sparkling water for its slaking.

And then—what had happened? Such a swift surefooted thing could surely not be trapped by a swarm of ants?

The boy bent curiously to the skeleton. Then he saw that the back leg that lay uppermost and strained out in the tension of death, was snapped midway in the thigh, so that broken bones jutted over each other uselessly. So that was it! Limping into the ant-masses it could not escape, once it had sensed the danger. Yes, but how had the leg been broken? Had it fallen, perhaps? Impossible, a buck was too light and graceful. Had some jealous rival horned it?

What could possibly have happened? Perhaps some Africans had thrown stones at it, as they do, trying to kill it for meat, and had broken its leg. Yes, that must be it.

Even as he imagined the crowd of running, shouting natives, and the flying stones, and the leaping buck, another picture came into his mind. He saw himself, on any one of these bright ringing mornings, drunk with excitement, taking a snap shot at some half-seen buck. He saw himself with the gun lowered, wondering whether he had missed or not; and thinking at last that it was late, and he wanted his breakfast, and it was not worth while to track miles after an animal that would very likely get away from him in any case.

For a moment he would not face it. He was a small boy again, kicking sulkily at the skeleton, hanging his head, refusing to accept the responsibility.

Then he straightened up, and looked down at the bones with an odd expression of dismay, all the anger gone out of him. His mind went quite empty; all around him he could see trickles of ants disappearing into the grass. The whispering noise was faint and dry, like the rustling of a cast snakeskin.

At last he picked up his gun and walked homewards. He was telling himself half defiantly that he wanted his breakfast. He was telling himself that it was getting very hot, much too hot to be out roaming the bush.

Really, he was tired. He walked heavily, not looking where he put his feet. When he came within sight of his home he stopped, knitting his brows. There was something he had to think out. The death of that small animal was a thing that concerned him, and he was by no means finished with it. It lay at the back of his mind uncomfortably.

Soon, the very next morning, he would get clear of everybody and go to the bush and think about it.

UNDERSTANDING THE STORY

1. Why is it important that the narrator is fifteen years old? How would the story change if he were younger or older?

2. How important is it that the narrator is alone for this experience? What might have happened if he had been with friends or with his father?

3. Explain the significance of the passage: "In the deep morning hush that held his future and his past, was a sound of pain." What is the boy's past? What is his future? In what way is this story about a rite of passage or an initiation?

4. Why is the buck described as "a figure from a dream"?

5. The narrator says, "For a moment he would not face it. He was . . . refusing to accept the responsibility." What responsibility is the boy evading?

6. At the end of the story, the boy says that he will think about this experience the next morning. Do you think that, in fact, he will do this? Explain the reasons for your point of view.

7. What **themes** do you find in this story?

ANALYZING LITERARY TECHNIQUE

1. How does Lessing use **contrast** in this story? What does contrast achieve?

2. What is the function of nature in this story?

3. What type of **epiphany** exists in this story? What profound revelation does the boy experience?

4. To what extent, if any, is the buck symbolic? What does Lessing's treatment of the buck accomplish?

5. What does Lessing accomplish by using a third-person limited omniscient **narrative perspective?** How would the story's impact be affected if it were told by a first-person narrator?

6. What does Lessing achieve by her use of **connotative** and **figurative language** to describe nature?

7. What **paradoxes** exist in this story, and what is their function?

WRITING ABOUT LITERATURE

1. Write an essay in which you analyze how Lessing uses connotative and figurative language to convey her feeling for the African landscape. What aspects of nature capture her interest? In what ways does her language function as a movie or video camera? Use quotations to support your ideas.

2. At the end of the story, the boy decides that "the very next morning, he would get clear of everybody and go to the bush and think about it." Consider the boy's situation, and try to express his thoughts about the experience of the previous day. Consider the following questions: What aspects of life and death would this experience bring to mind? Would it cause the boy to have a new attitude toward living things? Given his thoughts, how long is his reaction likely to last? How long does the boy expect to remember this experience?

Good Climate, Friendly Inhabitants

NADINE GORDIMER

ADINE GORDIMER (1923–), an important and influential South African writer, is known for her sensitive and perceptive writing about the racial problems of her country. In 1975 she won the French International Literary Prize, and her novel *The Conservationist* shared the United Kingdom's Booker Prize. Two novellas and a novel were published in the 1980s. In 1991 Gordimer was awarded the Nobel Prize for literature.

The child of Jewish immigrants, Gordimer grew up in a gold-mining town in what was then the Union of South Africa. She graduated from the University of the Witwatersrand in Johannesburg and has continued to live in that city. The first of her nine volumes of short stories, *Face to Face* (1949), was published when she was twenty-six; her first novel was published four years later.

All of Gordimer's fiction reflects some aspect of apartheid (the former official policy of racial segregation in South Africa) because, as she has explained, "In South Africa, society is the political situation." Viewing fiction as "a way of exploring possibilities present but undreamt of in the living of a single life," Gordimer focuses on the attitudes and emotions of the protagonist in each of her short stories. Some of these stories deal with the white society's sense of fear, distrust, isolation, and powerlessness. Others, such as "Good Climate, Friendly Inhabitants," reveal the lack of understanding and communication that apartheid fostered. Gordimer's best stories achieve her goal to "express from a situation in the exterior or interior world the life-giving drop . . . that will spread an intensity on the page; burn a hole in it." Gordimer chose "Good Climate, Friendly Inhabitants," from *Not for Publication* (1965), to be reprinted in *Selected Stories* (1975).

I n the office at the garage eight hours a day I wear mauve linen overalls—those snappy uniforms they make for girls who aren't really nurses. I'm forty-nine but I could be twenty-five except for my face and my legs. I've got that very fair skin and my legs have gone mottled, like Roquefort cheese.[1] My hair used to look pretty as a chickens' fluff, but now it's been bleached and permed too many times. I wouldn't admit this to anyone else, but to myself I admit everything. Perhaps I'll get one of those wigs everyone's wearing. You don't have to be short of hair, any more, to wear a wig.

I've been years at the garage—service station, as it's been called since it was rebuilt all steel and glass. That's at the front, where the petrol[2] pumps are; you still can't go into the workshop without getting grease on your things. But I don't have much call to go there. Between doing the books you'll see me hanging about in front for a breath of fresh air, smoking a cigarette and keeping an eye on the boys. Not the mechanics—they're all white chaps of course (bunch of ducktails they are, too, most of them)—but the petrol attendants. One boy's been with the firm twenty-three years—sometimes you'd think he owns the place; gets my goat. On the whole they're not a bad lot of natives, though you get a cheeky bastard now and then, or a thief, but he doesn't last long, with us.

We're just off the Greensleeves suburban shopping centre with the terrace restaurant and the fountain, and you get a very nice class of person coming up and down. I'm quite friends with some for the people from the luxury flats round about; they wouldn't pass without a word to me when they're walking their dogs or going to the shops. And of course you get to know a lot of the regular petrol customers, too. We've got two Rolls[3] and any amount of sport cars who never go anywhere else. And I only have to walk down the block to Maison Claude when I get my hair done, or in to Mr. Levine at the Greensleeves Pharmacy if I feel a cold coming on.

I've got a flat in one of the old buildings that are still left, back in town. Not too grand, but for ten quid[4] a month and right on the bus route . . . I was married once and I've got a lovely kid—married since she was seventeen and living in Rhodesia;[5] I couldn't stop her. She's very happy with him and they've got twin boys, real little toughies! I've seen them once.

There's a woman friend I go to the early flicks with every Friday, and the Versfelds' where I have a standing invitation for Sunday lunch. I think they depend on me, poor old things; they never see anybody. That's the trouble when you

---

[1] *Roquefort cheese:* A blue cheese.

[2] *petrol:* Gasoline.

[3] *Rolls:* Rolls Royce automobile.

[4] *quid:* A pound; a unit of money in the United Kingdom.

[5] *Rhodesia:* A country in southern Africa, now known as Zimbabwe.

work alone in an office, like I do, you don't make friends at your work. Nobody to talk to but those duckies in the workshop, and what can I have in common with a lot of louts in black leather jackets? No respect, either, you should hear the things they come out with. I'd sooner talk to the blacks, that's the truth, though I know it sounds a strange thing to say. At least they call you missus. Even old Madala knows he can't come into my office without taking his cap off, though heaven help you if you ask that boy to run up to the Greek for a packet of smokes, or round to the Swiss Confectionery. I had a dust-up with him once over it, the old monkey-face, but the manager didn't seem to want to get rid of him, he's been here so long. So he just keeps out of my way and he has his half-crown[6] from me at Christmas, same as the other boys. But you get more sense out of the boss-boy, Jack, than you can out of some whites, believe me, and he can make you laugh, too, in his way—of course they're like children, you see them yelling with laughter over something in their own language, noisy lot of devils; I don't suppose we'd think it funny at all if we knew what it was all about. This Jack used to get a lot of phone calls (I complained to the manager on the quiet and he's put a stop to it, now) and the natives on the other end used to be asking to talk to Mpanza and Makiwane and I don't know what all, and when I'd say there wasn't anyone of that name working here they'd come out with it and ask for Jack. So I said to him one day, why do you people have a hundred and one names, why don't these uncles and aunts and brothers-in-law come out with your name straight away and stop wasting my time? He said, "Here I'm Jack because Mpanza Makiwane is not a name, and there I'm Mpanza Makiwane because Jack is not a name, but I'm the only one who knows who I am wherever I am." I couldn't help laughing. He hardly ever calls you missus, I notice, but it doesn't sound cheeky, the way he speaks. Before they were allowed to buy drink for themselves, he used to ask me to buy a bottle of brandy for him once a week and I didn't see any harm.

Even if things are not too bright, no use grumbling. I don't believe in getting old before my time. Now and then it's happened that some man's taken a fancy to me at the garage. Every time he comes to fill up he finds some excuse to talk to me; if a chap likes me, I begin to feel it just like I did when I was seventeen, so that even if he was just sitting in his car looking at me through the glass of the office, I would know that he was waiting for me to come out. Eventually he'd ask me to the hotel for a drink after work. Usually that was as far as it went. I don't know what happens to these blokes, they are married, I suppose, though their wives don't still wear a perfect size fourteen,[7] like I do. They enjoy talking to another woman once in a while, but they quickly get nervous. They are businessmen and well off; one sent me a present, but it was one of those old-fashioned compacts, we used to call them flapjacks, meant for loose powder, and I use the solid kind everyone uses now.

Of course you get some funny types, and, as I say, I'm alone there in the front most of the time, with only the boys, the manager is at head office in town, and

---

[6] *half-crown:* Coin worth $^{30}/_{100}$ of a pound.

[7] *size fourteen:* Size eight in American sizes.

the other white men are all at the back. Little while ago a fellow came into my office wanting to pay for his petrol with Rhodesian money. Well, Jack, the boss-boy, came first to tell me that this fellow had given him Rhodesian money. I sent back to say we didn't take it. I looked through the glass and saw a big, expensive American car, not very new, and one of those men you recognize at once as the kind who move about a lot—he was poking out his cheek with his tongue, looking round the station and out into the busy street like, in his head, he was trying to work out his way around in a new town. Some people kick up hell with a native if he refuses them something, but this one didn't seem to; the next thing was he got the boy to bring him to me. "Boss says he must talk to you," Jack said, and turned on his heel. But I said, you wait here. I know Johannesburg;[8] my cash-box was there in the open safe. The fellow was young. He had that very tanned skin that has been sunburnt day after day, the tan you see on lifesavers at the beach. His hair was the thick streaky blond kind, waste on men. He says, "Miss, can't you help me out for half an hour?" Well, I'd had my hair done, it's true, but I don't kid myself you could think of me as a miss unless you saw my figure, from behind. He went on, "I've just driven down and I haven't had a chance to change my money. Just take this while I get hold of this chap I know and get him to cash a cheque for me."

I told him there was a bank up the road but he made some excuse. "I've got to tell my friend I'm in town anyway. Here, I'll leave this—it's a gold one." And he took the big fancy watch off his arm. "Go on, please, do me a favour." Somehow when he smiled he looked not so young, harder. The smile was on the side of his mouth. Anyway, I suddenly said okay, then, and the native boy turned and went out of the office, but I knew it was all right about my cash, and this fellow asked me which was the quickest way to get to Kensington and I came out from behind my desk and looked it up with him on the wall map. I though he was a fellow of about twenty-nine or thirty; he was so lean, with a snakeskin belt around his hips and a clean white open-neck shirt.

He was back on the dot. I took the money from the petrol and said, here's your watch, pushing it across the counter. I'd seen, the moment he'd gone and I'd picked up the watch to put it in the safe, that it wasn't gold: one of those Jap fakes that men take out of their pockets and try to sell you on street-corners. But I didn't say anything, because maybe he'd been had? I gave him the benefit of the doubt. What'd it matter? He'd paid for his petrol, anyway. He thanked me and said he supposed he'd better push off and find some hotel. I said the usual sort of thing, was he here on a visit and so on, and he said, yes, he didn't know how long, perhaps a couple of weeks, it all depended, and he'd like somewhere central. We had quite a little chat—you know how it is, you always feel friendly if you've done someone a favour and it's all worked out okay—and I mentioned a couple of hotels. But it's difficult if you don't know what sort of place a person wants, you may send him somewhere too expensive, or on the other hand you might

---

[8] *Johannesburg:* Capital of South Africa.

recommend one of the small places that he'd consider just a joint, such as the New Park, where I live.

A few days later I'd been down to the shops at lunch hour and when I came by where some of the boys were squatting over their lunch in the sun, Jack said, "That man came again." Thinks I can read his mind; what man, I said, but they never learn. "The other day, with the money that was no good." Oh, you mean the Rhodesian, I said. Jack didn't answer but went on tearing chunks of bread out of half a loaf and stuffing them into his mouth. One of the other boys began telling, in their own language with bits of English thrown in, what I could guess was the story of how the man had tried to pay with money that was no good; big joke, you know; but Jack didn't take any notice, I suppose he'd heard it once too often.

I went into my office to fetch a smoke, and when I was enjoying it outside in the sun Jack came over to the tap near me. I heard him drinking from his hand, and then he said, "He went and looked in the office window." Didn't he buy petrol? I said. "He pulled up at the pump but then he didn't buy, he said he will come back later." Well, that's all right, what're you getting excited about, we sell people as much petrol as they like, I said. I felt uncomfortable. I don't know why; you'd think I'd been giving away petrol at the garage's expense or something.

"You can't come from Rhodesia on those tyres," Jack said. No? I said. "Did you look at those tyres?" Why should I look at tyres? "No-no, you look at the tyres on that old car. You can't drive six hundred miles or so on those tyres. Worn out! Down to the tread!" But who cares where he came from, I said, it's his business. "But he had that money," Jack said to me. He shrugged and I shrugged; I went back into my office. As I say, sometimes you find yourself talking to that boy as if he was a white person.

Just before five that same afternoon the fellow came back. I don't know how it was, I happened to look up like I knew the car was going to be there. He was taking petrol and paying for it, this time; Old Madala was serving him. I don't know what got into me, curiosity maybe, but I got up and came to my door and said, how's Jo'burg treating you? "Ah, hell, I've had bad luck," he says. "The place I was staying had another booking for my room from today. I was supposed to go to my friend in Berea, but now his wife's brother has come. I don't mind paying for a decent place, but you take one look at some of them . . . Don't you know somewhere?" Well yes, I said, I was telling you that day. And I mentioned the Victoria, but he said he'd tried there, so then I told him about the New Park, near me. He listened, but looking round all the time, his mind was somewhere else. He said, "They'll tell me they're full, it'll be the same story." I told him that Mrs. Douglas who runs the place is a nice woman—she would be sure to fix him up. "You couldn't ask her?" he said. I said well, all right, from my place she was only round the corner, I'd pop in on my way home from work and tell her he'd be getting in touch with her.

When he heard that he said he'd give me a lift in his car, and so I took him to Mrs. Douglas myself, and she gave him a room. As we walked out of the hotel together he seemed wrapped up in his own affairs again, but on the pavement he suddenly suggested a drink. I thought he meant we'd go into the hotel lounge, but he said, "I've got a bottle of gin in the car," and he brought it up to my place. He was telling me about the time he was in the Congo[9] a few years ago, fighting for that native chief, whats's-name—Tshombe[10]—against the Irishmen who were sent out there to put old whats's-name down. The stories he told about Elisabethville![11] He was paid so much he could live like a king. We only had two gins each out of the bottle, but when I wanted him to take it along with him, he said, "I'll come for it sometime when I get a chance." He didn't say anything, but I got the idea he had come up to Jo'burg about a job.

I was frying a slice of liver next evening when he turned up at the door. The bottle was still standing where it'd been left. You feel uncomfortable when the place's full of the smell of frying and anyone can tell you're about to eat. I gave him the bottle but he didn't take it; he said he was on his way to Vereeniging[12] to see someone, he would just have a quick drink. I had to offer him something to eat, with me. He was one of those people who eat without noticing what it is. He never took in the flat, either; I mean he didn't look round at my things the way it's natural you do in someone else's home. And there was a lovely photo of my kid on the built-in fixture round the electric fire. I said to him while we were eating, is it a job you've come down for? He smiled the way youngsters smile at an older person who won't understand, anyway. "On business." But you could see that he was not a man who had an office, who wore a suit and sat in a chair. He was like one of those men you see in films, you know, the stranger in town who doesn't look as if he lives anywhere. Somebody in a film, thin and burned red as a brick and not saying much. I mean he did talk but it was never really anything about himself, only about things he'd seen happen. He never asked me anything about myself, either. It was queer; because of this, after I'd seen him a few times, it was just the same as if we were people who know each other so well they don't talk about themselves any more.

Another funny thing was, all the time he was coming in and out of the flat, I was talking about him with the boy—with Jack. I don't believe in discussing white people with natives, as a rule, I mean, whatever I think of a white, it encourages disrespect if you talk about it to a black. I've never said anything in front of the boys about the behaviour of that crowd of ducktails in the workshop, for instance. And of course I wouldn't be likely to discuss my private life with a native boy. Jack didn't know that this fellow was coming to the flat, but he'd heard me say I'd fix him up at the New Park Hotel, and he'd seen me take a lift home that afternoon. The boy's remark about tyres seemed to stick in my mind; I said to him: That man came all the way from the Congo.

"In the car?" Jack said; he's got such a serious face, for a native. The car goes all right, I said, he's driving all over with it now.

---

[9] *the Congo:* Here, the Congo is the region in central Africa that is now part of the Democratic Republic of the Congo.

[10] *Tshombe:* Political leader and rebel in the Congo.

[11] *Elisabethville:* A city in the Congo, now known as Lubumbashi.

[12] *Vereeniging:* A city near Johannesburg.

"Why doesn't he bring it in for retreads?"

I said he was just on holiday, he wouldn't have it done here.

The fellow didn't appear for five or six days and I thought he'd moved on, or made friends, as people do in this town. There was still about two fingers left in his bottle. I don't drink when I'm on my own. Again I meant to look at the tyres for myself, but I forgot. He took me home just like it had been an arranged thing; you know, a grown-up son calling for his mother not because he wants to, but because he has to. We hardly spoke in the car. I went out for pies, which wasn't much of a dinner to offer to anyone, but, as I say, he didn't know what he was eating, and he didn't want the gin, he had some cans of beer in the car. He leaned his chair back with all the weight on two legs and said, "I think I must clear out of this lousy dump, I don't know what you've got to be to get along here with these sharks." I said, you kids give up too easy, have you still not landed a job? "A job!" he said. "They owe me *money*, I'm trying to get *money* out of them." What's it all about, I said, what money? He didn't take any notice, as if I wouldn't understand. "Smart alecks and swindlers. I been here nearly three lousy weeks, now." I said, everybody who comes here finds Jo'burg tough compared with their home.

He'd had his head tipped back and he lifted it straight and looked at me. "I'm not such a kid." No? I said, feeling a bit awkward because he never talked about himself before. He was looking at me all the time, you'd have thought he was going to find his age written on my face. "I'm thirty-seven," he said. "Did you know that? Thirty-seven. Not so much younger."

Forty-nine. It was true, not so much. But he looked so young, with that hair always slicked back longish behind the ears as if he'd just come out of the shower, and that brown neck in the open-neck shirt. Lean men wear well, you can't tell. He did have false teeth, though, that was why his mouth made him look hard. I supposed he could have been thirty-seven; I didn't know, I didn't know.

It was like the scars on his body. There were scars on his back and other scars on his stomach, and my heart was in my mouth for him when I saw them, still pink and raw-looking, but he said that the ones on his back were from strokes he'd had in a boys' home as a kid and the others were from the fighting in Katanga.[13]

I know nobody would believe me, they would think I was just trying to make excuses for myself, but in the morning everything seemed just the same, I didn't feel I knew him any better. It was just like it was that first day when he came in with his Rhodesian money. He said, "Leave me the key. I might as well use the place while you're out all day." But what about the hotel, I said. "I've taken my things," he says. I said, you mean you've moved out? And something in his face, the bored sort of look, made me ask, you've told Mrs. Douglas? "She's found out by now," he said, it was unusual for him to smile. You mean you went without paying? I said. "Look, I told you I can't get my money out of those bastards."

---

[13] *Katanga:* A region in southern Congo that includes Elisabethville; the region is now known as Shaba.

Well, what could I do? I'd taken him to Mrs. Douglas myself. The woman'd given him a room on my recommendation. I had to go over to the New Park and spin her some yarn about him having to leave suddenly and that he'd left the money for me to pay. What else could I do? Of course, I didn't tell him.

But I told Jack. That's the funny thing about it. I told Jack that the man had disappeared, run off without paying my friend who ran the hotel where he was staying. The boy clicked his tongue the way they do, and laughed. And I said that was what you got for trying to help people. Yes, he said, Johannesburg was full of people like that, but you learn to know their faces, even if they were nice faces.

I said, you think that man had a nice face?

"You see he has a nice face," the boy said.

I was afraid I'd find the fellow there when I got home, and he was there. I said to him, that's my daughter, and showed him the photo, but he took no interest, not even when I said she lived in Gwelo[14] and perhaps he knew the town himself. I said why didn't he go back to Rhodesia to his job but he said Central Africa was finished, he wasn't going to be pushed around by a lot of blacks running the show—from what he told me, it's awful, you can't keep them out of hotels or anything.

Later on he went out to get some smokes and I suddenly thought, I'll lock the door and I won't let him into the flat again. I had made up my mind to do it. But when I saw his shadow on the other side of the frosty glass I just got up and opened it, and I felt like a fool, what was there to be afraid of? He was such a clean, good-looking fellow standing there; and anybody can be down on his luck. I sometimes wonder what'll happen to me—in some years, of course—if I can't work and I'm here alone, and nobody comes. Every Sunday you read in the paper about women dead alone in flats, no one discovers it for days.

He smoked night and day, like the world had some bad smell that he had to keep out of his nose. He was smoking in bed at the weekend and I made a remark about Princess Margaret[15] when she was here as a kid in 1947—I was looking at a story about the Royal Family, in the Sunday paper. He said he'd supposed he'd seen her, it was the year he went to the boys' home and they were taken to watch the procession.

One of the few things he'd told me about himself was that he was eight when he was sent to the home; I lay there and worked out that if he was thirty-seven, he should have been twenty in 1947, not eight years old.

But by then I found it hard to believe he was only twenty-five. You could always get rid of a boy of twenty-five. He wouldn't have the strength inside to make you afraid to try it.

I'd've felt safer if someone had known about him and me but of course I couldn't talk to anyone. Imagine the Versfelds. Or the woman I go out with on Fridays, I don't think she's had a cup of tea with a man since her husband died!

---

[14] *Gwelo:* A city in central Rhodesia, now known as Gwero, Zimbabwe.

[15] *Princess Margaret:* Princess Margaret was the sister of Queen Elizabeth II of England.

I remarked to Jack, the boss-boy, how old did he think the man had been, the one with the Rhodesian money who cheated the hotel? He said, "He's still here?" I said no, no, I just wondered. "He's young, that one," he said, but I should have remembered that half the time natives don't know their own age, it doesn't matter to them the way it does to us. I said to him, wha'd'you call young? He jerked his head back at the workshop. "Same like the mechanics." That bunch of kids! But this fellow wasn't cocky like them, wrestling with each other all over the place, calling after girls, fancying themselves the Beatles[16] when they sing in the washroom. The people he used to go off to see about things—I never saw any of them. If he had friends, they never came around. If only *somebody* else had known he was in the flat!

Then he said he was having the car overhauled because he was going off to Durban.[17] He said he had to leave the next Saturday. So I felt much better; I also felt bad, in a way, because there I'd been, thinking I'd have to find some way to make him go. He put his hand on my waist, in the daylight, and smiled right out at me and said, "Sorry, got to push on and get moving sometime, you know," and it was true that in a way he was right, I couldn't think what it'd be like without him, though I was always afraid he would stay. Oh he was nice to me then, I can tell you; he could be nice if he wanted to, it was like a trick that he could do, so real you couldn't believe it when it stopped just like that. I told him he should've brought the car into our place, I'd've seen to it that they did a proper job on it, but no, a friend of his was doing it free, in his own workshop.

Saturday came, he didn't go. The car wasn't ready. He sat about most of the week, disappeared for a night, but was there again in the morning. I'd given him a couple quid to keep him going. I said to him, what are you mucking about with that car in somebody's back yard for? Take it to a decent garage. Then—I'll never forget it—cool as anything, a bit irritated, he said, "Forget it. I haven't got the car any more." I said, wha'd'you mean, you mean you've sold it?—I suppose because in the back of my mind I'd been thinking, why doesn't he sell it, he needs money. And he said, "That's right. It's sold," but I knew he was lying, he couldn't be bothered to think of anything else to say. Once he'd said the car was sold, he said he was waiting for the money; he did pay me back three quid, but he borrowed again a day or so later. He'd keep his back to me when I came into the flat and he wouldn't answer when I spoke to him; and then just when he turned on me with that closed, half-asleep face and I'd think, this is it, now this is it—I can't explain how finished, done-for I felt, I only know that he had on his face exactly the same look I can remember on the face of a man, once, who was drowning some kittens one after the other in a bucket of water—just as I knew it was coming, he would burst out laughing at me. It was the only time he laughed. He would laugh until, nearly crying, I would begin to laugh too. And we would pretend it was kidding, and he would be nice to me, oh, he would be nice to me.

---

[16] *the Beatles:* British rock group, immensely popular in the 1960s and 1970s.

[17] *Durban:* A city on east coast of South Africa.

I used to sit in my office at the garage and look round at the car adverts and the maps on the wall and the elephant ear[18] growing in the oil drum and that was the only place I felt: but this is nonsense, what's got into me? The flat, and him in it—they didn't seem real. Then I'd go home at five and there it would all be.

I said to Jack, what's a '59 Chrysler worth? He took his time, he was cleaning his hands on some cotton waste. He said, "With those tyres, nobody will pay much."

Just to show him that he mustn't get too free with a white person, I asked him to send up to Mr. Levine for a headache powder for me. I joked, I'm getting a bit like Old Madala there, I feel so tired today.

D'you know what that boy said to me then? They've got more feeling than whites sometimes, that's the truth. He said, "When my children grow up they must work for me. Why don't you live there in Rhodesia with your daughter? The child must look after the mother. Why must you stay here alone in this town?"

Of course I wasn't going to explain to him that I like my independence. I always say I hope when I get old I die before I become a burden on anybody. But that afternoon I did something I should've done long ago, I said to the boy, if ever I don't turn up to work, you must tell them in the workshop to send someone to my flat to look for me. And I wrote down the address. Days could go by before anyone'd find what had become of me; it's not right.

When I got home that same evening, the fellow wasn't there. He'd gone. Not a word, not a note; nothing. Every time I heard the lift[19] rattling I thought, here he is. But he didn't come. When I was home on Saturday afternoon I couldn't stand it any longer and I went up to the Versfelds and asked the old lady if I couldn't sleep there a few days, I said my flat was being painted and the smell turned my stomach. I thought, if he comes to the garage, there are people around, at least there are the boys. I was smoking nearly as much as *he* used to and I couldn't sleep. I had to ask Mr. Levine to give me something. The slightest sound and I was in a cold sweat. At the end of the week I had to go back to the flat, and I bought a chain for the door and made a heavy curtain so's you couldn't see anyone standing there. I didn't go out, once I'd got in from work—not even to the early flicks—so I wouldn't have to come back into the building at night. You know how it is when you're nervous, the funniest things comfort you: I'd just tell myself, well, if I shouldn't turn up to work in the morning, the boy'd send somebody to see.

Then slowly I was beginning to forget about it. I kept the curtain and the chain and I stayed at home, but when you get used to something, no matter what it is, you don't think about it all the time, any more, though you still believe you do. I hadn't been to Maison Claude for about two weeks and my hair was a sight. Claude advised a soft perm and so it happened that I took a couple of hours off in the afternoon to get it done. The boss-boy Jack says to me when I come back, "He was here."

---

[18] *elephant ear:* A kind of plant.

[19] *lift:* Elevator.

I didn't know what to do, I couldn't help staring quickly all around. When, I said. "Now-now, while you were out." I had the feeling I couldn't get away. I knew he would come up to me with that closed, half-asleep face—burned as a good-looker lifesaver, burned like one of those tramps who are starving and lousy and pickled with cheap booze but have a horrible healthy look that comes from having nowhere to go out of the sun. I don't know what that boy must have thought of me, my face. He said, "I told him you're gone. You don't work here any more. You went to Rhodesia to your daughter. I don't know which place." And he put his nose back in one of the newspapers he's always reading whenever things are slack; I think he fancies himself quite the educated man and he likes to read about all these blacks who are becoming prime ministers and so on in other countries these days. I never remark on it; if you take any notice of things like that with them, you begin to give them big ideas about themselves.

That fellow's never bothered me again. I never breathed a word to anybody about it—as I say, that's the trouble when you work alone in an office like I do, there's no one you can speak to. It just shows you, a woman on her own has always got to look out; it's not only that it's not safe to walk about alone at night because of the natives, this whole town is full of people you can't trust.

UNDERSTANDING THE STORY

1. Describe the narrator's appearance. What does her appearance reveal about her personality?

2. What does the narrator's choice of friends reveal about the narrator?

3. What does that narrator's relationship with her daughter reveal about the narrator?

4. Describe the narrator's attitude and behavior toward blacks. How does it affect her relationship with Jack? How does she assert her social position?

5. What kind of person is the Rhodesian?

6. Why does the narrator initially find the Rhodesian appealing? Why does she later become afraid of him?

7. Why would the narrator have felt safer if she could have told someone about her relationship with the Rhodesian?

8. Why does Jack get rid of the Rhodesian?

9. "Know thyself" is a concept that was important to the ancient Greeks. Explain the significance of this concept and apply the concept to the narrator.

ANALYZING LITERARY TECHNIQUE

1. How does the setting of this story contribute to character development and plot?

2. What is Jack's function in the story?

3. Discuss why two of the three principal characters have no names. Given the narrative technique, how could the author have revealed their names? What did she accomplish by not doing so?

4. Describe the **tone** of the story. How does Gordimer achieve it?

5. What is the **climax** of the story?

6. What is the relationship between the narrator's last sentence and the title of the story?

7. What does the **narrative perspective** accomplish in this story?

WRITING ABOUT LITERATURE

1. Write an essay in which you analyze the function of the narrative perspective of this story. Choose what you consider to be the three most revealing examples of how this technique reinforces the impact of the story. For each example, first quote its use in the story and then explain its impact on the story.

2. Write a character sketch of the Rhodesian. What do you learn about him from his statements and his behavior? Choose an adjective that accurately describes him and then find at least three examples from the story that support your choice of adjective. Explain how each example contributes to understanding his character.

3. Tell this story from the perspective of one of the two males in the story. If you choose Jack, include his perceptions of both the narrator and the Rhodesian. If you choose the Rhodesian, focus on his personality, his evaluation of the narrator, and his motivation.

Marriage Is a Private Affair

CHINUA ACHEBE

*C*HINUA ACHEBE (1930–), the Nigerian author, is one of the most famous African writers. Writing in English, Achebe is a novelist, short-story writer, and poet. He is best known for *Things Fall Apart* (1958), the first major novel from tropical Africa. The work has become a classic. This novel is the second in a series of four novels that depicts seventy-five years in the life of the Ibo people. The other novels (in the order they tell the Ibo story) are *Arrow of God* (1964), *No Longer at Ease* (1960), and *A Man of the People* (1966).

Achebe was born into the Ibo tribe in Ogidi, in eastern Nigeria. His father was a Christian convert who became a teacher of Christianity. After attending Government College Achebe became one of the first graduates of the University College at Ibadan (1953). As an adult, he became interested in the pre-Christian past of his people, a study that resulted in his series of novels. From 1960 until 1967, Achebe worked for the Nigerian Broadcasting Service. In 1970 he began an academic career as a professor of English. He has taught at universities in Nigeria and the United States.

Achebe is dedicated to the principle that education is the key to the future well-being of Africa. He believes that the African peoples must know and value their heritage, understand their history, and possess a strong ethical code that condemns injustice and corruption everywhere. In a literary style that is direct and clear, Achebe's stories depict the changing nature of Nigerian society, with the inevitable conflicts between African tradition and modern European society. In "Marriage Is a Private Affair," Achebe reveals the universal significance of these conflicts. The story is from *Girls at War and Other Stories* (1972), which was written after the Nigerian civil war (1967–1970).

"Have you written to your dad yet?" asked Nene one afternoon as she sat with Nnaemeka in her room at 16 Kasanga Street, Lagos.[1]

"No. I've been thinking about it. I think it's better to tell him when I get home on leave!"

"But why? Your leave is such a long way off yet—six whole weeks. He should be let into our happiness now."

Nnaemeka was silent for a while, and then began very slowly as if he groped for his words: "I wish I were sure it would be happiness to him."

"Of course it must," replied Nene, a little surprised. "Why shouldn't it?"

"You have lived in Lagos all your life, and you know very little about people in remote parts of the country."

"That's what you always say. But I don't believe anybody will be so unlike other people that they will be unhappy when their sons are engaged to marry."

"Yes. They are most unhappy if the engagement is not arranged by them. In our case it's worse—you are not even an Ibo."[2]

This was said so seriously and so bluntly that Nene could not find speech immediately. In the cosmopolitan atmosphere of the city it had always seemed to her something of a joke that a person's tribe could determine whom he married.

At last she said, "You don't really mean that he will object to your marrying me simply on that account? I had always thought you Ibos were kindly disposed to other people."

"So we are. But when it comes to marriage, well, it's not quite so simple. And this," he added, "is not peculiar to the Ibos. If your father were alive and lived in the heart of Ibibio-land he would be exactly like my father."

"I don't know. But anyway, as your father is so fond of you, I'm sure he will forgive you soon enough. Come on then, be a good boy and send him a nice lovely letter. . . ."

"It would not be wise to break the news to him by writing. A letter will bring it upon him with a shock. I'm quite sure about that."

"All right, honey, suit yourself. You know your father."

As Nnaemeka walked home that evening he turned over in his mind the different ways of overcoming his father's opposition, especially now that he had gone and found a girl for him. He had thought of showing his letter to Nene but decided on second thought not to, at least for the moment. He read it again when he got home and couldn't help smiling to himself. He remembered Ugoye quite well, an Amazon[3] of a girl who used to beat up all the boys, himself included, on the way to the stream, a complete dunce at school.

---

[1] *Lagos:* Capital of Nigeria.

[2] *Ibo:* A people in southern Nigeria.

[3] *Amazon:* A strong, aggressive woman. The Amazons were a race of warrior women in Greek mythology.

I have found a girl who will suit you admirably—Ugoye Nweke, the eldest daughter of our neighbour, Jacob Nweke. She has a proper Christian upbringing. When she stopped schooling some years ago her father (a man of sound judgment) sent her to live in the house of a pastor where she has received all the training a wife could need. Her Sunday School teacher has told me that she reads her Bible very fluently. I hope we shall begin negotiations when you come home in December.

On the second evening of his return from Lagos Nnaemeka sat with his father under a cassia tree. This was the old man's retreat where he went to read his Bible when the parching December sun had set and a fresh, reviving wind blew on the leaves.

"Father," began Nnaemeka suddenly, "I have come to ask forgiveness."

"Forgiveness? For what, my son?" he asked in amazement.

"It's about the marriage question."

"Which marriage question?"

"I can't—we must—I mean it is impossible for me to marry Nweke's daughter."

"Impossible? Why?" asked his father.

"I don't love her."

"Nobody said you did. Why should you?" he asked.

"Marriage today is different. . . ."

"Look here, my son," interrupted his father, "nothing is different. What one looks for in a wife are a good character and a Christian background."

Nnaemeka saw there was no hope along the present line of argument.

"Moreover," he said, "I am engaged to marry another girl who has all of Ugoye's good qualities, and who . . ."

His father did not believe his ears. "What did you say?" he asked slowly and disconcertingly.

"She is a good Christian," his son went on, "and a teacher in a Girls' School in Lagos."

"Teacher, did you say? If you consider that a qualification for a good wife I should like to point out to you, Emeka, that no Christian woman should teach. St. Paul in his letter to the Corinthians says that women should keep silence."[4] He rose slowly from his seat and paced forwards and backwards. This was his pet subject, and he condemned vehemently those church leaders who encouraged women to teach in their schools. After he had spent his emotion on a long homily he at last came back to his son's engagement, in a seemingly milder tone.

"Whose daughter is she, anyway?"

"She is Nene Atang."

"What!" All the mildness was gone again. "Did you say Neneatanga, what does that mean?"

---

[4] *St. Paul . . . should keep silence:* St. Paul was an early Christian apostle and author of several books in the Christian Bible. In his first letter to the early church in Corinth, he criticized the Corinthians' practice of allowing women to preach.

"Nene Atang from Calabar.[5] She is the only girl I can marry." This was a very rash reply and Nnaemeka expected the storm to burst. But it did not. His father merely walked away into his room. This was most unexpected and perplexed Nnaemeka. His father's silence was infinitely more menacing than a flood of threatening speech. That night the old man did not eat.

When he sent for Nnaemeka a day later he applied all possible ways of dissuasion. But the young man's heart was hardened, and his father eventually gave him up as lost.

"I owe it to you, my son, as a duty to show you what is right and what is wrong. Whoever put this idea into your head might as well have cut your throat. It is Satan's work." He waved his son away.

"You will change your mind, Father, when you know Nene."

"I shall never see her," was the reply. From that night the father scarcely spoke to his son. He did not, however, cease hoping that he would realize how serious was the danger he was heading for. Day and night he put him in his prayers.

Nnaemeka, for his own part, was very deeply affected by his father's grief. But he kept hoping that it would pass away. If it had occurred to him that never in the history of his people had a man married a women who spoke a different tongue, he might have been less optimistic. "It has never been heard," was the verdict of an old man speaking a few weeks later. In that short sentence he spoke for all of his people. This man had come with others to commiserate with Okeke when news went round about his son's behaviour. By that time the son had gone back to Lagos.

"It has never been heard," said the old man again with a sad shake of his head.

"What did Our Lord[6] say?" asked another gentlemen. "Sons shall rise against their Fathers; it is there in the Holy Book."

"It is the beginning of the end," said another.

The discussion thus tending to become theological, Madubogwu, a highly practical man, brought it down once more to the ordinary level.

"Have you thought of consulting a native doctor about your son?" he asked Nnaemeka's father.

"He isn't sick," was the reply.

"What is he then? The boy's mind is diseased and only a good herbalist can bring him back to his right senses. The medicine he requires is *Amalile*, the same the women apply with success to recapture their husbands' straying affection."

"Madubogwu is right," said another gentleman. "This thing calls for medicine."

"I shall not call in a native doctor." Nnaemeka's father was known to be obstinately ahead of his more superstitious neighbours in these matters. "I will not be another Mrs. Ochuba. If my son wants to kill himself let him do it with his own hands. It is not for me to help him."

---

[5] *Calabar:* City in southeastern Nigeria.
[6] *Our Lord:* Christ.

"But it wasn't her fault," said Madubogwu. "She ought to have gone to an honest herbalist. She was a clever woman, nevertheless."

"She was a wicked murderess," said Jonathon who rarely argued with his neighbours because, he often said, they were incapable of reasoning. "The medicine was prepared for her husband, it was his name they called in its preparation and I am sure it would have been perfectly beneficial to him. It was wicked to put it in the herbalist's food, and say you were only trying it out."

Six months later, Nnaemeka was showing his young wife a short letter from his father:

> *It amazes me that you could be so unfeeling as to send me your wedding picture. I would have sent it back. But on further thought I decided just to cut off your wife and send it back to you because I have nothing to do with her. How I wish that I had nothing to do with you either.*

When Nene read through this letter and looked at the mutilated picture her eyes filled with tears and she began to sob.

"Don't cry, my darling," said her husband. "He is essentially good-natured and will one day look more kindly on our marriage." But years passed and that one day did not come.

For eight years, Okeke would have nothing to do with his son, Nnaemeka. Only three times (when Nnaemeka asked to come home and spend his leave) did he write to him.

"I can't have you in my house," he replied on one occasion. "It can be of no interest to me where or how you spend your leave—or your life, for that matter."

The prejudice against Nnaemeka's marriage was not confined to his little village. In Lagos, especially among his people who worked there, it showed itself in a different way. Their women, when they met at their village meeting were not hostile to Nene. Rather, they paid her such excessive deference as to make her feel she was not one of them. But as time went on, Nene gradually broke through some of this prejudice and even began to make some friends among them. Slowly and grudgingly they began to admit that she kept her home much better than most of them.

The story eventually got to the little village in the heart of the Ibo country that Nnaemeka and his young wife were a most happy couple. But his father was one of the few people who knew nothing about this. He always displayed so much temper whenever his son's name was mentioned that everyone avoided it in his presence. By a tremendous effort of will he had succeeded in pushing his son to the back of his mind. The strain had nearly killed him but he had persevered, and won.

Then one day he received a letter from Nene, and in spite of himself he began to glance through it perfunctorily until all of a sudden the expression on his face changed and he began to read more carefully.

> *. . . Our two sons, from the day they learnt that they have a grandfather, have insisted on being taken to him. I find it impossible to tell them that you will*

*not see them. I implore you to allow Nnaemeka to bring them home for a short
time during his leave next month. I shall remain here in Lagos . . .*

The old man at once felt the resolution he had built up over so many years
falling in. He was telling himself that he must not give in. He tried to steel
his heart against all the emotional appeals. It was a re-enactment of that other
struggle. He leaned against a window and looked out. The sky was overcast with
heavy black clouds and a high wind began to blow filling the air with dust and
dry leaves. It was one of those rare occasions when even Nature takes a hand in
a human fight. Very soon it began to rain, the first rain in the year. It came down
in large sharp drops and was accompanied by the lightning and thunder which
mark a change of season. Okeke was trying hard not to think of his two grandsons.
But he knew he was now fighting a losing battle. He tried to hum a favourite
hymn but the pattering of large rain drops on the roof broke up the tune. His
mind immediately returned to the children. How could he shut his door against
them? By a curious mental process he imagined them standing, sad and forsaken,
under the harsh angry weather—shut out from his house.

That night he hardly slept, from remorse—and a vague fear that he might
die without making it up to them.

UNDERSTANDING THE STORY

1. Why does Okeke object to Nnaemeka's marriage?
2. To what extent, if any, is Nnaemeka to blame for the destruction of his
   relationship with Okeke?
3. What does Nnaemeka's attitude toward Okeke revel about Nnaemeka?
4. What does Okeke's reaction to the suggestion about the native doctor
   reveal about Okeke?
5. Why does Okeke react to Nene's letter as he does?
6. What attitude does the title convey?
7. What effect does the last sentence have on the impact of the story?
8. What **themes** do you find in the story?

ANALYZING LITERARY TECHNIQUE

1. Find three examples of **contrast** in this story.
2. How does Achebe use **foreshadowing** in the story?
3. What is the **tone** of the story? How is the tone achieved?
4. Which view more accurately depicts the outcome of the story: "Character
   determines fate," or "Fate determines character"? Explain your choice.
5. In what ways is this story **ironic?**

WRITING ABOUT LITERATURE

1. Write an essay in which you analyze how Achebe's use of contrast enhances one of the story's themes. Examine two or three examples of contrast. Use quotations for each example and explain how each example relates to the theme.

2. Write a letter from Okeke to Nene after Okeke's grandsons have visited him. Consider the following questions: What does Okeke say about his grandchildren? How does he feel about Nene? To what extent, if any, have his attitudes changed?

The Rain Came

GRACE OGOT

*G*RACE OGOT (1930–) is a well-known African writer and politician from Kenya. Her works include the short-story collection *Land Without Thunder* (1968) and the novels *The Promised Land* (1966), *The Graduate* (1980), and *The Island of Tears* (1980). Ogot was the first female African writer to be published in English; she was also a founding member of the Writer's Association of Kenya.

Grace Ogot was born and reared in Nyanza Province of central Kenya. After training as a nurse in Uganda and England, she lived in London from 1955 to 1961 where she was the first African to qualify in England as a midwife. With the encouragement of her husband, Ogot began writing articles. Her career led to writing scripts and to broadcasting on the British Broadcasting Corporation's East African Service. She then moved to Makerere College in Uganda, where she worked in community development and public relations. President Daniel Moi nominated Ogot to the Kenyan Parliament in 1983. She eventually resigned from Parliament but was later elected assistant minister for culture and social services. She has used her high-profile political life to fight poverty and sexual discrimination in Kenya and to improve education. She has also represented her country at both the United Nations and the United Nations Education, Scientific, and Cultural Organization (UNESCO).

Her tales, such as "The Rain Came," usually deal with the life of the Luo people before the introduction of European ways.

The chief was still far from the gate when his daughter Oganda saw him. She ran to meet him. Breathlessly she asked her father, "What is the news, great Chief? Everyone in the village is anxiously waiting to hear when it will rain." Labong'o held out his hands for his daughter but he did not say a word. Puzzled by her father's cold attitude Oganda ran back to the village to warn the others that the chief was back.

The atmosphere in the village was tense and confused. Everyone moved aimlessly and fussed in the yard without actually doing any work. A young woman whispered to her co-wife, "If they have not solved this rain business today, the chief will crack." They had watched him getting thinner and thinner as the people kept on pestering him. "Our cattle lie dying the fields," they reported. "Soon it will be our children and then ourselves. Tell us what to do to save our lives, oh great Chief." So the chief had daily pleaded with the Almighty through the ancestors to deliver them from their great distress.

Instead of calling the family together and giving them the news immediately, Labong'o went to his own hut, a sign that he was not to be disturbed. Having replaced the shutter, he sat in the dimly-lit hut to contemplate.

It was no longer a question of being the chief of hunger-stricken people that weighed Labong'o's heart. It was the life of his only daughter that was at stake. At the time when Oganda came to meet him, he saw the glittering chain shining around her waist. The prophecy was complete. "It is Oganda, Oganda, my only daughter, who must die so young." Labong'o burst into tears before finishing the sentence. The chief must not weep. Society had declared him the bravest of men. But Labong'o did not care any more. He assumed the position of a simple father and wept bitterly. He loved his people, the Luo,[1] but what were the Luo for him without Oganda? Her life had brought a new life in Labong'o's world and he ruled better than he could remember. How would the spirit of the village survive his beautiful daughter? "There are so many homes and so many parents who have daughters. Why choose this one? She is all I have." Labong'o spoke as if the ancestors were there in the hut and he could see them face to face. Perhaps they were there, warning him to remember his promise on the day he was enthroned when he said aloud, before the elders, "I will lay down my life, if necessary, and the life of my household, to save this tribe from the hands of the enemy." "Deny! Deny!" he could hear the voice of his forefathers mocking him.

When Labong'o was made chief he was only a young man. Unlike his father he ruled for many years with only one wife. But people mocked him secretly because his only wife did not bear him a daughter. He married a second, a third and a fourth wife. But they all gave birth to male children. When Labong'o married a fifth wife, she bore him a daughter. They called her Oganda, meaning "beans," because her skin was very smooth. Out of Labong'o's twenty children, Oganda was the only girl. Though she was the chief's favorite, her mother's co-wives swallowed their jealous feelings and showered her with love. After all, they said, Oganda was a girl whose days in the royal family were numbered. She would soon marry at a tender age and leave the enviable position to someone else.

Never in his life had he been faced with such an impossible decision. Refusing to yield to the rain-maker's request would mean sacrificing the whole

---

[1] *Luo:* A people in Kenya.

tribe, putting the interests of the individual above those of the society. More than that. It would mean disobeying the ancestors, and most probably wiping the Luo people from the surface of the earth. On the other hand, to let Oganda die as a ransom for the people would permanently cripple Labong'o spiritually. He knew he would never be the same chief again.

The words of Nditi, the medicine-man, still echoed in his ears. "Podho, the ancestor of the Luo, appeared to me in a dream last night and he asked me to speak to the chief and the people," Nditi had said to the gathering of tribesmen. "A young woman who has not known a man must die so that the country may have rain. While Podho was still talking to me, I saw a young woman standing at the lakeside, her hands raised above her head. Her skin was as a tender young deer's. Her tall slender figure stood like a lonely reed at the river bank. Her sleepy eyes wore a sad look like that of a bereaved mother. She wore a gold ring on her left ear and a glittering brass chain around her waist. As I still marvelled at the beauty of this young woman, Podho told me, 'Out of all the women in this land, we have chosen this one. Let her offer herself a sacrifice to the lake monster! And on that day, the rain will come down in torrents. Let everyone stay at home on that day, lest he be carried away by the floods.'"

Outside, there was a strange stillness, except for the thirsty birds that sang lazily on the dying trees. The blinding midday heat had forced the people into their huts. Not far away from the chief's hut two guards were snoring away quietly. Labong'o removed his crown and the large eagle-head that hung loosely on his shoulders. He left the hut and, instead of asking Nyabogo the messenger to beat the drum, he went straight and beat it himself. In no time the whole household had assembled under the *siala* tree where he usually addressed them. He told Oganda to wait a while in her grandmother's hut.

When Labong'o stood to address his household his voice was hoarse and tears choked him. He started to speak but words refused to leave his lips. His wives and sons knew there was danger, perhaps their enemies had declared war on them. Labong'o's eyes were red and they could see he had been weeping. At last he told them, "One whom we love and treasure will be taken away from us. Oganda is to die." Labong'o's voice was so faint that he could not hear it himself. But he continued, "The ancestors have chosen her to be offered as a sacrifice to the lake monster in order that we may have rain."

For a moment there was dead silence among the people. They were completely stunned; and as some confused murmur broke out Oganda's mother fainted and was carried off to her own hut. But the other people rejoiced. They danced around singing and chanting, "Oganda is the lucky one to die for the people; if it is to save the people, let Oganda go."

In her grandmother's hut Oganda wondered what the whole family was discussing about her that she could not hear. Her grandmother's hut was well away from the chief's court and much as she strained her ears, she could not hear what they were saying. "It must be marriage," she concluded. It was an accepted custom for the family to discuss their daughter's future marriage behind her back. A faint smile played on Oganda's lips as she thought of the several young men who swallowed saliva at the mere mention of her name.

There was Kech, the son of an elder in a neighbouring clan. Kech was very handsome. He had sweet, meek eyes and roaring laughter. He could make a wonderful father, Oganda thought. But they would not be a good match. Kech was a bit too short to be her husband. It would humiliate her to have to look down at Kech each time she spoke to him. Then she thought of Dimo, the tall young man who had already distinguished himself as a brave warrior and an outstanding wrestler. Dimo loved Oganda, but Oganda thought he would make a cruel husband, always quarrelling and ready to fight. No, she did not like him. Oganda fingered the glittering chain on her waist as she thought of Osinda. A long time ago when she was quite young Osinda had given her that chain and, instead of wearing it around her neck several times, she wore it round her waist where it could permanently stay. She heard her heart pounding so loudly as she thought of him. She whispered, "Let it be you they are discussing, Osinda the lovely one. Come now and take me away. . . ."

The lean figure in the doorway startled Oganda who was rapt in thought about the man she loved. "You have frightened me, Grandma," said Oganda laughing. "Tell me, is it my marriage you were discussing? You can take it from me that I won't marry any of them." A smile played on her lips again. She was coaxing her grandma to tell her quickly, to tell her they were pleased with Osinda.

In the open space outside the excited relatives were dancing and singing. They were coming to the hut now, each carrying a gift to put at Oganda's feet. As their singing got nearer Oganda was able to hear what they were saying: "If it is to save the people, if it is to give us rain, let Oganda go. Let Oganda die for her people and for her ancestors." Was she mad to think that they were singing about her? How could she die? She found the lean figure of her grandmother barring the door. She could not get out. The look on her grandmother's face warned her that there was danger around the corner. "Mother, it is not marriage then?" Oganda asked urgently. She suddenly felt panicky, like a mouse cornered by a hungry cat. Forgetting that there was only one door in the hut, Oganda fought desperately to find another exit. She must fight for her life. But there was none.

She closed her eyes, leapt like a wild tiger through the door, knocking her grandmother flat to the ground. There outside in mourning garments Labong'o stood motionless, his hands folded at the back. He held his daughter's hand and led her away from the excited crowd to the little red-painted hut where her mother was resting. Here he broke the news officially to his daughter.

For a long time the three souls who loved each other dearly sat in darkness. It was no good speaking. And even if they tried, the words could not have come out. In the past they had been like three cooking-stones, sharing their burdens. Taking Oganda away from them would leave two useless stones which would not hold a cooking-pot.

News that the beautiful daughter of the chief was to be sacrificed to give the people rain spread across the country like wind. And at sunset the chief's village was full of relatives and friends who had come to congratulate Oganda. Many more were on their way, coming, carrying their gifts. They would dance till morning to keep her company. And in the morning they would prepare her a big farewell feast. All these relatives thought it a great honour to be selected by the spirits to die in order that the society might live. "Oganda's name will always remain a living name among us," they boasted.

Of course it was an honour, a great honour, for a woman's daughter to be chosen to die for the country. But what could the mother gain once her only daughter was blown away by the wind? There were so many other women in the land, why choose her daughter, her only child? Had human life any meaning all?—other women had houses full of children while Oganda's mother had to lose her only child!

In the cloudless sky the moon shone brightly and the numerous stars glittered. The dancers of all age groups assembled to dance before Oganda, who sat close to her mother sobbing quietly. All these years she had been with her people she thought she understood them. But now she discovered that she was a stranger among them. If they really loved her as they had always professed, why were they not sympathetic? Why were they not making any attempt to save her? Did her people really understand what it felt like to die young? Unable to restrain her emotions any longer, she sobbed loudly as her age-group got up to dance. They were young and beautiful and very soon they would marry and have their own children. They would have husbands to love and little huts for themselves. They would have reached maturity. Oganda touched the chain around her waist as she thought of Osinda. She wished Osinda were there too, among her friends. "Perhaps he is ill," she thought gravely. The chain comforted Oganda—she would die with it around her waist and wear it in the underground world.

In the morning a big feast of many different dishes was prepared for Oganda so that she could pick and choose. "People don't eat after death," they said. The food looked delicious but Oganda touched none of it. Let the happy people eat. She contented herself with sips of water from a little calabash.[2]

The time for her departure was drawing near and each minute was precious. It was a day's journey to the lake. She was to walk all night, passing through the great forest. But nothing could touch her, not even the denizens of the forest. She was already anointed with sacred oil. From the time Oganda received the sad news she had expected Osinda to appear any moment. But he was not there. A relative told her that Osinda was away on a private visit. Oganda realized that she would never see her dear one again.

In the afternoon the whole village stood at the gate to say good-bye and to see her for the last time. Her mother wept on her neck for a long time. The great chief in a mourning skin came to the gate barefooted and mingled with the people— a simple father in grief. He took off his wrist bracelet and put it on his daughter's wrist, saying, "You will always live among us. The spirit of our forefathers is with you."

Tongue-tied and unbelieving Oganda stood there before the people. She had nothing to say. She looked at her home once more. She could hear her heart beating so painfully within her. All her childhood plans were coming to an end.

---

[2] *calabash:* Drinking utensil made from a gourd.

She felt like a flower nipped in the bud never to enjoy the morning dew again. She looked at her weeping mother and whispered, "Whenever you want to see me, always look at the sunset. I will be there."

Oganda turned southwards to start her trek to the lake. Her parents, relatives, friends and admirers stood at the gate and watched her go. Her beautiful, slender figure grew smaller and smaller till she mingled with the thin dry trees in the forest.

As Oganda walked the lonely path that wound its way in the wilderness, she sang a song and her own voice kept her company.

> "The ancestors have said Oganda must die;
> The daughter of the chief must be sacrificed.
> When the lake monster feeds on my flesh,
> The people will have rain;
> Yes, the rain will come down in torrents.
> The wind will blow, the thunder will roar.
> And the floods will wash away the sandy beaches
> When the daughter of the chief dies in the lake.
> My age-group has consented,
> My parents have consented,
> So have my friends and relatives;
> Let Oganda die to give us rain.
> My age-group are young and ripe,
> Ripe for womanhood and motherhood;
> But Oganda must die young,
> Oganda must sleep with the ancestors.
> Yes, rain will come down in torrents."

The red rays of the setting sun embraced Oganda and she looked like a burning candle in the wilderness.

The people who came to hear her sad song were touched by her beauty. But they all said the same thing: "If it is to save the people, if it is to give us rain, then be not afraid. Your name will for ever live among us."

At midnight Oganda was tired and weary. She could walk no more. She sat under a big tree and, having sipped water from her calabash, she rested her head on the tree trunk and slept.

When she woke up in the morning the sun was high in the sky. After walking for many hours she reached the *tong*, a strip of land that separated the inhabited part of the country from the sacred place—*kar lamo*. No lay man could enter this place and come out alive—only those who had direct contact with the spirits and the Almighty were allowed to enter his holy of holies. But Oganda had to pass through this sacred land on her way to the lake, which she had to reach at sunset.

A large crowd gathered to see her for the last time. Her voice was now hoarse and painful but there was no need to worry any more. Soon she would not have to sing. The crowd looked at Oganda sympathetically, mumbling words she could not hear. But none of them pleaded for her life. As Oganda opened the gate a child, a young child, broke loose from the crowd and ran toward her. The child took a small ear-ring from her sweaty hands and gave it to Oganda, saying, "When you reach the world of the dead, give this ear-ring to my sister. She died last week. She forgot this ring." Oganda, taken aback by this strange request, took the little ring and handed her precious water and food to the child. She did not need them now. Oganda did not know whether to laugh or cry. She had heard mourners sending love to their sweethearts, long dead, but this idea of sending gifts was new to her.

Oganda held her breath as she crossed the barrier to enter the sacred land. She looked appealingly at the crowd but there was no response. Their minds were too preoccupied with their own survival. Rain was the precious medicine they were longing for and the sooner Oganda could get to her destination the better.

A strange feeling possessed the princess as she picked her way in the sacred land. There were strange noises that often started her and her first reaction was to take to her heels. But she remembered that she had to fulfill the wish of her people. She was exhausted, but the path was still winding. Then suddenly the path ended on sandy land. The water had retreated miles away from the shore, leaving a wide stretch of sand. Beyond this was the vast expanse of water.

Oganda felt afraid. She wanted to picture the size and shape of the monster, but fear would not let her. The people did not talk about it, nor did the crying children who were silenced at the mention of its name. The sun was still up but it was no longer hot. For a long time Oganda walked ankle-deep in the sand. She was exhausted and longed desperately for her calabash of water. As she moved on she had a strange feeling that something was following her. Was it the monster? Her hair stood erect and a cold paralysing feeling ran along her spine. She looked behind, sideways and in front, but there was nothing except a cloud of dust.

Oganda began to hurry but the feeling did not leave her and her whole body seemed to be bathing in its perspiration.

The sun was going down fast and the lake shore seemed to move along with it.

Oganda started to run. She must be at the lake before sunset. As she ran she heard a noise coming from behind. She looked back sharply and something resembling a moving bush was frantically running after her. It was about to catch up with her.

Oganda ran with all her strength. She was now determined to throw herself into the water even before sunset. She did not look back but the creature was upon her. She made an effort to cry out, as in a nightmare, but she could not hear her own voice. The creature caught up with Oganda. A strong hand grabbed her. But she fell flat on the sand and fainted.

When the lake breeze brought her back to consciousness a man was bending over her.

"O . . . !" Oganda opened her mouth to speak, but she had lost her voice. She swallowed a mouthful of water poured into her mouth by the stranger.

"Osinda, Osinda! Please let me die. Let me run, the sun is going down. Let me die. Let them have rain."

Osinda fondled the glittering chain around Oganda's waist and wiped tears from her face. "We must escape quickly to an unknown land," Osinda said urgently. "We must run away from the wrath of the ancestors and the retaliation of the monster."

"But the curse is upon me, Osinda, I am no good for you any more. And moreover the eyes of the ancestors will follow us everywhere and bad luck will befall us. Nor can we escape from the monster."

Oganda broke loose, afraid to escape, but Osinda grabbed her hands again. "Listen to me, Oganda! Listen! Here are two coats!" He then covered the whole of Oganda's body, except her eyes, with a leafy attire made from the twigs of bwombwe. "These will protect us from the eyes of the ancestors and the wrath of the monster. Now let us run out of here." He held Oganda's hand and they ran from the sacred land, avoiding the path that Oganda had followed.

The bush was thick and the long grass entangled their feet as they ran. Half-way through the sacred land they stopped and looked back. The sun was almost touching the surface of the water. They were frightened. They continued to run, now faster, to avoid the sinking sun.

"Have faith, Oganda—that thing will not reach us."

When they reached the barrier and looked behind them, trembling, only the tip of the sun could be seen above the water's surface.

"It is gone! It is gone!" Oganda wept, hiding her face in her hands.

"Weep not, the daughter of the chief. Let us run, let us escape."

There was a lightning flash in the distance. They looked up, frightened.

That night it rained in torrents as it had not done for a long, long time.

UNDERSTANDING THE STORY

1. Why was Oganda the most acceptable sacrifice?

2. What is the attitude of the villagers toward human sacrifice?

3. What choice does Labong'o have with regard to Oganda's sacrifice?

4. What choice does Oganda have with regard to being sacrificed?

5. What is special about the protective coats that Osinda supplies?

6. What is significant about the rain's arrival?

7. Does the author present Osinda as a hero or a villain? How does Oganda view him? How would Labong'o view him? How would the villagers view him?

8. What aspects of Oganda's behavior are heroic?

9. How might the villagers react if they knew that Oganda had escaped?

10. What does the story say about the role of tradition in a community?

ANALYZING LITERARY TECHNIQUE

1. What is significant about Ogot's **characterization** of the chief?

2. What is the significance of the story's title?

3. What is the function of **irony** in the story? How would the story be different without it?

4. What does Ogot achieve by using a third-person omniscient **narrative perspective?**

5. Find two or three examples of **figurative language** in the story. How is each example appropriate to the setting and subject matter of the story?

WRITING ABOUT LITERATURE

1. "The Rain Came" contains elements that are often found in myths that explain the relationship between human beings and the supernatural beings who control the forces of nature. The story also contains elements of a short story.

   Consider both the ways "The Rain Came" is a myth and the ways it is a short story. Write a brief essay in which you show how Ogot transformed a myth into a short story. Use quotations from the story to support your ideas.

2. Write a continuation of the story that begins with the onset of the rain. Consider the following questions: Do Osinda and Oganda return to the village? If so, why? How do the villagers now feel about human sacrifice? If Osinda and Oganda do not return, where do they go? How do the members of a different village receive them?

The Trials of Brother Jero

WOLE SOYINKA

OLE SOYINKA (1934–), the preeminent Nigerian
writer, was the first African writer to receive the Nobel
Prize for literature. In the words of the 1986 Nobel committee, Soyinka is one who "with wide cultural perspective and with
poetic overtones, fashions the drama of existence." A prolific and versatile writer, Soyinka is best known for his plays *The Trials of Brother
Jero* (1964), *Death and the King's Horseman* (1975), and *Requiem for a
Futurologist* (1985); for his prison poetry *A Shuttle in the Crypt* (1972);
for his African version of John Gay's *The Beggar's Opera, Opera
Wonyosi* (1981); for his autobiographical works *The Man Died: Prison
Notes* (1972) and *Aké: The Years of Childhood* (1981); for the fictional
biography of his father, *Ìsarà* (1989); and for *The Open Sore of a
Continent: A Personal Narrative of the Nigerian Crisis* (1996), a work
that looks at political unrest in Nigeria.

Soyinka was born in Abeokuta in western Nigeria. His parents were
both Yoruba. His mother passed on to him traditional Yoruba culture,
and his father, who was headmaster in a local Christian grammar
school, introduced him to modern European culture. After attending
Nigerian schools, he studied at the University of Leeds in England
from 1954 to 1957, graduating with honors in English. For the next
three years, he read plays and wrote scripts for the Royal Court
Theatre in London. Here his first dramatic sketches, poems, and songs
were performed. He returned to Nigeria in 1960, where he taught
drama at Ibadan, Ife, and Lagos Universities and worked at developing
a Nigerian theater. At Ibadan he was an actor, director, and dramatist.
He published his first volume of plays in 1963.

In 1967, while Soyinka was the director of the School of Drama
at Ibadan University, Nigeria was involved in a civil war. Soyinka
believed in intellectual freedom and political commitment. When he
opposed the military dictatorship in Nigeria and supported the seces-
sion of Biafra (an eastern region of Nigeria that was an independent
republic's from 1967 to 1970), he was arrested, denied a trial, and placed
in solitary confinement for twenty-two months. Determined not to let

this tactic destroy his mind, Soyinka secretly used whatever he had at hand to record his thoughts and to describe "the landscape of the loss of human contact." Once he was freed, he spent the next five years in Europe and in Ghana; he did not return to Nigeria until 1976. He then resumed living in Abeokuta, where he was a professor of comparative literature at the University of Ife and also the chairperson of the drama department.

In 1994 political pressure forced Soyinka to leave Nigeria again. The totalitarian regime that had lately come to power was persecuting anyone who sold his works and was threatening to cancel a conference at which he was to speak. Soyinka escaped to the United States, where he briefly taught at Harvard University. In 1996 he moved to Atlanta, Georgia, to teach at Emory University. He has since been able to return to Nigeria, although he continues to live in the United States.

Soyinka believes that a writer should not evade the present by glorying in the past. In his words, "The artist has always functioned as the record of the mores and experiences of his society and as the voice of vision in his own time." Soyinka is a man of broad African interests whose writings reflect his prison experiences, the study of the relationship between African myth and African literature, the importance of Yoruba tradition and the power of superstition over human life, the tension between traditional Yoruba culture and modern European culture, and the complexity and corruption of city life in Nigeria. His works also reveal his interest in the dual nature of the human personality. Often his characters are both creative and destructive, teetering between being master and victim and courting success while risking personal disaster. Soyinka often uses satire as a way of presenting excessive ambition, intrigue, and corruption. In this vein, he published the comic farce *The Trials of Brother Jero* and a darker sequel, *Jero's Metamorphosis* (1973).

CHARACTERS

JEROBOAM, a Beach Divine

OLD PROPHET, his mentor

CHUME, assistant to Jeroboam

AMOPE, his wife

A TRADER

MEMBER OF PARLIAMENT

DRUMMER BOY

PENITENT

NEIGHBOURS

WORSHIPPERS

A TOUGH MAMMA

A YOUNG GIRL

SCENE I

The stage is completely dark. A spotlight reveals the Prophet, a heavily but neatly bearded man; his hair is thick and high, but well-combed, unlike that of most prophets. Suave is the word for him. He carries a canvas pouch and a divine rod.[1] He speaks directly and with his accustomed loftiness to the audience.

JERO: I am a Prophet. A prophet by birth and by inclination. You have probably seen many of us on the streets, many with their own churches, many inland, many on the coast, many leading processions, many looking for processions to lead, many curing the deaf, many raising the dead. In fact, there are eggs and there are eggs. Same thing with prophets. I was born a Prophet. I think my parents found that I was born with rather thick and long hair. It was said to come right down to my eyes and down to my neck. For them, this was a certain sign that I was born a natural prophet. And I grew to love the trade. It used to be a very respectable one in those days and competition was dignified. But in the last few years, the beach has become fashionable, and the struggle for land has turned the profession into a thing of ridicule. Some prophets I could name gained their present beaches by getting women penitents to shake their bosoms in spiritual ecstasy. This prejudiced the councillors who came to divide the beach among us.

Yes, it did come to the point where it became necessary for the Town Council to come to the beach and settle the Prophets' territorial warfare once and for all. My Master, the same one who brought me up in prophetic ways, staked his claim and won a grant of land. . . . I helped him, with a campaign led by six dancing girls from the French territory, all dressed as Jehovah's Witnesses.[2] What my old Master did not realize was that I was really helping myself.

Mind you, the beach is hardly worth having these days. The worshippers have dwindled to a mere trickle and we really have to fight for every new convert. They all prefer High Life to the rhythm of celestial hymns. And television too is keeping our wealthier patrons at home. They used to come in the evening when they would not easily be recognized. Now they stay at home and watch television. However, my whole purpose in coming here is to show you one rather eventful day in my life, a day when I thought for a moment that the curse of my old Master was about to be fulfilled. It shook me quite a bit, but . . . the Lord protects his own. . . .

---

[1] *divine rod:* A metal rod about eighteen inches long, bent into a ring at one end. A symbol of authority.

[2] *Jehovah's Witnesses:* Jehovah's Witnesses believe in one God, Jehovah, and use a unique interpretation of the Bible as their guide to faith. They are known for their missionary outreach.

[*Enter* OLD PROPHET *shaking his fist.*]

OLD PROPHET: Ungrateful wretch! Is this how you repay the long years of training I have given you? To drive me, your old Tutor, off my piece of land . . . telling me I have lived beyond my time. Ha! May you be rewarded in the same manner. May the Wheel[3] come right round and find you just as helpless as you make me now. . . .

[*He continues to mouth curses, but inaudibly.*]

JERO [*ignoring him*]: He didn't move me one bit. The old dodderer had been foolish enough to imagine that when I organized the campaign to acquire his land in competition with [*ticking them off on his fingers*]—The Brotherhood of Jehu, the Cherubims and Seraphims, the Sisters of Judgement Day, the Heavenly Cowboys,[4] not to mention the Jehovah's Witnesses whom the French girls impersonated—well, he must have been pretty conceited to think that I did it all for him.

OLD PROPHET: Ingrate! Monster! I curse you with the curse of the Daughters of Discord. May they be your downfall. May the Daughters of Eve[5] bring ruin down on your head!

[OLD PROPHET *goes off, shaking his fist.*]

JERO: Actually that was a very cheap curse. He knew very well that I had one weakness—women. Not my fault, mind you. You must admit that I am rather good-looking . . . no, don't be misled, I am not at all vain. Nevertheless, I decided to be on my guard. The call of Prophecy is in my blood and I would not risk my calling with the fickleness of women. So I kept away from them. I am still single and since that day when I came into my own, no scandal has ever touched my name. And it was a sad day indeed when I woke up one morning and the first thing to meet my eyes was a Daughter of Eve. You may compare that feeling with waking up and finding a vulture crouched on your bedpost.

Blackout.

---

[3] *Wheel:* Fortune's wheel, sometimes called the wheel of life, which turns an individual's luck from good to bad or from bad to good.

[4] *The Brotherhood of Jehu . . . Heavenly Cowboys:* Imaginary religious sects.

[5] *Daughters of Discord . . . Daughters of Eve:* Women, especially women who entrap or seduce men.

SCENE II

Early morning. A few poles with nets and other litter denote a fishing village. Downstage right is the corner of a hut, window on one side, door on the other.

A cycle bell is heard ringing. Seconds after, a cycle is ridden on stage towards the hut. The rider is a shortish man; his feet barely touch the pedals. On the cross-bar is a woman; the cross-bar itself is wound round with a mat, and on the carrier is a large travelling sack, with a woman's household stool hanging from a corner of it.

AMOPE: Stop here. Stop here. That's his house.

[*The man applies the brakes too suddenly. The weight leans towards the woman's side, with the result that she props up the bicycle with her feet, rather jerkily. It is in fact no worse than any ordinary landing, but it is enough to bring out her sense of aggrievement.*]

AMOPE [*Her tone of martyrdom is easy, accustomed to use.*]: I suppose we all do our best, but after all these years one would think you could set me down a little more gently.

CHUME: You didn't give me much notice. I had to brake suddenly.

AMOPE: The way you complain—anybody who didn't see what happened would think you were the one who broke an ankle. [*She has already begun to limp.*]

CHUME: Don't tell me that was enough to break your ankle.

AMOPE: Break? You didn't hear me complain. You did your best, but if my toes are to be broken one by one just because I have to monkey on your bicycle, you must admit it's a tough life for a woman.

CHUME: I did my . . .

AMOPE: Yes, you did your best. I know. Didn't I admit it? Please . . . give me that stool . . . You know yourself that I'm not one to make much of a little thing like that, but I haven't been too well. If anyone knows that, it's you. Thank you. [*Taking the stool.*] . . . I haven't been well, that's all, otherwise I wouldn't have said a thing.

[*She sits down near the door of the hut, sighing heavily, and begins to nurse her feet.*]

CHUME: Do you want me to bandage it for you?

AMOPE: No, no. What for?

[CHUME *hesitates, then begins to unload the bundle.*]

CHUME: You're sure you don't want me to take you back? If it swells after I've gone . . .

AMOPE: I can look after myself. I've always done, and looked after you too. Just help me unload the things and place them against the wall . . . you know I wouldn't ask if it wasn't for the ankle.

[CHUME *had placed the bag next to her, thinking that was all. He returns now to untie the bundle. Brings out a small brazier covered with paper which is tied down, two small saucepans* . . .]

AMOPE: You haven't let the soup pour out, have you?

CHUME [*with some show of exasperation*]: Do you see oil on the wrapper? [*Throws down the wrapper.*]

AMOPE: Abuse me. All right, go on, begin to abuse me. You know that all I asked was if the soup had poured away, and it isn't as if that was something no one ever asked before. I would do it all myself if it wasn't for my ankle—anyone would think it was my fault . . . careful . . . careful now . . . the cork nearly came off that bottle. You know how difficult it is to get any clean water in this place . . .

[CHUME *unloads two bottles filled with water, two little parcels wrapped in paper, another tied in a knot, a box of matches, a piece of yam, two tins, one probably an* Ovaltine[6] *tin but containing something else of course, a cheap breakable spoon, a knife, while* AMOPE *keeps up her patient monologue, spoken almost with indifference.*]

AMOPE: Do, I beg you, take better care of that jar. . . . I know you didn't want to bring me, but it wasn't the fault of the jar, was it?

CHUME: Who said I didn't want to bring you?

AMOPE: You said it was too far away for you to bring me on your bicycle. . . . I suppose you really wanted me to walk. . . .

CHUME: I . . .

AMOPE: And after you'd broken my foot, the first thing you asked was if you should take me home. You were only too glad it happened . . . in fact if I wasn't the kind of person who would never think evil of anyone—even you—I would have said that you did it on purpose.

[*The unloading is over.* CHUME *shakes out the bag.*]

AMOPE: Just leave the bag here. I can use it for a pillow.

CHUME: Is there anything else before I go?

AMOPE: You've forgotten the mat. I know it's not much, but I would like something to sleep on. There are women who sleep in beds of course, but I'm not complaining. They are just lucky with their husbands, and we can't all be lucky I suppose.

---

[6] *Ovaltine:* A brand of cocoa.

CHUME: You've got a bed at home.

[*He unties the mat which is wound round the cross-bar.*]

AMOPE: And so I'm to leave my work undone. My trade is to suffer because I have a bed at home? Thank God I am not the kind of woman who . . .

CHUME: I am nearly late for work.

AMOPE: I know you can't wait to get away. You only use your work as an excuse. A Chief Messenger in the Local Government Office—do you call that work? Your old school friends are now Ministers,[7] riding in long cars. . . .

[CHUME *gets on his bike and flees.* AMOPE *shouts after him, craning her neck in his direction.*]

AMOPE: Don't forget to bring some more water when you're returning from work. [*She relapses and sighs heavily.*] He doesn't realize it is all for his own good. He's no worse than other men, but he won't make the effort to become something in life. A Chief Messenger. Am I to go to my grave as the wife of a Chief Messenger?

[*She is seated so that the Prophet does not immediately see her when he opens the window to breathe some fresh air. He stares straight out for a few moments, then shuts his eyes tightly, clasps his hands together above his chest, chin uplifted for a few moments' meditation. He relaxes and is about to go in when he sees* AMOPE's *back. He leans out to try to take in the rest of her but this proves impossible. Puzzled, he leaves the window and goes round to the door which is then seen to open about a foot and shut rapidly.* AMOPE *is calmly chewing cola.[8] As the door shuts she takes out a notebook and a pencil and checks some figures.*
    BROTHER JEROBOAM, *known to his congregation as* BROTHER JERO, *is seen again at the window, this time with his canvas pouch and divine stick. He lowers the bag to the ground, eases one leg over the window.*]

AMOPE [*without looking back*]: Where do you think you're going?

[BROTHER JERO *practically flings himself back into the house.*]

AMOPE: One pound, eight shillings, and ninepence[9] for three months. And he calls himself a man of God.

[*She puts the notebook away, unwraps the brazier, and proceeds to light it preparatory to getting breakfast.*
    The door opens another foot.]

---

[7] *Ministers:* Government officials.

[8] *cola:* Kola nuts, caffeine-containing seeds of the kola tree. They are chewed or used in beverages.

[9] *One pound . . . ninepence:* The pound is the unit of money in the United Kingdom. Shillings and pence are subunits of the pound.

JERO [*Coughs.*]: Sister . . . my dear sister in Christ . . .

AMOPE: I hope you slept well, Brother Jero. . . .

JERO: Yes, thanks be to God. [*Hems and coughs.*] I—er—I hope you have not come to stand in the way of Christ and his work.

AMOPE: If Christ doesn't stand in the way of me and my work.

JERO: Beware of pride, sister. That was a sinful way to talk.

AMOPE: Listen, you bearded debtor. You owe me one pound, eight and nine. You promised you would pay me three months ago but of course you have been too busy doing the work of God. Well, let me tell you that you are not going anywhere until you do a bit of my own work.

JERO: But the money is not in the house. I must get it from the post office before I can pay you.

AMOPE [*fanning the brazier*]: You'll have to think of something else before you call me a fool.

[BROTHER JEROBOAM *shuts the door.*
A *woman* TRADER *goes past with a deep calabash bowl*[10] *on her head.*]

AMOPE: Ei, what are you selling?

[*The* TRADER *hesitates, decides to continue on her way.*]

AMOPE: Isn't it you I'm calling? What have you got there?

TRADER [*stops, without turning round*]: Are you buying for trade or just for yourself?

AMOPE: It might help if you first told me what you have.

TRADER: Smoked fish.

AMOPE: Well, let's see it.

TRADER [*hesitates*]: All right, help me to set it down. But I don't usually stop on the way.

AMOPE: Isn't it money you are going to the market for, and isn't it money I'm going to pay you?

TRADER [*as* AMOPE *gets up and unloads her*]: Well, just remember it is early in the morning. Don't start me off wrong by haggling.

AMOPE: All right, all right. [*Looks at the fish.*] How much a dozen?

TRADER: One and three, and I'm not taking a penny less.

AMOPE: It is last week's, isn't it?

TRADER: I've told you, you're my first customer, so don't ruin my trade with the ill-luck of the morning.

---

[10] *calabash bowl:* Food or water container made from a gourd.

AMOPE [holding one up to her nose]: Well, it does smell a bit, doesn't it?

TRADER [putting back the wrappings]: Maybe it is you who haven't had a bath for a week.

AMOPE: Yeh! All right, go on. Abuse me. Go on and abuse me when all I wanted was a few of your miserable fish. I deserve it for trying to be neighbourly with a cross-eyed wretch, pauper that you are. . . .

TRADER: It is early in the morning. I am not going to let you infect my luck with your foul tongue by answering you back. And just you keep your cursed fingers from my goods because that is where you'll meet with the father of all devils if you don't.

[She lifts the load to her head all by herself.]

AMOPE: Yes, go on. Carry the burden of your crimes and take your beggar's rags out of my sight. . . .

TRADER: I leave you in the hands of your flatulent belly, you barren sinner. May you never do good in all your life.

AMOPE: You're cursing me now, are you?

[She leaps up just in time to see BROTHER JERO escape through the window.]

Help! Thief! Thief! You bearded rogue. Call yourself a prophet? But you'll find it easier to get out than to get in. You'll find that out or my name isn't Amope. . . .

[She turns on the TRADER who has already disappeared.]

Do you see what you have done, you spindle-leg toad? Receiver of stolen goods, just wait until the police catch up with you . . .

[Towards the end of this speech the sound of "gangan" drums is heard, coming from the side opposite the hut. A BOY enters carrying a drum on each shoulder. He walks towards her, drumming. She turns almost at once.]

AMOPE: Take yourself off, you dirty beggar. Do you think my money is for the likes of you?

[The BOY flees, turns suddenly, and beats a parting abuse on the drums.]

AMOPE: I don't know what the world is coming to. A thief of a Prophet, a swindler of a fish-seller and now that thing with lice on his head comes begging for money. He and the Prophet ought to get together with the fish-seller their mother.

Lights fade.

SCENE III

A short while later. The beach. A few stakes and palm leaves denote the territory of BROTHER JEROBOAM'*s church. To one side is a palm tree, and in the centre is a heap of sand with assorted empty bottles, a small mirror, and hanging from one of the bottles is a rosary[11] and cross.* BROTHER JERO *is standing as he was last seen when he made his escape—white flowing gown and a very fine velvet cape, white also. Stands upright, divine rod in hand, while the other caresses the velvet cape.*

JERO: I don't know how she found out my house. When I bought the goods off her, she did not even ask any questions. My calling was enough to guarantee payment. It is not as if this was a well-paid job. And it is not what I would call a luxury, this velvet cape which I bought from her. It would not have been necessary if one were not forced to distinguish himself more and more from these scum who degrade the calling of the Prophet. It becomes important to stand out, to be distinctive. I have set my heart after a particular name. They will look at my velvet cape and they will think of my goodness. Inevitably they must begin to call me . . . the Velvet-hearted Jeroboam. [*Straightens himself.*] Immaculate Jero, Articulate Hero of Christ's Crusade . . .

Well, it is out. I have not breathed it to a single soul, but that has been my ambition. You've got to have a name that appeals to the imagination—because the imagination is a thing of the spirit—it must catch the imagination of the crowd. Yes, one must move with modern times. Lack of colour gets one nowhere even in the Prophet's business. [*Looks all round him.*] Charlatans! If only I had this beach to myself. [*With sudden violence.*] But how does one maintain his dignity when the daughter of Eve forces him to leave his own house through a window? God curse that woman! I never thought she would dare affront the presence of a man of God. One pound eight for this little cape. It is sheer robbery.

[*He surveys the scene again. A young girl passes, sleepily, clothed only in her wrapper.*]

JERO: She passes here every morning, on her way to take a swim. Dirty-looking thing.

[*He yawns.*]

I am glad I got here before any customers—I mean worshippers—well, customers if you like. I always get that feeling every morning that I am a shopkeeper waiting for customers. The regular ones come at definite times. Strange, dissatisfied people. I know they are dissatisfied because I keep them dissatisfied. Once they are full, they won't come again. Like my good apprentice, Brother Chume. He wants to beat his wife, but I won't let him. If I do, he will become contented, and then that's another of my flock gone for ever. As long as he doesn't beat her, he comes here feeling helpless, and

---

[11] *rosary:* A string of beads used for counting prayers.

so there is no chance of his rebelling against me. Everything, in fact, is planned.

[*The young girl crosses the stage again. She has just had her swim and the difference is remarkable. Clean, wet, shiny face and hair. She continues to wipe herself with her wrapper as she walks.*]

JERO [*following her all the way with his eyes*]: Every morning, every day I witness this divine transformation, O Lord.

[*He shakes his head suddenly and bellows.*]

Pray Brother Jeroboam, pray! Pray for strength against temptation.

[*He falls on his knees, face squeezed in agony and hands clasped.* CHUME *enters, wheeling his bike. He leans it against the palm tree.*]

JERO [*not opening his eyes*]: Pray with me, brother. Pray with me. Pray for me against this one weakness . . . against this one weakness, O Lord . . .

CHUME [*falling down at once*]: Help him, Lord. Help him, Lord.

JERO: Against this one weakness, this weakness, O Abraham[12] . . .

CHUME: Help him, Lord. Help him, Lord.

JERO: Against this one weakness, David, David, Samuel, Samuel.[13]

CHUME: Help him. Help him. Help am. Help am.

JERO: Job Job, Elijah Elijah.[14]

CHUME [*getting more worked up*]: Help am God. Help am God. I say make you help am. Help am quick quick.

JERO: Tear the image from my heart. Tear this love for the Daughters of Eve . . .

CHUME: Adam, help am. Na[15] your son, help am. Help this your son.

JERO: Burn out this lust for the Daughters of Eve.

CHUME: Je-e-esu, Je-e-esu, Je-e-esu. Help am one time Je-e-e-su.

JERO: Abraka, Abraka, Abraka.

[CHUME *joins in.*]

Abraka, Abraka, Hebra, Hebra, Hebra, Hebra, Hebra, Hebra, Hebra, Hebra . . .

JERO [*rising*]: God bless you, brother. [*Turns around.*] Chume!

---

[12] *Abraham:* In the Bible, the founder of the Hebrew people.

[13] *David . . . Samuel:* Two historic figures from the Bible. David was the second king of Israel. Samuel was an early Hebrew leader who proclaimed David's kingship.

[14] *Job . . . Elijah:* Two Biblical figures. Job endured trials and kept his faith in God. Elijah was a prophet who opposed the worship of gods other than God.

[15] *Na:* Now.

CHUME: Good morning, Brother Jeroboam.

JERO: Chume, you are not at work. You've never come before in the morning.

CHUME: No, I went to work but I had to report sick.

JERO: Why, are you unwell, brother?

CHUME: No, Brother Jero . . . I . . .

JERO: A-ah, you have troubles and you could not wait to get them to God. We shall pray together.

CHUME: Brother Jero . . . I . . . I [He stops altogether.]

JERO: Is it difficult? Then let us commune silently for a while.

[CHUME folds his arms, raises his eyes to heaven.]

JERO: I wonder what is the matter with him. Actually I knew it was he the moment he opened his mouth. Only Brother Chume reverts to that animal jabber when he gets his spiritual excitement. And that is much too often for my liking. He is too crude, but then that is to my advantage. It means he would think of setting himself up as my equal.

[He joins CHUME in his meditative attitude, but almost immediately discards it, as if he has just remembered something.]

Christ my Protector! It is a good job I got away from that wretched woman as soon as I did. My disciple believes that I sleep on the beach, that is, if he thinks I sleep at all. Most of them believe the same but, for myself, I prefer my bed. Much more comfortable. And it gets rather cold on the beach at nights. Still, it does them good to believe that I am something of an ascetic. . . .

[He resumes his meditative pose for a couple of moments.]

[Gently.] Open your mind to God, brother. This is the tabernacle of Christ. Open your mind to God.

[CHUME is silent for a while, then bursts out suddenly.]

CHUME: Brother Jero, you must let me beat her!

JERO: What!

CHUME [desperately]: Just once, Prophet. Just once.

JERO: Brother Chume!

CHUME: Just once. Just one sound beating, and I swear not to ask again.

JERO: Apostate.[16] Have I not told you the will of God in this matter?

CHUME: But I've got to beat her, Prophet. You must save me from madness.

---

[16] Apostate: Unbeliever.

JERO: I will. But only if you obey me.

CHUME: In anything else, Prophet. But for this one, make you let me just beat am once!

JERO: Apostate!

CHUME: I n' go beat am too hard. Jus' once small small.

JERO: Traitor!

CHUME: Jus' this one time. I no' go ask again. Jus' do me this one favour, make a beat am today.

JERO: Brother Chume, what were you before you came to me?

CHUME: Prophet . . .

JERO [sternly]: What were you before the grace of God?

CHUME: A labourer, Prophet. A common labourer.

JERO: And did I not prophesy you would become an office boy?

CHUME: You do am, brother. Na so.

JERO: And then a messenger?

CHUME: Na you do am, brother. Na you.

JERO: And then quick promotion? Did I not prophesy it?

CHUME: Na true, prophet. Na true.

JERO: And what are you now? What are you?

CHUME: Chief Messenger.

JERO: By the grace of God! And by the grace of God, have I not seen you at the table of the Chief Clerk? And you behind the desk, giving orders?

CHUME: Yes, Prophet . . . but . . .

JERO: With a telephone and a table bell for calling the Messenger?

CHUME: Very true, Prophet, but . . .

JERO: But? But? Kneel! [pointing to the ground.] Kneel!

CHUME [wringing his hands]: Prophet!

JERO: Kneel, sinner, kneel. Hardener of heart, harbourer of Ashtoreth, Protector of Baal,[17] kneel, kneel.

[CHUME *falls on his knees.*]

CHUME: My life is a hell . . .

JERO: Forgive him, Father, forgive him.

CHUME: This woman will kill me . . .

---

[17] *Ashtoreth . . . Baal:* Goddess and god worshipped by the ancient Phoenicians. Chume is being accused of worshiping false gods.

JERO: Forgive him, Father, forgive him.

CHUME: Only this morning I . . .

JERO: Forgive him, Father, forgive him.

CHUME: All the way on my bicycle . . .

JERO: Forgive . . .

CHUME: And not a word of thanks . . .

JERO: Out Ashtoreth. Out Baal . . .

CHUME: All she gave me was abuse, abuse, abuse . . .

JERO: Hardener of the heart . . .

CHUME: Nothing but abuse . . .

JERO: Petrifier of the soul . . .

CHUME: If I could only beat her once, only once . . .

JERO [*shouting him down*]: Forgive this sinner, Father. Forgive him by day, forgive
   him by night, forgive him in the morning, forgive him at noon . . .

[*A man enters. Kneels at once and begins to chorus "Amen," or "Forgive him,
Lord," or "In the name of Jesus (pronounced Je-e-e-sus)." Those who follow later do
the same.*]

   . . . This is the son whom you appointed to follow in my footsteps. Soften
   his heart. Brother Chume, this woman whom you so desire to beat is your
   cross—bear it well. She is your heaven-sent trial—lay not your hands on
   her. I command you to speak no harsh word to her. Pray, Brother Chume,
   for strength in this hour of your trial. Pray for strength and fortitude.

[JEROBOAM *leaves them to continue their chorus,* CHUME *chanting, "Mercy, Mercy"
while he makes his next remarks.*]

   They begin to arrive. As usual in the same order. This one who always
   comes earliest, I have prophesied that he will be made a chief in his home
   town. That is a very safe prophecy. As safe as our most popular prophecy,
   that a man will live to be eighty. If it doesn't come true,

[*Enter an old couple, joining chorus as before.*]

   that man doesn't find out until he's on the other side. So everybody is
   quite happy. One of my most faithful adherents—unfortunately, he can
   only be present at week-ends—firmly believes that he is going to be the
   first Prime Minister of the new Mid-North-East-State—when it is created.
   That was a risky prophecy of mine, but I badly needed more worshippers
   around that time.

[*He looks at his watch.*]

The next one to arrive is my most faithful penitent. She wants children, so she is quite a sad case. Or you would think so. But even in the midst of her most self-abasing convulsions, she manages to notice everything that goes on around her. In fact, I had better get back to the service. She is always the one to tell me that my mind is not on the service. . . .

[Altering his manner—]

Rise, Brother Chume. Rise and let the Lord enter into you. Apprentice of the Lord, are you not he upon whose shoulders my mantle must descend?

[A woman (the PENITENT) enters and kneels at once in an attitude of prayer.]

CHUME: It is so, Brother Jero.

JERO: Then why do you harden your heart? The Lord says that you may not beat the good woman whom he has chosen to be your wife, to be your cross in your period of trial, and will you disobey him?

CHUME: No, Brother Jero.

JERO: Will you?

CHUME: No, Brother Jero.

JERO: Praise be to God.

CONGREGATION: Praise be to God.

JERO: Allelu . . .

CONGREGATION: Alleluia.

[To the clapping of hands, they sing "I will follow Jesus," swaying and then dancing as they get warmer.
 BROTHER JERO, as the singing starts, hands two empty bottles to CHUME who goes to fill them with water from the sea. CHUME has hardly gone out when the drummer boy enters from upstage, running. He is rather weighed down by two "gangan" drums, and darts fearful glances back in mortal terror of whatever it is that is chasing him. This turns out, some ten or so yards later, to be a woman, sash tightened around her waist, wrapper pulled so high up that half the length of her thigh is exposed. Her sleeves are rolled above her shoulder and she is striding after the DRUMMER in no unmistakable manner. JEROBOAM, who has followed the woman's exposed limbs with quite distressed concentration, comes suddenly to himself and kneels sharply, muttering.
 Again the DRUMMER appears, going across the state in a different direction, running still. The woman follows, distance undiminished, the same set pace. JEROBOAM calls to him.]

JERO: What did you do to her?

DRUMMER [without stopping]: Nothing. I was only drumming and then she said I was using it to abuse her father.

JERO [as the woman comes into sight]: Woman!

[*She continues out.* CHUME *enters with filled bottles.*]

JERO [*shaking his head*]: I know her very well. She's my neighbour. But she ignored me. . . .

[JEROBOAM *prepares to bless the water when once again the procession appears,* DRUMMER *first and the woman after.*]

JERO: Come here. She wouldn't dare touch you.

DRUMMER [*increasing his pace*]: You don't know her . . .

[*The woman comes in sight.*]

JERO: Neighbour, neighbour. My dear sister in Moses[18] . . .

[*She continues her pursuit offstage.* JERO *hesitates, then hands over his rod to* CHUME *and goes after them.*]

CHUME [*suddenly remembering*]: You haven't blessed the water, Brother Jeroboam.

[JERO *is already out of hearing.* CHUME *is obviously bewildered by the new responsibility. He fiddles around with the rod and eventually uses it to conduct the singing, which has gone on all this time, flagging when the two contestants come in view, and reviving again after they had passed.*

CHUME *has hardly begun to conduct his band when a woman detaches herself from the crowd in the expected* PENITENT's *paroxysm.*[19]]

PENITENT: Echa, echa, echa, echa, echa . . . eei, eei, eei, eei.

CHUME [*taken aback*]: Ngh? What's the matter?

PENITENT: Efie, efie, efie, efie, enh, enh, enh, enh . . .

CHUME [*dashing off*]: Brother Jeroboam, Brother Jeroboam . . .

[CHUME *shouts in all directions, returning confusedly each time in an attempt to minister to the* PENITENT. *As* JEROBOAM *is not forthcoming, he begins, very uncertainly, to sprinkle some of the water on the* PENTINENT, *crossing her on the forehead. This has to be achieved very rapidly in the brief moment when the* PENITENT's *head is lifted from beating on the ground.*]

CHUME [*stammering*]: Father . . . forgive her.

CONGREGATION [*strongly*]: Amen.

[*The unexpectedness of the response nearly throws* CHUME, *but then it also serves to bolster him up, receiving such support.*]

---

[18] Moses: In the Bible, the Hebrew prophet who led the Israelites out of slavery in Egypt and delivered the Ten Commandments to them.

[19] penitent's paroxysm: A fit brought on by religious feeling.

CHUME: Father, forgive her.

CONGREGATION: Amen.

[*The* PENITENT *continues to moan.*]

CHUME: Father forgive her.

CONGREGATION: Amen.

CHUME: Father forgive am.

CONGREGATION: Amen.

CHUME [*warming up to the task*]: Make you forgive am, Father.

CONGREGATION: Amen.

[*They rapidly gain pace,* CHUME *getting quite carried away.*]

CHUME: I say make you forgive am.

CONGREGATION: Amen.

CHUME: Forgive am one time.

CONGREGATION: Amen.

CHUME: Forgive am quick quick.

CONGREGATION: Amen.

CHUME: Forgive am, Father.

CONGREGATION: Amen.

CHUME: Forgive us all.

CONGREGATION: Amen.

CHUME: Forgive us all.

[*And then, punctuated regularly with Amens . . .*]

Yes, Father, make you forgive us all. Make you save us from palaver.[20] Save us from trouble at home. Tell our wives not to give us trouble . . .

[*The* PENITENT *has become placid. She is stretched out flat on the ground.*]

. . . Tell our wives not to give us trouble. And give us money to have a happy home. Give us money to satisfy our daily necessities. Make you no forget those of us who dey struggle daily. Those who be clerk today, make them Chief Clerk tomorrow. Those who are Messenger today, make them Senior Service tomorrow. Yes Father, those who are Messenger today, make them Senior Service tomorrow.

[*The Amens grow more and more ecstatic.*]

---

[20] *palaver*: Argument, dispute.

Those who are petty trader today, make them big contractor tomorrow. Those who dey sweep street today, give them their own big office tomorrow. If we dey walka today, give us our own bicycle tomorrow. I say those who dey walka today, give them their own bicycle tomorrow. Those who have bicycle today, they will ride their own car tomorrow.

[*The enthusiasm of the response, becomes, at this point, quite overpowering.*]

I say those who dey push bicycle, give them big car tomorrow. Give them big car tomorrow. Give them big car tomorrow, give them big car tomorrow.

[*The angry woman comes again in view, striding with the same gait as before, but now in possession of the drums. A few yards behind, the* DRUMMER *jog-trots wretchedly, pleading.*]

DRUMMER: I beg you, give me my drums. I take God's name beg you, I was not abusing your father. . . . For God's sake I beg you . . . I was not abusing your father. I was only drumming . . . I swear to God I was only drumming. . . .

[*They pass through.*]

PENITENT [*who has become much alive from the latter part of the prayers, pointing*]: Brother Jeroboam!

[BROTHER JERO *has just come in view. They all rush to help him back into the circle. He is a much altered man, his clothes torn and his face bleeding.*]

JERO [*slowly and painfully*]: Thank you, brother, sisters. Brother Chume, kindly tell these friends to leave me. I must pray for the soul of that sinful woman. I must say a personal prayer for her.

[CHUME *ushers them off. They go reluctantly, chattering excitedly.*]

JERO: Prayers this evening, as usual. Late afternoon.

CHUME [*shouting after*]: Prayers late afternoon as always. Brother Jeroboam says God keep you till then. Are you all right, Brother Jero?

JERO: Who would have thought that she would dare lift her hand against a prophet of God!

CHUME: Women are a plague, brother.

JERO: I had a premonition this morning that women would be my downfall today. But I thought of it only in the spiritual sense.

CHUME: Now you see how it is, Brother Jero.

JERO: From the moment I looked out of my window this morning, I have been tormented one way or another by the Daughters of Discord.

CHUME [*eagerly*]: That is how it is with me, Brother. Every day. Every morning and night. Only this morning she made me take her to the house of some poor man, whom she says owes her money. She loaded enough on my bicycle to lay siege for a week, and all the thanks I got was abuse.

JERO: Indeed, it must be a trial, Brother Chume . . . and it requires great . . .

[*He becomes suddenly suspicious.*]

Brother Chume, did you say that your wife went to make camp only this morning at the house of a . . . of someone who owes her money?

CHUME: Yes, I took her there myself.

JERO: Er . . . indeed, indeed. [*Coughs.*] Is . . . your wife a trader?

CHUME: Yes. Petty trading, you know. Wool, silk, cloth, and all that stuff.

JERO: Indeed. Quite an enterprising woman. [*Hems.*] Er . . . where was the house of this man . . . I mean, this man who owes her money?

CHUME: Not very far from here. Ajete settlement, a mile or so from here. I did not even know the place existed until today.

JERO [*to himself*]: So that is your wife . . .

CHUME: Did you speak, Prophet?

JERO: No, no. I was only thinking how little women have changed since Eve, since Delilah, since Jezebel.[21] But we must be strong of heart. I have my own cross too, Brother Chume. This morning alone I have been thrice in conflict with the Daughters of Discord. First there was . . . no, never mind that. There is another who crosses my path every day. Goes to swim just over there and then wait for me to be in the midst of my meditation before she swings her hips across here, flaunting her near nakedness before my eyes. . . .

CHUME [*to himself, with deep feeling*]: I'd willingly change crosses with you.

JERO: What, Brother Chume?

CHUME: I was only praying.

JERO: Ah. That is the only way. But er . . . I wonder really what the will of God would be in this matter. After all, Christ himself was not averse to using the whip when occasion demanded it.

CHUME [*eagerly*]: No, he did not hesitate.

JERO: In that case, since, Brother Chume, your wife seems such a wicked, wilful sinner, I think . . .

CHUME: Yes, Holy One . . . ?

---

[21] *Eve . . . Jezebel:* Three women from the Bible, all of whom were believed to have betrayed men. Eve tempted Adam to disobey God; as a result, Eve and Adam were forced to leave paradise and live in the world. Delilah tempted the hero Samson to reveal the source of his strength, which was his long uncut hair; she then cut off his hair and turned him over to his enemies. Jezebel encouraged the worship of Phoenician gods instead of the God of Israel.

JERO: You must take her home tonight . . .

CHUME: Yes. . . .

JERO: And beat her.

CHUME [*kneeling, clasps* JERO's *hand in his*]: Prophet!

JERO: Remember, it must be done in your own house. Never show the discord within your family to the world. Take her home and beat her.

[CHUME *leaps up and gets his bike.*]

JERO: And Brother Chume . . .

CHUME: Yes, Prophet . . .

JERO: The Son of God appeared to me again this morning, robed just as he was when he named you my successor. And he placed his burning sword on my shoulder and called me his knight. He gave me a new title . . . but you must tell it to no one—yet.

CHUME: I swear, Brother Jero.

JERO [*staring into space*]: He named me the Immaculate Jero, Articulate Hero of Christ's Crusade.

[*Pauses, then, with a regal dismissal—*] You may go, Brother Chume.

CHUME: God keep you, Brother Jero—the Immaculate.

JERO: God keep you, brother. [*He sadly fingers the velvet cape.*]

Lights fade.

SCENE IV

As Scene II, i.e., in front of the Prophet's home. Later that day. CHUME *is just wiping off the last crumbs of yams on his plate.* AMOPE *watches him.*

AMOPE: You can't say I don't try. Hounded out of house by debtors, I still manage to make you a meal.

CHUME [*sucking his fingers, sets down his plate*]: It was a good meal too.

AMOPE: I do my share as I've always done. I cooked you your meal. But when I ask you to bring me some clean water, you forget.

CHUME: I did not forget.

AMOPE: You keep saying that. Where is it then? Or perhaps the bottles fell off your bicycle on the way and got broken.

CHUME: That's a child's lie, Amope. You are talking to a man.

AMOPE: A fine man you are then, when you can't remember a simple thing like a bottle of clean water.

CHUME: I remembered. I just did not bring it. So that is that. And now pack up your things because we're going home.

[AMOPE *stares at him unbelieving.*]

CHUME: Pack up your things; you heard what I said.

AMOPE [*scrutinizing*]: I thought you were a bit early to get back. You haven't been to work at all. You've been drinking all day.

CHUME: You may think what suits you. You know I never touch any liquor.

AMOPE: You needn't say it as if it was a virtue. You don't drink only because you cannot afford to. That is all the reason there is.

CHUME: Hurry. I have certain work to do when I get home and I don't want you delaying me.

AMOPE: Go then. I am not budging from here till I get my money.

[CHUME *leaps up, begins to throw her things into the bag.* **BROTHER JERO** *enters, hides, and observes them.*]

AMOPE [*quietly*]: I hope you have ropes to tie me on the bicycle, because I don't intend to leave this place unless I am carried out. One pound eight shillings is no child's play. And it is my money not yours.

[CHUME *has finished packing the bag and is now tying it on to the carrier.*]

AMOPE: A messenger's pay isn't that much you know—just in case you've forgotten you're not drawing a minister's pay. So you better think again if you think I am letting my hard-earned money stay in the hands of that good-for-nothing. Just think, only this morning while I sat here, a Sanitary Inspector came along. He looked me all over and he made some notes in his book. Then he said, I suppose, woman, you realize that this place is marked down for slum clearance. This to me, as if I lived here. But you sit down and let your wife be exposed to such insults. And the Sanitary Inspector had a motor-cycle too, which is one better than a bicycle.

CHUME: You'd better be ready soon.

AMOPE: A Sanitary Inspector is a better job anyway. You can make something of yourself one way or another. They all do. A little here and a little there, call it bribery if you like, but see where *you've* got even though you don't drink or smoke or take bribes. He's got a motor-bike . . . anyway, who would want to offer cola to a Chief Messenger?

CHUME: Shut your big mouth!

AMOPE [*aghast*]: What did you say?

CHUME: I said shut your big mouth.

AMOPE: To me?

CHUME: Shut your big mouth before I shut it for you. [*Ties the mat round the cross-bar.*] And you'd better start to watch your step from now on. My period of abstinence is over. My cross has been lifted off my shoulders by the Prophet.

AMOPE [*genuinely distressed*]: He's mad.

CHUME [*viciously tying up the mat*]: My period of trial is over. [*Practically strangling the mat.*] If you so much as open your mouth now . . . [*Gives a further twist to the string.*]

AMOPE: God help me. He's gone mad.

CHUME [*imperiously*]: Get on the bike.

AMOPE [*backing away*]: I'm not coming with you.

CHUME: I said get on the bike!

AMOPE: Not with you. I'll find my own way home.

[CHUME *advances on her.* AMOPE *screams for help.* BROTHER JERO *crosses himself.* CHUME *catches her by the arm but she escapes, runs to the side of the house and beats on the door.*]

AMOPE: Help! Open the door for God's sake. Let me in. Let me in . . .

[BROTHER JERO *grimaces.*]

Is anyone in? Let me in for God's sake! Let me in or God will punish you!

JERO [*sticking his fingers in his ears*]: Blasphemy![22]

AMOPE: Prophet! Where's the Prophet?

[CHUME *lifts her bodily.*]

AMOPE: Let me down! Police! Police!

CHUME [*setting her down*]: If you shout just once more I'll . . . [*He raises a huge fist.*]

[BROTHER JERO *gasps in mock-horror, tut-tuts, covers his eyes with both hands, and departs.*]

AMOPE: Ho! You're mad. You're mad.

CHUME: Get on the bike.

AMOPE: Kill me! Kill me!

CHUME: Don't tempt me, woman!

AMOPE: I won't get on that thing unless you kill me first.

CHUME: Woman!

[*Two or three neighbours arrive, but keep a respectful distance.*]

---

[22] *Blasphemy:* Showing a lack of respect for God.

AMOPE: Kill me. You'll have to kill me. Everybody come and bear witness. He's going to kill me so come and bear witness. I forgive everyone who has ever done me evil. I forgive all my debtors especially the Prophet who has got me into all this trouble. Prophet Jeroboam, I hope you will pray for my soul in heaven. . . .

CHUME: You have no soul, wicked woman.

AMOPE: Brother Jeroboam, curse this man for me. You may keep the velvet cape if you curse this foolish man. I forgive you your debt. Go on, foolish man, kill me. If you don't kill me you won't do well in life.

CHUME [*suddenly*]: Shut up!

AMOPE [*warming up as more people arrive*]: Bear witness all of you. Tell the Prophet I forgive him his debt but he must curse this foolish man to hell. Go on, kill me!

CHUME [*who has turned away, forehead knotted in confusion*]: Can't you shut up, woman!

AMOPE: No, you must kill me . . .

[*The crowd hub-bubs all the time, scared as always at the prospect of interfering in man-wife palaver, but throwing in half-hearted tokens of concern—*]

"What's the matter, eh?" "You two keep quiet." "Who are they?" "Where is Brother Jero?" "Do you think we ought to send for the Prophet?" "These women are so troublesome! Somebody go and call Brother Jero."

CHUME [*lifting up* AMOPE's *head. She has, in the tradition of the "kill me" woman, shut her eyes tightly and continued to beat her fists on the prophet's doorstep.*]: Shut up and listen: Did I hear you say Prophet Jeroboam?

AMOPE: See him now. Let you bear witness. He's going to kill me. . . .

CHUME: I'm not touching you but I will if you don't answer my question.

AMOPE: Kill me . . . Kill me . . .

CHUME: Woman, did you say it was the Prophet who owed you money?

AMOPE: Kill me . . .

CHUME: Is this his house? [*Gives her head a shake.*] Does he live here . . . ?

AMOPE: Kill me . . . Kill me . . .

CHUME [*pushing her away in disgust and turning to the crowd. They retreat instinctively.*]: Is Brother Jeroboam . . . ?

NEAREST ONE [*hastily*]: No, no. I'm not Brother Jero. It's not me.

CHUME: Who said you were? Does the Prophet live here?

SAME MAN: Yes. Over there. That house.

CHUME [*Turns around and stands stock still. Stares at the house for quite some time.*]: So . . . so . . . so . . . so . . .

[*The crowd is puzzled over his change of mood. Even* AMOPE *looks up wonderingly.* CHUME *walks towards his bicycle, muttering to himself.*]

So . . . so . . . Suddenly he decided I may beat my wife, eh? For his own convenience. At his own convenience.

[*He releases the bundle from the carrier, pushing it down carelessly. He unties the mat also.*]

BYSTANDER: What next is he doing now?

CHUME [*mounting his bicycle*]: You stay here and don't move. If I don't find you here when I get back . . .

[*He rides off. They all stare at him in bewilderment.*]

AMOPE: He is quite mad. I have never seen him behave like that.

BYSTANDER: You are sure?

AMOPE: Am I sure? I'm his wife, so I ought to know, shouldn't I?

A WOMAN BYSTANDER: Then you ought to let the Prophet see to him. I had a brother once who had the fits and foamed at the mouth every other week. But the Prophet cured him. Drove the devils out of him, he did.

AMOPE: This one can't do anything. He's a debtor and that's all he knows. How to dodge his creditors.

[*She prepares to unpack her bundle.*]

Lights fade.

SCENE V

The beach. Nightfall.

A man in an elaborate "agbada" outfit, with long train and a cap is standing right, downstage, with a sheaf of notes in his hand. He is obviously delivering a speech, but we don't hear it. It is undoubtedly a fire-breathing speech.

The PROPHET JEROBOAM *stands bolt upright as always, surveying him with lofty compassion.*

JERO: I could teach him a trick or two about speech-making. He's a member of the Federal House, a back-bencher but with one eye on a ministerial post.[23] Comes here every day to rehearse his speeches. But he never makes them. Too scared.

[*Pause. The Prophet continues to study the* MEMBER.]

---

[23] *member of the Federal House . . . ministerial post:* A minor politician looking for a prestigious government appointment.

Poor fish. [*Chuckles and looks away.*] Oho, I had almost forgotten Brother Chume. By now he ought to have beaten his wife senseless. Pity! That means I've lost him. He is fulfilled and no longer needs me. True, he still has to become a Chief Clerk. But I have lost him as the one who was most dependent on me. . . . Never mind, it was a good price to pay for getting rid of my creditor. . . .

[*Goes back to the* MEMBER.]

Now he . . . he is already a member of my flock. He does not know it of course, but he is a follower. All I need do is claim him. Call him and say to him, My dear Member of the House, your place awaits you . . . Or do you doubt it? Watch me go to work on him. [*Raises his voice.*] My dear brother in Jesus!

[*The* MEMBER *stops, looks round, and resumes his speech.*]

Dear brother, do I not know you?

[*The* MEMBER *stops, looks round again.*]

Yes, you. In God's name, do I not know you?

[MEMBER *approaches slowly.*]

Yes indeed. It is you. And you come as it was predicted. Do you not perhaps remember me?

[MEMBER *looks at him scornfully.*]

Then you cannot be of the Lord. In another world, in another body, we met, and my message was for you . . .

[*The* MEMBER *turns his back impatiently.*]

MEMBER [*with great pomposity*]: Go and practise your fraudulences on another person of greater gullibility.

JERO [*very kindly, smiling*]: Indeed the matter is quite plain. You are not of the Lord. And yet such is the mystery of God's ways that his favour has lighted upon you . . . Minister . . . Minister by the grace of God . . .

[*The* MEMBER *stops dead.*]

Yes, brother, we have met. I saw this country plunged into strife. I saw the mustering of men, gathered in the name of peace through strength. And at a desk, in a large gilt room, great men of the land awaited your decision. Emissaries of foreign nations hung on your word, and on the door leading into your office, I read the words, Minister for War. . . .

[*The* MEMBER *turns round slowly.*]

. . . It is a position of power. But are you of the Lord? Are you in fact worthy? Must I, when I have looked into your soul, as the Lord has commanded me to do, must I pray to the Lord to remove this mantle from your shoulders and place it on a more God-fearing man?

[*The* MEMBER *moves forward unconsciously. The Prophet gestures him to stay where he is. Slowly—*]

Yes . . . I think I see Satan in your eyes. I see him entrenched in your eyes . . .

[*The* MEMBER *grows fearful, raises his arms in half-supplication.*]

The Minister for War would be the most powerful position in the Land. The Lord knows best, but he has empowered his lieutenants on earth to intercede where necessary. We can reach him by fasting and by prayer . . . we can make recommendations. . . . Brother, are you of God or are you ranged among his enemies . . . ?

[JEROBOAM's *face fades away and the light also dims on him as another voice—* CHUME's—*is heard long before he is seen.* CHUME *enters from left, downstage, agitated, and talking to himself.*]

CHUME: . . . What for . . . why, why, why, why 'e do am? For two years 'e no let me beat that woman. Why? No because God no like am. That one no fool me any more. 'E no be man of God. 'E say 'in sleep for beach whether 'e rain or cold but that one too na big lie. The man get house and 'e sleep there every night. But 'in get peace for 'in house, why 'en no let me get peace for mine? Wetin I do for am? Anyway, how they come meet? Where? When? What time 'e know say na my wife? Why 'e dey protect am from me? Perhaps na my woman dey give am chop[24] and in return he promise to see say 'in husband no beat am. A-a-a-ah, give am clothes, give am food and all comforts and necessities, and for exchange, 'in go see that 'in husband no beat am . . . Mmmmmm.

[*He shakes his head.*]

No, is not possible. I no believe that. If na so, how they come quarrel then. Why she go sit for front of 'in house demand all 'in money. I no beat am yet . . .

[*He stops suddenly. His eyes slowly distend.*]

Almighty! Chume, fool! O God, my life done spoil. My life done spoil finish. O God a no' get eyes for my head. Na lie. Na big lie. Na pretence 'e de pretend that wicked woman! She no' go collect nutin! She no' mean to sleep for outside house. The Prophet na 'in lover. As soon as 'e dark, she

---

[24] *give am chop:* Makes a bargain.

go in go meet 'in man. O God, wetin a do for you wey you go spoil my life so? Wetin make you vex for me so? I offend you? Chume, foolish man, your life done spoil. Your life done spoil. Yeah, ye . . . ah ah, ye-e-ah, they done ruin Chume for life . . . ye-e-ah, ye-e-ah, . . .

[*He goes off, his cries dying offstage.*

Light up slowly on JERO. *The* MEMBER *is seen kneeling now at* BROTHER JERO'S *feet, hands clasped, and shut eyes raised to heaven . . .*]

JERO [*his voice gaining volume*]: Protect him therefore. Protect him when he must lead this country as his great ancestors have done. He comes from the great warriors of the land. In his innocence he was not aware of this heritage. But you know everything and you plan it all. There is no end, no beginning. . . .

[CHUME *rushes in, brandishing a cutlass.*]

CHUME: Adulterer! Woman-thief! Na today a go finish you!

[JERO *looks round.*]

JERO: God save us! [*Flees.*]

MEMBER [*unaware of what is happening*]: Amen.

[CHUME *follows out* JERO, *murder-bent.*]

MEMBER: Amen. Amen. [*Opens his eyes.*] Thank you, Proph . . .

[*He looks right, left, back, front, but he finds the Prophet has really disappeared.*]

Prophet! Prophet! [*Turns sharply and rapidly in every direction, shouting.*] Prophet, where are you? Where have you gone? Prophet! Don't leave me, Prophet, don't leave me!

[*He looks up slowly, with awe.*]

Vanished. Transported. Utterly transmuted.[25] I knew it. I knew I stood in the presence of God. . . .

[*He bows his head, standing.* JEROBOAM *enters quite collected, and points to the convert.*]

JEROBOAM: You heard him. With your own ears you heard him. By tomorrow, the whole town will have heard about the miraculous disappearance of Brother Jeroboam. Testified to and witnessed by no less a person than one of the elected Rulers of the country. . . .

MEMBER [*goes to sit on the mound*]: I must await his return. If I show faith, he will show himself again to me. . . . [*Leaps up as he is about to sit.*] This is

---

[25] *transmuted:* Taken out of the world to be with God.

holy ground. [*Takes off his shoes and sits. Gets up again.*] I must hear further from him. Perhaps he has gone to learn more about this ministerial post. . . . [*Sits.*]

JEROBOAM: I have already sent for the police. It is a pity about Chume. But he has given me a fright, and no prophet likes to be frightened. With the influence of that nincompoop I should succeed in getting him certified with ease. A year in the lunatic asylum would do him good anyway.

[*The* MEMBER *is already nodding.*]

Good . . . He is falling asleep. When I appear again to him he'll think I have just fallen from the sky. Then I'll tell him that Satan just sent one of his emissaries into the world under the name of Chume, and that he had better put him in a strait-jacket at once . . . And so the day is saved. The police will call on me here as soon as they catch Chume. And it looks as if it is not quite time for the fulfilment of that spiteful man's prophecy.

[*He picks up a pebble and throws it at the* MEMBER. *At the same time a ring of red or some equally startling colour plays on his head, forming a sort of halo. The* MEMBER *wakes with a start, stares open-mouthed, and falls flat on his face, whispering in rapt awe—*]

MEMBER: "Master!"

Blackout

UNDERSTANDING THE PLAY

1. Describe Brother Jero's character.
2. Describe Chume's character.
3. Describe Amope's character.
4. Evaluate the extent to which each of the major characters behaves like a real person. To what extent, if any, do people like Brother Jero exist in modern society?
5. What is humorous about the unrevealed identities of Brother Jero and Amope?
6. Is it likely that Chume will be committed to an asylum? Find evidence in the play to support your point of view.
7. What are Brother Jero's trials? What is ironic about them?
8. Serious subjects often exist beneath the surface of the greatest comedies. What serious subjects are beneath the comedy in this play?
9. What appears to be Soyinka's goal in writing this play?

ANALYZING LITERARY TECHNIQUE

1. Soyinka uses language as a way of revealing important aspects of character. What do Brother Jero's and Chume's speech patterns and vocabulary reveal about their characters?

2. Find two examples of **dramatic irony** in the play, and explain what they contribute to the play.

3. Find two examples of **discovery** and explain how they function in the play.

4. Do you think **plot** or **characterization** is more important in this play? Explain.

5. To what degree, if any, is this play a **satire?**

6. To what extent is this play a **farce?** Do the farcical elements reinforce or undercut Soyinka's message? Explain.

WRITING ABOUT LITERATURE

1. In *The Trials of Brother Jero*, Soyinka criticizes a wide range of human behaviors, including hypocrisy, dishonesty, greed, ambition, lust, and marital violence. Consider which behavior you think receives the strongest criticism in the play. Then write a brief essay explaining why you think that behavior is a focus of criticism and analyzing the means suggested in the play for reforming that behavior. (For example, if you focus on marital violence, look closely at Chume and Amope's relationship and at Jero's advice to Chume. What does Soyinka seem to suggest about how married people *should* behave toward each other?) Use quotations from the play to support your arguments.

2. Write an essay in which you analyze how Soyinka creates humor through the use of the following literary techniques: (a) dramatic irony, (b) verbal irony, (c) repetition, (d) discovery, and (e) reversal. Choose two or three of these techniques and describe how they are used in the play. Use quotations to support your points.

3. Create a dialogue in which the conflicts between Brother Jero, Amope, and Chume are resolved. (You may focus on just two of the characters, for example, Jero and Chume.) Consider the following issues: Does Brother Jero pay his debt to Amope? Does Chume beat Amope? Does Chume confront Brother Jero and Amope with his hypothesis about their relationship? If so, how do they react? Does the relationship between Amope and Chume change? Does the relationship between Brother Jero and Chume change?

The Lovers

BESSIE HEAD

*B*ESSIE HEAD (1937–1986) is one of the major South
African writers. She is known for her novels *When Rain
Clouds Gather* (1969), *Maru* (1971), and *A Question of
Power* (1973); her collection of interconnected short stories, *The
Collector of Treasures and Other Botswana Village Tales* (1977); and for
her reconstruction of the history of a Botswana village, *Serowe: Village
of the Rain Wind* (1981).

Head was born in Pietermaritzburg, in the Union of South
Africa, the child of a white mother and a black father. Until the age
of thirteen, she lived with a foster family. After attending a mission
school, she trained to become a teacher. As a young adult, working as
a teacher and then as a journalist for *Drum* magazine in Cape Town,
Head lived in a political and social environment that dehumanized
her by classifying her as racially "mixed." In 1964, when she realized
that the newly named Republic of South Africa would be a nation of
apartheid rather than multiracial democracy, she emigrated to
Botswana, in south-central Africa. She became a citizen of Botswana
in 1979. Although Head was technically living in exile, she felt that
Botswana was where she could put down her roots; to her this meant
acquiring a sense of self and a connection with the land. She believed
that living among people "in a kind of social order, shaped from centuries past, by the ancestors of the tribe" nourished her creativity and
enabled her to become a writer.

Head's works reflect her attitudes and personal experiences. They
explore the experience of being an exile, the observance of social customs in an African society, the need of the individual to make independent decisions, the conflict between African and Western values,
and the tragedy of racial separation and hatred. The history, legends,
and myths of Botswana figure prominently in her stories, which she
calls "tales" because of their emphasis on narrative rather than character. "The Lovers," one her later and best tales, is typical in that it
focuses on the plight of the individual within the tribal community.

The love affair began in the summer. The love affair began in those dim dark days when young men and women did not have love affairs. It was one of those summers when it rained in torrents. Almost every afternoon towards sunset the low-hanging, rain-filled clouds would sweep across the sky in packed masses and suddenly, with barely a warning, the rain would pour down in blinding sheets.

The young women and little girls were still out in the forest gathering wood that afternoon when the first warning signs of rain appeared in the sky. They hastily gathered up their bundles of wood and began running home to escape the approaching storm. Suddenly, one of the young women halted painfully. In her haste she had trodden on a large thorn.

"Hurry on home, Monosi!" she cried to a little girl panting behind her. "I have to get this thorn out of my foot. If the rain catches me I shall find some shelter and come home once it is over."

Without a backward glance the little girl sped on after the hard-running group of wood gatherers. The young woman was quite alone with the approaching storm. The thorn proved difficult to extract. It had broken off and embedded itself deeply in her heel. A few drops of rain beat down on her back. The sky darkened.

Anxiously she looked around for the nearest shelter and saw a cavern in some rocks at the base of a hill nearby. She picked up her bundle of wood and limped hastily towards it, with the drops of rain pounding down faster and faster. She had barely entered the cavern when the torrent unleashed itself in a violent downpour. Her immediate concern was to seek its sanctuary but a moment later her heart lurched in fear as she realized that she was not alone. The warmth of another human filled the interior. She swung around swiftly and found herself almost face to face with a young man.

"We can shelter here together from the storm," he said with a quiet authority.

His face was as kind and protective as his words. Reassured, the young woman set down her bundle of sticks in the roomy interior of the cavern and together they seated themselves near its entrance. The roar of the rain was deafening so that even the thunder and lightening was muffled by its intensity. With quiet, harmonious movements the young man undid a leather pouch tied at his waist. He spent all his time cattle-herding and to while away the long hours he busied himself with all kinds of leather work, assembling skins into all kinds of clothes and blankets. He had a large number of sharpened implements in his pouch. He indicated to the young woman that he wished to extract the thorn. She extended her foot towards him and for some time he busied himself with this task, gently whittling away the skin around the thorn until he had exposed it sufficiently to extract it.

The young woman looked at his face with interest and marvelled at the ease and comfort she felt in his presence. In their world men and women lived strictly apart, especially the young and unmarried. This sense of apartness and separateness continued even throughout married life and marriage itself seemed to have no significance beyond a union for the production of children. This wide gap between the sexes created embarrassment on the level of personal contact; the young men often slid their eyes away uneasily or giggled at the sight of a woman. The young man did none of this. He had stared her directly in the eyes; all his movements were natural and unaffected. He was also very pleasing to look at. She thanked him with a smile once he had extracted the thorn and folded her extended foot beneath her. The violence of the storm abated a little but the heavily-laden sky continued to pour forth a steady downpour.

She had seen the young man around the village; she could vaguely place his family connections.

"Aren't you the son of Rra-Keaja?" she asked. She had a light chatty voice with an undertone of laughter in it, very expressive of her personality. She liked above all to be happy.

"I am the very Keaja he is named after," the young man replied with a smile. "I am the firstborn in the family."

"I am the firstborn in the family, too," she said. "I am Tselane, the daughter of Mma-Tselane."

His family ramifications were more complicated then hers. His father had three wives. All the firstborn of the first, second and third houses were boys. The children totalled eight in number, three boys and five girls, he explained. It was only when the conversation moved into deep water that Tselane realized that a whole area of the young man's speech had eluded her. He was the extreme opposite of her light chatty tone. He talked from deep rhythms within himself as though he had specifically invented language for his own use. He had an immense range of expression and feeling at his command; now his eyes lit up with humour, then they were absolutely serious and in earnest. He swayed almost imperceptibly as he talked. He talked like no one she had ever heard talking before, yet all his utterances were direct, simple and forthright. She bent forward and listened more attentively to his peculiar manner of speech.

"I don't like my mother," he said, shocking her. "I am her only son simply because my father stopped cohabitating with her after I was born. My father and I are alike. We don't like to be controlled by anyone and she made his life a misery when they were newly married. It was as if she had been born with a worm eating at her heart because she is satisfied with nothing. The only way my father could control the situation was to ignore her completely . . ."

He remained silent for a while, concentrating on his own thoughts. "I don't think I approve of all the arranged marriages we have here," he said finally. "My father would never have married her had he had his own choice. He was merely presented with her one day by his family and told they were to be married and there was nothing he could do about it."

He kept silent about the torture he endured from his mother. She hated him deeply and bitterly. She had hurled stones at him and scratched him on the arms and legs in her wild frustration. Like his father, he eluded her. He rarely spent time at home but kept the cattle-post as his permanent residence. When he approached home it was always with some gift of clothes or blankets. On that particular day he had an enormous gourd filled with milk.

The young woman, Tselane, floundered out of her depth in the face of such stark revelations. They lived in the strictest of traditional ways of life; all children were under the control of their parents until they were married, therefore it was taboo to discuss their elders. In her impulsive chatty way and partly out of embarrassment, it had been on the tip of her tongue to say that she liked her mother, that her mother was very kind-hearted. But there was a disturbing undertone in her household too. Her mother and father—and she was sure of it due to her detailed knowledge of her mother's way of life—had not cohabited for years either. A few years ago her father had taken another wife. She was her mother's only child. Oh, the surface of their household was polite and harmonious but her father was rarely at home. He was always irritable and morose when he was home.

"I am sorry about all the trouble in your home," she said at last, in a softer, more thoughtful tone. She was shaken at having been abruptly jolted into completely new ways of thought.

The young man smiled and then quite deliberately turned and stared at her. She stared back at him with friendly interest. She did not mind his close scrutiny of her person; he was easy to associate with, comfortable, truthful and open on his every gesture.

"Do you approve of arranged marriages?" he asked, still smiling.

"I have not thought of anything," she replied truthfully.

The dark was approaching rapidly. The rain had trickled down to a fine drizzle. Tselane stood up and picked up her bundle of wood. The young man picked up his gourd of milk. They were barely visible as they walked home together in the dark. Tselane's home was not too far from the hill. She lived on the extreme western side of the village, he on the extreme eastern side.

A bright fire burned in the hut they used as a cooking place on rainy days. Tselane's mother was sitting bent forward on her low stool, listening attentively to a visitor's tale. It was always like this—her mother was permanently surrounded by women who confided in her. The whole story of life unfolded daily around her stool: the ailments of children, women who had just had miscarriages, women undergoing treatment for barren wombs—the story was endless. It was the great pleasure of Tselane to seat herself quietly behind her mother's stool and listen with fascinated ears to this endless tale of woe. Her mother's visitor that evening was on the tail-end of a description of one of her children's ailments: chronic epilepsy, which seemed beyond cure. The child seemed in her death throes and the mother was just at the point of demonstrating the violent seizures when Tselane entered. Tselane quietly set her bundle of wood down in a corner and the conversation continued uninterrupted. She took her favoured place behind her mother's stool. Her father's second wife, Mma-Monosi, was seated on the opposite side of the fire, her face composed and serious. Her child, the little girl, Monosi, fed and attended to, lay fast asleep on a sleeping mat in one corner of the hut.

Tselane loved the two women of the household equally. They were both powerful independent women but with sharply differing personalities. Mma-Tselane was a queen who vaguely surveyed the kingdom she ruled with an abstracted, absent-minded air. Over the years of her married life she had built up a way of life for herself that filled her with content. She was reputed to be very delicate in health as after the birth of Tselane she had suffered a number of miscarriages and seemed incapable of bearing any more children. Her delicate health was a source of extreme irritation to her husband and at some stage he had abandoned her completely and taken Mma-Monosi as his second wife, intending to perpetuate his line and name through her healthy body. The arrangement suited Mma-Tselane. She was big-hearted and broadminded and yet, conversely, she prided herself in being the meticulous upholder of all the traditions the community adhered to. Once Mma-Monosi became of part of the household, Mma-Tselane did no work but entertained and paid calls the day long. Mma-Monosi ran the household.

The two women complemented each other, for, if Mma-Tselane was a queen, then Mma-Monosi was a humble worker. On the surface, Mma-Monosi appeared as sane and balanced as Mma-Tselane, but there was another side of personality that was very precariously balanced. Mma-Monosi took her trembling way through life. If all was stable and peaceful, then Mma-Monosi was stable and peaceful. If there was any disruption or disorder, Mma-Monosi's precarious inner balance registered every wave and upheaval. She hungered for approval of her every action and could be upset for days if criticized or reprimanded.

So, between them, the two women achieved a very harmonious household. Both were entirely absorbed in their full busy daily round; both were unconcerned that they received scant attention from the man of the household for Rra-Tselane was entirely concerned with his own affairs. He was a prominent member of the chief's court and divided his time between the chief's court and his cattle-post. He was rich in cattle and his herds were taken care of by servants. He was away at his cattle-post at that time.

It was with Mma-Monosi that the young girl, Tselane, enjoyed a free and happy relationship. They treated each other as equals, they both enjoyed hard work and whenever they were alone together, they laughed and joked all the time. Her own mother regarded Tselane as an object to whom she lowered her voice and issued commands between clenched teeth. Very soon Mma-Tselane stirred in her chair and said in that lowered voice: "Tselane, fetch me my bag of herbs."

Tselane obediently stood up and hurried to her mother's living-quarters for the bag of herbs. Then another interval followed during which her mother and the visitor discussed the medicinal properties of the herbs. Then Mma-Monosi served the evening meal. Then the visitor departed with assurances that Mma-Tselane would call on her the following day. Then they sat for a while in companionable silence. At one stage, seeing that the fire was burning low, Mma-Tselane arose and selected a few pieces of wood from Tselane's bundle to stoke up the fire.

"Er, Tselane," she said. "Your wood is quite dry. Did you shelter from the storm?"

"There is a cave in the hill not far from here, mother," Tselane replied. "And I sheltered there." She did not think it wise to add that she had shared the shelter with a young man; a lot of awkward questions of the wrong kind might have followed.

The mother cast her eyes vaguely over her daughter as if to say all was in order in her world; she always established simple facts about any matter and turned peacefully to the next task at hand. She suddenly decided that she was tired and would retire. Tselane and Mma-Monosi were left alone seated near the fire. Tselane was still elated by her encounter with the young man; so many pleasant thoughts were flying through her head.

"I want to ask you some questions, Mma-Monosi," she said eagerly.

"What is it you want to say, my child?" Mma-Monosi said, stirring out of a reverie.

"Do you approve of arranged marriages, Mma-Monosi?" she asked earnestly.

Mms-Monosi drew in her breath between her teeth with a sharp, hissing sound, then she lowered her voice in horror and said: "Tselane, you know quite well that I am your friend but if anyone else heard you talking like that you would be in trouble! Such things are never discussed here! What put that idea into your head because it is totally unknown to me?"

"But you question life when you begin to grow up," Tselane said defensively.

"That is what you never, never do," Mma-Monosi said severely. "If you question life you will upset it. Life is always in order." She looked thoroughly startled and agitated. "I know of something terrible that once happened to someone who questioned life," she added grimly.

"Who was it? What terrible thing happened?" Tselane asked, in her turn agitated.

"I can't tell you," Mma-Monosi said firmly. "It is too terrible to mention."

Tselane subsided into silence with a speculative look in her eye. She understood Mma-Monosi well. She couldn't keep a secret. She could always be tempted into telling a secret, if not today then some other day. She decided to find out the terrible story.

When Keaja arrived home his family was eating the evening meal. He first approached the women's quarters and offered them the gourd of milk.

"The cows are calving heavily," he explained. "There is a lot of milk and I can bring some home every day."

He was greeted joyously by the second and third wives of his father who anxiously inquired after their sons who lived with him at the cattle-post.

"They are quite well," he said politely. "I settled them and the cattle before I left. I shall return again in the early morning because I am worried about the young calves."

He avoided his mother's baleful stare and tight, deprived mouth. She never had anything to say to him, although, on his approach to the women's quarters, he had heard her voice, shrill and harsh, dominating the conversation. His meal was handed to him and he retreated to his father's quarters. He ate alone and apart from the women. A bright fire burned in his father's living quarters.

"Hello, Father-Of-Me," his father greet him, making affectionate play on the name Keaja. Keaja meant: I am eating now because I have a son to take care of me.

His father doted on him. In his eyes there was no greater son than Keaja. After an exchange of greetings his father asked: "And what is your news?"

He gave his father the same information about the cows calving heavily and the rich supply of milk; that his other two sons were quite well. They ate for a while in companionable silence. His mother's voice rose shrill and penetrating in the silent night. Quite unexpectedly his father looked up with a twinkle in his eye and said: "Those extra calves will put us in good stead, Father-Of-Me. I have just started negotiations about your marriage."

A spasm of chill, cold fear almost constricted Keaja's heart. "Who am I to marry, father?" he asked, alarmed.

"I cannot mention the family name just yet," his father replied carefully, not sensing his son's alarm. "The negotiations are still at a very delicate stage."

"Have you committed yourself in this matter, father?" he asked, a sharp angry note in his voice.

"Oh, yes," his father replied. "I have given my honour in this matter. It is just that these things take a long time to arrange as there are many courtesies to be observed."

"How long?" the son asked.

"About six new moons may have to pass," his father replied. "It may even be longer than that. I cannot say at this stage."

"I could choose a wife for myself," the son said with deadly quietude. "I could choose my own wife and then inform you of my choice."

His father stared at him in surprise.

"You cannot be different from everyone else," he said. "I must be a parent with a weakness that you can talk to me so."

His father knew that he indulged his son, that they had free and easy exchanges beyond what was socially permissible; even that brief exchange was more than most parents allowed their children. They arranged all details of their children's future and on the fatal day merely informed them that they were to be married to so-and-so. There was no point in saying: "I might not be able to live with so-and-so. She might be unsuited to me," so that when Keaja lapsed into silence, his father merely smiled indulgently and engaged him in small talk.

Keaja was certainly of a marriageable age. The previous year he had gone through his initiation ceremony. Apart from the other trials endured during the ceremony, detailed instruction had been given to the young men of his age group about sexual relations between men and women. They were hardly private and personal but affected by a large number of social regulations and taboos. If he broke the taboos at a personal and private level, death, sickness and great misfortune would fall upon his family. If he broke the taboos at a social level, death and disaster would fall upon the community. There were many periods in a man's life when abstinence from sexual relations was required; often this abstinence had to be practised communally, as in the period preceding the harvest of crops and only broken on the day of the harvest thanksgiving ceremony.

These regulations and taboos applied to men and women alike but the initiation ceremony for women, which Tselane had also experienced the previous year, was much more complex in their instruction. A delicate balance had to be preserved between a woman's reproductive cycle and the safety of the community; at almost every stage in her life a woman was a potential source of danger to the community. All women were given careful instruction in precautions to be observed during times of menstruation, childbirth and accidental miscarriages. Failure to observe the taboos could bring harm to animal life, crops and the community.

It could be seen then that the community held no place for people wildly carried away by their passions, that there was a logic and order in the carefully arranged sterile emotional and physical relationships between men and women. There was no one to challenge the established order of things; if people felt any personal unhappiness it was smothered and subdued and so life for the community proceeded from day to day in peace and harmony.

As all lovers do, they began a personal and emotional dialogue that excluded all life around them. Perhaps its pattern and direction is the same for all lovers, painful and maddening by turns in its initial insecurity. Who looked for who? They could not say, except that the far-western unpolluted end of the river where women drew water and the forests where they gathered firewood became Keaja's favorite hunting grounds. Their work periods coincided at that time. The corn had just been sowed and the women were idling in the village until the heavy soaking rains raising the weeds in their fields, then their next busy period would follow when they hoed out the weeds between their corn.

Kaeja returned every day to the village with gourds of milk for his family and it did not take Tselane long to note that he delayed and lingered in her work area until he had caught some glimpse of her. She was always in a crowd of gaily chattering young women. The memory of their first encounter had been so fresh and stimulating, so full of unexpected surprises in dialogue that she longed to approach him. One afternoon, while out wood gathering with her companions, she noticed him among the distant bushes and contrived to remove herself from her companions. As she walked towards him, he quite directly approached her and took hold of her hand. She made no effort to pull her hand free. It rested in his as though it belonged there. They walked on some distance, then he paused, and turning to face her told her all that he had on his mind in his perfect, simple way. This time he did not smile at all.

"My father will arrange a marriage for me after about six new moons have passed," he said. "I do not want that. I want a wife of my own choosing but all the things I want can only cause trouble."

She looked away into the distance, not immediately knowing what she ought to say. Her own parents had given her no clue of their plans for her future; indeed she had not had cause to think about it but she did not like most of the young men in the village. They had a hang-dog air as though the society and its oppressive ways had broken their will. She liked everything about Keaja and she felt safe with him as on the stormy afternoon in the cavern when he had said: "We can shelter here together from the storm . . . ."

"My own thoughts are not complicated," he went on, still holding on to her hand. "I thought I would find out how you felt about this matter. I thought I would like to choose you as my wife. If you do not want to choose me in turn, I shall not pursue my own wants any longer. I might even marry the wife my father chooses for me."

She turned around and faced him and spoke with a clarity of thought that startled her.

"I am afraid of nothing," she said. "Not even trouble or death but I need some time to find out what I am thinking."

Of his own accord, he let go of her hand and so they parted and went their separate ways. From that point onwards right until the following day, she lived in a state of high elation. Her thought processes were not all coherent; indeed she had not a thought in her head. Then the illogic of love took over. Just as she was about to pick up the pitcher in the late afternoon, she suddenly felt desperately ill, so ill that she was almost brought to the point of death. She experienced a paralysing lameness in her arms and legs. The weight of the pitcher with which she was to draw water was too heavy for her to endure.

She appealed to Mma-Monosi.

"I feel faint and ill today," she said. "I cannot draw water."

Mma-Monosi was only too happy to take over her chores but at the same time consulted anxiously with her mother about this sudden illness. Mma-Tselane, after some deliberation, decided that it was the illness young girls get in the limbs when they are growing too rapidly. She spent a happy three days doctoring her daughter with warm herb drinks, for Mma-Tselane liked nothing better than to concentrate on illness. Still, the physical turmoil the young girl felt continued unabated; at night she trembled violently from head to toe. It was so shocking and new that for two days she succumbed completely to the blow. It wasn't any coherent thought processes that made her struggle desperately to her feet on the third day but a need to quieten the anguish. She convinced her mother and Mma-Monosi that she felt well enough to perform her wood-gathering chores. Towards the afternoon she hurried to the forest area, carefully avoiding her gathering companions.

She was relieved, on meeting Keaja, to see that his face bore the same anguished look that she felt. He spoke first.

"I felt so ill and disturbed," he said. "I could do nothing but wait for your appearance."

They sat down on the ground together. She was so exhausted by her two-day struggle that for a moment she leaned forward and rested her head on his knees. Her thought processes seemed to awaken once more because she smiled peacefully and said: "I want to think."

Eventually she raised herself and looked at the young man with shining eyes.

"I felt so ill," she said. "My mother kept giving me herb drinks. She said it was normal to feel faint and dizzy when one is growing. I know now what made me feel so ill. I was fighting my training. My training has told me that people are not important in themselves but you so suddenly became important to me, as a person. I did not know how to tell my mother all this. I did not know how to tell her anything yet she was so kind and took care of me. Eventually I thought I would lose my mind so I came here to find you. . . ."

It was as if, from that moment onwards, they quietly and of their own willing, married each other. They began to plan together how they should meet and when they should meet. The young man was full of forethought and planning. He knew that, in the terms of his own society, he was starting a terrible mess, but then his society only calculated along the lines of human helplessness in the face of overwhelming odds. It did not calculate for human inventiveness and initiative. He only needed the young girl's pledge and from then onwards he took the initiative in all things. He was to startle and please her from that very day with his forethought. It was as if he knew that she would come at some time, that they would linger in joy with their love-making, so that when Tselane eventually expressed agitation at the lateness of the hour, he, with a superior smile, indicated a large bundle of wood nearby that he had collected for her to take home.

A peaceful interlude followed and the community innocently lived out its day-by-day life, unaware of the disruption and upheaval that would soon fall upon it. The women were soon out in the fields, hoeing weeds and tending their crops, Tselane among them, working side by side with Mma-Monosi, as she had always done. There was not even a ripple of the secret life she now lived; if anything, she worked harder and with greater contentment. She laughed and joked as usual with Mma-Monosi but sound instinct made her keep her private affair to herself.

When the corn was already high in the fields and about to ripen, Tselane realized that she was expecting a child. A matter that had been secret could be a secret no longer. When she confided this news to Keaja, he quite happily accepted it as a part of all the plans he had made, for as he said to her at that time: "I am not planning for death when we are so happy. I want it that we should live."

He had only one part of all his planning secure, a safe escape route outside the village and on to a new and unknown life they would make for themselves. They had made themselves outcasts from the acceptable order of village life and he presented her with two alternatives from which she could choose. The one alternative was simpler for them. They could leave the village at any moment and without informing anyone of their intentions. The world was very wide for a man. He had travelled great distances, both alone and in the company of other men, while on his hunting and herding duties. The area was safe for travel for some distance. He had sat around firesides and heard stories about wars and fugitives and other hospitable tribes who lived distances away and whose customs differed from theirs. Keaja had not been idle all this while. He had prepared all they would need for their journey and hidden their provisions in a secret place.

The alternative was more difficult for the lovers. They could inform their parents of their love and ask that they be married. He was not sure of the outcome but it was to invite death or worse. It might still lead to the escape route out of the village as he was not planning for death.

So after some thought Tselane decided to tell her parents because as she pointed out the first plan would be too heartbreaking for their parents. They therefore decided on that very day to inform their parents of their love and name the date on which they wished to marry.

It was nearing dusk when Tselane arrived home with her bundle of wood. Her mother and Mma-Monosi were seated out in the courtyard, engaged in some quiet conversation of their own. Tselane set down her bundle, approached the two women and knelt down quietly by her mother's side. Her mother turned towards her, expecting some request or message from a friend. There was no other way except for Tselane to convey her own message in the most direct way possible.

"Mother," she said. "I am expecting a child by the son of Rra-Keaja. We wish to be married by the next moon. We love each other. . . ."

For a moment her mother frowned as though her child's words did not make sense. Mma-Monosi's body shuddered several times as though she were cold but she maintained a deathly silence. Eventually Tselane's mother lowered her voice and said between clenched teeth: "You are to go to your hut and remain there. On no account are you to leave it without the supervision of Mma-Monosi."

For a time Mma-Tselane sat looking into the distance, a broken woman. Her social prestige, her kingdom, her self-esteem crumbled around her.

A short while later her husband entered the yard. He had spent an enjoyable day at the chief's court with other men. He now wished for his evening meal and retirement for the night. The last thing he wanted was conversation with women, so he looked up irritably as his wife appeared without his evening meal. She explained herself with as much dignity as she could muster. She was almost collapsing with shock. He listened in disbelief and gave a sharp exclamation of anger.

Just at this moment Keaja's father announced himself in the yard. "Rra-Tselane, I have just heard from my own son the offense he has committed against your house, but he desires nothing more than to marry your child. If this would remove the offense, then I am agreeable to it."

"Rra-Keaja," Tselane's father replied. "You know as well as I that this marriage isn't in the interests of your family or mine." He stood up and walked violently into the night.

Brokenly, Keaja's father also stood up and walked out of the yard.

It was her husband's words that shook Mma-Tselane out of her stupor of self-pity. She hurried to her living quarters for her skin shawl, whispered a few words to Mma-Monosi about her mission. Mma-Monosi too sped off into the night after Rra-Keaja. On catching up with him she whispered urgently: "Rra-Keaja! You may not know me. I approach you because we now share this trouble which has come upon us. This matter will never be secret. Tomorrow it will be a public affair. I therefore urge you to do as Mma-Tselane has done and make an appeal for your child at once. She has gone to the woman's compound of the chief's house as she has many friends there."

Her words lightened the old man's heavy heart. With a promise to send her his news, he turned and walked in the direction of the chief's yard.

Mma-Monosi sped back to her own yard.

"Tselane," she said, earnestly. "It is no light matter to break custom. You may pay for it with your life. I should have told you the story that night we discussed custom. When I was a young girl we had a case such as this but not such a deep mess. The young man had taken a fancy to a girl and she to him. He therefore refused the girl his parents had chosen for him. They could not break him and so they killed him. They killed him even though he had not touched the girl. But there is one thing I want you to know. I am your friend and I will die for you. No one will injure you while I am alive."

Their easy, affectionate relationship returned to them. They talked for some time about the love affair, Mma-Monosi absorbing every word with delight. A while later Mma-Tselane re-entered the yard. She was still too angry to talk to her own child but she called Mma-Monosi to one side and informed her that she had won an assurance in high places that no harm would come to her child.

And so began a week of raging storms and wild irrational deliberations. It was a family affair. It was a public affair. As a public affair, it would bring ruin and disaster upon the community and public anger was high. Two parents showed themselves up in a bad light, the father of Tselane and the mother of Keaja. Rra-Tselane was adamant that the marriage would never take place. He preferred to sound death warnings all the time. The worm that had been eating at the heart of Keaja's mother all this while finally arose and devoured her heart. She too could be heard to sound death warnings. Then a curious and temporary solution was handed down from high places. It was said that if the lovers removed themselves from the community for a certain number of days, it would make allowance for public anger to die down. Then the marriage of the lovers would be considered.

So appalling was the drama to the community that on the day Keaja was released from his home and allowed to approach the home of Tselane, all the people withdrew to their own homes so as not to witness the fearful sight. Only Mma-Monosi, who had supervised the last details of the departure, stood openly watching the direction in which the young lovers left the village. She saw them begin to ascend the hill not far from the home of Tselane. As darkness was approaching, she turned and walked back to her yard. To Mma-Tselane, who lay in a state of nervous collapse in her hut, Mma-Monosi made her last sane pronouncement on the whole affair.

"The young man is no fool," she said. "They have taken the direction of the hill. He knows that the hilltop is superior to any other. People are angry and someone might think of attacking them. An attacker will find it a difficult task as the young man will hurtle stones down on him before he ever gets near. Our child is quite safe with him."

Then the story took a horrible turn. Tension built up towards the day the lovers were supposed to return to community life. Days went by and they did not return. Eventually search parties were sent out to look for them but they had disappeared. Not even their footmarks were visible on the bare rock faces and tufts of grass on the hillside. At first the searchers returned and did not report having seen any abnormal phenomena, only baffled surprise. Then Mma-Monosi's precarious imaginative balance tipped over into chaos. She was seen walking grief-stricken towards the hill. As she reached its base she stood still and the whole drama of the disappearance of the lovers was re-created before her eyes. She first heard loud groans of anguish that made her blood run cold. She saw that as soon as Tselane and Keaja set foot on the hill, the rocks parted and a gaping hole appeared. The lovers sank into its depths and the rocks closed over them. As she called, "Tselane! Keaja!" their spirits arose and floated soundlessly with unseeing eyes to the top of the hill.

Mma-Monosi returned to the village and told a solemn and convincing story of all the phenomena she had seen. People only had to be informed that such phenomena existed and they all began seeing them too. Then Mma-Tselane, maddened and distraught by the loss of her daughter, slowly made her way to the hill. With sorrowful eyes she watched the drama re-create itself before her. She returned home and died. The hill from then onwards became an unpleasant embodiment of sinister forces which destroy life. It was no longer considered a safe dwelling place for the tribe. They packed up their belongings on the backs of their animals, destroyed the village and migrated to a safer area.

The deserted area remained unoccupied from then onwards until 1875 when people of the Bamalete tribe settled there. Although strangers to the area, they saw the same phenomena, they heard the loud groans of anguish and saw the silent floating spirits of the lovers. The legend was kept alive from generation unto generation and so the hill stands until this day in the village of Otse in southern Botswana as an eternal legend of love. Letswe La Baratani, The Hill of the Lovers, it is called.

UNDERSTANDING THE STORY

1. Why do the villagers unquestioningly accept the tribal regulations and taboos? How have the villagers adapted to these regulations?

2. Why does the tribe ignore the possibility of individual initiative?

3. What does Rra-Tselane's reply to Rra-Keaja's proposal reveal about Rra-Tselane? How does Rra-Tselane differ from Rra-Keaja?

4. What makes Mma-Tselane forget her self-pity and take action? What does she have to lose? What does she have to gain?

5. What connection, if any, exists between Mma-Monosi and the story that she tells Tselane? What elements in the story support your conclusion?

6. Why don't Keaja and Tselane return to the village?

7. What factors in the nature of the tribe affect the development of the legend of The Hill of the Lovers? What other legends could have developed from Mma-Monosi's report?

8. What **themes** do you find in this story?

ANALYZING LITERARY TECHNIQUE

1. What is the relationship between the **setting** and the **plot?** How does one element enhance the other?

2. Who or what is the **antagonist** in this story?

3. What does Head achieve by her **characterization** of Mma-Monosi?

4. What is the **climax** of the story? To what does it owe its power?

5. How does Head use **foreshadowing** in the story?

6. What does Head achieve by using a **third-person omniscient narrative perspective?**

7. To what extent, if any, can this story be considered a **folktale?** A legend? A **romance?**

WRITING ABOUT LITERATURE

1. Write an essay in which you analyze Head's choice of narrative perspective for this story. Begin by explaining the nature of the third-person omniscient point of view. Then discuss what is achieved and what is lost by this perspective. Give examples from the story to support your ideas. Do you think Head's choice of narrative perspective was a good one? Explain.

2. Tell this story from Mma-Monosi's point of view. Consider the following questions: Why is Mma-Monosi the one to help Tselane? Why does she relate her vision to the villagers? What does she hope to gain? What risks is she taking?

Asia and the South Pacific

THROUGH THEIR WRITINGS, the authors of Asia and the South Pacific reveal their thoughts on everything from the power of human relationships to the power of language and from politics to the discovery of the rare, beautiful moments of life.

In this section, several authors explore the meaning of life and the relationship of humans to the universe. In his poignant play "The Post Office," Rabindranath Tagore creates a memorable character in Amal, a little boy who lives life to its fullest in spite of his worsening illness. In "Not all the sum of earthly happiness," the poet and mystic Hafiz considers the question of whether possessions and riches equal a life of happiness. In the poem "The Rich Eat Three Full Meals," the Vietnamese poet Nguyen Binh Khiem reveals the peace he finds in nature. In the poem "Say Who I Am," the mystic Rumi explores the nature of the universe and his relationship to it. And Yasunari Kawabata describes a transcendent moment of beauty and discovery in the short story "The Grasshopper and the Bell Cricket."

A number of writers, through poems and short stories, explore various aspects of human relationships. "Prince Huo's Daughter," by Jiang Fang, is a well-told story of love gone awry. R. K. Narayan's short story "Forty-Five a Month" shows

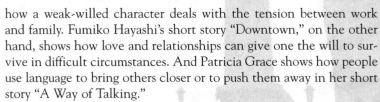

how a weak-willed character deals with the tension between work and family. Fumiko Hayashi's short story "Downtown," on the other hand, shows how love and relationships can give one the will to survive in difficult circumstances. And Patricia Grace shows how people use language to bring others closer or to push them away in her short story "A Way of Talking."

The loss of human relationships are explored in several other selections in this section. In "Wuling Chun," the poet Li Qingzhao lyrically describes her grief at the loss of her husband. On a larger scale, in his poem "Fighting South of the Ramparts," Li Po reveals the human cost of war. Ting Ling contrasts the grief and anger of political prisoners with the hope they hold for a new day politically in "A Certain Night." Katherine Mansfield exposes the character of a father who has never learned how to accept his son's death in the short story "The Fly." And an elderly puppeteer's secret is revealed in the surprise ending of "Life" by Shen Congwen.

The power of social relationships and restraints is explored in other selections. In Ryūnosuke Akutagawa's mystery "In a Grove," each character takes responsibility for the crime in order to save face. Lu Hsün describes the hypocrisy of those who seek divine blessings by adhering to old customs while ignoring the needs of others around them in "The New Year's Sacrifice." Anita Desai explores the tension between a mother and her son in a highly charged social setting in her short story "Pineapple Cake."

Fighting South
of the Ramparts

LI PO

L I PO (701–762), one of China's greatest poets, lived during
the golden age of the T'ang dynasty. Handsome, charming,
and brilliant, he spent the greater part of his life traveling
throughout China. For two brief periods he was a court poet, employed
first by the emperor and then, much later, by a prince. The later years
of Li Po's life were darkened by a devastating civil war, which began
when An Lu-shan, a Turkish general in command of a group of Chinese
imperial border armies, led a rebellion against the emperor in 755.

The subjects of Li Po's poetry reflect his varied life experiences.
Many of his poems are based on folk songs, which Li Po admired for
their effective, simple, and direct style. "Fighting South of the
Ramparts," written about 751, is based on a folk song that originated
during the Han dynasty, in the first century A.D.

Details in the poem refer to the reign of the Han emperor Wu Ti
(141–87 B.C.), whose armies doubled the size of the Chinese empire.
Wu Ti's armies fought border wars to acquire new territory and give
Wu Ti control over trade routes through central Asia. These armies
pushed the Huns (northern Mongolian tribes) and the Tartars
(central-Asian Turkish tribes) north beyond the Gobi Desert; northwest
into central Asia; and west into the T'ien Shan, the mountains that
today divide China from Russia. Under Wu Ti, other frontier armies
extended Chinese rule to the south and southwest.

In choosing to write a poem about the earlier Han border wars,
Li Po was tactfully protesting similar T'ang imperial policies. Not
long before Li Po was born, a T'ang emperor who ruled from 627 to
650 conscripted thousands of young peasants. These men were forced
off their farms to settle and defend remote border lands. They never
returned to their families.

In addition to expressing Li Po's criticism of T'ang expansionism,
"Fighting South of the Ramparts" reflects Li Po's sympathy with

Taoism, an important fourth-century-B.C. Chinese philosophy. The last two lines of the poem paraphrase the following verses from the *Tao-te Ching:*

> Arms are unblest among tools and not the superior man's tools. Only when it is unavoidable he uses them. . . . Rejoicing at a conquest means to enjoy the slaughter of men. He who enjoys the slaughter of men will most assuredly not obtain his will in the empire.

Last year we were fighting at the source of the Sang-kan;[1]
This year we are fighting on the Onion River[2] road.
We have washed our swords in the surf of Parthian seas;[3]
We have pastured our horses among the snows of the T'ien Shan.
The King's armies have grown grey and old   5
Fighting ten thousand leagues away from home.
The Huns have no trade but battle and carnage;
They have no fields or ploughlands,
But only wastes where white bones lie among yellow sands.
Where the House of Ch'in[4] built the Great Wall that was to keep away
    the Tartars,   10
There, in its turn, the House of Han[5] lit beacons of war.
The beacons are always alight, fighting and marching never stop.
Men die in the field, slashing sword to sword;
The horses of the conquered neigh piteously to Heaven.
Crows and hawks peck for human guts,   15
Carry them in their beaks and hang them on the branches of withered trees.
Captains and soldiers are smeared on the bushes and grass;
The general schemed in vain.
Know therefore that the sword is a cursed thing
Which the wise man uses only if he must.   20

---

[1] *Sang-kan:* River north of the Great Wall of China.

[2] *Onion River:* River in Turkestan, in central Asia.

[3] *Parthian seas:* Probably the Caspian Sea and the Aral Sea. Parthia was an ancient kingdom in what is now northeastern Iran.

[4] *House of Ch'in:* The Ch'in dynasty ruled the first Chinese empire from 221–206 B.C. The first emperor, Ch'in Shih-huang, was responsible for the building of the Great Wall between China and Mongolia.

[5] *House of Han:* The Han dynasty (206 B.C.–A.D. 220) succeeded the Ch'in dynasty in ruling China.

UNDERSTANDING THE POEM

1. Why does Li Po devote four lines to stating the locations of the battles?
2. Why does Li Po discuss the Huns although the poem is about Chinese soldiers?
3. What is the difference between the behavior of the House of Ch'in and the House of Han?
4. What is meant by line 18, "The general schemed in vain"?
5. If the speaker's point of view is shared by the other soldiers on the frontiers, what could occur?

ANALYZING LITERARY TECHNIQUE

1. Who is the speaker in the poem? What does Li Po accomplish by relating the poem from his point of view?
2. How does Li Po use **contrast** in the poem?
3. What **irony** about war does Li Po stress?
4. How does Li Po's use of **connotative language** contribute to his theme?
5. What is the function of the last two lines of the poem?

WRITING ABOUT LITERATURE

1. Analyze the ways in which Li Po conveys the theme of the poem to the reader. Choose two or three of Li Po's literary techniques that enhance the theme and write an essay that examines each technique. Using quotations from the poem as examples, explain how each technique enhances the theme.
2. Li Po's beliefs were grounded in the Taoist philosophy. The last two lines of the poem are a paraphrase of lines from the *Tao-te Ching,* a Chinese book of philosophy that dates from the fourth or third century B.C. (The lines are quoted in the introductory material.) The *Tao-te Ching* combines political advice and teachings about the Tao, or Way, which is the basis of the Taoist religion.

   Consult reference books to learn more about the principles of Taoism and then write a brief essay in which you relate Taoist philosophy to Li Po's point of view in this poem.
3. Write a poem about war. Consider the causes, effects, and consequences of war. Use figurative language to vividly convey your ideas and attitudes. You may choose to write from the perspective of a soldier or an officer or from the perspective of a civilian.

   If you wish, start by writing your ideas in paragraph form. Then pare your ideas down to essential phrases and words and arrange those phrases and words in a poetic form that pleases you.

Prince Huo's Daughter

JIANG FANG

*J*IANG FANG (c. 780–830) is one of the famous Chinese writers of the T'ang dynasty. One volume of his poetry and the following short story survive to this day.

It was during the T'ang dynasty (618–907) that the short story developed in China. Until then, Chinese fiction had consisted of fairy tales, ghost stories, myths, and legends. This early fiction had short simple plots, with no characterization and little description. However, during the T'ang dynasty writers became interested in fiction as an art form. They began to write tales with more complex structure and plot, adding realistic characterization and detailed description.

A popular theme in the T'ang short stories was the love between a man and a woman. This theme had many variations because social life at the time was complex. Male-female relationships included formally arranged marriages, which were often loveless, and love outside marriage. Courtesans, socially inferior women who sang in brothels and in teahouses, were often loved by men who were obligated to women of their own social class. Thus, the intricacies of courtship, unrequited love, and betrayed love became common subjects of the new fiction. "Prince Huo's Daughter" is based on the true story of the love affair between the famous poet Li Yi and the courtesan Xiaoyu.

During the Da Li Period[1] (766–779), there was a young man of Longxi[2] whose name was Li Yi. At the age of twenty he passed one of the civil service examinations and the following year the best scholars of his rank were to be chosen for official posts through a further

---

[1] *Da Li Period*: Da Li, also known as Ta-li, was the center of a powerful eighth-century state in the southern Yunnan province of China.

[2] *Longxi*: Town in southeastern China, now know as Zhengzhou.

examination at the Ministry of Civil Affairs. In the sixth month he arrived at the capital[3] and took lodgings in the Xinchang quarter. He came from a good family, showed brilliant promise, and was acknowledged by his contemporaries as unsurpassed in literary craftsmanship. Thus even senior scholars looked up to him. Having no mean opinion of his own gifts, he hoped for a beautiful and accomplished wife. But long and vainly did he search among the famous courtesans of the capital.

In Chang'an there was a match-maker named Bao, who was the eleventh child in her family. She had been a maidservant in the prince consort's family, but a dozen years before this had redeemed herself and married. Clever and with a ready tongue, she knew all the great families and was a past master at arranging matches. Li gave her rich gifts and asked her to find him a wife, and she was very well disposed towards him.

One afternoon, some months later, Li was sitting in the south pavilion of his lodgings when he heard insistent knocking and Bao was announced. Gathering up the skirt of his gown, he hurried to meet her. "What brings you here so unexpectedly, madam?" he asked.

Bao laughed and responded, "Have you been having sweet dreams? A fairy has come down to earth who cares nothing for wealth but who admires wit and gallantry. She is made for you!"

When Li heard this he leaped for joy and felt as if he were walking on air. Taking Bao's hand he bowed and thanked her, saying: "I shall be your slave as long as I live!"

Asked where the girl lived and what her name was, Bao replied: "She is the youngest daughter of Prince Huo. Her name is Jade, and the prince doted on her. Her mother, Qinchi, was his favourite slave. When the prince died, his sons refused to keep the child because her mother was of humble birth, so they gave her a portion and made her leave. She has changed her name to Zheng, and people do not know that the prince was her father. But she is the most beautiful creature you ever saw, with a sensibility and grace beyond compare. She is well versed too in music and the classics. Yesterday she asked me to find a good match for her, and when I mentioned your name she was delighted, for she knows you by reputation. They live in Old Temple Lane in the Shengye quarter, in the house at the entrance to the carriage drive. I have already made an appointment for you. Go tomorrow at noon to the end of the lane, and look for a maid called Guizi. She will show you the house."

As soon as the match-maker left, Li started to prepare for the great occasion, sending his servant Qiuhong to borrow a black charger with a gilt bit from his cousin Shang who was the adjutant general of the capital. That evening he washed his clothes, had a bath, and shaved. He could not sleep all night for joy. At dawn he put on his cap and examined himself in the mirror, fearing all might not go well. Having frittered away the time till noon, he called for the horse and galloped to the Shengye quarter. When he reached the place appointed, he saw

---

[3] *capital:* Chang'an, a city in central China on the Wai He River, now known as Xi'an.

a maid standing there waiting for him, who asked, "Are you Master Li?" He dismounted, told the maid to stable the horse, and went quickly in, bolting the gate behind him.

The match-maker came out from the house, smiling at him from a distance as she cried, "Who is this gate-crasher?" While they were joking with each other, he found himself led through the inner gate into a courtyard where there were four cherry trees and a parrot cage hanging on the northwest side.

At the sight of Li, the parrot squawked, "Here's a guest! Lower the curtain!"

Naturally bashful, Li had felt some scruples about going in, and now the parrot startled him and brought him to a standstill until Bao led the girl's mother down the steps to welcome him, and he was asked to go inside and take a seat opposite her. The mother, little more than forty, was a slender, attractive woman with charming manners.

"We have heard of your brilliance as a scholar," she said to Li, "and now that I see what a handsome young man you are too, I am sure your fame is well deserved. I have a daughter who, though lacking education, is not ill-favoured. She should be a suitable match for you. Madame Bao has already proposed this, and today I would like to offer my daughter to you in marriage."

"I am a clumsy fellow," he replied, "and do not deserve such a distinction. If you accept me, I shall count it as a great honour as long as I live."

Then a feast was laid, Jade was called by her mother from the east chamber, and Li bowed to greet her. At her entrance, he felt as if the room had been transformed into a bower of roses, and when their eyes met he was dazzled by her glance. The girl sat down beside her mother, who said to her, "You like to repeat those lines:

> 'When the wind in the bamboos rustles the curtain,
> I fancy my old friend is near.'

Here is the author of the poem. You have been reading his works so often—what do you think of him now you see him?"

Jade lowered her head and answered with a smile: "He doesn't live up to my expectations. Shouldn't a poet be more handsome?"

Then Li got up and made several bows. "You love talent and I admire beauty," he said. "Between us we have both!"

Jade and her mother looked at each other and smiled.

When they had drunk several cups of wine together, Li stood up and asked the girl to sing. At first she declined, but her mother insisted, and in a clear voice she sang an intricate melody. By the time they had drunk their fill it was evening, and the match-maker led the young man to the west wing to rest. The rooms were secluded in a quiet courtyard, and the hangings were magnificent. Bao told the maids Guizi and Wansha to take off Li's boots and belt. Then Jade herself appeared. With sweet archness and charming coyness she put off her clothes. Then they lowered the bed-curtains, lay down on the pillows and enjoyed each other to their hearts' content. The young man felt that he was in bed with a goddess.

During the night, however, the girl suddenly gazed at him through tears and said, "As a courtesan, I know I am no match for you. You love me now for my looks, but I fear that when I lose them your feelings will change, and then I shall be like a vine with nothing to cling to, or a fan discarded in the autumn. So at the height of my joy I cannot help grieving."

Li was touched, and putting his arm around her neck said gently, "Today I have attained the dream of my life. I swear I would rather die than leave you. Why do you talk like that? Let me have some white silk to pledge you my faith in writing."

Drying her tears, Jade called her maid Yingtao to raise the curtain and hold the candle, while she gave Li brush and ink. When not occupied with music, Jade was fond of reading, and her writing-case, brushes, and ink all came from the palace. Now she brought out an embroidered case and from it took three feet of white silk lined with black for him to write on. The young man had a gift for contemporary composition, and taking up the brush wrote rapidly. He swore by the mountains and rivers, by the sun and the moon, that he would be true. He wrote passionately and movingly, and when he had finished he gave Jade his pledge to keep in her jewel box.

After that they lived happily for two years like a pair of kingfishers soaring on high, together day and night. But in the spring of the third year, Li came first in his examination and was appointed secretary-general of Zheng County. In the fourth month, before leaving to take up his post and to visit his parents in Luoyang,[4] he gave a farewell party to all his relatives at the capital. It was the season between spring and summer. When the feast was over and the guest had gone, the young man and the girl were filled with grief at their coming separation.

"With your talents and fame," said Jade, "you have many admirers who would like to be related to you by marriage. And your old parents at home have no daughter-in-law to look after them. So when you go to take up this post, you are bound to find a good wife. The pledge you made me is not binding. But I have a small request to make, which I hope you will consider. May I tell you what it is?"

Li was startled and protested, "In what way have I offended you, that you speak like this? Tell me what is on you mind, and I promise to do whatever you ask."

"I am eighteen," said the girl, "and you are only twenty-two. There are still eight years before you reach thirty, the age at which a man should marry. I would like to crowd into these eight years all the love and happiness of my life. After that you can choose some girl of good family for a wife—it will not be too late. Then I shall retire from the world, cutting my hair short and becoming a nun. This is the wish of my life and I ask no more."

Cut to the heart, Li could not hold back his tears. "I swear by the bright sun," he assured the girl, "as long as I live I shall be true to you. My only fear is that I may fail to please you—how can I think of anything else? I beg you not to doubt me, but rest assured. I shall reach Huazhou in the eighth month and send to fetch

---

[4] *Luoyang:* City in central China.

you. We shall be together again before very long." A few days later he said good-bye to her and went east.

Ten days after Li's arrival at his post, he asked leave to go to Luoyang to see his parents. Before he reached home, his mother had arranged a match for him with a cousin in the Lu family—a verbal agreement had already been reached. His mother was so strict that Li, though hesitating, dared not decline; accordingly he went through with the ceremonies and arranged a date for the wedding. Since the girl's family was a powerful one, they demanded over a million cash betrothal money and would call off the marriage if this were not forthcoming. Because Li's family was poor he had to borrow this sum; and he took advantage of his leave to look up distant friends, traveling up and down the Huai and Yangtse River[5] valleys from the autumn till the next summer. Knowing that he had broken his promise to fetch Jade at the appointed time he sent no message to her, hoping that she would give him up. He also asked his friends not to disclose the truth.

When Li failed to return at the appointed time, Jade tried to find out what had become of him, only to receive contradictory reports. She also consulted many fortune-tellers and oracles. This went on for more than a year, until at last she fell ill of sorrow; and, lying in her lonely room, went from bad to worse. Though no tidings had come from Li, her love for him did not falter, and she gave presents to friends and acquaintances to persuade them to find news of him. This she did so persistently that soon all her money had gone and she often had to send her maid out secretly to sell dresses and trinkets through an innkeeper in the West Market.

One day Jade sent Wansha to sell an amethyst hairpin, and on her way to the inn the maid met an old jade-smith who worked in the palace. When he saw what she was carrying, he recognized it. "This hair-pin is one I made," he said. "Many years ago, when Prince Huo's youngest daughter first put up her hair, he ordered me to make this pin and gave me ten thousand cash for the job. I have always remembered it. Who are you? And how did you come by this?"

"My mistress is the prince's daughter," replied the maid. "She has come down in the world, and the man she married went to Luoyang and deserted her. So she fell ill of grief, and has been in a decline for two years. Now she wants me to sell this, so that she can bribe someone to get news of her husband."

The jade-smith shed tears, exclaiming, "Can the children of nobles fall on such evil times? My days are nearly spent, but this ill-fated lady's story wrings my heart."

Then the old man led Wansha to the house of Princess Yanxian, and when the princess heard this story she too heaved sigh after sigh. Finally she gave the maid one hundred and twenty thousand cash for the hair-pin.

Now the girl to whom Li was engaged was in the capital. After raising the sum he needed for his marriage, he returned to his post in Zheng County; but at the end of the year he again asked for leave to go to Chang'an to get married. And he found quiet lodgings, so that his whereabouts would not be known. A

---

[5] *Huai and Yangtse River:* The Huai River flows through eastern China into the Hongze Lake. The Yangtse, or Yangtze, flows through eastern China into the East China Sea.

young scholar, named Cui Yunming, who was Li's cousin and a kind-hearted man, had formerly drunk with Li in Jade's room and laughed and talked with her until they were on the best of terms. Whenever he received news of Li, he would tell Jade truthfully, and she had helped him so often with money and clothing that he felt quite indebted to her.

When Li came to the capital, Cui told Jade, who sighed and exclaimed indignantly, "How can he be so faithless?" She begged all her friends to ask Li to come to her; but knowing that he had broken his promise and that the girl was dying, he felt too ashamed to see her. He took to going out early and coming back late in order to avoid callers. Though Jade wept day and night, unable to eat or sleep in her longing to see him, he never came. And indignation and grief made her illness worse. When the story became known in the capital, all of the young scholars were moved by the girl's love while all the young gallants resented Li's heartlessness.

It was then spring, the season for pleasure trips, and Li went one day with five or six friends to Chongqing Temple to see the peonies in bloom. Strolling in the west corridor, they composed poems together. A close friend of Li's named Wei Xiaqing, a native of Chang'an, was one of the party. "Spring is beautiful and flowers are in bloom," he told Li. "But your old love nurses her grief in her lonely room. It is really cruel of you to abandon her. A true man would not do this. Think it over again!"

As Wei was sighing and reproaching Li, up came a young gallant wearing a yellow shirt and carrying a crossbow.

He was handsome and splendidly dressed, but attended only by a Central Asian boy with cropped hair. Walking behind them, he overheard their conversation; and presently he stepped forward and bowed to Li, saying, "Is your name not Li? My family comes from the east, and we are related to the royal house. Though I have no literary talent myself, I value it in others. I have long been an admirer of yours and hoped to make your acquaintance, and today I am lucky enough to meet you. My humble house is not far from here, and I have musicians to entertain you. I have eight or nine beautiful girls too, and a dozen good horses, all of them, at your disposal. I only hope you will honor me with a visit."

When Li's friends heard this, they were delighted. They rode along after this young gallant, who swiftly turned corner after corner until they reached the Shengye quarter. Since they were approaching Jade's house, Li was reluctant to go any farther and made some excuse to turn back.

But the stranger said, "My humble home is only a stone's throw away from here. Don't leave us now!" He took hold of Li's bridle and pulled his horse along.

In a moment they had reached the girl's house. Li was dismayed and tried to turn back, but the other quickly ordered attendants to help him dismount and lead him inside. They pushed him through the gate and bolted it, calling out, "Master Li is here!" Then the exclamations of joy and surprise could be heard from the whole house.

The night before, Jade had dreamed that Li was brought to her bedside by a man in a yellow shirt and that she was told to take off her shoes. When she woke up she told her mother this dream, and said, "Shoes symbolize union. That means that husband and wife will meet again. But to take them off means separation. We shall be united then parted again—for ever. Judging by this dream, I shall see him once more and after that I shall die."

In the morning she asked her mother to dress her hair for her. Her mother thought she was raving and paid no attention, but when Jade insisted she consented. And no sooner was her hair done than Li arrived.

Jade had been ill so long that she could not even turn in bed without help. But on hearing that her lover had come she got up swiftly, changed her clothes and hurried out like one possessed. Confronting Li in silence, she fixed angry eyes on him. So frail she could hardly stand, she kept averting her face and then, against her will, looking back, till all present were moved to tears.

Soon several dozen dishes of food and wine were brought in. And when the company asked in astonishment where this feast had come from, they found it had been ordered by the young gallant. The table spread, they sat down. Jade, though she had turned away from Li, kept stealing long glances at him; and finally raising her cup of wine, she poured a libation on the ground and said, "I am the unhappiest of women, and you are the most heartless of men. Dying young of a broken heart, I shall not be able to look after my mother; and I must bid farewell for ever to my silk dresses and music, to suffer torments in hell. This is your doing, sir! Farewell! After death I shall become an avenging spirit and give your wives and concubines no peace."

Grasping Li's arm with her left hand, she threw her cup to the ground. Then, after crying out several times, she fell dead. Her mother placed her body on Li's knee and told him to call her, but he could not revive her.

Li put on mourning and wept bitterly during the wake. The night before the obsequies she appeared to him within the funeral curtain, as beautiful as in life. She was wearing a pomegranate-red skirt, purple tunic, and red and green cape. Leaning against the curtain and fingering the embroidered tassels, she looked at him and said, "You must still have some feeling for me, to see me off. That is a comfort to me here among the shades." With that she vanished. The next day she was buried at Yusuyuan near the capital. After mourning by her grave, Li went back; and a month later he married his cousin. But he was in low spirits after all that had happened.

In the fifth month, Li went with his wife to his post in Zheng County. About ten days after their arrival, he was sleeping with his wife when he heard soft hoots outside the curtain, and looking out he saw a very handsome young man hiding behind the hangings and beckoning repeatedly to his wife. Li leaped up in agitation and went round the curtain several times to look for the intruder, but no one was there. This made him so suspicious that he gave his wife no peace until some friends persuaded him to make it up and he began to feel a little better. About ten days later, however, he came home to find his wife playing her lute on the couch, when an engraved rhinoceros-horn case, little over an inch in diameter and tied with a flimsy silk love-knot, was thrown into the room. This case fell on his wife's lap. When Li opened it, he found two love-peas, one Spanish fly, as well as other aphrodisiacs and love-charms. Howling like a wild beast in his anger, he seized the lute and beat his wife with it as he demanded the truth. But she could not clear herself. After that he often beat her savagely and treated her with great cruelty; and finally he denounced her in the court and divorced her.

After Li divorced his wife, he soon became suspicious of the maidservants and women slaves whom he had favoured, and some he even killed in his jealously. Once he went to Yangzhou and bought a famous courtesan named Ying, who was the eleventh child of her family. She was so charming and beautiful that Li was very fond of her. But when they were together he liked to tell her about another girl he had purchased, and how he had punished her for various faults. He told her such things every day to make her fear him, so that she would not dare to take other lovers. Whenever he went out, he would leave her on the bed covered up with a bath-tub which was sealed all round; and upon his return he would examine the tub carefully before letting her out. He also kept a very sharp dagger and would say to his maids, "This is Gexi steel. It's good for cutting the throats of unfaithful women!"

Whatever women he had, he would soon grow suspicious of them, and he was a jealous husband to the two other wives he married later.

UNDERSTANDING THE STORY

1. Why is this story called "Prince Huo's Daughter" instead of "Li Yi"?
2. What kind of person is Li Yi?
3. Why doesn't Li tell Jade the truth?
4. Who is responsible for Jade's illness? Explain.
5. To what extent does Li's shame excuse his callous behavior?
6. What is the significance of Jade's dream and her curse?
7. What motivates Li's attitude toward the women he loves after Jade's death?
8. What does this story reveal about life in China during the T'ang dynasty?
9. To what extent is intelligence more important than moral character in this story?
10. What **themes** do you find in the story?

ANALYZING LITERARY TECHNIQUE

1. To what extent is this story a **tragedy?** To what extent is it a **melodrama?**
2. What does the **narrative perspective** contribute to the story?
3. How does the **setting** affect the **plot?**
4. There are numerous references in this story to Li's "contemporaries," other scholars who take note of Li's career and personal life. What function do these scholars serve?

5. How does Jiang Fang use **foreshadowing** in this story?

6. At what point does the catharsis in this story occur?

7. What is the **resolution** of the story?

WRITING ABOUT LITERATURE

1. Analyze the character traits of Li and Jade. What traits are important for the development of the plot? What effect do Li's and Jade's personalities have on the reader? How does the author achieve this effect?

2. Tell this story (or one episode of it) from Li's point of view. Consider his treatment of Jade, his attitude toward his mother's choice of a bride, and his successive marriages. Remember that people often find justification for behavior that others criticize.

Wuling chun

LI QINGZHAO

LI QINGZHAO (1084–1151) is the well-known poet of *ci*, the Chinese poems that set new words to old or popular song melodies. Li Qingzhao, also known as Li Ch'ing-chao, published seven books of traditional poetry *(shi)* as well as six books of *ci* and a prose study of *ci*. About fifty of her *ci* and seventeen of her *shi* still survive. They can be found in English translation in *Li Ching-Chao: Complete Poems* (1979) and *The Complete Ci-poems of Li Qingzhao: A New English Translation* (1989).

Li Qingzhao was born to an aristocratic family during the Song dynasty. Her father was a professor and her mother was a poet; as a result she received an unusually liberal upbringing. She was already known for her poetry when she married Zhao Mingcheng, a scholar and government official, in 1101. The couple lived simply and collected books and antiques; together they compiled *Records on Metal and Stone*, a catalog of ancient texts and inscriptions. In 1126 their province was invaded by the Jurchen from Manchuria. When the couple fled to the south, they lost much of their antique collection. In 1129 Zhao Mingcheng was reassigned to a new post in Hu Zhou, but he died before he could reach it. Li Qingzhao continued to write poetry until she died in 1151.

The poetry of Li Qingzhao chronicles the various stages of her life. Her earlier poetry celebrates her life with Zhao Mingcheng; in fact, Li Qingzhao and her husband often wrote poems to each other. After his death, Li Qingzhao's poetry shows her grief and loneliness. "Wuling chun" (or "Wuling Spring"), to the tune "Spring in Wuling," was written about six years after the death of Zhao Mingcheng; it demonstrates that she still mourns the loss of her husband.

The wind subsides—the dust carries a fragrance of fallen petals;
It's late in the day—I'm too tired to comb my hair.
Things remain but he is gone, and with him everything.
On the verge of words, tears flow.

I hear at Twin Creek spring's still lovely;   5
How I long to float there on a small boat—
But I fear that at Twin Creek my frail grasshopper boat
Could not carry this load of grief.

UNDERSTANDING THE POEM

1. Why is the speaker "too tired to comb [her] hair" (line 2)?
2. What does the speaker mean when she says, "Things remain but he is gone, and with him everything" (line 3)?
3. What does the speaker wish she could do?

ANALYZING LITERARY TECHNIQUE

1. What concrete **images** does the poet use in the poem? What do these images convey?
2. What is the **tone** of the poem?
3. What is the effect of **contrast** in this poem?

WRITING ABOUT LITERATURE

1. Write an essay analyzing the use of imagery in this poem. Use quotations from the poem to support your ideas.
2. Write a poem to the tune of a popular song. Your lyrics may express joy or sadness. Be sure to use concrete images to convey the emotions you are expressing.

Say Who I Am

JALAL AD-DIN AR-RUMI

Persia

JALAL AD-DIN AR-RUMI (1207–1273), a Persian poet whose works remain modern in tone and thought, continues to be one of the world's most popular poets. His best-known works include *Divan-e-Shams*, a collection of poetry in praise of his spiritual mentor Shams al Din Tabrizi; *Masnavi*, a seven-volume book of meditations, fables, and anecdotes; and *Fihi ma Fihi*, a discourse on metaphysics.

Rumi was born in Balkh, a region in what is now Afghanistan. His father, Bahauddin, was a well-known religious teacher. When Rumi was five, his family was forced to flee Balkh under the threat of an invasion from the Mongol army of Genghis Khan; the family went on a pilgrimage to Mecca and finally settled in Konya (in modern Turkey). After the death of his father, Rumi received spiritual guidance from his father's friend Sayyid Burhaneddin—guidance that began with a forty-day retreat and eventually led to meditation and periods of fasting. Rumi became a renowned religion professor and Muslim mystic.

When Rumi was thirty-seven, he met Shams al Din Tabrizi, a follower of Sufism—a school of Islam founded on the belief that a true understanding of reality leads to an understanding of God and the divine. Rumi became a Sufi, and his subsequent friendship with Shams played a key role his life. Rumi formed the Mevlevi order of Sufism, which preached humility, charity, and religious tolerance. The Mevlevi included dance in its rituals, leading to the nickname "the whirling dervishes" ("whirling" describes the pattern of the circular dance, while "dervish" is the Persian word for beggar). It is rumored that when Rumi died in 1273, men of five faiths carried his funeral bier.

The *Masnavi*, from which many of Rumi's most popular poems are taken, was composed by Rumi when he was in his early fifties. This was his second collection of works. Though it was written many years after the death of Rumi's spiritual leader Shams, the ideas and the spirituality Rumi gained from that friendship run throughout the work. The text was written down by Rumi's friend Husameddin

Chelebi as Rumi recited his thoughts aloud. Chelebi never went out without his pen, and he would write for Rumi no matter where the two went. The *Masnavi's* enormous range of topics includes the political, religious, romantic, historical, and cultural aspects of human life.

In his writing, Rumi explores the spirituality of human life and of the environment. The mystical belief that knowledge of God can be achieved through subjective experience is apparent in many of Rumi's works, including "Say Who I Am."

I am dust particles in sunlight.
I am the round sun.

To the bits of dust I say, *Stay.*
To the sun, *Keep moving.*

I am morning mist,   5
and the breathing of evening.

I am wind in the top of a grove,
and surf on the cliff.

Mast, rudder, helmsman, and keel,
I am also the coral reef they founder on.   10

I am a tree with a trained parrot in its branches.
Silence, thought, and voice.

The musical air coming through a flute,
a spark off a stone, a flickering

in metal. Both candle,   15
and the moth crazy around it.

Rose, and the nightingale
lost in the fragrance.

I am all orders of being, the circling galaxy,
the evolutionary intelligence, the lift,   20

and the falling away. What is,
and what isn't. You who know

Jelaluddin, You the One
in all, say who

I am. Say I   25
am You.

UNDERSTANDING THE POEM

1. Who is the speaker addressing?
2. Why might the speaker tell the dust "Stay" (line 3)? Why might he tell the sun "Keep moving" (line 4)?
3. What is the meaning of the lines "Mast, rudder, helmsman, and keel, / I am also the coral reef they founder on" (lines 9–10)?
4. What is "evolutionary intelligence" (line 20)?
5. What is the **theme** of the poem?

ANALYZING LITERARY TECHNIQUE

1. What is the **tone** of this poem? How is this tone achieved?
2. What does Rumi's use of **apostrophe** contribute to the poem? How would the poem be different if Rumi had not used apostrophe?
3. How does **contrast** function in the poem?

WRITING ABOUT LITERATURE

1. Write an expository essay analyzing Rumi's use of **imagery** in the poem. He writes about objects of nature (such as the sun and a grove) and objects of human invention (such as ships and candles). How do these two aspects of the world function in the poem? Why might Rumi have used both objects of nature and objects of invention?
2. Rumi once wrote, "Know . . . that each thing in the universe is a vessel full to the brim with wisdom and beauty. It is a drop from the river of His Beauty. . . . It is a hidden treasure because of its fullness." Write an essay analyzing this quotation and its relationship to the theme of "Say Who I Am." Does the quotation reflect the ideas found in the poem? If so, how? What does Rumi seem to believe about the nature of the universe and his relation to it? What do you think he means when he says that all things are filled with "wisdom and beauty"?
3. Write a poem using apostrophe to illuminate a personal belief or a way in which you view the world. Picture whom you would like to address as you write.

Not all the
sum of earthly
happiness

HAFIZ

*S*HAMSEDDIN MOHAMMAD (c. 1320–c. 1389), known as Hafiz, is both a beloved Persian poet and a spiritual guide for many people around the world. "Hafiz" means "one who can recite the Koran"; the title is bestowed on people who have memorized the entire Koran. Hafiz's best-known work is *Divan-e-Hafiz,* a collection of his works that was compiled by his friend Mohammad Golandaam. The text was completed more than twenty years after Hafiz's death.

Hafiz was born to a coal merchant and his wife. The family moved from Isfahan, Persia (modern Iran), to Shiraz, Persia, when Hafiz was young. He loved Shiraz so dearly that he rarely left it, despite numerous invitations to travel abroad. His father died when Hafiz was a teenager, and Hafiz and his mother moved in with his uncle. Hafiz worked as a copyist and a baker's assistant before becoming a celebrated poet. According to legend, Hafiz began writing poetry when he fell in love with Shakh-e-Nabat (Branch of Sugarcane), a girl whom he first saw while delivering bread in a prosperous district of Shiraz. He was so enamored of her that he sat in vigil at the tomb of Baba Kuhi for forty days and nights. On his way back from the vigil, Hafiz met Attar, a shop-owner who became his spiritual master. Many of Hafiz's poem are dedicated to Shakh-e-Nabat, though he married another woman and had a son with her. Forty years after Hafiz first met Attar, Attar helped Hafiz achieve "cosmic consciousness," a true understanding of God.

"Not all the sum of earthly happiness" encapsulates Hafiz's beliefs about the nature of wealth and the differences between material and spiritual wealth. Hafiz's striking language probes many facets of the question he seeks to answer and captures the realities of life and the concerns of humanity.

Not all the sum of earthly happiness
Is worth the bowed head of a moment's pain,
And if I sell for wine my dervish[1] dress,
Worth more than what I sell is what I gain!
Land where my Lady dwells, thou holdest me   5
Enchained; else Fars[2] were but a barren soil,
Not worth the journey over land and sea,
                    Not worth the toil!

Down in the quarter where they sell red wine,
My holy carpet scarce would fetch a cup—   10
How brave a pledge of piety is mine,
Which is not worth a goblet foaming up!
Mine enemy heaped scorn on me and said:
"Forth from the tavern gate!" Why am I thrust
From off the threshold? is my fallen head   15
                    Not worth the dust?

Wash white that travel-stained sad robe of thine!
Where word and deed alike one colour bear,
The grape's fair purple garment shall outshine
Thy many-coloured rags and tattered gear.   20
Full easy seemed the sorrow of the sea
Lightened by hope of gain—hope flew too fast!
A hundred pearls were poor indemnity,
                    Not worth the blast.

The Sultan's crown, with priceless jewels set,   25
Encircles fear of death and constant dread;
It is a head-dress much desired—and yet
Art sure 'tis worth the dangers to the head?
'Twere best for thee to hide thy face from those
That long for thee; the Conqueror's reward   30
Is never worth the army's long-drawn woes,
                    Worth fire and sword.

Ah, seek the treasure of a mind at rest
And store it in the treasury of Ease;
Not worth a loyal heart, a tranquil breast,   35

---

[1] *dervish:* Persian for "beggar"; a member of a Muslim order known for devotional dances.
[2] *Fars:* A province in Iran; home to the powerful Achaemenid dynasty (550–420 B.C.) of Persia.

Were all the riches of thy lands and seas!
Ah, scorn, like Hafiz, the delights of earth,
Ask not one grain of favour from the base,
Two hundred sacks of jewels were not worth
                              Thy soul's disgrace!   40

UNDERSTANDING THE POEM

1. Why does the speaker value wine more than his "dervish dress" (line 3)?

2. Why might the speaker feel his "pledge of piety" (line 11) is brave?

3. What is "the sorrow of the sea" (line 21)?

4. Why does the speaker question the value of "the Sultan's crown" (line 25)?

5. What does the speaker mean by "Thy soul's disgrace" (line 40)?

ANALYZING LITERARY TECHNIQUE

1. How does the **repetition** of the phrase "not worth" function in the poem?

2. What is the function of the **metaphor** "the grape's fair purple garment" (line 19)?

3. Examine Hafiz's use of **personification** and its contribution to the poem.

4. What does the speaker mean by "the treasure of a mind at rest" (line 33)? What does the word "treasure" contribute to the meaning of the line?

5. Hafiz mentions a number of people in his poem (his Lady, his enemy, and the Sultan), and he refers to himself in the third person. Why might he have mentioned these people, and what does their inclusion add to the poem's meaning? Why might he mention himself last?

WRITING ABOUT LITERATURE

1. Write an expository essay analyzing one **stanza** in the poem. Could the stanza stand on its own, separate from the rest of the poem? What would this separation add to or detract from the poem? What is the main **theme** of the stanza?

2. Numerous religious and spiritual leaders throughout history—including Jesus Christ and Siddhartha Gautama—have taught that material possessions do not guarantee happiness on earth. Write an expository essay analyzing why you think this teaching may be so prevalent among spiritual teachers. Do you agree that wealth does not contribute greatly to earthly happiness? Can a person have both wealth and spirituality?

3. Write a letter to a friend explaining a facet of your life that is very important to you. Do you put your family first? Are you a loyal and true friend? Do you believe that artistic or athletic ability is important to who you are as a person? Use **imagery** and **figurative language** to help convey the meaning of the letter to your friend.

The Rich Eat
Three Full Meals

NGUYEN BINH KHIEM

GUYEN BINH KHIEM (1491–1585) was Vietnam's first poet as well as a preeminent teacher, advisor, and oracle. He—along with the French poet Victor Hugo and the Chinese revolutionary leader Sen—is considered one of the saints of the Vietnamese religion Cao Dai. Writing under the pen name Bach Van, Nguyen Binh Khiem wrote in the *nôm* style, in which Chinese characters are altered (often by combining characters) to make a distinctly Vietnamese language. His *nôm* poems were published as *Bach Van quoc-ngu thi-tap* (*Poems in National Language by Bach Van*). Translations of his poems can be found in *A Thousand Years of Vietnamese Poetry*.

Nguyen Binh Khiem was born in 1491 in the village of Trung An. In 1535 he received a doctorate of the first rank and came in first on his regional exams. He served as a government official in the court of the unpopular king of the Mac dynasty during a time of political unrest, but his wisdom and gentleness kept him above the political fray. He retired to his home village in 1542 and founded the Bach Van shrine, a collective school where students and poets gathered from all over Vietnam. Despite his retirement, the king of the Mac dynasty continued to call upon Nguyen Binh Khiem for advice during difficult times. Nguyen Binh Khiem always returned to Trung An after these sessions, to teach and to write poetry.

The poetry of Nguyen Binh Khiem reflects his enjoyment of the simple pleasures in life and his appreciation of nature. While many of his poems hint at the political unrest of his time or disparage the shallowness of life in society, he returns again and again to the rewarding life of *otium*, the life of cultivated leisure. "The Rich Eat Three Full Meals" is a good example of Nguyen Binh Khiem's preference for communing with nature rather than reflecting on the world.

The rich eat three full meals, the poor two small bowls,
But peace is what matters.
Thirsty, I drink sweet plum tea;
Warm, I lie in the shade, in the breeze;
My paintings are mountains and rivers all around me,   5
My damask, embroidered, the grass.
I rest at night, rest easy,
Am awake with the sun
And enjoying Heaven's heaped-up favors.

UNDERSTANDING THE POEM

1. What societal problems does the speaker acknowledge?

2. What does the speaker take pleasure in?

3. What are "Heaven's heaped-up favors"?

ANALYZING LITERARY TECHNIQUE

1. What two groups does the speaker **contrast** in the poem?

2. What **metaphors** does the poet use? How do these metaphors criticize one of the groups from question 1?

3. How does the poet use **imagery** to convey his point?

WRITING ABOUT LITERATURE

1. Write an essay analyzing the poet's use of metaphors and imagery to convey his message.

2. Write a poem in which you describe what brings you contentment. Use imagery and metaphors to convey your feelings of happiness and to describe what has created those feelings.

The Post Office

RABINDRANATH TAGORE

$\mathcal{R}$ABINDRANATH TAGORE (1861–1941), an internationally famous Indian poet, won the Nobel Prize for literature in 1913 for "his profoundly sensitive, fresh, and beautiful verse, by which, with consummate skill, he has made his poetic thought . . . a part of the literature of the West." Tagore, often referred to as "the Sun of India," personified Indian culture; through his work, he introduced the West to certain cultural values of his people. Mahatma Gandhi called him "the Great Teacher" and said of him, "In common with thousands of his countrymen, I owe much to one who by his poetic genius and singular purity of life has raised India in the estimation of the world."

In Europe and the United States, Tagore is best known for his poetry collection *Song Offerings* (1909). However, in India he is cherished as a prominent painter; an accomplished musician; the founder of an innovative educational institution; and a writer of short stories, novels, and dramas, as well as poetry. Tagore was knighted in 1915, but he renounced the title in 1919 following the Amritsar Massacre, in which British troops suppressed an Indian demonstration.

Tagore was born in Bengal, then a province of British India. His family included many famous individuals: musicians and artists as well as those who pursued religious and social reforms. Tagore's parents provided him with a private education in a literary environment.

After briefly studying law in England, Tagore returned to India at the age of twenty-four to manage his father's huge estate and to pursue his interest in writing. There he came to know many impoverished villagers, observing their suffering as well as their nobility. Choosing to live and write near them, Tagore became a prodigious author, publishing more than sixty volumes of poetry, twenty-four plays, eight novels, and eight short-story collections.

In 1901 Tagore founded Visva-Bharati, an innovative educational institution that operated outdoors amidst the beauty of nature. The school was built upon "the ideal of the spiritual unity of all races."

Students could learn from working artists and visiting Western scholars, and they could help local villagers. The school has become an international institute.

In 1911, Tagore wrote *The Post Office*, the first of his more symbolic and philosophical plays, after a five-year period (1902–1907) in which his wife, his daughter, and his youngest son had died. In 1913, an English translation of the play was performed at the Abbey Theater in Dublin. Later that year the Abbey Theater Company performed the play in London. *The Post Office* was also successfully performed in Paris and Berlin. However, the original play, written in the Bengali language, was not performed in India until the end of 1917.

The Post Office is characteristic of Tagore's work in that it reflects his humane values as well as his love of children and his appreciation of the beauty of the universe. He often gently criticized those who let tradition limit their lives and those who allowed wealth and power to stifle their human potential. His ability to express these profound values in a charmingly simple style has endeared Tagore to the world.

The Post Office, which has been translated into many languages, holds a special place among Tagore's plays. Andre Gide's French translation was read over the radio on the night before the Nazis invaded Paris in 1940. In 1942 a Polish version of this play was the last play performed in an orphanage in the Warsaw ghetto because, in the words of the director of the orphanage, "eventually one had to learn to accept serenely the angel of death."

Despite the angel of death hovering over this play, the play is more about life than about death. Amal, the young protagonist, is the model of what it is to be human, and his influence upon others extends far beyond the limits of the stage. It crosses oceans and spans countless years, touching the hearts and lives of all who come to know him.

DRAMATIS PERSONAE

MADHAV DUTTA

AMAL, *a small boy and Madhav's adopted child*

DOCTOR

CURDSELLER

WATCHMAN

THAKURDA, *a wanderer; Fakir*

VILLAGE HEADMAN, *a bully*

SHUDHA, *a flower girl*

VILLAGE BOYS

RAJA'S (KING'S) HERALD

RAJA'S (KING'S) PHYSICIAN

ACT I

[MADHAV's *house*]

MADHAV DUTTA: What a mess I'm in. Before he came, he meant nothing to me—I had no worries. Then he came here out of nowhere and filled my entire home; if he leaves me now this house will no longer seem like my home. Doctor, do you think he will—

DOCTOR: If the child is fated for a long life, then he shall have it, but it is written in the *Ayurveda*[1] that—

MADHAV: What? Please tell me!

DOCTOR: The scriptures say, "Bile and fever, palsy and phlegm all—"

MADHAV: Stop, stop, please don't recite those *slokas;*[2] they just make me more anxious. Tell me instead what must be done.

DOCTOR: [*taking snuff*] Great care must be observed.

MADHAV: That I know, but what kind of care? You must tell me.

DOCTOR: I have told you before: on no account should he be allowed out of doors.

MADHAV: But he's so young! To keep him inside all day is really cruel.

DOCTOR: What choice do you have? The autumn sun and wind are both like venom to the boy, for as the scriptures say, "In epilepsy, fever or wheezing fit, in jaundice or in swelling—"

MADHAV: Enough, that's enough scripture. So we have to shut him indoors—is there really no other cure?

DOCTOR: None at all, for in the wind and the sun—

MADHAV: Oh cease with your "this, that and the other." Please, stop it—just tell me what I have to do. Your remedies are so harsh. The poor boy is already putting up with a lot without complaining—but it breaks my heart to see how your prescription makes him suffer further.

DOCTOR: The greater the suffering, the happier the outcome. As the great sage Chyabana says, "In medication as in good counsel, the bitterest brings the speediest results." Well, I must be going, Mr. Dutta.

[*He goes.* THAKURDA *enters.*]

MADHAV: Oh no, Thakurda's back! Looks like trouble.

THAKURDA: Why? Why should a fellow like me scare you?

MADHAV: Because you make children run wild.

---

[1] *Ayurveda:* Ancient system of medicine recorded in the Vedas (the earliest and most sacred Hindu texts).

[2] *slokas:* Sanskirt verses in which each line contains sixteen syllables.

THAKURDA: You are not a boy, you have no child in your house, and you are past the age for running away—why do you worry?

MADHAV: Because I have brought a child to the house.

THAKURDA: Indeed!

MADHAV: My wife wanted to adopt a boy.

THAKURDA: I've known that for a long time, but I thought you didn't want to.

MADHAV: You know I was making a lot of money by hard work, and I used to think how terrible it would be if some boy turned up and wasted all my money without any effort. But this one has somehow charmed me so much that—

THAKURDA: —that no wealth is too much for him. And you now feel that the more you spend, the merrier your money's fate.

MADHAV: Before, I was addicted to making money—I couldn't help myself. But now my reward is the knowledge that whatever I earn will be his.

THAKURDA: And where did you find him?

MADHAV: He's a sort of nephew of my wife through some village connection. He lost his mother very early, poor boy. And just recently, he lost his father, too.

THAKURDA: How sad! Maybe I could be of some help to him.

MADHAV: The doctor says that he is so sick with fever that there isn't much hope. Now the only cure is somehow to keep him inside, away from the autumn sunshine and breezes. But you always come along and gaily lead children outside—that's why you scare me.

THAKURDA: Yes, I admit it, I have become a free spirit, like the autumn sun and wind. But I also know how to play games indoors. Let me finish a few errands of mine, then I will make friends with this boy of yours.

[*He goes.* AMAL *enters.*]

AMAL: Uncle!

MADHAV: What is it, Amal?

AMAL: Can't I even go out into the courtyard?

MADHAV: No, Amal.

AMAL: Look, over there, where Auntie is grinding lentils, there's a squirrel, balancing on its tail and munching the broken bits between its paws—can't I please go and see?

MADHAV: No, my son.

AMAL: I wish I could be a squirrel—Uncle, why can't I go out?

MADHAV: The doctor says that if you go out you will get ill.

AMAL: How does the doctor know that?

MADHAV: What do you mean, Amal! Of course he knows! He has read so many huge old books.

AMAL: Does reading make you know everything?

MADHAV: Of course! Don't you know?

AMAL: [with a sigh] I have not read a single book, so I guess I don't know anything.

MADHAV: But you are just like the greatest of pundits—you know, they never leave their houses.

AMAL: Don't they?

MADHAV: No, they don't, how can they? They only sit and read books, and never glance in any other direction. Amal, young fellow, you too will become a pundit—you will sit and read all those books, and everyone will gaze at you in wonder.

AMAL: No! Uncle, please no, I beg you, I don't want to be a pundit, I don't want to be one, Uncle.

MADHAV: Why not, Amal! If I could have been a pundit, my life would have been totally different.

AMAL: I want to see everything—everything there is to see.

MADHAV: What are you talking about? See what?

AMAL: Those faraway hills, for instance, which I can see from my window—I would so love to cross over them.

MADHAV: What a crazy idea! Just like that, for nothing, on a whim, you want to cross those hills? You are not talking sense. Those hills stand up so tall because they are forbidding you to go beyond them—otherwise, why would stone have been piled upon stone to form such a huge heap?

AMAL: Uncle, are you sure they are really forbidding us? To me, it looks like the earth is mute, and so she is raising up her hands towards the sky and calling us. Distant people sitting beside their windows in the heat of mid-day are also hearing the call. Don't the pundits hear it?

MADHAV: They are not mad like you—they don't want to listen.

AMAL: Yesterday I met someone as mad as me.

MADHAV: Really? Tell me.

AMAL: There was a bamboo pole across one of his shoulders. At the top of it was tied a small bundle. He held a small brass pot in his left hand. There was an old pair of curly-toed slippers on his feet, and he walked along the path through the fields towards the hills. I called out, "Where are you going?" He said, "I don't know—wherever I happen to go." So I asked him, "Why are you going?" And he replied, "I'm seeking work." Uncle, does everyone have to seek work?

MADHAV: Of course. People are always looking for work.

AMAL: All right, I'll be like them and go searching for work, too.

MADHAV: What if you seek and don't find?

AMAL: I will keep on searching. When the man with the slippers walked away, I watched him from the doorway. Not far off, where the stream flows past the fig tree, he put his pole down and gently washed his feet. Then he opened his sack, took out some maize flour, kneaded it with water and *chhatu*.[3] When he was finished, he picked up the sack again and put it on his shoulder, hitched up his clothes, waded into the stream and made his way across. I said to Auntie that I'm going to go to the stream some time and eat *chhatu*.

MADHAV: What did she say?

AMAL: She said, "Get well first, then I myself will take you to the stream and feed you with *chhatu*." When will I get better?

MADHAV: It won't be much longer, young fellow.

AMAL: Not long? You know, as soon as I get well I must be off.

MADHAV: Where to?

AMAL: There are so many winding streams I want to dip my feet in. And at noontime, when everyone is resting behind shuttered doors, I want to walk and walk in search of work, further and further.

MADHAV: All right, but first get better, then you—

AMAL: You won't tell me to become a pundit, Uncle, will you?

MADHAV: What will you become then?

AMAL: I can't think of anything yet—I will tell you when I've thought.

MADHAV: But you shouldn't talk to strangers like that.

AMAL: I like strangers very much.

MADHAV: What if one were to snatch you away?

AMAL: That would be fun. But no one ever takes me away; everyone wants me to sit right here.

MADHAV: I have some work to do, so I must go. But son, don't wander outside, all right?

AMAL: I won't. But Uncle, you must let me sit here in this room next to the road.

[MADHAV *goes.*]

---

[3] chhatu: Fine flour made of maize or barley.

ACT 2

CURDSELLER: *Dai—dai—good dai!*[4]

AMAL: Daiwallah,[5] Daiwallah, oh Daiwallah!

CURDSELLER: What do you want? To buy *dai?*

AMAL: How can I? I have no money.

CURDSELLER: What kind of a child are you? If you're not buying, why are you wasting my time?

AMAL: I just want to talk with you.

CURDSELLER: With me?

AMAL: When I hear your cry in the distance, it makes me so restless.

CURDSELLER: [*taking off his yoke*] Young fellow, what are you doing sitting there like that?

AMAL: The doctor's forbidden me to go outdoors, so I must sit here all day every day.

CURDSELLER: You poor child. What's wrong?

AMAL: I don't know. I haven't read any books, so I can't know what is the matter with me. Daiwallah, where do you come from?

CURDSELLER: I come from our village.

AMAL: Your village? Is it far away?

CURDSELLER: Our village is at the foot of the Panchmura hills, beside the Shamli river.

AMAL: Panchmura Hills, Shamli River—I think I've seen your village, although I don't remember when.

CURDSELLER: You have been there? Have you been to the foot of the hills?

AMAL: No, I've never been there. But I feel as if I have. Doesn't your village lie beneath some ancient sprawling trees, next to a red road?

CURDSELLER: You are right, son.

AMAL: And there are cows grazing on the hillside.

CURDSELLER: Right again! In our village, cows do graze, yes indeed.

AMAL: And women come to fetch water from the river and carry it in pitchers on their heads—and they wear red saris.

CURDSELLER: Yes, yes, that's it. All of our dairywomen come to the river for their water. But not all of them wear red saris. You must have visited the place sometime.

---

[4] dai: Curds.
[5] *Daiwallah:* Curdseller.

AMAL: No, I assure you, I have never been there. As soon as the doctor lets me go out, will you take me to your village?

CURDSELLER: Of course I will, with pleasure.

AMAL: Teach me how to sell *dai* as you do—walking all those far-off roads with your harness across your shoulder.

CURDSELLER: But my son, why sell *dai?* You should read books and become a pundit.

AMAL: No, no, I will never become a pundit. I will take some *dai* from your village beneath the old banyan tree beside the red road and I will sell it in distant villages. How does your call go? *"Dai—dai—good dai!"* Teach me the tune, won't you, please?

CURDSELLER: Heavens! Is such a tune worth teaching?

AMAL: Don't say that, I like it. You know when you hear a hawk shrieking high up in the sky, the cry gives you a strange feeling? Well, your distant call—which seems to float through the trees from some far bend in the road—has the same effect on me.

CURDSELLER: Son, please have a pot of my *dai.*

AMAL: But I have no money.

CURDSELLER: It doesn't matter, don't mention money. I would be ever so pleased if you ate some of my *dai.*

AMAL: Have I delayed you much?

CURDSELLER: No, not at all, son, it's no loss at all. For you have shown me the joy in selling *dai.*

[*He goes.*]

AMAL: [*chanting*] *Dai, dai,* good *dai! Dai* from the dairies beside the Shamli river in the Panchmura Hills. *Dai—dai!* Every dawn the dairywomen milk the cows under the trees, and every evening they set the *dai*—and what *dai* it is! *Dai, dai, dai-i,* delicious *dai!* Ah, look, there's the watchman doing his rounds. Watchman, oh Watchman, won't you come and listen to me for just a minute?

[WATCHMAN *enters.*]

WATCHMAN: What's all this shouting for? Aren't you afraid of me?

AMAL: Why should I be afraid of you?

WATCHMAN: What if I arrest you, take you away?

AMAL: Where will you take me? Far away, over the hills?

WATCHMAN: I might take you straight to the Raja!

AMAL: To the Raja! Would you really? But the doctor has forbidden me to go out. No one can take me anywhere. I must just sit here all day and night.

WATCHMAN: Doctor's order? Ah, I can see your face is quite pale. There are dark rings under your eyes. The veins are sticking out in both of your arms.

AMAL: Are you going to sound your gong?

WATCHMAN: The time is not yet right.

AMAL: Some people say, "time flies," while others say that "time is not yet ripe." But if you strike your gong, won't the time be right?

WATCHMAN: How so? I sound the gong only when the time is right.

AMAL: I do like your gong. I love listening to it, especially at noon after everyone's eaten and my uncle has gone out somewhere to work and Auntie dozes off reading the *Ramayana*,[6] and our small dog curls up into its tail in some shadow of the courtyard—then I hear your gong strike *dhong dhong, dhong dhong dhong!* But why do you strike it?

WATCHMAN: It tells everyone that time does not stand still, that time always moves onwards.

AMAL: Where is time going? To what land?

WATCHMAN: Nobody knows that.

AMAL: You mean nobody's been there? I would love to run away with time to this land that nobody knows.

WATCHMAN: All of us will go there one day, young man.

AMAL: Me too?

WATCHMAN: Of course.

AMAL: But the doctor has forbidden me to go out.

WATCHMAN: Some day perhaps the doctor will hold your hand and take you there.

AMAL: No, you don't know him, all he does is keep me locked up here.

WATCHMAN: But there is a greater doctor than he, a doctor who can set you free.

AMAL: When will this Great Doctor come for me? I'm so tired of staying here.

WATCHMAN: Shouldn't say such things, son.

AMAL: But I have to sit here all the time never going out, doing as I am told, and when your gong goes *dhong dhong dhong,* I feel so frustrated. Watchman—?

WATCHMAN: What is it?

AMAL: Tell me, over there across the road, that big house with a flag on top, with lots of people going in and out of it—what is it?

WATCHMAN: It's the new post office.

AMAL: Post office? Whose post office?

---

[6] Ramayana: One of the two ancient epics of India.

WATCHMAN: The Raja's, of course—who else could have a post office? [*Aside*] He's a strange boy.

AMAL: Do letters come to the post office from the Raja himself?

WATCHMAN: Yes, of course. Some day there may even be a letter addressed to you.

AMAL: A letter with my name on it? But I am only a child.

WATCHMAN: The Raja sends his littlest letters to children.

AMAL: Really? When will I get my letter? And how do you know that he's going to write to me?

WATCHMAN: Why else would he bother to set up a post office with a splendid golden flag outside your open window? [*Aside*] But I rather like the boy.

AMAL: When the Raja's letter comes, who will give it to me?

WATCHMAN: The Raja has many messengers—surely you have seen them running about with gold badges pinned to their chests.

AMAL: Where do they go?

WATCHMAN: From door to door, country to country. [*Aside*] The boy's questions really are amusing.

AMAL: When I grow up, I want to be a Raja's messenger.

WATCHMAN: Ha ha ha! A Raja's messenger! Now there's a responsible job. Come rain, come shine, among rich, among poor, wherever you are you must deliver your letters—it's a tremendous job!

AMAL: Why are you smiling that way? It's the best job there could be. Oh, I don't mean that your job isn't good too—you strike your gong during the heat of noon, *dhong dhong dhong,* and also in the dead of night—sometimes I suddenly wake up and find that the lamp has gone out and I hear a deep, dark, *dhong dhong dhong!*

WATCHMAN: Uh-oh, here comes the big boss—time to run. If he catches me chatting with you, he's sure to cause trouble.

AMAL: Where's the boss, which one is he?

WATCHMAN: Over there, way down the road. Don't you see his big umbrella— the one made of palm leaves—bobbing up and down?

AMAL: Has the boss been appointed by the Raja?

WATCHMAN: Oh no—he's been appointed by himself. But if you don't obey him, he'll cause endless difficulties—that's why people are afraid of him. Our Headman's entire job seems to be trouble-making, for everyone. So that's enough talk for today, time to leave. I'll be back tomorrow morning to bring you the news of the town.

[*He goes.*]

AMAL: If I receive a letter every day from the Raja, that would be wonderful. I'll sit here by the window and read them. Oh, but I don't know how to read. I wonder who can read them for me? Auntie reads *Ramayana*. Maybe she can read the Raja's writing? If nobody can read the letters, I'll keep them and read them all later, when I grow up. But what if the Raja's messengers don't know about me? Mr. Headman, oh dear Mr. Headman, could I talk to you for a minute?

HEADMAN: Who's this? Bellowing at me in the road! Who's this monkey?

AMAL: You are the Headman. I hear that everyone pays attention to you.

HEADMAN: [*flattered*] Yes, yes, they do. They do, or else.

AMAL: Do the Raja's messengers listen to you, too?

HEADMAN: Of course! Would they dare to ignore me?

AMAL: Will you tell the messengers that my name is Amal, and that I am always here, sitting by the window?

HEADMAN: Why should I do that?

AMAL: In case there is a letter addressed to me.

HEADMAN: A letter for you! Who would write *you* a letter?

AMAL: If the Raja writes to me then—

HEADMAN: Well now, aren't you a mighty fellow! Ho ho ho! So the Raja will write to you, will he? Of course he will, for you are his dear friend. In fact, he's getting sadder by the day because he's not seen you lately, so I hear. Well, your waiting's almost over; I bet that your letter will come any day now.

AMAL: Mr. Headman, why is your voice so harsh? Are you angry with me?

HEADMAN: Goodness me. Why should I be angry with you? Could I be so bold? After all, you are a correspondent of the Raja. [*Aside*] I can see that Madhav Dutta thinks he can drop the names of rajas and maharajas, just because he has made a little money. We'll soon see that he gets his comeuppance. [*To Amal*] Yes my lad, you'll soon get a royal letter at your house, I shall see to it myself.

AMAL: No no, please, you don't have to go to any trouble for me.

HEADMAN: And why not? I will tell our Raja about you, and I am sure he will not keep you waiting long. In fact, I bet he will send a footman at once to hear your news. [*Aside*] Really, Madhav Dutta's arrogance is too much. Just as soon as this reaches the ears of the Raja, there'll be trouble, that's for sure.

[*He goes.*]

AMAL: Who is that, with her jingling anklets? Please stop awhile.

[*A girl enters.*]

GIRL: How can I stop? The day's already passing.

AMAL: You don't want to stop, even for a moment—and I don't want to sit here a moment longer.

GIRL: To look at you reminds me of the fading morning star. What's the matter with you, tell me?

AMAL: I don't know, but the doctor has forbidden me to go out.

GIRL: Then don't go out, obey Doctor's words—if you don't, people will say you are naughty. I can see that just looking outside makes you restless. Let me close this window a bit.

AMAL: No no, don't close it! Everything is closed to me except this window. Tell me who you are, I don't seem to know you.

GIRL: I am Shudha.

AMAL: Shudha?

SHUDHA: Don't you know? I am the daughter of the local flower seller.

AMAL: And what do you do?

SHUDHA: I fill a wicker basket with plucked flowers and make garlands. Just now I'm off to pick some.

AMAL: You're going to pick flowers? Is that why your feet are so lively, and your anklets go jingle-jangle with each step? If I could go with you, I would pick flowers for you from the highest branches, beyond your sight.

SHUDHA: Would you now?! So you know where the flowers are better than I do?

AMAL: Yes, I know a lot. For example, I know all about the seven *champak*-flower[7] brothers. If I were well I would go deep into the forest where there is no path to be seen. There I would blossom as a *champak* flower on the tallest tip of the thinnest twig, where the hummingbird gets drunk on honey. Will you be my Parul,[8] my *champak*-flower sister?

SHUDHA: How silly! How could I be your Parul *didi?*[9] I am Shudha, daughter of Shashi, the flower seller. Every day I have to string many flower garlands. If I could spend the day sitting like you, then I would be very happy.

AMAL: What would you do if you had all day?

SHUDHA: First, I would play with my *bene-bou*[10] doll and marry her off, and then there's my pussycat Meni. I would love to—but it's getting late, and there won't be any flowers left if I dawdle here.

AMAL: Please talk to me a little longer, I'm enjoying it.

---

[7] champak-*flower:* The orange flowers of the champak, a Magnolia tree found in India.
[8] *Parul:* Species of trumpet-flower, well known in Bengali folk literature.
[9] didi: Elder sister.
[10] bene-bou: Clay doll.

SHUDHA: All right, if you are a good boy and stay here quietly, on my way back with the flowers I'll stop for another chat.

AMAL: Will you bring me a flower?

SHUDHA: How can I? Can you pay?

AMAL: I'll pay you when I grow up, when I've gone out seeking work beyond the stream over there—then I'll repay you.

SHUDHA: I accept.

AMAL: So you will return after picking flowers?

SHUDHA: I will return.

AMAL: Promise?

SHUDHA: I promise.

AMAL: You won't forget me? My name is Amal. Will you remember it?

SHUDHA: No, I won't forget. You will be remembered.

[*She goes. Some boys enter.*]

AMAL: Brothers. where are you going? Stop for a while.

BOYS: We're off to play.

AMAL: What game are you going to play?

BOYS: The ploughman's game.

FIRST BOY: [*waving a stick*] This is our ploughshare.

SECOND BOY: And we two will be the oxen.

AMAL: Will you play all day?

BOYS: Yes, the entire day.

AMAL: After that, will you come back home along the path by the river?

A BOY: Yes we will, when it's evening.

AMAL: Please drop by here, in front of my house.

A BOY: You can come with us now, come and play.

AMAL: Doctor's ordered me not to go out.

A BOY: Doctor! Why do you listen to him? Come on, let's go, it's getting late.

AMAL: Please, friends, won't you play in the road outside my window, just for a little while?

A BOY: But there's nothing here to play with.

AMAL: All my toys are lying right here, take them all. It's no fun playing indoors all alone—the toys are just lying here, doing nothing, scattered in the dust.

BOYS: Oh, what wonderful toys! Look at this ship! And this one with the matted hair is the old witch, Jatai. And here's a terrific sepoy[11] to play soldiers with. Are you really giving us these? Won't you miss them?

AMAL: No, I won't miss them, you can have them all.

A BOY: So we don't have to give them back?

AMAL: No, you don't need to.

A BOY: Nobody will scold you?

AMAL: No, nobody will. But promise me that you will come and play with them outside my house for a while each morning. When they get worn out, I'll get you some new ones.

A BOY: All right, friend, we'll come and play here every day. Now let's take the sepoys and have a battle. Where can we get muskets? Over there, there's a large piece of reed—that'll do if we cut it up into pieces. But friend, you are dozing off!

AMAL: Yes, I'm very sleepy. Why I feel sleepy so often, I don't know. But I've been sitting up a long time and I can't sit any longer; my back is aching.

A BOY: It's only the beginning of the day—why are you sleepy already? Listen, there goes the gong.

AMAL: Yes—*dhong dhong dhong*; it lulls me to sleep.

BOYS: We're going now, but we'll be back in the morning.

AMAL: Before you go, let me ask you something. You go about a lot. Do you know the Raja's messengers?

BOYS: Yes we do, quite well.

AMAL: Who are they? What are their names?

BOYS: One's called Badal, another's called Sharat, and there are others.

AMAL: Well, if a letter comes for me, will they know who I am?

A BOY: Why not? If your name is on the letter, they will certainly find you.

AMAL: When you come back in the morning, please ask one of them to stop by and meet me, will you?

BOYS: Yes, we will.

ACT 3

[AMAL *in bed.*]

AMAL: Uncle, can't I even sit near the window today? Doctor really forbids it?

MADHAV: Yes, he does. He says that sitting there every day is making your illness worse.

---

[11] *sepoy:* A native of India who served in the British army.

AMAL: But Uncle, that's not right—I don't know about my illness, but I know I feel better when I sit there.

MADHAV: Sitting there you have become friends with half the town—young and old alike. The area outside my door looks like a fairground. How will you stand the strain? Look at your face today—so wan!

AMAL: If my friend the fakir[12] comes by my window, he will miss me and go away again.

MADHAV: Who is this fakir?

AMAL: Every day he drops in and tells me tales of lands far and wide; he's so much fun to listen to.

MADHAV: I don't know of any fakir.

AMAL: He usually comes along about now. Uncle, I beg you, please ask him to come and sit with me.

[**THAKURDA** *enters, dressed as a fakir.*]

AMAL: There you are, Fakir. Come and sit on my bed.

MADHAV: What! Is that your—

THAKURDA: [*winking*] I am the fakir.

MADHAV: Of course you are.

AMAL: Where have you been this time, Fakir?

FAKIR: To the Island of Parrots. I just got back.

MADHAV: Parrot Island, eh?

FAKIR: Why so sceptical? Am I like you? When I travel, there are no expenses. I can go wherever I please.

AMAL: [*clapping in delight*] You have so much fun. When I get well, you promised I could be your disciple, remember?

THAKURDA: Of course. I will initiate you in my travel mantras, so that neither ocean nor mountain nor forest will bar your way.

MADHAV: What is all this crazy talk?

THAKURDA: Dearest Amal, there is nothing in mountain or ocean that frightens me—but if the doctor and your uncle get together, my mantras will be powerless.

AMAL: You won't tell Doctor about all of this, will you Uncle? Now I promise I will lie here, sleep and do nothing. But the day I get well I will swear by Fakir's mantras, and then I shall cross the rivers, mountains and oceans.

---

[12] *fakir:* A Muslim or Hindu beggar who travels from place to place and is often thought to be able to perform wondrous deeds.

MADHAV: Hush, son, don't keep on talking about leaving—just to hear you makes me feel so sad.

AMAL: Tell me, Fakir, what is Parrot Island like?

THAKURDA: It is a rather weird place, a land of birds without any human beings. The birds do not speak or come to land, they only sing and fly around.

AMAL: How fantastic! And is there ocean all around?

THAKURDA: Yes, of course.

AMAL: And are there green hills?

THAKURDA: Yes, in the hills, the birds make their nests. In the evening, as the rays of the setting sun make the green hillsides glow, the parrots flock to their nests in a green swarm—and then the hills and the parrots become one single mass of green. It's indescribable.

AMAL: And what about streams and waterfalls?

THAKURDA: Absolutely! How could there not be?! They flow like molten diamonds, and how the drops dance! The small pebbles in the streams hum and murmur as the waters gush over them, until finally they plunge into the ocean. No one, not even a doctor, can restrain them for even a single second. I tell you, if the birds did not ostracize me as a mere man, I would make myself a small hut among the thousands of nests beside some waterfall and pass my days watching the waters and the ocean waves below.

AMAL: If I were a bird then—

THAKURDA: Then there would be a problem. I hear you have already arranged with the Daiwallah to sell *dai* when you grow up. I don't think your business would do to well among the parrots. Who knows, you might even take a loss.

MADHAV: I can't take this nonsense any longer! You two will drive me mad. I am going.

AMAL: Uncle, has my Daiwallah come and gone yet?

MADHAV: Of course he has. He won't make ends meet by carrying things for you and your fancy fakir friend, or by flitting around Parrot Island, will he? But he left a pot of *dai* for you, and he said to tell you that his youngest niece is getting married in his village—so he's rather busy, because he has to go and book the flute players from Kalmipara.

AMAL: But he promised that his youngest niece would marry me.

THAKURDA: Now we *are* in trouble.

AMAL: He said she would be a delicious bride, with a nose ring and a red-striped sari. With her own hands she would milk a black cow in the mornings and bring me an earthenware bowl full of frothy, fresh milk. And at evening time, after taking a lamp to the cowshed, she would settle down with me and tell me tales of the seven *champak*-flower brothers.

THAKURDA: Well, she sounds like a wonderful bride. Even a fakir like me feels tempted. But don't lose heart, my child, let him marry off this niece. I give you my word that when your time comes, there will be no shortage of nieces in his family.

MADHAV: Be off with you! This time you really have gone too far.

[MADHAV *goes.*]

AMAL: Fakir, now that Uncle's gone, tell me secretly—has the Raja sent a letter in my name to the post office?

THAKURDA: I hear that his letter has been dispatched—it is on its way.

AMAL: On its way? Which way? Is it coming by that path through the dense forest that you see when the sky clears after rain?

THAKURDA: Yes. You seem to know it.

AMAL: I know a lot, Fakir.

THAKURDA: So I see—but how?

AMAL: I can't say. I can see everything before my eyes, as if I have really seen it many times, but long ago—how long ago I cannot recall. Shall I describe it to you? I can see the Raja's messenger coming down the hillside alone, a lantern in his left hand and on his back a bag of letters, descending for days and nights; and then at the foot of hills, where the waterfall becomes a winding stream, he follows the footpath along the bank and walks on through the corn; then comes the sugar cane field and he disappears into the narrow lane that cuts through the tall stems of sugar canes; and then he reaches the open meadow where the cricket chirps and where there is no one to be seen, only the snipe wagging their tails and poking at the mud with their beaks. I can picture it all. And the nearer he gets, the gladder I feel.

THAKURDA: Though I do not have your fresh vision, still I see it.

AMAL: Tell me Fakir, do you know the Raja?

THAKURDA: I certainly do. I often go to his court to seek alms.

AMAL: I see! When I get better I will go with you and seek alms from him. Can I go with you?

THAKURDA: Son, you do not need to seek—he will give without your asking.

AMAL: But I would rather seek. I'll go to the road outside his palace chanting "Victory to the Raja!" and begging alms—maybe I will also dance with a cymbal. What do you think?

THAKURDA: It sounds good; and if I accompany you, I will receive gifts, too. What will you ask him for?

AMAL: I will ask him to make me a Raja's messenger, who will go all over the land with a lantern in his hand delivering messages from door to door. You know, Fakir, someone has told me that as soon as I am well, he will teach me how to beg. I will go out begging with him wherever I please.

THAKURDA: And who is this person?

AMAL: Chidam.

THAKURDA: Which Chidam?

AMAL: Blind and lame Chidam. Every day he comes to my window. A boy just like me pushes him around in a cart with wheels. I've often told Chidam that when I'm better, I will push him around, too.

THAKURDA: That would be interesting, I can see.

AMAL: He is going to teach me all about begging. I tell Uncle that we should give Chidam something, but Uncle says that he's not really blind or lame. Perhaps he is not totally blind, but I know he does not see very well—I am sure of that.

THAKURDA: You are right. Whether you call him blind or not, it is true that he does not see well. But if he gets no alms from you, why does he like to sit with you?

AMAL: Because he hears all about different places from me. The poor fellow cannot see, but he listens when I tell him about all the lands that you tell me about. The other day you told me of the Land of No Weight, where everything weighs nothing and even a tiny hop will send you sailing over a hill. He really liked hearing about that place. Fakir, how do you reach that land?

THAKURDA: There's an inner road, but it's hard to find.

AMAL: Since the poor man is blind, he will never see any place, and will have to go on begging alms. Sometimes he moans to me about it, and I tell him that at least he visits a lot of places as a beggar—not everyone can do that.

THAKURDA: Son, why do you feel so sad to stay at home?

AMAL: Not sad, not now. Until now, my days did drag endlessly—but I have seen the Raja's post office and I am happier, I even like sitting indoors. I know my letter will come, and the thought keeps me company, so I wait quite happily. But I have no idea what the Raja will write in his letter.

THAKURDA: You do not need to know. As long as your name is there, that is enough.

[MADHAV enters.]

MADHAV: Do you two realize what trouble you have got us into?

THAKURDA: Why, what's up?

MADHAV: Rumour has it that you are saying that the Raja has established his post office only to correspond with you.

THAKURDA: So?

MADHAV: And so the Headman has sent an anonymous letter about this to the Raja.

THAKURDA: We all know that most things reach the Raja's ears.

MADHAV: Then why didn't you watch yourself! Why did you take the names of rajas and maharajas in vain? You'll pull me in, too.

AMAL: Fakir, will the Raja be angry?

THAKURDA: Who says so? Why should he be? How can he rule his kingdom with majesty if he becomes mad at a child like you and a fakir like me?

AMAL: You know, Fakir, since this morning there has been a kind of darkness in my mind; sometimes things look as if in a dream. I feel like being totally silent. I don't want to talk any more. Won't the Raja's letter ever come? Just now, this room seemed to vanish, as if everything—as if all—

THAKURDA: [fanning AMAL] It will come, my dear, the letter will come today.

[DOCTOR enters.]

DOCTOR: So how do you feel today?

AMAL: Doctor, I am now feeling comfortable, all my pain seems to be going away.

DOCTOR: [aside to MADHAV] I don't like the look of that smile very much. When he says he feels better there is danger in store. As the great Chakradhar Dutta says—

MADHAV: Please, Doctor, spare me Chakradhar Dutta. Just tell me what is the matter?

DOCTOR: It looks as if we cannot hold on to him much longer. I recommended certain precautions, but he seems to have been exposed to the outside air.

MADHAV: No, Doctor, I have done my utmost to keep him from such exposure. He has been kept indoors, and most of the time the place was kept shut.

DOCTOR: The air has turned rather strange today, and I notice a severe draught blowing through your door. That is not at all good. You must shut the door at once. Try not to have any visitors for a few days. If people drop in, they can come through the back door. And you should get rid of this glare that comes through the window when the sun sets—it disturbs the patient's mind.

MADHAV: Amal's eyes are closed. I think he's asleep. When I look at his face, it's as if—oh Doctor! this child who is not my own but whom I have loved as my own, will he be taken from me?

DOCTOR: Who's coming now? It's the Headman, coming here. Drat! I must go, my friend. Go inside and shut your door tight. When I get home, I'll send over a strong dose—give it to the boy. If he can resist its power, he may yet pull through.

[DOCTOR and MADHAV go. HEADMAN enters.]

HEADMAN: Hey, boy!

THAKURDA: [*suddenly standing up*] Ssh ssh . . . be quiet!

AMAL: No, Fakir, you thought I was sleeping, but I wasn't. I heard everything. And I also heard faraway talk; my parents were talking beside my bed.

[MADHAV *enters.*]

HEADMAN: So, Madhav Dutta, these days you are rubbing shoulders with people in high places!

MADHAV: What you do mean, Headman? Don't make fun of us. We are very humble folk.

HEADMAN: But isn't your boy awaiting a letter from the Raja?

MADHAV: He's a mere child, and sick and confused at that. Why do you listen to him?

HEADMAN: On the contrary. Where else could our Raja find a worthier correspondent than your boy? That must be why he has built his new royal post office outside your window. Hey little fellow, there is a letter from the Raja addressed to you.

AMAL: [*startled*] Really?

HEADMAN: And why not?—with your royal friendship! [*Hands him a blank sheet*] Ha ha ha, here's your letter.

AMAL: Are you teasing? Fakir, Fakir, tell me, is it really the letter?

THAKURDA: Yes, my boy, you have your Fakir's word, it is indeed the letter.

AMAL: But my eyes can't see anything—everything looks blank to me! Headman, sir, tell me what's in the letter.

HEADMAN: His Majesty writes, "I will be visiting your home shortly. Prepare me a meal of puffed rice and parched paddy[13] with molasses. I don't like to stay in the palace for one minute more than I have to." Ha ha ha!

MADHAV: [*with folded hands*] I beg you, sir, I implore you, do not ridicule us.

THAKURDA: Ridicule! What ridicule? Who would dare to ridicule!

MADHAV: What! Thakurda, are you out of your mind?

THAKURDA: Maybe I am. But I also see letters on this blank sheet. The Raja writes that he will personally visit Amal, and that his royal physician will accompany him.

AMAL: Fakir—it is true! I hear his herald! Can you hear the call?

HEADMAN: Ha ha ha! Let him become a bit more demented, then he'll hear it.

---

[13] *paddy:* Rice in its husk.

AMAL: Headman, sir, I thought that you were angry with me, that you disliked me. I never imagined that you would bring me the Raja's letter—it never occurred to me. I must wash the dust from your feet.

HEADMAN: Well, I'll say this much, the boy certainly has good manners. Not too bright, but he has a good heart.

AMAL: The day is nearly over, I can feel it. There goes the evening gong— *dhong dhong dhong, dhong dhong dhong.* Has the evening star appeared yet, Fakir? Why don't I see it?

THAKURDA: They have shut all your windows. I will open them.

[*A banging at the outside door*]

MADHAV: What's that! Who's there? What an annoyance!

[*from outside*] Open the door.

MADHAV: Who are you?

[*from outside*] Open the door.

MADHAV: Headman, could it be robbers?

HEADMAN: Who's there? Panchanan Morhal, Headman, speaking. Aren't you scared? [*To* **MADHAV**] Listen! The banging has stopped. Even the toughest thieves know to fear Panchanan's voice!

MADHAV: [*looking out of the window*] Look! They have smashed the door, that's why the banging has ceased.

[**RAJA'S HERALD** *enters.*]

RAJA'S HERALD: His Majesty will arrive tonight.

HEADMAN: Disaster!

AMAL: When in the night, Herald? At what hour?

RAJA'S HERALD: In the dead of night.

AMAL: When my friend the watchman strikes his gong at the town's Lion Gate, *dhong dhong dhong, dhong dhong dhong*—at that hour?

RAJA'S HERALD: Yes, at that hour. In the meantime, the Raja has sent his finest physician to attend to his little friend.

[**RAJA'S PHYSICIAN** *enters.*]

RAJA'S PHYSICIAN: What's this! All closed up?! Open up, open up, open all the doors and windows. [*He feels* **AMAL'S** *body.*] How are you feeling, young fellow?

AMAL: Quite well, very well, Doctor. My illness is gone, my pain is gone. Now everything is open—I can see all the stars, shining on the far side of darkness.

PHYSICIAN: When the Raja comes in the dead of night, will you rise and go forth with him?

AMAL: I will, I have the will. I long to go forth. I will ask the Raja to show me the Pole Star in the heavens. Perhaps I have seen it many times, but have not recognized it.

PHYSICIAN: The Raja will show you all things. [To MADHAV] Please make the room clean and decorate it with flowers to greet our Raja. [Pointing to the HEADMAN] That man should not be permitted here.

AMAL: Oh no, Doctor, he is my friend. Before you came, he brought me the Raja's letter.

PHYSICIAN: All right, my boy, since he is your friend, he may remain.

MADHAV: [whispering in AMAL's ear] My son, the Raja loves you, and he is coming here in person. Please entreat him to give us something. You know our condition—we are not well off.

AMAL: Uncle, I have already thought about it—do not worry.

MADHAV: What will you request?

AMAL: I will beg him to make me a royal messenger in his post office. I will deliver his messages to homes everywhere.

MADHAV: [striking his forehead] Alas, such is my fate!

AMAL: Uncle, when the Raja comes, what shall we offer him?

RAJA'S HERALD: The Raja has commanded a meal of puffed rice and parched paddy with molasses.

AMAL: Headman, those were your very words! You knew everything about the Raja, and we knew nothing!

HEADMAN: If you would send someone to my house, we will endeavour to provide His Majesty with good—

PHYSICIAN: No need for it. Now you must all be calm. It is coming, coming, his sleep is coming. I will sit beside his pillow as he drifts off. Blow out the lamp; let the starlight come in; his sleep has arrived.

MADHAV: [to THAKURDA] Thakurda, why so hushed, with your palms pressed together like a statue? I feel a kind of dread. These do not seem like good omens. Why has the room been darkened? What use is starlight?

THAKURDA: Be quiet, unbeliever! Do not speak.

[SHUDHA enters.]

SHUDHA: Amal?

PHYSICIAN: He has fallen asleep.

SHUDHA: I have brought flowers for him. Can I put them in his hand?

PHYSICIAN: Yes, you may give him your flowers.

SHUDHA: When will he awake?

PHYSICIAN: Directly the Raja comes and calls him.

SHUDHA: Will you whisper a word in his ear for me?

PHYSICIAN: What shall I say?

SHUDHA: Tell him, "Shudha has not forgotten you."

UNDERSTANDING THE PLAY

1. Why does Tagore create a **protagonist** (Amal) who does not know how to read?

2. The doctor tells Madhav Dutta that "the greater the suffering, the happier the outcome." To what extent, if any, does illness cause Amal to have a happier life?

3. Amal declares that he would love to cross over the faraway hills and that the earth "is raising up her hands towards the sky and calling us." In contrast, Madhav declares, "Those hills stand up so tall because they are forbidding you to go beyond them." What do these remarks reveal about the two people who make them?

4. The Watchman's gong functions like a clock. Why does he view his job as important?

5. The Watchman speaks to Amal of a doctor who will hold Amal's hand, take him to the land that nobody knows, and set him free. Who is this great doctor? Why does the Watchman tell Amal that it is wrong to wish for the doctor to come?

6. What is significant about the post office?

7. Why does Thakurda pretend to be a fakir? What does his deception accomplish? To what extent, if any, is Madhav correct when he views the fakir's words as "crazy talk"?

8. Evaluate the letter that the Headman brings to Amal. What does Amal see on the sheet of paper? Why does the Headman laugh at what he reads? Why does Thakurda see a different message on the sheet?

9. Explain the Headman's reaction to the arrival of the Raja's herald.

10. Explain the royal physician's reaction to the Headman.

11. Explain the three demands that the royal physician makes.

12. Why is Madhav dismayed by what Amal intends to request of the Raja?

13. What do Madhav's final questions reveal about him? What is Thakurda's response?

14. What is the significance of the last line of the play?

15. To what extent, if any, do magical or miraculous events occur in connection with the Raja's letter?

ANALYZING LITERARY TECHNIQUE

1. How does Tagore reveal the **setting** of this play? Find examples that reveal the location of the action.

2. Find examples of **irony** and explain how each example contributes to the play.

3. Describe the **tone** of this play. How does Tagore create it?

4. How does Tagore mark the passage of time in this play?

5. Find examples of Tagore's use of **foreshadowing** and explain what each example contributes to the play.

6. Find examples of Tagore's use of **repetition** in this play. Explain the purpose of each example.

7. What ideas, or **themes,** does Tagore convey in this play?

WRITING ABOUT LITERATURE

1. Write an essay in which you analyze Tagore's techniques for unifying the action in this play. Consider his use of repetition, foreshadowing and variations on a theme.

2. Write an essay in which you analyze the thematic content of this play. Choose three themes and show how Tagore uses the action to reveal each theme.

3. Write an essay in which you characterize one character (for example, Amal or the Headman). How does Tagore enable the audience or reader to learn about that character from what the character says? From what others say about the character? Find examples in the play that reveal the traits of this character. For each example, use a quotation and explain what it reveals.

4. Write a story or a poem in which you use words to paint a portrait of a person who leads a life that inspires others. Be sure to convey the connection between what the person does and how those actions inspire others.

The Fly

KATHERINE MANSFIELD

KATHERINE MANSFIELD (1888–1923), an important short-story writer, deeply admired Anton Chekhov's work. She was the first writer in English to use his short stories as a model. Like Chekhov, Mansfield ignores exposition and immediately immerses the reader in the action of the story. She also reveals character through multiple perspectives and through seemingly trivial details and actions. Admiring the quality of her stories, other writers have adopted Mansfield's techniques. Mansfield is best known for four collections of stories: *Bliss* (1920); *The Garden Party* (1922); and two posthumously published volumes, *The Dove's Nest* (1923) and *Something Childish* (1924).

Mansfield was born Kathleen Mansfield Beauchamp in Wellington, New Zealand. Her father sent her to Queen's College in London from 1903 to 1906. She returned to New Zealand for two years to study music, but she preferred London and returned there in 1908 to become a professional writer. She wrote only sketches and short stories. Her first collection of sketches, *In a German Pension*, was published in 1911. In 1917 she developed tuberculosis, which ended her writing career. The disease eventually killed her.

Mansfield was interested in the complexity of the human personality. She uses language as a painter uses color, carefully choosing each word for its contribution to the total design. A character's deeds may belie his or her words, revealing the private person beneath the public one; objects become symbols with the same purpose. After the traumatic death of her brother during World War I, she wrote in her journal: "All must be told with a sense of mystery, a radiance, an afterglow. . . ." These qualities shine forth even in the dark story "The Fly," which typifies Mansfield's fascination with psychology and her masterful literary technique.

"**Y**'are very snug in here," piped old Mr. Woodifield, and he peered out of the great, green leather arm-chair by his friend, the boss's desk, as a baby peers out of its pram. His talk was over; it was time for him to be off. But he did not want to go. Since he had retired, since his . . . stroke, the wife and the girls kept him boxed up in the house every day of the week except Tuesday. On Tuesday he was dressed up and brushed and allowed to cut back to the City[1] for the day. Though what he did there the wife and girls couldn't imagine. Made a nuisance of himself to his friends, they supposed. . . . Well, perhaps so. All the same, we cling to our last pleasures as the tree clings to its last leaves. So there sat old Woodifield, smoking a cigar and staring almost greedily at the boss, who rolled in his office chair, stout, rosy, five years older than he, and still going strong, still at the helm. It did one good to see him.

Wistfully, admiringly, the old voice added, "It's snug in here, upon my word!"

"Yes, it's comfortable enough," agreed the boss, and he flipped the *Financial Times* with a paper-knife. As a matter of fact he was proud of his room; he liked to have it admired, especially by old Woodifield. It gave him a feeling of deep, solid satisfaction to be planted there in the midst of it in full view of that frail old figure in the muffler.

"I've had it done up lately," he explained, as he had explained for the past— how many?—weeks. "New carpet," and he pointed to the bright red carpet with a pattern of large white rings. "New furniture," and he nodded towards the massive bookcase and the table with legs like twisted treacle.[2] "Electric heating!" He waved almost exultantly towards the five transparent, pearly sausages glowing so softly in the tilted copper pan.

But he did not draw old Woodifield's attention to the photograph over the table of a grave-looking boy in uniform standing in one of those spectral photographers' parks with photographers' storm-clouds behind him. It was not new. It had been there for over six years.

"There was something I wanted to tell you," said old Woodifield, and his eyes grew dim remembering. "Now what was it? I had it in my mind when I started out this morning." His hands began to tremble, and patches of red showed above his beard.

Poor old chap, he's on his last pins, thought the boss. And, feeling kindly, he winked at the old man, and said jokingly, "I tell you what. I've got a little drop of something here that'll do you good before you go out into the cold again. It's beautiful stuff. It wouldn't hurt a child." He took a key off his watch-chain, unlocked a cupboard below his desk, and drew forth a dark, squat bottle. "That's

---

[1] *the City:* Financial district of London.
[2] *treacle:* Molasses.

the medicine," said he. "And the man from whom I got it told me on the strict Q. T.[3] it came from the cellars at Windsor Castle."[4]

Old Woodifield's mouth fell open at the sight. He couldn't have looked more surprised if the boss had produced a rabbit.

"It's whisky, ain't it?" he piped, feebly.

The boss turned the bottle and lovingly showed him the label. Whisky it was.

"D'you know," said he, peering up at the boss wonderingly, "they won't let me touch it at home." And he looked as though he was going to cry.

"Ah, that's where we know a bit more than the ladies," cried the boss, swooping across for two tumblers that stood on the table with the water-bottle, and pouring a generous finger into each. "Drink it down. It'll do you good. And don't put any water with it. It's sacrilege to tamper with stuff like this. Ah!" He tossed off his, pulled out his handkerchief, hastily wiped his moustaches, and cocked an eye at old Woodifield, who was rolling his in his chaps.

The old man swallowed, was silent a moment, and then said faintly, "It's nutty!"

But it warmed him; it crept into his chill old brain—he remembered.

"That was it," he said, heaving himself out of his chair. "I thought you'd like to know. The girls were in Belgium last week having a look at poor Reggie's grave, and they happened to come across your boy's. They are quite near each other, it seems."

Old Woodifield paused, but the boss made no reply. Only a quiver of his eyelids showed that he heard.

"The girls were delighted with the way the place is kept," piped the old voice. "Beautifully looked after. Couldn't be better if they were at home. You've not been across, have yer?"

"No, no!" For various reasons the boss had not been across.

"There's miles of it," quavered old Woodifield, "and it's all as neat as a garden. Flowers growing on all the graves. Nice broad paths." It was plain from his voice how much he liked a nice broad path.

The pause came again. Then the old man brightened wonderfully.

"D'you know what the hotel made the girls pay for a pot of jam?" he piped. "Ten francs![5] Robbery, I call it. It was a little pot, so Gertrude says, no bigger than a half-crown. And she hadn't taken more than a spoonful when they charged her ten francs. Gertrude brought the pot away with her to teach 'em a lesson. Quite right, too; it's trading on our feelings. They think because we're over there having a look around we're ready to pay anything. That's what it is." And he turned towards the door.

"Quite right, quite right!" cried the boss, though what was quite right he hadn't the least idea. He came around by his desk, followed the shuffling footsteps to the door, and saw the old fellow out. Woodifield was gone.

---

[3] *on the strict Q.T.:* Privately.

[4] *Windsor Castle:* The main residence of the British royal family.

[5] *franc:* Belgian unit of money.

For a long moment the boss stayed, staring at nothing, while the grey-haired office messenger, watching him, dodged in and out of his cubbyhole like a dog that expects to be taken for a run. Then: "I'll see nobody for half an hour, Macey," said the boss. "Understand? Nobody at all."

"Very good, sir."

The door shut, the firm, heavy steps recrossed the bright carpet, the fat body plumped down in the spring chair, and leaning forward, the boss covered his face with his hands. He wanted, he intended, he had arranged to weep. . . .

It had been a terrible shock to him when old Woodifield sprang that remark upon him about the boy's grave. It was exactly as though the earth had opened and he had seen the boy lying there with Woodifield's girls staring down at him. For it was strange. Although over six years had passed away, the boss never thought of the boy except as lying unchanged, unblemished in his uniform; asleep for ever. "My son!" groaned the boss. But no tears came yet. In the past, in the first months and even years after the boy's death, he had only to say those words to be overcome by such grief that nothing short of a violent fit of weeping could relieve him. Time, he had declared then, he had told everybody, could make no difference. Other men perhaps might recover, might live their loss down, but not he. How was it possible? His boy was an only son. Ever since his birth the boss had worked at building up this business for him; it had no other meaning if it was not for the boy. Life itself had come to have no other meaning. How on earth could he have slaved, denied himself, kept going all those years without the promise for ever before him of the boy's stepping into his shoes and carrying on where he left off?

And that promise had been so near being fulfilled. The boy had been in the office learning the ropes for a year before the war. Every morning they had started off together; they had come back by the same train. And what congratulations he had received as the boy's father! No wonder; he had taken to it marvellously. As to his popularity with the staff, every man jack of them down to old Macey couldn't make enough of the boy. And he wasn't in the least spoiled. No, he was just his bright, natural self, with the right word for everybody, with that boyish look and his habit of saying, "Simply splendid!"

But all that was over and done with as though it never had been. The day had come when Macey had handed him the telegram that brought the whole place crashing about his head. "Deeply regret to inform you . . ." And he had left the office a broken man, with his life in ruins.

Six years ago, six years . . . How quickly time passed! It might have happened yesterday. The boss took his hands from his face; he was puzzled. Something seemed to be wrong with him. He wasn't feeling as he wanted to feel. He decided to get up and have a look at the boy's photograph. But it wasn't a favorite photograph of his; the expression was unnatural. It was cold, even stern-looking. The boy had never looked like that.

At that moment the boss noticed that a fly had fallen into his broad inkpot, and was trying feebly but desperately to clamber out again. Help! help! said those struggling legs. But the sides of the inkpot were wet and slippery; it fell back again and began to swim. The boss took up a pen, picked the fly out of the ink, and shook it on to a piece of blotting-paper. For a fraction of a second it lay still on the dark patch that oozed round it. Then the front legs waved, took hold, and, pulling its small sodden body up, it began the immense task of cleaning the ink from its wings. Over and under, over and under, went a leg along a wing, as the stone goes over and under the scythe. Then there was a pause, while the fly, seeming to stand on the tips of its toes, tried to expand first one wing and then the other. It succeeded at last, and sitting down, it began, like a minute cat, to clean its face. Now one could imagine that the little front legs rubbed against each other lightly, joyfully. The horrible danger was over; it had escaped; it was ready for life again.

But just then the boss had an idea. He plunged his pen back into the ink, leaned his thick wrist on the blotting-paper, and as the fly tried its wings, down came a great, heavy blot. What would it make of that? What indeed! The little beggar seemed absolutely cowed, stunned, and afraid to move because of what would happen next. But then, as if painfully, it dragged itself forward. The front legs waved, caught hold, and, more slowly, the task began again.

He's a plucky little devil, thought the boss, and he felt a real admiration for the fly's courage. That was the way to tackle things; that was the right spirit. Never say die; it was only a question of . . . But the fly had again finished its laborious task, and the boss had just time to refill his pen, to shake fair and square on the new-cleaned body yet another drop. What about it this time? A painful moment of suspense followed. But, behold, the front legs were again waving; the boss felt a rush of relief. He leaned over the fly and said to it tenderly. "You artful little b . . ." And he actually had the brilliant notion of breathing on it to help the drying process. All the same, there was something timid and weak about its efforts now, and the boss decided that this time should be the last, as he dipped the pen into the inkpot.

It was. The last blot fell on the soaked blotting-paper, and the draggled fly lay in it and did not stir. The back legs were stuck to the body; the front legs were not to be seen.

"Come on," said the boss. "Look sharp!" And he stirred it with his pen—in vain. Nothing happened or was likely to happen. The fly was dead.

The boss lifted the corpse on the end of the paper-knife and flung it into the waste-paper basket, but such a grinding feeling of wretchedness seized him that he felt positively frightened. He started forward and pressed the bell for Macey.

"Bring me some fresh blotting-paper," he said, sternly, "and look sharp about it." And while the old dog padded away he fell to wondering what it was he had been thinking about before. What was it? It was . . . He took out his handkerchief and passed it inside his collar. For the life of him he could not remember.

UNDERSTANDING THE STORY

1. Why doesn't Mansfield give the boss a name? In what ways does the boss reveal the appropriateness of his title?

2. Why does the boss keep a photo he dislikes of his son on his desk?

3. Why does the boss call his son "the boy" instead of using his son's name?

4. Why hasn't the boss gone to see his son's grave?

5. Why can't the boss cry?

6. Why does the boss rescue the fly only to kill it?

7. What **themes** do you find in this story?

ANALYZING LITERARY TECHNIQUE

1. What is the function of Mr. Woodifield?

2. To what extent, if any, is the photograph of the boss's son a **symbol?** Consider why the photograph is so different from the boss's memory of his son.

3. To what extent, if any, is the fly a symbol?

4. What role does memory play in the story?

5. To what extent, if any, does Mansfield achieve **psychological realism** in this story? Consider her choice of **narrative perspective.**

6. James Joyce defined an **epiphany** as "a sudden spiritual manifestation." An epiphany occurs when an insignificant event brings one to understanding the essential nature of an object or situation. To what extent, if any, is the incident involving the boss and the fly an epiphany?

7. What **paradoxes** do you find in this story?

WRITING ABOUT LITERATURE

1. Write an essay in which you discuss whether "the boss" is an appropriate title for the principal character. Choose two or three incidents from the story that support your ideas.

2. Apply the narrator's thought "we cling to our last pleasures as the tree clings to its last leaves" to a theme of the story. Consider the boss, Mr. Woodifield, and the fly. Use quotations from the story to support your ideas.

3. Express what it would be like to be the son who was being trained to inherit his father's business. Alternatively, assume that the son survived the war; create a conversation in which he and his father discuss whether he will return to the family business.

The New Year's Sacrifice

ˑLU HSÜN

L U HSÜN (1881–1936), the pen name of Chou Shu-jen, is among the greatest Chinese writers of the twentieth century. He is considered to be the founder of modern Chinese literature and is best known for two collections of short stories, *Call to Arms* (1923) and *Hesitation* (1926).

Lu Hsün was born in Shaoh-sing, in Chekiang Province. During his childhood, his family lost its wealth, but his parents continued to value knowledge and education. From 1898 to 1901, he attended a modern school in Nanking (now Nanjing), and in 1902 he went to Japan, where he attended the Naval Academy and studied Western medicine. While he was in Japan, he discovered the short stories of Russian authors Nicolai Gogol and Anton Chekhov. In 1909 Lu Hsün returned to China, where he taught biology and practiced medicine.

Meanwhile Western literature was beginning to enter China and to invite unfavorable comparisons between Chinese society and Western society. For centuries Chinese society had been remarkably inhumane in its treatment of the lower classes and of women. People of wealth and power believed in the Confucian values of respect, kindness, and generosity, but they did not apply these values to the common people.

Lu Hsün decided to become a writer in order to inspire social change. In 1918 he joined Hu Shih's literary revolution. Hu Shih believed in incorporating aspects of foreign culture and life into Chinese literature. Lu Hsün's first short story, "Diary of a Madman," was published in 1918 in the magazine *New Youth* as the first piece of fiction of the new literature. The story was a scathing criticism of Chinese society, challenging the traditional view that society rewarded good and punished evil. Lu Hsün attacked the unqualified respect with which the Chinese had always viewed their past.

In the early 1920s Lu Hsün became convinced that only revolution could solve China's social problems. By 1929 he supported the Communist Party and actively criticized the government of Chiang

Kai-shek. He was treated as a national hero by Mao Tse-tung and the Communists, but his writing during this later period lacks the quality of his earlier writing.

With reference to his short stories, Lu Hsün is quoted as saying, "My themes were usually the unfortunates in this abnormal society. My aim was to expose the disease and draw attention to it so that it might be cured." "The New Year's Sacrifice," published in *Call to Arms*, addresses the issues of women's rights and presents Lu Hsün at his best.

New Year's Eve of the old calendar[1] seems after all more like the real New Year's Eve; for, to say nothing of the villages and towns, even in the air there is a feeling that New Year is coming. From the pale, lowering evening clouds issue frequent flashes of lightning, followed by a rumbling sound of firecrackers celebrating the departure of the Hearth God; while, nearer by, the firecrackers explode even more violently, and before the deafening report dies away the air is filled with a faint smell of powder. It was on such a night that I returned to Luchen, my native place. Although I call it my native place, I had had no home there for some time, so I had to put up temporarily with a certain Mr. Lu, the fourth son of his family. He is a member of our clan, and belongs to the generation before mine, so I ought to call him "Fourth Uncle." An old student of the imperial college who went in for Neo-Confucianism,[2] I found him very little changed in any way, simply slightly older, but without any moustache as yet. When we met, after exchanging a few polite remarks he said I was fatter, and after saying that immediately started a violent attack on the revolutionaries. I knew this was not meant personally, because the object of the attack was still Kang Yu-wei.[3] Nevertheless, conversation proved difficult, so that in a short time I found myself alone in the study.

The next day I got up very late, and after lunch went out to see some relatives and friends. The day after I did the same. None of them was greatly changed, simply slightly older; but every family was busy preparing for "the sacrifice." This is the great end-of-year ceremony in Luchen, when people reverently welcome the God of Fortune and solicit good fortune for the coming year. They kill chickens and geese and buy pork, scouring and scrubbing until all the women's arms turn red in the water. Some of them still wear twisted silver bracelets. After the meat is cooked some chopsticks are thrust into it at random, and this is called the "offering." It is

---

[1] *old calendar:* The Chinese lunar calendar.

[2] *imperial college . . . Neo-Confucianism:* The imperial college was the highest institute of learning in China in the nineteenth century. Confucius (551–479 B.C.) was a Chinese philosopher who emphasized devotion to family and friends, ancestor worship, and the importance of justice and peace. His teachings have been very influential on Chinese religion and society.

[3] *Kang Yu-wei:* A reformer who lived from 1858 to 1927. He advocated constitutional monarchy, which would have limited the emperor's power.

set out at dawn when incense and candles are lit, and they reverently invite the God of Fortune to come and partake of the offering. Only men can be worshippers, and after the sacrifice they naturally continue to let off firecrackers as before. This happens every year, in every family, provided they can afford to buy the offering and firecrackers; and this year they naturally followed the old custom.

The day grew overcast. In the afternoon it actually started to snow, the biggest snow-flakes as large as plum blossom petals fluttered about the sky; and this, combined with the smoke and air of activity, made Luchen appear in a ferment. When I returned to my uncle's study the roof of the house was already white with snow. The room also appeared brighter, the great red rubbing hanging on the wall showing up very clearly the character for Longevity written by the Taoist saint Chen Tuan.[4] One of a pair of scrolls had fallen down and was lying loosely rolled up on the long table, but the other was still hanging there, bearing the words: "By understanding reason we achieve tranquility of mind." Idly, I went to turn over the books on the table beneath the window, but all I could find was a pile of what looked like an incomplete set of *Kang Hsi's Dictionary*, a volume of Chiang Yung's *Notes to Chu Hsi's Philosophical Writings* and a volume of *Commentaries on the Four Books*.[5] At all events, I made up my mind to leave the next day.

Besides, the very thought of my meeting with Hsiang Lin's Wife the day before made me uncomfortable. It happened in the afternoon. I had been visiting a friend in the eastern part of the town. As I came out I met her by the river, and seeing the way she fastened her eyes on me I knew very well she meant to speak to me. Of all the people I had seen this time at Luchen none had changed as much as she: her hair, which had been streaked with white five years before, was now completely white, quite unlike someone in her forties. Her face was fearfully thin and dark in its sallowness, and had moreover lost its former expression of sadness, looking as if carved out of wood. Only an occasional flicker of her eyes showed she was still a living creature. In one hand she carried a wicker basket, in which was a broken bowl, empty; in the other she held a bamboo pole longer than herself, split at the bottom: it was clear she had become a beggar.

I stood still, waiting for her to come and ask for money.

"You have come back?" she asked me first.

"Yes."

"That is very good. You are a scholar, and have travelled too and seen a lot. I just want to ask you something." Her lustreless eyes suddenly gleamed.

I never guessed she would talk to me like this. I stood there taken by surprise.

"It is this." She drew two paces nearer, and whispered very confidentially: "After a person dies, does he turn into a ghost or not?"

---

[4] *Taoist saint Chen Tuan:* Taoism is a Chinese religion based on the Tao, or Way, that teaches simplicity and selflessness. Chen Tuan was a hermit who lived at the beginning of the tenth century.

[5] *Kang Hsi's Dictionary . . . Four Books:* A Chinese dictionary from the seventeenth century and two books on Confucian philosophy.

As she fixed her eyes on me I was seized with foreboding. A shiver ran down my spine and I felt more nervous than during an unexpected examination at school, when unfortunately the teacher stands by one's side. Personally, I had never given the least thought to the question of the existence of spirits. In this emergency how should I answer her? Hesitating for a moment, I reflected: "It is the tradition here to believe in spirits, yet she seems to be sceptical—perhaps it would be better to say she hopes: hopes that there is immortality and yet hopes that there is not. Why increase the sufferings of the wretched? To give her something to look forward to, it would be better to say there is."

"There may be, I think," I told her hesitantly.

"Then, there must also be a Hell?"

"What, Hell?" Greatly startled, I could only try to evade the question. "Hell? According to reason there should be one too—but not necessarily. Who cares about it anyway? . . ."

"Then will all the people of one family who have died see each other again?"

"Well, as to whether they will see each other again or not . . ." I realized now that I was a complete fool; for all my hesitation and reflection I had been unable to answer her three questions. Immediately I lost confidence and wanted to say the exact opposite of what I had previously said. "In this case . . . as a matter of fact, I am not sure. . . . Actually, regarding the question of ghosts, I am not sure either."

In order to avoid further importunate questions, I walked off, and beat a hasty retreat to my uncle's house, feeling exceedingly uncomfortable. I thought to myself: "I am afraid my answer will prove dangerous to her. Probably it is just that when other people are celebrating she feels lonely by herself, but could there be another reason? Could she have had some premonition? If there is another reason, and as a result something happens, then, through my answer, I shall be held responsible to a certain extent." Finally, however, I ended by laughing at myself, thinking that such a chance meeting could have no great significance, and yet I was taking it so to heart; no wonder certain educationalists called me a neurotic. Moreover I had distinctly said, "I am not sure," contradicting my previous answer; so that even if anything did happen, it would have nothing at all to do with me.

"I am not sure" is a most useful phrase.

Inexperienced and rash young men often take it upon themselves to solve people's problems for them or choose doctors for them, and if by any chance things turn out badly, they are probably held to blame; but by simply concluding with this phrase "I am not sure," one can free oneself of all responsibility. At this time I felt even more strongly the necessity for such a phrase, since even in speaking with a beggar woman there was no dispensing with it.

However, I continued to feel uncomfortable, and even after a night's rest my mind kept running on this, as if I had a premonition of some untoward development. In that oppressive snowy weather, in the gloomy study, this discomfort increased. It would be better to leave: I should go back to town the next day. The boiled shark's fins in the Fu Hsing Restaurant used to cost a dollar for a large portion, and I wondered if this cheap and delicious dish had increased in price or not. Although the friends who had accompanied me in the old days had scattered, even if I was alone the shark's fins still had to be tasted. At all events, I made up my mind to leave the next day.

After experiencing many times that things which I hoped would not happen and felt should not happen invariably did happen, I was desperately afraid this would prove another such case. And, indeed, strange things did begin to happen. Towards evening I heard talking—it sounded like a discussion—in the inner room; but soon the conversation ended, all I heard was my uncle saying loudly as he walked out: "Not earlier nor later, but just at this time—sure sign of a bad character!"

At first I felt astonished, then very uncomfortable, thinking these words must refer to me. I looked outside the door, but no one was there. I contained myself with difficulty till their servant came in before dinner to brew a pot of tea, when at last I had a chance to make some enquiries.

"With whom was Mr. Lu angry just now?" I asked.

"Why, still with Hsiang Lin's Wife," he replied briefly.

"Hsiang Lin's Wife? How was that?" I asked again.

"She's dead."

"Dead?" My heart suddenly missed a beat. I started, and probably changed colour too. But since he did not raise his head, he was probably quite unaware of how I felt. Then I controlled myself, and asked:

"When did she die?"

"When? Last night, or else today, I'm not sure."

"How did she die?"

"How did she die? Why, of poverty of course." He answered placidly and, still without having raised his head to look at me, went out.

However, my agitation was only short-lived, for now that something I had felt imminent had already taken place, I no longer had to take refuge in my "I'm not sure," or the servant's expression "dying of poverty" for comfort. My heart already felt lighter. Only from time to time something still seemed to weigh on it. Dinner was served, and my uncle solemnly accompanied me. I wanted to ask about Hsiang Lin's Wife, but knew that although he had read, "Ghosts and spirits are properties of Nature,"[6] he had retained many superstitions, and on the eve of this sacrifice it was out of the question to mention anything like death or illness. In case of necessity one could use veiled allusions, but unfortunately I did not know how to, so although questions kept rising to the tip of my tongue, I had to bite them back. From his solemn expression I suddenly suspected that he looked on me as choosing not earlier nor later but just this time to come and trouble him, and that I was also a bad character; therefore to set his mind at rest I told him at once that I intended to leave Luchen the next day and go back to the city. He did not press me greatly to stay. So we quietly finished the meal.

In winter the days are short and, now that it was snowing, darkness already enveloped the whole town. Everybody was busy beneath the lamplight, but outside the windows it was very quiet. Snow-flakes fell on the thickly piled snow, as if

---

[6] "Ghosts . . . of Nature": A Confucian saying.

they were whispering, making me feel even more lonely. I sat by myself under the yellow gleam of the vegetable oil lamp and thought, "This poor woman, abandoned by people in the dust as a tiresome and worn-out toy, once left her own imprint in the dust, and those who enjoy life must have wondered at her for wishing to prolong her existence; but now at least she has been swept clear by eternity. Whether spirits exist or not I do not know; but in the present world when a meaningless existence ends, so that someone whom others are tired of seeing is no longer seen, it is just as well, both for the individual concerned and for others." I listened quietly to see if I could hear the snow falling outside the window, still pursuing this train of thought, until gradually I felt less ill at ease.

Fragments of her life, seen or heard before, now combined to form one whole.

She did not belong to Luchen. One year at the beginning of winter, when my uncle's family wanted to change their maidservant, Old Mrs. Wei brought her in and introduced her. Her hair was tied with white bands, she wore a black skirt, blue jacket and pale green bodice, and was about twenty-six, with a pale skin but rosy cheeks. Old Mrs. Wei called her Hsiang Lin's Wife, and said that she was a neighbour of her mother's family, and because her husband was dead she wanted to go out to work. My uncle knitted his brows and my aunt immediately understood that he disapproved of her because she was a widow. She looked very suitable, though, with big strong feet and hands, and a meek expression; and she had said nothing but showed every sign of being tractable and hard-working. So my aunt paid no attention to my uncle's frown, but kept her. During the period of probation she worked from morning till night, as if she found resting dull, and she was so strong that she could do a man's work; accordingly on the third day it was settled, and each month she was to be paid five hundred cash.

Everybody called her Hsiang Lin's Wife. They did not ask her her own name; but since she was introduced by someone from Wei Village who said she was a neighbour, presumably her name was also Wei. She was not very talkative, only answering when other people spoke to her, and her answers were brief. It was not until a dozen days or so had passed that they learned little by little that she still had a severe mother-in-law at home and a younger brother-in-law more than ten years old, who could cut wood. Her husband, who had been a woodcutter too, had died in the spring. He had been ten years younger than she. This little was all that people learned from her.

The days passed quickly. She worked as hard as ever; she would eat anything, and did not spare herself. Everybody agreed that the Lu family had found a very good maidservant, who really got through more work than a hard-working man. At the end of the year she swept, mopped, killed chickens and geese and sat up to boil the sacrificial meat, single-handed, so the family did not have to hire extra help. Nevertheless, she, on her side, was satisfied; gradually the trace of a smile appeared at the corner of her mouth. She became plumper and her skin whiter.

New Year was scarcely over when she came back from washing rice by the river looking pale, and said that in the distance she had just seen a man wandering on the opposite bank who looked very like her husband's cousin, and probably he had come to look for her. My aunt, much alarmed, made detailed enquiries, but failed to get any further information. As soon as my uncle learned of it he frowned and said, "This is bad. She must have run away from her husband's family."

Before long this inference that she had run away was confirmed.

About a fortnight later, just as everybody was beginning to forget what had happened, Old Mrs. Wei suddenly called, bringing with her a woman in her thirties who, she said, was the maidservant's mother-in-law. Although the woman looked like a villager, she behaved with great self-possession and had a ready tongue in her head. After the usual polite remarks she apologized for coming to take her daughter-in-law home, saying there was a great deal to be done at the beginning of spring, and since there were only old people and children at home they were short-handed.

"Since it is her mother-in-law who wants her to go back, what is there to be said?" was her uncle's comment.

Thereupon her wages were reckoned up. They amounted to one thousand seven hundred and fifty cash, all of which she had left with her mistress without using a single coin. My aunt gave the entire amount to her mother-in-law. The latter also took her clothes, thanked Mr. and Mrs. Lu and went out. By this time it was already noon.

"Oh, the rice! Didn't Hsiang Lin's Wife go to wash the rice?" my aunt exclaimed some time later. Probably she was rather hungry, so that she remembered lunch.

Thereupon everybody set about looking for the rice basket. My aunt went first to the kitchen, then to the hall, then to the bedroom, but not a trace of it was to be seen anywhere. My uncle went outside, but could not find it either; only when he went right down to the riverside did he see it, set down fair and square on the bank, with a bundle of vegetables beside it.

Some people there told him that a boat with a white awning had moored there in the morning, but since the awning covered the boat completely they did not know who was inside, and before this incident no one had paid any attention to it. But when Hsiang Lin's Wife came to wash rice, two men looking like country people jumped off the boat just as she was kneeling down and seizing hold of her carried her on board. After several shouts and cries, Hsiang Lin's Wife became silent; they had probably stopped her mouth. Then two women walked up, one of them a stranger and the other Old Mrs. Wei. When the people who told this story tried to peep into the boat they could not see very clearly, but Hsiang Lin's Wife seemed to be lying bound on the floor of the boat.

"Disgraceful! Still . . ." said my uncle.

That day my aunt cooked the midday meal herself, and my cousin Ah Niu lit the fire.

After lunch Old Mrs. Wei came again.

"Disgraceful!" said my uncle.

"What is the meaning of this? How dare you come here again!" My aunt, who was washing dishes, started scolding as soon as she saw her. "You recommended her yourself, and then plotted to have her carried off, causing all this stir. What will people think? Are you trying to make a laughing-stock of our family?"

"Aiya, I was really taken in! Now I have come specially to clear up this business. When she asked me to find her work, how was I to know that she had left home without her mother-in-law's consent? I am very sorry, Mr. Lu, Mrs. Lu. Because I am so old and foolish and careless, I have offended my patrons. However, it is lucky for me that your family is always so generous and kind, and unwilling to be hard on your inferiors. This time I promise to find you someone good to make up for my mistake."

"Still . . ." said my uncle.

Thereupon the business of Hsiang Lin's Wife was concluded, and before long it was also forgotten.

O nly my aunt, because the maidservants taken on afterwards were all lazy or fond of stealing food, or else both lazy and fond of stealing food, with not a good one in the lot, still often spoke of Hsiang Lin's Wife. On such occasions she would always say to herself, "I wonder what has become of her now?" meaning that she would like to have her back. But by the following New Year she too gave up hope.

The New Year's holiday was nearly over when Old Mrs. Wei, already half tipsy, came to pay her respects and said it was because she had been back to Wei Village to visit her mother's family and stayed a few days that she had come late. During the course of conversation they naturally came to speak of Hsiang Lin's Wife.

"She?" said Mrs. Wei cheerfully, "She is in luck now. When her mother-in-law dragged her home, she had already promised her to the sixth son of the Ho family in Ho village. Not long after she reached home they put her in the bridal chair and sent her off."

"Aiya! What a mother-in-law!" exclaimed my aunt in amazement.

"Ah madam, you really talk like a great lady! We country folk, poor women, think nothing of that. She still had a younger brother-in-law who had to be married. And if they hadn't found her a husband, where would they have found the money for his wedding? But her mother-in-law is a clever and capable woman, who knows how to drive a good bargain, so she married her off into the mountains. If she had married her to someone in the same village, she wouldn't have got so much money; but since very few women were willing to marry someone living deep in the mountains, she got eighty thousand cash. Now the second son is married, the presents only cost her fifty thousand, and after paying the wedding expenses she still has over ten thousand left. Just think, doesn't this show she knows how to drive a good bargain? . . ."

"But was Hsiang Lin's Wife willing?"

"It wasn't a question of being willing or not. Of course anyone would have protested. They just tied her up with a rope, stuffed her into the bridal chair, carried her to the man's house, put on the bridal headdress, performed the ceremony in the hall and locked them in their room; and that was that. But Hsiang Lin's Wife is quite a character. I heard she really put up a great struggle, and everybody said she was different from other people because she had worked in a scholar's family. We go-betweens, madam, see a great deal. When widows remarry, some cry and shout, some threaten to commit suicide, some when they have been carried to the man's house won't go through the ceremony, and some even smash the wedding candlesticks. But Hsiang Lin's Wife was different from the rest. They said she shouted and cursed all the way, so that by the time they had carried her to Ho Village she was completely hoarse. When they dragged her out of the chair, although the two chairbearers and her young brother-in-law used all their strength, they couldn't force her to go through the ceremony. The moment they were careless enough to loosen their grip—gracious Buddha![7]—she threw herself against a corner of the table and knocked a big hole in her head. The blood poured out; and although they used two handfuls of incense ashes and bandaged her with two pieces of red cloth, they still couldn't stop the bleeding. Finally it took all of them together to get her shut up with her husband in the bridal chamber, where she went on cursing. Oh, it was really dreadful!" She shook her head, cast down her eyes and said no more.

"And after that what happened?" asked my aunt.

"They said the next day she still didn't get up," said Old Mrs. Wei, raising her eyes.

"And after?"

"After? She got up. At the end of the year she had a baby, a boy, who was two this New Year.[8] These few days when I was at home some people went to Ho Village, and when they came back they said they had seen her and her son, and that both mother and baby are fat. There is no mother-in-law over her, the man is a strong fellow who can earn a living, and the house is their own. Well, well, she is really in luck."

After this even my aunt gave up talking of Hsiang Lin's Wife.

But one autumn, two New Years after they heard how lucky Hsiang Lin's Wife had been, she actually reappeared on the threshold of my uncle's house. On the table she placed a round bulb-shaped basket, and under the eaves a small roll of bedding. Her hair was still wrapped in white bands, and she wore a black skirt, blue jacket and pale green bodice. But her skin was sallow and her cheeks had lost their colour; she kept her eyes downcast, and her eyes, with their tear-stained rims, were no longer bright. Just as before, it was Old Mrs. Wei, looking very benevolent, who brought her in, and who explained at length to my aunt:

"It was really a bolt from the blue. Her husband was so strong nobody could have guessed that a young fellow like that would die of typhoid fever.[9] First he seemed better, but then he ate a bowl of cold rice and the sickness came back. Luckily she had the boy, and she can work, whether it is chopping wood, picking tea-leaves or raising silkworms; so at first she was able to carry on. Then who could

---

[7] *Buddha:* Gautama Siddhartha (c. 563–483 B.C.), Indian philosopher and teacher who founded the Buddhist religion.

[8] *two this New Year:* In China children were considered one year old at their first New Year after their birth; another year was added at the following New Year, and so on.

[9] *typhoid fever:* An infectious disease characterized by high fever, headache, and diarrhea.

believe that the child, too, would be carried off by a wolf? Although it was nearly the end of spring, still wolves came to the village—how could anyone have guessed that? Now she is all on her own. Her brother-in-law came to take the house, and turned her out; so she has really no way open to her but to come and ask help from her former mistress. Luckily this time there is nobody to stop her, and you happen to be wanting a new servant, so I have brought her here. I think someone who is used to your ways is much better than a new hand. . . ."

"I was really stupid, really . . ." Hsiang Lin's Wife raised her listless eyes to say. "I only knew that when it snows the wild beasts in the glen have nothing to eat and may come to the villages; I didn't know that in spring they came too. I got up at dawn and opened the door, filled a small basket with beans and called our Ah Mao to go and sit on the threshold and shell the beans. He was very obedient and always did as I told him: he went out. Then I chopped wood at the back of the house and washed the rice, and when the rice was in the pan and I wanted to boil the beans I called Ah Mao, but there was no answer; and when I went out to look, all I could see was beans scattered on the ground, but no Ah Mao. He never went to other families to play; and in fact at each place where I went to ask, there was no sign of him. I became desperate, and begged people to go to look for him. Only in the afternoon, after looking everywhere else did they go to look in the glen and see one of his little shoes caught on a bramble. 'That's bad,' they said, 'he must have met a wolf.' And sure enough when they went further in there he was, lying in the wolf's lair, with all his entrails eaten away, his hand still tightly clutching that little basket . . ." At this point she started crying, and was unable to complete the sentence.

My aunt had been undecided at first, but by the end of this story the rims of her eyes were rather red. After thinking for a moment she told her to take the round basket and bedding into the servants' quarters. Old Mrs. Wei heaved a long sigh as if relieved of a great burden. Hsiang Lin's Wife looked a little more at ease than when she first came and, without having to be told the way, quietly took away her bedding. From this time on she worked again as a maidservant in Luchen.

Everybody still called her Hsiang Lin's Wife.

However, she had changed a great deal. She had not been there more than three days before her master and mistress realized that she was not as quick as before. Since her memory was much worse, and her impassive face never showed the least trace of a smile, my aunt already expressed herself very far from satisfied. When the woman first arrived, although my uncle frowned as before, because they invariably had such difficulty in finding servants he did not object very strongly, only secretly warned my aunt that while such people may seem very pitiful they exert a bad moral influence. Thus although it would be all right for her to do ordinary work she must not join the preparations for sacrifice; they would have to prepare all the dishes themselves, for otherwise they would be unclean and the ancestors would not accept them.

The most important event in my uncle's household was the ancestral sacrifice, and formerly this had been the busiest time for Hsiang Lin's Wife; but now she had very little to do. When the table was placed in the centre of the hall and the curtain fastened, she still remembered how to set out the winecups and chopsticks in the old way.

"Hsiang Lin's Wife, put those down!" said my aunt hastily. "I'll do it!"

She sheepishly withdrew her hand and went to get the candlesticks.

"Hsiang Lin's Wife, put those down!" cried my aunt hastily again. "I'll fetch them."

After walking round several times without finding anything to do, Hsiang Lin's Wife could only go hesitantly away. All she did that day was to sit by the stove and feed the fire.

The people in the town still called her Hsiang Lin's Wife, but in a different tone from before; and although they talked to her still, their manner was colder. She did not mind this in the least, only, looking straight in front of her, she would tell everybody her story, which night or day was never out of her mind.

"I was really stupid, really," she would say. "I only knew that when it snows the wild beasts in the glen have nothing to eat and may come to the villages; I didn't know that in spring they came too. I got up at dawn and opened the door, filled a small basket with beans and called our Ah Mao to go and sit on the threshold and shell them. He was very obedient and always did as I told him: he went out. Then I chopped wood at the back of the house and washed the rice, and when the rice was in the pan and I wanted to boil the beans I called Ah Mao, but there was no answer; and when I went out to look, all I could see was beans scattered on the ground, but no Ah Mao. He never went to other families to play; and in fact at each place where I went to ask, there was no sign of him. I became desperate, and begged people to go to look for him. Only in the afternoon, after looking everywhere else, did they go to look in the glen and see one of his little shoes caught on a bramble. 'That's bad,' they said, 'he must have met a wolf.' And sure enough when they went further in there he was, lying in the wolf's lair, with all his entrails eaten away, his hand still tightly clutching that small basket. . . ." At this point she would start crying and her voice would trail away.

This story was rather effective, and when men heard it they often stopped smiling and walked away disconcerted, while the women not only seemed to forgive her but their faces immediately lost their contemptuous look and they added their tears to hers. There were some old women who had not heard her speaking in the street, who went specially to look for her, to hear her sad tale. When her voice trailed away and she started to cry, they joined in, shedding the tears which had gathered in their eyes. Then they sighed, and went away satisfied, exchanging comments.

She asked nothing better than to tell her sad story over and over again, often gathering three or four hearers. But before long everybody knew it by heart, until even in the eyes of the most kindly, Buddha-fearing old ladies not a trace of tears could be seen. In the end, almost everyone in the town could recite her tale, and it bored and exasperated them to hear it.

"I was really stupid, really . . ." she would begin.

"Yes, you only knew that in snowy weather the wild beasts in the mountains had nothing to eat and might come down to the villages." Promptly cutting short her recital, they walked away.

She would stand there open-mouthed, looking at them with a dazed expression, and then go away too, as if she also felt disconcerted. But she still brooded over it, hoping from other topics such as small baskets, beans and other people's children, to lead up to the story of her Ah Mao. If she saw a child of two or three, she would say, "Oh dear, if my Ah Mao were still alive, he would be just as big. . . ."

Children seeing the look in her eyes would take fright and, clutching the hems of their mothers' clothes, try to tug them away. Thereupon she would be left by herself again, and finally walk away disconcerted. Later everybody knew what she was like, and it only needed a child present for them to ask her with an artificial smile, "Hsiang Lin's Wife, if your Ah Mao were alive, wouldn't he be just as big as that?"

She probably did not realize that her story, after having been turned over and tasted by people for so many days, had long since become stale, only exciting disgust and contempt; but from the way people smiled she seemed to know that they were cold and sarcastic, and that there was no need for her to say any more. She would simply look at them, not answering a word.

In Luchen people celebrate New Year in a big way; preparations start from the twentieth day of the twelfth month onwards. That year my uncle's household found it necessary to hire a temporary manservant, but since there was still a great deal to do they also called in another maidservant, Liu Ma, to help. Chickens and geese had to be killed; but Liu Ma was a devout woman who abstained from meat, did not kill living things, and would only wash the sacrificial dishes. Hsiang Lin's Wife had nothing to do but feed the fire. She sat there, resting, watching Liu Ma as she washed the sacrifical dishes. A light snow began to fall.

"Dear me, I was really stupid," began Hsiang Lin's Wife, as if to herself, looking at the sky and sighing.

"Hsiang Lin's Wife, there you go again," said Liu Ma, looking at her impatiently. "I ask you: that wound on your forehead, wasn't it then you got it?"

"Uh, huh," she answered vaguely.

"Let me ask you: what made you willing after all?"

"Me?"

"Yes. What I think is, you must have been willing; otherwise . . ."

"Oh dear, you don't know how strong he was."

"I don't believe it. I don't believe he was so strong that you really couldn't keep him off. You must have been willing, only you put the blame on his being so strong."

"Oh dear, you . . . you try for yourself and see." She smiled.

Liu Ma's lined face broke into a smile too, making it wrinkled like a walnut; her small beady eyes swept Hsiang Lin's Wife's forehead and fastened on her eyes. As if rather embarrassed, Hsiang Lin's Wife immediately stopped smiling, averted her eyes and looked at the snow-flakes.

"Hsiang Lin's Wife, that was really a bad bargain," continued Liu Ma mysteriously. "If you had held out longer or knocked yourself to death, it would have been better. As it is, after living with your second husband for less than two years, you are guilty of a great crime. Just think, when you go down to the lower world in future, these two men's ghosts will fight over you. To which will you go? The King of Hell will have no choice but to cut you in two and divide you between them. I think, really . . ."

Then terror showed in her face. This was something she had never heard in the mountains.

"I think you had better take precautions beforehand. Go to the Tutelary God's Temple[10] and buy a threshold to be your substitute, so that thousands of people can walk over it and trample on it, in order to atone for your sins in this life and avoid torment after death."

At the time Hsiang Lin's Wife said nothing, but she must have taken this to heart, for the next morning when she got up there were dark circles beneath her eyes. After breakfast she went to the Tutelary God's Temple at the west end of the village, and asked to buy a threshold. The temple priests would not agree at first, and only when she shed tears did they give a grudging consent. The price was twelve thousand cash.

She had long since given up talking to people, because Ah Mao's story was received with such contempt; but news of her conversation with Liu Ma that day spread, and many people took a fresh interest in her and came again to tease her into talking. As for the subject, that had naturally changed to deal with the wound on her forehead.

"Hsiang Lin's Wife, I ask you: what made you willing after all that time?" one would cry.

"Oh, what a pity, to have had this knock for nothing," another looking at her scar would agree.

Probably she knew from their smiles and tone of voice that they were making fun of her, for she always looked steadily at them without saying a word, and finally did not even turn her head. All day long she kept her lips tightly closed, bearing on her head the scar which everyone considered a mark of shame, silently shopping, sweeping the floor, washing vegetables, preparing rice. Only after nearly a year did she take from my aunt her wages which had accumulated. She changed them for twelve silver dollars, and asking for leave went to the west end of the town. In less time than it takes for a meal she was back again, looking much comforted, and with an unaccustomed light in her eyes. She told my aunt happily that she had bought a threshold in the Tutelary God's Temple.

When the time came for the ancestral sacrifice at the winter equinox, she worked harder than ever, and seeing my aunt take out the sacrificial utensils and with Ah Niu carry the table into the middle of the hall, she went confidently to fetch the winecups and chopsticks.

"Put those down, Hsiang Lin's Wife!" my aunt called out hastily.

She withdrew her hand as if scorched, her face turned ashen-grey, and instead of fetching the candlesticks she just stood there dazed. Only when my uncle came to burn incense and told her to go, did she walk away. This time the change in

---

[10] *Tutelary God's Temple*: Temple of the guardian god of the village.

her was very great, for the next day not only were her eyes sunken, but even her spirit seemed broken. Moreover she became very timid, not only afraid of the dark and shadows, but also of the sight of anyone. Even her own master or mistress made her look as frightened as a little mouse that has come out of its hole in the daytime. For the rest, she would sit stupidly, like a wooden statue. In less than half a year her hair began to turn grey, and her memory became much worse, reaching a point when she was constantly forgetting to go and prepare the rice.

"What has come over Hsiang Lin's Wife? It would really have been better not to have kept her that time." My aunt would sometimes speak like this in front of her, as if to warn her.

However, she remained this way, so that it was impossible to see any hope of her improving. They finally decided to get rid of her and tell her to go back to Old Mrs. Wei. While I was at Luchen they were still only talking of this; but judging by what happened later, it is evident that this was what they must have done. Whether after leaving my uncle's household she became a beggar, or whether she went first to Old Mrs. Wei's house and later became a beggar, I do not know.

I was woken up by firecrackers exploding noisily close at hand, saw the glow of the yellow oil lamp as large as a bean, and heard the splutter of fireworks as my uncle's household celebrated the sacrifice. I knew that it was nearly dawn. I felt bewildered, hearing as in a dream the confused continuous sound of distant crackers which seemed to form one dense cloud of noise in the sky, joining the whirling snow-flakes to envelop the whole town. Wrapped in this medley of sound, relaxed and at ease, the doubt which had preyed on me from dawn to early night was swept clean away by the atmosphere of celebration, and I felt only that the saints of heaven and earth had accepted the sacrifice and incense and were all reeling with intoxication in the sky, preparing to give the people of Luchen boundless good fortune.

UNDERSTANDING THE STORY

1. How would Lu Hsün define the attitudes and actions of a good person? Given Lu Hsün's construction of this story, what relationship should exist between a person's day-to-day life and his or her religious life?

2. Why does Hsiang Lin's Wife ask the narrator three questions? Why is the narrator worried about the effect of his answers?

3. Why does Fourth Uncle think that Hsiang Lin's Wife is "a bad character"?

4. Why does Hsiang Lin's Wife choose to die during the time of the New Year's sacrifice? Relate your response to the meaning of the story.

5. Why won't Fourth Uncle let Hsiang Lin's Wife participate in the religious rites connected with the New Year's festival?

6. Why do the people in Luchen view Hsiang Lin's Wife with contempt?

7. To what extent does Lu Hsün appear to be criticizing Fouth Uncle and his household?

8. In presenting Hsiang Lin's Wife as a victim of social injustice, what social attitudes in the rural China of his day does Lu Hsün portray?

9. "The New Year's Sacrifice" is called "Benediction" in another translation. How do these two titles relate to the **theme?**

ANALYZING LITERARY TECHNIQUE

1. Why does Lu Hsün begin and end the story with the current New Year's holiday?

2. What function does the **flashback** serve in the story? Why does Lu Hsün choose this way to tell his story?

3. What do the depictions of Fourth Uncle and Fourth Aunt contribute to the story?

4. To what extent is this story a **satire?**

5. What is the function of **irony** in this story? Consider both the character of Liu Ma and the final paragraph of the story.

6. What **paradox** does Lu Hsün present in this story?

WRITING ABOUT LITERATURE

1. Write an essay in which you analyze Lu Hsün's use of satire. Consider the characterizations of Fourth Uncle, Fourth Aunt, and Liu Ma as well as the story's title and final paragraph. Support your ideas with at least three examples, explaining the function of each example. Use quotations as part of your examples. Conclude with an evaluation of what satire contributes to the story as a whole.

2. Write a contemporary version of Lu Hsün's story. Include one or two characters who live their lives as Fourth Uncle and Fourth Aunt live theirs. Focus your story on a character who suffers from an injustice that relates to the personality of your other main character or characters. Set your story in a real or imaginary place at the present time.

In a Grove

RYŪNOSUKE AKUTAGAWA

*R*YŪNOSUKE AKUTAGAWA (1892–1927) is the first
modern Japanese writer to gain wide appreciation in the
Western world. The author of 150 short stories, he is famous
for his early stories, which have become classics in Japan. He is best
known for "Rashōmon" (1915) and "In a Grove" (1922), which director Akira Kurosawa combined in the prize-winning film *Rashōmon*
(1950). However, some scholars consider Akutagawa's masterpiece to
be "Cogwheels," an autobiographical "nightmare" written shortly
before he committed suicide and published posthumously in 1927.

Born in Tokyo, Akutagawa was the son of a milkman and of a
woman who became incurably insane when he was still an infant.
The boy was adopted by his maternal uncle and the uncle's wife, who
gave him their family name. He received affection and culture, but he
longed for the mother he never had. Moreover, because insanity was
thought to be inherited, Akutagawa lived in fear that he would share
his mother's fate. His late autobiographical stories reveal that he felt
insecure and alienated all his life. Until his college years, books often
substituted for real experiences, and he did not acquire friends until
his intellectual excellence drew others to him. Despite his great success as a writer, he committed suicide at the age of thirty-five.

In 1914, during his second year at Tokyo Imperial University,
Akutagawa published his first original story. His knowledge of the literatures of Europe, China, and Japan was instrumental in his development
as a stylist, and he was recognized as much for his literary style as for the
content of his fiction. At the time when naturalism led other Japanese
authors to write personal confessions as fiction, and the proletarian
movement led them to write slice-of-life fiction about the working class,
Akutagawa refused to deal directly with personal experience. Instead,
he adopted early historical settings for his stories, many of which he
based on the ancient tales in *Stories of Times Now Long Ago*.

An eclectic reader, Akutagawa often combined ideas from many literary sources into one of his own stories. However, he was more than a
talented borrower with a poet's gift with language. Psychology fascinated

him, and often in his stories a detached, impersonal narrator illuminates the human mind and soul. With penetrating vision, he saw the dark side of even virtuous and heroic behavior, and he conveyed psychological reality in a variety of literary styles that ranged from realism in his early stories to surrealism in his last great works.

"In a Grove" is one of Akutagawa's most striking stories. The original version is found in *Stories of Times Now Long Ago*, but the psychological focus of the story is Akutagawa's unique and provocative contribution.

THE TESTIMONY OF A WOODCUTTER QUESTIONED BY A HIGH POLICE COMMISSIONER

Yes sir. Certainly, it was I who found the body. This morning, as usual, I went to cut my daily quota of cedars, when I found the body in a grove in a hollow in the mountains. The exact location? About 150 meters off the Yamashina stage road.[1] It's an out-of-the-way grove of bamboo and cedars.

The body was lying flat on its back dressed in a bluish silk kimono and a wrinkled head-dress of the Kyōto style. A single sword-stroke had pierced the breast. The fallen bamboo-blades around it were stained with bloody blossoms. No, the blood was no longer running. The wound had dried up, I believe. And also, a gad-fly was stuck fast there, hardly noticing my footsteps.

You ask me if I saw a sword or any such thing?

No, nothing sir. I found only a rope at the root of a cedar near by. And . . . well, in addition to a rope, I found a comb. That was all. Apparently he must have made a battle of it before he was murdered, because the grass and fallen bamboo-blades had been trampled down all around.

"A horse was near by?"

No, sir. It's hard enough for a man to enter, let alone a horse.

THE TESTIMONY OF A TRAVELING BUDDHIST[2] PRIEST QUESTIONED BY A HIGH POLICE COMMISSIONER

The time? Certainly, it was about noon yesterday, sir. The unfortunate man was on the road from Sekiyama to Yamashina. He was walking toward Sekiyama with a woman accompanying him on horseback, who I have since learned was his wife. A scarf hanging from her head hid her face from view. All I saw was the color of her clothes, a lilac-colored suit. Her horse was a sorrel with a fine mane. The lady's height? Oh, about four feet five inches. Since I am a Buddhist priest,

---

[1] *Yamashina stage road:* A road outside of Kyōto, a city in central Honshu in Japan. All the action takes place around Kyōto.

[2] *Buddhist:* A follower of the religion founded by Gautama Siddhartha (c. 563–483 B.C.), an Indian philosopher and teacher. Buddhism emphasizes self-denial and a code of thought and behavior that lead believers to nirvana, a release from earthly suffering.

I took little notice about her details. Well, the man was armed with a sword as well as a bow and arrows. And I remember that he carried some twenty odd arrows in a quiver.

Little did I expect that he would meet such a fate. Truly human life is as evanescent as the morning dew or a flash of lightning. My words are inadequate to express my sympathy for him.

THE TESTIMONY OF A POLICEMAN QUESTIONED
BY A HIGH POLICE COMMISSIONER

The man that I arrested? He is a notorious brigand called Tajomaru. When I arrested him, he had fallen off his horse. He was on the bridge at Awataguchi. The time? It was in the early hours of last night. For the record, I might say that the other day I tried to arrest him, but unfortunately he escaped. He was wearing a dark blue silk kimono and a large plain sword. And, as you see, he got a bow and arrows somewhere. You say that this bow and these arrows look like the ones owned by the dead man? Then Tajomaru must be the murderer. The bow wound with leather strips, the black lacquered quiver, the seventeen arrows with hawk feathers—these were all in his possession I believe. Yes, sir, the horse is as you say, a sorrel with a fine mane. A little beyond the stone bridge I found the horse grazing by the roadside, with his long rein dangling. Surely there is some providence in his having been thrown by the horse.

Of all the robbers prowling around Kyōto, this Tajomaru has given the most grief to the women in town. Last autumn a wife who came to the mountain back of the Pindora of the Toribe Temple, presumably to pay a visit, was murdered, along with a girl. It has been suspected that it was his doing. If this criminal murdered the man, you cannot tell what he may have done with the man's wife. May it please your honor to look into this problem as well.

THE TESTIMONY OF AN OLD WOMAN QUESTIONED
BY A HIGH POLICE COMMISSIONER

Yes, sir, that corpse is the man who married my daughter. He does not come from Kyōto. He was a samurai in the town of Kokufu in the province of Wakasa.[3] His name was Kanazawa no Takehiko, and his age was twenty-six. He was of a gentle disposition, so I am sure he did nothing to provoke the anger of others.

My daughter? Her name is Masago, and her age is nineteen. She is a spirited, fun-loving girl, but I am sure she has never known any man except Takehiko. She has a small, oval, dark-complected face with a mole at the corner of her left eye.

Yesterday, Takehiko left for Wakasa with my daughter. What bad luck it is that things should have come to such a sad end! What has become of my daughter? I am resigned to giving up my son-in-law as lost, but the fate of my daughter worries me sick. For heaven's sake leave no stone unturned to find her. I hate that

---

[3] *samurai . . . province of Wakasa:* A samurai was a member of the military class in feudal Japan. Wakasa is the area north of Kyōto.

robber Tajomaru, or whatever his name is. Not only my son-in-law, but my daughter . . . (Her later words were drowned in tears.)

TAJOMARU'S CONFESSION

I killed him, but not her. Where's she gone? I can't tell. Oh, wait a minute. No torture can make me confess what I don't know. Now things have come to such a head, I won't keep anything from you.

Yesterday a little past noon I met that couple. Just then a puff of wind blew, and raised her hanging scarf, so that I caught a glimpse of her face. Instantly it was again covered from my view. That may have been one reason; she looked like a Bodhisattva.[4] At that moment I made up my mind to capture her even if I had to kill her man.

Why? To me killing isn't a matter of such great consequence as you might think. When a woman is captured, her man has to be killed anyway. In killing, I use the sword I wear at my side. Am I the only one who kills people? You, you don't use swords. You kill people with your power, with your money. Sometimes you kill them on the pretext of working for their good. It's true they don't bleed. They are in the best of health, but all the same you've killed them. It's hard to say who is a greater sinner, you or me. (An ironical smile.)

But it would have been good if I could capture a woman without killing her man. So, I made up my mind to capture her, and do my best not to kill him. But it's out of the question on the Yamashina stage road. So I managed to lure the couple into the mountains.

It was quite easy. I became their traveling companion, and I told them there was an old mound in the mountain over there, and that I had dug it open and found many mirrors and swords. I went on to tell them I'd buried the things in a grove behind the mountain, and that I'd like to sell them at a low price to anyone who would care to have them. Then . . . you see, isn't greed terrible? He was beginning to be moved by my talk before he knew it. In less than half an hour they were driving their horse toward the mountain with me.

When he came in front of the grove, I told them that the treasures were buried in it, and I asked them to come and see. The man had no objection—he was blinded by greed. The woman said she would wait on horseback. It was natural for her to say so, at the sight of a thick grove. To tell you the truth, my plan worked just as I wished, so I went into the grove with him, leaving her behind alone.

The grove is only bamboo for some distance. About fifty yards ahead there's a rather open clump of cedars. It was a convenient spot for my purpose. Pushing my way through the grove, I told him a plausible lie that the treasures were buried under the cedars. When I told him this, he pushed his laborious way toward the slender cedar visible through the grove. After a while the bamboo thinned out, and we came to where a number of cedars grew in a row. As soon as we got there, I seized him from behind. Because he was a trained, sword-bearing warrior, he was quite strong, but he was taken by surprise, so there was no help for him. I soon

---

[4] *Bodhisattva:* A Buddhist holy person.

tied him up to the root of a cedar. Where did I get the rope? Thank heaven, being a robber, I had a rope with me, since I might have to scale a wall at any moment. Of course it was easy to stop him from calling out by gagging his mouth with fallen bamboo leaves.

When I disposed of him, I went to his woman and asked her to come and see him, because he seemed to have been suddenly taken sick. It's needless to say that this plan also worked well. The woman, her sedge hat[5] off, came into the depths of the grove, where I led her by the hand. The instant she caught sight of her husband, she drew a small sword. I've never seen a woman of such violent temper. If I'd been off guard, I'd have got a thrust in my side. I dodged, but she kept on slashing at me. She might have wounded me deeply or killed me. But I'm Tajomaru. I managed to strike down her small sword without drawing my own. The most spirited woman is defenseless without a weapon. At least I could satisfy my desire for her without taking her husband's life.

Yes, . . . without taking his life. I had no wish to kill him. I was about to run away from the grove, leaving the woman behind in tears, when she frantically clung to my arm. In broken fragments of words, she asked that either her husband or I die. She said it was more trying than death to have her shame known to two men. She gasped out that she wanted to be the wife of whichever survived. Then a furious desire to kill him seized me. (Gloomy excitement.)

Telling you in this way, no doubt I seem a crueler man than you. But that's because you didn't see her face. Especially her burning eyes at that moment. As I saw her eye to eye, I wanted to make her my wife even if I were to be struck by lightning. I wanted to make her my wife . . . this single desire filled my mind. This was not only lust, as you might think. At that time if I'd had no other desire than lust, I'd surely not have minded knocking her down and running away. Then I wouldn't have stained my sword with his blood. But the moment I gazed at her face in the dark grove, I decided not to leave there without killing him.

But I didn't like to resort to unfair means to kill him. I untied him and told him to cross swords with me. (The rope that was found at the root of the cedar is the rope I dropped at the time.) Furious with anger, he drew his thick sword. And quick as thought, he sprang at me ferociously, without speaking a word. I needn't tell you how our fight turned out. The twenty-third stroke . . . please remember this. I'm impressed with this fact still. Nobody under the sun has ever clashed swords with me twenty strokes. (A cheerful smile.)

When he fell, I turned toward her, lowering my blood-stained sword. But to my great astonishment she was gone. I wondered to where she had run away. I looked for her in the clump of cedars. I listened, but heard only a groaning sound from the throat of the dying man.

As soon as we started to cross swords, she may have run away through the grove to call for help. When I thought of that, I decided it was a matter of life and death to me. So, robbing him of his sword, and bow and arrows, I ran out to the mountain road. There I found her horse still grazing quietly. It would be a mere waste of words to tell you the later details, but before I entered town I had already

---

[5] *sedge hat:* Straw hat.

parted with the sword. That's all my confession. I know that my head will be hung in chains anyway, so put me down for the maximum penalty. (A defiant attitude.)

THE CONFESSION OF A WOMAN WHO HAS COME TO THE *SHIMIZU* TEMPLE[6]

That man in the blue silk kimono, after forcing me to yield to him, laughed mockingly as he looked at my bound husband. How horrified my husband must have been! But no matter how hard he struggled in agony, the rope cut into him all the more tightly. In spite of myself I ran stumblingly toward his side. Or rather I tried to run toward him, but the man instantly knocked me down. Just at that moment I saw an indescribable light in my husband's eyes. Something beyond expression . . . his eyes make me shudder even now. That instantaneous look of my husband, who couldn't speak a word, told me all his heart. The flash in his eyes was neither anger nor sorrow . . . only a cold light, a look of loathing. More struck by the look in his eyes than by the blow of the thief, I called out in spite of myself and fell unconscious.

In the course of time I came to, and found that the man in blue silk was gone. I saw only my husband still bound to the root of the cedar. I raised myself from the bamboo-blades with difficulty, and looked into his face; but the expression in his eyes was just the same as before.

Beneath the cold contempt in his eyes, there was hatred. Shame, grief, and anger . . . I didn't know how to express my heart at that time. Reeling to my feet, I went up to my husband.

"Takejiro," I said to him, "since things have come to this pass, I cannot live with you. I'm determined to die, . . . but you must die, too. You saw my shame. I can't leave you alive as you are."

This was all I could say. Still he went on gazing at me with loathing and contempt. My heart breaking, I looked for his sword. It must have been taken by the robber. Neither his sword nor his bow and arrows were to be seen in the grove. But fortunately my small sword was lying at my feet. Raising it over head, once more I said, "Now give me your life. I'll follow you right away."

When he heard these words, he moved his lips with difficulty. Since his mouth was stuffed with leaves, of course his voice could not be heard at all. But at a glance I understood his words. Despising me, his look said only, "Kill me." Neither conscious nor unconscious, I stabbed the small sword through his lilac-colored kimono into his breast.

Again at this time I must have fainted. By the time I managed to look up, he had already breathed his last—still in bonds. A streak of sinking sunlight streamed through the clump of cedars and bamboos, and shone on his pale face. Gulping down my sobs, I untied the rope from his dead body. And . . . and what has become of me since I have no more strength to tell you. Anyway I hadn't the strength to die. I stabbed my own throat with the small sword, I threw myself into a pond at the foot of the mountain, and I tried to kill myself in many ways.

---

[6] Shimizu *Temple:* Famous temple in Shimizu, a town in south-central Honshu.

Unable to end my life, I am still living in dishonor. (A lonely smile.) Worthless as I am, I must have been forsaken even by the most merciful Kwannon.[7] I killed my own husband. I was violated by the robber. Whatever can I do? Whatever can I . . . I . . . (Gradually, violent sobbing.)

THE STORY OF THE MURDERED MAN, AS TOLD THROUGH A MEDIUM

After violating my wife, the robber, sitting there, began to speak comforting words to her. Of course I couldn't speak. My whole body was tied fast to the root of a cedar. But meanwhile I winked at her many times, as much as to say "Don't believe the robber." I wanted to convey some such meaning to her. But my wife, sitting dejectedly on the bamboo leaves, was looking hard at her lap. To all appearances, she was listening to his words. I was agonized by jealousy. In the meantime the robber went on with his clever talk, from one subject to another. The robber finally made his bold, brazen proposal. "Once your virtue is stained, you won't get along well with your husband, so won't you be my wife instead? It's my love for you that made me be violent toward you."

While the criminal talked, my wife raised her face as if in a trance. She had never looked so beautiful as at that moment. What did my beautiful wife say in answer to him while I was sitting bound there? I am lost in space, but I have never thought of her answer without burning with anger and jealousy. Truly she said, . . . "Then take me away with you wherever you go."

This is not the whole of her sin. If that were all, I would not be tormented so much in the dark. When she was going out of the grove as if in a dream, her hand in the robber's, she suddenly turned pale, and pointed at me tied to the root of the cedar, and said, "Kill him! I cannot marry you as long as he lives." "Kill him!" she cried many times, as if she had gone crazy. Even now these words threaten to blow me into the bottomless abyss of darkness. Has such a hateful thing come out of a human mouth ever before? Have such cursed words ever struck a human ear, even once? Even once such a . . . (A sudden cry of scorn). At these words the robber himself turned pale. "Kill him," she cried, clinging to his arms. Looking hard at her, he answered neither yes or no . . . but hardly had I thought about his answer before she had been knocked down into the bamboo leaves. (Again a cry of scorn.) Quietly folding his arms, he looked at me and said, "What will you do with her? Kill her or save her? You have only to nod. Kill her?" For these words alone I would like to pardon his crime.

While I hesitated, she shrieked and ran into the depths of the grove. The robber instantly snatched at her, but he failed even to grasp her sleeve.

After she ran away, he took up my sword, and my bow and arrows. With a single stroke he cut one of my bonds. I remember his mumbling, "My fate is next." Then he disappeared from the grove. All was silent after that. No, I heard some-one crying. Untying the rest of my bonds, I listened carefully, and I noticed that it was my own crying. (Long silence.)

---

[7] *Kwannon:* Buddhist goddess of mercy.

I raised my exhausted body from the root of the cedar. In front of me there was shining the small sword which my wife had dropped. I took it up and stabbed it into my breast. A bloody lump rose to my mouth, but I didn't feel any pain. When my breast grew cold, everything was silent as the dead in their graves. What profound silence! Not a single bird-note was heard in the sky over this grave in the hollow of the mountains. Only a lonely light lingered on the cedars and mountains. By and by the light gradually grew fainter, till the cedars and bamboo were lost to view. Lying there, I was enveloped in deep silence.

Then someone crept up to me. I tried to see who it was. But darkness had already been gathering round me. Someone . . . that someone drew the small sword softly out of my breast in its invisible hand. At the same time once more blood flowed into my mouth. And once and for all I sank down into the darkness of space.

UNDERSTANDING THE STORY

1. Why do the husband, the wife, and the thief all claim to have done the stabbing?

2. Consider the testimony of (a) the thief, (b) the wife, and (c) the husband. Do you believe each character's testimony? What does he or she have to gain from the testimony? What does he or she have to lose? How would you have expected him or her to have reacted?

3. What **themes** do you find in the story?

ANALYZING LITERARY TECHNIQUE

1. Why does Akutagawa choose to tell the story from various points of view? What does his choice of **narrative perspective** achieve?

2. Why does the author leave the mystery unsolved?

3. What is the function of **irony** in the story?

4. Why does the author include the testimonies of minor characters: the woodcutter, the priest, the policeman, and the old woman?

WRITING ABOUT LITERATURE

1. Take one of the three participants (husband, wife, or thief) and analyze the extent to which his or her story is a reliable account of the incident.

2. Create an objective version of the story that explains what occurred and why. For example, the film director Kurosawa tells the story from the perspective of a woodcutter who observes the series of events while concealed behind some bushes.

The Grasshopper
and the
Bell Cricket

YASUNARI KAWABATA

*Y*ASUNARI KAWABATA (1899–1972) was the first
Japanese writer to win the Nobel Prize for literature (1968).
He is known for his miniature *Palm-of-the-Hand Stories*
(1930, 1950, 1964); his short stories "Of Birds and Beasts" (1933) and
"One Arm" (1964); and three novels, *The Izu Dancer* (1926), which
brought him lasting fame as the author of one of the first modern
Japanese novels; *The Snow Country* (1937), which some consider to
be his most important work; and *The Sound of the Mountain* (1952),
which others consider to be his masterpiece.

Kawabata was born in Osaka. His father, a doctor, died when he
was two; his mother died when he was three, his grandmother when
he was eight, and his older sister when he was ten. He lived with his
grandfather until his grandfather died when Kawabata was sixteen.
Kawabata considered himself to be a "master of funerals," and his
lonely childhood left lasting effects upon his life.

Kawabata was fifteen years old when he decided that he would
become a novelist. The diary that he kept a during his grandfather's
last days received critical acclaim when he published it eleven years
later under the title "Diary of a Sixteen-Year-Old." Throughout his
high-school and college years, his stories were published in literary
magazines.

In 1924 Kawabata graduated from the Tokyo Imperial University
with a major in English literature. He wrote monthly book reviews
from 1922 until 1938, becoming an important literary critic who
influenced the careers of many young writers. In his own fiction, he
revolted against the style called Japanese naturalism that was popular
in the 1920s because he believed that literature should record the
beauty in the world and that a more lyrical and subjective style was
necessary to achieve this goal.

Kawabata's *Palm-of-the-Hand Stories* (stories that are small enough to fit into the palm of one's hand) reflect his preoccupation with beauty. In these stories, Kawabata takes the essence of haiku and sets it in prose. He captures a moment in time—with its single emotion, idea, or atmosphere—and fashions it into an epiphany, a sudden and profound revelation that emanates from the moment but moves beyond it. "The Grasshopper and the Bell Cricket," written in 1924, is a fine example of Kawabata's ability to create atmosphere and tone. In his words, it is a story where "the poetic spirit of my young days lives on."

Walking along the tile-roofed wall of the university, I turned aside and approached the upper school. Behind the white board fence of the school playground, from a dusky clump of bushes under the black cherry trees, an insect's voice could be heard. Walking more slowly and listening to that voice, and feeling reluctant to part with it, I turned right so as not to leave the playground behind. When I turned to the left, the fence gave way to an embankment planted with orange trees. At the corner, I exclaimed with surprise. My eyes gleaming at what they saw up ahead, I hurried forward with short steps.

At the base of the embankment was a bobbing cluster of beautiful varicolored lanterns, such as one might see at a festival in a remote country village. Without going any farther, I knew that it was a group of children on an insect chase among the bushes of the embankment. There were about twenty lanterns. Not only were there crimson, pink, indigo, green, purple, and yellow lanterns, but one lantern glowed with five colors at once. There were even some little red store-bought lanterns. But most of the lanterns were beautiful square ones that the children had made themselves with love and care. The bobbing lanterns, the coming together of children on this lonely slope—surely it was a scene from a fairy tale?

One of the neighborhood children had heard an insect sing on this slope one night. Buying a red lantern, he had come back the next night to find the insect. The night after that, there was another child. This new child could not buy a lantern. Cutting out the back and front of a small carton and papering it, he placed a candle on the bottom and fastened a string to the top. The number of children grew to five, and then to seven. They learned how to color the paper that they stretched over the windows of the cutout cartons, and to draw pictures on it. Then these wise child-artists, cutting out round, three cornered, and lozenge leaf shapes in the cartons, coloring each little window a different color, with circles and diamonds, red and green, made a single and whole decorative pattern. The child with the red lantern discarded it as a tasteless object that could be bought at a store. The child who had made his own lantern threw it away because the design was too simple. The pattern of light that one had had in hand the night before was unsatisfactory the morning after. Each day, with cardboard, paper, brush, scissors, penknife, and glue, the children made new lanterns out of their hearts and minds. Look at my lantern! Be the most unusually beautiful!

And each night, they had gone out on their insect hunts. These were the twenty children and their beautiful lanterns that I now saw before me.

Wide-eyed, I loitered near them. Not only did the square lanterns have old-fashioned patterns and flower shapes, but the names of the children who had made them were cut in squared letters of the syllabary.[1] Different from the painted-over red lanterns, others (made of thick cutout cardboard) had their designs drawn onto the paper windows, so that the candle's light seemed to emanate from the form and color of the design itself. The lanterns brought out the shadows of the bushes like dark light. The children crouched eagerly on the slope wherever they heard an insect's voice.

"Does anyone want a grasshopper?" A boy, who had been peering into a bush about thirty feet away from the other children, suddenly straightened up and shouted.

"Yes! Give it to me!" Six or seven other children came running up. Crowding behind the boy who had found the grasshopper, they peered into the bush. Brushing away their outstretched hands and spreading out his arms, the boy stood as if guarding the bush where the insect was. Waving the lantern in his right hand, he called again to the other children.

"Does anyone want a grasshopper? A grasshopper!"

"I do! I do!" Four or five more children came running up. It seemed you could not catch a more precious insect than a grasshopper. The boy called out a third time.

"Doesn't anyone want a grasshopper?"

Two or three more children came over.

"Yes. I want it."

It was a girl, who just now had come up behind the boy who'd discovered the insect. Lightly turning his body, the boy gracefully bent forward. Shifting the lantern to his left hand, he reached his right hand into the bush.

"It's a grasshopper."

"Yes. I'd like to have it."

The boy quickly stood up. As if to say "Here!" he thrust out his fist that held the insect at the girl. She, slipping her left wrist under the string of her lantern, enclosed the boy's fist with both hands. The boy quietly opened his fist. The insect was transferred to between the girl's thumb and index finger.

"Oh! It's not a grasshopper. It's a bell cricket!" The girl's eyes shone as she looked at the small brown insect.

"It's a bell cricket! It's a bell cricket!" The children echoed in an envious chorus.

"It's a bell cricket. It's a bell cricket."

Glancing with her bright intelligent eyes at the boy who had given her the cricket, the girl opened the little insect cage hanging at her side and released the cricket in it.

---

[1] *syllabary:* A set of written characters, each of which represents a syllable rather than a letter.

"It's a bell cricket."

"Oh, it's a bell cricket," the boy who'd captured it muttered. Holding up the insect cage close to his eyes, he looked inside it. By the light of his beautiful many-colored lantern, also held up at eye level, he glanced at the girl's face.

Oh, I thought, I felt slightly jealous of the boy, and sheepish. How silly of me not to have understood his actions until now! Then I caught my breath in surprise. Look! It was something on the girl's breast that neither the boy who had given her the cricket, nor she who had accepted it, nor the children who were looking at them noticed.

In the faint greenish light that fell on the girl's breast, wasn't the name "Fujio" clearly discernable? The boy's lantern, which he held up alongside the girl's insect cage, inscribed his name, cut out in the green papered aperture, onto her white cotton kimono. The girl's lantern, which dangled loosely from her wrist, did not project its pattern so clearly, but still one could make out, in a trembling patch of red on the boy's waist, the name "Kiyoko." This chance interplay of red and green—if it was chance or play—neither Fujio nor Kiyoko knew about.

Even if they remembered forever that Fujio had given her the cricket and that Kiyoko had accepted it, not even in dreams would Fujio ever know that his name had been written in green on Kiyoko's breast or that Kiyoko's name had been inscribed in red on his waist, nor would Kiyoko ever know that Fujio's name had been inscribed in green on her breast or that her own name had been written in red on Fujio's waist.

Fujio! Even when you have become a young man, laugh with pleasure at a girl's delight when, told that it's a grasshopper, she is given a bell cricket; laugh with affection at a girl's chagrin when, told that it's a bell cricket, she is given a grasshopper.

Even if you have the wit to look by yourself in a bush away from the other children, there are not many bell crickets in the world. Probably you will find a girl like a grasshopper whom you think is a bell cricket.

And finally, to your clouded, wounded heart, even a true bell cricket will seem like a grasshopper. Should that day come, when it seems to you that the world is only full of grasshoppers, I will think it a pity that you have no way to remember tonight's play of light, when your name was written in green by your beautiful lantern on a girl's breast.

UNDERSTANDING THE STORY

1. What is the role of surprise in the story?

2. Why is the story about children? To what extent, if any, would adults serve just as well?

3. What does the children's attitude about their lanterns reveal about them?

4. What does Fujio's repeated question ("Does anyone want a grasshopper?") reveal about him? What does this repeated question contribute to the story?

5. How does Fujio feel when Kiyoko reveals that the grasshopper is actually a bell cricket?

6. Consider Kawabata's three uses of lantern light (a) bobbing; (b) illuminating; and (c) reflecting. What does each use contribute to the story?

7. What does the narrator's point of view add to the story?

ANALYZING LITERARY TECHNIQUE

1. How does the story's setting contribute to its **tone?**

2. How does Kawabata's choice of **narrative perspective** contribute to the tone of the story?

3. How does the narrator's use of **apostrophe** contribute to the tone of the story?

4. How does **irony** function in the story?

5. How does Kawabata's use of **symbols** relate to his **theme?**

6. What is the function of **repetition** in the story? Consider two or three examples.

WRITING ABOUT LITERATURE

1. Write an essay in which you analyze how Kawabata uses the play of light in this story. Consider (a) bobbing lanterns; (b) illuminating light; and (c) reflected light. Use quotations from the story to support your ideas.

2. Write an essay in which you analyze how Kawabata achieves the tone of this story. Consider his use of three of the following techniques: (a) setting; (b) narrative perspective; (c) apostrophe; and (d) irony. Use quotations from the story to support your ideas.

3. Describe your real or imagined observation of a special moment. It may involve people, an aspect of nature, or an aspect of your community. Use detail to convey what you see so that your readers will react as you reacted to your experience.

Life

SHEN CONGWEN

*S*HEN CONGWEN (1902–1988), otherwise known as Shen Ts'ung-wen, is one of China's greatest writers. He is renowned both for his depiction of the rural peoples and countryside of Hunan Province and for his beautiful prose, which many people consider to be the finest literary Chinese ever written. It was Shen Congwen's goal to transform modern spoken Chinese into a literary language. He succeeded by creating a broad vocabulary and new literary styles that would convey both lyricism and satire in prose. He wrote more than thirty-five volumes of short stories and novellas as well as travelogues, personal essays, literary criticism, and poetry. Among his works best known in China are *The Long River* (1945) and the short-story collections *Lamp of Spring* (1943) and *Black Phoenix* (1943). Two English translations of his work appeared later, *The Chinese Earth* (1947) and *The Border Town and Other Stories* (1981). A collection of short stories that is representative of Shen Congwen's entire literary career, *Imperfect Paradise,* appeared in 1995.

Shen Congwen was born Shen Yuehuan, in the western province of Hunan. He trained for a career in the military and became a foot soldier. In this capacity, he was able to observe, with the eye of a born storyteller, the rich landscape of Southern China as well as the local color—the customs and the way of speaking—of the various ethnic groups who lived in Hunan.

Shen Congwen arrived in Peking (now Beijing), in northeastern China, at the age of twenty. He began his career as a writer by publishing short pieces in Peking's magazines and newspapers. In the 1920s and 1930s, a new generation of urban young people, the first to view themselves as "modern," became his enthusiastic readers. The literary work of major Western writers, available in translation, was causing intellectuals like himself to become more aware of the social conditions that prevailed in his nation, particularly in rural areas where people lived in poverty and continued to practice old customs. His stories reveal his deep sympathy for these rural people as he depicts their emotional responses to their struggles. The world is one in which Fate often determines whether love and joy can take root and flower or whether the buds are doomed to die on the vine.

It is a tragedy for world literature that Shen Congwen became a victim of political oppression. He lived through the Communist revolution (the red terror), the National counterrevolution (the white terror), and the war with Japan. Beginning in 1928 and continuing through the Sino-Japanese War (1937–45), Congwen taught "exercises in composition" in universities. Although his fiction continued to reveal his enduring empathy with the poor and downtrodden, he never joined a political party.

Nevertheless, when the Communists came into power in China in 1949, they snuffed out Shen Congwen's brilliant literary life. The Chinese Nationalists, in Taiwan, were quick to follow. Until Mao Ze-dong's (Mao Tse-tung's) death in 1976, Shen Congwen's name was obliterated from all textbooks, his literary work was banned, and he was forbidden to teach. Both the Communist and the Nationalist parties viewed him as being disloyal to China because he would not use his influence on their behalf.

When the Communist government forced Shen Congwen to undergo "thought reform" by participating in a political reeducation program, he found that he was unable to write in a politically correct manner. Therefore in 1949 he gave up his career as a writer. The emotional toll on Shen Congwen resulted in a complete mental breakdown; however, he finally recovered, and in 1955 he began his new career as a research scholar at the National Palace Museum in Beijing, where he became the chief curator in charge of the study of the material culture of ancient China—a pursuit that was conveniently remote from contemporary politics.

After the death of Mao Ze-dong, Shen Congwen's name and his literary work were reinstated, and he acquired international fame. In 1980, at the age of seventy-eight, he traveled abroad for the first time. At this time, in preparation for the 1983 publication of his collected works, he began a careful revision of the fiction that he had not touched for at least thirty years.

Shen Congwen's characteristic insight into human nature as well as his gifts as a stylist are evident in the short story "Life," written in 1933. It is set at Shisha Lakes, an old area on the north side of Peking where visitors could watch performers, such as jugglers and acrobats. On the surface, the story reflects Shen Congwen's sympathy for the poor person who needs to muster whatever ability he possesses in the hope of winning a meager reward to purchase an equally meager meal. However, the story concludes with a set of surprises that permits a second related story to surface. Subject and style are so inextricably interwoven in this story that a close analysis of character, plot, and literary technique will enable the reader to understand and appreciate the extraordinary nature of Shen Congwen's talent and accomplishment.

In the Shisha Lakes district of Peking there was a landfill area at the southern end of the Qianhai where residents dumped cinders from their stoves. A band of people with time on their hands had gathered there in the sun to see what was going on, for the least bit of commotion was enough to collect a crowd.

Sssss. . . .

The sound was like the ripping of silk or a firecracker going off. A toy with wings of brightly colored paper spiraled into the air, lofted on a wire held by the vendor. All the different faces turned skyward to watch. It was a tiny airplane, flying up and coming down. In the air it caught the attention of those standing farther away. For this little plane had especially bright colors, characteristic of toys made in Peking.

After reaching a certain height, the toy plane would slowly descend, like a parachute. Usually it landed somewhere on the field, where it could be collected and sent up on another mission. But, if the angle of the launch was askew, it would land elsewhere; sometimes a breeze would get it entangled in the tops of the willow trees, or land it on the white awning of one of the many stalls, or even on the straw hat of an innocent bystander. It was so light that the person could be unaware of it and continue walking. A group of noisy children would then follow him like a pack of dogs, laughing and yelling until he finally caught on. And then he would snatch the object from his hat and throw it on the ground, whereupon the children would fight over it and forget the passerby completely.

It cost three cents to send this little airplane into the air. Anyone willing to pay the price could do it and could do it over and over again until the little plane was lost.

As more people reached into their pockets for coins to fly the plane, a smile appeared on the toy vendor's face. He soon disappeared, counting his money, into the Lake View Teahouse, a place to drink tea and listen to Peking opera. The crowd disappeared as quickly as it had gathered. Soon only lotus pods littered the site. The pods were normally light green on the outside and pale green on the inside, but some were also brown on the outside.

An old man past sixty walked onto the grounds carrying two large puppets, half life size and joined to each other. He looked around at the empty site and knew that this was not a good place to put on his show. But he had little choice.

Laying his puppets down under the bright sun, he picked up a lotus pod and felt its contents, then coughed a little to test his voice. He didn't have a gong or drum. He had only those two joined puppet bodies, crudely made and stiff as boards, one with a black face, the other with a white face. That was all. Nor did he have an audience.

The old man looked around the landfill with his bloodshot little eyes. It was so hot and the location so bad, he knew that, without a few tricks to attract an audience, he could never hope to get anyone to watch his show. The old man looked at the white face and spoke to it gently in a low voice, as if comforting himself.

"Wang Jiu,[1] don't you worry. People will come. Look at these lotus pods; they're signs that our honored guests are on their way. We'll wait a while and then perform for them. If we do a good job, there's no need to worry that these gentlemen won't spare us a few coppers. If the show is good, the gentlemen will go home and tell their children, Hey, Wang Jiu and Zhao Si[2] are really good wrestlers. They grapple with each other, trip each other up, and throw each other around, all under the hot July sun, and they don't even sweat."

"It's true, you don't sweat," he said, mumbling to Wang Jiu. "Hot as all get out, and still you don't sweat, or even get tired. Good fellow!"

Finally a single person came over, looking like he was testing the waters before a dive. He wore a striped shirt with his shirttails hanging out, like he was one of those sloppy college students from the city. And he had that frail, sickly look of a scholar from bygone days.

The old man gave the Peking student the once-over and smiled at him, thinking that his savior had arrived. His whole body came alive, like a young person's. He moved his arms up and down while the college student stood there looking the puppets in the face, as if studying them. The old man started muttering again, speaking to the white-faced character as devotedly as a father to his son.

"Look, Wang Jiu, the honored young masters and mistresses haven't arrived yet, but this gentleman is here. All right, let's begin, for I'm sure this gentleman won't leave. You better be careful; don't let Zhao Si get the better of you. This gentleman will be on your side, watching you trip up bad old Zhao Si. This gentleman won't go away."

The old man stood the puppet body up and smoothed its tattered old gown. Next, he took out two wooden puppet legs and tied them so they hung down from his own belt. When everything was set, he lifted up the puppet torso, hunched over, and crawled inside its outfit. Hidden under the puppets' clothing, he then put his arms into the false legs, one for each character, adjusted their position, and began to act out the part of two men wrestling there in the ash field. He jumped, he slid, and used his own feet to try to trip the false legs of the other puppet. Though he could not see the puppet outfit he was wearing or even his audience, the result was extremely lifelike.

The college student flashed a sad smile. And, quite a distance away, someone else noticed what was going on here. He came over out of curiosity. The second member of the audience had arrived.

Soon the third had rushed over, and so on, up to thirteen.

The crowd of people come to watch the puppets fight grew bigger, until the performers were surrounded on all four sides.

The crowd was roaring with laughter. From under his clothing the old man could barely make out the feet and legs of the people who had gathered around to watch. Then he used Wang Jiu's real leg and tripped up Zhao Si. The outer

---

[1] *Wang Jiu:* Wang the Ninth.
[2] *Zhao Si:* Zhao the Fourth.

puppet and the old man who was acting out the other puppet by hiding under his clothes both fell into a heap on the dusty ground. There was a burst of laughter on the field, and this comic little scene came to an end.

The old man slowly crawled out of the dirty, tattered clothing, revealing a head of graying hair. His face was all red and sweating, but there was a smile written across it, a tired smile.

After he was out of the puppets' clothing, he stood the puppets up again and mumbled to himself, "Good work, Wang Jiu! You did it. Look, I told you that honored guests were on their way over to watch you, and don't you see them all before you now. Now that you have played your part so well and thrown Zhao Si, our honored guests are sure to favor us with fistfuls of their spare change, and we'll be able to satisfy ourselves with some *wowotou*.[3] Look at your face—you look like a young lady. Are you tired? Is the sun too hot for you?"

Wiping his brow with a corner of his shirt as he spoke, he said, "Come on, how about another round if you're so good. Some day we'll go to Nanjing[4] for the national boxing competition and show those Southerners a thing or two."

The crowd burst into laughter again.

As he was about to step into the puppet suit again, a pock-faced policeman responsible for assessing sideshow concession fees pushed his way up from behind.

The policeman thought this act of one man wrestling himself was interesting, so he kept quiet and watched from the front row. But, as the old man turned around in his hunched-over position, he saw those thick leather boots and quickly assessed the position and importance of this member of the audience. The old man immediately pretended that Zhao Si was out of breath. He went limp and slid to the ground in a pile.

The old man quickly stepped out of his suit and smiled ingratiatingly at the policeman, as if to say, "Sir, how do you do, how do you do, *nin hao, nin hao*." He took his hands out of the false legs and said softly to Wang Jiu, with self-deprecating humor, "See, our honored guest has indeed come. He wears a brown uniform and holds a pad of receipts for collecting his four-cent fees on floating concessions. He knows very well that we can't afford a simple wheatcake to fill our stomachs."

Looking at the people, he continued, "These people have come to watch us wrestle. It's really hot. But our honored guests are just standing there. Wait just one moment, and we'll begin."

He eyed the policeman, but he didn't have a cent on him, so, after a moment, he looked at the sizable crowd that had gathered and began to bow and solicit money. "Honored guests, my apologies for the delay in this hot weather. Those who have some change on you, please spare us a little. Those whose wallets are empty, please stay around and give us moral support."

Some in the crowd threw him a coin or two, but the others just stood still and looked on. Then a young army officer tossed a handful of coins before walking away with a frown on his face. The old man had to walk to the edge of the crowd

---

[3] wowotou: Cornmeal muffins of the coarsest grade.
[4] *Nanjing:* City in Eastern China on the Chang River.

to pick them up. Because he still had the legs of the puppet tied to his waist, they moved this way and that as he walked, which the crowd found uproarious.

The policeman had already made a mark on the piece of paper and was preparing to give it to the old man. The puppeteer looked it over, quickly counted out four coins in his hand, and gave them to the policeman. Murmuring, "Wang Jiu, Wang Jiu," the policeman went away with a smirk on his face. When he had left, the old man rolled up the receipt and stuck it behind his ear. He said to the puppet, "Wang Jiu, four cents isn't much, is it? You're hot, are you? You aren't even sweating. But look at the poor policeman. He sweats a lot because he has to walk all over the place!" At this point, he thought about the sweat on his own head. He crouched down and used Wang Jiu's shirt to wipe his own sweat, hoping to elicit a laugh from his audience. But no one laughed.

The old man belonged to that class of people in society that performed for others. They acted and sang, not because they were especially good, but because people came to watch them, out of curiosity and pity. When it came time to pay, those who could afford it paid without hesitation, but in every case, as soon as something new began elsewhere, the crowd would suddenly dissolve and move on.

At a concession selling lotus fruits under the shade of the willows, a person had fallen down unconscious from heat stroke. No one knew what had happened, but, because someone had run over there, a crowd of people followed. In a moment, half the crowd that was watching the puppet show disappeared. Those remaining also seemed to notice the hot sun beating down on their heads. They, too, began to leave.

The college student who looked as if he were testing the waters before a dive also seemed to remember that he had something to do. He disappeared into the crowd along the road.

Now there were only seven people left.

The old man looked around and smiled. Without a word, he clasped his hands together and crouched down again to pick up his puppet. He put the puppet clothing over his head, placed his arms through the puppet's legs, then shook his shoulders and began the same act all over again. His strange motions attracted four more people, but soon five others left. When a real fight broke out elsewhere, the rest of the people left in a hurry.

The old man continued with his act. He lifted up the false legs, making it look as if Wang Jiu had lifted Zhao Si's entire body. He energetically tipped his shoulders to the right and to the left, as if the two puppets were viciously attacking each other. Finally, after the fierce struggle, he would fall down, always in the same way. It was, of course, Wang Jiu who had defeated Zhao Si.

When the old man emerged from the heap of old, tattered clothing, there was only one observer left, a short policeman who stood there with a smile on his face. But he loomed especially large and appeared particularly happy, for he was the only one there.

The old man went up to him, bowed, and felt for the receipt he had stuck behind his ear. It had disappeared. Searching for it in the pile of clothing where the puppets were, he found it on the ground. Instead of inspecting it, the policeman just looked with a silly grin at the pair of false legs tied to the old man's waist and walked away, shaking his head.

The old man sat down on the ground in the same posture as the puppets and counted the money in his can. He smiled at the white-faced puppet, Wang Jiu, speaking to him in the same tone of voice he had used to capture his audience, and with the same self-deprecating humor. His voice was affectionate and tender. He did not want people to know that he had had a son named Wang Jiu, a son who died in a fight with Zhao Si. He never told anyone. He only let the people see the fight between them. Although he kept Wang Jiu at a disadvantage, giving Zhao Si the upper hand at first, it was Wang Jiu who always won in the end.

Wang Jiu had been dead for ten years now, and the old man had been performing this act all over Peking for about as long. As to the real Zhao Si, he had died of hepatitis in Baoding prefecture five long years ago.

UNDERSTANDING THE STORY

1. What qualities does the puppeteer possess? How does the author reveal each quality?

2. What role do the puppets perform in the puppeteer's life?

3. How does the final paragraph affect the story?

4. In the final sentence, how does the author imply that the puppeteer is unaware that Zhao Si has been dead for five years?

5. In what way is "Life" an appropriate title?

6. What **themes** do you find in this story?

ANALYZING LITERARY TECHNIQUE

1. Why does the author begin with the toy vendor if his story is about the puppeteer?

2. From whose **point of view** is this story told? What is the advantage of this point of view? How would this story be different if it were told from the point of view of the puppeteer? Of a member of the audience?

3. Analyze the author's use of detail. Consider the following descriptions: (a) the toy vendor's airplanes; (b) the person collapsing from heat stroke; (c) the young army officer who leaves with a frown on his face and the pock-faced policeman who leaves with a smirk on his face. What does each contribute to the story?

4. What is the **climax** of the story?

5. How does the author **foreshadow** the climax? What effect does foreshadowing have upon the **characterization** of the puppeteer?

6. Find two examples of the author's use of **irony** and explain what each example contributes to the story.

7. Describe the **tone** of this story. How does the author achieve it?

WRITING ABOUT LITERATURE

1. Write an expository essay in which you analyze the story as it would be told from three points of view: (a) the omniscient author, (b) the puppeteer, and (c) a member of audience. In your introductory paragraph, explain the significance of point of view. In the next three paragraphs, discuss the three possible points of view, noting the similarities and differences as well as the advantages and disadvantages. In your concluding paragraph, explain the advantages of the point of view from which this story is told.

2. Write an expository essay in which you analyze the author's use of foreshadowing in this story. In your opening paragraph, discuss the technique of foreshadowing. In the body of your essay, use quotations from the story that foreshadow the conclusion. Conclude your essay by explaining how foreshadowing enriches the author's characterization of the puppeteer.

3. Write a character sketch of the puppeteer. Choose three adjectives that describe his personality and use quotations from the story to support each adjective. In your introductory paragraph, state the subject of your essay. In a second sentence, mention the three aspects of the puppeteer's personality that you will be discussing. Devote one paragraph to your analysis of each quality. As part of your analysis, explain the way in which the quotation that you have chosen supports the quality that you have chosen. In your concluding paragraph, evaluate the puppeteer on the basis of the three qualities that you have analyzed.

4. Write a story in which a personal tragedy affects the way a person lives. Give the story a surprise ending; however, foreshadow whatever surprise you devise.

A Certain Night

TING LING

*T*ING LING (1904–1985), who also wrote under the pen name Chiang Ping-chih, is one of modern China's most famous writers. She is known for her commitment to women's rights and for her courageous stand against all forms of social injustice. She is best known for "Miss Sophie's Diary" (1928); "When I Was in Xia Village" (1940); "In the Hospital" (1941), a criticism of communist corruption; and *The Sun Shines over the Sangkan River* (1949), a prize-winning novel about land reform.

Ting Ling (or Ding Ling) was born into an upper-class well-educated family in Linli, in the province of Hunan; she was named Jiang Bingzhi. After her father died when she was four, her mother broke with tradition and trained to become a teacher in a new education system that advocated a more democratic society and gender equality. Ting Ling was educated in girls' schools that were a product of this new system. She was fifteen years old when the May Fourth Movement of 1919 introduced Western thought and literature to China. In the foreword to the English edition of her short stories, she states:

> If I had not been influenced by Western literature I would probably not have been able to write fiction. . . . My earliest stories followed the path of Western realism, and not only in their form: the thinking behind them was to some extent influenced by Western democracy. A little later, as the Chinese revolution developed, my fiction changed with the needs of the age and of the Chinese people.

The publication of "Miss Sophie's Diary" brought Ting Ling national fame. In 1930 she joined the League of Left-Wing Writers and edited its magazine. Then, after joining the Communist Party, she introduced an early form of social realism into her stories about the lives of peasants and workers. In 1942, following the publication of an essay in which she advocated women's rights, Mao Tse-tung proclaimed that communist ideology must be the major principle in the arts. Ting Ling was then removed from all positions of authority in literary and women's organizations. In 1958 she became the principal target in a major campaign against dissident writers. Her famous stories "When I Was in Xia Village" and "In the Hospital" were now condemned as "poisonous weeds." She was declared a political nonperson and sent to a "reform-through-labor camp" in the northern wilds of Manchuria, where she remained for twenty years. At first she was permitted to continue her writing. However, in 1966 Red Guards destroyed all her work, subjected her to public humiliation, and put her into solitary confinement for several years.

In 1978, two years after the deaths of Chou En-Lai and Mao Tse-tung, Ting Ling was released from the labor camp. She was suffering from malnourishment and cancer. The heroines in her last works are women who achieve a sense of identity and self-esteem by serving in the Communist Party.

"A Certain Night," written in 1933, is Ting Ling's fictional account of the death of her husband. Having become a communist activist, he was executed by the nationalist police early in 1931.

A muffled tramp of feet.

A group of figures, too many to be counted, came into the square from the hall that was lit with bluish electric lights. The heavy tramp of boots and shoes in the thick snow. The ferocious wind of a winter's night lashing their faces with the rain that had been falling for a fortnight and with large snowflakes. The sudden onslaught of the cold wind made them all shiver in their hearts, but they tramped on.

Another howling blast of wind mercilessly flailed their bodies and faces. In the middle of them all, surrounded and driven along by a huge escort, came one man, a slight young man looking handsome and at the same time drawn. The shock seemed to wake him up. Everything that had happened in the past or just a moment ago seemed set out before him, at a great distance and very clearly. That cunning face, malicious and smug, a round face, a face with a revolting moustache of the sort imperialists wear; and an evil voice giving a forced laugh. From where he sat up on high he had given him such an arrogant and uninhibited stare. "Have you anything else to say?" he had asked, then continued, "You have been given your sentences and they will be executed immediately." When the young man remembered this a fire that could have consumed him started up in his heart. He had wanted to rip that face to shreds and smash the voice to smithereens. In his wild fury he almost longed to push his way out through the men crowding round him and start walking fast and vigorously. Just now, when he had been suddenly condemned to death without any trial, he had not stayed calm like the rest of his comrades, but had passed out, overwhelmed by extreme anger and pain.

He was a passionate poet, loyal and hard-working.

A rifle butt thudded hard into his chest, which was even more emaciated than usual after twenty days of being kept on short rations and going hungry in the dark and sunless prison.

"What are you in such a hurry for, . . . you? Death's waiting for you. You'll get yours." A murderous-looking soldier started swearing at him after breaking the silence by hitting him.

The manacles and fetters on his hands and feet clanked repulsively, as did those on other hands and feet. Then there was even more noise around him as iron-soled boots tramped harder in the snow.

He now understood some more, and realized where he was now being taken. A strange thought came into his head. Above his eyes he could see another pair of eyes, a pair of beloved and unforgettable eyes that could always see his soul. He was very clearly aware of something deep in his heart that was pricking him then agonizingly tearing his flesh and blood inch by inch.

The sky was black, boundlessly black, and from it fell rain and snow while the north wind howled. The world was grey, like fog, and the deathly grey was reflected in the night by the snow. The people were black figures moving silently across the snow. Amid the sound of shackles and bayonets none of the escorts or prisoners spoke, groaned, sighed, or wept. They moved without interruption to the square that had been secretly turned into a temporary execution ground.

". . . the swine," thought some of them. "Where are they taking us to bump us off?"

A woman comrade in the second rank kept shaking her thick mop of hair as if she were angry. It was because the wind kept blowing her short hair across her forehead and eyes.

The young man forced himself by biting his lips hard not to give a wild and rending final shout. He was shaking with a fury that he could not express and glaring all around with a look of hatred so fierce that it hurt him, looking for something as if he wished he could devour it all, looking at one person and then at another.

The dim light of the snow shone on the man next to him, a fierce-browed soldier, and on another stupid soldier with his mouth and nostrils open wide, and on . . . Suddenly he saw a familiar and friendly face, which showed him a calm, kindly expression, an expression that spoke volumes, an expression of consolation and encouragement that only comrades can give each other as they face their death. Most of his hatred and regrets disappeared. Affection and something else that can only be called life filled his wounded chest. All he wanted to do was to hug that face and kiss it. He replied to the expression with a much braver and a more resolute nod.

The tramp of feet, a loud and untidy noise in the darkness, was like the irregular pounding of victory drums crowded all around them, and the twenty-five of them, as they walked ahead. Above their heads the wind was roaring and soughing, as if a great red banner were waving above them.

"Halt! This is the place. Where d'you think you're going, you . . . ?" The chief executioner was armed and struck his Mauser pistol hard as he shouted in a firm voice with all his intimidating might.

"We're there," was the thought that echoed in many minds.

"Line the criminals up! Tie them up," The loathsome and vicious order came from the chief executioner's throat, and the soldiers in their padded greatcoats pushed them clumsily and hard, hitting them with rifle butts and putting ropes round their chests to tie them to the stakes behind them. There was an even louder noise of leather boots and shoes in the snow.

They said not a word, holding hard to their anger and their silence because they could no longer find any way of expressing their hatred for these enemies. Their hands and feet were now shackled and they were each tied fast to a wooden post that had been driven in days earlier.

Darkness stretched out in front of them, wind, rain and snow kept blowing into their faces, and the bone-chilling cold was mercilessly lashing their bodies, from which the warm scholars' gowns and overcoats had been ripped off in the hall. But they did not feel cold.

They were standing in a close-packed row.

"Here, over here a bit. Aim straight. . . ."

In the darkness of the night a group of men could just be made out in front of them carrying and moving around something heavy.

"Right. Here will do. Count the criminals."

"One, two, three. . . ." A soldier walked up to them and started counting.

The chief executioner, his face set in an ugly cast, followed the soldier along the row of prisoners, bending his fingers as he counted.

At the sight of that ugly and vicious face, which seemed to symbolize the cruelty of all the rulers to the oppressed, an angry fire started to burn in his heart again. The fire hurt his eyes and his whole body. He longed to be able to punch and kill the cur, but he had been tied up tightly with his hands behind him. All he could do was to grind his teeth in hatred, his whole body shaking with fury.

"Courage, comrade," said a comrade standing to his right.

He turned and saw that it was a familiar face: the man with whom he had talked a great deal at supper.

"It's not that. I'm rather worked up."

". . . twenty-three, twenty-four, twenty-five. Correct. Right. . . ."

The men who were counting started yelling and stamping hard in the snow as they moved towards the object that had been set up.

Boundless emptiness, wind, snow, grey, darkness. . . .

Human forms looked big and heavy against the deathly pale grey.

"Very well. Ready. Wait for my order."

So shouted the chief executioner.

All hearts tensed, pulled like bowstrings. The heavy death-like thing stood in front of them, carefully guarded by several soldiers. The sky was about to fall and the darkness to crush them, the twenty-five.

Someone started shouting in a loud voice:

"Arise, comrades. Don't forget that although we're going to die now a great congress is being held elsewhere today, and our government is going to be formed today. We must celebrate the creation of our government. Long live our government!"

With that they all broke out into wild shouts. There had been many things in their minds that they had forgotten to say or express. Only now did they suddenly realize, which was why they were all shouting at the tops of their voices the slogans they wanted to shout, dispelling the darkness. What spread out in front of them was the brilliance of a new state being founded.

As a whistle blew shrilly a mighty sound rose from twenty-five voices starting to sing:

"Arise, ye prisoners of starvation. . . ."[1]

There was a rattle of fire as the heavy object raked along the whole length of the row, firing several dozen rounds.

The singing was quieter, but some voices were now even louder:

"It is the final struggle. . . ."

The whistle blew again.

Another rattle of fire as the row was raked for a second time with several more rounds.

The more bullets that were fired, the quieter was the singing. There were now only a few voices still shouting.

"The Interna . . ."

The whistle blew for the third time and the third burst of firing began. With the sounds of the bullets the singing stopped.

"Try singing now, . . . you bastards." The chief executioner swore at them with an air of satisfaction, then walked back the way they had come, giving his orders:

"Put the gun away, and get back to the barracks as soon as you can. The bodies can be buried tomorrow morning. The dead can't run away."

With that he walked back towards the hall.

Several dozen soldiers once again tramped noisily through the snow as they returned.

The night was silent, hushed, solemn. Large snowflakes and fine drops of rain were swirling around. The wild, winter wind blew first one way then another. Snow piled up on the head that hung forward, only to be dispersed by the wind. None of them said anything, tied there in silence. In a few places, in one, two, three . . . places, blood was flowing and falling on the snow in the darkness.

When will it be light?

---

[1] "*Arise . . . starvation*": Lines from "Internationale," a revolutionary socialist hymn.

UNDERSTANDING THE STORY

1. To what extent, if any, does the narrator think that these men and women deserve to die?

2. How does the narrator distinguish between the nationalists and the communists so that the reader knows who is to be admired?

3. How do the nationalists regard the condemned prisoners? Why?

4. How does the young poet's attitude toward his death change in the course of the story?

5. Why did Ting Ling write this story? To what extent, if any, did she honor the memory of her husband?

6. What **themes** do you find in this story?

ANALYZING LITERARY TECHNIQUE

1. What is the **tone** of the story? How does Ting Ling achieve it?

2. How does the **setting** of the story contribute to the tone?

3. What are the main **symbols** in this story? How do they function?

4. What do the trampling feet **connote?** Why does Ting Ling repeat this image?

WRITING ABOUT LITERATURE

1. Write an essay in which you analyze the ways in which this story reflects a political bias. Conclude with an evaluation of the story's effectiveness as propaganda. Use quotations from the story to support your ideas.

2. Tell this story from the point of view of a nationalist soldier. How does the soldier justify his attitudes and his behavior?

Downtown

FUMIKO HAYASHI

*F*UMIKO HAYASHI (1904–1951) was the most popular female writer in Japan from 1932 until her death. She was a talented, prodigious writer of short stories and novels, publishing nine full-length novels and numerous short stories in the last two years of her life. Her last novel, *Floating Clouds* (1951), and the short stories "Late Chrysanthemum" (1948) and "Downtown"[1] (1949) are considered her best works.

Hayashi was the child of an itinerant dry-goods peddler and his wife. Her childhood was spent moving from place to place. In spite of her abject poverty and rootless life, Hayashi possessed a vitality and a love of life that remained with her throughout her life.

With a high-school education, Hayashi moved to Tokyo and tried unsuccessfully to support herself. She worked as a waitress in cheap cafes, a children's maid, a clerk in the office of a stockbroker, a painter of plastic toys in a factory, an assistant in a maternity hospital, a street vendor, and an itinerant peddler. Often she was so poor that she was homeless and close to starvation. Nevertheless, in her spare time, she wrote short stories, poems, and tales for children.

Hayashi's first novel, *A Vagabond's Story*, was published in 1930, after appearing serially in *Women and the Arts* magazine. It was realistic, effective, and autobiographical. In 1931 Hayashi used the money she earned for the novel to buy a ticket to Paris by way of the Trans-Siberian Railway. During the following months, she wrote travel articles for leading Japanese magazines. During World War II, Hayashi worked as a correspondent in Southeast Asia. After returning home in 1943, she adopted a little boy; she moved with him to Tokyo soon after the war ended. Her writing after the war created her literary reputation. By the time she died, Hayashi had achieved popularity, high critical regard, and wealth. She had written over 270 books.

---

[1] *Downtown:* The title of this story, as translated by Ivan Morris, is "Downtown." This story has appeared elsewhere under the title "Tokyo."

Hayashi always wrote about poor people, whom she depicted with realism and compassion. Her principal characters are usually humble women from the lower classes in Tokyo who, despite their hardships, are determined to survive and have faith in the future. Ryo, in "Downtown," is a typical Hayashi protagonist.

It was a bitter, windy afternoon. As Ryo hurried down the street with her rucksack, she kept to the side where the pale sun shone down over the roofs of the office buildings. Every now and then she looked about curiously—at a building, at a parked car—at one of those innumerable bomb sites scattered through downtown Tokyo.

Glancing over a boarding, Ryo saw a huge pile of rusty iron, and next to it a cabin with a glass door. A fire was burning within, and the warm sound of the crackling wood reached where she was standing. In front of the cabin stood a man in overalls with a red kerchief about his head. There was something pleasant about this tall fellow, and Ryo screwed up her courage to call out, "Tea for sale! Would you like some tea, please?"

"Tea?" said the man.

"Yes," said Ryo with a nervous smile. "It's Shizuoka tea."[2]

She stepped in through an opening in the boarding and, unfastening the straps of her rucksack, put it down by the cabin. Inside she could see a fire burning in an iron stove; from a bar above hung a brass kettle with a wisp of steam rising from the spout.

"Excuse me," said Ryo, "but would you mind if I came in and warmed myself by your stove a few minutes? It's freezing out, and I've been walking for miles."

"Of course you can come in," said the man. "Close the door and get warm."

He pointed towards the stool, which was his only article of furniture, and sat down on a packing case in the corner. Ryo hesitated a moment. Then she dragged her rucksack into the cabin and, crouching by the stove, held up her hands to the fire.

"You'll be more comfortable on that stool," said the man, glancing at her attractive face, flushed in the sudden warmth, and at her shabby attire.

"Surely this isn't what you usually do—hawk tea from door to door?"

"Oh yes, it's how I make my living," Ryo said. "I was told that this was a good neighborhood, but I've been walking around here since early morning and have only managed to sell one packet of tea. I'm about ready to go home now, but I thought I'd have my lunch somewhere on the way."

"Well, you're perfectly welcome to stay here and eat your lunch," said the man. "And don't worry about not having sold your tea," he added, smiling. "It's all a matter of luck, you know! You'll probably have a good day tomorrow."

---

[2] *Shizuoka tea:* Tea from a major tea-producing region of Honshu in Japan.

The kettle came to a boil with a whistling sound. As he unhooked it from the bar, Ryo had a chance to look about her. She took in the boarded ceiling black with soot, the blackboard by the window, the shelf for family gods on which stood a potted sakaki tree. The man took a limp-looking packet from the table, and unwrapping it, disclosed a piece of cod. A few minutes later the smell of baking fish permeated the cabin.

"Come on," said the man. "Sit down and have your meal."

Ryo took her lunch box out of the rucksack and seated herself on the stool.

"Selling things is never much fun, is it?" remarked the man, turning the cod over on the grill. "Tell me, how much do you get for a hundred grams of that tea?"

"I should get thirty-five yen[3] to make any sort of a profit. The people who send me the stuff often mix in bad tea, so I'm lucky if I can get thirty yen."

In Ryo's lunch box were two small fish covered with some boiled barley and a few bean-paste pickles. She began eating.

"Where do you live?" the man asked her.

"In the Shitaya district. Actually, I don't know one part of Tokyo from another! I've only been here a few weeks and a friend's putting me up until I find something better."

The cod was ready now. He cut it in two and gave Ryo half, adding potatoes and rice from a platter. Ryo smiled and bowed slightly in thanks, then took out a bag of tea from her rucksack and poured some into a paper handkerchief.

"Do put this into the kettle," she said, holding it out to him.

He shook his head and smiled, showing his white teeth.

"Good Lord no! It's far too expensive."

Quickly Ryo removed the lid and poured the tea in before he could stop her. Laughing, the man went to fetch a teacup and a mug from the shelf.

"What about your husband?" he asked, while ranging them on the packing case. "You're married, aren't you?"

"Oh yes, I am. My husband's still in Siberia.[4] That's why I have to work like this."

Ryo's thoughts flew to her husband, from whom she had not heard for six years; by now he had come to seem so remote that it required an effort to remember his looks, or the once-familiar sound of his voice. She woke up each morning with a feeling of emptiness and desolation. At times it seemed to Ryo that her husband had frozen into a ghost in the subarctic Siberia—a ghost, or a thin white pillar, or just a breath of frosty air. Nowadays no one any longer mentioned the war and she was almost embarrassed to let people know that her husband was still a prisoner.

"It's funny," the man said. "The fact is, I was in Siberia myself! I spent three years chopping wood near the Amur River[5]—I only managed to get sent home

---

[3] *yen:* Japanese unit of money.

[4] *Siberia:* Ryo's husband is a prisoner of war being held in the Soviet Union.

[5] *Amur River:* The river forms part of the border between the Soviet Union and Manchuria in northeastern China and flows through the eastern part of Siberia.

last year. Well, it's all in a matter of luck! It's tough on your husband. But it's just as tough on you."

"So you've really been repatriated from Siberia! You don't seem any the worse for it," Ryo said.

"Well, I don't know about that!" the man shrugged his shoulders. "Anyway, as you see, I'm still alive."

Ryo closed her lunch box, and as she did so, she studied him. There was a simplicity and directness about this man that made her want to talk openly in a way that she found difficult with more educated people.

"Got any kids?" he said.

"Yes, a boy of six. He should be at school, but I've had difficulty getting him registered here in Tokyo. These officials certainly know how to make life complicated for people!"

The man untied his kerchief, wiped the cup and the mug with it, and poured out the steaming tea.

"It's good stuff this!" he said, sipping noisily.

"Do you like it? It's not the best quality, you know: only two hundred and ten yen a kilo wholesale. But you're right—it's quite good."

The wind had grown stronger while they were talking; it whistled over the tin roof of the cabin. Ryo glanced out the window, steeling herself for her long walk home.

"I'll have some of your tea—seven hundred and fifty grams," the man told her, extracting two crumbled hundred-yen notes from the pocket of his overalls.

"Don't be silly," said Ryo. "You can have it for nothing."

"Oh no, that won't do. Business is business!" He forced the money into her hand. "Well, if you're ever in this part of the world again, come in and have another chat."

"I should like to," said Ryo, glancing around the tiny cabin. "But you don't live here, do you?"

"Oh, but I do! I look after that iron out there and help load the trucks. I'm here most of the day."

He opened a door under the shelf, disclosing a sort of cubbyhole containing a bed neatly made up. Ryo noticed a colored postcard of the Fifty Bells of Yamada tacked to the back of the door.

"My, you've fixed it up nicely," she said smiling. "You're really quite snug here, aren't you?"

She wondered how old he could be.

2

From that day on, Ryo came regularly to the Yotsugi district to sell tea; each time she visited the cabin on the bomb site. She learned that the man's name was Tsuruishi Yoshio. Almost invariably he had some small delicacy waiting for her to put in her lunch box—a pickled plum, a piece of beef, a sardine. Her business began to improve and she acquired a few regular customers in the neighborhood.

A week after their first meeting, she brought along her boy, Ryukichi. Tsuruishi chatted with the child for a while and then took him out for a walk. When they returned, Ryukichi was carrying a large caramel cake.

"He's got a good appetite, this youngster of yours," said Tsuruishi, patting the boy's close-cropped head.

Ryo wondered vaguely whether her new friend was married; in fact she found herself wondering about various aspects of her life. She was now twenty-nine, and she realized with a start that this was the first time she had been seriously interested in any man but her husband. Tsuruishi's easy, carefree temperament somehow appealed to her, though she took great care not to let him guess that.

A little later Tsuruishi suggested taking Ryo and Ryukichi to see Asakusa[6] on his next free day. They met in front of the information booth in Ueno Station, Tsuruishi wearing an ancient gray suit that looked far too tight, Ryo clad in a blue dress of kimono material and a light-brown coat. In spite of her cheap clothes, she had about her something youthful and elegant as she stood there in the crowded station. Beside the tall, heavy Tsuruishi, she looked like a schoolgirl off on a holiday. In her shopping bag lay their lunch: bread, oranges, and seaweed stuffed with rice.

"Well, let's hope it doesn't rain," said Tsuruishi, putting his arm lightly round Ryo's waist as he steered her through the crowd.

They took the subway to Asakusa Station, then walked from the Matsuya Department Store to the Niten Shinto Gate past hundreds of tiny stalls. The Asakusa district was quite different from what Ryo had imagined. She was amazed when Tsuruishi pointed to a small red-lacquered temple and told her that this was the home of the famous Asakusa Goddess of Mercy. In the distance she could hear the plaintive wail of a trumpet and a saxophone emerging from some loud-speaker; it mingled strangely with the sound of the wind whistling through the branches of the ancient sakaki trees.

They made their way through the old-clothes market, and came to a row of food-stalls squeezed tightly against each other beside the Asakusa Pond; here the air was redolent with the smell of burning oil. Tsuruishi went to one of the stalls and bought Ryukichi a stick of yellow candy-floss. The boy nibbled at it, as the three of them walked down a narrow street plastered with American-style billboards advertising restaurants, movies, revues. It was less than a month since Ryo had first noticed Tsuruishi by his cabin, yet she felt as much at ease with him as if she had known him all her life.

"Well, it's started raining after all," he said, holding out his hand. Ryo looked up, to see scattered drops of rain falling from the gray sky. So their precious excursion would be ruined, she thought.

"We'd better go in there," said Tsuruishi, pointing to one of the shops, outside which hung a garish lantern with characters announcing the "Merry Teahouse." They took seats at a table underneath a ceiling decorated with artificial cherry blossoms. The place had a strangely unhomelike atmosphere, but they were

---

[6] *Asakusa:* A shopping and entertainment district of Tokyo.

determined to make the best of it and ordered a pot of tea; Ryo distributed her stuffed seaweed, bread, and oranges. It was not long before the meal was finished and by then it had started raining in earnest.

"We'd better wait till it lets up a bit," suggested Tsuruishi. "Then I'll take you home."

Ryo wondered if he was referring to her place or his. She was staying in the cramped apartment of a friend from her home town and did not even have a room to call her own; rather than go there, she would have preferred returning to Tsuruishi's cabin, but that too was scarcely large enough to hold three people. Taking out her purse, she counted her money under the table. The seven hundred yen should be enough to get shelter for a few hours at an inn.

"D'you know what I'd really like?" she said. "I'd like us to go to a movie and then find some inn and have a dish of food before saying good-bye to each other. But I suppose that's all rather expensive!"

"Yes, I suppose it is," said Tsuruishi, laughing. "Come on! We'll do it all the same."

Taking his overcoat off the peg, he threw it over Ryukichi's head, and ran through the downpour to a movie theatre. Of course there were no seats! Standing watching the film, the little boy went sound asleep, leaning against Tsuruishi. The air in the theatre seemed to get thicker and hotter every moment; on the roof they could hear the rain beating down.

It was getting dark as they left the theatre and hurried through the rain, which pelted down with the swishing sound of banana leaves in a high wind. At last they found a small inn where the landlord led them to a carpeted room at the end of a drafty passage. Ryo took off her wet socks. The boy sat down in a corner and promptly went back to sleep.

"Here, he can use this as a pillow," said Tsuruishi, picking up an old cushion from a chair and putting it under Ryukichi's head.

From an overflowing gutter above the window the water poured in a steady stream onto the courtyard. It sounded like a waterfall in some faraway mountain village.

Tsuruishi took out a handkerchief and began wiping Ryo's wet hair. A feeling of happiness coursed through her as she looked up at him. It was as if the rain had begun to wash away all the loneliness which had been gathering within her year after year.

She went to see if they could get some food and in the corridor met a maid in Western clothes carrying a tea tray. After Ryo had ordered two bowls of spaghetti, she and Tsuruishi sat down to drink their tea, facing each other across an empty brazier. Later Tsuruishi came and sat on the floor beside Ryo. Leaning their backs against the wall they gazed out at the darkening, rainy sky.

"How old are you, Ryo?" Tsuruishi asked her. "I should guess twenty-five."

Ryo laughed. "I'm afraid not, Tsuru, I'm already an old woman! I'm twenty-eight."

"Oh, so you're a year older than me."

"My goodness, you're young!" said Ryo, "I thought you must be at least thirty."

She looked straight at him, into his dark, gentle eyes with their bushy brows. He seemed to be blushing slightly. Then he bent forward and took off his wet socks.

The rain continued unabated. Presently the maid came with some cold spaghetti and soup. Ryo woke the boy and gave him a plate of soup; he was half asleep as he sipped it.

"Look, Ryo," Tsuruishi said, "we might as well all stay the night at this inn. You can't go home in this rain, can you?"

"No," said Ryo. "No, I suppose not."

Tsuruishi left the room and returned with a load of quilted bedrolls which he spread on the floor. At once the whole room seemed to be full of bedding. Ryo tucked up her son in one of the rolls, the boy sleeping soundly as she did so. Then she turned out the light, undressed, and lay down. She could hear Tsuruishi settling down at the other end of the room.

"I suppose the people in this inn think we're married," said Tsuruishi after a while.

"Yes, I suppose so. It's not very nice of us to fool them!"

She spoke in jest, but now that she lay undressed on her bedroll, she felt for the first time vaguely disturbed and guilty. Her husband for some reason seemed much closer than he had for years. But of course she was only here because of the rain, she reminded herself. . . . And gradually her thoughts began to wander pleasantly afield, and she dozed off.

When she awoke it was still dark. She could hear Tsuruishi whispering her name from his corner, and she sat up with a start.

"Ryo, Ryo, can I come and talk to you for a while?"

"No, Tsuru," she said, "I don't think you should."

On the roof the rain was still pattering down, but the force of the storm was over; only a trickle was dropping from the gutter into the yard. Under the sound of the rain she thought she could hear Tsuruishi sigh softly.

"Look Tsuru," she said after a pause. "I've never asked you before, but are you married?"

"No. Not now," Tsuruishi said.

"You used to be?"

"Yes. I used to be. When I got back from the army, I found that my wife was living with another man."

"Were you—angry?"

"Angry? Yes, I suppose I was. Still, there wasn't much I could do about it. She'd left me, and that was that."

They were silent again.

"What shall we talk about?" Ryo asked.

Tsuruishi laughed. "Well, there really doesn't seem to be anything special to talk about. That spaghetti wasn't very good, was it?"

"No, one certainly couldn't call it good. And they charged us a hundred yen each for it!"

"It would be nice if you and Ryukichi had your own room to live in, wouldn't it?" Tsuruishi remarked.

"Oh yes, it would be marvelous! You don't think we might find a room near you? I'd really like to live near you, Tsuru, you know."

"It's pretty hard to find rooms these days, especially downtown. But I'll keep a lookout and let you know. . . . You're such a wonderful person, Ryo!"

"Me?" said Ryo laughing. "Don't be silly!"

"Yes, yes, you're wonderful! . . . really wonderful!"

Ryo lay back on the floor. Suddenly she wanted to throw her arms around Tsuruishi, to feel his body close to hers. She did not dare speak for fear that her voice might betray her; her breath came almost painfully; her whole body tingled. Outside the window an early morning truck clattered past.

"Where are your parents, Tsuru?" she asked after a while.

"In the country near Fukuoka."[7]

"But you have a sister in Tokyo?"

"Yes. She's all alone, like you, with two kids to take care of. She's got a sewing machine and makes Western-style clothing. Her husband was killed several years ago in the war in China. War, always war!"

Outside the window Ryo could make out the first glimmer of dawn. So their night together was almost over, she thought unhappily. In a way she wished that Tsuruishi hadn't given up so easily, and yet she was convinced that it was best like this. If he had been a man she hardly knew, or for whom she felt nothing, she might have given herself to him with no afterthought. With Tsuruishi it would have been different—quite different.

"Ryo, I can't get to sleep." His voice reached her again. "I'm wide awake, you know. I suppose I'm not used to this sort of thing."

"What sort of thing?"

"Why—sleeping in the same room with a girl."

"Oh Tsuru, don't tell me that you don't have girl friends occasionally!"

"Only professional girl friends."

Ryo laughed. "Men have it easy! In some ways, at least. . . ."

She heard Tsuruishi moving about. Suddenly he was beside her, bending over her. Ryo did not move, not even when she felt his arms around her, his face against hers. In the dark her eyes were wide open, and before them bright lights seemed to be flashing. His hot lips were pressed to her cheek.

"Ryo . . . Ryo."

"It's wrong, you know," she murmured. "Wrong to my husband. . . ."

But almost at once she regretted the words. As Tsuruishi bent over her, she could make out the silhouette of his face against the lightening sky. Bowed forward like that, he seemed to be offering obeisance to some god. Ryo hesitated for a moment. Then she threw her warm arms about his neck.

---

[7] *Fukuoka:* Japanese town at the north end of Honshu.

3

Two days later Ryo set out happily with her boy to visit Tsuruishi. When she reached the bomb site, she was surprised not to see him before his cabin, his red kerchief tied about his head. Ryukichi ran ahead to find out if he were home and came back in a moment.

"There are strangers there, Mamma!"

Seized with panic, Ryo hurried over to the cabin and peered in. Two workmen were busy piling up Tsuruishi's effects in a corner.

"What is it, ma'am?" one of them said, turning his head.

"I'm looking for Tsuruishi."

"Oh, don't you know? Tsuruishi died yesterday."

"Died," she said. She wanted to say something more but no words would come.

She had noticed a small candle burning on the shelf for family gods, and now she was aware of its somber meaning.

"Yes," went on the man, "he was killed about eight o'clock last night. He went in a truck with one of the men to deliver some iron bars in Omiya,[8] and on their way back the truck overturned on a narrow bridge. He and the driver were both killed. His sister went to Omiya today with one of the company officials to see about the cremation."

Ryo stared vacantly before her. Vacantly she watched the two men piling up Tsuruishi's belongings. Beside the candle on the shelf, she caught sight of the two bags of tea he had bought from her that first day—could it be only two weeks ago? One of them was folded over halfway down; the other was still unopened.

"You were a friend of his, ma'am, I imagine? He was a fine fellow, Tsuru! Funny to think that he needn't have gone to Omiya at all. The driver wasn't feeling well and Tsuru said he'd go along to Omiya to help him unload. Crazy, isn't it—after getting through the war and Siberia and all the rest of it, to be killed like that!"

One of the men took down the postcard of the Fifty Bells of Yamada and blew the dust off it. Ryo stood looking at Tsuruishi's belongings piled on the floor—the kettle, the frying pan, the rubber boots. When her eyes reached the blackboard, she noticed for the first time a message scratched awkwardly in red chalk: "Ryo— I waited for you till two o'clock. Back this evening."

Automatically she bowed to the two men and swung the rucksack on her back. She felt numb as she left the cabin, holding Ryukichi by the hand, but as they passed the bomb site, the burning tears welled into her eyes.

"Did that man die, Mamma?"

"Yes, he died," Ryo said.

"Why did he die?"

"He fell into a river."

The tears were running down her cheeks now; they poured out uncontrollably as she hurried through the downtown streets. They came to an arched bridge over

---

[8] *Omiya*: Town just north of Tokyo.

the Sumida River,[9] crossed it, and walked along the bank in the direction of Hakuho.

"Don't worry if you get pregnant," Tsuruishi had told her that morning in Asakusa, "I'll look after you whatever happens, Ryo!" And later on, just before they parted, he had said, "I haven't got much money, but you must let me help you a bit. I can give you two thousand yen a month out of my salary." He had taken Ryukichi to a shop that specialized in foreign goods and bought him a baseball cap with his name written on it. Then the three of them had walked gaily along the streetcar lines, skirting the enormous puddles left by the rain. When they came to a milk bar, Tsuruishi had taken them in and ordered them each a big glass of milk. . . .

Now an icy wind seemed to have blown up from the dark river. A flock of waterfowl stood on the opposite bank, looking frozen and miserable. Barges moved slowly up and down the river.

"Mamma, I want a sketchbook. You said I could have a sketchbook."

"Later," answered Ryo, "I'll get you one later."

"But Mamma, we just passed a stall with hundreds of sketchbooks. I'm hungry, Mamma. Can't we have something to eat?"

"Later. A little later!"

They were passing a long row of barrack-like buildings. They must be private houses, she thought. The people who lived there probably all had rooms of their own. From one of the windows a bedroll had been hung out to air and inside a woman could be seen tidying the room.

"Tea for sale!" called out Ryo softly. "Best quality Shizuoka tea!"

There was no reply and Ryo repeated her call a little louder.

"I don't want any," said the woman. She pulled in the bedroll and shut the window with a bang.

Ryo went from house to house down the row calling her ware, but nobody wanted any tea. Ryukichi followed behind, muttering that he was hungry and tired. Ryo's rucksack dug painfully into her shoulders, and occasionally she had to stop to adjust the straps. Yet in a way she almost welcomed the physical pain.

4

The next day she went downtown by herself, leaving Ryukichi at home. When she came to the bomb site, she noticed that a fire was burning inside the cabin. She ran to the door and walked in. By Tsuruishi's stove sat an old man in a short workman's overcoat, feeding the flames with firewood. The room was full of smoke and it was billowing out of the window.

"What do you want?" said the old man, looking round.

"I've come to sell some Shizuoka tea."

"Shizuoka tea? I've got plenty right here."

---

[9] *Sumida River:* The Sumida flows through Tokyo into Tokyo Bay.

Ryo turned without a word and hurried off. She had thought of asking for the address of Tsuruishi's sister and of going to burn a stick of incense in his memory, but suddenly this seemed quite pointless. She walked back to the river, which reflected the late afternoon sun, and sat down by a pile of broken concrete. The body of a dead kitten was lying upside down a few yards away. As her thoughts went to Tsuruishi, she wondered vaguely whether it would have been better never to have met him. No, no, certainly not that! She could never regret knowing him, nor anything that had happened with him. Nor did she regret having come to Tokyo. When she had arrived, a month or so before, she had planned to return to the country if her business was unsuccessful, but now she knew that she would be staying on here in Tokyo—yes, probably right here in downtown Tokyo where Tsuruishi had lived.

She got up, swung the rucksack on her back, and walked away from the river. As she strolled along a side street, she noticed a hut which seemed to consist of old boards nailed haphazardly together. Going to the door, she called out, "Tea for sale! Would anyone like some tea?" The door opened and in the entrance appeared a woman dressed far more poorly than Ryo herself.

"How much does it cost?" asked the woman. And, then, seeing the rucksack, she added, "Come in and rest a while, if you like. I'll see how much money we've got left. We may have enough for some tea."

Ryo went in and put down her rucksack. In the small room four sewing women were sitting on the floor around an oil stove, working on a mass of shirts and socks. They were women like herself, thought Ryo, as she watched their busy needles moving in and out of the material. A feeling of warmth came over her.

UNDERSTANDING THE STORY

1. Describe the world in which Ryo lives. To what extent, if any, does this story reflect the situation of other people in other times and places?

2. What values remain in Ryo's world?

3. Why is Ryo "almost embarrassed" to tell people that her husband is still a prisoner of war?

4. Why does Ryo decide to remain in Tokyo after Tsuruishi dies?

5. To what extent, if any, would it have been better if Ryo had never met Tsuruishi?

6. To what extent, if any, is Ryo a sympathetic character?

7. What role does luck or fate play in the story?

8. What is Hayashi's attitude toward war?

9. What **themes** do you find in this story?

ANALYZING LITERARY TECHNIQUE

1. Relate the setting of the story to its **plot.**
2. What is the function of Tsuruishi in the story?
3. How does Hayashi use **irony?** What does it contribute to the story?
4. Describe the **tone** of the story. How does Hayashi create it?
5. Why did Hayashi call this story "Downtown" instead of "Ryo"?

WRITING ABOUT LITERATURE

1. Write a **characterization** of Ryo in which you show how Hayashi makes her a sympathetic character. Think of three adjectives to describe Ryo and include incidents from the story that support each of your choices. Be sure to relate Ryo's character to the time and place in which she lived.
2. Create a story that reveals what happens to Ryo after Hayashi's story ends. Consider the following questions: Does her husband return? Does she continue to live with her friend? Does she continue to sell tea? Is her son able to enter school?

Forty-Five a Month

R. K. NARAYAN

ASIPURAM KRISHNASWAMI NARAYAN (1906–2001) is India's most famous novelist and short-story writer. In addition to having written fourteen novels and five collections of short stories, Narayan has retold Indian legends in *Gods, Demons, and Others* (1964); *The Ramayana* (1972); and *The Mahabharata* (1978). His greatest novel, *The Guide* (1958), won India's highest literary prize. He also published several collections of short stories, including *Under the Banyan Tree* (1985) and *The Grandmother's Tale and Other Stories* (1993); and many novels, including his breakthrough autobiographical novel, *The English Teacher* (1945), and *The World of Nagaraj* (1990).

Born in Madras, in southern India, Narayan, a Hindu Brahman, was always interested in the myths and legends of the Indian people. For most of his life, he lived in Mysore, where he wrote in English about Malgudi, a fictional town in southern India. His first book, *Swami and Friends*, was published in 1935.

In writing about "the human comedy," Narayan reflects the mixture of tragic and comic that he believes characterizes human behavior and life. His compassion for ordinary people softens the ironic aspects of their lives. In his introduction to *Malgudi Days* (1982), the collection of short stories that includes "Forty-Five a Month," Narayan states:

> The material available to a story writer in India is limitless. Within a broad climate of inherited culture there are endless variations. . . . Under such conditions the writer has only to look out of the window to pick up a character (and thereby a story).

"Forty-Five a Month" reflects Narayan's humane values and his literary talent.

Shanta could not stay in her class any longer. She had done clay-modelling, music, drill, a bit of alphabets and numbers and was now cutting coloured paper. She would have to cut till the bell rang and the teacher said, "Now you may all go home," or "Put away the scissors and take up your alphabets—" Shanta was impatient to know the time. She asked her friend sitting next to her, "Is it five now?"

"Maybe," she replied.

"Or is it six?"

"I don't think so," her friend replied, "because night comes at six."

"Do you think it is five?"

"Yes."

"Oh, I must go. My father will be back at home now. He has asked me to be ready at five. He is taking me to the cinema this evening. I must go home." She threw down her scissors and ran up to the teacher. "Madam, I must go home."

"Why, Shanta Bai?"

"Because it is five o'clock now."

"Who told you it was five?"

"Kamala."

"It is not five now. It is—do you see the clock there? Tell me what the time is. I taught you to read the clock the other day." Shanta stood gazing at the clock in the hall, counted the figures laboriously and declared, "It is nine o'clock."

The teacher called the other girls and said, "Who will tell me the time from that clock?" Several of them concurred with Shanta and said it was nine o'clock, till the teacher said, "You are seeing only the long hand. See the short one, where is it?"

"Two and a half."

"So what is the time?"

"Two and a half."

"It is two forty-five, understand? Now you may all go to your seats—" Shanta returned to the teacher in about ten minutes and asked, "Is it five, madam, because I have to be ready at five. Otherwise my father will be very angry with me. He asked me to return home early."

"At what time?"

"Now." The teacher gave her permission to leave, and Shanta picked up her books and dashed out of the class with a cry of joy. She ran home, threw her books on the floor and shouted, "Mother, Mother," and Mother came running from the next house, where she had gone to chat with her friends.

Mother asked, "Why are you back so early?"

"Has Father come home?" Shanta asked. She would not take her coffee or tiffin[1] but insisted on being dressed first. She opened the trunk and insisted on wearing the thinnest frock and knickers, while her mother wanted to dress her

---

[1] *tiffin:* Midday snack.

in a long skirt and thick coat for the evening. Shanta picked out a gorgeous ribbon from a cardboard soap box in which she kept pencils, ribbons and chalk bits. There was a heated argument between mother and daughter over the dress, and finally Mother had to give in. Shanta put on her favourite pink frock, braided her hair and flaunted a green ribbon on her pigtail. She powdered her face and pressed a vermilion mark on her forehead. She said, "Now Father will say what a nice girl I am because I'm ready. Aren't you also coming, Mother?"

"Not today."

Shanta stood at the little gate looking down the street.

Mother said, "Father will come only after five; don't stand in the sun. It is only four o' clock."

The sun was disappearing behind the house on the opposite row, and Shanta knew that presently it would be dark. She ran in to her mother and asked, "Why hasn't Father come home yet, Mother?"

"How can I know? He is perhaps held up in the office."

Shanta made a wry face. "I don't like these people in the office. They are bad people—"

She went back to the gate and stood looking out. Her mother shouted from inside, "Come in, Shanta. It is getting dark, don't stand there." But Shanta would not go in. She stood at the gate and a wild idea came into her head. Why should she not go to the office and call out Father and then go to the cinema? She wondered where his office might be. She had no notion. She had seen her father take the turn at the end of the street every day. If one went there, perhaps one went automatically to Father's office. She threw a glance about to see if Mother was anywhere and moved down the street.

It was twilight. Everyone going about looked gigantic, walls of houses appeared very high and cycles and carriages looked as though they would bear down on her. She walked on the very edge of the road. Soon the lamps were twinkling, and the passers-by looked like shadows. She had taken two turns and did not know where she was. She sat down on the edge of the road biting her nails. She wondered how she was to reach home. A servant employed in the next house was passing along, and she picked herself up and stood before him.

"Oh, what are you doing here all alone?" he asked. She replied, "I don't know. I came here. Will you take me to our house?" She followed him and was soon back in her house.

Venkat Rao, Shanta's father, was about to start for his office that morning when a *jutka*[2] passed along the street distributing cinema handbills. Shanta dashed to the street and picked up a handbill. She held it up and asked, "Father, will you take me to the cinema today?" He felt unhappy at the question. Here was the child growing up without having any of the amenities and the simple life of pleasures of life. He had hardly taken her twice to the cinema. He had no time for the child. While children of her age in other houses had all the dolls, dresses and

---

[2] jutka: A two-wheeled horse-drawn carriage.

outings that they wanted, this child was growing up all alone and like a barbarian more or less. He felt furious with his office. For forty rupees[3] a month they seemed to have purchased him outright.

He reproached himself for neglecting his wife and child—even the wife could have her own circle of friends and so on: she was after all a grown-up, but what about the child? What a drab, colourless existence was hers! Every day they kept him at the office until seven or eight in the evening, and when he came home the child was asleep. Even on Sundays they wanted him at the office. Why did they think he had no personal life, a life of his own? They gave him hardly any time to take the child to the park or the pictures. He was going to show them that they weren't to toy with him. Yes, he was prepared even to quarrel with his manager if necessary.

He said with resolve, "I will take you to the cinema this evening. Be ready at five."

"Really! Mother!" Shanta shouted. Mother came out of the kitchen.

"Father is taking me to a cinema in the evening."

Shanta's mother smiled cynically. "Don't make false promises to the child—" Venkat Rao glared at her. "Don't talk nonsense. You think you are the only person who keeps promises—"

He told Shanta, "Be ready at five, and I will come and take you positively. If you are not ready, I will be very angry with you."

He walked to his office full of resolve. He would do his normal work and get out at five. If they started any old tricks of theirs, he was going to tell the boss, "Here is my resignation. My child's happiness is more important to me than these horrible papers of yours."

All day the usual stream of papers flowed onto his table and off it. He scrutinized, signed and drafted. He was corrected, admonished and insulted. He had a break of only five minutes in the afternoon for his coffee.

When the office clock struck five and the other clerks were leaving, he went up to the manager and said, "May I go, sir?" The manager looked up from his paper. "You!" It was unthinkable that the cash and account section should be closing at five. "How can you go?"

"I have some urgent private business, sir," he said, smothering the lines he had been rehearsing since this morning: "Herewith my resignation." He visualized Shanta standing at the door, dressed and palpitating with eagerness.

"There shouldn't be anything more urgent than the office work; go back to your seat. You know how many hours I work?" asked the manager. The manager came to the office nearly three hours before opening time and stayed nearly three hours after closing, even on Sundays. The clerks commented among themselves, "His wife must be whipping him whenever he is seen at home; that is why the old owl seems so fond of his office."

"Did you trace the source of that ten-eight difference?" asked the manager.

"I shall have to examine two hundred vouchers. I thought we might do it tomorrow."

---

[3] *rupees:* Indian unit of money.

"No, no, this won't do. You must rectify it immediately."

Venkat Rao mumbled, "Yes, sir," and slunk back to his seat. The clock showed 5:30. Now it meant two hours of excruciating search among vouchers. All the rest of the office had gone. Only he and another clerk in his section were working, and of course, the manager was there. Venkat Rao was furious. His mind was made up. He wasn't a slave who had sold himself for forty rupees outright. He could make that money easily; and if he couldn't, it would be more honourable to die of starvation.

He took a sheet of paper and wrote: "Herewith my resignation. If you people think you have bought me body and soul for forty rupees, you are mistaken. I think it would be far better for me and my family to die of starvation than slave for this petty forty rupees on which you have kept me for years and years. I suppose you have not the slightest notion of giving me an increment. You give yourselves heavy slices frequently, and I don't see why you shouldn't think of us occasionally. In any case it doesn't interest me now, since this is my resignation. If I and my family perish of starvation, may our ghosts come and haunt you all your life—" He folded the letter, put it in an envelope, sealed the flap and addressed it to the manager. He left his seat and stood before the manager. The manager mechanically received the letter and put it on his pad.

"Venkat Rao," said the manager, "I'm sure you will be glad to hear this news. Our officer discussed the question of increments today, and I've recommended you for an increment of five rupees. Orders are not yet passed, so keep this to yourself for the present." Venkat Rao put out his hand, snatched the envelope from the pad and hastily slipped it in his pocket.

"What is that letter?"

"I have applied for a little casual leave, sir, but I think . . ."

"You can't get any leave for at least a fortnight to come."

"Yes, sir, I realize that. That is why I am withdrawing my application, sir."

"Very well. Have you traced that mistake?"

"I'm scrutinizing the vouchers, sir. I will find it out within an hour. . . ."

It was nine o'clock when he went home. Shanta was already asleep. Her mother said, "She wouldn't even change her frock, thinking at any moment you might be coming and taking her out. She hardly ate any food; and wouldn't lie down for fear of crumpling her dress. . . ."

Venkat Rao's heart bled when he saw his child sleeping in her pink frock, hair combed and face powdered, dressed and ready to be taken out. "Why should I not take her to the night show?" He shook her gently and called, "Shanta, Shanta." Shanta kicked her legs and cried, irritated at being disturbed. Mother whispered, "Don't wake her," and patted her back to sleep.

Venkat Rao watched the child for a moment. "I don't know if it is going to be possible for me to take her out at all—you see, they are giving me an increment—" he wailed.

UNDERSTANDING THE STORY

1. Why does Venkat Rao agree to take Shanta to the movies?

2. To what extent, if any, does Venkat Rao think that Shanta is more deprived than she is?

3. If Venkat Rao is so unhappy about his financial situation, why doesn't he either quit or demand a larger increase in salary?

4. How does Venkat Rao's personality contribute to his problems?

5. What if Venkat Rao had taken the risk, resigned from his job, and found a job that gave him more free time but paid him less? Should he have taken it if it involved living less well? What if his family preferred the higher standard of living?

6. What **themes** do you find in this story?

ANALYZING LITERARY TECHNIQUE

1. Why does Narayan begin the story by focusing on Shanta instead of on the father?

2. What **narrative perspective** does Narayan use, and what does this perspective contribute to the story?

3. Give two examples of **foreshadowing** and explain their function.

4. How does Narayan use **irony** in this story?

5. Describe the **tone** of the story. How does Narayan achieve it?

WRITING ABOUT LITERATURE

1. Narayan states that his short stories either reveal a "pattern of existence" in someone's life or focus on a moment in time in which a "central character faces some kind of crisis and either resolves it or lives with it." To what extent, if any, does one of these descriptions apply to this story? Write a brief essay defending your point of view. Use quotations from the story to support your position.

2. Tell the story from Shanta's mother's point of view. What is her attitude toward her husband's job? Does she think that he is earning enough? Does she think that he should be working as hard as he does? Would she prefer that he quit and look for another job? Does she view herself and Shanta as deprived?

Pineapple Cake

ANITA DESAI

NITA DESAI (1937–) is India's preeminent imagist writer. Writing in English, she evokes the atmosphere of contemporary Indian society through concrete descriptions that rely on figurative language and visual images. Desai combines an insider's knowledge of Indian society with an outsider's objectivity. As she focuses on her characters' struggles with the situations they find themselves in, she alternates between objective photographic descriptions and subjective monologues that reveal her characters' inner thoughts and feelings. Desai is best known for her novels *Clear Light of Day* (1980), which is about an unhappy woman who gains insight into her own imperfection, and *Baumgartner's Bombay* (1989), which is about a German-Jewish refugee; her short story collection *Games at Twilight* (1978); and her children's book *The Village by the Sea* (1982), which is noted for its description of poverty.

Anita Desai was born Anita Mazumdar, in Mussoorie, India, in 1937 to a German-Jewish mother and a Bengali father. She graduated with honors from Delhi University in 1957, married in 1958, and became the mother of four children. In 1987 Desai came to the United States; she is currently a professor of English at Mount Holyoke College.

As a writer, Desai sets her fiction in modern India and focuses on the inner thoughts and feelings of her protagonists, who are usually women trying to cope with the complexities of Indian society. Some of these women are filled with despair because they feel smothered in a society that denies them independence. Some experience a conflict between themselves and their families or their communities as they search for identity. Others suffer because they live in a society where class distinction and social status are important.

"Pineapple Cake," which appears in *Games at Twilight*, is a fine introduction to Desai's thematic material as well as to her complex literary style. A mother and her young son are attending a wedding in India. Like a cinematographer who turns a camera on her subject,

Desai uses language to create living portraits of her two subjects from a double perspective—the objective perspective of an observer and the subjective opinion of the characters themselves. Desai creates a story that goes beyond the characters, the settings, and the situations. She combines character, setting, and plot to reveal how one event affects two participants. The following story is appealing because it reflects Desai's eye for significant detail, her wit, and her sympathy for her characters.

Victor was a nervous rather than rebellious child. But it made no difference to his mother: she had the same way of dealing with nerves and rebels.

"You like pineapple cake, don't you? Well, come along, get dressed quickly—yes, yes, the velvet shorts—the new shoes, yes—hurry—pineapple cake for good boys. . . ."

So it had gone all afternoon and, by holding out the bait of pineapple cake, his favourite, Mrs. Fernandez had the boy dressed in his new frilled shirt and purple velvet shorts and new shoes that bit his toes and had him sitting quietly in church right through the long ceremony. Or so she thought, her faith in pineapple cake being matched only by her faith in Our Lady of Mount Mary, Bandra Hill, Bombay. Looking at Victor, trying hard to keep his loud breathing bottled inside his chest and leaning down to see what made his shoes so vicious, you might have thought she had been successful, but success never satisfies and Mrs. Fernandez sighed to think how much easier it would have been if she had had a daughter instead. Little girls love weddings, little girls play at weddings, little girls can be dressed in can-can petticoats and frocks like crêpe-paper bells of pink and orange, their oiled and ringleted hair crowned with rustling wreaths of paper flowers. She glanced around her rather tiredly to hear the church rustling and crepitating with excited little girls, dim and dusty as it was, lit here and there by a blazing afternoon window of red and blue glass, a flare of candles or a silver bell breathless in the turgid air. This reminded her how she had come to this church to pray and light candles to Our Lady when she was expecting Victor, and it made her glance down at him and wonder why he was perspiring so. Yes, the collar of the frilled shirt was a bit tight and the church was airless and stuffy but it wasn't very refined of him to sweat so. Of course all the little boys in her row seemed to be in the same state—each one threatened or bribed into docility, their silence straining in their chests, soundlessly clamouring. Their eyes were the eyes of prisoners, dark and blazing at the ignominy and boredom and injustice of it all. When they shut their eyes and bowed their heads in prayer, it was as if half the candles in church had gone out, and it was darker.

Relenting, Mrs. Fernandez whispered, under cover of the sonorous prayer led by the grey padre in faded purple, "Nearly over now, Victor. In a little while we'll be going to tea—pineapple cake for you."

Victor hadn't much faith in his mother's promises. They had a way of getting postponed or cancelled on account of some small accidental lapse on his part. He might tear a hole in his sleeve—no pocket money. Or stare a minute too long at Uncle Arthur who was down on a visit from Goa and had a wen[1] on the back of his bald head—no caramel custard for pudding. So he would not exchange looks with her but stared stolidly down at his polished shoes, licked his dry lips and wondered if there would be Fanta or Coca-Cola at tea.

Then the ceremony came to an end. How or why, he could not tell, sunk so far below eye-level in that lake of breathless witnesses to the marriage of Carmen Maria Braganza of Goa and George de Mello of Byculla, Bombay. He had seen nothing of it, only followed, disconsolately and confusedly, the smells and sounds of it, like some underground creature, an infant mole, trying to make out what went on outside its burrow, and whether it was alarming or enticing. Now it was over and his mother was digging him in the ribs, shoving him out, hurrying him by running into his heels, and now they were streaming out with the tide. At the door he made out the purple of the padre's robes, he was handed a pink paper flower by a little girl who held a silver basket full of them and whose face gleamed with fanatic self-importance, and then he was swept down the stairs, held onto by his elbow and, once on ground level, his mother was making a din about finding a vehicle to take them to the reception at Green's. "The tea will be at Green's, you know," she had been saying several times a day for weeks now. "Those de Mellos must have money—they can't be so badly off—tea at Green's, after all."

It was no easy matter, she found, to be taken care of, for although there was a whole line of cabs at the kerb, they all belonged to the more important members of the de Mello and Braganza families. When Mrs. Fernandez realized this, she set her lips together and looked dangerously wrathful, and the party atmosphere began quickly to dissolve in the acid of bad temper and the threat to her dignity. Victor stupidly began a fantasy of slipping out of her hold and breaking into a toy shop for skates and speeding ahead of the whole caravan on a magic pair, to arrive at Green's before the bride, losing his mother on the way . . . But she found two seats, in the nick of time, in a taxi that already contained a short, broad woman in a purple net frock and a long thin man with an adam's apple that struggled to rise above his polka-dotted bow tie and then slipped down again with an audible croak. The four of them sat squeezed together and the women made little remarks about how beautiful Carmen Maria had looked and how the de Mellos couldn't be badly off, tea at Green's, after all. "Green's," the woman in the purple net frock yelled into the taxi driver's ear and gave her bottom an important shake that knocked Victor against the door. He felt that he was being shoved out, he was not wanted, he had no place here. This must have made him look peaked for his mother squeezed his hand and whispered, "You've been a good boy—pineapple cake for you." Victor sat still, not breathing. The man with the adam's apple stretched his neck longer and longer, swivelled his head about on the top of it and said nothing, but the frog in his throat gurgled to itself.

---

[1] *wen:* a growth or cyst.

Let out of the taxi, Victor looked about him at the wonders of Bombay harbour while the elders tried to be polite and yet not pay the taxi. Had his father brought him here on a Sunday outing, with a ferry boat ride and a fresh coconut drink for treats, he would have enjoyed the Arab dhows[2] with their muddy sails, the ships and tankers and seagulls and the Gateway of India like a coloured version of the photograph in his history book, but it was too unexpected. He had been promised pineapple cake at Green's, sufficiently overwhelming in itself—he hadn't the wherewithal to cope with the Gateway of India as well.

Instinctively he put out his hand to find his mother's and received another shock—she had slipped on a pair of gloves, dreadfully new ones of crackling nylon lace, like fresh bandages on her purple hands. She squeezed his hand, saying "If you want to do soo-soo, tell me, I'll find the toilet. Don't you go and wet your pants, man." Horrified, he pulled away but she caught him by the collar and led him into the hotel and up the stairs to the tea room where refreshments were to be served in celebration of Carmen Maria's and George de Mello's wedding. The band was still playing "Here Comes The Bride" when Victor and his mother entered.

Here there was a repetition of the scene over the taxi: this time it was seats at a suitable table that Mrs. Fernandez demanded, could not find, then spotted, was turned away from and, finally, led to two others by a slippery-smooth waiter used to such scenes. The tables had been arranged in the form of the letter E, and covered with white cloths. Little vases marched up the centres of the tables, sprouting stiff zinnias and limp periwinkles. The guests, chief and otherwise, seemed flustered by the arrangements, rustled about, making adjustments and readjustments, but the staff showed no such hesitations over protocol. They seated the party masterfully, had the tables laid out impeccably and, when the band swung into the "Do Re Mi" song from *The Sound of Music*, brought in the wedding cake. Everyone craned to see Carmen Maria cut it, and Victor's mother gave him a pinch that made him half-rise from his chair, whispering, "Stand up if you can't see, man, stand up to see Carmen Maria cut the cake." There was a burst of laughter, applause and raucous congratulation with an undertone of ribaldry that unnerved Victor and made him sink down on his chair, already a bit sick.

The band was playing a lively version of "I Am Sixteen, Going on Seventeen" when Victor heard a curious sound, as of a choked drain being forced. Others heard it too for suddenly chairs were being scraped back, people were standing up, some of them stepped backwards and nearly fell on top of Victor who hastily got off his chair. The mother of the bride, in her pink and silver gauzes, ran up, crying "Oh no, oh no, no, no!"

Two seats down sat the man with the long, thin neck in which an adam's apple rose and fell so lugubriously. Only he was no longer sitting. He was sprawled over his chair, his head hanging over the back in a curiously unhinged way, as though dangling at the end of a rope. The woman in the purple net dress was leaning over him and screaming "Aub, Aub, my darling Aubrey! Help my darling

---

[2] *dhows:* boats.

Aubrey!" Victor gave a shiver and stepped back and back till someone caught and held him.

Someone ran past—perhaps one of those confident young waiters who knew all there was to know—shouting "Phone for a doctor, quick! Call Dr. Patel," and then there was a long, ripping groan all the way down the tables which seemed to come from the woman in the purple net dress or perhaps from the bride's mother, Victor could not tell—"Oh, why did it have to happen *today?* Couldn't he have gone into another day?" Carmen Maria, the bride, began to sob frightenedly. After that someone grasped the long-necked old man by his knees and armpits and carried him away, his head and his shoes dangling like stuffed paper bags. The knot of guests around him loosened and came apart to make way for what was obviously a corpse.

Dimly, Victor realized this. The screams and sobs of the party-dressed women underlined it. So did the slow, stunned way in which people rose from the table, scraped back their chairs and retreated to the balcony, shaking their heads and muttering, "An omen, I tell you, it must be an omen." Victor made a hesitant move towards the balcony—perhaps he would see the hearse arrive.

But Victor's mother was holding him by the arm and she gave it an excited tug. "Sit *down,* man," she whispered furtively, "here comes the pineapple cake," and, to his amazement, a plate of pastries was actually on the table now—iced, coloured and gay. "Take it, take the pineapple cake," she urged him, pushing him towards the plate, and when the boy didn't move but stared down at the pastry dish as though it were the corpse on the red rexine sofa, her mouth gave an impatient twitch and she reached out to fork the pineapple cake onto her own plate. She ate it quickly. Wiping her mouth primly, she said, "I think we'd better go now."

UNDERSTANDING THE STORY

1. Note the opening sentence. Why does the author alert the reader to Victor's being "a nervous rather than rebellious child"?

2. Why does success never satisfy Mrs. Fernandez?

3. What do Mrs. Fernandez's experiences with the cab and at the wedding reception reveal about her?

4. Why does Mrs. Fernandez address her little boy as "man"?

5. How realistic is the response of the bride's mother to the crisis?

6. What is the role of the pineapple cake in this story? Why does Mrs. Fernandez eat the pineapple cake? What is revealed about Mrs. Fernandez and Victor by their responses to the cake?

7. Choose four scenes that characterize Victor and explain what each scene reveals about him.

8. Which character does Desai feel greater sympathy for? Why?

ANALYZING LITERARY TECHNIQUE

1. What does the opening sentence suggest about the presence of a **protagonist** and an **antagonist** in this story?

2. Why does the author give such a detailed picture of the various **settings** in this story?

3. Analyze Desai's **narrative perspective.** Note where she is objective and where she is subjective. What does her use of **interior monologue** achieve?

4. Analyze why Desai is called an **imagist** writer. List two examples of each of the following: (a) **similes,** (b) **metaphors,** (c) colors, (d) adjectives, and (e) verbs. Explain what these images contribute to the story.

5. What event marks the **crisis** in the story? The **climax?** The **resolution?** What is ironic about the end of the story?

6. What is the significance of the title? What does the closing **irony** contribute to the story as a whole?

7. Find two examples of each of the following techniques: (a) **humor,** (b) **satire,** and (c) **black humor.**

WRITING ABOUT LITERATURE

1. Write an expository essay in which you analyze Desai's **tone** in "Pineapple Cake." Find two examples of each of the following: (a) humor, (b) satire, and (c) black humor. Explain what each technique contributes to the tone of the story.

2. Write an expository essay in which you discuss why Desai is called an imagist. Examine the ways in which she uses language to describe a scene in the story. Consider her use of similes, metaphors, colors, adjectives, and verbs. Choose five examples of each category and explain why each example is effective.

3. Write a story in which a character attends a social function. Imagine that you are photographing or videotaping the scene. Use **figurative language** and effective adjectives and verbs to convey the atmosphere that you are observing. Try to make your description so vivid that your readers will be able to visualize the social function that you are describing.

A Way of Talking

PATRICIA GRACE

*P*ATRICIA GRACE (1937–) is a prizewinning Maori
author from New Zealand. Her short stories and novels
reflect the culture and values of the Maori people. Grace
has published four anthologies of short stories and five novels.
Waiariki, her first published work and the first collection of short stories by a female Maori author, appeared in 1975. Her first novel,
Mutuwhenua, followed in 1978. Her latest novel, *Dogside Story*, was
published in 2001. She has also written books for Maori children. Her
work, written in English, has been translated into several languages.

Grace was born in Wellington, New Zealand, in 1937. She has
taught in elementary and high schools; her interest is in teaching
English as a second language. Grace lives with her husband in
Plimmerton, near Wellington, and she is the mother of seven children.

The Maori, the native people of New Zealand, are Polynesian.
They probably arrived in New Zealand by canoe in the fourteenth
century. In her novels and stories, Grace focuses on the contemporary
lives of the Maori, both at home and in the broader world.

The following story, "A Way of Talking," demonstrates ways
people use and interpret language. Life at home is placed alongside
life in the outside world, and the story becomes a way of letting the
Maori people reveal something about themselves and their interaction with outsiders. The reader listens as the Maori speak among
themselves in a mixed language that reflects their oral tradition. To
enable "Pakeha" readers to gain an insight into what it is to be an outsider, Grace does not translate their Maori expressions.

Rose came back yesterday; we went down to the bus to meet her. She's just the same as ever, Rose. Talks all the time flat out and makes us laugh with her way of talking. On the way home we kept saying, "E Rohe, you're just the same as ever." It's good having my sister back and knowing she hasn't changed. Rose is the hard-case one in the family, the kamakama one, and the one with the brains.

Last night we stayed up talking till all hours, even Dad and Nanny who usually go to bed after tea. Rose made us laugh telling about the people she knows, and taking off professor this and professor that from varsity.[1] Nanny, Mum, and I had tears running down from laughing; e ta Rose, we laughed all night.

At last Nanny got out of her chair and said, "Time for sleeping. The mouths steal the time of the eyes." That's the lovely way she has of talking, Nanny, when she speaks in English. So we went to bed and Rose and I kept our mouths going for another hour or so before falling asleep.

This morning I said to Rose that we'd better go and get her measured for the dress up at Mrs. Frazer's. Rose wanted to wait a day or two but I reminded her the wedding was only two weeks away and that Mrs. Frazer had three frocks to finish.

"Who's Mrs. Frazer anyway?" she asked. Then I remembered Rose hadn't met these neighbours though they'd been in the district a few years. Rose had been away at school.

"She's a dressmaker," I looked for words. "She's nice."

"What sort of nice?" asked Rose.

"Rose, don't you say anything funny when we go up there," I said. I know Rose, she's smart. "Don't you get smart." I'm older than Rose but she's the one that speaks out when something doesn't please her. Mum used to say, Rohe, you've got the brains but you look to your sister for the sense. I started to feel funny about taking Rose up to Jane Frazer's because Jane often says the wrong thing without knowing.

We got our work done, had a bath and changed, and when Dad came back from the shed we took the station-wagon to drive over to Jane's. Before we left we called out to Mum, "Don't forget to make us a Maori bread for when we get back."

"What's wrong with your own hands," Mum said, but she was only joking. Always when one of us comes home one of the first things she does is make a big Maori bread.

Rose made a good impression with her kamakama ways, and Jane's two nuisance kids took a liking to her straight away. They kept jumping up and down on the sofa to get Rose's attention and I kept thinking what a waste of a good sofa it was, what a waste of a good house for those two nuisance things. I hope when I have kids they won't be so hoha.

---

[1] *varsity:* University.

I was pleased about Jane and Rose. Jane was asking Rose all sorts of questions about her life in Auckland. About varsity and did Rose join in the marches and demonstrations. Then they went on to talking about fashions and social life in the city, and Jane seemed deeply interested. Almost as though she was jealous of Rose and the way she lived, as though she felt Rose had something better than a lovely house and clothes and everything she needed to make life good for her. I was pleased to see that Jane liked my sister so much, and proud of my sister and her entertaining and friendly ways.

Jane made a cup of coffee when she'd finished measuring Rose for the frock, then packed the two kids outside with a piece of chocolate cake each. We were sitting having coffee when we heard a truck turn in at the bottom of Frazers' drive.

Jane said, "That's Alan. He's been down the road getting the Maoris for scrub cutting."

I felt my face get hot. I was angry. At the same time I was hoping Rose would let the remark pass. I tried hard to think of something to say to cover Jane's words though I'd hardly said a thing all morning. But my tongue seemed to thicken and all I could think of was, Rohe don't.

Rose was calm. Not all red and flustered like me. She took a big pull on the cigarette she had lit, squinted her eyes up and blew the smoke out gently. I knew something was coming.

"Don't they have names?"

"What. Who?" Jane was surprised and her face was getting pink.

"The people from down the road whom your husband is employing to cut scrub." Rose, the stink thing, she was talking all Pakehafied.

"I don't know any of their names."

I was glaring at Rose because I wanted her to stop but she was avoiding my looks and pretending to concentrate on her cigarette.

"Do they know yours?"

"Mine?"

"Your name."

"Well . . . Yes."

"Yet you have never bothered to find out their names or to wonder whether or not they have any."

The silence seemed to bang around in my head for ages and ages. Then I think Jane muttered something about difficulty, but that touchy sister of mine stood up and said, "Come on, Hera." And I with my red face and shut mouth followed her out to the station-wagon without a goodbye or anything.

I was so wild with Rose. I was wild. I was determined to blow her up about what she had done, I was determined. But now that we were alone together I couldn't think what to say. Instead I felt an awful big sulk coming on. It has always been my trouble, sulking. Whenever I don't feel sure about something I go into a big fat sulk. We had a teacher at school who used to say to some of us girls, "Speak, don't sulk." She'd say, "You only sulk because you haven't learned how and when to say your minds."

She was right that teacher, yet here I am a young woman about to be married and haven't learned yet how to get the words out. Dad used to say to me, "Look out, girlie, you'll stand on your lip."

At last I said, "Rose, you're a stink thing." Tears were on the way. "Gee Rohe, you made me embarrassed." Then Rose said, "Don't worry, Honey, she's got a thick hide."

These words of Rose's took me by surprise and I realised something about Rose then. What she said made all my anger go away and I felt very sad because it's not our way of talking to each other. Usually we'd say, "Never mind, Sis," if we wanted something to be forgotten. But when Rose said, "Don't worry, Honey, she's got a thick hide," it made her seem a lot older than me, and tougher, and as though she knew much more than me about the world.

It made me realise too that underneath her jolly and forthright ways Rose is very hurt. I remembered back to when we were both little and Rose used to play up at school if she didn't like the teacher. She'd get smart and I used to be ashamed and tell Mum on her when we got home, because although she had the brains I was always the well-behaved one.

Rose was speaking to me in a new way now. It made me feel sorry for her and for myself. All my life I had been sitting back and letting her do the objecting. Not only me, but Mum and Dad and the rest of the family too. All of us too scared to make known when we had been hurt or slighted. And how can the likes of Jane know, when we go round pretending all is well? How can Jane know us?

But then I tried to put another thought into words. I said to Rose, "We do it too. We say, 'the Pakeha doctor,' or 'the Pakeha at the post office,' and sometimes we mean it in a bad way."

"Except that we talk like this to each other only. It's not so much what is said, but when and where and in whose presence. Besides, you and I don't speak in this way now, not since we were little. It's the older ones: Mum, Dad, Nanny who have this habit."

Then Rose said something else: "Jane Frazer will still want to be your friend and mine in spite of my embarrassing her today; we're in the fashion."

"What do you mean?"

"It's fashionable for a Pakeha to have a Maori for a friend." Suddenly Rose grinned. Then I heard Jane's voice coming out of that Rohe's mouth and felt a grin of my own coming. "I have friends who are Maoris. They're lovely people. The eldest girl was married recently and I did the frocks. The other girl is at varsity. They're all so *friendly* and so *natural* and their house is absolutely *spotless*."

I stopped the wagon in the drive and when we'd got out Rose started strutting up the path. I saw Jane's way of walking and felt a giggle coming on. Rose walked up Mum's scrubbed steps, "Absolutely spotless." She left her shoes in the porch and bounced into the kitchen. "What did I tell you? Absolutely spotless. And a friendly natural woman taking new bread from the oven."

Mum looked at Rose then at me. "What have you two been up to? Rohe, I hope you behaved yourself at that Pakeha place?" But Rose was setting the table. At the sight of Mum's bread she'd forgotten all about Jane and the events of the morning.

When Dad, Heke, and Matiu came in for lunch, Rose, Mum, Nanny and I were already into the bread and the big bowl of hot corn.

"E ta," Dad said. "Let your hardworking father and your two hardworking brothers starve. Eat up."

"The bread's terrible. You men better go down to the shop and get you a shop bread," said Rose.

"Be the day," said Heke.

"Come on, my fat Rohe. Move over and make room for your daddy. Come on my baby shift over."

Dad squeezed himself round behind the table next to Rose. He picked up the bread Rose had buttered for herself and started eating. "The bread's terrible all right," he said. Then Mat and Heke started going on about how awful the corn was and who cooked it and who grew it, who watered it all summer and who pulled out the weeds.

So I joined in the carryings on and forgot about Rose and Jane for the meantime. But I'm not leaving it at that. I'll find some way of letting Rose know I understand, and I know it will be difficult for me because I'm not clever the way she is. I can't say things the same and I've never learnt to stick up for myself.

But my sister won't have to be alone again. I'll let her know that.

UNDERSTANDING THE STORY

1. How does Rose's being at university affect her attitudes and behavior?

2. What is significant about Mrs. Frazer's not knowing the names of the scrub cutters?

3. Why does Rose tell Mrs. Frazer what she thinks?

4. How does Rose view those who find it fashionable to have a Maori for a friend? Why does she react as she does to this attitude?

5. What bothers Hera about Rose's ways? What makes Hera self-conscious?

6. What is significant about Rose's remarks to Hera concerning Maori attitudes toward Pakehas?

7. Why does Hera sulk?

8. What causes Hera to change her mind about how to deal with prejudice?

9. Why does Hera think that it will be difficult for her to change?

10. What forms of prejudice exist in this story? What other forms exist?

ANALYZING LITERARY TECHNIQUE

1. How does the first paragraph of the story lead the reader into the tale that follows? What does it **foreshadow?**

2. How does Grace reveal the **setting** of this story? Find examples of local color that reveal the story's location.

3. How does Grace take the reader into the Maori world? From whose **point of view** is this story told? To what extent, if any, is this technique successful?

4. How does Grace **characterize** the members of the Maori family in this story? What does the reader learn about these characters from their attitudes, values, and decisions? What does the reader learn about these characters from the way outsiders respond to them?

5. Find two examples of **irony** in the story. What is often ironic about prejudice?

6. Describe the **tone** of this story. How does Grace achieve it?

7. What is the significance of the story's title?

8. What ideas, or **themes,** does Grace convey in this story?

9. To what extent, if any, does Grace resolve the issues set forth in this story? To what extent does she leave the story open-ended?

WRITING ABOUT LITERATURE

1. Write an expository essay in which you analyze the significance of the title of this story. Consider all the ways in which the characters use language. Use quotations and explain the significance of each example.

2. Write a story in which a character is both an insider and an outsider. Contrast the two worlds in which that character lives. Use conversation to reflect the differences.

South and Central America

$\mathcal{T}$HE SELECTIONS OF THE LITERATURE of South and Central America in this section explore various aspects of human relationships, from ideal love to the fragility of friendship.

Many of the literary selections explore romantic relationships. In the sonnet "Vicarious Love," the poet and nun Sor Juana Inés de la Cruz contrasts infatuation with real love. In the play *Crossroads*, Carlos Solórzano describes a man and a woman whose inability to recognize and reveal their true selves costs them a chance at love. A young woman revisits her earlier loveless marriage in María Luisa Bombal's short story "The Tree." Octavio Paz, in the poem "Two Bodies," describes both the limitations and the satisfactions of an intimate relationship.

Other human relationships are described by other writers in this section. In "The Third Bank of the River," João Guimarães Rosa describes the reaction of a boy whose father inexplicably deserts the family in a most unusual way. Rosario Castellanos, in her poem "Chess," describes the threat to friendships that come from competitive situations. And in Gabriel García Márquez's short story "A Very Old Man with Enormous Wings," the intolerance that ordinary people have toward people who are not like themselves is gently satirized.

The theme of coming of age is explored in two of the stories in this section. In Julio Cortázar's "End of the Game," the disappointments of the real world intrude on the fantasy world that three young girls have created for themselves. Jorge Luis Borges, in "The Story from Rosendo Juárez," shows how even an adult can change his life and become more self-confident and independent.

The remaining pieces in this section deal with the power of language. Gabriela Mistral honors the beauty of both language and nature in her poem "Serene Words." Pablo Neruda, in his poem "The Word," celebrates the nature and power of figurative language through a tribute to metaphor.

Vicarious Love

SOR JUANA INÉS DE LA CRUZ

*S*OR JUANA INÉS DE LA CRUZ (1651–1695) was an intellectual and a feminist ahead of her time—the seventeenth century Mexico in which she lived. She joined a convent, most likely to allow her to retain her intellectual freedom; there she was able to read and write extensively. She wrote poems, songs, and plays—both with and without a religious bent. Her secular plays *The Trials of a Noble House* (1683) and *Love the Greater Labyrinth* (1689) and her sacramental play *The Divine Narcissus* (1690) are examples of her work. She is, however, best known for her essay *Reply to Sor Philothea* (1690), a vigorous defense of women's right to education.

Juana Inés de Asbaje y Ramírez was born in 1651, probably illegitimately, to Pedro Manuel de Asbaje and Isabel Ramirez in the Mexican village of San Miguel Nepantla. Her father left when she was still young. Juana was sent to live with her mother's relatives in Mexico City when she was about eight years old. Her grandfather had an extensive library where, despite her lack of formal education, she read voraciously.

In 1664 Juana was presented to the new viceroy of Mexico City and became a maid-in-waiting to his wife, the Marquise de Mancera. Soon she was known for her great learning. After five years at court, Juana entered the Convent of the Discalced (Barefoot) Carmelites of St. Joseph, but she left after three months because the rules were too strict. A year and a half later Sor Juana joined the Convent of the Order of St. Jerome, where she lived until she died. The living conditions at the convent were very comfortable, and Sor Juana had an apartment, servants, and her own private library. She continued to be popular with the courtiers, entertaining them at intellectual gatherings at the convent.

In 1690 the Bishop of Puebla persuaded Sor Juana to write down her criticism of a famous sermon, the "Sermon del mandato," by the Jesuit priest Antonio de Vieira. Without her knowledge, the Bishop published her criticism under the title *Missive Worthy of Athena;* he also published his response, under the pseudonym Sor Philothea de la Cruz, which criticized her intellectualism. In 1691 Sor Juana published her famous response, the *Reply to Sor Philothea*, defending the right of women to education and describing her own intellectual history. However, the damage was already done. The Archbishop of Mexico, a known misogynist, pressured her to stop writing, and she was forced to turn over her books and scientific instruments. She died of the plague in 1695.

The writings of Sor Juana cover a range of subjects, including love—an interesting choice of topic for a nun. The sonnet "Vicarious Love" is an excellent introduction to her poetry.

Fabio, what pretty women covet most
is worship from every man who comes along.
Altars are strictly useless in their eyes
unless the weight of victims makes them groan.
    Therefore, should one man only pay them court,   5
they'll protest to Fortune they've been cheated,
convinced the gist of being a deity
lies not in beauty but in being entreated.
    Yet, prizing moderation in such matters,
for throngs of suitors I've a strong distaste.   10
I only wish to grant my love's increase
    to one who feels it cannot be replaced.
Love's delicacy consists in being loved;
one pinch too much or little spoils love's taste.

UNDERSTANDING THE POEM

1. According to the speaker, when do "pretty women" feel cheated?

2. What is the "gist of being a deity" (line 7)?

3. What does the speaker value?

4. What is "love's increase" (line 11)?

5. Why is "Vicarious Love" an appropriate title for this poem?

ANALYZING LITERARY TECHNIQUE

1. Analyze the structure of this **sonnet.** Is it a Petrarchan or a Shakespearian sonnet?

2. What is the **tone** of this poem? How is this tone related to its structure as a sonnet?

3. What related **metaphors** does the poet use?

4. How does the speaker draw **contrasts** between herself and the other women?

5. What is the function of **apostrophe** in this poem?

WRITING ABOUT LITERATURE

1. Write an essay analyzing the structure of the sonnet. How does the tone relate to the structure of the sonnet? How does the message of the sonnet relate to its structure? Use quotations from the poem to demonstrate your ideas.

2. Write a sonnet or a poem in response to Sor Juana's sonnet in which you tell a friend about your preferences for being loved. Do you want many admirers, or would you prefer a sole suitor? Do you agree with the speaker of the poem that "Love's delicacy consists in being loved; / one pinch too much or little spoils love's taste" (lines 13–14)?

Serene Words

GABRIELA MISTRAL

*G*ABRIELA MISTRAL (1889–1957), the Chilean poet, was the first Latin American writer to win the Nobel Prize for literature. The 1945 Nobel committee commended "her lyric poetry, which, inspired by powerful emotions, has made her name a symbol of the idealistic aspirations of the entire Latin American world." She is best known for three collections of poetry: *Desolation* (1922), *Felling* (1938), and *Wine Press* (1954).

Mistral was born Lucila Godoy Alcayaga. Her family was poor and rural, and in the absence of available formal schooling, she had to educate herself. By the time she was fifteen, she was determined to teach children like herself. By 1922 Mistral was so highly esteemed as a teacher that the Mexican government invited her to work on Mexico's educational reform. Today schools are named after her in every South American country. As a person actively involved in the welfare of the people of her country, Mistral was chosen to represent Chile in the League of Nations and later in the United Nations. She was also the Chilean consul to many countries.

Mistral's fame as a poet began in 1914, when she won a national poetry contest for her three "Sonnets of Death." She adopted her pen name from two sources: *Gabriela* from the archangel Gabriel, whose name means "God is my strength" and who, in Christian tradition, is God's chief messenger; and *Mistral* from the strong, cold mistral—a wind that comes down from the north and blows through southern France. Mistral became the most popular Latin American poet of her time, receiving many honors, including the Chilean National Prize for literature in 1951.

In her poems, such as "Serene Words," Mistral often reflects on what her experiences have taught her about life. She responds to love and loss, joy and suffering, and she finds emotional support in her faith in God. Her style reflects the sights and sounds of her childhood in an isolated village in northern Chile, the love of nature, and the simple language of ordinary people. "Serene Words" appeared in *Desolation*, Mistral's first collection of poetry.

Now in the middle of my days I glean
this truth that has a flower's freshness:
life is the gold and sweetness of wheat,
hate is brief and love immense.

Let us exchange for a smiling verse   5
that verse scored with blood and gall.
Heavenly violets open, and through the valley
the wind blows a honeyed breath.

Now I understand not only the man who prays;
now I understand the man who breaks into song.   10
Thirst is long-lasting and the hillside twisting;
but a lily can ensnare our gaze.

Our eyes grow heavy with weeping,
yet a brook can make us smile.
A skylark's song bursting heavenward   15
makes us forget it is hard to die.

There is nothing now that can pierce my flesh.
With love, all turmoil ceased.
The gaze of my mother still brings me peace.
I feel that God is putting me to sleep.   20

UNDERSTANDING THE POEM

1. In "Serene Words" the speaker expresses her personal view of life. What is her attitude toward good and evil?

2. In the poem what experiences shape the ideas and values of people? What sources provide emotional support?

3. What is the connection between a person's age and attitudes? To what extent, if any, does the speaker's age affect her feelings? Compare her point of view with that of a child and that of a senior citizen.

ANALYZING LITERARY TECHNIQUE

1. What is the function of **contrast** in this poem? Which contrasts are most effective? Why does Mistral avoid contrast in the last stanza?

2. Find examples of Mistral's use of **connotative language** and explain what each example contributes to the poem.

3. Find two or three examples of **figurative language** and explain their contribution to the poem.

4. Why is this considered to be a **lyric** poem?

WRITING ABOUT LITERATURE

1. Write an essay in which you analyze Mistral's use of contrast. Consider the poet's use of connotative and figurative language. Using quotations, give two or three examples of contrast and explain what each example contributes to the poem. In your conclusion, evaluate what the technique of contrast contributes to the poem as a whole.

2. Write a poem that expresses how a person finds comfort. Possible sources of comfort might include a friend or family member, a pet, a book, a piece of music, or an aspect of nature. Think about why the speaker in your poem needs to be comforted, and try to create a clear link between the speaker's need for comfort and the source of that comfort. Express your ideas in figurative language (**similes, metaphors, personification**).

The Tree

MARÍA LUISA BOMBAL

ARÍA LUISA BOMBAL (1910–1980), the Chilean writer, is a pioneer in surrealist literature in Latin America and one of the most important Latin American novelists of the twentieth century. She is best known for *The Final Mist* (1935), *The Shrouded Woman* (1938), and "The Tree" (1939).

Bombal was born in Viña del Mar, a resort community in Chile. After her father's death when she was thirteen, her family moved to Paris, where she attended high school and then the Sorbonne. In 1931 she returned to Chile, and in 1933 she moved to Buenos Aires, Argentina, to be a part of the avant garde literary movement that centered on Jorge Luis Borges and Victoria Ocampo and their literary journal *South*. During her years in Argentina, Bombal wrote screenplays and fiction. Between 1940 and 1970, she lived in the United States with her second husband, returning to South America after his death.

Bombal had no illusions about the plight of women in Chilean society in the 1930s. At that time, a woman could not open a bank account in her own name, could not vote, and could not leave the country without her husband's permission. Bombal expressed her own attitudes in *The Shrouded Woman*, where the protagonist asks:

> Why, why is a woman's nature such that man must always be in the center of her life?
> Men succeed in applying their passion to other things. But women's desire is to brood over love pain in an orderly house, surrounded by an unfinished tapestry.

In each of her works, Bombal's protagonist is a defeated woman who tells her story from the depths of solitude and frustration.

Bombal is considered a surrealist because of her subject matter and her style. At the time she was writing fiction, it was unusual in Latin America to emphasize an individual rather than a social group or a philosophy. Bombal's interest in the subconscious and in the dream world of her female protagonists reflects the influence of Sigmund Freud. Her style includes stream of consciousness (a structure based in associative thinking) and striking figurative language. In "The Tree," Bombal interweaves music, literature, and water in a way that is the equivalent of counterpoint in musical composition.

The pianist sits down, coughs affectedly, and concentrates for a moment. The cluster of lights illuminating the hall slowly diminishes to a soft, warm glow, as a musical phrase begins to rise in the silence, and to develop, clear, restrained and judiciously capricious.

"Mozart,[1] perhaps," thinks Brígida. As usual, she has forgotten to ask for the program. "Mozart, perhaps, or Scarlatti."[2] She knew so little about music! And it wasn't because she had no ear for it, or interest. As a child it was she who had demanded piano lessons; no one needed to force them on her, as with her sisters. Her sisters, however, played correctly now and read music at sight, while she. . . . She had given up her studies within a year after she began them. The reason for her inconsistency was as simple as it was shameful; she had never succeeded in learning the key of F; never. "I don't understand; my memory is incapable of going beyond the key of G." How indignant her father was! "Oh, how I'd love to give up this job of being a man alone with several daughters to raise. Poor Carmen! She surely must have suffered because of Brígida. This child is retarded."

Brígida was the youngest of six girls, all different in character. When the father finally came to his sixth daughter, he was so perplexed and tired out by the first five that he preferred to simplify matters by declaring her retarded. "I'm not going to struggle any longer, it's useless. Let her be. If she doesn't want to study, let her not study. If she likes to spend time in the kitchen listening to ghost stories, that's up to her. If she likes dolls at sixteen, let her play with them." And Brígida had kept her dolls and remained completely ignorant.

How pleasant it is to be ignorant! Not to know exactly who Mozart was, where he came from, who influenced him, the details of his technique! How nice to just let him lead you by the hand, as now.

And, indeed, Mozart is leading her. He leads her across a bridge suspended over a crystalline stream which runs over a bed of rosy sand. She is dressed in white, with a lace parasol—intricate and fine as a spider web—open over her shoulder.

"You look younger every day, Brígida. I met your husband yesterday, your ex-husband, I mean. His hair is all white."

But she doesn't answer, she doesn't stop, she continues to cross the bridge which Mozart has improvised for her to the garden of her youthful years when

---

[1] *Mozart:* Wolfgang Amadeus Mozart (1756–1791), Austrian composer.
[2] *Scarlatti:* Domenico Scarlatti (1685–1757), Italian composer.

she was eighteen: tall fountains in which the water sings; her chestnut braids, which when undone reach her ankles, her golden complexion, her dark eyes opened wide as if questioning; a small mouth with full lips, a sweet smile and the most slender, most graceful body in the world. What was she thinking about as she sat on the edge of the fountain? Nothing. "She is as stupid as she is pretty," they said. But it never mattered to her that she was stupid, or unsought after at dances. One by one, her sisters were asked to marry. No one proposed to her.

Mozart! Now he offers her a staircase of blue marble which she descends, between a double row of icy cold lilies. And now he opens for her a gate of thick iron bars with gilded tips so that she can throw her arms around the neck of Luis, her father's close friend. Ever since she was a very small child, when they all used to abandon her, she would run to Luis. He would pick her up and she would hug him, laughing with little warbling sounds, and shower him with kisses like a downpour of rain, haphazardly, upon his eyes, his forehead and his hair, already gray (had he ever been young?).

"You are a necklace," Luis would say to her. "You are like a necklace of birds."

That is why she married him. Because, with that solemn and taciturn man, she didn't feel guilty of being as she was: silly, playful, and lazy. Yes; now that so many years have passed she understands that she did not marry Luis for love; nevertheless, she doesn't quite understand why, why she went away one day suddenly. . . .

But at this point Mozart takes her nervously by the hand, and dragging her along at a pace which becomes more urgent by the second, compels her to cross the garden in the opposite direction, to recross the bridge at a run, almost in headlong flight. And after having deprived her of the parasol and the transparent skirt, he closes the door of her past with a chord at once gentle and firm, and leaves her in the concert hall, dressed in black, mechanically applauding while the glow of the artificial lights increases.

Once more the half-shadow, and once more the foreboding silence.

And now Beethoven's[3] music begins to stir up the warm waves of his notes under a spring moon. How far the sea has withdrawn! Brígida walks across the beach toward the sea now recoiled in the distance, shimmering and calm, but then, the sea swells, slowly grows, comes to meet her, envelops her, and with gentle waves, gradually pushes her, pushes her from behind until it makes her rest her cheek upon the body of a man. And then it recedes, leaving her forgotten upon Luis's breast.

"You don't have a heart, you don't have a heart," she used to tell Luis. Her husband's heart beat so deep inside him that she could rarely hear it, and then only in an unexpected way. "You are never with me when you are beside me," she protested in the bedroom when he ritually opened the evening papers before going to sleep. "Why did you marry me?"

"Because you have the eyes of a frightened little doe," he answered and kissed her. And she, suddenly happy, proudly welcomed on her shoulder the weight of his gray head. Oh, his shiny, silver hair!

---

[3] *Beethoven:* Ludwig van Beethoven (1770–1827), German composer.

"Luis, you have never told me exactly what color your hair was when you were a boy, and you have never told me either what your mother said when you began to get gray at fifteen. What did she say? Did she laugh? Did she cry? And were you proud or ashamed? And at school, your friends, what did they say? Tell me, Luis, tell me. . . ."

"Tomorrow I'll tell you. I'm sleepy, Brígida. I'm very tired. Turn off the light."

Unconsciously he moved away from her to fall asleep, and she unconsciously, all night long, pursued her husband's shoulder, sought his breath, tried to live beneath his breath, like a plant shut up and thirsty that stretches out its branches in search of a more favorable climate.

In the morning, when the maid opened the blinds, Luis was no longer at her side. He had gotten up stealthily without saying good morning to her for fear that his "necklace of birds" would insist on holding him firmly by the shoulders. "Five minutes, just five minutes. Your office won't disappear because you stay five minutes longer with me, Luis."

Her awakenings. Ah, how sad her awakenings! But—it was strange—scarcely did she step into her dressing room than her sadness vanished, as if by magic.

Waves toss and break in the distance, murmuring like a sea of leaves. Is it Beethoven? No.

It is the tree close to the window of the dressing room. It was enough for her to enter to feel a wonderfully pleasant sensation circulating within her. How hot it always was in the bedroom, in the mornings! And what a harsh light! Here, on the other hand, in the dressing room, even one's eyes felt rested, refreshed. The drab cretonnes,[4] the tree that cast shadows on the walls like rough, cold water, the mirrors that reflected the foliage and receded into an infinite, green forest. How pleasant that room was! It seemed like a world submerged in an aquarium. How that huge rubber tree chattered! All the birds of the neighborhood came to take shelter in it. It was the only tree on that narrow, sloping street which dropped down directly to the river from one corner of the city.

"I'm busy. I can't accompany you. . . . I have a lot to do. I won't make it for lunch. . . . Hello, yes, I'm at the Club. An engagement. Have your dinner and go to bed. . . . No. I don't know. You better not wait for me, Brígida."

"If only I had some girl friends!" she sighed. But everybody was bored with her. If she would only try to be a little less stupid! But how to gain at one stroke so much lost ground? To be intelligent you should begin from childhood, shouldn't you?

Her sisters, however, were taken everywhere by their husbands, but Luis— why shouldn't she confess it to herself?—was ashamed of her, of her ignorance, her timidity, and even her eighteen years. Had he not asked her to say she was at least twenty-one, as if her extreme youth were a secret defect?

And at night, how tired he always was when he went to bed! He never listened to her attentively. He did smile at her, yes, with a smile which she knew was mechanical. He showered her with caresses from which he was absent. Why

---

[4] *cretonnes:* Heavy cloth curtains.

do you suppose he had married her? To keep up a habit, perhaps to strengthen the old friendly relationship with her father. Perhaps life consisted, for men, of a series of ingrained habits. If one should be broken, probably confusion, failure would result. And then they would begin to wander through the streets of the city, to sit on the benches of the public squares, each day more poorly dressed and more in need of a shave. Luis's life, therefore, consisted of filling every minute of the day with some activity. Why hadn't she understood that before! Her father was right when he declared her retarded.

"I should like to see it snow some time, Luis."

"This summer I'll take you to Europe, and since it is winter there, you will be able to see snow."

"I know it is winter in Europe when it is summer here. I'm not that ignorant!"

Sometimes, as if to awaken him to the emotion of real love, she would throw herself upon her husband and cover him with kisses, weeping, calling him Luis, Luis, Luis. . . .

"What? What's the matter with you? What do you want?"

"Nothing."

"Why are you calling me that way then?"

"No reason, just to call you. I like to call you." And he would smile, taking kindly to that new game.

Summer arrived, her first summer as a married woman. New duties kept Luis from offering her the promised trip.

"Brígida, the heat is going to be terrible this summer in Buenos Aires.[5] Why don't you go to the ranch with your father?"

"Alone?"

"I would go to see you every weekend."

She had sat down on the bed, ready to insult him. But she sought in vain for cutting words to shout at him. She didn't know anything, anything at all. Not even how to insult.

"What's the matter with you? What are you thinking about, Brígida?"

For the first time, Luis retraced his steps and bent over her, uneasy, letting the time of his arrival at the office pass by.

"I'm sleepy," Brígida had replied childishly, while she hid her face in the pillows.

For the first time he had called her from the Club at lunch time. But she had refused to go to the telephone, furiously wielding that weapon she had found without thinking: silence.

That same evening she ate opposite her husband without raising her eyes, all her nerves taut.

"Are you still angry, Brígida?"

But she did not break the silence.

---

[5] *Buenos Aires:* Capital of Argentina.

"You certainly know that I love you, my necklace of birds. But I can't be with you all the time. I'm a very busy man. One reaches my age a slave to a thousand commitments."

". . ."

"Do you want to go out tonight?"

". . ."

"You don't want to? Patience. Tell me, did Robert call from Montevideo?"[6]

". . ."

"What a pretty dress! Is it new?"

". . ."

"Is it new, Brígida? Answer, answer me."

But she did not break the silence this time either. And a moment later the unexpected, the astonishing, the absurd happens. Luis gets up from his chair, throws the napkin violently on the table, and leaves the house, slamming doors behind him.

She too had gotten up, stunned, trembling with indignation at such injustice. "And me, and me," she murmured, confused: "What about me who for almost a year . . . when for the first time I allow myself one reproach. . . . Oh, I'm leaving, I'm leaving, this very night! I'll never set foot in this house again." And she furiously opened the closets of her dressing room, wildly threw the clothes on the floor.

It was then that someone rapped with his knuckles on the window panes.

She had run, she knew not how or with what unaccustomed courage, to the window. She had opened it. It was the tree, the rubber tree which a great gust of wind was shaking, which was hitting the glass with its branches, which summoned her from outside as if she should see it writhing like an impetuous black flame beneath the fiery sky of that summer evening.

A heavy shower would soon beat against its cold leaves. How delightful! All night long she would be able to hear the rain whipping, trickling through the leaves of the rubber tree as if along the ducts of a thousand imaginary gutters. All night long she would hear the old trunk of the rubber tree creak and groan, telling her of the storm, while she snuggled up very close to Luis, voluntarily shivering between the sheets of the big bed.

Handfuls of pearls that rain buckets upon a silver roof. Chopin. *Études* by Frédéric Chopin.[7]

How many weeks did she wake up suddenly, very early, when she scarcely perceived that her husband, now also stubbornly silent, had slipped out of bed?

The dressing room: the window wide open, and odor of river and pasture floating in that kindly room, and the mirrors veiled by a halo of mist.

Chopin and the rain that slips through the leaves of the rubber tree with the noise of a hidden waterfall that seems to drench even the roses on the cretonnes, become intermingled in her agitated nostalgia.

---

[6] *Montevideo:* Capital of Uruguay.

[7] Études *by* Frédéric Chopin: Music for piano written by Chopin (1810–1849), Polish pianist and composer.

What does one do in the summertime when it rains so much? Stay in one's room the whole day feigning convalescence or sadness? Luis had entered timidly one afternoon. He had sat down very stiffly. There was a silence.

"Brígida, then it is true? You no longer love me?"

She had become happy all of a sudden, stupidly. She might have cried out: "No, no; I love you, Luis; I love you," if he had given her time, if he had not added, almost immediately, with his habitual calm:

"In any case, I don't think it is wise for us to separate, Brígida. We have to think it over a great deal."

Her impulses subsided as abruptly as they had arisen. Why become excited uselessly! Luis loved her with tenderness and moderation: if some time he should come to hate her, he would hate her justly and prudently. And that was life. She approached the window, rested her forehead against the icy glass. There was the rubber tree calmly receiving the rain that struck it, softly and steadily. The room stood still in the shadow, orderly and quiet. Everything seemed to come to a stop, eternal and very noble. That was life. And there was a certain greatness in accepting it as it was, mediocre, as something definitive, irremediable. And from the depths of things there seemed to spring forth and rise a melody of grave, slow words to which she stood listening: "Always." "Never." And thus the hours, the days and the years go by. Always! Never! Life, life!

On regaining her bearings she realized that her husband had slipped out of the room. Always! Never!

And the rain, secretly and constantly, continued to murmur in the music of Chopin.

Summer tore the leaves from its burning calendar. Luminous and blinding pages fell like golden swords, pages of an unwholesome humidity like the breath of the swamps; pages of brief and violent storms, and pages of hot winds, of the winds that bring the "carnation of the air" and hang it in the immense rubber tree.

Children used to play hide-and-seek among the enormous twisted roots that raised the paving stones of the sidewalk, and the tree was filled with laughter and whispering. Then she appeared at the window and clapped her hands; the children dispersed, frightened, without noticing her smile, the smile of a girl who also wanted to take part in the game.

Alone, she would lean for a long time on her elbows at the window watching the trembling of the foliage—some breeze always blew along that street which dropped straight down to the river—and it was like sinking one's gaze in shifting water or in the restless fire of a hearth. One could spend one's idle hours this way, devoid of all thought, in a stupor of well-being.

Scarcely did the room begin to fill with the haze of twilight when she lit the first lamp, and the first lamp shone in the mirrors, multiplied like a firefly wishing to precipitate the coming of night.

And night after night she dozed next to her husband, suffering at intervals. But when her pain increased to the point of wounding her like a knife thrust, when she was beset by too urgent a desire to awaken Luis in order to hit him or caress him, she slipped away on tiptoe to the dressing room and opened the window.

The room instantly filled with discreet sounds and presences, with mysterious footfalls, the fluttering of wings, the subtle crackling of vegetation, the soft chirping of a cricket hidden under the bark of the rubber tree submerged in the stars of a hot summer night.

Her fever passed as her bare feet gradually became chilled on the matting. She did not know why it was so easy for her to suffer in that room.

Chopin's melancholy linking one *Étude* after another, linking one melancholy after another, imperturbably.

And autumn came. The dry leaves whirled about for a moment before rolling on the grass of the narrow garden, on the sidewalk of the steep street. The leaves shook loose and fell. . . . The top of the rubber tree remained green, but underneath, the tree turned red, darkened like the worn-out lining of a sumptuous evening cape. And the room now seemed to be submerged in a goblet of dull gold.

Lying on the divan, she patiently waited for suppertime, for Luis's improbable arrival. She had resumed speaking to him, she had become his wife again without enthusiasm and without anger. She no longer loved him. But she no longer suffered. On the contrary, an unexpected feeling of plentitude, of placidity had taken hold of her. Now no one or nothing could hurt her. It may be that true happiness lies in the conviction that happiness has been irremediably lost. Then we begin to move through life without hope or fear, capable of finally enjoying all the small pleasures, which are the most lasting.

A terrible din, then a flash of light that throws her backward, trembling all over.

Is it the intermission? No. It is the rubber tree, she knows it.

They had felled it with a single stroke of the ax. She could not hear the work that began very early in the morning. "The roots were raising the pavement stones of the sidewalk and then, naturally, the neighborhood committee. . . ."

Blinded, she has lifted her hands to her eyes. When she recovers her sight, she stands up and looks around her. What is she looking at? The hall suddenly lighted, the people who are dispersing? No. She has remained imprisoned in the web of her past, she cannot leave the dressing room. Her dressing room invaded by a white, terrifying light. It was as if they ripped off the roof; a harsh light came in everywhere, seeped through her pores, burned her with cold. And she saw everything in the light of that cold light; Luis, his wrinkled face, his hands crossed by coarse, discolored veins, and the gaudy colored cretonnes. Frightened, she has run to the window. The window now opens directly on a narrow street, so narrow that her room almost crashes against the front of a dazzling skyscraper. On the ground floor, show windows and more show windows, full of bottles. On the street corner, a row of automobiles lined up in front of a service station painted red. Some boys in shirt sleeves are kicking a ball in the middle of the street.

And all that ugliness had entered her mirrors. Now in her mirrors there were nickel-plated balconies and shabby clotheslines and canary cages.

They had taken away her privacy, her secret; she found herself in the middle of the street, naked beside an old husband who turned his back on her in bed, who had given her no children. She does not understand how until then she had not wanted to have children, how she had come to the idea that she was going to live without children all her life. She does not understand how she could endure for one year Luis's laughter, that over-cheerful laughter, that false laughter of a man who has become skilled in laughter because it is necessary to laugh on certain occasions.

A lie! Her resignation and her serenity were a lie; she wanted love, yes, love; and trips and madness, and love, love. . . .

"But Brígida, why are you going? Why did you stay?" Luis had asked.

Now she would have known how to answer him:

"The tree, Luis, the tree! They have cut down the rubber tree."

UNDERSTANDING THE STORY

1. Brígida's father treated Brígida as though she were retarded. What effect does this have on her life?

2. To what extent, if any, is Brígida correct that "to be intelligent you should begin from childhood"?

3. Why does Brígida refuse to confront Luis with her anger about the change in their summer plans? What message does her silence give Luis, and what effect does it have on their marriage?

4. What disturbs Brígida about her relationship with Luis? Why is she happy when Luis asks her about her love for him? What quickly snuffs out these emotions?

5. What do the words "always" and "never" mean to Brígida?

6. To what extent, if any, does Brígida believe that

   > true happiness lies in the conviction that happiness has been irremediably lost. Then we begin to move through life without hope or fear, capable of finally enjoying all the small pleasures, which are the most lasting.

ANALYZING LITERARY TECHNIQUE

1. Explain the connection between the setting and structure of the story. What connection exists between Mozart's, Beethoven's, and Chopin's music and Brígida's thoughts during the playing of these compositions?

2. What does Bombal's choice of **narrative perspective** add to the story?

3. What is the important **irony** in the story?

4. Explain Bombal's use of music as a **symbol.**

5. How does Bombal use water as a symbol?

6. How does the tree function as a symbol? Why do you think Bombal chose "The Tree" as the title of this story?

7. Why is Luis's description of Brígida as "a necklace of birds" important?

8. What is significant about the mirrors and the window in Brígida's dressing room?

WRITING ABOUT LITERATURE

1. Write an essay in which you analyze Bombal's use of symbolism in "The Tree." Examine her use of two or three of the following symbols: the tree, the music, the water, and the "necklace of birds." You may chose to organize your essay according to the three stages of Brígida's thoughts or according to the symbols you choose. Use quotations from the story to support your ideas.

2. Write a sequel to this story in which you describe Brígida's life after her divorce. Choose whatever form you wish for the sequel (for example, a diary, a letter to a sister, a conversation with Luis, or a story).

3. Tell this story from Luis's point of view. Consider questions such as the following: Why does Luis marry Brígida? What does she contribute to his life? Why does he treat her as he does? How does he feel about the divorce?

The Story from Rosendo Juárez

JORGE LUIS BORGES

ORGE LUIS BORGES (1899–1986), the Argentine author, is considered by many to be the most important and influential Latin American writer of the twentieth century. His short stories, poetry, and essays are famous for their philosophical ideas as well as for their style. His favorite form of fiction was the short story. His major works—*Ficciones* (1944) and *The Aleph and Other Stories* (1949)—brought him international fame and led to the development of the fantastic in Latin American literature by influencing such writers as Gabriel García Márquez.

Borges was born in Buenos Aires, Argentina. His father taught psychology in English and introduced Borges both to poetry and to philosophy. His mother translated English and American literature into Spanish. Borges described himself as a frail, lonely child whose most important friend and teacher was his father's English library. In 1914, when the family moved to Geneva, Switzerland, Borges learned French and Latin in high school and German on his own. He returned to Buenos Aires in 1921. Between 1921 and 1930, he wrote four books of essays and three books of poetry. He became director of the National Library of Argentina in 1955 and professor of English and American literature at the University of Buenos Aires in 1956. By then a hereditary eye disease had caused him to become blind. As his vision failed, his mother became his secretary, writing out the essays, poems, and short stories that he dictated to her.

Borges had no interest in writing about national issues or regional life. Instead, his short stories are dramatic presentations of his worldview—the absurd nature of human life in an absurd universe. In many of his stories, personal identity is illusory, reality is a dream, and time and space are self-deceptions of the imagination. A number of his stories focus on knife fights and violent deaths because these subjects involve questions of courage, personal identity, success and fame, and time and human existence.

"The Story from Rosendo Juárez" (1969) appears in the collection *Dr. Brodie's Report* (1970). Borges describes it as "a sequel and an antidote" to his first famous short story, "Streetcorner Man" (1933), which has been adapted for ballet, drama, and film. "The Story from Rosendo Juárez" repeats the earlier plot from the point of view of a different character. The story is set at a time in Argentina's history when the police condoned the activities of the toughs and killers who, as bodyguards for leading politicians, intimidated voters during elections.

It was about eleven o'clock one night; I had gone into the old-fashioned general-store-and-bar, which is now simply a bar, on the corner of Bolívar and Venezuela.[1] As I went in, I noticed that over in a corner, sitting at one of the little tables, was a man I had never seen before. He hissed to catch my eye and motioned me to come over. He must have looked like a man that one didn't want to cross, because I went at once toward his table. I felt, inexplicably, that he had been sitting there for some time, in that chair, before that empty glass. He was neither tall nor short; he looked like an honest craftsman, or perhaps an old-fashioned country fellow. His sparse mustache was grizzled. A bit stiff, as Porteños tend to be, he had not taken off his neck scarf. He offered to buy me a drink; I sat down and we chatted. All this happened in nineteen-thirty-something.

"You've heard of me, sir, though we've never met," the man began, "but I know you. My name is Rosendo Juárez. It was Nicolás Paredes, no doubt, God rest his soul, that told you about me. That old man was something. I'll tell you—the stories he'd tell. . . . Not so as to fool anyone, of course—just to be entertaining. But since you and I are here with nothing else on our hands just now, I'd like to tell you what really happened that night . . . the night the Yardmaster was murdered. You've put the story in a novel, sir—and I'm hardly qualified to judge that novel—but I want you to know the truth behind the lies you wrote."

He paused, as though to put his recollections in order, and then he began. . . .

Things happen to a man, you see, and a man only understands them as the years go by. What happened to me that night had been waiting to happen for a long time. I was brought up in the neighborhood of the Maldonado, out beyond Floresta. It was one big open sewage ditch back then, if you know what I mean; but fortunately they've run sewer lines in there now. I've always been of the opinion that nobody has the right to stand in the way of progress. You just do the best you can with the hand you're dealt. . . .

It never occurred to me to find out the name of the father that begot me. Clementina Juárez, my mother, was a good honest woman that earned her living with her iron. If you were to ask me, I'd say she was from Entre Ríos or the Banda

---

[1] *Bolívar and Venezuela*: Street corner in Buenos Aires, the capital of Argentina.

Oriental, what people now call Uruguay;[2] be that as it may, she would always talk about her relatives over in Uruguay, in Concepción.[3] For myself, I grew up the best I could. I learned to knife fight with the other boys, using a charred piece of stick. That was before we were all taken over by soccer, which back at that time was still just something the English did.

Anyway, while I was sitting in the bar one night, this fellow named Garmendia started trying to pick a fight with me. I ignored him for a while—playing deaf, you might say—but this Garmendia, who was feeling his liquor, kept egging me on. We finally took it outside; out on the sidewalk, Garmendia turned back a second, pushed the door open again a little, and announced—"Not to worry, boys, I'll be right back."

I had borrowed a knife. We walked down toward the Maldonado, slow, watching each other. He was a few years older than I was; he and I had practiced knife fighting together lots of times, and I had a feeling I was going to get positively gutted. I was walking down the right-hand side of the alley, and him down the left. Suddenly, he tripped over some big chunks of cement that were lying there. The second he tripped, I jumped him, almost without thinking about it. I cut his cheek open with one slash, then we locked together—there was a second when anything could've happened—and then I stabbed him once, which was all it took. . . . It was only sometime later that I realized he'd left his mark on me, too—scratches, though, that was about it. I learned that night that it isn't hard to kill a man, or get killed yourself. The creek was down; to keep the body from being found too soon, I half-hid it behind a brick kiln. I was so stunned I suppose I just stopped thinking, because I slipped off the ring Garmendia always wore and put it on. Then I straightened my hat and went back to the bar. I walked in as easy as you please.

"Looks like it's me that's come back," I said.

I ordered a shot of brandy, and the truth is, I needed it. That was when somebody pointed out the bloodstain.

That night I tossed and turned on my bunk all night; I didn't fall asleep till nearly dawn. About the time of early mass, two cops came looking for me. You should have seen the way my mother carried on, may she rest in peace, poor thing. I was dragged off like a criminal. Two days and two nights I sat in that stinking cell. Nobody came to visit me—except for Luis Irala, a true friend if ever there was one. But they wouldn't let him see me. Then one morning the captain sent for me. He was sitting there in his chair; he didn't even look at me at first, but he did speak.

"So you put Garmendia out of his misery?" he said.

"If you say so," I answered.

---

[2] *Entre Ríos or the Banda Oriental . . . Uruguay:* Entre Ríos is a northeastern province of Argentina, located just north of Buenos Aires; it borders on the country of Uruguay. Uruguay was formerly known as the Banda Oriental.

[3] *in Uruguay, in Concepción:* also Concepcíon del Uruguay, a city in Entre Ríos.

"It's 'sir' to you. And we'll have no ducking or dodging, now. Here are the statements from the witnesses, and here's the ring that was found in your house. Just sign the confession and get this over with."

He dipped the pen in the inkwell and handed it to me.

"Let me think about this, captain.—Sir," I added.

"I'll give you twenty-four hours to think about it real good, in your very own cell. I won't rush you. But if you decide not to see things in a reasonable way, you'd best start getting used to the idea of a vacation down on Calle Las Heras."

As you might imagine, I didn't understand that right away.

"If you decide to come around, you'll be in for a few days. I'll let you go— don[4] Nicolás Paredes has promised me he'll fix it for you."

But it was *ten* days. I'd almost given up hope when they finally remembered me. I signed what they put in front of me to sign and one of the cops took me over to Calle Cabrera. . . .

There were horses tied to the hitching post, and standing out on the porch and all inside the place there were more people than a Saturday night at the whorehouse. It looked like a party committee headquarters. Don Nicolás, who was sipping at a *mate*,[5] finally called me over. As calm as you please, he told me he was going to send me out to Morón,[6] where they were setting up for the elections. He told me to look up a certain Sr. Laferrer; he'd try me out, he said. The letter I was to take was written by a kid in black that wrote poems about tenement houses and riffraff—or anyway, that's what I was told. I can't imagine that educated people would be much interested in that sort of thing, much less if it's told in poetry. Anyway, I thanked Paredes for the favor, and I left. The cop didn't stay so infernally glued to me on the way back.

So it all turned out for the best. Providence knows what it's doing. Garmendia's killing, which at first had got me in such hot water, was now starting to open doors for me. Of course the cops had me over a barrel—if I didn't work out, if I didn't toe the line for the party, I'd be hauled in again. But I'd got some heart back, and I had faith in myself.

Laferrer warned me right off that I was going to have to walk the straight and narrow with him, but if I did, he said, he might make me his bodyguard. The work I did for 'em was all anyone could ask. In Morón, and later on in the neighborhood too, I gradually won my bosses' trust. The police and the party gradually spread the word that I was a man to be reckoned with; I was an important cog in the wheels of the elections in Buenos Aires, and out in the province too. Elections were fierce back then; I won't bore you, señor, with stories about the blood that would be shed. I did all I could to make life hard on the radicals, though to this day they're still riding on Alem's coattails. But as I say, there was no man that didn't show me respect. I got myself a woman, La Lujanera we called her, and a handsome copper sorrel. For years I pretended to be some kind of Moreira—who

---

[4] *don:* Title of respect.

[5] mate: Kind of tea served in South America.

[6] *Morón:* Suburb of Buenos Aires.

in his day was probably imitating some other stage show gaucho. I played a lot of cards and drank a lot of absinthe. . . .

We old folks talk and talk and talk, I know, but I'm coming to what I wanted to tell you. I don't know if I mentioned Luis Irala. A true friend, the likes of which you'll not often find. . . . He was getting on in years when I knew him, and he'd never been afraid of hard work; for some reason he took a liking to me. He'd never set foot in a committee room—he earned his living carpentering. He didn't stick his nose in anybody else's business, and he didn't let anybody stick their nose in his. One morning he came to see me.

"I guess you've heard Casilda left me," he said. "Rufino Aguilera is the man that took her away from me."

I'd had dealing with that particular individual in Morón.

"I know Rufino," I told him. "I'd have to say that of all the Aguileras, he's the least disgusting."

"Disgusting or not, I've got a bone to pick with him."

I thought for a minute.

"Listen," I finally told him, "nobody takes anything away from anybody. If Casilda left you, it's because it's Rufino she wants, and she's not interested in you."

"But what'll people say? That I'm yellow? That I don't stand up to a man that wrongs me?"

"My advice to you is not to go looking for trouble because of what people might say, let alone because of a woman that doesn't love you anymore."

"I couldn't care less about her," he said. "A man that thinks longer than five minutes running about a woman is no man, he's a pansy. And Casilda's heartless, anyway. The last night we spent together she told me I was getting old."

"She was telling you the truth."

"And it hurts, but it's besides the point—Rufino's the one I'm after now."

"You want to be careful there," I told him. "I've seen Rufino in action, in the Merlo elections. He's like greased lightning."

"You think I'm afraid of Rufino Aguilera?"

"I know you're not afraid of him, but think about it—one of two things will happen: either you kill him and you get sent off to stir, or he kills you and you get sent off to Chacarita."

"One of two things. So tell me, what would you do in my place?"

"I don't know, but then I'm not exactly the best example to follow. I'm a guy that to get his backside out of jail has turned into a gorilla for the party."

"I'm not planning to turn into a gorilla for the party, I'm planning to collect a debt a man owes me."

"You mean you're going to stake your peace of mind on a stranger you've never met and a woman you don't even love anymore?"

But Luis Irala wasn't interested in hearing what I had to say, so he left. The next day we heard that he'd picked a fight with Rufino in some bar over in Morón and Rufino had killed him.

He went off to get killed, and he got himself killed right honorably, too—man to man. I'd done the best I could, I'd given him a friend's advice, but I still felt guilty.

A few days after the wake, I went to the cockfights. I'd never been all that keen on cockfights, but that Sunday, I'll tell you the truth, they made me sick. What in the world's wrong with those animals, I thought, that they tear each other to pieces this way, for no good reason?

The night of this story I'm telling you, the night of the end of the story, the boys and I had all gone to a dance over at the place that a black woman we called La Parda ran. Funny—all these years, and I still remember the flowered dress La Lujanera was wearing that night. . . . The party was out in the patio. There was the usual drunk trying to pick a fight, but I made sure things went the way they were supposed to go. It was early, couldn't have been midnight yet, when the strangers showed up. One of them—they called him the Yardmaster, and he was stabbed in the back and killed that very night, just the way you wrote it, sir— anyway, this one fellow bought a round of drinks for the house. By coincidence this Yardmaster and I were dead ringers for each other. He had something up his sleeve that night: he came up to me and started laying it on pretty thick—he was from up north, he said, and he'd been hearing about me. He couldn't say enough about my reputation. I let him talk, but I was beginning to suspect what was coming. He was hitting the gin hard, too, and I figured it was to get his courage up— and sure enough, pretty soon he challenged me to a fight. That was when it happened—what nobody wants to understand. I looked at that swaggering drunk just spoiling for a fight, and it was like I was looking at myself in a mirror, and all of a sudden I was ashamed of myself. I wasn't afraid of him; if I had been, I might've gone outside and fought him. I just stood there. This other guy, this Yardmaster, who by now had his face about this far from mine, raised his voice so everybody could hear him:

"You know what's wrong with you? You're yellow, that's what's wrong with you!"

"That may be," I said. "I can live with being called yellow. You can tell people you called me a son of a whore, too, and say I let you spit in my face. Now then, does that make you feel better?"

La Lujanera slipped her hand up my sleeve and pulled out the knife I always carried there and slipped it into my hand. And to make sure I got the message, she also said, "Rosendo, I think you're needing this." Her eyes were blazing.

I dropped the knife and walked out—taking my time about it. People stepped back to make way for me. They couldn't believe their eyes. What did I care what they thought.

To get out of that life, I moved to Uruguay and became an oxcart driver. Since I came back, I've made my place here. San Telmo has always been a peaceful place to live.

UNDERSTANDING THE STORY

1. Rosendo remarks that "things happen to a man, you see, and a man only understands them as the years go by." How might the passage of time help one's understanding of the past?

2. What effect did Rosendo's experience with Garmendia have on Rosendo's attitudes and behavior?

3. Rosendo remarks, "Providence knows what it's doing." To what extent does this remark conflict with Rosendo's attitude toward Garmendia's death?

4. Evaluate the effect of Luis Irala's death on Rosendo's attitudes and behavior.

5. Why did the Yardmaster make Rosendo feel ashamed of himself?

6. Why did Rosendo decide to make a clean break from the life that he had been leading?

7. How has Rosendo changed as he has grown from youth through adolescence to adulthood?

8. What **themes** do you find in this story?

9. Borges wrote a group of stories about knife fighters. What do you think interested him about these people?

ANALYZING LITERARY TECHNIQUE

1. "The Story from Rosendo Juárez" begins with a paragraph of **exposition** narrated by the author. What function does the exposition serve?

2. Rosendo's telling of his own story is built on a **flashback.** What advantages exist in this technique?

3. Find two examples of **foreshadowing** and explain their function in the story.

4. Find one or two examples of **situational irony** and explain their function in the story.

5. In what ways is the Yardmaster both a mirror image and a **doppelgänger** for Rosendo?

6. What does the cockfight **symbolize?**

7. What function does the **narrative perspective** perform in the story?

8. What is the central **paradox** in the story?

WRITING ABOUT LITERATURE

1. Write an essay in which you apply the following two quotations from Borges's "Streetcorner Man" to "The Story from Rosendo Juárez": (a) "All it takes to die is being alive," and (b) "a man's so full of pride and now look—all he's good for is gathering flies." Find quotations from "The Story from Rosendo Juárez" that support or contradict the point of view expressed in these quotations. How do you think "The Story from Rosendo Juárez" expresses Borges's view about how an adult should act?

2. Write a character sketch of Rosendo in which you trace his development from youth to maturity. Choose three adjectives, one for each period of his life, and use quotations from the story to support your ideas.

3. Create a dialogue between two bystanders who were at La Parda's the night the Yardman got killed and Rosendo walked out. Have them argue about whether Rosendo is, in fact, a coward.

The Word

PABLO NERUDA

*P*ABLO NERUDA (1904–1973), the preeminent
Chilean poet, won the Nobel Prize for literature in 1971
"for a poetry that with the action of an elemental force
brings alive a continent's destiny and dreams." Neruda's twenty-nine
volumes of poetry have been translated into eighty languages. His surrealistic, symbolic, and visionary writing changed the style of modern
Latin American poetry. Neruda is best known for *Twenty Love Poems
and a Song of Despair* (1924) and for *General Song* (1950), a collection
of poetry that includes his great poem "The Heights of Machu Picchu."

Neruda was born Ricardo Neftali Reyes in the small town of
Temuco in southern Chile. His father, a railroad worker, thought so little of poetry that Neruda wrote under a pseudonym that he later adopted
as his name. In 1921 Neruda left home for Santiago, where he joined a
group of avant garde poets. He published his first book of poetry in 1923.

In 1927 Neruda became a career Chilean diplomat. In 1934, he
joined a group of Latin American poets in Spain, where the Spanish
poet and dramatist Federico García Lorca became his mentor. Neruda
was the Chilean consul to Spain when the Fascists executed García
Lorca early in the Spanish civil war. The fact that the nonpolitical
poet was murdered because he sympathized with the Republican government had a profound influence on Neruda's life. Thereafter Neruda
was active in politics, and social issues became important themes in
his poetry. His support of the Republican side in the Spanish civil war
made it necessary for him to resign his diplomatic post. However, when
he returned to Chile in 1938, he actively supported the Communist
Party there. In 1948 his criticism of the Chilean government forced
Neruda to flee to Argentina. Leftist values continued to inspire his
poetry until he died.

In his poetry, Neruda celebrated life while emphasizing social
issues. He passionately loved language, the tool of his trade. In his
autobiography, *Memoirs* (1974), he included the prose poem "The
Word," which is about words. In it he says:

Words fell like pebbles out of the boots of the barbarians, out of their beards, their helmets, their horseshoes, luminous words that were left glittering here. . . . They carried off the gold and left us the gold. . . . They left us the words.

The following poem, also titled "The Word," is from *Fully Empowered* (1962). It is another eloquent tribute to language.

The word
was born in the blood,
grew in the dark body, beating,
and flew through the lips and the mouth.

Farther away and nearer   5
still, still it came
from dead fathers and from wandering races,
from lands that had returned to stone
weary of their poor tribes,
because when pain took to the roads   10
the settlements set out and arrived
and new lands and water reunited
to sow their words anew.

And so, this is the inheritance—
this is the wavelength which connects us   15
with the dead man and the dawn
of new beings not yet come to light.

Still the atmosphere quivers
with the initial word
dressed up   20
in terror and sighing.
It emerged
from the darkness
and until now there is no thunder
that rumbles yet with all the iron   25
of that word,
the first
word uttered—
perhaps it was only a ripple, a drop,
and yet its great cataract falls and falls.   30

Later on, the word fills with meaning.
It remained gravid and it filled up with lives.
Everything had to do with births and sounds—
affirmation, clarity, strength,
negation, destruction, death—   35
the verb took over all the power
and blended existence with essence
in the electricity of its beauty.

Human word, syllable, combination
of spread light and the fine art of the silversmith,   40
hereditary goblet which gathers
the communications of the blood—
here is where silence was gathered up
in the completeness of the human word
and, for human beings, not to speak is to die—   45
language extends even to the hair,
the mouth speaks without the lips moving—
all of a sudden the eyes are words.

I take the word and go over it
as though it were nothing more than a human shape,   50
its arrangements awe me and I find my way
through each variation in the spoken word—
I utter and I am and without speaking I approach
the limit of words and the silence.

I drink to the word, raising   55
a word or a shining cup,
in it I drink
the pure wine of language
or inexhaustible water,
maternal source of words,   60
and cup and water and wine
give rise to my song
because the verb is the source
and vivid life—it is blood,
blood which expresses its substance   65
and so implies its own unwinding—
words give glass-quality to glass, blood to blood,
and life to life itself.

UNDERSTANDING THE POEM

1. What type of situations motivated the first word?
2. What is "the inheritance" of words (line 14)?
3. Why does the speaker value verbs most highly?
4. To what extent is it true that "not to speak is to die" (line 45)?
5. What is the **theme** of "The Word"? Which lines reveal the theme?

ANALYZING LITERARY TECHNIQUE

1. What **metaphor** is used for the word in stanza 1? What is the advantage of this choice?
2. Evaluate Neruda's use of metaphor in stanza 2. Consider (a) "lands that had returned to stone" (line 8), (b) "when pain took to the roads" (line 10), and (c) "new lands and water reunited / to sow their word anew" (lines 12–13).
3. In stanza 7, Neruda alludes to French philosopher René Descartes's statement "I think; therefore, I am." What does the allusion add to Neruda's own statement?
4. How does Neruda use the metaphor of "a shining cup" in stanza 8? Why is it appropriate?
5. How does blood function as a metaphor in the poem?
6. How does water function as a metaphor in the poem?

WRITING ABOUT LITERATURE

1. Write an essay in which you analyze Neruda's use of metaphor. Choose three metaphors, explain their use in the poem, and evaluate their contribution. Consider what each contributes to the importance of language and quote from the poem to support your ideas. Conclude with a general statement about the role of metaphor in the poem.
2. Create your own poem about words. Choose a common verb that has many synonyms, such as *walk* or *talk*. Use a dictionary to learn the verb's history and, if you wish, a thesaurus to find more synonyms. Express your ideas in visual language by using **similes** and metaphors. Use rhyme if it enhances your poem or write in free verse. (If you prefer, write a paragraph first; then remove all extraneous words, and finally arrange the remaining words in a pattern that pleases your ear.)

The Third Bank
of the River

JOÃO GUIMARÃES ROSA

OÃO GUIMARÃES ROSA (1908–1967), the twentieth-century Brazilian author, is one of Latin America's most important and influential writers. Many scholars and critics rank his novel *The Devil to Pay in the Backlands* (1956) among the greatest in world literature. His poetic treatment of narrative in his first published collection of short stories, *Sagarana* (1946), was so striking that it replaced social realism as the predominant literary style in Brazil. Three other collections of Rosa's short stories were published in the 1960s, including *The Third Bank of the River and Other Stories* (1962).

Rosa was born into an old patrician family in a small town in the state of Minas Gerais, the vast barren high plateau region in the interior of Brazil that provides the setting for most of his stories. In 1930 he became a doctor, and for four years he practiced medicine in the same area in which he had grown up. Often instead of payment he would ask his patients to tell him a story. The oral tales that he collected influenced the stories he wrote. Rosa participated in the 1930 revolution in Brazil as an army doctor. In 1934 he became a career diplomat in the Brazilian Ministry of Foreign Affairs, a position that took him to Germany, Colombia, and France. When speaking about his life, he is quoted as saying, "As a physician, I came to know the mystical greatness of suffering; as a rebel, the value of consciousness; and as a soldier, the importance of the proximity of death."

Rosa transformed regional tales into lyrical prose that reflects the universal human condition. "I have always been a mystic," he announced, believing that reality is multifaceted, that logic is only one possible way to analyze the nature of reality, and that people see only fragments or surfaces of what actually exists. As Rosa's characters search for meaning in their lives, they may discard the traditionally logical way of looking at life and may experience what is extraordinary and even miraculous.

Rosa developed his revolutionary, highly poetic, and lyrical style to express his unusual view of the world. Since he views life as a mystery, with many valid interpretations of reality, it is not surprising that he chooses a style that will force his readers to make of each story what they will. "The Third Bank of the River" exemplifies this style.

My father was a dutiful, orderly, straightforward man. And according to several reliable people of whom I inquired, he had had these qualities since adolescence or even childhood. By my own recollection, he was neither jollier nor more melancholy than the other men we knew. Maybe a little quieter. It was Mother, not Father, who ruled the house. She scolded us daily—my sister, my brother, and me. But it happened one day that Father ordered a boat.

He was very serious about it. It was to be made specially for him, of mimosa wood. It was to be sturdy enough to last twenty or thirty years and just large enough for one person. Mother carried on plenty about it. Was her husband going to become a fisherman all of a sudden? Or a hunter? Father said nothing. Our house was less than a mile from the river, which around there was deep, quiet, and so wide you couldn't see across it.

I can never forget the day the rowboat was delivered. Father showed no joy or other emotion. He just put on his hat as he always did and said goodby to us. He took along no food or bundle of any sort. We expected Mother to rant and rave, but she didn't. She looked very pale and bit her lip, but all she said was: "If you go away, stay away. Don't ever come back!"

Father made no reply. He looked gently at me and motioned me to walk along with him. I feared Mother's wrath, yet I eagerly obeyed. We headed toward the river together. I felt bold and exhilarated, so much so that I said: "Father, will you take me with you in your boat?"

He just looked at me, gave me his blessing, and by a gesture, told me to go back. I made as if to do so but, when his back was turned, I ducked behind some bushes to watch him. Father got into the boat and rowed away. Its shadow slid across the water like a crocodile long and quiet.

Father did not come back. Nor did he go anywhere, really. He just rowed and floated across and around, out there in the river. Everyone was appalled. What had never happened, what could not possibly happen, was happening. Our relatives, neighbors, and friends came over to discuss the phenomenon.

Mother was ashamed. She said little and conducted herself with great composure. As a consequence, almost everyone thought (though no one said it) that Father had gone insane. A few, however, suggested that Father might be fulfilling a promise he had made to God or to a saint, or that he might have some horrible disease, maybe leprosy,[1] and that he left for the sake of the family, at the same time wishing to remain fairly near them.

---

[1] *leprosy:* A disfiguring skin disease.

Travelers along the river and people living near the bank on one side or the other reported that Father never put foot on land, by day or night. He just moved about the river, solitary, aimless, like a derelict. Mother and our relatives agreed that the food which he had doubtless hidden in the boat would soon give out and that then he would either leave the river and travel off somewhere (which would be at least a little more respectable) or he would repent and come home.

How far from the truth they were! Father had a secret source of provisions: me. Every day I stole food and brought it to him. The first night after he left, we all lit fires on the shore and prayed and called to him. I was deeply distressed and felt a need to do something more. The following day I went down to the river with a loaf of corn bread, a bunch of bananas, and some bricks of raw brown sugar. I waited impatiently a long, long hour. Then I saw the boat, far off, alone, gliding almost imperceptibly on the smoothness of the river. Father was sitting in the bottom of the boat. He saw me but he did not row toward me or make any gesture. I showed him the food and then I placed it in a hollow rock on the river bank; it was safe there from animals, rain, and dew. I did this day after day, on and on and on. Later I learned, to my surprise, that Mother knew what I was doing and left food around where I could easily steal it. She had a lot of feelings she didn't show.

Mother sent for her brother to come and help on the farm and in business matters. She had the school teacher come and tutor us children at home because of the time we had lost. One day, at her request, the priest put on his vestments, went down to the shore, and tried to exorcise the devils that had got into my father. He shouted that Father had a duty to cease his unholy obstinacy. Another day she arranged to have two soldiers come and try to frighten him. All to no avail. My father went by in the distance, sometimes so far away he could barely be seen. He never replied to anyone and no one ever got close to him. When some newspapermen came in a launch to take his picture, Father headed his boat to the other side of the river and into the marshes, which he knew like the palm of his hand but in which other people quickly got lost. There in his private maze, which extended for miles, with heavy foliage overhead and rushes on all sides, he was safe.

We had to get accustomed to the idea of Father's being out on the river. We had to but we couldn't, we never could. I think I was the only one who understood to some degree what our father wanted and what he did not want. The thing I could not understand at all was how he stood the hardship. Day and night, in sun and rain, in heat and in terrible midyear cold spells, with his old hat on his head and very little other clothing, week after week, month after month, year after year, unheedful of the waste and emptiness in which his life was slipping by. He never set foot on earth or grass, on isle or mainland shore. No doubt he sometimes tied up the boat at a secret place, perhaps the tip of some island, to get a little sleep. He never lit a fire or even struck a match and he had no flashlight. He took only a small part of the food that I left in the hollow—not enough, it seemed to me, for survival. What could his state of health have been? How about the continual drain on his energy, pulling and pushing oars to control the boat? And how did he survive the annual floods, when the river rose and swept along with it all sorts of dangerous objects—branches of trees, dead bodies of animals— that might suddenly crash against his little boat?

He never talked to a living soul. And we never talked about him. We just thought. No, we could never put our father out of mind. If for a short time we seemed to, it was just a lull from which we would be sharply awakened by the realization of his frightening situation.

My sister got married, but Mother didn't want a wedding party. It would have been a sad affair, for we thought of him every time we ate some especially tasty food. Just as we thought of him in our cozy beds on a cold, stormy night—out there, alone and unprotected, trying to bail out the boat with only his hands and a gourd. Now and then someone would say that I was getting to look more and more like my father. But I knew that by then his hair and beard must have been shaggy and his nails long. I pictured him thin and sickly, black with hair and sunburn, and almost naked despite the articles of clothing I occasionally left for him.

He didn't seem to care about us at all. But I felt affection and respect for him, and, whenever they praised me because I had done something good, I said: "My father taught me to act that way."

It wasn't exactly accurate but it was a truthful sort of lie. As I said, Father didn't seem to care about us. But then why did he stay around there? Why didn't he go up the river or down the river, beyond the possibility of seeing us or being seen by us? He alone knew the answer.

My sister had a baby boy. She insisted on showing Father his grandson. One beautiful day we all went down to the riverbank, my sister in her white wedding dress, and she lifted the baby high. Her husband held a parasol above them. We shouted to Father and waited. He did not appear. My sister cried; we all cried in each other's arms.

My sister and her husband moved far away. My brother went to live in a city. Times changed, with their usual imperceptible rapidity. Mother finally moved too; she was old and went to live with her daughter. I remained behind, a leftover. I could never think of marrying. I just stayed there with the impedimenta of my life. Father, wandering alone and forlorn on the river, needed me. I knew he needed me, although he never even told me why he was doing it. When I put the question to people bluntly and insistently, all they told me was that they heard that Father had explained it to the man who made the boat. But now this man was dead and nobody knew or remembered anything. There was just some foolish talk, when the rains were especially severe and persistent, that my father was wise like Noah and had the boat built in anticipation of a new flood;[2] I dimly remember people saying this. In any case, I would not condemn my father for what he was doing. My hair was beginning to turn gray.

I have only sad things to say. What bad had I done, what was my great guilt? My father always away and his absence always with me. And the river, always the river, perpetually renewing itself. The river, always. I was beginning to suffer from old age, in which life is just a sort of lingering. I had attacks of illness and of anxiety. I had a nagging rheumatism. And he? Why, why was he doing it? He must

---

[2] *Noah . . . new flood:* A figure in the Bible. Noah was warned by God that there would be a great flood. He built an ark (ship) to save his family and one pair of every living creature.

have been suffering terribly. He was so old. One day, in his failing strength, he might let the boat capsize; or he might let the current carry it downstream, on and on, until it plunged over the waterfall to the boiling turmoil below. It pressed upon my heart. He was out there and I was forever robbed of my peace. I am guilty of I know not what, and my pain is an open wound inside me. Perhaps I would know—if things were different. I began to guess what was wrong.

Out with it! Had I gone crazy? No, in our house that word was never spoken, never through all the years. No one called anybody crazy, for nobody is crazy. Or maybe everybody. All I did was go there and wave a handkerchief so he would be more likely to see me. I was in complete command of myself. I waited. Finally he appeared in the distance, there, then over there, a vague shape sitting in the back of the boat. I called to him several times. And I said what I was so eager to say, to state formally and under oath. I said it as loud as I could:

"Father, you have been out there long enough. You are old. . . . Come back, you don't have to do it anymore. . . . Come back and I'll go instead. Right now, if you want. Any time. I'll get into the boat. I'll take your place."

And when I had said this my heart beat more firmly.

He heard me. He stood up. He maneuvered with his oars and headed the boat toward me. He had accepted my offer. And suddenly, I trembled, down deep. For he had raised his arm and waved—the first time in so many, so many years. And I couldn't. . . . In terror, my hair on end, I ran, I fled madly. For he seemed to come from another world. And I'm begging forgiveness, begging, begging.

I experienced the dreadful sense of cold that comes from deadly fear, and I became ill. Nobody ever saw or heard about him again. Am I a man, after such a failure? I am what never should have been. I am what must be silent. I know it is too late. I must stay in the deserts and unmarked plains of my life, and I fear I shall shorten it. But when death comes I want them to take me and put me in a little boat in this perpetual water between the long shores; and I, down the river, lost in the river, inside the river . . . the river . . .

UNDERSTANDING THE STORY

1. Why does the narrator begin by describing his father as "dutiful, orderly, straightforward"?

2. Why does the father abandon his family? To what extent is his behavior like that of parents who live at home but remove themselves emotionally from their families?

3. Why does the father remain visible to his family?

4. What, if anything, would have made it possible for the father to return home?

5. What right does the father have to treat his family in this way?

6. Why does the narrator feel affection and respect for his father when it is difficult to accept his father's strange behavior?

7. Why does the narrator tell "a truthful sort of lie" and attribute his own good behavior to his father's teachings?

8. Why does the narrator choose to never marry and to remain near his father?

9. What is significant about the narrator's remark "Nobody is crazy. Or maybe everybody"?

10. Why does the narrator volunteer to exchange places with his father? Why does his father accept his offer? What terrifies the narrator about changing places with his father?

11. What does the narrator mean by his concluding remarks?

12. Who is most responsible for the course of the narrator's life? Evaluate the narrator's own responsibility and the responsibility of his mother and his father.

ANALYZING LITERARY TECHNIQUE

1. Describe the relationship between the setting and the **plot.**

2. Why is the **narrative perspective** important in this story? To what extent is a first-person narrator appropriate? Contrast the effect of a third-person **omniscient narrator.**

3. How does Rosa's use of **realism** contribute to the story?

4. What is the **climax** of the story? Evaluate its significance.

5. Explain the meaning and function of the river as a **symbol.** What is the "third bank of the river"?

WRITING ABOUT LITERATURE

1. Write an essay in which you either justify or criticize the narrator's change of mind about his offer to take his father's place. Consider the following questions: What does the narrator owe his father? What does the narrator owe himself? Which obligation is the more important of the two? Why?

2. Tell this story from the father's point of view. Consider the following questions: Why does the father act as he does? How does he feel about his family and his life? Under what conditions, if any, would he have returned home?

End of the Game

JULIO CORTÁZAR

*J*ULIO CORTÁZAR (1914–1984) is an internationally acclaimed Latin American author from Argentina. Although he was a novelist, a poet, a playwright, an essayist, a literary critic, and a translator of Edgar Allan Poe's complete prose works, he is known as a master of the short story. His best-known works are his short-story collections: *Blow Up and Other Stories* (1956; 1967); *All Fires the Fire*, (1966; 1973); *A Change of Light* (1974; 1978; 1980); and *We Love Glenda So Much* (1981; 1983). He is also known for the following novels: *Hopscotch* (1963; 1966), the novel that is considered his masterpiece; *The Winners* (1965; 1973), a social allegory about passengers on a sea voyage; and *62: A Model Kit* (1968; 1972). *Hopscotch* and the film *Blow Up*, (based on Cortázar's short story and directed by Michelangelo Antonini) brought him international fame.

Cortázar was born in Brussels, Belgium, to Argentine parents. His family moved back to Buenos Aires when he was six years old, but he grew up with a lasting interest in French culture and literature. Cortázar was still very young when his father deserted his family and left his mother to rear and educate him.

After teaching high school in Buenos Aries for five years, Cortázar began to teach courses in French literature at local universities. However, the values espoused by the Peronist government conflicted with his own values. The Argentine government made it so difficult for him to continue teaching that he resigned in 1951 and emigrated to Paris, France, where he spent the rest of his life writing and working as a freelance translator for UNESCO. Although he had avoided radical politics in Argentina, he became a socialist in Paris. He supported Castro's government in Cuba, Allende's government in Chile, and the Sandinista government in Nicaragua, to which he contributed the royalties from his literary works.

Cortázar began to write short stories in 1934. However, his first story was not published until 1946, when his mentor Jorge Luis Borges published it in the magazine *The Annals of Buenos Aires*. Cortázar published his first short-story collection, *Bestiario,* in 1951, the year he left Argentina.

Like the work of Borges, Cortázar's early work deals with life and death, with the quest for identity, and with the nature of time. His later work depicts everyday life on a surrealist level, where he blends fantasy with reality in a technique known as magic realism. In Cortázar's words, "Nothing is ordinary when submitted to a silent and sustained scrutiny." His focus is often on social consciousness, and a principal theme is the isolation—and therefore the estrangement—of the individual in the modern world.

Cortázar speaks of himself as follows:

> I refer to my own experience as a story writer, and I see a relatively happy and unremarkable man, caught up in the same trivialities and trips to the dentist as any inhabitant of a large city . . . who suddenly, instantaneously, in the subway, in a cafe, in a dream, in the office . . . stops being him-and-his-circumstances and, for no reason, without warning . . . without anything that gives him a chance to clench his teeth and take a deep breath, *he is a story,* a shapeless mass without words or faces or beginning or end, but still a story, something that can only be a story, and then, suddenly, . . . he puts a paper in the typewriter and begins to write, even if his bosses and the whole United Nations scream in his ears.

"End of the Game" is one of Cortázar's most famous short stories. Although the story takes place in Argentina, the attitudes and behavior of the characters are universal.

Letitia, Holanda and I used to play by the Argentine Central tracks during the hot weather, hoping that Mama and Aunt Ruth would go up to their siesta so that we could get out past the white gate. After washing the dishes, Mama and Aunt Ruth were always tired, especially when Holanda and I were drying, because it was then that there were arguments, spoons on the floor, secret words that only we understood, and in general, an atmosphere in which the smell of grease, José's yowling, and the dimness of the kitchen would end up in an incredible fight and the subsequent commotion. Holanda specialized in rigging this sort of brawl, for example, letting an already clean glass slip into the pan of dirty water, or casually dropping a remark to the effect that the Loza house had two maids to do all the work. I had other systems: I liked to suggest to Aunt Ruth that she was going to get an allergy rash on her hands if she kept scrubbing the pots instead of doing the cups and plates once in a while, which were exactly what Mama liked to wash, and over which they would confront one another soundlessly in a war of advantage to get the easy item. The heroic expedient, in case the bits of advice and the drawn-out family recollections began to bore us, was to upset some boiling water on the cat's back. Now that's a big lie about a scalded cat, it really is, except that you have to take the reference to cold water literally; because José never backed away from hot water, almost insinuating himself under it, poor animal, when we spilled a half-cup of it somewhere around 220°F., or less, a good deal less, probably, because his hair never fell out. The whole point was to get Troy burning, and in the confusion, crowned by a splendid G-flat from Aunt Ruth and Mama's sprint for the whipstick, Holanda and I would take no time at all to get lost in the long porch, toward the empty rooms off the back, where Letitia would be waiting for us, reading Ponson de Terrail, or some other equally inexplicable book.

Normally, Mama chased us a good part of the way, but her desire to bust in our skulls evaporated soon enough, and finally (we had barred the door and were begging for mercy in emotion-filled and very theatrical voices), she got tired and went off, repeating the same sentence: "Those ruffians'll end up on the street."

Where we ended up was by the Argentine Central tracks, when the house had settled down and was silent, and we saw the cat stretched out under the lemon tree to take its siesta also, a rest buzzing with fragrances and wasps. We'd open the white gate slowly, and when we shut it again with a slam like a blast of wind, it was a freedom which took us by the hands, seized the whole of our bodies and tumbled us out. Then we ran, trying to get the speed to scramble up the low embankment of the right-of-way, and there spread out upon the world, we silently surveyed our kingdom.

Our kingdom was this: a long curve of the tracks ended its bend just opposite the back section of the house. There was just the gravel incline, the crossties, and the double line of track; some dumb sparse grass among the rubble where mica, quartz, and feldspar—the components of granite—sparkled like real diamonds in the two o'clock afternoon sun. When we stooped down to touch the rails (not wasting time because it would have been dangerous to spend much time there, not so much from the trains as for fear of being seen from the house), the heat off the stone roadbed flushed our faces, and facing into the wind from the river there was a damp heat against our cheeks and ears. We liked to bend our legs and squat down, rise, squat again, move from one kind of hot zone to the other, watching each other's faces to measure the perspiration—a minute or two later we would be sopping with it. And we were always quiet, looking down the track into the distance, or at the river on the other side, that stretch of coffee-and-cream river.

After this first inspection of the kingdom, we'd scramble down the bank and flop in the meager shadow of the willows next the wall enclosing the house where the white gate was. This was the capital city of the kingdom, the wilderness city and the headquarters of our game. Letitia was the first to start the game; she was the luckiest and the most privileged of the three of us. Letitia didn't have to dry dishes or make the beds, she could laze away the day reading or pasting up pictures, and at night they let her stay up later if she asked to, not counting having a room to herself, special hot broth when she wanted it, and all kinds of other advantages. Little by little she had taken more and more advantage of these privileges, and had been presiding over the game since the summer before, I think really she was presiding over the whole kingdom; in any case she was quicker at saying things, and Holanda and I accepted them without protest, happy almost. It's likely that Mama's long lectures on how we ought to behave toward Letitia had had their effect, or simply that we loved her enough and it didn't bother us that she was boss. A pity that she didn't have the looks for the boss, she was the shortest of the three of us and very skinny. Holanda was skinny, and I never weighed over 110, but Letitia was scragglier than we were, and even worse, that kind of skinniness you can see from a distance in the neck and ears. Maybe it was the stiffness of her back that made her look so thin, for instance she could hardly move her head from side to side, she was like a folded-up ironing board, one of those kind they had in the Loza house, with a cover of white material. Like an ironing board with the wide part up, leaning closed against the wall. And she led us.

The best satisfaction was to imagine that someday Mama or Aunt Ruth would find out about the game. If they managed to find out about the game there would be an unbelievable mess. The G-flat and fainting fits, incredible protests of devotion and sacrifice ill-rewarded, and a string of words threatening the more celebrated punishments, closing the bid with a dire prediction of our fates, which consisted of the three of us ending up on the street. This final prediction always left us somewhat perplexed, because to end up in the street always seemed fairly normal to us.

First Letitia had us draw lots. We used to use pebbles hidden in the hand, count to twenty-one, any way at all. If we used the count-to-twenty-one system, we would pretend two or three more girls and include them in the counting to prevent cheating. If one of them came out 21, we dropped her from the group and started drawing again, until one of us won. Then Holanda and I lifted the stone and we got out the ornament-box. Suppose Holanda had won, Letitia and I chose the ornaments. The game took two forms: Statues and Attitudes. Attitudes did not require ornaments but an awful lot of expressiveness, for Envy you could show your teeth, make fists and hold them in a position so as to seem cringing. For Charity the ideal was an angelic face, eyes turned up to the sky, while the hands offered something—a rag, a ball, a branch of willow—to a poor invisible orphan. Shame and Fear were easy to do; Spite and Jealousy required a more conscientious study. The Statues were determined, almost all of them, by the choice of ornaments, and here absolute liberty reigned. So that a statue would come out of it, one had to think carefully of every detail in the costume. It was a rule of the game that the one chosen could not take part in the selection; the two remaining argued out the business at hand and then fitted the ornaments on. The winner had to invent her statue taking into account what they'd dressed her in, and in this way the game was much more complicated and exciting because sometimes there were counterplots, and the victim would find herself rigged out in adornments which were completely hopeless; so it was up to her to be quick then in composing a good statue. Usually when the game called for Attitudes, the winner came up pretty well outfitted, but there were times when the Statues were horrible failures.

Well, the story I'm telling, lord knows when it began, but things changed the day the first note fell from the train. Naturally the Attitudes and Statues were not for our own consumption, we'd have gotten bored immediately. The rules were that the winner had to station herself at the foot of the embankment, leaving the shade of the willow trees, and wait for the train from Tigre that passed at 2:08. At that height above Palermo the trains went by pretty fast and we weren't bashful doing the Statue or the Attitude. We hardly saw the people in the train windows, but with time, we got a bit more expert, and we knew that some of the passengers were expecting to see us. One man with white hair and tortoise-shell glasses used to stick his head out the window and wave at the Statue or the Attitude with a handkerchief. Boys sitting on the steps of the coaches on their way back from school shouted things as the train went by, but some of them remained serious and watching us. In actual fact, the Statue or the Attitude saw nothing at all, because she had to concentrate so hard on holding herself stock-still, but the other two under the willows would analyze in excruciating detail the great success produced, or the audience indifference. It was a Wednesday when the note dropped as the second coach went by. It fell very near Holanda (she did Malicious Gossip that day) and ricocheted toward me. The small piece of paper was tightly folded up and had been shoved through a metal nut. In a man's handwriting, and pretty bad too, it said: "The Statues very pretty. I ride in the third window of the second coach. Ariel B." For all the trouble of stuffing it through the nut and tossing it, it seemed to us a little dry, but it delighted us. We chose lots to see who would keep it, and I won. The next day nobody wanted to play because we all wanted to see what Ariel B. was like, but we were afraid he would misinterpret our interruption, so finally we chose lots and Letitia won. Holanda and I were very happy because Letitia did Statues very well, poor thing. The paralysis wasn't noticeable when she was still, and she was capable of gestures of enormous nobility. With Attitudes she always chose Generosity, Piety, Sacrifice and Renunciation. With Statues she tried for the style of the Venus in the parlor which Aunt Ruth called the Venus de Nilo. For that reason we chose ornaments especially so that Ariel would be very impressed. We hung a piece of green velvet on her like a tunic, and a crown of willow on her hair. As we were wearing short sleeves, the Greek effect was terrific. Letitia practiced a little in the shade, and we decided that we'd show ourselves also and wave at Ariel, discreetly, but very friendly.

Letitia was magnificent, when the train came she didn't budge a finger. Since she couldn't turn her head, she threw it backward, bringing her arms against her body almost as though she were missing them; except for the green tunic, it was like looking at the Venus de Nilo. In the third window we saw a boy with blond curly hair and light eyes, who smiled brightly when he saw that Holanda and I were waving at him. The train was gone in a second, but it was 4:30 and we were still discussing whether he was wearing a dark suit, a red tie, and if he were really nice or a creep. On Thursday I did an Attitude, Dejection, and we got another note which read: "The three of you I like very much. Ariel." Now he stuck his head and one arm out the window and laughed and waved at us. We figured him to be eighteen (we were sure he was no older than sixteen) and we decided that he was coming back every day from some English school, we couldn't stand the idea of any of the regular peanut factories. You could see that Ariel was super.

As it happened, Holanda had the terrific luck to win three days running. She surpassed herself, doing the attitudes Reproach and Robbery, and a very difficult

Statue of The Ballerina, balancing on one foot from the time the train hit the curve. The next day I won, and the day after that too; when I was doing Horror, a note from Ariel almost caught me on the nose; at first we didn't understand it: "The prettiest is the laziest." Letitia was the last to understand it; we saw that she blushed and went off by herself, and Holanda and I looked at each other, just a little furious. The first judicial opinion it occurred to us to hand down was that Ariel was an idiot, but we couldn't tell Letitia that, poor angel, with the disadvantage she had to put up with. She said nothing, but it seemed to be understood that the paper was hers, and she kept it. We were sort of quiet going back to the house that day, and didn't get together that night. Letitia was very happy at the supper table, her eyes shining, and Mama looked at Aunt Ruth a couple of times as evidence of her own high spirits. In those days they were trying out a new strengthening treatment for Letitia, and considering how she looked, it was miraculous how well she was feeling.

Before we went to sleep, Holanda and I talked about the business. The note from Ariel didn't bother us so much, thrown from a train going its own way, that's how it is, but it seemed to us that Letitia from her privileged position was taking too much advantage of us. She knew we weren't going to say anything to her, and in a household where there's someone with some physical defect and a lot of pride, everyone pretends to ignore it starting with the one who's sick, or better yet, they pretend they don't know that the other one knows. But you don't have to exaggerate it either, and the way Letitia was acting at the table, or the way she kept the note, was just too much. That night I went back to having nightmares about trains, it was morning and I was walking on enormous railroad beaches covered with rails filled with switches, seeing in the distance the red glows of locomotives approaching, anxiously trying to calculate if the train was going to pass to my left and threatened at the same time by the arrival of an express back of me or—what was even worse—that one of the trains would switch off onto one of the sidings and run directly over me. But I forgot it by morning because Letitia was all full of aches and we had to help her get dressed. It seemed to us that she was a little sorry for the business yesterday and we were very nice to her, telling her that's what happens with walking too much and that maybe it would be better for her to stay in her room reading. She said nothing but came to the table for breakfast, and when Mama asked, she said she was fine and her back hardly hurt at all. She stated it firmly and looked at us.

That afternoon I won, but at that moment, I don't know what came over me, I told Letitia that I'd give her my place, naturally without telling her why. That this guy clearly preferred her and would look at her until his eyes fell out. The game drew to Statues, and we selected simple items so as not to complicate life, and she invented a sort of Chinese Princess, with a shy air, looking at the ground, and the hands placed together as Chinese princesses are wont to do. When the train passed, Holanda was lying on her back under the willows, but I watched and saw that Ariel had eyes only for Letitia. He kept looking at her until the train disappeared around the curve, and Letitia stood there motionless and didn't know that he had just looked at her that way. But when it came to resting under the trees again, we saw that she knew all right, and that she'd have been pleased to keep the costume on all afternoon and all night.

Wednesday we drew between Holanda and me, because Letitia said it was only fair she be left out. Holanda won, darn her luck, but Ariel's letter fell next to me. When I picked it up I had the impulse to give it to Letitia who didn't say a word, but I thought, then, that neither was it a matter of catering to everybody's wishes, and I opened it slowly. Ariel announced that the next day he was going to get off at the nearby station and that he would come by the embankment to chat for a while. It was all terribly written, but the final phrase was handsomely put: "Warmest regards to the three Statues." The signature looked like a scrawl though we remarked on its personality.

While we were taking the ornaments off Holanda, Letitia looked at me once or twice. I'd read them the message and no one had made any comments, which was very upsetting because finally, at last, Ariel was going to come and one had to think about this new development and come to some decision. If they found out about it at the house, or if by accident one of the Loza girls, those envious little runts, came to spy on us, there was going to be one incredible mess. Furthermore, it was extremely unlike us to remain silent over a thing like this; we hardly looked at one another, putting the ornaments away and going back through the white gate to the house.

Aunt Ruth asked Holanda and me to wash the cat, and she took Letitia off for the evening treatment and finally we could get our feelings off our chests. It seemed super that Ariel was going to come, we'd never had a friend like that, our cousin Tito we didn't count, a dumbbell who cut out paper dolls and believed in first communion. We were extremely nervous in our expectation and José, poor angel, got the short end of it. Holanda was the braver of the two and brought up the subject of Letitia. I didn't know what to think, on the one hand it seemed ghastly to me that Ariel should find out, but also it was only fair that things clear themselves up, no one had to out and out put herself on the line for someone else. What I really would have wanted was that Letitia not suffer; she had enough to put up with and now the new treatment and all those things.

That night Mama was amazed to see us so quiet and said what a miracle, and had the cat got our tongues, then looked at Aunt Ruth and both of them thought for sure we'd been raising hell of some kind and were conscience-stricken. Letitia ate very little and said that she hurt and would they let her go to her room to read Rocambole. Though she didn't much want to, Holanda gave her a hand, and I sat down and started some knitting, something I do only when I'm nervous. Twice I thought to go down to Letitia's room, I couldn't figure out what the two of them were doing there alone, but then Holanda came back with a mysterious air of importance and sat next to me not saying a word until Mama and Aunt Ruth cleared the table. "She doesn't want to go tomorrow. She wrote a letter and said that if he asks a lot of questions we should give it to him." Half-opening the pocket of her blouse she showed me the lilac-tinted envelope. Then they called us in to dry the dishes, and that night we fell asleep almost immediately, exhausted by all the high-pitched emotion and from washing José.

The next day it was my turn to do the marketing and I didn't see Letitia all morning, she stayed in her room. Before they called us to lunch I went in for a moment and found her sitting on the window with a pile of pillows and a new Rocambole novel. You could see she felt terrible, but she started to laugh and told me about a bee that couldn't find its way out and about a funny dream she had had. I said it was a pity she wasn't coming out to the willows, but I found it difficult to put it nicely. "If you want, we can explain to Ariel that you feel upset," I suggested, but she said no and shut up like a clam. I insisted for a little while, really, that she should come, and finally got terribly gushy and told her she shouldn't be afraid, giving as an example that true affection knows no barriers and other fat ideas we'd gotten from *The Treasure of Youth,* but it got harder and harder to say anything to her because she was looking out the window and looked as if she were going to cry. Finally I left, saying that Mama needed me. Lunch lasted for days, and Holanda got a slap from Aunt Ruth for having spattered some tomato sauce from the spaghetti onto the tablecloth. I don't even remember doing the dishes, right away we were out under the willows hugging one another, very happy, and not jealous of one another in the slightest. Holanda explained to me everything we had to say about our studies so that Ariel would be impressed, because high school students despised girls who'd only been through grade school and studied just home ec and knew how to do raised needlework. When the train went past at 2:08, Ariel waved his arms enthusiastically, and we waved a welcome to him with our embossed handkerchiefs. Some twenty minutes later we saw him arrive by the embankment; he was taller than we had thought and dressed all in grey.

I don't even remember what we talked about at first; he was somewhat shy in spite of having come and the notes and everything, and said a lot of considerate things. Almost immediately he praised our Statues and Attitudes and asked our names, and why had the third one not come. Holanda explained that Letitia had not been able to come, and he said that that was a pity and that he thought Letitia was an exquisite name. Then he told us stuff about the Industrial High School, it was not the English school, unhappily, and wanted to know if we would show him the ornaments. Holanda lifted the stone and we let him see the things. He seemed to be very interested in them, and at different times he would take one of the ornaments and say, "Letitia wore this one day," or "This was for the Oriental statue," what he meant was the Chinese Princess. We sat in the shade under a willow and he was happy but distracted, and you could see that he was only being polite. Holanda looked at me two or three times when the conversation lapsed into silence, and that made both of us feel awful, made us want to get out of it, or wish that Ariel had never come at all. He asked again if Letitia were ill and Holanda looked at me and I thought she was going to tell him, but instead she answered that Letitia had not been able to come. Ariel drew geometric figures in the dust with a stick and occasionally looked at the white gate and we knew what he was thinking, and because of that Holanda was right to pull out the lilac envelope and hand it up to him, and he stood there surprised with the envelope in his hand; then he blushed while we explained to him that Letitia had sent it to him, and he put the letter in an inside jacket pocket, not wanting to read it in front of us. Almost immediately he said that it had been a great pleasure for him and that he was delighted to have come, but his hand was soft and unpleasant in a way it'd have been better for the interview to end right away, although later we could only think of his grey eyes and the sad way he had of smiling. We also agreed on how he had said goodbye: "Until always," a form we'd never heard at home and which seemed to us so godlike and poetic. We told all this to Letitia who was waiting for us under the lemon tree in the patio, and I would have liked to have asked her what she had said in the letter, but I don't know what, it was because she'd sealed the envelope before giving to Holanda, so I didn't say anything about that and only told her what Ariel was like and how many times he'd asked for her. This was not at all an easy thing to do because it was a nice thing and a terrible thing at the same time; we noticed that Letitia was feeling very happy and at the same time she was almost crying, and we found ourselves saying that Aunt Ruth wanted us now and we left her looking at the wasps in the lemon tree.

When we were going to sleep that night, Holanda said to me, "The game's finished from tomorrow on, you'll see." But she was wrong though not by much, and the next day Letitia gave us the regular signal when dessert came around. We went out to wash the dishes somewhat astonished, and a bit sore, because that was sheer sauciness on Letitia's part and not the right thing to do. She was waiting for us at the gate, and we almost died of fright when we got to the willows for she brought out of her pocket Mama's pearl collar and all her rings, even Aunt Ruth's big one with the ruby. If the Loza girls were spying on us and saw us with the jewels, sure as anything Mama would learn about it right away and kill us, the nasty little creeps. But Letitia wasn't scared and said if anything happened she was the only one responsible. "I would like you to leave it to me today," she added without looking at us. We got the ornaments out right away, all of a sudden we wanted to be very kind to Letitia and give her all the pleasure, although at the bottom of everything we were still feeling a little spiteful. The game came out Statues, and we chose lovely things that would go well with the jewels, lots of peacock feathers to set in the hair, and a fur that from a distance looked like silver fox, and a pink veil that she put on like a turban. We saw that she was thinking, trying the Statue out, but without moving, and when the train appeared on the curve she placed herself at the foot of the incline with all the jewels sparkling in the sun. She lifted her arms as if she were going to do an Attitude instead of a Statue, her hands pointed at the sky with her head thrown back (the only direction she could, poor thing) and bent her body backwards so far it scared us. To us it seemed terrific, the most regal statue she'd ever done; then we saw Ariel looking at her, hung halfway out the window he looked just at her, turning his head and looking at her without seeing us, until the train carried him out of sight all at once. I don't know why, the two of us started running at the same time to catch Letitia who was standing there, still with her eyes closed and enormous tears all down her face. She pushed us back, not angrily, but we helped her stuff the jewels in her pocket, and she went back to the house alone while we put the ornaments away in their box for the last time. We knew almost what was going to happen, but just the same we went out to the willows the next day, just the two of us, after

Aunt Ruth imposed absolute silence so as not to disturb Letitia who hurt and who wanted to sleep. When the train came by, it was no surprise to see the third window empty, and while we were grinning at one another, somewhere between relief and being furious, we imagined Ariel riding on the other side of the coach, not moving in his seat, looking off toward the river with his grey eyes.

UNDERSTANDING THE STORY

1. What is the real game that the girls play? Why do the girls hide their game from Mama and Aunt Ruth?

2. Why does Letitia choose the Attitudes and the Statues that she does?

3. How do the girls feel toward Letitia?

4. What effect does Ariel have on the game?

5. How does Letitia feel about Ariel's interest in her? What do you think she tells Ariel in her letter?

6. Why does Letitia want to be the actress on the last day? Why does Letitia choose to be a regal statue? Why does she keep her eyes closed? Why does she return home alone?

7. Why does Ariel stop looking for the girls after he sees Letitia's last Statue? Why does Letitia stop playing the game?

8. Why does the game end? Why does Holanda know that the game will end?

9. What makes the title appropriate?

10. Find five references to Letitia's intelligence or to the education of Ariel or Letitia's family. What is the significance of these references?

11. In what ways does this story depict a coming of age or a rite of passage? What does the story reveal about fantasy and reality?

ANALYZING LITERARY TECHNIQUE

1. From whose **point of view** is this story told? How would the story be different if Cortázar, as omniscient author, narrated it? If Letitia narrated it? Why did Cortázar choose this point of view?

2. Note the narrator's use of **figurative language.** (a) What does the **allusion** to the burning of Troy contribute to the story? (b) Why does the narrator **personify** freedom by saying that freedom can take the girls by the hands? (c) Why does the narrator use the **metaphor** of a kingdom when referring to the play area? (d) What **simile** is used to describe Letitia, and why is it effective? (e) Why is the **hyperbole** "Lunch lasted for days" appropriate?

3. How does the author use **foreshadowing** in the story? Note two events that lead readers to suspect the inevitable conclusion.

4. Consider the narrator's use of **irony.** (a) What is ironic about the statement that "Letitia didn't have to dry dishes or make the beds, she could laze away the day reading"? (b) What is ironic about the narrator's "gushy" remark to Letitia, which she hopes will encourage Letitia to join in their play?

WRITING ABOUT LITERATURE

1. Write an expository essay in which you analyze Cortázar's use of point of view. Introduce your essay with a paragraph in which you describe the significance of point of view. In the body of your essay, devote one paragraph to each of the following alternatives: (a) an omniscient author's point of view; (b) Letitia's point of view; (c) the present narrator's point of view. Conclude your essay with a paragraph in which you explain why Cortázar chose the present narrator's point of view.

2. Write a story in which a character comes of age by discovering that fantasy is different from reality.

3. Retell this story from Letitia's point of view.

Two Bodies

OCTAVIO PAZ

*O*CTAVIO PAZ (1914–1998), Mexico's preeminent poet-essayist and a major twentieth-century poet, won the Nobel Prize for literature in 1990 "for impassioned writing with wide horizons, characterized by sensuous intelligence and humanistic integrity." Although he wrote more than forty books of poetry and prose, he is best known for *The Labyrinth of Solitude* (1950), a classic that defines the essence of Latin American culture through essays on Mexican history, culture, and identity. Paz is also known as a master stylist. "Sun Stone" (1958), his best-known poem, retells Aztec myths using surrealistic imagery, a technique that the Nobel Prize committee commended.

Paz was born in Mexico City. His father, a lawyer and politician who was devoted to social reform, was a supporter of Emiliano Zapata, the Mexican revolutionary. Because of his political views, Paz's father was forced to live in exile in Los Angeles, California, where Paz joined him for a few years. When Paz became a young adult, he fought on the Republican side in the Spanish civil war. A Marxist until the Nazi-Soviet Pact of 1938, he refers to himself as "a disillusioned leftist." Between 1945 and 1968, he was a career diplomat, serving as the Mexican ambassador to France, Switzerland, Japan, and India.

Paz was an adolescent when his first volume of poetry was published. Throughout his adult life, he was always a poet and an author; his diplomatic posts enriched his artistic knowledge. In Paris he was influenced by existentialism (with its focus on alienation) and by surrealism (with its focus on the unconscious). Alienation became one of the major themes in his writing, and surrealism the foundation of his poetic style. While in Japan and India, his exposure to Asian culture led him to incorporate aspects of Asian culture into his own worldview. From 1976 until his death in 1998, Paz was the publisher of the monthly literary magazine *Vuelta*.[1]

---

[1] Vuelta: *Vuelta* means "return."

According to Paz, "A poem is a shell that echoes the music of the world." Paz also stated, "If it happens that what you write for yourself becomes something for others as well, especially for a young reader, then you have achieved something." "Two Bodies" is an early lyric poem that first appeared in *Nature of Cloud*. It expresses an existentialist view of the universe with the skill and power for which Paz is known.

Two bodies face to face
are at times two waves
and night is an ocean.

Two bodies face to face
are at times two stones
and night a desert.   5

Two bodies face to face
are at times two roots
laced into night.

Two bodies face to face
are at times two knives   10
and night strikes sparks.

Two bodies face to face
are two stars falling
in an empty sky.   15

UNDERSTANDING THE POEM

1. Why does Paz place the bodies "face to face"?
2. Why does Paz describe the bodies at night?
3. What is significant about the phrase "at times"? Why is it omitted from the last stanza?
4. What is the speaker saying about human beings and the universe?

ANALYZING LITERARY TECHNIQUE

1. What does night symbolize in the poem?

2. Paz creates various **metaphors** in the first four stanzas of the poem to comment on human relationships. Choose two or more of these metaphors and explain what they suggest about relationships and the world.

3. In stanza 5, what do the metaphors of "two stars" and "an empty sky" suggest?

4. To what extent, if any, can the order of the five stanzas be rearranged without changing the meaning or impact of the poem?

5. What is the function of **repetition** in the poem?

6. **Existentialism** claims that the process of striving to create meaning is a valid end in itself. How does "Two Bodies" reflect existential beliefs?

WRITING ABOUT LITERATURE

1. Write an essay in which you analyze Paz's use of metaphor in "Two Bodies." Show the connection between the metaphors that he chooses and the ideas that he wishes to convey. Use quotations to support your ideas.

2. Create a poem in which you describe a human relationship, for example, between two sisters, a father and a son, an older person and a young person, or a teacher and a student. Find two or three striking images that suggest that relationship. Arrange your images into a logical or aesthetically pleasing order. You may add any additional details or images that you need to complete your poem.

Crossroads
A Sad Vaudeville

CARLOS SOLÓRZANO

ARLOS SOLÓRZANO (1922–), Guatemalan drama-
tist, artistic director, and scholar, is known both for his work
in Latin American theater and for his introduction of
European avant garde theater into Mexico. Solórzano's plays include
Doña Beatriz, the Hapless (1951); *The Magician* (1954); *The Hands of
God* (1956); *The Puppets* (1958); and *Crossroads* (1958). He has also
edited the books *Hispanic-American Contemporary Theater* (1964) and
Guatemalan Theater (1967) and written the novel *False Demons*
(1966).

Solórzano was born in San Marcos, Guatemala. In 1939, at the age
of seventeen, he moved to Mexico City. He attended the National
University of Mexico, earning a degree in architecture in 1944 and a
doctorate in literature in 1948. From 1949 to 1951, he studied drama
at the Sorbonne; while in Paris, Albert Camus became his "great friend
and teacher." After Solórzano returned to Mexico, he became a professor of Hispanic-American literature at the National University of
Mexico, and he directed the university's theater from 1952 to 1962.

In his plays, Solórzano expresses the anguish of modern life in a sick
society where humanity is absent and human dignity is not valued.
His characters are often torn between their desire to conform and
their desire to be free. Solórzano believes that people must overcome
the constraints of society even though such freedom can be terrifying.
Stylistically, he is innovative and versatile, employing different realistic and symbolic techniques for different plays.

Crossroads, or *Crossing*, is one of a group of three one-act plays.
It was first produced in 1966. Like Solórzano's other dramas, it is
modern and universal in its themes and avant garde in its technique.
In this play, Solórzano examines the nature of reality. The anguish that
his characters experience arises from their personal expectations and
their interpersonal relations rather than from their internal conflicts.

CHARACTERS

THE FLAGMAN

THE TRAIN

THE MAN

THE WOMAN

Setting: Stage empty, dark. At one end, a semaphore that alternately flashes a green light and a red one. In the center, hanging from the ceiling, a big clock whose hands show five o'clock sharp.

    [*The characters will move mechanically, like characters in the silent movies. The* MAN *in fast motion; the* WOMAN, *in slow motion. As the curtain rises, the* FLAGMAN *is at the end of the stage, opposite the semaphore, with a lighted lantern in his hand. He is standing very stiffly and indifferently.*]

FLAGMAN [*staring into space, in an impersonal voice*]: The trains from the North travel toward the South, the trains from the North travel toward the South, the trains from the North travel toward the South. [*He repeats the refrain several times while the* TRAIN *crosses the back of the stage. The* TRAIN *will be formed by men dressed in gray. As they pass by, they each mechanically perform a pantomime with one arm extended, the hand on the shoulder of the man in front, and the other arm making a circular motion, synchronized with the rhythm of the* FLAGMAN's *words.*] The trains from the North travel toward the South [*etc.*]. [*Loud train whistle. The* MAN *who comes at the end of the* TRAIN *breaks free of it by making a movement as though he were jumping off. The* TRAIN *disappears on the right.*]

MAN [*carrying small valise. He glances around the place, then looks at the clock, which he compares with his watch. He is young, serene of face, approximately twenty-five years old. He addresses the* FLAGMAN]: Good afternoon. [*As a reply, he receives the latter's refrain.*] Is this the place this ticket indicates? [*He places it in front of the* FLAGMAN's *eyes. The* FLAGMAN *nods.*] A train stops here, just about now, doesn't it?

FLAGMAN [*without looking at him*]: Trains never stop here.

MAN: Are you the flagman?

FLAGMAN: They call me by many names.

MAN: Then, perhaps you've seen a woman around here.

FLAGMAN: I've seen no one.

MAN [*approaching him*]: Do you know? The woman I'm looking for is . . .

FLAGMAN [*interrupting*]: They all look alike.

MAN: Oh, no! She's different. She's the woman that I've been waiting for for many years. She'll be wearing a white flower on her dress. Or is it yellow? [*He searches nervously in his pockets and takes out a paper that he reads.*] No, it's white . . . that's what she says in her letter. [*The* FLAGMAN *takes a few steps, feeling ill at ease.*] Pardon me for telling you all this, but now you'll be able to understand how important it is for me to find this woman, because . . .

FLAGMAN [*interrupting again*]: What woman?

MAN: The one that I'm looking for.

FLAGMAN: I don't know what woman you're looking for.

MAN: The one that I've just told you about.

FLAGMAN: Ah. . . .

MAN: Perhaps she has passed by and you didn't see her. [*The* FLAGMAN *shrugs his shoulders.*] Well, I guess that I have to tell you everything to see if you can remember. She's tall, slender, with black hair and big blue eyes. She's wearing a white flower on her dress. . . . [*Anxiously.*] Hasn't she been around here?

FLAGMAN: I can't know if someone I don't know has been around.

MAN: Excuse me. I know that I'm nervous but I have the impression that we aren't speaking the same language, that is, that you aren't answering my questions. . . .

FLAGMAN: That's not my job.

MAN: Nevertheless, I believe that a flagman ought to know how to answer questions. [*Transition.*] She wrote to me that she'd be here at five, at the railroad crossing of . . . [*He reads the ticket.*] I'll never know how to pronounce this name, but I know that it's here. We chose this point because it's halfway between our homes. Even for this kind of date, a romantic one, one must be fair. [*The* FLAGMAN *looks at him without understanding.*] Yes, romantic. [*With ingenuous pride:*] Maybe I'll bore you, but I must tell you that one day I saw an ad in a magazine. It was hers. How well written that ad was! She said that she needed a young man like me, to establish relations with so as not to live so alone. [*Pause.*] I wrote to her and she answered me. Then I sent her my photo and she sent me hers. You can't imagine what a beauty!

FLAGMAN [*who has not heard most of the account*]: Is she selling something?

MAN [*surprised*]: Who?

FLAGMAN: The woman who placed the ad.

MAN: No, for heaven's sake! She placed that ad because she said that she was shy, and she thought it might help and . . .

FLAGMAN: Everyone sells something.

MAN [*impatiently*]: You just don't understand me.

FLAGMAN: It's possible. . . .

MAN: Well, I mean . . . understand how excited I am on coming to meet someone whom I don't know but who . . .

FLAGMAN: How's that?

MAN [*upset*]: That is, I know her well, but I haven't seen her.

FLAGMAN: That's very common.

MAN: Do you think so?

FLAGMAN: The contrary's also common.

MAN: I don't understand.

FLAGMAN: It isn't necessary.

MAN: But you only speak nonsense! I should warn you that although I've an inclination toward romantic things, I'm a man who isn't pleased by jokes in bad taste. [*The* FLAGMAN *shrugs his shoulders again.*] Besides, this delay upsets me as does this dark place with that clock that doesn't run. It seems like a timeless place.

[*Suddenly a loud train whistle is heard. The semaphore comes to life flashing the green light. The* FLAGMAN *again adopts his rigid posture; staring into space, he repeats his refrain.*]

FLAGMAN [*loudly*]: The trains from the South travel toward the North. The trains from the South travel toward the North. The trains from the South travel toward the North [*etc.*].

[*The* TRAIN *passes across the back of the stage, from right to left.*]

MAN [*shouting*]: There, on that train! . . . She should be on it. [*He rushes to meet the* TRAIN *which passes by without stopping, almost knocking him down. The* MAN *remains at stage center, his arms at his sides. Disillusioned:*] She wasn't on it.

FLAGMAN: It's only natural.

MAN: What do you mean?

FLAGMAN: He's never coming. . . .

MAN: Who?

FLAGMAN: The man we're waiting for.

MAN: But it's a question of a woman.

FLAGMAN: It's the same.

MAN: How is a man going to be the same as a woman?

FLAGMAN: He isn't the same, but in a certain way he is.

MAN: You change your mind quickly.

FLAGMAN: I don't know.

MAN [*furiously*]: Then, what is it that you do know?

FLAGMAN [*indifferently*]: Where they're going.

MAN: The trains?

FLAGMAN: They all go to the same place.

MAN: What do you mean?

FLAGMAN: They come and go, but they end by meeting one another. . . .

MAN: That would be impossible.

FLAGMAN: But it's true. The impossible is always true.

MAN [*as if these last words brought him back to reality, he abandons his furious attitude and calms down*]: You're right in what you say. [*Hesitating.*] For example, my meeting with that woman seems impossible and it's the only certain thing of my whole existence. [*Suddenly, with an unexpected tone of anguish:*] But it's five ten. [*He looks at his watch.*] And she isn't coming. [*He takes the arm of the* FLAGMAN *who remains indifferent.*] Help me, do all that is possible to remember! I'm sure that if you want to, you can tell me if you saw her or not. . . .

FLAGMAN: One can't know by just seeing a person whether it was the one who placed an ad in the newspaper.

MAN [*once again containing his ill humor*]: But I already described what she's like to you! . . .

FLAGMAN [*imperturbably*]: I'm sorry. I forgot . . .

[*Meanwhile a* WOMAN *dressed in black has come in behind the* MAN. *She is tall and slim. Her face is covered by a heavy veil. She walks softly with a pantomime motion. On her dress she wears a very large white flower. On seeing her the* FLAGMAN *raises his lantern and examines her. The* MAN, *blinded by the light, covers his eyes. On seeing herself discovered, the* WOMAN *tears the white flower violently from her dress. She puts it in her purse and turns her back, remaining motionless.*]

MAN [*still covering his eyes*]: Ooh! You're going to blind me with that lantern.

FLAGMAN [*returning to his habitual stiffness*]: I beg your pardon. . . .

MAN [*to the* FLAGMAN]: Someone has come in, right?

FLAGMAN: It's not important.

MAN [*recovering from the glare, he notices the presence of the* WOMAN *and runs toward her. He stops suddenly*]: Ah . . . [*Timidly*] I beg you to. . . .

WOMAN [*her back turned*]: Yes?

MAN [*embarrassed*]: I thought that you . . . were someone . . .

WOMAN: Yes . . .

MAN [*with determination*]: Someone I'm looking for. [*She does not move. Pause.*] Will you permit me to see you from the front?

WOMAN: From the front?

MAN [*upset*]: Yes . . . it's absolutely necessary that I see you . . .

WOMAN [*without turning*]: But . . . why? [*She begins to turn slowly.*]

MAN: Well . . . in order to . . . [*On seeing that her face is covered, he backs away.*] You aren't wearing anything on your dress . . . and nevertheless . . .

WOMAN [*trembling*]: And nevertheless?

MAN: You have the same stature and build. . . .

WOMAN [*with a jesting tone*]: Really?

MAN [*with distrust*]: Could you tell me how you got here? I didn't see a train.

WOMAN [*interrupting, stammering*]: I arrived . . . ahead of time . . . and I waited.

MAN: Ahead of what time?

WOMAN: We all wait for a time. Aren't you waiting for it?

MAN [*sadly*]: Yes.

WOMAN: I believe that there is but one moment to recognize one another, to extend our hands. One mustn't let it pass us by.

MAN: What do you mean by that? Who are you?

WOMAN: Now I'm the woman I've always wanted to be.

MAN [*timidly*]: Will you let me see your face?

WOMAN [*frightened*]: Why?

MAN: I need to find that one face, the special one, the different one.

WOMAN [*moving away*]: I am sorry. I can't.

MAN [*following her with a tortured motion*]: Excuse me. I'm stupid, I know. For a moment I thought that you could be she. But it's absurd. If it were so, you'd come straight to me, for we have called one another from afar.

WOMAN [*trembling*]: Perhaps she's more afraid of finding the one she seeks than of letting him pass by without stopping.

MAN: No, that would also be absurd. [*Transition.*] In any case, I beg your pardon. [*He moves away and sits down on his small suitcase, his back to the* WOMAN.] I'll wait here.

[*In the meantime, while the* MAN *is not looking at her, the* WOMAN *has raised her veil with long slow movements. When she uncovers her face, it is obvious that she is old. Her forehead is furrowed by deep wrinkles. She is like the mask of old age. This face contrasts obviously with her body, still slender, ageless.*]

WOMAN [*to the* FLAGMAN *who stares at her*]: You saw me from the beginning, didn't you? Why didn't you tell him?

FLAGMAN [*indifferently*]: Whom?

WOMAN [*pointing to the* MAN]: Him, the only one.

FLAGMAN: I'd forgotten him.

WOMAN [*in a surge of anguish*]: Shall I tell him that I'm that woman he's waiting for? Will he recognize in this old face the unsatisfied longing still in this body of mine? How can I tell him that I need him even more than when I was young, as young as I am in that touched-up photo that he's looking at?

[*In the meantime, the* MAN *studies the photograph with fascination. The* WOMAN *covers her face again with the veil and goes up to the* MAN.]

WOMAN: Is she very late?

MAN [*his back turned*]: Of course. . . .

WOMAN: It would hurt you a great deal if she wouldn't come!

MAN [*turning forcefully*]: She has to come.

WOMAN: Nevertheless, you must realize that perhaps she's afraid to reveal herself, that maybe she's waiting for you to discover her.

MAN: I don't understand.

WOMAN [*very close to the* MAN]: I have a friend . . . who always lived alone, thinking nevertheless that the best thing for her was to get together with someone. [*She pauses. The* MAN *listens to her, interested.*] She was ugly, very ugly, perhaps that was why she dreamed of a man instead of looking for him. She liked to have her pictures taken. She had the photographs touched up, so that the picture turned out to be hers, but at the same time it was someone else's. She used to write to young men, sending them her photograph. She called them close to her house, with loving words. . . . When they arrived, she'd wait behind the windows; she wouldn't let herself be seen. . . .

MAN: Why are you telling me all this?

WOMAN [*without hearing*]: She'd see them. She knew that they were there on account of her. Each day, a different one. She accumulated many memories, the faces, the bodies of those strong men who had waited for her.

MAN: How absurd! I think. . . .

WOMAN: You're also strong and young.

MAN [*confused*]: Yes, but . . .

WOMAN: And today she's one day older than yesterday.

MAN [*after allowing a pause*]: Really I don't see what relation all this can have to . . .

WOMAN [*drawing near and placing her hand on the* MAN's *head*]: Perhaps you'll understand now. Close your eyes. [*She passes her hand over the eyes of the* MAN *in a loving manner.*] Have you never felt fear?

MAN: Fear? Of what?

WOMAN: Of living, of being . . . as if all your life you'd been waiting for something that never comes?

MAN: No. . . . [*He opens his eyes.*]

WOMAN: Tell me the truth. Close your eyes, those eyes that are separating us now. Have you been afraid?

[*The* MAN *closes his eyes.*]

MAN [*hesitatingly*]: Well, a little. . . .

WOMAN [*with an absent voice*]: A suffering . . . in solitude . . .

MAN: Yes, at times. . . . [*He takes the* WOMAN's *hand.*]

WOMAN: Above all when you begin to fall asleep. The solitude of your body, a body alone, that inevitably ages.

MAN: Yes, but . . .

WOMAN: The solitude of the heart that tries hard every night to prolong its cry against silence.

MAN: I've felt something like that . . . but . . . not so clearly . . . not so pointedly.

WOMAN: It's that . . . perhaps you were waiting for that voice, the one of someone invented by you, to your measure. . . .

MAN: Yes . . . I think that's it.

WOMAN: Would you be able to recognize that voice with your eyes open?

MAN: I'm sure that I could. . . .

WOMAN: Even if it were a voice invented many years before, in the dark inmost recesses of time?

MAN: It wouldn't matter. I'd know how to recognize it.

WOMAN: Then, is that what you're waiting for?

MAN: Yes. I'm here for her sake, looking for her.

WOMAN: She's waiting for you also. [*The* WOMAN *raises the veil little by little until she leaves her withered face in the open.*] She'll be only a memory for you, if you don't allow yourself to be overcome by time. Time is her worst enemy. Will you fight it?

[*They are seated very close to one another.*]

MAN: Yes.

WOMAN: All right. . . . Open your eyes.

[*The* MAN *opens his eyes slowly and is surprised to find himself held by the* WOMAN's *two hands. He stands up with a brusque movement.*]

MAN [*bewildered*]: Excuse me, I'm confused . . .

WOMAN [*entreatingly*]: Oh, no! . . . Don't tell me that . . .

MAN: It was a stupidity of mine . . .

WOMAN [*imploringly*]: But you said . . .

MAN: It's ridiculous! For a moment I thought that you were she. Understand me. It was a wild dream.

WOMAN [*grieved*]: Yes, yes . . .

MAN: I don't know how I could . . .

WOMAN [*calming herself*]: I understand you. A wild dream and nothing more . . .

MAN: You're really very kind to pardon me. . . . [*Looking at his watch, astonished:*] It's five thirty! . . . [*Pause.*]

WOMAN [*sadly*]: Yes. . . . Now I believe that she won't come.

MAN: How would that be possible?

WOMAN: It's better that way.

MAN: Who are you to tell me that?

WOMAN: No one. [*She opens her purse.*] Do you want this white flower?

MAN [*snatching it from her*]: Where did you get it? Why are you giving it to me?

WOMAN: I picked it up . . . in passing . . .

MAN [*with great excitement*]: But then, she has been here. Perhaps she has gotten lost or mistaken the place. Or perhaps, while I was here talking with you, she has passed by without stopping.

WOMAN [*covering her face*]: I already told you that there is but a moment to recognize oneself, to close one's eyes . . .

MAN: But now . . . what can I do in order to . . . find her?

WOMAN: Wait . . . as everyone does. . . . Wait . . . [*She takes the flower again.*]

MAN: But, what about you?

WOMAN: I'll continue searching, calling them, seeing them pass by. When you're old, you'll understand. [*The train whistle is heard. The* WOMAN *moves away from the* MAN, *with sorrowful movements.*] Good-bye, good-bye . . .

MAN [*to himself*]: Who can this woman be who speaks to me as if she knew me? [*He runs toward her. He checks himself.*] Good-bye . . .

[*The semaphore flashes the green light. The* FLAGMAN *becomes stiff in order to repeat his refrain.*]

FLAGMAN: The trains from the North travel toward the South, the trains from the North travel toward the South, the trains from the North travel toward the South, the trains from the North travel toward the South [*etc.*].

[*The* TRAIN *crosses the back of the stage. The* WOMAN *waves the flower sadly and with long movements approaches the* TRAIN. *She gets on it. The* FLAGMAN *repeats his refrain while the* TRAIN *leaves dragging the* WOMAN, *who goes off with writhing and anguished pantomime movements.*]

MAN [*with a certain sadness, to the* FLAGMAN *who remains indifferent*]: There was something in her that . . . anyhow, I believe it's better that that woman has left.

FLAGMAN: Which one, sir?

MAN: That one, the one who had picked up a white flower . . .

FLAGMAN: I didn't notice that. . . .

MAN: No? [*He looks at the* FLAGMAN *dejectedly.*] But, really, haven't you seen the other one?

FLAGMAN: What other one?

MAN: The one that I'm looking for.

FLAGMAN: I don't know who it can be. . . .

MAN: One who is wearing a white flower, but who isn't the one that you saw a moment ago.

FLAGMAN [*harshly*]: I saw the one that you aren't looking for, and the one you're looking for I didn't see!

MAN [*irritated*]: Can't you be useful for anything? What the devil are you good for?

[*Loud train whistle.*]

FLAGMAN: What did you say?

MAN [*shouting*]: What the devil are you good for!

[*Green light of the semaphore. The* TRAIN *crosses the back of the stage very slowly.*]

FLAGMAN [*in a distant voice*]: The trains from the North travel toward the South, the trains from the North travel toward the South, the trains from the North travel toward the South, the trains from the North travel toward the South [*etc.*].

[*The* MAN *covers his head with his hands, desperate. The* FLAGMASTER *repeats his refrain while the* TRAIN *passes by slowly. Before it leaves the stage, the curtain falls gently.*]

Curtain

UNDERSTANDING THE PLAY

1. Why doesn't Solórzano give the Man and the Woman particular names?

2. Why does the Flagman tell the Man "they call me by many names"?

3. To what extent is the Flagman correct when he says, "The impossible is always true"?

4. Why is the Woman "more afraid of finding the one she seeks than of letting him pass by without stopping"?

5. Why doesn't the Woman reveal her identity to the Man? Why does she offer the Man the white flower?

6. Why does the Man feel that the woman he awaits must come?

7. What does the Woman's story about her "friend" and the Man's reaction to the story reveal about the Woman and the Man?

8. Why is the Man angry at the Flagman at the end of the play? To what extent, if any, do you think the Man's response is appropriate?

9. What does the Man's final line—"What the devil are you good for!"—reveal about the Man?

10. The Woman says, "There is but one moment to recognize one another, to extend our hands. One mustn't let it pass us by." To what extent do you think that the statement is accurate?

11. Solórzano depicts an experience in the life-journey of both the Man and the Woman. As the characters journey along the path of self-discovery, what does each character learn?

12. What **themes** do you find in this play?

ANALYZING LITERARY TECHNIQUE

1. Why does Solórzano set the play in a location where no train stops?

2. Analyze the role of the Flagman.

3. Why does Solórzano make the Woman old rather than young? Why doesn't he choose the combination of an old man and a young woman?

4. Find an example of **foreshadowing** and explain its function.

5. Find examples of **dramatic irony** and **verbal irony** and explain what they contribute to the play.

6. How does Solórzano use **symbolism** in this play? Find one or two examples and explain their function.

7. What **paradoxes** do you find in this play?

8. Why do you think that Solórzano calls this play "A Sad Vaudeville"?

WRITING ABOUT LITERATURE

1. Write an essay in which you analyze the role of the Flagman. For example, is he a symbol of the impersonal modern world, a foil for the Man, or a philosopher of modern life? Use quotations to support your position and explain how each quotation contributes to Solórzano's goals in the play. Conclude by evaluating the success of the Flagman as a character.

2. Write an essay in which you analyze Solórzano's use of irony in the play. Consider both verbal irony and dramatic irony. Discuss two or three examples of irony, using quotations to support your ideas and explaining what each example contributes to the play. Conclude with an evaluation of what irony contributes to the play as a whole.

3. Write a brief description of how this experience affects the Man's life. Consider the following questions: Does the Man write to the Woman again? Does she respond? How? How does the Man proceed with his quest for a romantic relationship? To what extent, if any, does he continue to respond to personal advertisements? What finally happens to him?

Chess

ROSARIO CASTELLANOS

Mexico

$\mathcal{R}$OSARIO CASTELLANOS (1925–1974), a major Mexican writer, is best known for *The Nine Guardians* (1957), a novel about the plight of Mexican women; *Office of Shadows* (1962), a realistic depiction of Mexican Indians; and two volumes of short stories, *The Guests of August* (1964) and *Family Album* (1971). In addition, she wrote twelve books of poetry, four volumes of essays, and one play.

Castellanos was born in Mexico City, but she spent much of her youth in Comitán, Chiapas, near Guatemala. Her childhood was marked by death, rejection, and solitude. Her younger brother died suddenly when she was very young. Her parents withdrew in grief, and they told her that they loved her only out of obligation. She was reared by an Indian nanny who inspired her later interest in the Indian population of Mexico and the plight of poor and uneducated Indians.

When Castellanos was an adolescent, her family lost its land, the source of its wealth. With the loss went the family's sense of social and economic superiority, so the family moved to Mexico City where life was simpler. In Mexico City, Castellanos attended the National University, where she studied philosophy and wrote literature as an avocation. She did not feel free to "dedicate [herself] professionally to literature" until her parents died in 1948. That year she published her first book of poetry.

Castellanos was interested in Mexican culture, particularly in the role of women in that culture. In the early 1960s, she wrote articles for the National University; in the late 1960s, she taught comparative literature there. In 1971 she became Mexico's ambassador to Israel, where she lectured on Latin American literature at the Hebrew University in Jerusalem. She died in 1974 as the result of an accident.

Castellanos's work is known for its depiction of ordinary domestic events. Her goal was to write about women in a way that would "destroy the myths inside and outside ourselves." Her love of poetry is reflected in her statement "The words of poetry constitute the only way to achieve permanence in this world." Her most mature poetry, that written after 1969, appears in the last three sections of her anthology *You Are Not Poetry* (1972). In an interview in 1974, Castellanos described her later poems as follows:

> I use a series of incidents or experiences which are not formally considered to be poetic. I feel I have the freedom to leave the poetic canon behind and to find something outside it which is valid for me. . . . They are vital experiences at a level of awareness and a level of maturity which I hope have become part of the poems.

"Chess" is an excellent illustration of Castellanos's poetic vision.

Because we were friends and sometimes loved each other,
perhaps to add one more tie
to the many that already bound us,
we decided to play games of the mind.

We set up a board between us: 5
equally divided into pieces, values,
and possible moves.
We learned the rules, we swore to respect them,
and the match began.

We've been sitting here for centuries, meditating   10
ferociously
how to deal the one last blow that will finally
annihilate the other one forever.

UNDERSTANDING THE POEM

1. To what extent does the actual spirit of the game appear to be different from what the speaker anticipated?

2. Examine the last line of the poem. To what extent, if any, does Castellanos seem to imply that competition endangers friendship?

3. What difference does the sex of the two players make to your understanding of the poem?

4. What **themes** do you find in the poem?

ANALYZING LITERARY TECHNIQUE

1. What does the chess game **symbolize?** Why is it an appropriate game for this purpose?
2. Analyze the structure of the poem. How do the three stanzas relate to each other? What is the function of the final line?
3. What is the function of **irony** in the poem?

WRITING ABOUT LITERATURE

1. Write an essay in which you analyze the structure of the poem in terms of its content and theme. Include an analysis of the symbolic and ironic aspects of the poem. Use quotations to support your ideas.
2. Write a conversation between the two people following the end of their chess game. Decide whether the man or the woman is the winner.

A Very Old Man with Enormous Wings
A Tale for Children

GABRIEL GARCÍA MÁRQUEZ

*G*ABRIEL GARCÍA MÁRQUEZ (1928–), a master storyteller from Colombia and the most famous Latin American writer, won the Nobel Prize for literature in 1982 "for his novels and short stories, in which the fantastic and realistic are combined in a richly composed world of imagination." He is best known for his novel *One Hundred Years of Solitude* (1967), the first Latin American book to become an international bestseller, and for his more recent novel *Love in the Time of Cholera* (1985). His other works include short stories, published in a complete collection in 1975, followed by editions of *Collected Stories* in 1984 and 1999 and a fictional biography of Simón Bolívar, *The General in His Labyrinth* (1989).

García Márquez was born into a poor family in Arcataca, a small town on the Caribbean coast of Colombia that he has immortalized in his fiction as the town of Macondo. His mother left him to be reared by his grandparents. With a university education in journalism and law, García Márquez became a journalist and a foreign correspondent. His first short story was published in 1947; his first novella, *Leaf Storm*, was published in 1955. In the early 1960s he settled in Mexico City, where he continues to keep his primary residence.

García Márquez is fond of saying that nothing interesting has happened to him since he left his grandmother's home. Her legacy of Caribbean-Colombian folklore infuses his fiction with an exuberance and an acceptance of wonder as part of reality. It is the source of his magic realism—which considers both the real and the fantastic, the believable and the incredible, to be part of one coherent and insepa-rable whole. In his words:

> It always amuses me that the biggest praise for my work comes for the imagination while the truth is that there's not

a single line in all my work that does not have a basis in reality. The problem is that Caribbean reality resembles the wildest imagination.

"A Very Old Man with Enormous Wings" appears in both *Leaf Storm and Other Stories* (1972) and *Collected Stories*. It exemplifies the content, style, and view of life that have made the fiction of García Márquez loved throughout the world.

On the third day of rain they had killed so many crabs inside the house that Pelayo had to cross his drenched courtyard and throw them into the sea, because the newborn child had a temperature all night and they thought it was due to the stench. The world had been sad since Tuesday. Sea and sky were a single ash-gray thing and the sands of the beach, which on March nights glimmered like powdered light, had become a stew of mud and rotten shellfish. The light was so weak at noon that when Pelayo was coming back to the house after throwing away the crabs, it was hard for him to see what it was that was moving and groaning in the rear of the courtyard. He had to go very close to see that it was an old man, a very old man, lying face down in the mud, who, in spite of his tremendous efforts, couldn't get up, impeded by his enormous wings.

Frightened by that nightmare, Pelayo ran to get Elisenda, his wife, who was putting compresses on the sick child, and he took her to the rear of the courtyard. They both looked at the fallen body with mute stupor. He was dressed like a rag picker. There were only a few faded hairs left on his bald skull and very few teeth in his mouth, and his pitiful condition of a drenched great-grandfather had taken away any sense of grandeur he might have had. His huge buzzard wings, dirty and half-plucked, were forever entangled in the mud. They looked at him so long and so closely that Pelayo and Elisenda very soon overcame their surprise and in the end found him familiar. Then they dared speak to him, and he answered in an incomprehensible dialect with a strong sailor's voice. That was how they skipped over the inconvenience of the wings and quite intelligently concluded that he was a lonely castaway from some foreign ship wrecked by the storm. And yet, they called in a neighbor woman who knew everything about life and death to see him, and all she needed was one look to show them their mistake.

"He's an angel," she told them. "He must have been coming for the child, but the poor fellow is so old that the rain knocked him down."

On the following day everyone knew that a flesh-and-blood angel was held captive in Pelayo's house. Against the judgment of the wise neighbor woman, for whom angels in those times were the fugitive survivors of a celestial conspiracy, they did not have the heart to club him to death. Pelayo watched over him all afternoon from the kitchen, armed with his bailiff's club, and before going to bed he dragged him out of the mud and locked him up with the hens in the wire chicken coop. In the middle of the night, when the rain stopped, Pelayo and Elisenda were still killing crabs. A short time afterward the child woke up without a fever and with a desire to eat. Then they felt magnanimous and decided to put the angel on a raft with fresh water and provisions for three days and leave him to his fate on the high seas. But when they went out into the courtyard with the first light of dawn, they found the whole neighborhood in front of the chicken coop having fun with the angel, without the slightest reverence, tossing him things to eat through the openings in the wires as if he weren't a supernatural creature but a circus animal.

Father Gonzaga arrived before seven o'clock, alarmed at the strange news. By that time onlookers less frivolous than those at dawn had already arrived and they were making all kinds of conjectures concerning the captive's future. The simplest among them thought that he should be named mayor of the world. Others of sterner mind felt that he should be promoted to the rank of five-star general in order to win all wars. Some visionaries hoped that he could be put to stud in order to implant on earth a race of winged wise men who could take charge of the universe. But Father Gonzaga, before becoming a priest, had been a robust woodcutter. Standing by the wire, he reviewed his catechism[1] in an instant and asked them to open the door so that he could take a close look at that pitiful man who looked more like a huge decrepit hen among the fascinated chickens. He was lying in a corner drying his open wings in the sunlight among the fruit peels and breakfast leftovers that the early risers had thrown him. Alien to the impertinences of the world, he only lifted his antiquarian eyes and murmured something in his dialect when Father Gonzaga went into the chicken coop and said good morning in Latin.[2] The parish priest had his first suspicion of an impostor when he saw that he did not understand the language of God or know how to greet His ministers. Then he noticed that seen close up he was much too human: he had an unbearable smell of the outdoors, the back side of his wings was strewn with parasites and his main feathers had been mistreated by terrestrial winds, and nothing about him measured up to the proud dignity of the angels. Then he came out of the chicken coop and in a brief sermon warned the curious against the risks of being ingenuous. He reminded them that the devil had the bad habit of making use of carnival tricks in order to confuse the unwary. He argued that if wings were not the essential element in determining the difference between a hawk and an airplane, they were even less so in the recognition of angels. Nevertheless, he promised to write a letter to his bishop so that the latter would write to his primate so that the latter would write to the Supreme Pontiff[3] in order to get the final verdict from the highest courts.

His prudence fell on sterile hearts. The news of the captive angel spread with such rapidity that after a few hours the courtyard had the bustle of a marketplace and they had to call in troops with fixed bayonets to disperse the mob that was about to knock the house down. Elisenda, her spine all twisted from sweeping up

---

[1] *Catechism:* Manual of religious instruction.

[2] *Latin:* The official language of the Roman Catholic Church.

[3] *bishop . . . Supreme Pontiff:* Bishops and primates are officials in the Roman Catholic Church. The Supreme Pontiff, the Pope, is the spiritual leader of the Roman Catholic Church.

so much marketplace trash, then got the idea of fencing in the yard and charging five cents admission to see the angel.

The curious came from far away. A travelling carnival arrived with a flying acrobat who buzzed over the crowd several times, but no one paid any attention to him because his wings were not those of an angel but, rather, those of a sidereal bat. The most unfortunate invalids on earth came in search of health: a poor woman who since childhood had been counting her heartbeats and had run out of numbers; a Portuguese man who couldn't sleep because the noise of the stars disturbed him; a sleepwalker who got up at night to undo the things he had done while awake; and many others with less serious ailments. In the midst of that shipwreck disorder that made the earth tremble, Pelayo and Elisenda were happy with fatigue, for in less than a week they had crammed their rooms with money and the line of pilgrims waiting their turn to enter still reached beyond the horizon.

The angel was the only one who took no part in his own act. He spent his time trying to get comfortable in his borrowed nest, befuddled by the hellish heat of the oil lamps and sacramental candles that had been placed along the wire. At first they tried to make him eat some mothballs, which, according to the wisdom of the wise neighbor woman, were the food prescribed for angels. But he turned them down, just as he turned down the papal lunches[4] that the penitents brought him, and they never found out whether it was because he was an angel or because he was an old man that in the end he ate nothing but eggplant mush. His only supernatural virtue seemed to be patience. Especially during the first days, when the hens pecked at him, searching for the stellar parasites that proliferated in his wings, and the cripples pulled out feathers to touch their defective parts with, and even the most merciful threw stones at him, trying to get him to rise so they could see him standing. The only time they succeeded in arousing him was when they burned his side with an iron for branding steers, for he had been motionless for so many hours that they thought he was dead. He awoke with a start, ranting in his hermetic language and with tears in his eyes, and he flapped his wings a couple of times, which brought on a whirlwind of chicken dung and lunar dust and a gale of panic that did not seem to be of this world. Although many thought that his reaction had been one not of rage but of pain, from then on they were careful not to annoy him, because the majority understood that his passivity was not that of a hero taking his ease but that of a cataclysm in repose.

Father Gonzaga held back the crowd's frivolity with formulas of maidservant inspiration while awaiting the arrival of a final judgment on the nature of the captive. But the mail from Rome[5] showed no sense of urgency. They spent their time finding out if the prisoner had a navel, if his dialect had any connection with Aramaic, how many times he could fit on the head of a pin,[6] or whether he wasn't

---

[4] *papal lunches:* Lunches blessed by or required by the pope.

[5] *Rome:* Location of the Vatican, the headquarters of the Roman Catholic Church.

[6] *navel . . . head of a pin:* Various tests to determine whether the angel is genuine. A navel would indicate the angel was human because he had been connected by an umbilical cord to his mother. Aramaic was the dialect spoken by Jesus Christ and his disciples. A question debated by medieval Christian theologians was how many angels could fit on the head of a pin.

just a Norwegian with wings. Those meager letters might have come and gone until the end of time if a providential event had not put an end to the priest's tribulations.

It so happened that during those days, among so many carnival attractions, there arrived in town the travelling show of the woman who had been changed into a spider for having disobeyed her parents. The admission to see her was not only less than the admission to see the angel, but people were permitted to ask her all manner of questions about her absurd state and to examine her up and down so that no one would ever doubt the truth of her horror. She was a frightful tarantula the size of a ram and with the head of a sad maiden. What was most heartrending, however, was not her outlandish shape but the sincere affliction with which she recounted the details of her misfortune. While still practically a child she had sneaked out of her parents' house to go to a dance, and while she was coming back through the woods after having danced all night without permission, a fearful thunderclap rent the sky in two and through the crack came the lightning bolt of brimstone that changed her into a spider. Her only nourishment came from the meatballs that charitable souls chose to toss into her mouth. A spectacle like that, full of so much human truth and with such a fearful lesson, was bound to defeat without even trying that of a haughty angel who scarcely deigned to look at mortals. Besides, the few miracles attributed to the angel showed a certain mental disorder, like the blind man who didn't recover his sight but grew three new teeth, or the paralytic who didn't get to walk but almost won the lottery, and the leper whose sores sprouted sunflowers. Those consolation miracles, which were more like mocking fun, had already ruined the angel's reputation when the woman who had been changed into a spider finally crushed him completely. That was how Father Gonzaga was cured forever of his insomnia and Pelayo's courtyard went back to being as empty as during the time it had rained for three days and crabs walked through the bedrooms.

The owners of the house had no reason to lament. With the money they saved they built a two-story mansion with balconies and gardens and high netting so that crabs wouldn't get in during the winter, and with iron bars on the windows so that angels wouldn't get in. Pelayo also set up a rabbit warren close to town and gave up his job as bailiff for good, and Elisenda bought some satin pumps with high heels and many dresses of iridescent silk, the kind worn on Sunday by the most desirable women in those times. The chicken coop was the only thing that didn't receive any attention. If they washed it down with creolin and burned tears of myrrh[7] inside it every so often, it was not in homage to the angel but to drive away the dungheap stench that still hung everywhere like a ghost and was turning the new house into an old one. At first, when the child learned to walk, they were careful that he not get too close to the chicken coop. But then they began to lose their fears and got used to the smell, and before the child got his second teeth he'd gone inside the chicken coop to play, where the wires were falling part. The angel was no less standoffish with him than with other mortals, but he tolerated the most ingenious infamies with the patience of a dog who had no illusions. They both came down with the chicken pox at the same time. The

---

[7] *creolin . . . myrrh:* Creolin is a disinfectant. Myrrh is a kind of incense.

doctor who took care of the child couldn't resist the temptation to listen to the angel's heart, and he found so much whistling in the heart and so many sounds in his kidneys that it seemed impossible for him to be alive. What surprised him most, however, was the logic of his wings. They seemed so natural on that completely human organism that he couldn't understand why other men didn't have them too.

When the child began school it had been some time since the sun and rain had caused the collapse of the chicken coop. The angel went dragging himself about here and there like a stray dying man. They would drive him out of the bedroom with a broom and a moment later find him in the kitchen. He seemed to be in so many places at the same time that they grew to think that he'd been duplicated, that he was reproducing himself all through the house, and the exasperated and unhinged Elisenda shouted that it was awful living in that hell full of angels. He could scarcely eat and his antiquarian eyes had also became so foggy that he went about bumping into posts. All he had left were the bare cannulae[8] of his last feathers. Pelayo threw a blanket over him and extended him the charity of letting him sleep in the shed, and only then did they notice that he had a temperature at night, and was delirious with the tongue twisters of an old Norwegian. That was one of the few times they became alarmed, for they thought he was going to die and not even the wise neighbor woman had been able to tell them what to do with dead angels.

And yet he not only survived his worst winter, but seemed improved with the first sunny days. He remained motionless for several days in the farthest corner of the courtyard, where no one would see him, and at the beginning of December some large, stiff feathers began to grow on his wings, the feathers of a scarecrow, which looked more like another misfortune of decrepitude. But he must have known the reason for those changes, for he was quite careful that no one should notice them, that no one should hear the sea chanteys that he sometimes sang under the stars. One morning Elisenda was cutting some bunches of onions for lunch when a wind that seemed to come from the high sea blew into the kitchen. Then she went to the window and caught the angel in his first attempts at flight. They were so clumsy that his fingernails opened a furrow in the vegetable patch and he was on the point of knocking the shed down with the ungainly flapping that slipped on the light and couldn't get a grip on the air. But he did manage to gain altitude. Elisenda let out a sigh of relief, for herself and for him, when she saw him pass over the last houses, holding himself up in some way with the risky flapping of a senile vulture. She kept watching him even when she was through cutting the onions and she kept on watching until it was no longer possible for her to see him, because then he was no longer an annoyance in her life but an imaginary dot on the horizon of the sea.

---

[8] *cannulae:* Quills.

UNDERSTANDING THE STORY

1. Why does the angel appear in the form of a very old man?
2. Why is the angel described as speaking like a Norwegian?
3. How do Pelayo and Elisenda feel about their guest? Why?
4. To what extent, if any, does it matter whether Pelayo's guest is an angel?
5. What does the villagers' treatment of the angel reveal about the villagers?
6. What is significant about the abilities and inabilities of the angel?
7. What is significant about the person who comes closest to determining who or what the angel is?
8. What is significant about the villagers' fascination with the spider-maiden?
9. Why does the angel spend so many years with Pelayo's family?
10. What is the narrator's attitude toward the whole experience?
11. What **themes** do you find in this story?

ANALYZING LITERARY TECHNIQUE

1. Do you find the story primarily humorous or sad? Which does García Márquez seem to intend the story to be? Why?
2. To what extent, if any, is this story a **satire?**
3. How is this story like a **folktale?**
4. How does the author use **irony** in the story?
5. Why does the author call the story "a tale for children"? What parts would a child enjoy? What parts, if any, are probably beyond a child's ability to appreciate?
6. How is this story an example of **magic realism?** How does García Márquez use both magic and realism?
7. What **paradoxes** do you find in this story?

WRITING ABOUT LITERATURE

1. García Márquez calls this story "a tale for children." Write an essay in which you analyze two or three aspects of the story that would appeal to children. Use quotations to support your ideas. As part of your analysis, explain the appeal of each element. In your conclusion, explain whether you think this is a children's tale.
2. This story includes an allusion to the Greek myth of Arachne. Arachne was an arrogant maiden who boasted that the quality of her weaving surpassed that of the goddess Athena. In a weaving contest between Arachne and Athena, Arachne wove a pictorial tapestry that ridiculed the behavior of the gods. Infuriated by the disrespect, Athena turned Arachne into a spider.

Write an essay in which you analyze why García Márquez includes the spider-maiden story. What does the mythological allusion add to the larger tale? Use quotations to support your ideas.

3. Taking the point of view of the angel, write a report that the angel might give to his superiors. Consider answering the following questions as part of his report: Why did he arrive? What opinions does he have about his visit? Why did he stay so long? Why did he leave when he did?

A North America

THE LITERATURE OF NORTH AMERICA reveals the range of human responses to events of daily life. From denial to affirmation, these reactions make for a rich collection of writings.

Many of the authors of the selections from North America show the struggles that humans face in making decisions about how they live their lives and how they interact with others. In "Day of the Butterfly," by Alice Munro, a sensitive girl walks a fine line as she befriends a girl who is an outsider. In Ernest Hemingway's "Soldier's Home," a young veteran caught between the expectations of his family and the person he has now become must make decisions about how to live his life. In Eugene O'Neill's one-act play *Ile,* a whaling captain must choose between his need for respect and self-fulfillment and his obligation to his wife. In "Roselily," Alice Walker depicts a woman revisiting her decision to better her life, even as the consequences of that decision become more and more of a reality. On another front, Walt Whitman describes the irony of being torn between his desire for the solitude of the country and his love for Manhattan in his poem "Give Me the Splendid Silent Sun."

Other writers in this section describe how characters make meaning out of life. On the one hand, the people in

T. S. Eliot's "The Hollow Men" respond to life with despair and passivity. On the other hand, Phoenix Jackson, in Eudora Welty's "A Worn Path," affirms life in spite of its obstacles. In Langston Hughes's poem "Mother to Son," a mother encourages her son to face life with dignity and pride, despite its difficulties. In Anne Hébert's poem "Hands," a woman's hands show the work and love she has put into her life. And in Emily Dickinson's poem "My life closed twice before its close," Dickinson grieves the loss of two people who were dear to her and struggles with the question of whether there is life after death.

Finally, the poem from a traditional Zuñi ritual, "Special Request for the Children of Mother Corn," reveals the ties the Zuñi feel to nature.

Special Request for the Children of Mother Corn

ZUÑI (Traditional)

The "Special Request for the Children of Mother Corn" is a ritual poem of the Zuñi. The Zuñi, a large Pueblo community that is more than eight hundred years old, are an agricultural tribe of western New Mexico. Today the Zuñi remain true to their cultural heritage.

In 1540 the Zuñi were the first Pueblo Indians to be discovered in the Southwest by the Spaniards. Despite centuries of Spanish control that followed, the Zuñi preserved their culture. In 1800 they became a self-governing community under Mexican rule; in 1848 their territory became part of the United States.

A Zuñi creation myth tells the origin of the first seven corn plants, which were the flesh of the seven Corn Maidens, immortal mothers of the Zuñi and members of the Corn Clan. Long ago, according to the myth, the Zuñi fell asleep while the Corn Maidens danced. In response the Corn Maidens disappeared, but they left behind their flesh (in the form of corn) for the people to eat. When the Zuñi awoke, they were terrified. They feared that they would have to travel far in search of food after the corn had been eaten. Finally a Zuñi god found the Corn Maidens and brought them back for one brief visit. Then the Corn Maidens went to live in the land of everlasting summer. Each spring the Corn Maidens' sweet-smelling breath—the south wind—brings warmth, rain, fertility, life, and health to their children, the corn plants, and to their family, the Zuñi.

The following request, or prayer, is recited by a religious leader in midwinter when the seed corn for the coming year is blessed.

Perhaps if we are lucky
Our earth mother
Will wrap herself in a fourfold robe
Of white meal,
Full of frost flowers;   5
A floor of ice will spread over the world,
The forests,
Because of the cold, will lean to one side,
Their arms will break beneath the weight of snow.
When the days are thus,   10
The flesh of our earth mother
Will crack with cold.
Then in the spring when she is replete with living waters,
Our mothers,[1]
All different kinds of corn,   15
In their earth mother
We shall lay to rest.
With their earth mother's living waters
They will be made into new beings;
Into their sun father's daylight   20
They will come out standing;
Yonder to all directions
They will stretch out their hands calling for rain.
Then with their fresh waters
[The rain makers] will pass us on our roads.   25
Clasping their young ones in their arms,
They will rear their children.
Gathering them into our houses,
Following these toward whom our thoughts bend,
With our thoughts following them,[2]   30
Thus we shall always live.

UNDERSTANDING THE POEM

1. Why is this poem recited?

2. What is important about the Zuñi's relationship to corn?

3. What do the lines "All different kinds of corn, / In their earth mother / We shall lay to rest" (lines 15–17) mean?

4. Explain the significance of the final lines of the poem, "With our thoughts following them, / Thus we shall always live."

---

[1] *mothers:* Cobs of seed corn.

[2] *them:* The corn spirits.

ANALYZING LITERARY TECHNIQUE

1. Find two examples of **personification** and explain their contribution to the poem.

2. Analyze the role of **metaphor** in this poem. What do the metaphors suggest about the lives of the Zuñi?

WRITING ABOUT LITERATURE

1. Write an essay in which you analyze the role of personification in the poem. Choose examples of personification and explain the contribution of each example to the work as a whole. Then evaluate the effectiveness of personification in the poem.

2. Write a letter or poem requesting assistance. For example, you might write to a parent or friend asking for help with a problem or to a political leader asking for information about antipoverty or antidiscrimination programs. Attempt to present the issue in a way that will elicit concern and aid from the person you are addressing. Use concrete supporting details, effective comparisons (**similes** and metaphors), and **connotative language.**

Give Me
the Splendid
Silent Sun

WALT WHITMAN

WALT WHITMAN (1819–1892) is often called America's national poet. He was the first American poet to acquire a significant international reputation. He revolutionized American poetry by deciding that a poem could have any structure and sound pattern and by choosing to write free verse in the language of common speech. Whitman is best known for his monumental life's work *Leaves of Grass* (1855–1891), a collection of poems that grew in number through the years from twelve to about three hundred. His four best-known poems are "Out of the Cradle Endlessly Rocking," "When Lilacs Last in the Dooryard Bloom'd," "Song of Myself," and "O Captain! My Captain!"

Walter Whitman Jr. was born near Huntington, Long Island, New York; he was one of ten children. His father was a farmer who became a carpenter when the family moved to Brooklyn. Whitman dropped out of school after five years to help support his family. By age fourteen he was involved in journalism, a career that sustained him for most of the next twenty years.

Early in the Civil War, in 1862, Whitman went to Virginia to try to locate one of his brothers, who had been declared missing in action. After finding his brother and seeing the war first hand, Whitman went to Washington, D.C., where he spent most of his time during the remainder of the war caring for hospitalized Confederate and Union soldiers. These experiences led him to write what many critics consider to be America's greatest Civil War poetry.

After the war, Whitman worked in the attorney general's office until 1873, when he was incapacitated by a stroke from which he never recovered. By the early 1880s he had gained a national reputation as "the good gray poet," and he continued to write poetry until he died.

Whitman attempted to project himself into the identities of ordinary Americans from all walks of life and to incorporate their lives into his own. He was a romantic in his view of himself as a prophet and in his belief in America as the great democracy where the sense of equality and community among all the people would inspire international brotherhood and sisterhood. However, he was a realist in his love for the details of daily life and in his meticulous presentation of these details. Both his romanticism and realism are evident in "Give Me the Splendid Silent Sun," written in 1865.

Give me the splendid silent sun with all his beams full-dazzling,
Give me juicy autumnal fruit ripe and red from the orchard,
Give me a field where the unmowed grass grows,
Give me an arbor, give me the trellised grape,
Give me fresh corn and wheat, give me serene-moving animals teaching
    content,   5
Give me nights perfectly quiet as on high plateaus west of the Mississippi,
    and I looking up at the stars,
Give me odorous at sunrise a garden of beautiful flowers where I can walk
    undisturbed,
Give me for marriage a sweet-breathed woman of whom I should never tire,
Give me a perfect child, give me, away aside from the noise of the world,
    a rural domestic life,
Give me to warble spontaneous songs recluse by myself,
    for my own ears only,   10
Give me solitude, give me Nature, give me again O Nature your primal
    sanities!
These demanding to have them, (tired with ceaseless excitement,
    and racked by the war-strife)
These to procure incessantly asking, rising in cries from my heart.
While yet incessantly asking still I adhere to my city,
Day upon day and year upon year, O city, walking your streets,   15
When you hold me enchained a certain time refusing to give me up,
Yet giving to make me glutted, enriched of soul, you give me forever faces;
(O I see what I sought to escape, confronting, reversing my cries,
I see my own soul trampling down what it asked for.)

Keep your splendid silent sun,   20
Keep your woods, O Nature, and the quiet places by the woods,
Keep your fields of clover and timothy, and your cornfields and orchards,
Keep the blossoming buckwheat fields where the Ninth-month bees hum;
Give me faces and streets—give me these phantoms incessant and endless
    along the trottoirs![1]

---

[1] *trottoirs:* Sidewalks.

Give me interminable eyes—give me women—give me comrades and
    lovers by the thousand!   25
Let me see new ones every day—let me hold new ones by the hand
    every day!
Give me such shows—give me the streets of Manhattan!
Give me Broadway, with the soldiers marching—give me the sound
    of the trumpets and drums!
(The soldiers in companies or regiments—some starting away flushed
    and reckless,
Some, their time up, returning with thinned ranks, young,
    yet very old, worn, marching, noticing nothing;)   30
Give me the shores and wharves heavy-fringed with black ships!
O such for me! O an intense life, full of repletion and varied!
The life of the theatre, bar-room, huge hotel, for me!
The saloon of the steamer! The crowded excursion for me!
    The torchlight procession!
The dense brigade bound for the war, with high-piled military wagons
    following;   35
People, endless, streaming, with strong voices, passions, pageants,
Manhattan streets with their powerful throbs, with beating
    drums as now,
The endless and noisy chorus, the rustle and clank of muskets
    (even the sight of the wounded),
Manhattan crowds, with their turbulent musical chorus!
Manhattan faces and eyes forever for me.   40

UNDERSTANDING THE POEM

1. Evaluate Whitman's view of nature and life in the country as being **romantic**
   or **realistic.**

2. Evaluate Whitman's view of urban life as being romantic or realistic.

3. To what extent, if any, does Whitman convince you that the country or
   the city is a fine place to live?

4. How does the fact that Whitman wrote this poem toward the end of the
   Civil War affect the poem's content?

ANALYZING LITERARY TECHNIQUE

1. What does Whitman achieve by the use of **free verse?**

2. What is the function of **contrast** in the poem?

3. What does Whitman's use of **apostrophe** contribute to the poem? Whom
   or what is Whitman addressing?

4. What is the function of **irony** in the poem? To what extent, if any, is the first line of the poem ironic?

5. What is the central **paradox** in this poem?

6. Analyze Whitman's use of **repetition.**

7. What is the **tone** of the poem? How does Whitman achieve it?

WRITING ABOUT LITERATURE

1. Write an essay in which you analyze Whitman's use of repetition in this poem. Consider his repeated use of phrases and sentence patterns. Use quotations to support your ideas.

2. Write your own poem about the place that you would prefer to live. List its appeals for you in a descriptive way. Consider how you might use repetition to emphasize your ideas.

My life closed
twice before
its close—

EMILY DICKINSON

&MILY DICKINSON (1830–1886), originally viewed as a
minor idiosyncratic poet, is now considered by many to be one
of the preeminent poets in the English language. Although
fewer than ten of her poems were published during her lifetime (and
those were published without her consent), nearly eighteen hundred
poems were discovered after her death, most of them short lyrics.
Among her best-known poems are "There's a certain Slant of light,"
"The Soul selects her own Society," "I heard a Fly buzz—when I died,"
"The Brain—is wider than the Sky," "Because I could not stop for
Death," and "My life closed twice before its close—."

Dickinson was born in Amherst, Massachusetts, where her father
was a prominent attorney. Because she was an artist, she chose to live
in an environment that her intellect and imagination could control.
For example, she refused to attend the funeral service for her father;
instead, she listened to the service from a secluded part of the stairway of the family home. Her isolation permitted her to develop her
own response to her father's death.

Because Dickinson lived the last twenty-four years of her life as a
recluse, many of her most important relationships were conducted by
correspondence. For nearly ten years, she corresponded with Charles
Wadsworth, a married minister in Philadelphia whose preaching had
impressed her. She considered him her "dearest earthly friend," and
her feelings for him determined the content of many of her poems. In
her mind, she transformed him into her great love, an imaginative
re-creation that inspired her to write fine love poetry. Their correspondence ended when he moved to San Francisco in 1862, but in the same
year she began a correspondence with Colonel Thomas Wentworth
Higginson, whose writing she had admired in the *Atlantic Monthly*.
They shared an extraordinary literary correspondence for the rest of

Dickinson's life. Higginson wrote the introduction to her first published volume of poetry in 1890.

Dickinson's poetry was as private as her life. After her death, poems were found written on brown paper bags, on the insides of envelopes, in the margins of newspapers, and on the backs of newspaper clippings. Despite her Puritan heritage, many of her poems reflect original ideas about life and death. Some of Dickinson's poems reflect her insights into her heart and mind; others reveal her enjoyment of her garden and the changing of the seasons. Writing about her art in a letter to Colonel Higginson in 1870, she stated:

> If I read a book and it makes my whole body so cold no fire can ever warm me, I know that is poetry. If I feel physically as if the top of my head were taken off, I know that is poetry. These are the only ways I know it.

Whatever the subject, Dickinson expressed her personal experience with conciseness and, a sense of immediacy. She wrote in conversational American English. "My life closed twice before its close" is thought to refer to the death of her father and to the departure of Wadsworth.

My life closed twice before its close—
It yet remains to see
If Immortality unveil
A third event to me

So huge, so hopeless to conceive   5
As these that twice befell.
Parting is all we know of heaven,
And all we need of hell.

UNDERSTANDING THE POEM

1. What does the speaker mean by the line "My life closed twice before its close" (line 1)?

2. How does the speaker view Immortality?

3. What is meant by the line "Parting is all we know of heaven" (line 7)?

4. What is meant by the lines "Parting is . . . all we need of hell" (lines 7–8)?

ANALYZING LITERARY TECHNIQUE

1. How does Dickinson use **connotative language** in the poem?
2. How does Dickinson use **paradox** in the poem?
3. In what sense is the last line the **climax** of the poem?
4. What is the **tone** of the poem? How does Dickinson achieve it?

WRITING ABOUT LITERATURE

1. Write an essay in which you analyze how Dickinson uses paradox in the poem. Consider her use of the words "close," "Immortality," "heaven," and "hell." Use quotations to support your ideas.

2. Dickinson is known for her ability to express complex ideas and deep feelings in a few well-chosen words. Write an essay in which you examine the specific ways in which Dickinson compresses a large idea into a few lines. Use quotations from this poem to support your ideas.

3. Write a poem or a short piece of prose about what the departure of a friend or relative takes away from life or what the presence of a loved one adds to life. Use connotative language to give your poetry or prose emotional power.

Ile

EUGENE O'NEILL

UGENE O'NEILL (1888–1953), considered by many to be the greatest American playwright, was awarded the Nobel Prize for literature in 1936 "for the power, honesty, and deep-felt emotions of his dramatic works, which embody an original concept of tragedy." O'Neill's serious and innovative approach to theater brought American drama into the mainstream of world theater. He was a master of both the one-act play and the full-length drama and a master of both realistic and expressionistic form. Influenced by the work of Sigmund Freud, O'Neill was always concerned with the human psyche's ability to handle illusion and reality and with the tragic aspects of the human condition. When necessary, he created dramatic techniques that would express psychological ideas. His best-known plays include *The Great God Brown* (1926), which uses masks to convey the conflicts between the public and the private personality; *Strange Interlude* (1928), which uses the aside as a soliloquy; *Mourning Becomes Electra* (1931), a Civil War trilogy, based on the Greek *Oresteia*, which uses a modern version of the Greek chorus; *The Iceman Cometh* (1946); and the autobiographical *Long Day's Journey into Night* (1956), which uses dream sequences as structure and interior monologue as content.

O'Neill was born in New York City to professional actors, with whom he toured until he was eight. "Home" was a succession of backstage dressing rooms, train compartments, and hotel rooms. His mother became a morphine addict and his older brother, also an actor, became an alcoholic. After attending Princeton University for a year (1906–7), O'Neill held a variety of jobs, including that of gold prospector in Honduras (1909) and seaman in the Merchant Marine (1910–11). The year 1912 was critical in his life. He suffered from alcoholism, attempted suicide, and held a job as a newspaper reporter; finally he was confined in a tuberculosis sanitarium, where he had time to read extensively and to begin writing plays. By the time he was released from the sanitarium in 1913, he had decided to become a professional writer.

While O'Neill convalesced during the winter of 1913–14, he wrote two full-length plays and eleven one-act plays, six of which he destroyed and five of which were published as *Thirst* in 1914. Determined "to be an artist or nothing," O'Neill successfully petitioned Professor George Baker to permit him to participate as a special student in his "Drama 47 Workshop" at Harvard College. From 1916 to 1920 he was associated with the Provincetown Players as both actor and writer, the company's modest operation being conducive to experimental theater. Their productions of ten of his one-act plays brought O'Neill critical acclaim. O'Neill won a Pulitzer Prize in 1920 for *Beyond the Horizon*, his first important full-length play. Ill health plagued O'Neill from 1934 to the end of his life, first limiting his writing and eventually preventing it.

O'Neill's one-act slice-of-life plays reflect aspects of his own experiences, interests, and attitudes. In *Ile*[1] (1917), perhaps the best of these plays, O'Neill combines his experiences as a seaman with the true story of a wife who sailed with her husband on a long and difficult voyage. *Ile* is typical of O'Neill in that its characters are common people who live on the periphery of society. *Ile* is also typical in that it focuses on "the impelling inscrutable forces behind life" and the tragic effect of these forces on the human soul. According to O'Neill:

> The subject is the same one that always was and always will be the one subject for drama, and that is man and his struggle with his fate. The struggle used to be with the gods, but is now with himself, his own past, his attempt to belong.

Ile offers O'Neill's special touches: psychological drama, symbolism, and effective theater.

CHARACTERS

BEN, *the cabin boy*

THE STEWARD

CAPTAIN KEENEY

SLOCUM, *second mate*

MRS. KEENEY

JOE, *a harpooner*

Members of the crew of the Atlantic Queen

Scene: **CAPTAIN KEENEY'**s *cabin on board the steam whaling ship* Atlantic Queen— *a small, square compartment about eight feet high, with a skylight in the center looking*

---

[1] Ile: Whale oil.

out on the poop deck.[2] On the left (the stern of the ship) a long bench with rough cushions is built in against the wall. In front of the bench a table. Over the bench, several curtained port-holes.

In the rear left, a door leading to the captain's sleeping quarters. To the right of the door a small organ, looking as if it were brand new, is placed against the wall.

On the right, to the rear, a marble-topped sideboard. On the sideboard, a woman's sewing basket. Farther forward, a doorway leading to the companionway, and past the officers' quarters to the main deck.

In the center of the room, a stove. From the middle of the ceiling a hanging lamp is suspended. The walls of the cabin are painted white.

There is no rolling of the ship, and the light which comes through the sky-light is sickly and faint, indicating one of those gray days of calm when ocean and sky are alike dead. The silence is unbroken except for the measured tread of someone walking up and down on the poop deck overhead.

It is nearing two bells—one o' clock—in the afternoon of a day in the year 1895.

At the rise of the curtain there is a moment of intense silence. Then THE STEWARD enters and commences to clear the table of the few dishes which still remain on it after the CAPTAIN's dinner. He is an old grizzled man, dressed in dungaree pants, a sweater, and a woolen cap with ear flaps. His manner is sullen and angry. He stops stacking up the plates and casts a quick glance upward at the skylight, then tiptoes over to the closed door in rear and listens with his ear pressed to the crack. What he hears makes his face darken, and he mutters a furious curse. There is a noise from the doorway on the right, and he darts back to the table.

BEN enters. He is an overgrown, gawky boy with a long, pinched face. He is dressed in sweater, fur cap, etc. His teeth are chattering with the cold, and he hurries to the stove, where he stands for a moment shivering, blowing on his hands, slapping them against his sides, on the verge of crying.

THE STEWARD [in relieved tones—seeing who it was]: Oh, 'tis you, is it? What're ye shiverin' 'bout? Stay by the stove where ye belong, and ye'll find no need of chatterin'.

BEN: It's c-c-cold. [Trying to control his chattering teeth—derisively] Who d'ye think it were—the Old Man?

THE STEWARD [makes a threatening move—BEN shrinks away]: None o' your lip, young un, or I'll learn ye. [More kindly] Where was it ye've been all o' the time—the fo'c'stle?[3]

BEN: Yes.

THE STEWARD: Let the Old Man see ye up for'ard monkeyshinin' with the hands, and ye'll get a hidin' ye'll not forget in a hurry.

---

[2] *poop deck*: A deck built over the cabin of the ship.

[3] *fo'c'stle*: Forecastle, the front upper deck of a ship; it contains the crew's quarters.

BEN: Aw, he don't see nothin'. [*A trace of awe in his tones—he glances upward.*] He jest walks up and down like he didn't notice nobody—and stares at the ice to the no'the'ard.

THE STEWARD [*the same tone of awe creeping into his voice*]: He's always starin' at the ice. [*In a sudden rage, shaking his fist at the skylight*] Ice, ice, ice! Damn him and damn the ice! Holdin' us in for nigh on a year—nothin' to see but ice—stuck in it like a fly in molasses!

BEN [*apprehensively*]: Ssshh! He'll hear ye.

THE STEWARD [*raging*]: Aye, damn, and damn the Arctic seas, and damn this rotten whalin' ship of his, and damn me for a fool to ever ship on it! [*Subsiding, as if realizing the uselessness of this outburst—shaking his head— slowly, with deep conviction.*] He's a hard man—as hard a man as ever sailed the seas.

BEN [*solemnly*]: Aye.

THE STEWARD: The two years we all signed up for are done this day! Two years o' this dog's life, and no luck in the fishin', and the hands half-starved with the food runnin' low, rotten as it is; and not a sign of him turnin' back for home! [*Bitterly*] Home! I begin to doubt if I'll set foot on land again. [*Excitedly*] What is it he thinks he's goin' to do? Keep us all up here after our time is worked out, till the last man of us is starved to death or frozen? We've grub enough hardly to last out the voyage back if we started now. What are the men goin' to do 'bout it? Did you hear any talk in the fo'c'stle?

BEN [*going over to him—in a half whisper*]: They said if he don't put back south for home today they're goin' to mutiny.

THE STEWARD [*with grim satisfaction*]: Mutiny? Aye, 'tis the only thing they can do; and serve him right after the manner he's treated them—'s if they weren't no better nor dogs.

BEN: The ice is all broken up to the s'uth'ard. They's clear water 'sfar's you can see. He ain't got no excuse for not turnin' back for home, the men says.

THE STEWARD [*bitterly*]: He won't look nowheres but no'the'ard, where they's only the ice to see. He don't want to see no clear water. All he thinks on is gettin' the ile—'s if it was our fault he ain't had good luck with the whales. [*Shaking his head*] I think the man's mighty nigh losin' his senses.

BEN [*awed*]: D'you really think he's crazy?

THE STEWARD: Aye, it's the punishment o' God on him. Did ye ever hear of a man who wasn't crazy do the things he does? [*Pointing to the door in rear*] Who but a man that's mad would take this woman—and as sweet a woman as ever was—on a rotten whalin' ship to the Arctic seas to be locked in by the ice for nigh on a year, and maybe lose her senses forever?—for it's sure she'll never be the same again.

BEN [*sadly*]: She useter be awful nice to me before—[*His eyes grow wide and frightened*]—she got like she is.

THE STEWARD: Aye, she was good to all of us. 'Twould have been hell on board without her; for he's a hard man—a hard, hard man—a driver, if there ever was one. [*With a grim laugh*] I hope he's satisfied now—drivin' her on til she's near lost her mind. And who could blame her? 'Tis a God's wonder we're not a ship full of crazed people—with the ice all the time, and the quiet so thick you're afraid to hear your own voice.

BEN [*with a frightened glance toward the door on right*]: She don't never speak to me no more—jest looks at me 's if she didn't know me.

THE STEWARD: She don't know no one—but him. She talks to him—when she does talk—right enough.

BEN: She does nothin' all day long now but sit and sew—and then she cries to herself without makin' no noise. I've see her.

THE STEWARD: Aye, I could hear her through the door a while back.

BEN [*tiptoes over to the door and listens*]: She's cryin' now.

THE STEWARD [*furiously—shaking his fist*]: God send his soul to hell for the devil he is! [*There is the noise of someone coming slowly down the companionway stairs.* THE STEWARD *hurries to his stacked-up dishes. He is so nervous from fright that he knocks off the top one, which falls and breaks on the floor. He stands aghast, trembling with dread.* BEN *is violently rubbing off the organ with a piece of cloth which he has snatched from his pocket.* CAPTAIN KEENEY *appears in the doorway on right and comes into the cabin, removing his fur cap as he does so. He is a man of about forty, around five ten in height, but looking much shorter on account of the enormous proportions of his shoulders and chest. His face is massive and deeply lined, with gray-blue eyes of a bleak hardness, and a tightly clenched, thin-lipped mouth. His thick hair is long and gray. He is dressed in a heavy blue jacket and blue pants stuffed into his sea boots. He is followed into the cabin by the* SECOND MATE, *a rangy six-footer with a lean, weatherbeaten face.* THE MATE *is dressed about the same as* THE CAPTAIN. *He is a man of thirty or so.*]

KEENEY [*comes toward* THE STEWARD *with a stern look on his face.* THE STEWARD *is visibly frightened, and the stack of dishes rattles in his trembling hands.* KEENEY *draws back his fist and* THE STEWARD *shrinks away. The fist is gradually lowered and* KEENEY *speaks slowly*]: 'Twould be like hitting a worm. It is nigh two bells, Mr. Steward, and this truck not cleared yet.

THE STEWARD [*stammering*]: Y-y-yes, sir.

KEENEY: Instead of doin' your rightful work ye've been below here gossipin' old women's talk with that boy. [*To* BEN, *fiercely*] Get out o' this, you! Clean up the chart room. [BEN *darts past* THE MATE *to the open doorway.*] Pick up that dish, Mr. Steward!

THE STEWARD [*doing so with difficulty*]: Yes, sir.

KEENEY: The next dish you break, Mr. Steward, you take a bath in the Bering Sea[4] at the end of a rope.

THE STEWARD [*trembling*]: Yes, sir. [*He hurries out.* **THE SECOND MATE** *walks slowly over to* **THE CAPTAIN.**]

MATE: I warn't 'specially anxious the man at the wheel should catch what I wanted to say to you, sir. That's why I asked you to come below.

KEENEY [*impatiently*]: Speak your say, Mr. Slocum.

MATE [*unconsciously lowering his voice*]: I'm afeared there'll be trouble with the hands, by the look o' things. They'll likely turn ugly, every blessed one o' them, if you don't put back. The two years they signed up for is up today.

KEENEY: And d'you think you're tellin' me something new, Mr. Slocum? I've felt it in the air this long time past. D'you think I've not seen their ugly looks and the grudgin' way they worked? [*The door in rear is opened and* **MRS. KEENEY** *stands in the doorway. She is a slight, sweet-faced little woman, primly dressed in black. Her eyes are red from weeping, and her face drawn and pale. She takes in the cabin with a frightened glance, and stands as if fixed to the spot by some nameless dread, clasping and unclasping her hands nervously. The two men turn and look at her.*]

KEENEY [*with rough tenderness*]: Well, Annie?

MRS. KEENEY [*as if awakening from a dream*]: David, I—[*She is silent.* **THE MATE** *starts for the doorway.*]

KEENEY [*turning to him—sharply*]: Wait!

MATE: Yes, sir.

KEENEY: D'you want anything, Annie?

MRS. KEENEY [*after a pause, during which she seems to be endeavoring to collect her thoughts*]: I thought maybe—I'd go up on deck, David, to get a breath of fresh air. [*She stands humbly awaiting his permission. He and* **THE MATE** *exchange a significant glance.*]

KEENEY: It's too cold, Annie. You'd best stay below. There's nothing to look at on deck—but ice.

MRS. KEENEY [*monotonously*]: I know—ice, ice, ice! But there's nothing to see down here but these walls. [*She makes gesture of loathing.*]

KEENEY: You can play the organ, Annie.

MRS. KEENEY [*dully*]: I hate the organ. It puts me in mind of home.

KEENEY [*a touch of resentment in his voice*]: I got it jest for you!

MRS. KEENEY [*dully*]: I know. [*She turns away from them and walks slowly to the bench on left. She lifts up one of the curtains and looks through a port-hole, then utters an exclamation of joy.*] Ah, water! Clear water! As far as I can see!

---

[4] *Bering Sea*: Part of the north Pacific between Alaska and Siberia.

How good it looks after all these months of ice! [*She turns round to them, her face transfigured with joy.*] Ah, now I must go up on deck and look at it, David!

KEENEY [*frowning*]: Best not today, Annie. Best wait for a day when the sun shines.

MRS. KEENEY [*desperately*]: But the sun never shines in this terrible place.

KEENEY [*a tone of command in his voice*]: Best not today, Annie.

MRS. KEENEY [*crumbling before this command—abjectly*]: Very well, David. [*She stands there, staring straight before her as if in a daze. The two men look at her uneasily.*]

KEENEY [*sharply*]: Annie!

MRS. KEENEY [*dully*]: Yes, David.

KEENEY: Me and Mr. Slocum has business to talk about—ship's business.

MRS. KEENEY: Very well, David. [*She goes slowly out, rear; and leaves the door three-quarters shut behind her.*]

KEENEY: Best not have her on deck if they's goin' to be any trouble.

MATE: Yes, sir.

KEENEY: And trouble they's goin' to be. I feel it in my bones. [*Takes a revolver from the pocket of his coat and examines it.*] Got your'n?

MATE: Yes, sir.

KEENEY: Not that we'll have to use 'em—not if I know their breed of dog—jest to frighten 'em up a bit. [*Grimly*] I ain't never been forced to use one yit; and trouble I've had by land and by sea s'long as I kin remember, and will have till my dyin' day, I reckon.

MATE [*hesitatingly*]: Then you ain't goin'—to turn back?

KEENEY: Turn back! Mr. Slocum, did you ever hear o' me pointin' s'uth for home with only a measly four hundred barrel of ile in the hold?

MATE [*hastily*]: But the grub's gettin' low.

KEENEY: They's enough to last a long time yit, if they're careful with it; and they's plenty of water.

MATE: They say it's not fit to eat—what's left; and the two years they signed on fur is up today. They might make trouble for you in the courts when we git home.

KEENEY: Let them make what law trouble they kin! I don't give a damn 'bout the money. I've got to git the ile! [*glancing sharply at* THE MATE] You ain't turnin' no sea lawyer, be you, Mr. Slocum?

MATE [*flushing*]: Not by a hell of a sight, sir.

KEENEY: What do the fools want to go home fur now? Their share o' the four hundred barrel wouldn't keep them chewin' terbacco.

MATE [*slowly*]: They wants to git back to their old folks an' things, I s'pose.

KEENEY [*looking at him searchingly*]: 'N you want to turn back, too. [THE MATE *looks down confusedly before his sharp gaze.*] Don't lie, Mr. Slocum. It's writ down plain in your eyes. [*With grim sarcasm*] I hope, Mr. Slocum, you ain't agoin' to jine the men agin me.

MATE [*indignantly*]: That ain't fair, sir, to say sich things.

KEENEY [*with satisfaction*]: I warn't much afeard o' that, Tom. You been with me nigh on ten year, and I've learned ye whalin'. No man kin say I ain't a good master, if I be a hard one.

MATE: I warn't thinkin' of myself, sir—'bout turnin' home, I mean. [*Desperately*] But Mrs. Keeney, sir—seems like she ain't jest satisfied up here, ailin'-like— what with the cold an' bad luck an' the ice an' all.

KEENEY [*his face clouding—rebukingly, but not severely*]: That's my business, Mr. Slocum. I'll thank you to steer a clear course o' that. [*A pause.*] The ice'll break up soon to no'the'ard. I could see it startin' today. And when it goes and we git some sun, Annie'll pick up. [*Another pause—then he bursts forth*] It ain't the damned money what's keepin' me in the northern seas, Tom. But I can't go back to Homeport with a measly four hundred barrel of ile. I'd die fust. I ain't never come back home in all my days with- out a full ship. Ain't that true?

MATE: Yes, sir; but this voyage you been icebound, an'—

KEENEY [*scornfully*]: And d'you s'pose any of 'em would believe that—any o' them skippers I've beaten voyage after voyage? Can't you hear 'em laughin' and sneerin'—Tibbots 'n' Harris 'n' Simms and the rest—and all o' Homeport makin' fun o' me? "Dave Keeney, what boasts he's the best whalin' skipper out o' Homeport, comin' back with a measly four hundred barrel of ile!" [*The thought of this drives him into a frenzy, and he smashes his fist down on the marble top of the sideboard.*] I got to git the ile, I tell you! How could I figure on this ice? It's never been so bad before in the thirty year I been a-comin' here. And now it's breakin' up. In a couple o' days it'll be all gone. And they's whale here, plenty of 'em. I know they is, and I ain't never gone wrong yit. I got to git the ile! I got to git it in spite of all hell, and by God, I ain't a-goin' home till I do git it! [*There is the sound of subdued sobbing from the door in rear. The two men stand silent for a moment, listening. Then* KEENEY *goes over to the door and looks in. He hesitates for a moment as if he were going to enter—then closes the door softly.* JOE, *the harpooner, an enormous six-footer with a battered, ugly face, enters from right and stands waiting for* THE CAPTAIN *to notice him.*]

KEENEY [*turning and seeing him*]: Don't be standin' there like a hawk, Harpooner. Speak up!

JOE [*confusedly*]: We want—the men, sir—they wants to send a depitation aft[5] to have a word with you.

---

[5] *aft*: Toward the back of the ship; from aft, the back part of a ship.

KEENEY [*furiously*]: Tell 'em to go to—[*Checks himself and continues grimly*]— Tell 'em to come. I'll see 'em.

JOE: Aye, aye, sir. [*He goes out.*]

KEENEY [*with a grim smile*]: Here it comes, the trouble you spoke of, Mr. Slocum, and we'll make short shift of it. It's better to crush such things at the start than to let them make headway.

MATE [*worriedly*]: Shall I wake up the First and Fourth, sir? We might need their help.

KEENEY: No, let them sleep. I'm well able to handle this alone, Mr. Slocum. [*There is the shuffling of footsteps from outside and five of the crew crowd into the cabin, led by* JOE. *All dressed alike—sweaters, sea boots, etc. They glance uneasily at* THE CAPTAIN, *twirling their fur caps in their hands.*]

KEENEY [*after a pause*]: Well? Who's to speak fur ye?

JOE [*stepping forward with an air of bravado*]: I be.

KEENEY [*eyeing him up and down coldly*]: So you be. Then speak your say and be quick about it.

JOE [*trying not to wilt before* THE CAPTAIN'*s glance, and avoiding his eyes*]: The time we signed up for is done today.

KEENEY [*icily*]: You're tellin' me nothin' I don't know.

JOE: You ain't p'intin' fur home yit, far 'swe kin see.

KEENEY: No, and I ain't agoin' to till this ship is full of ile.

JOE: You can't go no further no'th with the ice before ye.

KEENEY: The ice is breaking up.

JOE [*after a slight pause, during which the others mumble angrily to one another*]: The grub we're gittin' now is rotten.

KEENEY: It's good enough fur ye. Better men than ye are have eaten worse. [*There is a chorus of angry exclamations from the crowd.*]

JOE [*encouraged by this support*]: We ain't agoin' to work no more 'less you puts back for home.

KEENEY [*fiercely*]: You ain't, ain't you?

JOE: No; and the law courts'll say we was right.

KEENEY: To hell with your law courts! We're at sea now, and I'm the law on this ship! [*Edging up toward the harpooner.*] And every mother's son of you what don't obey my orders goes in irons. [*There are more angry exclamations from the crew.* MRS. KEENEY *appears in the doorway in rear and looks on with startled eyes. None of the men notice her.*]

JOE [*with bravado*]: Then we're a-goin' to mutiny and take the old hooker[6] home ourselves. Ain't we, boys? [*As he turns his head to look at the others,* KEENEY'*s*

---

[6] *hooker*: Old ship.

fist shoots out to the side of his jaw. JOE *goes down in a heap and lies there.* MRS. KEENEY *gives a shriek and hides her face in her hands. The men pull out their sheath knives and start a rush, but stop when they find themselves confronted by the revolvers of* KEENEY *and* THE MATE.]

KEENEY [*his eyes and voice snapping*]: Hold still! [*The men stand huddled together in a sullen silence.* KEENEY'*s voice is full of mockery.*] You's found out it ain't safe to mutiny on this ship, ain't you? And now git for'ard where ye belong, and—[*he gives* JOE'*s body a contemptuous kick*]—drag him with you. And remember, the first man of ye I see shirkin' I'll shoot dead as sure as there's a sea under us, and you can tell the rest the same. Git for'ard now! Quick! [*The men leave in cowed silence, carrying* JOE *with them.* KEENEY *turns to* THE MATE *with a short laugh and puts his revolver back in his pocket.*] Best get up on deck, Mr. Slocum, and see to it they don't try none of their skulkin' tricks. We'll have to keep an eye peeled from now on. I know 'em.

MATE: Yes, sir. [*He goes out, right.* KEENEY *hears his wife's hysterical weeping and turns around in surprise—then walks slowly to her side.*]

KEENEY [*putting an arm around her shoulder—with gruff tenderness*]: There, there, Annie. Don't be feared. It's all past and gone.

MRS. KEENEY [*shrinking away from him*]: Oh, I can't bear it! I can't bear it any longer!

KEENEY [*gently*]: Can't bear what, Annie?

MRS. KEENEY [*hysterically*]: All this horrible brutality, and these brutes of men, and this terrible ship and this prison cell of a room, and the ice all around and the silence. [*After this outburst she calms down and wipes her eyes with her handkerchief.*]

KEENEY [*after a pause, during which he looks down at her with a puzzled frown*]: Remember, I warn't hankerin' to have you come on this voyage, Annie.

MRS. KEENEY: I wanted to be with you, David, don't you see? I didn't want to wait back there in the house all alone as I've been doing these last six years since we were married—waiting, and watching, and fearing—with nothing to keep my mind occupied—not able to go back teaching school on account of being Dave Keeney's wife. I used to dream of sailing on the great, wide, glorious ocean. I wanted to be by your side in the danger and vigorous life of it all. I wanted to see you the hero they make you out to be in Homeport. And instead [*her voice grows tremulous*] all I find is ice and cold—and brutality! [*Her voice breaks.*]

KEENEY: I warned you what it'd be like, Annie. "Whalin' ain't no ladies' tea party," I says to you, "and you better stay to home where you've got all your woman's comforts." [*Shaking his head*] But you was so set on it.

MRS. KEENEY [*wearily*]: Oh, I know it isn't your fault, David. You see, I didn't believe you. I guess I was dreaming about the old Vikings[7] in the story books, and I thought you were one of them.

KEENEY [*protestingly*]: I done my best to make it as cozy and comfortable as could be. [MRS. KEENEY *looks around her in wild scorn.*] I even sent to the city for that organ for ye, thinkin' it might be soothin' to ye to be playin' it times when they was calms and things was dull-like.

MRS. KEENEY [*wearily*]: Yes, you were very kind, David. I know that. [*She goes to left and lifts the curtains from the port-hole and looks out—then suddenly bursts forth*]: I won't stand it—I can't stand it—pent up by these walls like a prisoner. [*She runs over to him and throws her arms around him, weeping. He puts his arm protectingly over her shoulders.*] Take me away from here, David! If I don't get away from here, out of this terrible ship, I'll go mad! Take me home, David! I can't think any more. I feel as if the cold and the silence were crushing down on my brain. I'm afraid. Take me home!

KEENEY [*holds her at arm's length and looks at her face anxiously*]: Best go to bed, Annie. You ain't yourself. You got fever. Your eyes look so strange-like. I ain't never seen you look this way before.

MRS. KEENEY [*laughing hysterically*]: It's the ice and the cold and the silence— they'd make anyone look strange.

KEENEY [*soothingly*]: In a month or two, with good luck, three at the most, I'll have her filled with ile, and then we'll give her everything she'll stand and p'int for home.

MRS. KEENEY: But we can't wait for that—I can't wait. I want to get home. And the men won't wait. They want to get home. It's cruel, it's brutal for you to keep them. You must sail back. You've got no excuse. There's clear water to the south now. If you've a heart at all you've got to turn back.

KEENEY [*harshly*]: I can't, Annie.

MRS. KEENEY: Why can't you?

KEENEY: A woman couldn't rightly understand my reason.

MRS. KEENEY [*wildly*]: Because it's a stubborn reason. Oh, I heard you talking with the second mate. You're afraid the other captains will sneer at you because you didn't come back with a full ship. You want to live up to your silly reputation even if you have to beat and starve men and drive me mad to do it.

KEENEY [*his jaw set stubbornly*]: It ain't that, Annie. Them skippers would never dare sneer to my face. It ain't so much what anyone'd say—but—[*he hesitates, struggling to express his meaning*] you see—I've always done it—since my first voyage as skipper. I always come back—with a full ship—and—it don't

---

[7] *Vikings:* Scandinavian sea explorers and pirates who lived from the eighth to the tenth centuries.

seem right not to—somehow. I been always first whalin' skipper out o' Homeport, and—don't you see my meanin', Annie? [*He glances at her. She is not looking at him, but staring dully in front of her, not hearing a word he is saying.*] Annie! [*She comes to herself with a start.*] Best turn in, Annie, there's a good woman. You ain't well.

MRS. KEENEY [*resisting his attempts to guide her to the door in rear*]: David! Won't you please turn back?

KEENEY [*gently*]: I can't Annie—not yet a while. You don't see my meanin'. I got to git the ile.

MRS. KEENEY: It'd be different if you needed the money, but you don't. You've got more than plenty.

KEENEY [*impatiently*]: It ain't the money I'm thinkin' of. D'you think I'm as mean as that?

MRS. KEENEY [*dully*]: No—I don't know—I can't understand. [*Intensely*] Oh, I want to be home in the old house once more, and see my own kitchen again, and hear a woman's voice talking to me and be able to talk to her. Two years! It seems so long ago—as if I'd been dead and could never go back.

KEENEY [*worried by her strange tone and the faraway look in her eyes*]: Best go to bed, Annie. You ain't well.

MRS. KEENEY [*not appearing to hear him*]: I used to think Homeport was a stupid, monotonous place. Then I used to go down on the beach, especially when it was windy and the breakers were rolling in, and I'd dream of the fine, free life you must be leading. [*She gives a laugh which is half a sob.*] I used to love the sea then. [*She pauses; then continues with slow intensity*] But now— I don't ever want to see the sea again.

KEENEY [*thinking to humor her*]: 'Tis no fit place for a woman, that's sure. I was a fool to bring ye.

MRS. KEENEY [*after a pause—passing her hand over her eyes with a gesture of pathetic weariness*]: How long would it take us to reach home—if we started now?

KEENEY [*frowning*]: 'Bout two months, I reckon, Annie, with fair luck.

MRS. KEENEY [*counts on her fingers—then murmurs with a rapt smile*]: That would be August, the latter part of August, wouldn't it? It was on the twenty-fifth of August we were married, David, wasn't it?

KEENEY [*trying to conceal the fact that her memories have moved him—gruffly*]: Don't you remember?

MRS. KEENEY [*vaguely—again passes her hand over her eyes*]: My memory is leaving me—up here in the ice. It was so long ago. [*A pause—then she smiles dreamily.*] It's June now. The lilacs will be all in bloom in the front yard—and the climbing roses on the trellis to the side of the house—they're budding— [*She suddenly covers her face with her hands and commences to sob.*]

KEENEY [*disturbed*]: Go in and rest, Annie. You're all worn out cryin' over what can't be helped.

MRS. KEENEY [*suddenly throwing her arms around his neck and clinging to him*]: You love me, don't you, David?

KEENEY [*in amazed embarrassment at this outburst*]: Love you? Why d'you ask me such a question, Annie?

MRS. KEENEY [*shaking him fiercely*]: But you do, don't you, David? Tell me!

KEENEY: I'm your husband, Annie, and you're my wife. Could there be aught but love between us after all these years?

MRS. KEENEY [*shaking him again—still more fiercely*]: Then you do love me. Say it!

KEENEY [*simply*]: I do, Annie.

MRS. KEENEY [*gives a sigh of relief—her hands drop to her sides. KEENEY regards her anxiously. She passes her hand across her eyes and murmurs half to herself*]: I sometimes think if we could only have had a child—[KEENEY *turns away from her, deeply moved. She grabs his arm and turns him around to face her—intensely.*] And I've always been a good wife to you, haven't I, David?

KEENEY [*his voice betraying his emotion*]: No man has ever had a better, Annie.

MRS. KEENEY: And I've never asked for much from you, have I, David? Have I?

KEENEY: You know you could have all I got the power to give ye, Annie.

MRS. KEENEY [*wildly*]: Then do this, this once, for my sake, for God's sake— take me home! It's killing me, this life—the brutality and cold and horror of it. I'm going mad. I can feel the threat in the air. I can't bear the silence threatening me—day after gray day and every day the same. I can't bear it. [*Sobbing*] I'll go mad, I know I will. Take me home, David, if you love me as you say. I'm afraid. For the love of God, take me home! [*She throws her arms around him, weeping against his shoulder. His face betrays the tremendous struggle going on within him. He holds her out at arm's length, his expression softening. For a moment his shoulders sag, he becomes old, his iron spirit weakens as he looks at her tearstained face.*]

KEENEY [*dragging out the words with an effort*]: I'll do it, Annie—for your sake— if you say it's needful for ye.

MRS. KEENEY [*wild with joy—kissing him*]: God bless you for that, David! [*He turns away from her silently and walks toward the companionway. Just at that moment there is a clatter of footsteps on the stairs and* THE MATE *enters the cabin.*]

MATE [*excitedly*]: The ice is breakin' up to the no'the'ard, sir. There's a clear passage through the floe, and clear water beyond, the lookout says. [KEENEY *straightens himself like a man coming out of a trance.* MRS. KEENEY *looks at* THE MATE *with terrified eyes.*]

KEENEY [*dazedly—trying to collect his thoughts*]: A clear passage? To no'the'ard?

MATE: Yes, sir.

KEENEY [*his voice suddenly grim with determination*]: Then get ready and we'll drive her through.

MATE: Aye, aye, sir.

MRS. KEENEY [*appealingly*]: David! David!

KEENEY [*not heeding her*]: Will the men turn to willin' or must we drag 'em out?

MATE: They'll turn to willin' enough. You put the fear o' God into 'em, sir. They're meek as lambs.

KEENEY: Then drive 'em—both watches. [*With grim determination*] They's whale t'other side o' this floe and we're agoin' to git 'em.

MATE: Aye, aye, sir. [*He goes out hurriedly. A moment later there is the sound of scuffling feet from the deck outside and* THE MATE's *voice shouting orders.*]

KEENEY [*speaking aloud to himself—derisively*]: And I was agoin' home like a yaller dog![8]

MRS. KEENEY [*imploringly*]: David!

KEENEY [*sternly*]: Woman, you ain't a-doin' right when you meddle in men's business and weaken 'em. You can't know my feelin's. I got to prove a man to be a good husband for ye to take pride in. I got to git the ile, I tell ye.

MRS. KEENEY [*supplicatingly*]: David! Aren't you going home?

KEENEY [*ignoring this question—commandingly*]: You ain't well. Go and lay down a mite. [*He starts for the door.*] I got to git on deck. [*He goes out. She cries after him in anguish, "David!" A pause. She passes her hand across her eyes— then commences to laugh hysterically and goes to the organ. She sits down and starts to play wildly an old hymn, "There Is Rest for the Weary."* KEENEY *re- enters from the doorway to the deck and stands looking at her angrily. He comes over and grabs her roughly by the shoulder.*]

KEENEY: Woman, what foolish mockin' is this? [*She laughs wildly, and he starts back from her in alarm.*] Annie! What is it? [*She doesn't answer him.* KEENEY's *voice trembles.*] Don't you know me, Annie? [*He puts both hands on her shoulders and turns her around so that he can look into her eyes. She stares up at him with a stupid expression, a vague smile on her lips. He stumbles away from her, and she commences softly to play the organ again.*]

KEENEY [*swallowing hard—in a hoarse whisper, as if he had difficulty in speaking*]: You said—you was a-goin' mad—God! [*A long wail is heard from the deck above, "Ah, bl-o-o-ow!" A moment later* THE MATE's *face appears through the skylight. He cannot see* MRS. KEENEY.]

MATE [*in great excitement*]: Whales, sir—a whole school of 'em—off the star-b'd[8] quarter, 'bout five miles away—big ones!

KEENEY [*galvanized into action*]: Are you lowerin' the boats?

MATE: Yes, sir!

---

[8] *like a yaller dog*: Like I was afraid.

[9] *star-b'd*: Starboard, the right-hand side of a ship.

KEENEY [*with grim decision*]: I'm a-comin' with ye.

MATE: Aye, aye, sir. [*Jubilantly*] You'll git the ile now right enough, sir. [*His head is withdrawn and he can be heard shouting orders.*]

KEENEY [*turning to his wife*]: Annie! Did you hear him? I'll git the ile. [*She doesn't answer or seem to know he is there. He gives a hard laugh which is almost a groan.*] I know you're foolin' me, Annie. You ain't out of your mind—[*anxiously*] be you? I'll git the ile now right enough—jest a little while longer, Annie— then we'll turn home'ard. I can't turn back now, you see that, don't you? I've got to git the ile. [*In sudden terror*] Answer me! You ain't mad, be you? [*She keeps on playing the organ, but makes no reply.* THE MATE's *face appears again through the skylight.*]

MATE: All ready, sir. [KEENEY *turns his back on his wife and strides to the doorway, where he stands for a moment and looks back at her in anguish, fighting to control his feelings.*]

MATE: Comin', sir?

KEENEY [*his face suddenly grows hard with determination*]: Aye. [*He turns abruptly and goes out.* MRS. KEENEY *does not appear to notice his departure. Her whole attention seems centered in the organ. She sits with half-closed eyes, her body swaying a little from side to side to the rhythm of the hymn. Her fingers move faster and faster and she is playing wildly and discordantly as the curtain falls.*]

UNDERSTANDING THE STORY

1. What are three major **conflicts** in *Ile*?

2. What factors makes these conflicts so powerful?

3. Who is more to blame for Mrs. Keeney's condition: Mrs. Keeney herself or Captain Keeney? Explain.

4. To what extent, if any, does O'Neill present one character more sympathetically than the others? Explain.

5. Which is the wiser decision for Captain Keeney to make? Explain.

6. To what extent, if any, do these characters have the power to control their fate?

7. How do the seamen react to their captain's decision?

8. What **themes** do you find in this play?

ANALYZING LITERARY TECHNIQUE

1. What function do Ben and the steward perform in *Ile*?
2. Give an example of **foreshadowing** and explain its function.
3. What is the function of fate in *Ile*?
4. Explain the connection between the **setting** of the play and the **tone.**
5. What action marks the **crisis** in the play? What is the **climax?**
6. What factors make *Ile* a **tragedy?** Consider Captain Keeney's actions and personality.
7. What **paradoxes** do you find in this play?
8. To what extent does O'Neill use **symbolism** in *Ile*? For what purpose?
9. Find examples of **repetition** and explain their function.

WRITING ABOUT LITERATURE

1. Write an essay in which you analyze Captain Keeney as a tragic figure. Consider to what extent, if any, Captain Keeney's personality and behavior reflect the psychological pattern seen in the traditional Greek hero, where *arete* (personal excellence) leads to **hubris** (excessive pride), which in turn leads to *ate* (blind, reckless behavior) and finally to **nemesis** (retribution). Support your ideas with quotations from the play.
2. Create a dialogue between another sea captain and his wife in which they discuss this voyage of Captain Keeney's. Have them consider the issues that are important to Captain Keeney and his wife. How does this couple evaluate the problems?

Soldier's Home

ERNEST HEMINGWAY

ERNEST HEMINGWAY (1899–1961), the American short-story writer and novelist, won the Nobel Prize for literature in 1954 "for his powerful and style-forming mastery of the art of modern narration and for the influence he exerted on contemporary style." Hemingway represented "the lost generation," those disillusioned by the inhumanity of World War I. Because the Hemingway hero accepts the postwar world and chooses to act with honesty, courage, and compassion, the Nobel committee described Hemingway as "one of the great writers of our time . . . who, honestly and undauntedly, reproduces the genuine features of the hard countenance of the age." Hemingway is best known for the novels *The Sun Also Rises* (1926), *A Farewell to Arms* (1929), *For Whom the Bell Tolls* (1940), and *The Old Man and the Sea* (1952). Each was made into a successful motion picture.

Hemingway was born into a doctor's family in Oak Park, Illinois. His father loved nature, and the family spent summers fishing and hunting in the woods of northern Michigan. Hemingway loved to write, and his short stories were published in his high-school newspaper and literary magazine. After graduating in 1917, he did not attend college. When a boxing injury prevented him from enlisting in the army in World War I, he volunteered first as a Red Cross ambulance driver in France and then as an infantry soldier in Italy, where he was seriously wounded. From 1920 to 1924, he was a foreign correspondent for the *Toronto Star* and the *Star Weekly*, where he covered the war between Greece and Turkey and the subsequent peace conference. During this period, he began his career as a writer under the tutelage of his friends Gertrude Stein and Ezra Pound. His first book, *Three Stories and Ten Poems*, was published in 1923. From 1928 to 1938, he lived in Key West, Florida, writing, fishing, and traveling abroad. He particularly enjoyed watching bullfights in Spain and hunting in Africa. In 1936 and 1937, he actively supported the Republican cause in the Spanish civil war, which he covered as a journalist. Hemingway's short stories and novels reflect his unusual and varied life experiences.

Many twentieth-century writers who have adopted Hemingway's style have ignored the worldview that exists beneath the surface simplicity of his characters' words. Hemingway's goal in his fiction was to reproduce an ordinary but significant situation so exactly that readers would identify with his characters' attitudes about life. Consequently, a Hemingway story functions on two levels. The surface realistic story is a way to understand a deeper and broader truth about the nature of the human condition. This dual dimension gives Hemingway's stories their interest; the underlying truths give them their depth and their power. In Hemingway's words:

> I always try to write on the principle of the iceberg. There is seven-eighths of it underneath for every part that shows. Anything you know, you can eliminate and it only strengthens your iceberg. It is the part that doesn't show.

The Hemingway hero lives in a universe that lacks all meaning and order. It is a world in which bad things happen to good people, a world in which those who mistreat others may not be punished for their words or deeds. Whatever external moral code the hero may have had is no longer valid. Once he views his universe to be amoral, any type of behavior becomes possible, since no valid external code—with its accompanying sanctions—exists. Nevertheless, the Hemingway hero insists on having positive moral values guide his decisions. He responds thoughtfully and courageously to the absurd world in which he finds himself by becoming inner-directed and creating his own strong moral code of behavior. He determines his own stature as a human being by how he thinks, speaks, and acts when under pressure and in crisis.

The Hemingway hero knows that to compromise his values is to destroy the essence of who he is. Therefore, where he finds himself surrounded by anarchy, he creates order for himself; where he finds dishonesty, he responds with honesty; where he finds cowardice, he behaves with courage; where he finds cruelty, he responds with compassion; and where he finds ineptitude, he acts with skill. Finally, when he finds that he has been emotionally or spiritually wounded, he has the courage and the self-confidence to put forth the effort to heal himself, and he expects that, with time, he will succeed.

In the following story, the Hemingway hero is a veteran who has recently returned from World War I. The story is typical of Hemingway's work in that he tells the important story indirectly, by implication. Because the surface story obliquely reveals the important truths that cause the protagonist to think, speak, and act as he does, readers who hope to discover what Hemingway is actually saying in this story—and who want to understand what is truly important about it—must look beyond the story to the experiences that have created the veteran's point of view.

Krebs went to the war from a Methodist college in Kansas. There is a picture which shows him among his fraternity brothers, all of them wearing exactly the same height and style collar. He enlisted in the Marines in 1917 and did not return to the United States until the second division returned from the Rhine in the summer of 1919.

There is a picture which shows him on the Rhine with two German girls and another corporal. Krebs and the corporal look too big for their uniforms. The German girls are not beautiful. The Rhine does not show in the picture.

By the time Krebs returned to his home town in Oklahoma the greeting of heroes was over. He came back much too late. The men from the town who had been drafted had all been welcomed elaborately on their return. There had been a great deal of hysteria. Now the reaction had set in. People seemed to think it was rather ridiculous for Krebs to be getting back so late, years after the war was over.

At first Krebs, who had been at Belleau Wood, Soissons, the Champagne, St. Mihiel and in the Argonne did not want to talk about the war at all. Later he felt the need to talk but no one wanted to hear about it. His town had heard too many atrocity stories to be thrilled by actualities. Krebs found that to be listened to at all he had to lie, and after he had done this twice he, too, had a reaction against the war and against talking about it. A distaste for everything that had happened to him in the war set in because of the lies he had told. All of the times that had been able to make him feel cool and clear inside himself when he thought of them; the times so long back when he had done the one thing, the only thing for a man to do, easily and naturally, when he might have done something else, now lost their cool, valuable quality and then were lost themselves.

His lies were quite unimportant lies and consisted in attributing to himself things other men had seen, done or heard of, and stating as facts certain apocryphal incidents familiar to all soldiers. Even his lies were not sensational at the pool room. His acquaintances, who had heard detailed accounts of German women found chained to machine guns in the Argonne forest and who could not comprehend, or were barred by their patriotism from interest in, any German machine gunners who were not chained, were not thrilled by his stories.

Krebs acquired the nausea in regard to experience that is the result of untruth or exaggeration, and when he occasionally met another man who had really been a soldier and they talked a few minutes in the dressing room at a dance he fell into the easy pose of the old soldier among other soldiers: that he had been badly, sickeningly frightened all the time. In this way he lost everything.

During this time, it was late summer, he was sleeping late in bed, getting up to walk down town to the library to get a book, eating lunch at home, reading on the front porch until he became bored and then walking down through the town to spend the hottest hours of the day in the cool dark of the pool room. He loved to play pool.

In the evening he practised on his clarinet, strolled down town, read and went to bed. He was still a hero to his two young sisters. His mother would have given him breakfast in bed if he had wanted it. She often came in when he was in bed and asked him to tell her about the war, but her attention always wandered. His father was non-committal.

Before Krebs went away to the war he had never been allowed to drive the family motor car. His father was in the real estate business and always wanted the car to be at his command when he required it to take clients out into the country to show them a piece of farm property. The car always stood outside the First National Bank building where his father had an office on the second floor. Now, after the war, it was still the same car.

Nothing was changed in the town except that the young girls had grown up. But they lived in such a complicated world of already defined alliances and shifting feuds that Krebs did not feel the energy or the courage to break into it. He liked to look at them, though. There were so many good-looking young girls. Most of them had their hair cut short. When he went away only the little girls wore their hair like that or girls that were fast. They all wore sweaters and shirt waists with round Dutch collars. It was a pattern. He liked to look at them from the front porch as they walked on the other side of the street. He liked to watch them walking under the shade of the trees. He liked the round Dutch collars above their sweaters. He liked their silk stockings and flat shoes. He liked their bobbed hair and the way they walked.

When he was in town their appeal to him was not very strong. He did not like them when he saw them in the Greek's ice cream parlor. He did not want them themselves really. They were too complicated. There was something else. Vaguely he wanted a girl but he did not want to have to work to get her. He would have liked to have a girl but he did not want to have to spend a long time getting her. He did not want to get into the intrigue and the politics. He did not want to have to do any courting. He did not want to tell any more lies. It wasn't worth it.

He did not want any consequences. He did not want any consequences ever again. He wanted to live along without consequences. Besides he did not really need a girl. The army had taught him that. It was all right to pose as though you had to have a girl. Nearly everybody did that. But it wasn't true. You did not need a girl. That was the funny thing. First a fellow boasted how girls mean nothing to him, that he never thought of them, that they could not touch him. Then a fellow boasted that he could not get along without girls, that he had to have them all the time, that he could not go to sleep without them.

That was all a lie. It was all a lie both ways. You did not need a girl unless you thought about them. He learned that in the army. Then sooner or later you always got one. When you were really ripe for a girl you always got one. You did not have to think about it. Sooner or later it would come. He had learned that in the army.

Now he would have liked a girl if she had come to him and not wanted to talk. But here at home it was all too complicated. He knew he could never get through it all again. It was not worth the trouble. That was the thing about French girls and German girls. There was not all this talking. You couldn't talk much and you did not need to talk. It was simple and you were friends. He thought about France and then he began to think about Germany. On the whole he had liked Germany better. He did not want to leave Germany. He did not want to come home. Still, he had come home. He sat on the front porch.

He liked the girls that were walking along the other side of the street. He liked the look of them much better than the French girls or the German girls. But the world they were in was not the world he was in. He would like to have one of them. But it was not worth it. They were such a nice pattern. He liked the pattern. It was exciting. But he would not go through all the talking. He did not want one badly enough. He liked to look at them all, though. It was not worth it. Not now when things were getting good again.

He sat there on the porch reading a book on the war. It was a history and he was reading about all the engagements he had been in. It was the most interesting reading he had ever done. He wished there were more maps. He looked forward with a good feeling to reading all the really good histories when they would come out with good detail maps. Now he was really learning about the war. He had been a good soldier. That made a difference.

One morning after he had been home about a month his mother came into his bedroom and sat on the bed. She smoothed her apron.

"I had a talk with your father last night, Harold," she said, "and he is willing for you to take the car out in the evenings."

"Yeah?" said Krebs, who was not fully awake. "Take the car out? Yeah?"

"Yes. Your father has felt for some time that you should be able to take the car out in the evenings whenever you wished but we only talked it over last night."

"I'll bet you made him," Krebs said.

"No. It was your father's suggestion that we talk the matter over."

"Yeah. I'll bet you made him," Krebs sat up in bed.

"Will you come down to breakfast, Harold?" his mother said.

"As soon as I get my clothes on," Krebs said.

His mother went out of the room and he could hear her frying something downstairs while he washed, shaved and dressed to go down into the dining-room for breakfast. While he was eating breakfast his sister brought in the mail.

"Well, Hare," she said. "You old sleepy-head. What do you ever get up for?"

Krebs looked at her. He liked her. She was his best sister.

"Have you got the paper?" he asked.

She handed him *The Kansas City Star* and he shucked off its brown wrapper and opened it to the sporting page. He folded *The Star* open and propped it against the water pitcher with his cereal dish to steady it, so he could read while he ate.

"Harold," his mother stood in the kitchen doorway, "Harold, please don't muss up the paper. Your father can't read his *Star* if it's been mussed."

"I won't muss it," Krebs said.

His sister sat down at the table and watched him while he read.

"We're playing indoor over at school this afternoon," she said. "I'm going to pitch."

"Good," said Krebs. "How's the old wing?"

"I can pitch better than lots of the boys. I tell them all you taught me. The other girls aren't much good."

"Yeah?" said Krebs.

"I tell them all you're my beau. Aren't you my beau, Hare?"

"You bet."

"Couldn't your brother really be your beau just because he's your brother?"

"I don't know."

"Sure you know. Couldn't you be my beau, Hare, if I was old enough and if you wanted to?"

"Sure. You're my girl now."

"Am I really your girl?"

"Sure."

"Do you love me?"

"Uh, huh."

"Will you love me always?"

"Sure."

"Will you come over and watch me play indoor?"

"Maybe."

"Aw, Hare, you don't love me. If you loved me, you'd want to come over and watch me play indoor."

Krebs's mother came into the dining-room from the kitchen. She carried a plate with two fried eggs and some crisp bacon on it and a plate of buckwheat cakes.

"You run along, Helen," she said. "I want to talk to Harold."

She put the eggs and bacon down in front of him and brought in a jug of maple syrup for the buckwheat cakes. Then she sat down across the table from Krebs.

"I wish you'd put down the paper a minute, Harold," she said.

Krebs took down the paper and folded it.

"Have you decided what you are going to do yet, Harold?" his mother said, taking off her glasses.

"No," said Krebs.

"Don't you think it's about time?" His mother did not say this in a mean way. She seemed worried.

"I hadn't thought about it," Krebs said.

"God has some work for every one to do," his mother said. "There can be no idle hands in His Kingdom."

"I'm not in His Kingdom," Krebs said.

"We are all of us in His Kingdom."

Krebs felt embarrassed and resentful as always.

"I've worried about you so much, Harold," his mother went on. "I know the temptations you must have been exposed to. I know how weak men are. I know what your own dear grandfather, my own father, told us about the Civil War and I have prayed for you. I pray for you all day long, Harold."

Krebs looked at the bacon fat hardening on his plate.

"Your father is worried, too," his mother went on. "He thinks you have lost your ambition, that you haven't got a definite aim in life. Charley Simmons, who is just your age, has a good job and is going to be married. The boys are all settling down; they're all determined to get somewhere; you can see that boys like Charley Simmons are on their way to being really a credit to the community."

Krebs said nothing.

"Don't look that way, Harold," his mother said. "You know we love you and I want to tell you for your own good how matters stand. Your father does not want to hamper your freedom. He thinks you should be allowed to drive the car. If you want to take some of the nice girls out riding with you, we are only too pleased. We want you to enjoy yourself. But you are going to have to settle down to work, Harold. Your father doesn't care what you start in at. All work is honorable as he says. But you've got to make a start at something. He asked me to speak to you this morning and then you can stop in and see him at his office."

"Is that all?" Krebs asked.

"Yes. Don't you love your mother, dear boy?"

"No," Krebs said.

His mother looked at him across the table. Her eyes were shiny. She started crying.

"I don't love anybody," Krebs said.

It wasn't any good. He couldn't tell her, he couldn't make her see it. It was silly to have said it. He had only hurt her. He went over and took hold of her arm. She was crying with her head in her hands.

"I didn't mean it," he said. "I was just angry at something. I didn't mean I didn't love you."

His mother went on crying. Krebs put his arm on her shoulder.

"Can't you believe me, mother?"

His mother shook her head.

"Please, please, mother. Please believe me."

"All right," his mother said chokily. She looked up at him. "I believe you, Harold."

Krebs kissed her hair. She put her face up to him.

"I'm your mother," she said. "I held you next to my heart when you were a tiny baby."

Krebs felt sick and vaguely nauseated.

"I know, Mummy," he said. "I'll try and be a good boy for you."

"Would you kneel and pray with me, Harold?" his mother asked.

They knelt down beside the dining-room table and Krebs's mother prayed.

"Now, you pray, Harold," she said.

"I can't," Krebs said.

"Try, Harold."

"I can't."

"Do you want me to pray for you?"

"Yes."

So his mother prayed for him and then they stood up and Krebs kissed his mother and went out of the house. He had tried so to keep his life from being complicated. Still, none of it had touched him. He had felt sorry for his mother and she had made him lie. He would go to Kansas City and get a job and she would feel all right about it. There would be one more scene maybe before he got away. He would not go down to his father's office. He would miss that one. He wanted his life to go smoothly. It had just gotten going that way. Well, that was all over now, anyway. He would go over to the schoolyard and watch Helen play indoor baseball.

UNDERSTANDING THE STORY

1. In what two ways can the title of the story be read? What is the significance of this dual interpretation?

2. What has Krebs experienced before his return home? What aspects of this experience have affected his life?

3. Why does Hemingway state in the opening sentences that Krebs went to a Methodist college and that he belonged to a fraternity?

4. How has the additional year Krebs spent in Germany affected him?

5. How does Krebs show himself to be a Hemingway hero?

6. How does Krebs cope with his return home?

7. What determines when Krebs is called Krebs and when he is called Harold or Hare? What is significant about this difference?

8. Describe the personalities of Krebs's parents. How does Hemingway convey the personality of each parent? What role do the parents play in the story?

9. Why does Krebs tell his mother that he does not love her or anyone else?

10. Why is it significant that Krebs permits his mother to pray for him?

11. Why does Hemingway include the conversation between Krebs and Helen?

12. What does each decision that Krebs makes at the end of the story reveal about his current state and about his future?

13. What **themes** do you find in this story?

ANALYZING LITERARY TECHNIQUE

1. From whose **point of view** is this story told? Why is point of view important here?

2. What is the **conflict** in the story?

3. What events mark the **crisis,** the **climax,** and the **resolution** of the story?

4. Find an example of **irony** in this story and explain its significance to the story.

5. What does Hemingway achieve through his use of short simple sentences? Give examples of when Hemingway uses this style.

6. Find examples of Hemingway's selective use of detail and explain what each example achieves.

7. Note Hemingway's use of **repetition** to reveal an important theme of the story.

8. What is the **tone** of the story?

WRITING ABOUT LITERATURE

1. Write an expository essay in which you analyze Krebs as a Hemingway hero. In your introductory paragraph, describe the qualities that a Hemingway hero possesses. In the body of your essay, use quotations from the story to show that Krebs possesses each of these qualities. In your concluding paragraph, explain the significance of a Hemingway hero.

2. Write an essay in which you analyze three aspects of Hemingway's style. Choices may include use of detail, repetition, and short simple sentences. In your opening paragraph, explain the subject of your essay. In the three paragraphs that form the body of your essay, devote one paragraph to each aspect of Hemingway's style that you are discussing. Use quotations from the text and explain what each quotation contributes to the story. In your concluding paragraph, explain what Hemingway's style contributes to the story as a whole.

3. Retell "Soldier's Home" from the point of view of either Krebs's mother or his father. Relate the values and attitudes of the parent who is telling the story.

4. Write a story in which a character has an experience that profoundly affects her or him. Reveal the importance of this experience by expressing the character's thoughts, comments, and actions as well as the comments and actions of those who respond to her or him. Choose a style that always reflects your character's state of mind.

The Hollow Men

T. S. ELIOT

*T*HOMAS STEARNS ELIOT (1888–1965) is considered by many to be the poetic voice of the twentieth century. In 1948, he won the Nobel Prize for literature "for his work as a trail-blazing pioneer of modern poetry." Eliot was the first major poet to focus on the sterility of the modern age. In spite of the wonders of technology and their material well-being, his characters are intelligent but ineffectual. They have lost their sense of identity, their sense of purpose, and their sense of community. The form of Eliot's poetry is as innovative as his point of view. His intellect united with his artistic genius to create a wealth of similes, metaphors, and allusions that have become symbols for the human condition in the twentieth century. He is best known for his poems "The Love Song of J. Alfred Prufrock" (1917), "The Waste Land" (1922), and "The Hollow Men" (1925) and for his play, *Murder in the Cathedral* (1935).

T. S. Eliot was born in St. Louis, Missouri, into a distinguished family of educators. He attended Milton Academy and Harvard College. While a Harvard student, he became fascinated by anthropology, mythology, and Jungian psychology. He also was well educated in the classics and philosophy and fluent in French and German. After discovering the French Symbolist and the American Imagist poets, he contributed poetry to the Harvard *Advocate* and wrote his major poem, "The Love Song of J. Alfred Prufrock." After graduating from Harvard in 1909, he attended the Sorbonne in Paris and Oxford University in England, thereafter settling in London. Eliot earned a living as a teacher, a banker, and an editor. In 1922, he became the founder and editor of the literary journal *The Criterion*. In 1925, he became a director of Faber and Faber and encouraged the publication of poetry by many who have since come to be regarded as great modern English poets. In 1928, the year after he became a British subject, he described himself as "a classicist in literature, a royalist in politics, and an Anglo-Catholic in religion." Thereafter, his perspective became less bleak and more serene. He continued to publish poems, plays, and literary criticism through the 1950s.

Eliot considered the poet's task to be "to express the greatest emotional intensity of his time, based on whatever his time happened to think." Unlike the poets of the nineteenth century, he felt that "the essential advantage for a poet is not to have a beautiful world with which to deal; it is to be able to see beneath both beauty and ugliness; to see the boredom, and the horror, and the glory." He was an astute observer of personality, lifestyle, and values. Eliot was the first poet writing in English to incorporate extensively into his poetry the interest of the Symbolists and Imagists in new subjects, free rhythms, and concrete images that evoke and suggest, rather than describe, some aspect of reality. With these ideas in mind, he fused content with style, intellect with emotion, and complexity with simplicity. "The Hollow Men," first published in *Poems 1909–1925* (1925), evokes the worldview for which Eliot is famous in language that has become part of the modern idiom.

Mistah Kurtz—he dead
A penny for the Old Guy[1]

I

We are the hollow men
We are the stuffed men
Leaning together
Headpiece filled with straw. Alas!
Our dried voices, when   5
We whisper together
Are quiet and meaningless
As wind in dry grass
Or rats' feet over broken glass
In our dry cellar   10

Shape without form, shade without colour,
Paralysed force, gesture without motion;

Those who have crossed
With direct eyes, to death's other Kingdom

---

[1] *Mistah Kurtz . . . Old Guy:* Kurtz is a character in Joseph Conrad's *Heart of Darkness.* An ivory trader in the Congo who is corrupted by power, Kurtz goes mad and dies. Guy Fawkes (1570–1606) helped lead an attempt to blow up Parliament and King James I of England. The failure of the plot is celebrated annually in England with figures of Fawkes ("Guys") burned in bonfires.

Remember us—if at all—not as lost   15
Violent souls, but only
As the hollow men
The stuffed men.

II

Eyes I dare not meet in dreams
In death's dream kingdom   20
These do not appear:
There, the eyes are
Sunlight on a broken column
There, is a tree swinging
And voices are   25
In the wind's singing
More distant and more solemn
Than a fading star.

Let me be no nearer
In death's dream kingdom   30
Let me also wear
Such deliberate disguises
Rat's coat, crowskin, crossed staves
In a field
Behaving as the wind behaves   35
No nearer—

Not that final meeting
In the twilight kingdom

III

This is the dead land
This is cactus land   40
Here the stone images
Are raised, here they receive
The supplication of a dead man's hand
Under the twinkle of a fading star.

Is it like this   45
In death's other kingdom
Waking alone
At the hour when we are
Trembling with tenderness
Lips that would kiss   50
Form prayers to broken stone.

IV

The eyes are not here
There are no eyes here
In this valley of dying stars
In this hollow valley   55
This broken jaw of our lost kingdoms

In this last of meeting places
We grope together
And avoid speech
Gathered on this beach of the tumid river   60

Sightless, unless
The eyes reappear
As the perpetual star
Multifoliate rose[2]
Of death's twilight kingdom   65
The hope only
Of empty men

V

Here we go round the prickly pear
Prickly pear prickly pear
Here we round the prickly pear   70
At five o'clock in the morning.

Between the idea
And the reality
Between the motion
And the act   75
Falls the Shadow
                    For Thine is the Kingdom[3]

Between the conception
And the creation
Between the emotion   80
And the response
Falls the Shadow
                    Life is very long

---

[2] *multifoliate rose:* An image from Dante Alighieri's (1265–1321) *Divine Comedy.* Dante
   envisioned God as the center of a rose, with the souls of saved persons clustered around
   God like petals.

[3] *For Thine is the Kingdom:* Line from the Lord's Prayer, taught by Jesus to his disciples.

Between the desire
And the spasm   85
Between the potency
And the existence
Between the essence
And the descent
Falls the Shadow   90
   For Thine is the Kingdom

For Thine is
Life is
For Thine is the

This is the way the world ends   95
This is the way the world ends
This is the way the world ends
Not with a bang but a whimper.

UNDERSTANDING THE POEM

1. Why is the adjective "hollow" appropriate for the people Eliot is describing?

2. What picture does the description "Shape without form, shade without colour, / Paralysed force, gesture without motion" (lines 11–12) bring to your mind? How does this description blend with other images in the poem? What does it contribute to the poem?

3. What is "death's other Kingdom" (line 14)? Is "death's dream kingdom" (line 20) the same place? What kind of place is it?

4. What are the "stone images" that "receive / The supplication of a dead man's hand" (lines 41–43)?

5. What lost kingdoms are referred to in the line "This broken jaw of our lost kingdoms" (line 56)?

6. What does the statement *"Life is very long"* (line 83) add to the poem's meaning?

7. Explain the connection between the lines "Remember us . . . not as lost / Violent souls, but only / As the hollow men / The stuffed men" (lines 15–18) with the final lines of the poem, *"This is the way the world ends / Not with a bang but a whimper"* (lines 97–98).

8. What **themes** do you find in the poem?

ANALYZING LITERARY TECHNIQUE

1. What object does the **metaphor** "stuffed men" (line 2) refer to? Why is this an appropriate metaphor?

2. Analyze Eliot's use of images of eyes and vision in this poem. What do the images contribute to the poem as a whole?

3. What is the effect of the **allusion** to the children's song "Here We Go 'Round the Mulberry Bush" (lines 68–71 and 95–98)?

4. The epigraph *"Mistah Kurtz—he dead"* alludes to Joseph Conrad's *Heart of Darkness*. In the novel Mr. Kurtz, a European who goes to central Africa to buy ivory, loses his civilized values. As he dies, he think about his deeds among the Africans, recognizes the darkness that inhabits his own soul, and exclaims "The horror! The horror!" How does this epigraph relate to the themes of this poem?

5. The epigraph *"A penny for the Old Guy"* alludes to Guy Fawkes Day, which is celebrated annually in England by burning figures of Guy in effigy and by having children collect pennies. How does this epigraph relate to the themes of this poem?

6. Find examples of various types of **figurative language** in the poem and explain what each example contributes to the poem.

7. What do sound devices—such as **repetition, parallelism,** and **rhythm**—contribute to the poem?

WRITING ABOUT LITERATURE

1. Write an essay in which you analyze Eliot's use of figurative language. Use quotations from the poem to examine examples of figurative language. In your conclusion, evaluate what the various types of figurative language contribute to the poem as a whole.

2. Eliot was familiar with the work of Carl Jung. According to Jung, the Shadow is an inherent part of each person's personality. It "personifies everything that the subject refuses to acknowledge about himself and yet is always thrusting itself upon him directly or indirectly." Jung believed that it was essential for individuals to acknowledge the dark aspects of their personalities—their Shadows—in order to keep these aspects under control. Write a brief essay in which you consider how Eliot's "The Hollow Men" relates to Jung's concept of the Shadow. How do the "hollow men" view themselves? What do they hide? What does the end of the poem suggest about the "hollow men's" chances of becoming whole? Use quotations to support your ideas.

3. The conception of twentieth-century men and women as "hollow" is simple yet evocative. One appropriate word can convey as much meaning as an essay. Decide whether or not today's men and women are "hollow." Defend your point of view with logical arguments; use as many specific examples as you can to support your ideas.

Mother to Son

LANGSTON HUGHES

L ANGSTON HUGHES (1902–1967), an African
American poet, is known for his insight into the character and lives of poor urban blacks. He is also known as
the creator of Simple, a fictional Harlem workingman who functions
as the spokesman for the urban African Americans of his time and
place. In addition to the four Simple books, Hughes wrote fifteen volumes of poetry; seven novels; thirty-six short stories; and many plays,
radio and television scripts, children's books, and works of nonfiction.
As a dramatist, he influenced black theater. As a translator and
anthologist, he brought African, Afro-Caribbean, and African
American literature into the American literary mainstream. For over
forty years, during the Harlem Renaissance and beyond, he was an
influential leader of the black cultural community, where he helped
many young writers.

James Langston Hughes was born in Joplin, Missouri. His parents
divorced when he was quite young, and his father moved to Mexico
to escape racism in the United States. Hughes lived alternately with
his grandmother and his mother in various Midwestern cities. While
in high school, he wrote poetry, preferring the style of the Americans
who wrote in free verse. After graduation, he lived in Mexico with his
father for a year, attended Columbia University for a year, and spent
time traveling and working in Africa and Paris, France. In 1925
Hughes joined his mother in Washington, D.C., where his job as a
busboy in a hotel dining room became the turning point in his life.

Hughes was working in the dining room when one of his favorite
poets, Vachel Lindsay, came in to eat. Hughes was too shy to speak
with the poet, but he put some of his poems beside Lindsay's plate.
That night Lindsay read Hughes's poetry to a distinguished audience,
bringing the young poet local fame. Hughes then took Lindsay's
advice and submitted his poetry to magazines for publication. When
"The Weary Blues" won first prize in a contest sponsored by
Opportunity, a magazine that encouraged creative works by African

Americans, Hughes's career began. When his first volume of poetry was published (*The Weary Blues*, 1926), Hughes was offered a scholarship to Lincoln University in Pennsylvania, from which he graduated in 1929.

Hughes's poetry can be divided into three categories: poems that are related to music; poems that protest racial injustice and oppression; and poems that affirm courage, racial dignity, and faith in the democratic process. "Mother to Son" is one of Hughes's most famous affirmative poems.

Well, son, I'll tell you:
Life for me ain't been no crystal stair.
It's had tacks in it,
And splinters,
And boards torn up,   5
And places with no carpet on the floor—
Bare,
But all the time
I'se been a-climbin' on,
And reachin' landin's,   10
And turnin' corners,
And sometimes goin' in the dark
Where there ain't been no light.
So boy, don't you turn back.
Don't you set down on the steps   15
'Cause you finds it's kinder hard.
Don't you fall now—
For I'se still goin', honey,
I'se still climbin',
And life for me ain't been no crystal stair.   20

UNDERSTANDING THE STORY

1. Describe the mother's background. Why are the circumstances of her life important?

2. Why is the mother describing her life to her son?

3. From the mother's advice to her son, describe the character of the mother.

4. What **themes** do you find in this poem?

ANALYZING LITERARY TECHNIQUES

1. Why is the stairway a good symbol of life?

2. Analyze the extended **metaphor** of the stairway. Explain what each of the following could represent in life: (a) tacks and splinters (lines 3–4); (b) "boards torn up" (line 5); (c) "no carpet" (line 6); (d) landings (line 10); (e) turning corners (line 11); and (f) being in the dark (line 12).

3. What does Hughes's use of **apostrophe** achieve in this poem?

4. What techniques does Hughes use to **characterize** the mother?

5. What does Hughes achieve by using **free verse?**

WRITING ABOUT LITERATURE

1. Write an essay in which you analyze Hughes's use of a staircase as an extended metaphor in the poem. How does the choice of this metaphor relate to the poem's themes?

2. Write a response from the son to his mother. Include his view of why he is receiving this advice, his response to his mother's life, and the effect of his mother's attitudes and behavior on his own life. You may choose to write the response as a poem or a letter.

A Worn Path

EUDORA WELTY

E UDORA WELTY (1909–2001) is known as an important Southern writer of short stories and novels. The characters in her fiction reflect her compassion and respect for people. Through her characters, Welty explores what is universal in humanity, and she exposes the mystery that is an inherent part of each individual's life. Her first book, *A Curtain of Green and Other Stories* (1941), includes such well-known stories as "Why I Live at the P.O.," "A Visit of Charity," "Powerhouse," and "A Worn Path." In 1980 *The Collected Stories of Eudora Welty* won the National Medal for Literature. *The Ponder Heart* (1954) was adapted for the stage in 1957, and *The Robber Bridegroom* (1942) was made into a musical in 1975.

Welty was born and reared in Jackson, Mississippi, where her father was president of an insurance company. After a brief part-time career in journalism, she became a publicity agent for the Works Progress Administration in Mississippi during the Depression years. As she traveled about interviewing and photographing people from all walks of life, she learned that "what I needed to find out about people and their lives had to be sought . . . through writing stories." Welty's first story was published in *Manuscript* magazine in 1936. Later her stories appeared in such magazines as the *Southern Review* and the *Atlantic Monthly*.

Welty found the sources for her stories in "the irresistible, the magnetic, the alarming (pleasant or disturbing), the overwhelming person, place, or thing." With a photographer's eye and an acute ear, she uses dialogue and action to imbue her characters with their distinctive values and goals. Many of her characters are ordinary people whose lives are grounded in the Natchez area of Mississippi. Many of her stories, including "A Worn Path," reflect her love of folktales, legends, and the literature of oral tradition; Welty's stories are enhanced by being read aloud. With each story, she creates "a little world in space, just as we can isolate one star in the sky by a concentrated vision."

The idea for "A Worn Path" originated when Welty observed a solitary old woman slowly crossing a distant field. "I couldn't see her up close," Welty explained, "but you could tell it was an old woman going somewhere, and I thought, she is bent on an errand. And I know it isn't for herself. It was just the look of her figure." That night Welty wrote about Phoenix Jackson, another "woman who would be in such desperate need and live so remotely away from help and who would have so far to go . . . with the same urgency about it."

It was December—a bright frozen day in the early morning. Far out in the country there was an old Negro woman with her head tied in a red rag, coming along a path through the pinewoods. Her name was Phoenix Jackson. She was very old and small and she walked slowly in the dark pine shadows, moving a little from side to side in her steps, with the balanced heaviness and lightness of a pendulum in a grandfather clock. She carried a thin, small cane made from an umbrella, and with this she kept tapping the frozen earth in front of her. This made a grave and persistent noise in the still air, that seemed meditative like the chirping of a solitary little bird.

She wore a dark striped dress reaching down to her shoe tops, and an equally long apron of bleached sugar sacks, with a full pocket: all neat and tidy, but every time she took a step she might have fallen over her shoelaces, which dragged from her unlaced shoes. She looked straight ahead. Her eyes were blue with age. Her skin had a pattern all its own of numberless branching wrinkles as though a whole little tree stood in the middle of her forehead, but a golden color ran underneath, and the two knobs of her cheeks were illumined by a yellow burning under the dark. Under the red rag her hair came down on her neck in the frailest of ringlets, still black, and with an odor like copper.

Now and then there was a quivering in the thicket. Old Phoenix said, "Out of my way, all you foxes, owls, beetles, jack rabbits, coon, and wild animals! . . . Keep out from under these feet, little bob-whites. . . . Keep the big wild hog out of my path. Don't let none of those come running my direction. I got a long way." Under her small black-freckled hand her cane, limber as a buggy whip, would switch at the brush as if to rouse up any hiding things.

On she went. The woods were deep and still. The sun made the pine needles almost too bright to look at, up where the wind rocked. The cones dropped as light as feathers. Down in the hollow was the mourning dove—it was not too late for him.

The path ran up a hill. "Seem like there is chains about my feet, time I get this far," she said, in the voice of argument old people keep to use with themselves. "Something always take a hold of me on this hill—pleads I should stay."

After she got to the top she turned and gave a full, severe look behind her where she had come. "Up through pines," she said at length. "Now down through oaks."

Her eyes opened their widest, and she started down gently. But before she got to the bottom of the hill a bush caught her dress.

Her fingers were busy and intent, but her skirts were full and long, so that before she could pull them free in one place they were caught in another. It was not possible to allow the dress to tear. "I in the thorny bush," she said. "Thorns, you doing your appointed work. Never want to let folks past, no sir. Old eyes thought you was a pretty little *green* bush."

Finally, trembling all over, she stood free, and after a moment dared to stoop for her cane.

"Sun so high!" she cried, leaning back and looking, while the thick tears went over her eyes. "The time getting all gone here."

At the foot of this hill was a place where a log was laid across the creek.

"Now comes the trial," said Phoenix.

Putting her right foot out, she mounted the log and shut her eyes. Lifting her skirt, leveling her cane fiercely before her, like a festival figure in some parade, she began to march across. Then she opened her eyes and she was safe on the other side.

"I wasn't as old as I thought," she said.

But she sat down to rest. She spread her skirts on the bank around her and folded her hands over her knees. Up above her was a tree in a pearly cloud of mistletoe. She did not dare to close her eyes, and when a little boy brought her a plate with a slice of marble-cake on it she spoke to him. "That would be acceptable," she said. But when she went to take it there was just her own hand in the air.

So she left that tree, and had to go through a barbed-wire fence. There she had to creep and crawl, spreading her knees and stretching her fingers like a baby trying to climb the steps. But she talked loudly to herself: she could not let her dress be torn now, so late in the day, and she could not pay for having arm or leg sawed off if she got caught where she was.

At last she was safe through the fence and risen up out in the clearing. Big dead trees, like black men with one arm, were standing in the purple stalks of the withered cotton field. There sat a buzzard.

"Who are you watching?"

In the furrow she made her way along.

"Glad this not the season for bulls," she said, looking sideways, "and the good Lord made his snakes to curl up and sleep in the winter. A pleasure I don't see no two-headed snake coming around that tree, where it come once. It took a while to get by him, back in the summer."

She passed through the old cotton and went into a field of dead corn. It whispered and shook and was taller than her head. "Through the maze now," she said, for there was no path.

Then there was something tall, black, and skinny there, moving before her.

At first she took it for a man. It could have been a man dancing in the field. But she stood still and listened, and it did not make a sound. It was as silent as a ghost.

"Ghost," she said sharply, "who be you the ghost of? For I have heard of nary death close by."

But there was no answer—only the ragged dancing in the wind.

She shut her eyes, reached out her hand, and touched a sleeve. She found a coat and inside that an emptiness, cold as ice.

"You scarecrow," she said. Her face lighted. "I ought to be shut up for good," she said with laughter. "My senses is gone. I too old. I the oldest people I ever know. Dance, old scarecrow," she said, "while I dancing with you."

She kicked her foot over the furrow, and with mouth drawn down, shook her head once or twice in a little strutting way. Some husks blew down and whirled in streamers about her skirts.

Then she went on, parting her way from side to side with the cane, through the whispering field. At last she came to the end, to a wagon track where the silver grass blew between the red ruts. The quail were walking around like pullets, seeming all dainty and unseen.

"Walk pretty," she said. "This is the easy place. This the easy going."

She followed the track, swaying through the quiet bare fields, through the little strings of trees silver in their dead leaves, past cabins silver from weather, with the doors and windows boarded shut, all like old women under a spell sitting there. "I walking in their sleep," she said, nodding her head vigorously.

In a ravine she went where a spring was silently flowing through a hollow log. Old Phoenix bent and drank. "Sweet-gum makes the water sweet," she said, and drank more. "Nobody know who made this well, for it was here when I was born."

The track crossed a swampy part where the moss hung as white as lace from every limb. "Sleep on, alligators, and blow your bubbles." Then the track went into the road.

Deep, deep the road went down between the high green-colored banks. Overhead the live-oaks met, and it was as dark as a cave.

A black dog with a lolling tongue came up out of the weeds by the ditch. She was meditating, and not ready, and when he came at her she only hit him a little with her cane. Over she went in the ditch, like a little puff of milkweed.

Down there, her sense drifted away. A dream visited her, and she reached her hand up, but nothing reached down and gave her a pull. So she lay there and presently went to talking. "Old woman," she said to herself, "that black dog come up out of the weeds to stall you off, and now there he sitting on his fine tail, smiling at you."

A white man finally came along and found her—a hunter, a young man, with his dog on a chain.

"Well, Granny!" he laughed. "What are you doing there?"

"Lying on my back like a June-bug waiting to be turned over, mister," she said, reaching up her hand.

He lifted her up, gave her a swing in the air, and set her down. "Anything broken, Granny?"

"No sir, them old dead weeds is springy enough," said Phoenix, when she got her breath. "I thank you for your trouble."

"Where do you live, Granny?" he asked, while the two dogs were growling at each other.

"Away back yonder, sir, behind the ridge. You can't even see it from here."

"On your way home?"

"No sir, I going to town."

"Why, that's too far! That's as far as I walk when I come out myself, and I get something for my trouble." He patted the stuffed bag he carried, and there hung down a little closed claw. It was one of the bob-whites, with its beak hooked bitterly to show it was dead. "Now you go on home, Granny!"

"I bound to go to town, mister," said Phoenix. "The time come around."

He gave another laugh, filling the whole landscape. "I know you old colored people! Wouldn't miss going to town to see Santa Claus!"

But something held old Phoenix very still. The deep lines in her face went into a fierce and different radiation. Without warning, she had seen with her own eyes a flashing nickel fall out of the man's pocket onto the ground.

"How old are you, Granny?" he was saying.

"There is no telling, mister," she said, "no telling."

Then she gave a little cry and clapped her hands and said, "Git on away from here, dog! Look! Look at that dog!" She laughed as if in admiration. "He ain't scared of nobody. He a big black dog." She whispered, "Sic him!"

"Watch me get rid of that cur," said the man. "Sic him, Pete! Sic him!"

Phoenix heard the dogs fighting and heard the man running and throwing sticks. She even heard a gunshot. But she was slowly bending forward by that time, further and further forward, the lids stretched down over her eyes, as if she were doing this in her sleep. Her chin was lowered almost to her knees. The yellow palm of her hand came out from the fold of her apron. Her fingers slid down and along the ground under the piece of money with the grace and care they would have in lifting an egg from under a setting hen. Then she slowly straightened up, she stood erect, and the nickel was in her apron pocket. A bird flew by. Her lips moved. "God watching me the whole time. I come to stealing."

The man came back, and his own dog panted about them. "Well, I scared him off that time," he said, and then he laughed and lifted his gun and pointed it at Phoenix.

She stood straight and faced him.

"Doesn't the gun scare you?" he said, still pointing it.

"No, sir, I seen plenty go off closer by, in my day, and for less than what I done," she said, holding utterly still.

He smiled, and shouldered the gun. "Well, Granny," he said, "you must be a hundred years old, and scared of nothing. I'd give you a dime if I had any money with me. But you take my advice and stay home, and nothing will happen to you."

"I bound to go on my way, mister," said Phoenix. She inclined her head in the red rag. Then they went in different directions, but she could hear the gun shooting again and again over the hill.

She walked on. The shadows hung from the oak trees to the road like curtains. Then she smelled wood-smoke, and smelled the river, and she saw a steeple and the cabins on their steep steps. Dozens of little black children whirled around her. There ahead was Natchez[1] shining. Bells were ringing. She walked on.

In the paved city it was Christmas time. There were red and green electric lights strung and crisscrossed everywhere, and all turned on in the daytime. Old

---

[1] *Natchez*: City in southwestern Mississippi.

Phoenix would have been lost if she had not distrusted her eyesight and depended on her feet to know where to take her.

She paused quietly on the sidewalk where people were passing by. A lady came along in the crowd, carrying an armful of red-, green-, and silver-wrapped presents; she gave off perfume like the red roses in hot summer, and Phoenix stopped her.

"Please, missy, will you lace up my shoe?" She held up her foot.

"What do you want, Grandma?"

"See my shoe," said Phoenix. "Do all right for out in the country, but wouldn't look right to go in a big building."

"Stand still then, Grandma," said the lady. She put her packages down on the sidewalk beside her and laced and tied both shoes tightly.

"Can't lace 'em with a cane," said Phoenix. "Thank you, missy. I doesn't mind asking a nice lady to tie up my shoe, when I gets out on the street."

Moving slowly and from side to side, she went into the big building, and into a tower of steps, where she walked up and around and around until her feet knew to stop.

She entered a door, and there she saw nailed up on the wall the document that had been stamped with the gold seal and framed in the gold frame, which matched the dream that was hung up in her head.

"Here I be," she said. There was a fixed and ceremonial stiffness over her body.

"A charity case, I suppose," said the attendant who sat at the desk before her.

But Phoenix only looked above her head. There was sweat on her face, the wrinkles in her skin shone like a bright net.

"Speak up, Grandma," the woman said. "What's your name? We must have your history, you know. Have you been here before? What seems to be the trouble with you?"

Old Phoenix only gave a twitch to her face as if a fly were bothering her.

"Are you deaf?" cried the attendant.

But then the nurse came in.

"Oh, that's just Old Aunt Phoenix," she said. "She doesn't come for herself—she has a little grandson. She lives away back off the Old Natchez Trace." She bent down. "Well, Aunt Phoenix, why don't you just take a seat? We won't keep you standing after your long trip." She pointed.

The old woman sat down, bolt upright in the chair.

"Now, how is the boy?" asked the nurse.

Old Phoenix did not speak.

"I said, how is the boy?"

But Phoenix only waited and stared straight ahead, her face very solemn and withdrawn into rigidity.

"Is his throat any better?" asked the nurse. "Aunt Phoenix, don't you hear me? Is your grandson's throat any better since the last time you came for the medicine?"

With her hands to her knees, the old woman waited, silent, erect and motionless, just as if she were in armor.

"You mustn't take up our time this way, Aunt Phoenix," the nurse said. "Tell us quickly about your grandson, and get it over. He isn't dead, is he?"

At last there came a flicker and then a flame of comprehension across her face, and she spoke.

"My grandson. It was my memory had left me. There I sat and forgot why I made my long trip."

"Forgot?" The nurse frowned. "After you came so far?"

Then Phoenix was like an old woman begging a dignified forgiveness for waking up frightened in the night. "I never did go to school, I was too old at the Surrender,"[2] she said in a soft voice. "I'm an old woman without an education. It was my memory fail me. My little grandson, he is just the same, and I forgot it in the coming."

"Throat never heals, does it?" said the nurse, speaking in a loud, sure voice to old Phoenix. By now she had a card with something written on it, a little list. "Yes. Swallowed lye. When was it?—January—two-three years ago—"

Phoenix spoke unasked now. "No, missy, he not dead, he just the same. Every little while his throat begin to close up again, and he not able to swallow. He not get his breath. He not able to help himself. So that time come around, and I go on another trip for soothing medicine."

"All right. The doctor said as long as you came to get it, you could have it," said the nurse. "But it's an obstinate case."

"My little grandson, he sit up there in the house all wrapped up, waiting by himself," Phoenix went on. "We is the only two left in the world. He suffer and it don't seem to put him back at all. He got a sweet look. He going to last. He wear a little patch quilt and peep out holding his mouth open like a little bird. I remembers so plain now. I not going to forget him again, no, the whole enduring time. I could tell him from all the others in creation."

"All right." The nurse was trying to hush her now. She brought her a bottle of medicine. "Charity," she said, making a check mark in a book.

Old Phoenix held the bottle close to her eyes, and then carefully put it into her pocket.

"I thank you," she said.

"It's Christmas time, Grandma," said the attendant. "Could I give you a few pennies out of my purse?"

"Five pennies is a nickel," said Phoenix stiffly.

"Here's a nickel," said the attendant.

Phoenix rose carefully and held out her hand. She received the nickel and then fished the other nickel out of her pocket and laid it beside the new one. She stared at her palm closely, with her head on one side.

Then she gave a tap with her cane on the floor.

"This is what come to me to do," she said. "I going to the store and buy my child a little windmill they sells, made out of paper. He going to find it hard to believe there such a thing in the world. I'll march myself back where he waiting, holding it straight up in this hand."

---

[2] *Surrender:* The surrender of the Confederate army to the Union army at the end of the American Civil War.

She lifted her free hand, gave a little nod, turned around, and walked out of the doctor's office. Then her slow step began on the stairs, going down.

UNDERSTANDING THE STORY

1. Why does Phoenix make the journey to Natchez?

2. Why does Welty create the kind of adventures that Phoenix experiences on her journey? What is the effect of Phoenix's running conversation with her environment? To what extent, if any, is Phoenix a heroic figure?

3. What is the significance of Phoenix's fantasy about the cake and her experience with the scarecrow?

4. What is important about Phoenix's meeting with the hunter? To what extent, if any, is her attitude evident in her treatment of him?

5. In what ways does Phoenix's behavior change once she arrives at the doctor's office? What do these changes reveal about Phoenix?

6. Compare the attitudes of the attendant, the nurse, and the doctor toward Phoenix. Why does Welty create such differences?

7. Do you think Phoenix's grandson is alive or dead? Why?

8. How does Welty feel about Phoenix? How does she reveal her attitude?

ANALYZING LITERARY TECHNIQUE

1. What effect does the technique of gradually revealing information have in this story? Consider the information that it is near Christmas, that Phoenix has a purpose for her journey, and that her grandson has been ill for several years.

2. Why is "Phoenix" an appropriate name for the story's protagonist?

3. In what ways is the paper windmill symbolic?

4. Why is the story called "A Worn Path"? What does the title symbolize?

5. Note Welty's use of sentence structure: the number of short sentences in which the verb follows the subject. What effect does this style have?

WRITING ABOUT LITERATURE

1. Write an essay in which you analyze Phoenix as a heroic figure. Choose three heroic qualities that Phoenix possesses. Find an adventure that reveals each quality and explain how each quality is heroic. Use quotations when describing Phoenix's adventures. Conclude your essay by evaluating what Phoenix's heroism contributes to the story.

2. Write two reports, each from a different point of view. First, write Phoenix's story as a medical report by the doctor. Second, write Phoenix's obituary as a Natchez newspaper columnist would approach her life. In both versions, discuss your analysis of Phoenix and her grandson.

Day of the Butterfly

ALICE MUNRO

ALICE MUNRO (1931–), a Canadian writer of short stories, is a gifted contemporary author. She is best known for her collections of short stories: *Dance of the Happy Shades* (1968); *The Beggar Maid*—also published as *Who Do You Think You Are?*—(1977); *The Moons of Jupiter* (1982); *Progress of Love* (1986); *Friend of My Youth* (1990); *Open Secrets* (1994); *Selected Stories* (1996); and *Hateship, Friendship, Courtship, Loveship, Marriage: Stories* (2001). She has also written one novel, *Lives of Girls and Women* (1971).

Munro was born in the small town of Wingham, in southern Ontario. She attended the nearby University of Western Ontario in London, Ontario, for two years. There she observed a variety of people by working as a waitress, a maid, a library clerk, and a tobacco picker. She then moved to British Columbia, where she spent the next twenty years living in Vancouver and Victoria, operating a bookstore and writing and publishing short stories. In 1976 she returned to southern Ontario, where she continues to live.

Munro began writing at the age of twelve. By the time she was fifteen, she expected to write a novel, but she explains, "I thought perhaps I wasn't ready so I would write a short story in the meantime." Since then she has published numerous short stories in literary magazines, ten collections of short stories, and one novel. Almost all of her stories are set in the towns and countryside of southern Ontario where her roots are.

The hallmarks of Munro's fiction are her ability to create distinctive sympathetic characters and to portray a dramatic situation in depth within the framework of a short story. She examines human relationships with an eye for critical details and an ear for revealing conversation. Her protagonists are usually intelligent and sensitive young girls or women.

Munro's characters are clearly aware of social and economic differences, but their stresses and strains involve a choice of moral values. Often the drama of the story focuses on the internal conflict between the way they wish to act and the way their peers expect them to act.

In discussing the issue of individuality versus community, Munro explains, "In small towns, you have no privacy at all. You have a role, a character, but one that other people have made up for you." In such an environment, conflicting needs, demands, and loyalties are common fare for sensitive souls. Munro's protagonists often find themselves surprised by a turn of events that gives them a moment of profound understanding. In achieving her goal of making the "mysterious touchable" and the "touchable mysterious," Munro reveals the underlying significance of ordinary events.

"Day of the Butterfly" is an early story that reveals Munro's focus and technique. An earlier version of the story was published in a literary magazine in 1956 as "Good-by Myra."

I do not remember when Myra Sayla came to town, though she must have been in our class at school for two or three years. I start remembering her in the last year, when her little brother Jimmy Sayla was in Grade One. Jimmy Sayla was not used to going to the bathroom by himself and he would have to come to the Grade Six door and ask for Myra and she would take him downstairs. Quite often he would not get to Myra in time and there would be a big dark stain on his little button-on cotton pants. Then Myra had to come and ask the teacher: "Please may I take my brother home, he has wet himself?"

That was what she said the first time and everybody in the front seats heard her—though Myra's voice was the lightest singsong—and there was a muted giggling which alerted the rest of the class. Our teacher, a cold gentle girl who wore glasses with thin gold rims and in the stiff solicitude of certain poses resembled a giraffe, wrote something on a piece of paper and showed it to Myra. And Myra recited uncertainly: "My brother has had an accident, please, teacher."

Everybody knew of Jimmy Sayla's shame and at recess (if he was not being kept in, as he often was, for doing something he shouldn't in school) he did not dare go out on the school grounds, where the other little boys, and some bigger ones, were waiting to chase him and corner him against the back fence and thrash him with tree branches. He had to stay with Myra. But at our school there were the two sides, the Boys' Side and the Girls' Side, and it was believed that if you so much as stepped on the side that was not your own you might easily get the strap. Jimmy could not go out on the Girls' Side and Myra could not go out on the Boys' Side, and no one was allowed to stay in the school unless it was raining or snowing. So Myra and Jimmy spent every recess standing in the little back porch between the two sides. Perhaps they watched the baseball games, the tag and skipping and building of leaf houses in the fall and snow forts in the winter; perhaps they did not watch at all. Whenever you happened to look at them their heads were slightly bent, their narrow bodies hunched in, quite still. They had long smooth oval faces, melancholy and discreet—dark, oily, shining hair. The little boy's was long, clipped at home, and Myra's was worn in heavy braids coiled on top of her head so that she looked, from a distance, as if she was wearing a turban too big for her. Over their dark eyes the lids were never fully raised; they had a weary look. But it was more than that. They were like children in a medieval painting, they were like small figures carved of wood, for worship or magic, with faces smooth and aged, and meekly, cryptically uncommunicative.

Most of the teachers at our school had been teaching for a long time and at recess they would disappear into the teachers' room and not bother us. But our own teacher, the young woman of the fragile gold-rimmed glasses, was apt to watch us from a window and sometimes come out, looking brisk and uncomfortable, to stop a fight among the little girls or start a running game among the big ones, who had been huddled together playing Truth or Secrets. One day she came out and called, "Girls in Grade Six, I want to talk to you!" She smiled persuasively, earnestly, and with dreadful unease, showing fine gold rims around her teeth. She said, "There is a girl in Grade Six called Myra Sayla. She *is* in your grade, isn't she?"

We mumbled. But there was a coo from Gladys Healey. "Yes, Miss Darling!"

"Well, why is she never playing with the rest of you? Every day I see her standing in the back porch, never playing. Do you think she looks happy standing back there? Do you think you would be very happy, if *you* were left back there?"

Nobody answered; we faced Miss Darling, all respectful, self-possessed, and bored with the unreality of her question. Then Gladys said, "Myra can't come out with us, Miss Darling. Myra has to look after her little brother!"

"Oh," said Miss Darling dubiously. "Well you ought to try to be nicer to her anyway. Don't you think so? Don't you? You will try to be nicer, won't you? I *know* you will." Poor Miss Darling! Her campaigns were soon confused, her persuasions turned to bleating and uncertain pleas.

When she had gone Gladys Healey said softly, "You will try to be nicer, won't you? I *know* you will!" and then drawing her lip back over her big teeth she yelled exuberantly, "I don't care if it rains or freezes."[1] She went through the whole verse and ended it with a spectacular twirl of her Royal Stuart tartan[2] skirt. Mr. Healey ran a Dry Goods and Ladies' Wear, and his daughter's leadership in our class was partly due to her flashing plaid skirts and organdie blouses and velvet jackets with brass buttons, but also to her early-maturing bust and the fine brutal force of her personality. Now we all began to imitate Miss Darling.

We had not paid much attention to Myra before this. But now a game was developed; it started with saying, "Let's be nice to Myra!" Then we would walk up to her in formal groups of three or four and at a signal, say together, "Hel-lo Myra, Hello My-ra!" and follow up with something like, "What do you wash your hair in, Myra, it's so nice and shiny, My-ra." "Oh she washes it in cod-liver oil, don't you, Myra, she washes it in cod-liver oil, can't you smell it?"

And to tell the truth there was a smell about Myra, but it was a rotten-sweetish smell as of bad fruit. That was what the Saylas did, kept a little fruit store. Her father sat all day on a stool by the window, with his shirt open over his swelling stomach and tufts of black hair showing around his belly button; he chewed garlic.

---

[1] "*I don't care . . . freezes*": Line from a popular song.

[2] *Royal Stuart tartan*: A red plaid.

But if you went into the store it was Mrs. Sayla who came to wait on you, appearing silently between the limp print curtains hung across the back of the store. Her hair was crimped in black waves and she smiled with her full lips held together, stretched as far as they would go; she told you the price in a little rapping voice, daring you to challenge her and, when you did not, handed you the bag of fruit with open mockery in her eyes.

One morning in the winter I was walking up the school hill very early; a neighbour had given me a ride into town. I lived about half a mile out of town, on a farm, and I should not have been going to the town school at all, but to a country school nearby where there were half a dozen pupils and a teacher a little demented since her change of life.[3] But my mother, who was an ambitious woman, had prevailed on the town trustees to accept me and my father to pay the extra tuition, and I went to school in town. I was the only one in the class who carried a lunch pail and ate peanut-butter sandwiches in the high, bare, mustard-coloured cloakroom, the only one who had to wear rubber boots in the spring, when the roads were heavy with mud. I felt a little danger, on account of this; but I could not tell exactly what it was.

I saw Myra and Jimmy ahead of me on the hill; they always went to school very early—sometimes so early that they had to stand outside waiting for the janitor to open the door. They were walking slowly, and now and then Myra half turned around. I had often loitered in that way, wanting to walk with some important girl who was behind me, and not quite daring to stop and wait. Now it occurred to me that Myra might be doing this with me. I did not know what to do. I could not afford to be seen walking with her, and I did not even want to—but, on the other hand, the flattery of those humble, hopeful turnings was not lost on me. A role was shaping for me that I could not resist playing. I felt a great pleasurable rush of self-conscious benevolence; before I thought what I was doing I called, "Myra! Hey, Myra, wait up, I got some Cracker Jack!"[4] and I quickened my pace as she stopped.

Myra waited, but she did not look at me; she waited in the withdrawn and rigid attitude with which she always met us. Perhaps she thought I was playing a trick on her, perhaps she expected me to run past and throw an empty Cracker Jack box in her face. And I opened the box and held it out to her. She took a little. Jimmy ducked behind her coat and would not take any when I offered the box to him.

"He's shy," I said reassuringly. "A lot of little kids are shy like that. He'll probably grow out of it."

"Yes," said Myra.

"I have a brother four," I said. "He's awfully shy." He wasn't. "Have some more Cracker Jack," I said. "I used to eat Cracker Jack all the time but I don't any more. I think it's bad for your complexion."

There was silence.

"Do you like Art?" said Myra faintly.

---

[3] *change of life:* Menopause.
[4] *Cracker Jack:* Caramel corn.

"No. I like Social Studies and Spelling and Health."

"I like Art and Arithmetic." Myra could add and multiply in her head faster than anyone else in the class.

"I wish I was as good as you. In Arithmetic," I said, and felt magnanimous.

"But I am no good at Spelling," said Myra. "I make the most mistakes, I'll fail maybe." She did not sound unhappy about this, but pleased to have such a thing to say. She kept her head turned away from me staring at the dirty snowbanks along Victoria Street, and as she talked she made a sound as if she was wetting her lips with her tongue.

"You won't fail," I said. "You are too good at Arithmetic. What are you going to be when you grow up?"

She looked bewildered. "I will help my mother," she said. "And work in the store."

"Well I am going to be an airplane hostess," I said. "But don't mention it to anybody. I haven't told many people."

"No, I won't," said Myra. "Do you read Steve Canyon[5] in the paper?"

"Yes." It was queer to think that Myra, too, read the comics, or that she did anything at all, apart from her role at the school. "Do you read Rip Kirby?"

"Do you read Orphan Annie?"

"Do you read Betsy and the Boys?"

"You haven't had hardly any Cracker Jack," I said. "Have some. Take a whole handful."

Myra looked into the box. "There's a prize in there," she said. She pulled it out. It was a brooch, a little tin butterfly, painted gold with bits of coloured glass stuck onto it to look like jewels. She held it in her brown hand, smiling slightly.

I said, "Do you like that?"

Myra said, "I like them blue stones. Blue stones are sapphires."

"I know. My birthstone is sapphire. What is your birthstone?"

"I don't know."

"When is your birthday?"

"July."

"Then yours is ruby."

"I like sapphire better," said Myra. "I like yours." She handed me the brooch.

"You keep it," I said. "Finders keepers."

Myra kept holding it out, as if she did not know what I meant. "Finders keepers," I said.

"It was your Cracker Jack," said Myra, scared and solemn. "You bought it."

"Well you found it."

"No—" said Myra.

"Go on!" I said. "Here, I'll *give* it to you." I took the brooch from her and pushed it back into her hand.

We were both surprised. We looked at each other; I flushed but Myra did not. I realized the pledge as our fingers touched; I was panicky, but *all right*. I thought,

---

[5] *Steve Canyon*: Newspaper comic strip. *Rip Kirby*, *Orphan Annie*, and *Betsy and the Boys* are also comic strips.

I can come early and walk with her other mornings. I can go and talk to her at recess. Why not? *Why not?*

Myra put the brooch in her pocket. She said, "I can wear it on my good dress. My good dress is blue."

I knew it would be. Myra wore out her good dresses at school. Even in mid-winter among the plaid wool skirts and serge tunics, she glimmered sadly in sky-blue taffeta, in dusty turquoise crepe, a grown woman's dress made over, weighted by a big bow at the V of the neck and folding empty over Myra's narrow chest.

And I was glad she had not put it on. If someone asked her where she got it, and she told them, what would I say?

It was the day after this, or the week after, that Myra did not come to school. Often she was kept at home to help. But this time she did not come back. For a week, then two weeks, her desk was empty. Then we had a moving day at school and Myra's books were taken out of her desk and put on a shelf in the closet. Miss Darling said, "We'll find a seat when she comes back." And she stopped calling Myra's name when she took attendance.

Jimmy Sayla did not come to school either, having no one to take him to the bathroom.

In the fourth week or the fifth, that Myra had been away, Gladys Healey came to school and said, "Do you know what—Myra Sayla is sick in the hospital."

It was true. Gladys Healey had an aunt who was a nurse. Gladys put up her hand in the middle of Spelling and told Miss Darling. "I thought you might like to know," she said. "Oh yes," said Miss Darling. "I do know."

"What has she got?" we said to Gladys.

And Gladys said, "Akemia,[6] or something. And she has blood transfusions." She said to Miss Darling, "My aunt is a nurse."

So Miss Darling had the whole class write Myra a letter, in which everybody said, "Dear Myra, We are all writing you a letter. We hope you will soon be better and be back to school, Yours truly. . . ." And Miss Darling said, "I've thought of something. Who would like to go up to the hospital and visit Myra on the twentieth of March, for a birthday party?"

I said, "Her birthday's in July."

"I know," said Miss Darling. "It's the twentieth of July. So this year she could have it on the twentieth of March, because she is sick."

"But her *birthday* is in July."

"Because she's sick," said Miss Darling, with a warning shrillness. "The cook at the hospital would make a cake and you could all give a little present, twenty-five cents or so. It would have to be between two and four, because that's visiting hours. And we couldn't all go, it'd be too many. So who wants to go and who wants to stay here and do supplementary reading?"

We all put up our hands. Miss Darling got out the spelling records and picked out the first fifteen, twelve girls and three boys. Then the three boys did not want

---

[6] *Akemia:* Mispronunciation of *leukemia,* a form of cancer that affects the blood.

to go so she picked out the next three girls. And I do not know when it was, but I think it was probably at this moment that the birthday party of Myra Sayla became fashionable.

Perhaps it was because Gladys Healey had an aunt who was a nurse, perhaps it was the excitement of sickness and hospitals, or simply the fact that Myra was so entirely, impressively set free of all the rules and conditions of our lives. We began to talk of her as if she were something we owned, and her party became a cause; with womanly heaviness we discussed it at recess, and decided that twenty-five cents was too low.

We all went up to the hospital on a sunny afternoon when the snow was melting, carrying our presents, and a nurse led us upstairs, single file, and down a hall past half-closed doors and dim conversations. She and Miss Darling kept saying, "Sh-sh," but we were going on tiptoe anyway; our hospital demeanor was perfect.

At this small country hospital there was no children's ward, and Myra was not really a child; they had put her in with two grey old women. A nurse was putting screens around them as we came in.

Myra was sitting up in bed, in a bulky stiff hospital gown. Her hair was down, the long braids falling over her shoulders and down the coverlet. But her face was the same, always the same.

She had been told something about the party, Miss Darling said, so the surprise would not upset her; but it seemed she had not believed, or had not understood what it was. She watched us as she used to watch in the school grounds when we played.

"Well, here we are!" said Miss Darling. "Here we are!"

And we said, "Happy birthday, Myra! Hello, Myra, happy birthday!" Myra said, "My birthday is in July." Her voice was lighter than ever, drifting, expressionless.

"Never mind when it is, really," said Miss Darling. "Pretend it's now! How old are you, Myra?"

"Eleven," Myra said. "In July."

Then we all took off our coats and emerged in our party dresses, and laid our presents, in their pale flowery wrappings on Myra's bed. Some of our mothers had made immense, complicated bows of fine satin ribbon, some of them had even taped on little bouquets of imitation roses and lilies of the valley. "Here Myra," we said, "here Myra, happy birthday." Myra did not look at us, but at the ribbons, pink and blue and speckled with silver, and the miniature bouquets; they pleased her, as the butterfly had done. An innocent look came into her face, a partial, private smile.

"Open them, Myra," said Miss Darling. "They're for you!"

Myra gathered the presents around her, fingering them, with this smile, and a cautious realization, an unexpected pride. She said, "Saturday I'm going to London[7] to St. Joseph's Hospital."

---

[7] *London:* City in Ontario.

"That's where my mother was at," somebody said. "We went and saw her. They've got all nuns there."

"My father's sister is a nun," said Myra calmly.

She began to unwrap the presents, with an air that not even Gladys could have bettered, folding the tissue paper and the ribbons, and drawing out books and puzzles and cutouts as if they were all prizes she had won. Miss Darling said that maybe she should say thank you, and the person's name with every gift she opened, to make sure she knew whom it was from, and so Myra said, "Thank you, Mary Louise, thank you, Carol," and when she came to mine she said, "Thank you, Helen." Everyone explained their presents to her and there was talking and excitement and a little gaiety, which Myra presided over, though she was not gay. A cake was brought in with *Happy Birthday Myra* written on it, pink on white, and eleven candles. Miss Darling lit the candles and we all sang Happy Birthday to You, and cried, "Make a wish, Myra, make a wish—" and Myra blew them out. Then we all had cake and strawberry ice cream.

At four o'clock a buzzer sounded and the nurse took out what was left of the cake, and the dirty dishes, and we put on our coats to go home. Everybody said, "Goodbye, Myra," and Myra sat in bed watching us go, her back straight, not supported by any pillow, her hands resting on the gifts. But at the door I heard her call; she called, "Helen!" Only a couple of others heard; Miss Darling did not hear, she had gone out ahead. I went back to the bed.

Myra said, "I got too many things. You take something."

"What?" I said. "It's for your birthday. You always get a lot at a birthday."

"Well you take something," Myra said. She picked up a leatherette case with a mirror in it, a comb and a nail file and a natural lipstick and a small handkerchief edged with gold thread. I had noticed it before. "You take that," she said.

"Don't you want it?"

"You take it." She put it into my hand. Our fingers touched again.

"When I come back from London," Myra said, "you can come and play at my place after school."

"Okay," I said. Outside the hospital window there was a clear carrying sound of somebody playing in the street, maybe chasing with the last snowballs of the year. This sound made Myra, her triumph and her bounty, and most of all her future in which she had found this place for me, turn shadowy, turn dark. All the presents on the bed, the folded paper and ribbons, those guilt-tinged offerings, had passed into this shadow, they were no longer innocent objects to be touched, exchanged, accepted without danger. I didn't want to take the case now but I could not think how to get out of it, what lie to tell. I'll give it away, I thought, I won't ever play with it. I would let my little brother pull it apart.

The nurse came back, carrying a glass of chocolate milk.

"What's the matter, didn't you hear the buzzer?"

So I was released, set free by the barriers which now closed about Myra, her unknown, exalted, ether-smelling hospital world, and by the treachery of my own heart. "Well thank you," I said. "Thank you for the thing. Goodbye."

Did Myra ever say goodbye? Not likely. She sat in her high bed, her delicate brown neck, rising out of a hospital gown too big for her, her brown carved face immune to treachery, her offering perhaps already forgotten, prepared to be set apart for legendary uses, as she was even in the back porch at school.

UNDERSTANDING THE STORY

1. What is the **conflict** in this story?

2. What is the relationship between Jimmy Sayla's problem and Myra's treatment by her peer group? How does Jimmy's social situation parallel Myra's?

3. Why are Myra and Jimmy "meekly, cryptically uncommunicative"?

4. Evaluate Miss Darling's role in Myra's life. To what extent, if any, should Miss Darling's behavior have been different?

5. What concern does Helen have about her life in school? How is this concern likely to affect her attitude toward Myra?

6. Why is Myra's birthday being celebrated in March when her birthday is in July? Why does Myra's party become fashionable?

7. Why does Myra insist that Helen accept one of her best gifts? Why does Helen consider Myra's gift a source of danger?

8. How do Myra's feelings change in the course of her party? What do the closing lines of the story reveal about Myra? To what extent would the party have been significant in Myra's life?

ANALYZING LITERARY TECHNIQUE

1. What does the **setting** contribute to the story?

2. What does the butterfly **symbolize?**

3. What does Munro accomplish with her choice of **narrative perspective?**

4. How can a reader tell whether Helen is a **reliable narrator?**

5. What is the central **paradox** of this story?

WRITING ABOUT LITERATURE

1. Write an essay in which you analyze what Munro reveals about human nature in this story. Consider the behavior of Helen, Myra, Gladys, and Miss Darling. Support each of your ideas with a quotation from the story.

2. Munro revised this story between the earliest published version and the version reprinted above by changing the last scene. How else might the story have ended? Consider several options and write a new ending for the story.

Hands

ANNE HÉBERT

*A*NNE HÉBERT (1916–2000), a versatile and well-known
Quebecois writer, wrote poems, novels, short stories, and
plays. She generated controversy regarding some of the subjects
she chose to write about, yet her writings helped show the Quebecois
that they were part of a modern society. Despite the controversies, she
won many awards, including the prestigious Prix de Libraires de
France in 1970 for her novel *Kamouraska* and the Prix Femina for her
novel *Les Fous de Bassan* (translated as *In the Shadow of the Wind*)
(1982). In addition to several novels, she has published several volumes of poetry, including her first collection, *Les Songes en équilibre*
(meaning "dreams in equilibrium") (1942) and *Le Tombeau des rois*
(translated as Tomb of the Kings) (1952). Her poetic collections *Day
Has No Equal but the Night* (1994) and *Anne Hébert: Selected Poems*
(1987) are available in English.

Anne Hébert was born in Catherine-de-Fossambault, Quebec, a
small town outside of Quebec City, in 1916. Her father, Maurice-Lang
Hébert, a government official and part-time literary critic, and her
cousin, poet Hector de Saint-Denis Garneau, encouraged her literary
development. At age twenty-six, she published her first collection of
poetry, which included many poems that had already been published
in other journals. Her second collection of poems and her story "The
Torrent" were rejected by Quebecois publishers as being too contro-
versial; Hébert and a friend later published them at their own
expense. Hébert moved to Paris, where she hoped to find a more
receptive audience for her works. Despite living in Paris for almost
forty years, Quebec remained the focus of her writings, and she often
returned there for visits. After learning that she was terminally ill,
Hébert returned to Quebec for good in the late 1990s. She died of
cancer in 2000.

Although Hébert's writings take many forms, several themes
emerge throughout her works. One theme is the revolt against and
the liberation from a restrictive society, such as the Quebecois society

of the mid-twentieth century. Another theme is the tension between past experiences and present realities, a theme that is explored in the poem "Hands."

She sits on the edge of seasons
And flashes her hands like rays.

She is strange
And looks at her hands colored by days.

The days on her hands   5
Occupy and arrest her.

She never closes them
And she always stretches them.

The signs of the world
Are etched on her fingers.   10

So many deep markings
Weighing her down with massive wrought rings.

Between her and us
There is no place for rest and love

Without this ruthless offering   15
Of hands adorned with pain
Opened to the sun.

UNDERSTANDING THE POEM

1. Who is the "she" of the poem?
2. Why is she sitting "on the edge of seasons"?
3. What are "etched on her fingers"?
4. Whom is the poet referring to as "us" in line 13?
5. What is the "ruthless offering / Of hands adorned with pain / Opened to the sun"?

ANALYZING LITERARY TECHNIQUE

1. Find two examples of **figurative language** in the poem and describe their effect.
2. What is the **tone** of the poem?
3. How does the poet reveal the woman's character?

WRITING ABOUT LITERATURE

1. Write an essay analyzing the poet's use of figurative language to reveal the woman's character. Use quotations from the poem to illustrate your points.
2. Write a poem or a short story in which a scar or another physical marking sums up a person's character or life—either yours or someone else's. Use figurative language to describe both the scar and the person's character.

Roselily

ALICE WALKER

ALICE WALKER (1944–) is an important African American poet, novelist, short-story writer, and essayist. With her novel *The Color Purple* (1982), Walker became the first black woman to win the Pulitzer Prize for fiction. *The Color Purple*, which also earned her an American Book Award, was adapted for film in 1985. Among Walker's other well-known works are a collection of short stories, *In Love and Trouble: Stories of Black Women* (1973), which includes "Everyday Use" and "Roselily"; the poetry collection *Revolutionary Petunias and Other Poems* (1973); two books of essays, *In Search of Our Mothers' Gardens* (1983) and *Living by the Word: Selected Writings, 1973–1987* (1988); and the novels *The Temple of My Familiar* (1989) and *Possessing the Secret of Joy* (1992).

Walker was born in Eatonton, Georgia, into a family of share-croppers. She attended Spelman College in Atlanta, where she participated in Civil Rights demonstrations, and Sarah Lawrence College, where she participated in a study-abroad program in Africa. After graduating from Sarah Lawrence College, Walker pursued a writing career, publishing her first short story in 1967. Her first volume of poems, *Once*, was published in 1968. Walker earned a Ph.D. from Russell Sage College in 1972 and has taught literature and creative writing at a number of schools, including Yale University and Wellesley College. She was also a contributing editor for *Ms.* magazine for a number of years.

Walker's writings often reflect her own life experiences, including her childhood in Georgia, her studies in Africa, and her participation in the Civil Rights movement. Many of her works point to the importance of family relationships for support and survival and to the importance of change in improving an individual's life. She is especially concerned about black women's struggle for self-fulfillment in an environment where both race and gender are major obstacles to be overcome. In "Roselily," Walker describes one woman's decision to make changes in her life.

Dearly Beloved,[1]

She dreams; dragging herself across the world. A small girl in her mother's white robe and veil, knee raised waist high through a bowl of quicksand soup. The man who stands beside her is against this standing on the front porch of her house, being married to the sound of cars whizzing by on highway 61.[2]

we are gathered here

Like cotton to be weighed. Her fingers at the last minute busily removing dry leaves and twigs. Aware it is a superficial sweep. She knows he blames Mississippi for the respectful way the men turn their heads up in the yard, the women stand waiting and knowledgeable, their children held from mischief by teachings from the wrong God.[3] He glares beyond them to the occupants of the cars, white faces glued to promises beyond a country wedding, noses thrust forward like dogs on a track. For him they usurp the wedding.

in the sight of God

Yes, open house. That is what country black folks like. She dreams she does not already have three children. A squeeze around the flowers in her hands chokes off three and four and five years of breath. Instantly she is ashamed and frightened in her superstition. She looks for the first time at the preacher, forces humility into her eyes, as if she believes he is, in fact, a man of God. She can imagine God, a small black boy, timidly pulling the preacher's coattail.

to join this man and this woman

She thinks of ropes, chains, handcuffs, his religion. His place of worship. Where she will be required to sit apart with covered head. In Chicago, a word she hears when thinking of smoke, from his description of what a cinder was, which they never had in Panther Burn. She sees hovering over the heads of the clean neighbors in her front yard black specks falling, clinging, from the sky. But in Chicago. Respect, a chance to build. Her children at last from underneath the detrimental wheel. A chance to be on top. What a relief, she thinks. What a vision, a view, from up so high.

---

[1] Dearly Beloved: The italicized words are from the Church of England wedding service, which has been adapted by many Christian denominations.

[2] *highway 61:* Highway that runs through eastern Mississippi.

[3] *wrong God:* Roselily's new husband is Muslim, not Christian.

in holy matrimony.

Her fourth child she gave away to the child's father who had some money. Certainly a good job. Had gone to Harvard. Was a good man but weak because good language meant so much to him he could not live with Roselily. Could not abide TV in the living room, five beds in three rooms, no Bach[4] except four to six on Sunday afternoons. No chess at all. She does not forget to worry about her son among his father's people. She wonders if the New England climate will agree with him. If he will ever come down to Mississippi, as his father did, to try to right the country's wrongs. She wonders if he will be stronger than his father. His father cried off and on throughout her pregnancy. Went to skin and bones. Suffered nightmares, retching and falling out of bed. Tried to kill himself. Later told his wife he found the right baby through friends. Vouched for, the sterling qualities that would make up his character.

It is not her nature to blame. Still, she is not entirely thankful. She supposes New England, the North, to be quite different from what she knows. It seems right somehow to her that people who move there to live return home completely changed. She thinks of the air, the smoke, the cinders. Imagines cinders big as hailstones; heavy, weighing on the people. Wonders how this pressure finds its way into the veins, roping the springs of laughter.

If there's anybody here that knows a reason why

But of course they know no reason why beyond what they daily have come to know. She thinks of the man who will be her husband, feels shut away from him because of the stiff severity of his plain black suit. His religion. A lifetime of black and white. Of veils. Covered head. It is as if her children are already gone from her. Not dead, but exalted on a pedestal, a stalk that has no roots. She wonders how to make new roots. It is beyond her. She wonders what one does with memories in a brand-new life. This had seemed easy, until she thought of it. "The reasons why . . . the people who" . . . she thinks, and does not wonder where the thought is from.

these two should not be joined

She thinks of her mother, who is dead. Dead, but still her mother. Joined. This is confusing. Of her father. A gray old man who sold wild mink, rabbit, fox skins to Sears, Roebuck. He stands in the yard, like a man waiting for a train. Her young sisters stand behind her in smooth green dresses, with flowers in their hands and hair. They giggle, she feels, at the absurdity of the wedding. They are ready for something new. She thinks the man beside her should marry one of them. She feels old. Yoked. An arm seems to reach out from behind her and snatch her backward. She thinks of cemeteries and the long sleep of grandparents mingling

---

[4] *Bach:* Johann Sebastian Bach (1685–1750), German composer.

in the dirt. She believes that she believes in ghosts. In the soil giving back what it takes.

together,

In the city. He sees her in a new way. This she knows, and is grateful. But is it new enough? She cannot always be a bride and virgin, wearing robes and veil. Even now her body itches to be free of satin and voile, organdy and lily of the valley. Memories crash against her. Memories of being bare to the sun. She wonders what it will be like. Not to have to go to a job. Not to work in a sewing plant. Not to worry about learning to sew straight seams in workingmen's overalls, jeans and dress pants. Her place will be in the home, he has said, repeatedly, promising her rest she has prayed for. But now she wonders. When she is rested, what will she do? They will make babies—she thinks practically about her fine brown body, his strong black one. They will be inevitable. Her hands will be full. Full of what? Babies. She is not comforted.

let him speak

She wishes she had asked him to explain more of what he meant. But she was impatient. Impatient to be done with sewing. With doing everything for three children, alone. Impatient to leave the girls she had known since childhood, their children growing up, their husbands hanging around her, already old, seedy. Nothing about them that she wanted, or needed. The fathers of her children driving by, waving, not waving; reminders of times she would just as soon forget. Impatient to see the South Side,[5] where they would live and build and be respectable and respected and free. Her husband would free her. A romantic hush. Proposal. Promises. A new life! Respectable, reclaimed, renewed. Free! In robe and veil.

or forever hold

She does not even know if she loves him. She loves his sobriety. His refusal to sing just because he knows the tune. She loves his pride. His blackness and his gray car. She loves his understanding of her *condition*. She thinks she loves the effort he will make to redo her into what he truly wants. His love of her makes her completely conscious of how unloved she was before. This is something; though it makes her unbearably sad. Melancholy. She blinks her eyes. Remembers she is finally being married, like other girls. Like other girls, women? Something strains upward behind her eyes. She thinks of the something as a rat trapped, cornered, scurrying to and fro in her head, peering through the windows of her eyes. She wants to live for once. But doesn't know quite what that means. Wonders if she

---

[5] *South Side:* Area of Chicago.

has ever done it. If she ever will. The preacher is odious to her. She wants to strike him out of the way, out of her light, with the back of her hand. It seems to her he has always been standing in front of her, barring her way.

his peace.

The rest she does not hear. She feels a kiss, passionate, rousing, within the general pandemonium. Cars driving up blowing their horns. Firecrackers go off. Dogs come from under the house and begin to yelp and bark. Her husband's hand is like the clasp of an iron gate. People congratulate. Her children press against her. They look with awe and distaste mixed with hope at their new father. He stands curiously apart, in spite of the people crowding about to grasp his free hand. He smiles at them all but his eyes are as if turned inward. He knows they cannot understand that he is not a Christian. He will not explain himself. He feels different, he looks it. The old women thought he was like one of their sons except that he had somehow got away from them. Still a son, not a son. Changed.

She thinks how it will be later in the night in the silvery gray car. How they will spin through the darkness of Mississippi and in the morning be in Chicago, Illinois. She thinks of Lincoln, the president. That is all she knows about the place. She feels ignorant, *wrong,* backward. She presses her worried fingers into his palm. He is standing in front of her. In the crush of well-wishing people, he does not look back.

UNDERSTANDING THE STORY

1. In what way is Roselily "like cotton to be weighed"?
2. What is Roselily's new husband's attitude toward marriage?
3. What was "weak" about the father of Roselily's fourth child?
4. Why are roots important to Roselily?
5. Why did Roselily decide to marry this man?
6. In what way might Roselily's Chicago experience mirror her past experience?
7. What is Roselily's view of the preacher? Why does she feel "he has always been standing in front of her, barring her way"?
8. Why does Roselily feel *"wrong"*? To what extent, if any, do you think that this marriage will be successful? Explain.
9. What kind of person is Roselily? Find examples to support your ideas.

ANALYZING LITERARY TECHNIQUE

1. Evaluate Walker's use of **narrative perspective.** How does she achieve **psychological realism,** the sense that the reader is inside a character's thoughts? What does psychological realism contribute to the story?

2. Examine the relationship between the words of the marriage ceremony and Roselily's thoughts. What does this interplay achieve?

3. Examine Walker's use of **contrast.** How does it enhance the story?

4. What kind of **symbols** does Walker use in the story? How does the symbolism enhance the story?

WRITING ABOUT LITERATURE

1. Write an essay in which you analyze Walker's use of symbols of constraint in this story. What does Roselily hope to be freed from? Choose three symbols and explain how each symbol enhances the meaning of the story. Use quotations as part of your analysis.

2. Write a character sketch of Roselily. Choose one adjective to describe her and find three quotations from the story that demonstrate this trait. Explain how each quotation supports your choice of adjective.

3. Write a letter from Roselily to a friend in which she describes details of her new life and her feelings about it.

Great Britain and Ireland

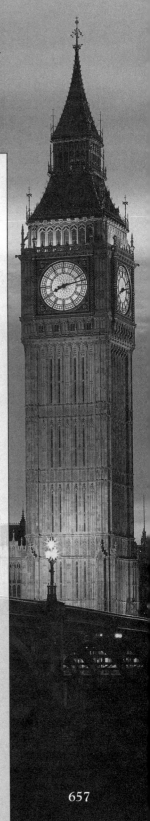

THE PLAY, POEMS, AND STORIES of Great Britain and Ireland demonstrate a deep understanding of human emotions, from love and delight to treachery and greed.

Several of the writers from Great Britain and Ireland explore various facets of love. Elizabeth Barrett Browning, in Sonnet 32, reveals her fear before making a lasting emotional commitment. In his poem "Dover Beach," Matthew Arnold expresses the power of human love in the face of an irrational universe. The poem "Goblin Market," by Christina Rossetti, is a heroic story of the triumph of love over adversity. In the Old English poem "A Woman's Message," an anonymous Anglo-Saxon woman laments the loss of her husband and rues the family treachery that brought her to her present circumstances. William Shakespeare's *Much Ado About Nothing* combines tragedy and comedy as the characters search for love and inner direction.

Three authors approach the workings of greed on the human psyche from different angles. In an excerpt from his *Canterbury Tales*, "The Pardoner's Tale," Geoffrey Chaucer rewrites a parable popular in his day about three greedy thieves and their encounter with Death. In the cautionary short story "An Outpost of Progress," Joseph Conrad decries colonialism while demonstrating the ill effects of greed on humans in an

unregulated environment. In contrast, Emily Brontë's "The Old Stoic" is a testament to the poet's desire for freedom and her rejection of love and wealth.

Two poets celebrate the beauty of the world around them. William Wordsworth, in his poem "My Heart Leaps Up," expresses his delight in the wonder and beauty of nature and his ability to appreciate it. William Butler Yeats, in "The Lake Isle of Innisfree," depicts the pastoral Irish countryside of his youth, a memory that brings him peace in his adult life.

Finally, James Joyce, in his classic coming-of-age story "Araby," describes a young boy's loss of childish innocence at a bazaar.

A Woman's Message

ANONYMOUS

"A Woman's Message," written between 600 and 940 in Anglo-Saxon England, projects a striking sense of immediacy and humanity that is still meaningful today despite the great difference in culture and the gap of centuries. The poem appears in the *Exeter Book,* one of the most important collections of Old English poetry.

The little that is known of the culture that produced this Anglo-Saxon work is surmised from the few manuscripts that survived the Viking invasion of Britain at the end of the eighth century and King Henry VIII's destruction of monasteries, including their large libraries, in 1536 and 1537. The poems in the *Exeter Book* were copied by monks and made into a book in about 940. In 1071, not long after the Norman Conquest, the book was given to the library of Exeter Cathedral by the cathedral's first bishop, Leofric. "A Woman's Message" complements the poems "The Husband's Message," "The Wanderer," and "The Seafarer" (also from the *Exeter Book*) and the epic *Beowulf* in depicting aspects of the culture of Germanic England.

"A Woman's Message," originally written in Anglo-Saxon or Old English, is often known by the title "A Wife's Lament." The poem reveals the vulnerable position of women in the northern European cultures of that time. Women depicted in other Anglo-Saxon, Scandinavian, and Germanic poetry of the period also experience the loss of love, the loneliness of separation, and the feeling of being the helpless victim of circumstance. What is most unusual is this poet's ability to describe a woman's poignant situation and to depict her suffering with sensitivity and power.

This song of journeys into sorrow
Is mine. I sing it. I alone
Can ravel out its misery, full-grown
When I was, and never worse than now.
The darkness of exile droops on my life.   5
His going began it, the tossing waves
Taking my lord. I was left in the dawn
Friendless where affection had been. I travelled
Seeking the sun of protection and safety,
Accepting exile as payment for hope.   10
         But the man's family was weaving plans
In the dark, intending to drive us apart
With a wedge the width of the world, condemning
Our love to a living death. I wept.
My new lord commanded me into a convent   15
Of wooden nuns, in a land where I knew
No lovers, no friends. So sadness was framed,
For I'd matched myself with a fitting man,
Born to misfortune, blessed with sorrow,
His mind closed to me, mulling on murder.   20
How gaily, how often, we'd fashioned oaths
Defying everything but death to endanger
Our love; now only the words are left
And our friendship's a fable that time has forgotten
And never tells. For my well-belovèd   25
I've been forced to suffer, far and near.
         I was ordered to live in a nun's-nest of leaves,
In an earthen cavern under an oak.
I writhe with longing in this ancient hole;
The valleys seem leaden, the hills reared aloft,   30
And the bitter towns all bramble patches
Of empty pleasure. The memory of parting
Rips at my heart. My friends are out there,
Savouring their lives, secure in their beds,
While at dawn, alone, I crawl miserably down   35
Under the oak growing out of my cave.
There I must squat the summer-long day,
There I can water the earth with weeping
For exile and sorrow, for sadness that can never
Find rest from grief nor from the famished   40
Desires that leap at unquenched life.
         May that man be always bent with misery,
With calloused thoughts; may he have to cling
To laughter and smiles when sorrow is clamouring

Wild for his blood; let him win his pleasures 45
Unfriended, alone; force him out
Into distant lands—as my lover dwells
In the shade of rocks the storm has frosted,
My downhearted lover, in a desolate hall
Lapped by floods. Christ, how he suffers, 50
Unable to smother swelling memories
Of a better place. There are few things more bitter
Than awaiting a love who is lost to hope.

UNDERSTANDING THE POEM

1. Analyze who is most responsible for the woman's fate: (a) the woman's husband, (b) her husband's family, (c) her new lord, or (d) the woman herself.

2. Analyze which aspect of the woman's life makes her most unhappy: (a) her loneliness, (b) her physical discomfort, (c) her danger, or (d) her memories.

3. Why does the poet choose not to name any of the characters?

4. What motivates the woman to tell her story?

5. To what extent, if any, does this poem transcend time and space?

ANALYZING LITERARY TECHNIQUE

1. What is the relationship between the **setting** and the **theme** of the poem?

2. How does the technique of **contrast** function in the poem?

3. How does the poet create the **tone** of the poem?

4. What does the poet's use of **metaphor** contribute to the theme of the poem?

5. Why is this poem called both a **lyric monologue** and an **elegy?**

6. How does the poet use **paradox** in the poem?

7. Find three **oxymorons** in the poem and explain their contribution.

8. What does the poem gain by telling this story from the woman's point of view? To what extent, if any, is she an unreliable **narrator?**

9. Find two examples of **irony** and explain their function in the poem.

10. How does the poet use **alliteration?** What does it contribute to the poem?

WRITING ABOUT LITERATURE

1. Analyze how the poet's use of metaphor enhances the theme of the poem. One way to begin is to write out the theme of the poem. Next, make a list of all the metaphors in the poem and put a star next to the metaphors

that relate to the theme. Now you will be able to write an introductory paragraph in which you briefly summarize the poem and its theme. In the next paragraph, which is the core of your essay, discuss the metaphors that relate to the theme. Quote each metaphor and explain its relation to the theme. In a concluding paragraph, evaluate what the use of metaphor contributes to the poem.

2. Write the man's story of his journey in either prose or poetry. Consider the following issues: What has caused the man to make this journey? Why didn't his wife accompany him? What role did his family play in his exile? Is his story a journey into sorrow or into good fortune? What might befall such a man who leaves his community? Does he become a slave or a warrior under another lord? Is he forced to wander from one community to another without a home? Is he, in fact, hoping that his wife will find him? For additional details about life in England at this time, read "The Husband's Message," "The Seafarer," and "The Wanderer."

The Pardoner's Tale

GEOFFREY CHAUCER

*G*EOFFREY CHAUCER (c. 1345-1400) is the father of English literature. He is best known for his masterpiece *The Canterbury Tales,* which includes "The Pardoner's Tale," a story about the three thieves. Chaucer did not create his stories; it was then the custom for authors to retell popular tales. A writer's merit depended on how good a storyteller he was, and for six hundred years Chaucer has been considered a genius of a storyteller. He gave the world a group of personalities who come to life under his pen and reveal Chaucer's own great psychological insight, his respect for human abilities, and his sense of humor. The artistic skill with which Chaucer rendered these tales has been an inspiration for generations of English poets who have followed him.

No record exists of Chaucer's life until 1357, when he was a page in the household of a countess. During his lifetime Chaucer held a variety of jobs, including soldier in the English army (a duty that took him to France); customs controller on hides, skins, wools, and wine in London; member of the British House of Commons; justice of the peace for the county of Kent; and deputy forester for the Crown. A commercial venture for the king introduced him to the intellectual and cultural life of Florence, Italy, the center of the Italian Renaissance and the capital of European art and literature at a time when English culture was still in the Middle Ages.

Chaucer appreciated all kinds of people and all styles of literature, which he read in French, Latin, and Italian. He took up creative writing as a hobby and continued to write for recreation. In 1386 he began *The Canterbury Tales,* a project that was so ambitious that he was still working on it when he died in 1400. He was buried in his family's vault in Westminster Abbey. Later other English poets chose to be buried near him, thus creating "The Poet's Corner."

A pilgrimage to Canterbury, England, to visit the shrine of Saint Thomas à Becket provides the structure for *The Canterbury Tales.* The long journey brings together people from many walks of life—rich and poor, learned and ignorant, old and young, female and male, religious and secular, aristocrat and commoner, honorable and disreputable. The pilgrims cope with the boredom of travel by telling stories, and the best storyteller will win a free dinner at the end of the trip. Chaucer intended that thirty-one pilgrims, including himself, would each tell four tales, two on the journey to Canterbury and two on the return trip. He left only twenty-three completed tales and one fragment.

People have enjoyed *The Canterbury Tales* for six hundred years because it is a collection of stories that combine excellent characterization with a fine plot. Although Chaucer did not create the idea that a group of people would gather together and tell stories, his decision to make each pilgrim interact with the others and to tell a tale that was consistent with his or her personality or life experiences was unique in its time.

These three young roisterers of whom I tell
Long before prime[1] had rung from any bell
Were seated in a tavern at their drinking,
And as they sat, they heard a bell go clinking
Before a corpse being carried to his grave.   5
One of these roisterers, when he heard it, gave
An order to his boy: "Go out and try
To learn whose corpse is being carried by.
Get me his name, and get it right. Take heed."
    "Sir," said the boy, "there isn't any need.   10
I learned before you came here, by two hours.
He was, it happens, an old friend of yours,
And all at once, there on his bench upright
As he was sitting drunk, he was killed last night.
A sly thief, Death men call him, who deprives   15
All the people in this country of their lives,
Came with his spear and smiting his heart in two
Went on his business with no more ado.
A thousand have been slaughtered by his hand
During this plague. And, sir, before you stand   20
Within his presence, it should be necessary,
It seems to me, to know your adversary.
Be evermore prepared to meet this foe.
My mother taught me thus; that's all I know."
    "Now by St. Mary," said the innkeeper,   25
"This child speaks truth. Man, woman, laborer,
Servant, and child the thief has slain this year

---

[1] *Prime:* An early morning hour, between seven and nine.

In a big village a mile or more from here.
I think it is his place of habitation.
It would be wise to make some preparation   30
Before he brought a man into disgrace."

"God's arms!" this roisterer said. "So that's the case!
Is it so dangerous with this thief to meet?
I'll look for him by every path and street,
I vow it, by God's holy bones! Hear me,   35
Fellows of mine, we are all one, we three.
Let each of us hold up his hand to the other
And each of us become his fellow's brother.
We'll slay this Death, who slaughters and betrays.
He shall be slain whose hand so many slays,   40
By the dignity of God, before tonight!"

The three together set about to plight
Their oaths to live and die each for the other
Just as though each had been to each born brother.
And in their drunken frenzy up they get   45
And toward the village off at once they set
Which the innkeeper had spoken of before,
And many were the grisly oaths they swore.
They rent Christ's precious body limb from limb—
Death shall be dead, if they lay hands on him!   50

When they had hardly gone the first half mile,
Just as they were about to cross a stile,
An old man, poor and humble, met them there.
The old man greeted them with a meek air
And said, "God bless you, lords, and be your guide."   55

"What's this?" the proudest of the three replied.
"Old beggar, I hope you meet with evil grace!
Why are you all wrapped up except your face?
What are you doing alive so many a year?"

The old man at these words began to peer   60
Into this gambler's face. "Because I can,
Though I should walk to India, find no man,"
He said, "in any village or any town,
Who for my age is willing to lay down
His youth. So I must keep my old age still   65
For as long a time as it may be God's will.
Nor will Death take my life from me, alas!
Thus like a restless prisoner I pass
And on the ground, which is my mother's gate,
I walk and with my staff both early and late   70
I knock and say, 'Dear mother, let me in!
See how I vanish, flesh, and blood, and skin!

Alas, when shall my bones be laid to rest?
I would exchange with you my clothing chest,
Mother, that in my chamber long has been   75
For an old haircloth rag to wrap me in.'
And yet she still refuses me that grace.
All white, therefore, and withered is my face.
    "But, sirs, you do yourselves no courtesy
To speak to an old man so churlishly   80
Unless he had wronged you either in word or deed.
As you yourselves in Holy Writ may read,
'Before an aged man whose head is hoar
Men ought to rise.'[2] I counsel you, therefore,
No harm nor wrong here to an old man do,   85
No more than you would have men do to you
In your old age, if you so long abide.
And God be with you, whether you walk or ride!
I must go yonder where I have to go."
    "No, you old beggar, by St. John, not so,"   90
Said another of these gamblers. "As for me,
By God, you won't get off so easily!
You spoke just now of that false traitor, Death,
Who in this land robs all our friends of breath.
Tell where he is, since you must be his spy,   95
Or you will suffer for it, so say I
By God and by the holy sacrament.
You are in league with him, false thief, and bent
On killing us young folk, that's clear to my mind."
    "If you are so impatient, sirs, to find   100
Death," he replied, "turn up this crooked way,
For in that grove I left him, truth to say,
Beneath a tree, and there he will abide.
No boast of yours will make him run and hide.
Do you see that oak tree? Just there you will find   105
This Death, and God, who bought again mankind,
Save and amend you!" So said this old man;
And promptly each of these three gamblers ran
Until he reached the tree, and there they found
Florins of fine gold, minted bright and round,   110
Nearly eight bushels of them, as they thought.
And after Death no longer then they sought.
Each of them was so ravished at the sight,
So fair the florins glittered and so bright,
That down they sat beside the precious hoard.   115

---

[2] *'Before . . . to rise'*: From Leviticus 19:32, in the Old Testament.

The worst of them, he uttered the first word.
    "Brothers," he told them, "listen to what I say.
My head is sharp, for all I joke and play.
Fortune has given us this pile of treasure
To set us up in lives of ease and pleasure.   120
Lightly it comes, lightly we'll make it go.
God's precious dignity! Who was to know
We'd ever tumble on such luck today?
If we could only carry this gold away,
Home to my house, or either one of yours—   125
For well you know that all this gold is ours—
We'd touch the summit of felicity.
But still, by daylight that can hardly be.
People would call us thieves, too bold for stealth,
And they would have us hanged for our own wealth.   130
It must be done by night, that's our best plan,
As prudently and slyly as we can.
Hence my proposal is that we should all
Draw lots, and let's see where the lot will fall,
And the one of us who draws the shortest stick   135
Shall run back to the town, and make it quick,
And bring us bread and wine here on the sly,
And two of us will keep a watchful eye
Over this gold; and if he doesn't stay
Too long in town, we'll carry this gold away   140
By night, wherever we all agree it's best."
    One of them held the cut out in his fist
And had them draw to see where it would fall,
And the cut fell on the youngest of them all.
At once he set off on his way to town,   145
And the very moment after he was gone
The one who urged this plan said to the other:
"You know that by sworn oath you are my brother.
I'll tell you something you can profit by.
Our friend has gone, that's clear to any eye,   150
And here is gold, abundant as can be,
That we propose to share alike, we three.
But if I worked it out, as I could do,
So that it could be shared between us two,
Wouldn't that be a favor, a friendly one?"   155
    The other answered, "How that can be done,
I don't quite see. He knows we have the gold.
What shall we do, or what shall he be told?"
    "Will you keep the secret tucked inside your head?
And in a few words," the first scoundrel said,   160

"I'll tell you how to bring this end about."

"Granted," the other told him. "Never doubt,
I won't betray you, that you can believe."

"Now," said the first, "we are two, as you perceive,
And two of us must have more strength than one.   165
When he sits down, get up as if in fun
And wrestle with him. While you play this game
I'll run him through the ribs. You do the same
With your dagger there, and then this gold shall be
Divided, dear friend, between you and me.   170
Then all that we desire we can fulfill,
And both of us can roll the dice at will."
Thus in agreement these two scoundrels fell
To slay the third, as you have heard me tell.

The youngest, who had started off to town,   175
Within his heart kept rolling up and down
The beauty of these florins, new and bright.
"O Lord," he thought, "were there some way I might
Have all this treasure to myself alone,
There isn't a man who dwells beneath God's throne   180
Could live a life as merry as mine should be!"
And so at last the fiend, our enemy,
Put in his head that he could gain his ends
If he bought poison to kill off his friends.
Finding his life in such a sinful state,   185
The devil was allowed to seal his fate.
For it was altogether his intent
To kill his friends, and never to repent.
So off he set, no longer would he tarry,
Into the town, to an apothecary,   190
And begged for poison; he wanted it because
He meant to kill his rats; besides, there was
A polecat living in his hedge, he said,
Who killed his capons; and when he went to bed
He wanted to take vengeance, if he might,   195
On vermin that devoured him by night.

The apothecary answered, "You shall have
A drug that as I hope the Lord will save
My soul, no living thing in all creation,
Eating or drinking of this preparation   200
A dose no bigger than a grain of wheat,
But promptly with his death-stroke he shall meet.
Die, that he will, and in a briefer while
Than you can walk the distance of a mile,
This poison is so strong and virulent."   205

Taking the poison, off the scoundrel went,
Holding it in a box, and next he ran
To the neighboring street, and borrowed from a man
Three generous flagons. He emptied out his drug
In two of them, and kept the other jug   210
For his own drink; he let no poison lurk
In that! And so all night he meant to work
Carrying off the gold. Such was his plan,
And when he had filled them, this accursed man
Retraced his path, still following his design,   215
Back to his friends with his three jugs of wine.
    But why dilate upon it any more?
For just as they had planned his death before,
Just so they killed him, and with no delay.
When it was finished, one spoke up to say: 220
"Now let's sit down and drink, and we can bury
His body later on. First we'll be merry,"
And as he said the words, he took the jug
That, as it happened, held the poisonous drug,
And drank, and gave his friend a drink as well,   225
And promptly they both died. But truth to tell,
In all that Avicenna[3] ever wrote
He never described in chapter, rule, or note
More marvelous signs of poisoning, I suppose,
Than appeared in these two wretches at the close.   230
Thus they both perished for their homicide,
And thus the traitorous poisoner also died.

UNDERSTANDING THE POEM

1. In "The Pardoner's Tale," how does the old man know that the three
   young men will find Death beneath the tree?

2. Would anyone else who found the gold also have found Death? Why or
   why not?

3. Why do the young men think that the old man is Death's spy?

4. What makes the young men think that they could kill Death?

---

[3] *Avicenna:* Arab philosopher, physician, and author of a medical textbook of the early
eleventh century.

ANALYZING LITERARY TECHNIQUE

1. Who is the old man? To what extent, if any, does **personification** enhance this tale?

2. What is **ironic** about the old man's comment about finding Death?

3. Why doesn't Chaucer describe the murder of the first young man?

4. In what way is the death of the three young men a fitting conclusion?

5. In what way is this tale a **parable** or an **allegory?** What lesson does it teach?

WRITING ABOUT LITERATURE

1. Examine the view of justice presented in this tale. Consider the depiction of the four major characters, the function of the old man, and the nature of the final deaths. Use quotations to support your ideas. Two possible points of view: (a) Justice exists when those who are evil are punished; or (b) Justice is actually a matter of luck.

2. Chaucer was a child during the great plague of 1347 to 1351, which was called Black Death. In *A Distant Mirror,* historian Barbara Tuchman describes the plague as "the most lethal disaster of recorded history . . . which killed an estimated one third of the population living between India and Iceland." Using quotations from the story to support your ideas, examine the role Death plays in the plot, setting, characters, and theme of this tale. Either begin or conclude with a general statement that summarizes your point of view.

3. Write a tale for one of Chaucer's other pilgrims. Follow Chaucer's example and choose one of the following story patterns that were popular in England in the Middle Ages: the tale of a saint's life, an animal epic, a romance, or a story that will teach a moral (such as "The Pardoner's Tale"). Chaucer created a psychological connection between the kind of person the pardoner was and the tale he told (a pardoner is a preacher who raised money for religious purposes by selling pardons and indulgences, official documents that released a sinner from punishment after death). Try to create some connection between the pilgrim you choose and the tale that person tells.

    Choose from the following list of Chaucer's pilgrims: a cook, a sailor, a farmer, a miller of flour, a carpenter, a weaver or a dyer of cloth, a weaver of tapestries, a dealer in clothing, a merchant, a doctor, a lawyer, a clerk from Oxford, a franklin (a landowner who was not a member of the nobility), a knight or a squire, a priest, a nun, a pardoner, a monk (who lived a secluded life in a monastery), and a friar (who combined living as a monk with religious activities in the secular world).

Much Ado About Nothing

WILLIAM SHAKESPEARE

ILLIAM SHAKESPEARE (1564–1616), the English poet and dramatist, is one of the greatest literary figures in history. He is considered the greatest writer in the English language. His works reveal insight into human psychology, deep respect for the human spirit, and profound awareness of the wonder and terror of human behavior. He is a master of the sonnet form in poetry, but he is best known for his plays, which combine exciting stories, superb characterizations, and poetic language that has no equal. Among his best-known plays are the tragedies *Romeo and Juliet* (1595–96), *Hamlet* (1600–1601), *Othello* (1604), *King Lear* (1605), and *Macbeth* (1606); the Roman plays *Julius Caesar* (1599) and *Antony and Cleopatra* (1606–7); the English historical plays *Richard III* (1592–93) and *Henry IV, Part 1* (1589–90); the comedies *Much Ado About Nothing* (1598–99), *The Taming of the Shrew* (1593–94), *A Midsummer Night's Dream* (1595–96), *As You Like It* (1599), and *Twelfth Night* (1601–2); and the romances *The Winter's Tale* (1610–11) and *The Tempest* (1611). Shakespeare's plays were successful because they appealed to people from all walks of life, the educated and the uneducated, the rich and the poor, and they continue to be performed throughout the world.

William Shakespeare was born in April 1564 to John Shakespeare, a locally prominent merchant, and his wife Mary in the English market town of Stratford-upon-Avon. Shakespeare attended the Stratford Grammar School, where he studied Latin and became familiar with the great writers of ancient Rome, including the playwrights Terence, Plautus, and Seneca. He also learned to read Italian, the most popular foreign language in England at that time. However, when his father's economic situation declined, Shakespeare had to quit school and go to work. In 1582 he married Anne Hathaway, who was seven or eight years older than he. They had three children: Susanna (christened May 26, 1583) and twins, Hamnet and Judith (February 2, 1585). Hamnet died during the summer of 1596.

Until the first public theater (The Theatre) was built in London in 1576, public entertainment consisted largely of performances by traveling acrobats, musicians, and magicians. However, in the early 1570s a group of scholars called the "University Wits" began to write plays and to perform them in town squares, inn yards, and large open theaters outside London. By the late 1500s and early 1600s, Londoners attended the theater as commonly as people today watch television, attend movies, or listen to the radio.

No one knows when William Shakespeare began to write or when he entered the London theater scene; however, by the late 1580s he had become both an actor and a playwright. In 1594 he became a charter member, shareholder, and principal actor with a theater company known as the Lord Chamberlain's Men, which became the leading theatrical company in London; after James I ascended the throne in 1603, the company was known as the King's Men. In 1608 he became part of a group that operated one of the new smaller and more expensive private theaters, the Second Blackfriars Theatre.

From 1598 to 1609, Shakespeare wrote his greatest plays. Some of the best actors of the time were members of Shakespeare's company, and he wrote for them. For the clown Will Kemp, he wrote *A Midsummer Night's Dream* and *Much Ado About Nothing*. For the tragic actor Richard Burbage, he wrote *Hamlet* and *Macbeth*. Shakespeare himself played the ghost in *Hamlet*. In about 1611 Shakespeare left the London theater scene and retired to Stratford, where he died on April 23, 1616.

Much Ado About Nothing is a wonderfully provocative play about two sets of lovers. It is typical of Shakespeare's work in that character, rather than fate or accident, determines how a person responds to a crisis. Individuals are responsible for their actions, and those who disrupt the moral order of society suffer adverse consequences. However, *Much Ado* is unusual in that three characters who would be punished in a tragedy are quickly forgiven here. The critical question is whether *Much Ado* is too tragic for a comedy and too comic for a tragedy or whether Shakespeare is using a pair of love stories to tell a serious tale about the nature of human beings. Audiences, readers, and critics have continued to find aspects of this play to be disturbing; often they dismiss the work as "much ado about nothing" rather than seek an explanation for its outrageous attitudes and actions.

The cuckold jokes in *Much Ado* are so numerous that an explanation is necessary. In Shakespeare's day, most women were economically dependent on a male provider, and love was not necessarily a factor in marriage. Gossip gave birth to humorous stories in which a wife would betray, or cuckold, her husband by contriving to be alone with a lover. (The word *cuckold*, which always refers to a man who has an unfaithful wife, is derived from the cuckoo, a bird that lays its eggs in the nests of other birds.) The cuckold jokes express both the male's fear and distrust of women (in the form of the husband) and the male's role as conqueror (in the form of the lover). The cuckold was thought to grow horns that symbolized his marital dishonor; he would wear a cap to hide those horns.

In *Much Ado About Nothing*, Shakespeare is at his best in revealing the beauty and versatility of the English language. To Benedick and Beatrice—and, of course, to Shakespeare, their creator—"wit" is a verbal expression of creative intelligence. Benedick expresses the priceless value of language when he declares that people who let others outwit them have nothing left that is of value (V.iv.102–3). Four hundred years later we still agree with Benedick, and we still appreciate the supreme writer who crafted this provocative pair of love stories.

DRAMATIS PERSONÆ

DON PEDRO, *prince of Arragon.*

DON JOHN, *his bastard brother.*

CLAUDIO, *a young lord of Florence.*

BENEDICK, *a young lord of Padua.*

LEONATO, *governor of Messina.*

ANTONIO, *his brother.*

BALTHASAR, *attendant on Don Pedro.*

CONRADE,
BORACHIO, } *followers of Don John.*

FRIAR FRANCIS.

DOGBERRY, *a constable.*

VERGES, *a headborough.*

A Sexton.

A Boy.

HERO, *daughter to Leonato.*

BEATRICE, *niece to Leonato.*

MARGARET,
URSULA, } *gentlewomen attending on Hero.*

Messengers, Watch, Attendants, &c.

Scene—*Messina.*

ACT I.

SCENE I. *Before* LEONATO's *house.*

Enter LEONATO, HERO, *and* BEATRICE, *with a* Messenger.

LEONATO: I learn in this letter that Don Pedro of Arragon comes this
night to Messina.

MESSENGER: He is very near by this: he was not three leagues off when
I left him.

LEONATO: How many gentlemen have you lost in this action?   5

MESSENGER: But few of any sort, and none of name.

LEONATO: A victory is twice itself when the achiever brings home full
numbers. I find here that Don Pedro hath bestowed much honour
on a young Florentine named Claudio.

MESSENGER: Much deserved on his part, and equally remembered by Don   10
Pedro: he hath borne himself beyond the promise of his age; doing,
in the figure of a lamb, the feats of a lion: he hath indeed better
bettered expectation than you must expect of me to tell you how.

LEONATO: He hath an uncle here in Messina will be very much glad of it.

MESSENGER: I have already delivered him letters, and there appears   15
much joy in him; even so much, that joy could not show itself
modest enough without a badge of bitterness.

LEONATO: Did he break out into tears?

MESSENGER: In great measure.

LEONATO: A kind overflow of kindness: there are no faces truer than
those that are so washed. How much better is it to weep at joy than   20
to joy at weeping!

BEATRICE: I pray you, is Signior Mountanto[1] returned from the wars or
no?

MESSENGER: I know none of that name, lady: there was none such in   25
the army of any sort.

LEONATO: What is he that you ask for, niece?

HERO: My cousin means Signior Benedick of Padua.

MESSENGER: O, he's returned; and as pleasant as ever he was.

BEATRICE: He set up his bills here in Messina and challenged Cupid at   30
the flight; and my uncle's fool, reading the challenge, subscribed for
Cupid, and challenged him at the bird-bolt.[2] I pray you, how many

---

[1] *Mountanto:* From a fencing term (*montant*) for an upward thrust or blow.
[2] *bird-bolt:* Blunt-headed arrow used for shooting birds at close range.

hath he killed and eaten in these wars? But how many hath he killed? for, indeed, I promised to eat all of his killing.

LEONATO: Faith, niece, you tax Signior Benedick too much; but he'll be meet with you, I doubt it not.   35

MESSENGER: He hath done good service, lady, in these wars.

BEATRICE: You had musty victual, and he hath holp to eat it: he is a very valiant trencher-man;[3] he hath an excellent stomach.

MESSENGER: And a good soldier too, lady.   40

BEATRICE: And a good soldier to a lady; but what is he to a lord?

MESSENGER: A lord to a lord, a man to a man; stuffed with all honourable virtues.

BEATRICE: It is so, indeed; he is no less than a stuffed man: but for the stuffing,—well, we are all mortal.   45

LEONATO: You must not, sir, mistake my niece. There is a kind of merry war betwixt Signior Benedick and her: they never meet but there's a skirmish of wit between them.

BEATRICE: Alas! he gets nothing by that. In our last conflict four of his five wits[4] went halting off, and now is the whole man governed with   50 one: so that if he have wit enough to keep himself warm, let him bear it for a difference between himself and his horse; for it is all the wealth that he hath left, to be known a reasonable creature. Who is his companion now? He hath every month a new sworn brother.

MESSENGER: Is't possible?   55

BEATRICE: Very easily possible: he wears his faith but as the fashion of his hat; it ever changes with the next block.

MESSENGER: I see, lady, the gentleman is not in your books.

BEATRICE: No; an[5] he were, I would burn my study. But, I pray you, who is his companion? Is there no young squarer[6] now that will   60 make a voyage with him to the devil?

MESSENGER: He is most in the company of the right noble Claudio.

BEATRICE: O Lord, he will hang upon him like a disease: he is sooner caught than the pestilence, and the taker runs presently mad. God help the noble Claudio! if he have caught the Benedick, it will cost   65 him a thousand pound ere a' be cured.

MESSENGER: I will hold friends with you, lady.

---

[3] *trencher-man:* Good eater; a *trencher* is a plate.

[4] *five wits:* Judgment, imagination, memory, common wit, and fantasy.

[5] *an:* If.

[6] *squarer:* Quarreler.

BEATRICE: Do, good friend.

LEONATO: You will never run mad, niece.

BEATRICE: No, not till a hot January. 70

MESSENGER: Don Pedro is approached.

Enter DON PEDRO, DON JOHN, CLAUDIO, BENEDICK, *and* BALTHASAR.

DON PEDRO: Good Signior Leonato, you are come to meet your trouble: the fashion of the world is to avoid cost, and you encounter it.

LEONATO: Never came trouble to my house in the likeness of your Grace: for trouble being gone, comfort should remain; but when 75 you depart from me, sorrow abides, and happiness takes his leave.

DON PEDRO: You embrace your charge too willingly. I think this is your daughter.

LEONATO: Her mother hath many times told me so.

BENEDICK: Were you in doubt, sir, that you asked her? 80

LEONATO: Signior Benedick, no; for then were you a child.

DON PEDRO: You have it full, Benedick: we may guess by this what you are, being a man. Truly, the lady fathers herself. Be happy, lady; for you are like an honourable father.

BENEDICK: If Signior Leonato be her father, she would not have his 85 head on her shoulders for all Messina, as like him as she is.

BEATRICE: I wonder that you will still be talking, Signior Benedick: nobody marks you.

BENEDICK: What, my dear Lady Disdain! are you yet living?

BEATRICE: Is it possible disdain should die while she hath such meet 90 food to feed it, as Signior Benedick? Courtesy itself must convert to disdain, if you come in her presence.

BENEDICK: Then is courtesy a turncoat. But it is certain I am loved of all ladies, only you excepted: and I would I could find in my heart that I had not a hard heart; for, truly, I love none. 95

BEATRICE: A dear happiness to women: they would else have been troubled with a pernicious suitor. I thank God and my cold blood, I am of your humour for that: I had rather hear my dog bark at a crow than a man swear he loves me.

BENEDICK: God keep your ladyship still in that mind! so some 100 gentleman or other shall 'scape a predestinate scratched face.

BEATRICE: Scratching could not make it worse, an 'twere such a face as yours were.

BENEDICK: Well, you are a rare parrot-teacher.

BEATRICE: A bird of my tongue is better than a beast of yours. 105

BENEDICK: I would my horse had the speed of your tongue, and so good a continuer. But keep your way, i' God's name; I have done.

BEATRICE: You always end with a jade's trick:[7] I know you of old.

DON PEDRO: That is the sum of all, Leonato. Signior Claudio and Signior Benedick, my dear friend Leonato hath invited you all. I 110 tell him we shall stay here at the least a month; and he heartily prays some occasion may detain us longer. I dare swear he is no hypocrite, but prays from his heart.

LEONATO: If you swear, my lord, you shall not be forsworn. [*To* DON JOHN] Let me bid you welcome, my lord: being reconciled to the 115 prince your brother, I owe you all duty.

DON JOHN: I thank you: I am not of many words, but I thank you.

LEONATO: Please it your Grace lead on?

DON PEDRO: Your hand, Leonato; we will go together.
[*Exeunt all except* BENEDICK *and* CLAUDIO.]

CLAUDIO: Benedick, didst thou note the daughter of Signior Leonato? 120

BENEDICK: I noted her not; but I looked on her.

CLAUDIO: Is she not a modest young lady?

BENEDICK: Do you question me, as an honest man should do, for my simple true judgement? or would you have me speak after my custom, as being a professed tyrant to their sex? 125

CLAUDIO: No; I pray thee speak in sober judgement.

BENEDICK: Why, i'faith, methinks she's too low for a high praise, too brown for a fair praise, and too little for a great praise: only this commendation I can afford her, that were she other than she is, she were unhandsome; and being no other but as she is, I do not like her. 130

CLAUDIO: Thou thinkest I am in sport: I pray thee tell me truly how thou likest her.

BENEDICK: Would you buy her, that you inquire after her?

CLAUDIO: Can the world buy such a jewel?

BENEDICK: Yea, and a case to put it into. But speak you this with a sad 135 brow? or do you play the flouting Jack, to tell us Cupid is a good hare-finder, and Vulcan a rare carpenter?[8] Come, in what key shall a man take you, to go in the song?

---

[7] *jade's trick:* A fatigued or ill-trained horse's "trick" of dropping out of a race.

[8] *Cupid . . . a rare carpenter:* Cupid is blind, and Vulcan is a blacksmith, not a carpenter; thus, Benedick thinks Claudio is mocking.

CLAUDIO: In mine eye she is the sweetest lady that ever I looked on.

BENEDICK: I can see yet without spectacles, and I see no such matter: 140
there's her cousin, an she were not possessed with a fury, exceeds
her as much in beauty as the first of May doth the last of December.
But I hope you have no intent to turn husband, have you?

CLAUDIO: I would scarce trust myself, though I had sworn the contrary,
if Hero would be my wife. 145

BENEDICK: Is't come to this? In faith, hath not the world one man but
he will wear his cap with suspicion?[9] Shall I never see a bachelor of
threescore again? Go to, i'faith; an thou wilt needs thrust thy neck
into a yoke, wear the print of it, and sigh away Sundays. Look; Don
Pedro is returned to seek you. 150

Re-enter DON PEDRO.

DON PEDRO: What secret hath held you here, that you followed not to
Leonato's?

BENEDICK: I would your Grace would constrain me to tell.

DON PEDRO: I charge thee on thy allegiance.

BENEDICK: You hear, Count Claudio: I can be secret as a dumb man; I 155
would have you think so; but, on my allegiance, mark you this, on
my allegiance. He is in love. With who? now that is your Grace's
part. Mark how short his answer is;—With Hero, Leonato's short
daughter.

CLAUDIO: If this were so, so were it uttered. 160

BENEDICK: Like the old tale, my lord: "it is not so, nor 'twas not so, but,
indeed, God forbid it should be so."

CLAUDIO: If my passion change not shortly, God forbid it should be
otherwise.

DON PEDRO: Amen, if you love her; for the lady is very well worthy. 165

CLAUDIO: You speak this to fetch me in, my lord.

DON PEDRO: By my troth, I speak my thought.

CLAUDIO: And, in faith, my lord, I spoke mine.

BENEDICK: And, by my two faiths and troths, my lord, I spoke mine.

CLAUDIO: That I love her, I feel. 170

DON PEDRO: That she is worthy, I know.

---

[9] *wear his cap with suspicion:* The first of many allusions to the joke that a cuckold (the
husband of an unfaithful wife) grew horns; wearing a cap would hide the horns.

BENEDICK: That I neither feel how she should be loved, nor know how she should be worthy, is the opinion that fire cannot melt out of me: I will die in it at the stake.

DON PEDRO: Thou wast ever an obstinate heretic in the despite of beauty. 175

CLAUDIO: And never could maintain his part but in the force of his will.

BENEDICK: That a woman conceived me, I thank her; that she brought me up, I likewise give her most humble thanks: but that I will have a recheat winded in my forehead, or hang my bugle in an invisible baldrick,[10] all women shall pardon me. Because I will not do them 180 the wrong to mistrust any, I will do myself the right to trust none; and the fine is, for the which I may go the finer, I will live a bachelor.

DON PEDRO: I shall see thee, ere I die, look pale with love.

BENEDICK: With anger, with sickness, or with hunger, my lord; not with love: prove that ever I lose more blood with love than I will get again 185 with drinking, pick out mine eyes with a ballad-maker's pen, and hang me up at the door of a brothel-house for the sign of blind Cupid.

DON PEDRO: Well, if ever thou dost fall from this faith, thou will prove a notable argument.

BENEDICK: If I do, hang me in a bottle like a cat, and shoot at me; and he 190 that hits me, let him be clapped on the shoulder and called Adam.[11]

DON PEDRO: Well, as time shall try:
"In time the savage bull doth bear the yoke."

BENEDICK: The savage bull may; but if ever the sensible Benedick bear it, pluck off the bull's horns, and set them in my forehead: and let 195 me be vilely painted; and in such great letters as they write "Here is good horse to hire," let them signify under my sign "Here you may see Benedick the married man."

CLAUDIO: If this should ever happen, thou wouldst be horn-mad.

DON PEDRO: Nay, if Cupid have not spent all his quiver in Venice, 200 thou wilt quake for this shortly.

BENEDICK: I look for an earthquake too, then.

DON PEDRO: Well, you will temporize with the hours. In the meantime, good Signior Benedick, repair to Leonato's: commend me to him, and tell him I will not fail him at supper; for indeed he hath made 205 great preparation.

---

10 *recheat . . . in an invisible baldrick:* A recheat is a call sounded on a hunting horn to gather the hounds; a baldrick is a strap from which a hunting horn (bugle) is hung; thus, Benedick is again referring to the cuckolded husband.

11 *hang me in a bottle . . . called Adam:* In archery contests, a cat was sometimes suspended in a wicker basket (bottle) as a target. Adam Bell was an archer in outlaw ballads.

BENEDICK: I have almost matter enough in me for such an embassage; and so I commit you—

CLAUDIO: To the tuition of God: From my house, if I had it,—

DON PEDRO: The sixth of July: Your loving friend, Benedick.[12]   210

BENEDICK: Nay, mock not, mock not. The body of your discourse is sometime guarded with fragments, and the guards are but slightly basted on neither: ere you flout old ends any further, examine your conscience: and so I leave you.   [*Exit.*]

CLAUDIO: My liege, your highness now may do me good.   215

DON PEDRO: My love is thine to teach: teach it but how,
And thou shalt see how apt it is to learn
Any hard lesson that may do thee good.

CLAUDIO: Hath Leonato any son, my lord?

DON PEDRO: No child but Hero; she's his only heir.   220
Dost thou affect her, Claudio?

CLAUDIO: O, my lord,
When you went onward on this ended action,
I look'd upon her with a soldier's eye,
That liked, but had a rougher task in hand
Than to drive liking to the name of love: 225
But now I am return'd and that war-thoughts
Have left their places vacant, in their rooms
Come thronging soft and delicate desires,
All prompting me how fair young Hero is,
Saying, I liked her ere I went to wars.   230

DON PEDRO: Thou wilt be like a lover presently,
And tire the hearer with a book of words.
If thou dost love fair Hero, cherish it;
And I will break[13] with her and with her father,
And thou shalt have her. Was't not to this end   235
That thou began'st to twist so fine a story?

CLAUDIO: How sweetly you do minister to love,
That know love's grief by his complexion!
But lest my liking might too sudden seem,
I would have salved it with a longer treatise.   240

---

[12] *To the tuition of God . . . Benedick:* Benedick's words sound like the closing of a letter, and Claudio and Don Pedro finish the "letter" in the style of the times, with place, date, and signature.

[13] *break:* Break the news; open up the subject.

DON PEDRO: What need the bridge much broader than the flood?
    The fairest grant is the necessity.
    Look, what will serve is fit: 'tis once, thou lovest,
    And I will fit thee with the remedy.
    I know we shall have revelling to-night: 245
    I will assume thy part in some disguise,
    And tell fair Hero I am Claudio;
    And in her bosom I'll unclasp my heart,
    And take her hearing prisoner with the force
    And strong encounter of my amorous tale: 250
    Then after to her father will I break;
    And the conclusion is, she shall be thine.
    In practice let us put it presently.   [*Exeunt.*]

SCENE II. *A room in* LEONATO's *house.*

Enter LEONATO *and* ANTONIO, *meeting.*

LEONATO: How now, brother! Where is my cousin, your son? hath he provided this music?

ANTONIO: He is very busy about it. But, brother, I can tell you strange news, that you yet dreamt not of.

LEONATO: Are they good?   5

ANTONIO: As the event stamps them: but they have a good cover; they show well outward. The prince and Count Claudio, walking in a thick-pleached alley[14] in mine orchard, were thus much overheard by a man of mine: the prince discovered[15] to Claudio that he loved my niece your daughter, and meant to acknowledge it this night in a   10 dance; and if he found her accordant, he meant to take the present time by the top, and instantly break with you of it.

LEONATO: Hath the fellow any wit that told you this?

ANTONIO: A good sharp fellow: I will send for him; and question him yourself.   15

LEONATO: No, no; we will hold it as a dream till it appear itself: but I will acquaint my daughter withal, that she may be the better prepared for an answer, if peradventure this be true. Go you and tell her of it. [*Enter* Attendants.] Cousins, you know what you have to do. O, I cry you mercy, friend; go you with me, and I will use your skill.   20 Good cousin, have a care this busy time.   [*Exeunt.*]

---

[14] *thick-pleached alley:* Walkway formed by densely interwoven branches.
[15] *discovered:* Revealed.

SCENE III. *The same.*

Enter DON JOHN *and* CONRADE.

CONRADE: What the good-year, my lord! why are you thus out of
measure sad?

DON JOHN: There is no measure in the occasion that breeds; therefore
the sadness is without limit.

CONRADE: You should hear reason.   5

DON JOHN: And when I have heard it, what blessing brings it?

CONRADE: If not a present remedy, at least a patient sufferance.

DON JOHN: I wonder that thou, being (as thou sayest thou art) born under
Saturn,[16] goest about to apply a moral medicine to a mortifying
mischief. I cannot hide what I am: I must be sad when I have cause,   10
and smile at no man's jests; eat when I have stomach, and wait for
no man's leisure; sleep when I am drowsy, and tend on no man's
business; laugh when I am merry, and claw no man in his humour.

CONRADE: Yea, but you must not make the full show of this till you
may do it without controlment. You have of late stood out against   15
your brother, and he hath ta'en you newly into his grace; where it is
impossible you should take true root but by the fair weather that
you make yourself; it is needful that you frame the season for your
own harvest.

DON JOHN: I had rather be a canker in a hedge than a rose in his grace; 20
and it better fits my blood to be disdained of all than to fashion a
carriage to rob love from any: in this, though I cannot be said to be
a flattering honest man, it must not be denied but I am a plain-
dealing villain. I am trusted with a muzzle, and enfranchised with a
clog;[17] therefore I have decreed not to sing in my cage. If I had my   25
mouth, I would bite; if I had my liberty, I would do my liking: in
the meantime let me be that I am, and seek not to alter me.

CONRADE: Can you make no use of your discontent?

DON JOHN: I make all use of it, for I use it only.
Who comes here?   30

Enter BORACHIO.

What news, Borachio?

---

[16] *born under Saturn:* Persons born under the sign of the planet Saturn were said to be
melancholy.

[17] *clog:* Heavy wooden block used to restrict the movement of animals.

BORACHIO: I came yonder from a great supper: the prince your brother is royally entertained by Leonato; and I can give you intelligence of an intended marriage.

DON JOHN: Will it serve for any model to build mischief on? What is   35
he for a fool that betroths himself to unquietness?

BORACHIO: Marry, it is your brother's right hand.

DON JOHN: Who? the most exquisite Claudio?

BORACHIO: Even he.

DON JOHN: A proper squire! And who, and who? which way looks he?   40

BORACHIO: Marry, on Hero, the daughter and heir of Leonato.

DON JOHN: A very forward March-chick![18] How came you to this?

BORACHIO: Being entertained for[19] a perfumer, as I was smoking a musty room, comes me the prince and Claudio, hand in hand, in sad conference: I whipt me behind the arras; and there heard it   45
agreed upon, that the prince should woo Hero for himself, and having obtained her, give her to Count Claudio.

DON JOHN: Come, come, let us thither: this may prove food to my displeasure. That young start-up hath all the glory of my overthrow: if I can cross him any way, I bless myself every way. You are both   50
sure, and will assist me?

CONRADE: To the death, my lord.

DON JOHN: Let us to the great supper: their cheer is the greater that I am subdued. Would the cook were of my mind! Shall we go prove what's to be done?   55

BORACHIO: We'll wait upon your lordship.   [*Exeunt.*]

ACT II.

SCENE I. *A hall in* LEONATO'*s house.*

Enter LEONATO, ANTONIO, HERO, BEATRICE, *and others.*

LEONATO: Was not Count John here at supper?

ANTONIO: I saw him not.

BEATRICE: How tartly that gentleman looks! I never can see him but I am heart-burned an hour after.

HERO: He is of a very melancholy disposition.   5

---

[18] *March-chick:* Prematurely born chick.
[19] *entertained for:* Hired as.

BEATRICE: He were an excellent man that were made just in the midway between him and Benedick: the one is too like an image and says nothing, and the other too like my lady's eldest son, evermore tattling.

LEONATO: Then half Signior Benedick's tongue in Count John's mouth, and half Count John's melancholy in Signior Benedick's face,— 10

BEATRICE: With a good leg and a good foot, uncle, and money enough in his purse, such a man would win any woman in the world, if a' could get her good-will.

LEONATO: By my troth, niece, thou wilt never get thee a husband, if thou be so shrewd[20] of thy tongue. 15

ANTONIO: In faith, she's too curst.

BEATRICE: Too curst is more than curst: I shall lessen God's sending that way; for it is said, "God sends a curst cow short horns;" but to a cow too curst he sends none.

LEONATO: So, by being too curst, God will send you no horns. 20

BEATRICE: Just, if he send me no husband; for the which blessing I am at him upon my knees every morning and evening. Lord, I could not endure a husband with a beard on his face: I had rather lie in the woollen.[21]

LEONATO: You may light on a husband that hath no beard. 25

BEATRICE: What should I do with him? dress him in my apparel, and make him my waiting-gentlewoman? He that hath a beard is more than a youth; and he that hath no beard is less than a man: and he that is more than a youth is not for me; and he that is less than a man, I am not for him: therefore I will even take sixpence in earnest 30 of the bear-ward, and lead his apes into hell.[22]

LEONATO: Well, then, go you into hell?

BEATRICE: No, but to the gate; and there will the devil meet me, like an old cuckold, with horns on his head, and say, "Get you to heaven, Beatrice, get you to heaven; here's no place for you maids:" so deliver 35 I up my apes, and away to Saint Peter for the heavens; he shows me where the bachelors sit, and there live we as merry as the day is long.

ANTONIO: [To HERO] Well, niece, I trust you will be ruled by your father.

BEATRICE: Yes, faith; it is my cousin's duty to make courtesy, and say, "Father, as it please you." But yet for all that, cousin, let him be a 40

---

[20] *shrewd:* Sharp.

[21] *lie in the woollen:* To sleep with blankets next to the skin; i.e., without sheets.

[22] *the bear-ward . . . into hell:* A bear-ward was a bear keeper and trainer; the ward also sometimes kept apes.

handsome fellow, or else make another courtesy, and say, "Father, as it please me."

LEONATO: Well, niece, I hope to see you one day fitted with a husband.

BEATRICE: Not till God make men of some other metal than earth. Would it not grieve a woman to be overmastered with a piece of valiant dust? to make an account of her life to a clod of a wayward marl? No, uncle, I'll none: Adam's sons are my brethren; and, truly, I hold it a sin to match in my kindred. 45

LEONATO: Daughter, remember what I told you: if the prince do solicit you in that kind, you know your answer. 50

BEATRICE: The fault will be in the music, cousin, if you be not wooed in good time: if the prince be too important, tell him there is measure in every thing, and so dance out the answer. For, hear me, Hero: wooing, wedding, and repenting, is as a Scotch jig, a measure, and a cinque pace:[23] the first suit is hot and hasty, like a Scotch jig, and full as fantastical; the wedding, mannerly-modest, as a measure, full of state and ancientry; and then comes repentance, and, with his bad legs, falls into the cinque pace faster and faster, till he sink into his grave. 55

LEONATO: Cousin, you apprehend passing shrewdly.

BEATRICE: I have a good eye, uncle: I can see a church by daylight. 60

LEONATO: The revellers are entering, brother: make good room.

[All put on their masks.]

Enter DON PEDRO, CLAUDIO, BENEDICK, BALTHASAR, DON JOHN, BORACHIO, MARGARET, URSULA, *and others, masked.*

DON PEDRO: Lady, will you walk about with your friend?

HERO: So you walk softly, and look sweetly, and say nothing, I am yours for the walk; and especially when I walk away.

DON PEDRO: With me in your company? 65

HERO: I may say so, when I please.

DON PEDRO: And when please you to say so?

HERO: When I like your favour; for God defend the lute should be like the case!

DON PEDRO: My visor is Philemon's roof; within the house is Jove.[24] 70

HERO: Why, then, your visor should be thatched.

---

[23] *cinque pace:* A lively dance; from the French *cinque* (five) *pas* (step).
[24] *Philemon's roof . . . Jove:* Philemon and his wife, Baucis, unknowingly played host to Jove in their humble cottage.

DON PEDRO: Speak low, if you speak love.   [*Drawing her aside.*]

BALTHASAR: Well, I would you did like me.

MARGARET: So would not I, for your own sake; for I have many ill qualities.   75

BALTHASAR: Which is one?

MARGARET: I say my prayers aloud.

BALTHASAR: I love you the better: the hearers may cry, Amen.

MARGARET: God match me with a good dancer!

BALTHASAR: Amen.   80

MARGARET: And God keep him out of my sight when the dance is done! Answer, clerk.

BALTHASAR: No more words: the clerk is answered.

URSULA: I know you well enough; you are Signior Antonio.

ANTONIO: At a word, I am not.   85

URSULA: I know you by the waggling of your head.

ANTONIO: To tell you true, I counterfeit him.

URSULA: You could never do him so ill-well, unless you were the very man. Here's his dry hand up and down: you are he, you are he.

ANTONIO: At a word, I am not.   90

URSULA: Come, come, do you think I do not know you by your excellent wit? can virtue hide itself? Go to, mum, you are he: graces will appear, and there's an end.

BEATRICE: Will you not tell me who told you so?

BENEDICK: No, you shall pardon me.   95

BEATRICE: Nor will you not tell me who you are?

BENEDICK: Not now.

BEATRICE: That I was disdainful, and that I had my good wit out of the "Hundred Merry Tales":[25]—well, this was Signior Benedick that said so.   100

BENEDICK: What's he?

BEATRICE: I am sure you know him well enough.

BENEDICK: Not I, believe me.

BEATRICE: Did he never make you laugh?

BENEDICK: I pray you, what is he?   105

---

[25] *"Hundred Merry Tales"*: A popular joke book.

BEATRICE: Why, he is the prince's jester: a very dull fool; only his gift is
in devising impossible slanders: none but libertines delight in him;
and the commendation is not in his wit, but in his villany; for he
both pleases men and angers them, and then they laugh at him and
beat him. I am sure he is in the fleet: I would he had boarded me. 110

BENEDICK: When I know the gentleman, I'll tell him what you say.

BEATRICE: Do, do: he'll but break a comparison or two on me; which,
peradventure not marked or not laughed at, strikes him into melancholy; and then there's a partridge wing saved, for the fool will eat
no supper that night. [*Music.*] We must follow the leaders. 115

BENEDICK: In every good thing.

BEATRICE: Nay, if they lead to any ill, I will leave them at the next
turning.

[*Dance. Then exeunt all except* DON JOHN, BORACHIO, *and* CLAUDIO.]

DON JOHN: Sure my brother is amorous on Hero, and hath withdrawn
her father to break with him about it. The ladies follow her, and
but one visor remains. 120

BORACHIO: And that is Claudio: I know him by his bearing.

DON JOHN: Are not you Signior Benedick?

CLAUDIO: You know me well; I am he.

DON JOHN: Signior, you are very near my brother in his love: he is 125
enamoured on Hero; I pray you, dissuade him from her: she is no
equal for his birth: you may do the part of an honest man in it.

CLAUDIO: How know you he loves her?

DON JOHN: I heard him swear his affection.

BORACHIO: So did I too; and he swore he would marry her to-night. 130

DON JOHN: Come, let us to the banquet.
                        [*Exeunt* DON JOHN *and* BORACHIO.]

CLAUDIO: Thus answer I in name of Benedick,
But hear these ill news with the ears of Claudio.
'Tis certain so; the prince wooes for himself.
Friendship is constant in all other things 135
Save in the office and affairs of love:
Therefore all hearts in love use their own tongues;
Let every eye negotiate for itself,
And trust no agent; for beauty is a witch,
Against whose charms faith melteth into blood. 140
This is an accident of hourly proof,
Which I mistrusted not. Farewell, therefore, Hero!

Re-enter BENEDICK.

BENEDICK: Count Claudio?

CLAUDIO: Yea, the same.

BENEDICK: Come, will you go with me?   145

CLAUDIO: Whither?

BENEDICK: Even to the next willow, about your own business, county.
What fashion will you wear the garland of? about your neck, like an
usurer's chain? or under your arm, like a lieutenant's scarf? You must
wear it one way, for the prince hath got your Hero.   150

CLAUDIO: I wish him joy of her.

BENEDICK: Why, that's spoken like an honest drovier;[26] so they sell
bullocks. But did you think the prince would have served you thus?

CLAUDIO: I pray you, leave me.

BENEDICK: Ho! now you strike like the blind man; 'twas the boy that   155
stole your meat, and you'll beat the post.

CLAUDIO: If it will not be, I'll leave you.   [*Exit.*]

BENEDICK: Alas, poor hurt fowl! now will he creep into sedges.[27] But,
that my Lady Beatrice should know me, and not know me! The
prince's fool! Ha? It may be I go under that title because I am merry.   160
Yea, but so I am apt to do myself wrong; I am not so reputed: it is
the base, though bitter, disposition of Beatrice that puts the world
into her person, and so gives me out. Well, I'll be revenged as I may.

Re-enter DON PEDRO.

DON PEDRO: Now, signior, where's the count? did you see him?

BENEDICK: Troth, my lord, I have played the part of Lady Fame. I found   165
him here as melancholy as a lodge in a warren:[28] I told him, and I
think I told him true, that your grace had got the good will of this
young lady; and I offered him my company to a willow-tree, either
to make him a garland, as being forsaken, or to bind him up a rod,
as being worthy to be whipped.   170

DON PEDRO: To be whipped! What's his fault?

BENEDICK: The flat transgression of a school-boy, who, being overjoyed
with finding a birds' nest, shows it his companion, and he steals it.

DON PEDRO: Wilt thou make a trust a transgression? The transgression
is in the stealer.   175

---

[26] *drovier:* Cattle dealer.

[27] *sedges:* A mass of plants along a river.

[28] *lodge in a warren:* The gamekeeper's cottage was necessarily isolated.

BENEDICK: Yet it had not been amiss the rod had been made, and the garland too; for the garland he might have worn himself, and the rod he might have bestowed on you, who, as I take it, have stolen his birds' nest.

DON PEDRO: I will but teach them to sing, and restore them to the owner.   180

BENEDICK: If their singing answer your saying, by my faith, you say honestly.

DON PEDRO: The Lady Beatrice hath a quarrel to you: the gentleman that danced with her told her she is much wronged by you.

BENEDICK: O, she misused me past the endurance of a block! an oak   185
but with one green leaf on it would have answered her; my very visor began to assume life and scold with her. She told me, not thinking I had been myself, that I was the prince's jester, that I was duller than a great thaw; huddling jest upon jest, with such impossible conveyance, upon me, that I stood like a man at a mark,   190
with a whole army shooting at me. She speaks poniards, and every word stabs: if her breath were as terrible as her terminations,[29] there were no living near her; she would infect to the north star. I would not marry her, though she were endowed with all that Adam had left him before he transgressed: she would have made Hercules   195
have turned spit, yea, and have cleft his club to make the fire too. Come, talk not of her: you shall find her the infernal Ate[30] in good apparel. I would to God some scholar would conjure her;[31] for certainly, while she is here, a man may live as quiet in hell as in a sanctuary; and people sin upon purpose, because they would go   200
thither; so, indeed, all disquiet, horror, and perturbation follows her.

DON PEDRO: Look, here she comes.

Re-enter CLAUDIO, BEATRICE, HERO, *and* LEONATO.

BENEDICK: Will your grace command me any service to the world's end? I will go on the slightest errand now to the Antipodes that you can devise to send me on; I will fetch you a toothpicker now   205
from the furthest inch of Asia; bring you the length of Prester John's[32] foot; fetch you a hair off the great Cham's[33] beard; do you any embassage to the Pigmies;[34] rather than hold three words' conference with this harpy. You have no employment for me?

---

[29] *terminations:* Terms, words.

[30] *Ate:* Greek goddess of mischief and destructive deeds.

[31] *scholar would conjure her:* Demons could only be exorcised in Latin; therefore, scholars were needed for exorcisms.

[32] *Prester John:* Legendary Christian king in Asia.

[33] *great Cham:* Khan of Tartary, ruler of the Mongols.

[34] *Pigmies:* Legendary tribe living in India.

DON PEDRO: None, but to desire your good company. 210

BENEDICK: O God, sir, here's a dish I love not: I cannot endure my
Lady Tongue. [*Exit.*]

DON PEDRO: Come, lady, come; you have lost the heart of Signior
Benedick.

BEATRICE: Indeed, my lord, he lent it me awhile; and I gave him use for 215
it, a double heart for his single one: marry, once before he won it of
me with false dice, therefore your Grace may well say I have lost it.

DON PEDRO: You have put him down, lady, you have put him down.

BEATRICE: So I would not he should do me, my lord, lest I should prove
the mother of fools. I have brought Count Claudio, whom you sent 220
me to seek.

DON PEDRO: Why, how now, count! wherefore are you sad?

CLAUDIO: Not sad, my lord.

DON PEDRO: How then? sick?

CLAUDIO: Neither, my lord. 225

BEATRICE: The count is neither sad, nor sick, nor merry, nor well;
but civil count, civil as an orange, and something of that jealous
complexion.

DON PEDRO: I'faith, lady, I think your blazon to be true; though, I'll be
sworn, if he be so, his conceit is false. Here, Claudio, I have wooed 230
in thy name, and fair Hero is won: I have broke with her father,
and his good will obtained: name the day of marriage, and God give
thee joy!

LEONATO: Count, take of me my daughter, and with her my fortunes:
his Grace hath made the match, and all grace say Amen to it. 235

BEATRICE: Speak, count, 'tis your cue.

CLAUDIO: Silence is the perfectest herald of joy: I were but little happy,
if I could say how much. Lady, as you are mine, I am yours: I give
away myself for you, and dote upon the exchange.

BEATRICE: Speak, cousin; or, if you cannot, stop his mouth with a kiss, 240
and let not him speak neither.

DON PEDRO: In faith, lady, you have a merry heart.

BEATRICE: Yea, my lord; I thank it, poor fool, it keeps on the windy
side of care. My cousin tells him in his ear that he is in her heart.

CLAUDIO: And so she doth, cousin. 245

BEATRICE: Good Lord, for alliance! Thus goes every one to the world but I, and I am sun-burnt;[35] I may sit in a corner, and cry heigh-ho for a husband!

DON PEDRO: Lady Beatrice, I will get you one.

BEATRICE: I would rather have one of your father's getting. Hath your Grace ne'er a brother like you? Your father got excellent husbands, if a maid could come by them. 250

DON PEDRO: Will you have me, lady?

BEATRICE: No, my lord, unless I might have another for working-days: your Grace is too costly to wear every day. But, I beseech your Grace, pardon me: I was born to speak all mirth and no matter. 255

DON PEDRO: Your silence most offends me, and to be merry best becomes you; for, out of question, you were born in a merry hour.

BEATRICE: No, sure, my lord, my mother cried; but then there was a star danced, and under that was I born. Cousins, God give you joy! 260

LEONATO: Niece, will you look to those things I told you of?

BEATRICE: I cry you mercy, uncle. By your Grace's pardon.   [*Exit.*]

DON PEDRO: By my troth, a pleasant-spirited lady.

LEONATO: There's little of the melancholy element in her, my lord: she is never sad but when she sleeps; and not ever sad then; for I have heard my daughter say, she hath often dreamed of unhappiness, and waked herself with laughing. 265

DON PEDRO: She cannot endure to hear tell of a husband.

LEONATO: O, by no means: she mocks all her wooers out of suit.

DON PEDRO: She were an excellent wife for Benedick. 270

LEONATO: O Lord, my lord, if they were but a week married, they would talk themselves mad.

DON PEDRO: County Claudio, when mean you to go to church?

CLAUDIO: To-morrow, my lord: time goes on crutches till love have all his rites. 275

LEONATO: Not till Monday, my dear son, which is hence a just seven-night; and a time too brief, too, to have all things answer my mind.[36]

DON PEDRO: Come, you shake the head at so long a breathing: but, I warrant thee, Claudio, the time shall not go dully by us. I will, in the interim, undertake one of Hercules' labours; which is, to bring Signior Benedick and the Lady Beatrice into a mountain of affection 280

---

[35] *sun-burnt:* Dark complexions were considered unattractive in the Renaissance.
[36] *answer my mind:* Suit my wishes.

the one with the other. I would fain have it a match; and I doubt not but to fashion it, if you three will but minister such assistance as I shall give you direction.

LEONATO: My lord, I am for you, though it cost me ten nights' watchings.   285

CLAUDIO: And I, my lord.

DON PEDRO: And you too, gentle Hero?

HERO: I will do any modest office, my lord, to help my cousin to a good husband.

DON PEDRO: And Benedick is not the unhopefullest husband that I   290
know. Thus far can I praise him; he is of a noble strain, of approved valour, and confirmed honesty. I will teach you how to humour your cousin, that she shall fall in love with Benedick; and I, with your two helps, will so practise on Benedick, that, in despite of his quick wit and his queasy stomach, he shall fall in love with   295
Beatrice. If we can do this, Cupid is no longer an archer: his glory shall be ours, for we are the only love-gods. Go in with me, and I will tell you my drift.   [*Exeunt.*]

SCENE II. *The same.*

Enter DON JOHN *and* BORACHIO.

DON JOHN: It is so; the Count Claudio shall marry the daughter of Leonato.

BORACHIO: Yea, my lord; but I can cross it.

DON JOHN: Any bar, any cross, any impediment will be medicinable to me: I am sick in displeasure to him; and whatsoever comes athwart   5
his affection ranges evenly with mine. How canst thou cross this marriage?

BORACHIO: Not honestly, my lord; but so covertly that no dishonesty shall appear in me.

DON JOHN: Show me briefly how.   10

BORACHIO: I think I told your lordship, a year since, how much I am in the favour of Margaret, the waiting gentlewoman to Hero.

DON JOHN: I remember.

BORACHIO: I can, at any unseasonable instant of the night, appoint her to look out at her lady's chamber window.   15

DON JOHN: What life is in that, to be the death of this marriage?

BORACHIO: The poison of that lies in you to temper. Go you to the prince your brother; spare not to tell him that he hath wronged his

honour in marrying the renowned Claudio—whose estimation do you
mightily hold up—to a contaminated stale,[37] such a one as Hero.   20

DON JOHN: What proof shall I make of that?

BORACHIO: Proof enough to misuse the prince, to vex Claudio, to undo
Hero, and kill Leonato. Look you for any other issue?

DON JOHN: Only to despite them I will endeavour any thing.

BORACHIO: Go, then; find me a meet hour to draw Don Pedro and the   25
Count Claudio alone: tell them that you know that Hero loves me;
intend[38] a kind of zeal both to the prince and Claudio, as,—in love
of your brother's honour, who hath made this match, and his friend's
reputation, who is thus like to be cozened with the semblance of a
maid,—that you have discovered thus. They will scarcely believe   30
this without trial: offer them instances; which shall bear no less
likelihood than to see me at her chamber-window; hear me call
Margaret, Hero; hear Margaret term me Claudio; and bring them to
see this the very night before the intended wedding,—for in the
meantime I will so fashion the matter that Hero shall be absent,—   35
and there shall appear such seeming truth of Hero's disloyalty, that
jealousy shall be called assurance and all the preparation overthrown.

DON JOHN: Grow this to what adverse issue it can, I will put it in practice.
Be cunning in the working this, and thy fee is a thousand ducats.

BORACHIO: Be you constant in the accusation, and my cunning shall   40
not shame me.

DON JOHN: I will presently go learn their day of marriage.   [*Exeunt.*]

SCENE III. LEONATO's *orchard.*

Enter BENEDICK.

BENEDICK: Boy!

Enter Boy.

BOY: Signior?

BENEDICK: In my chamber-window lies a book: bring it hither to me in
the orchard.

BOY: I am here already, sir.   5

BENEDICK: I know that; but I would have thee hence, and here again.
[*Exit* Boy.] I do much wonder that one man, seeing how much
another man is a fool when he dedicates his behaviours to love,

---

[37] *stale:* Prostitute.
[38] *intend:* Pretend.

will, after he hath laughed at such shallow follies in others, become
the argument of his own scorn by falling in love: and such a man is   10
Claudio. I have known when there was no music with him but the
drum and the fife; and now had he rather hear the tabor and the
pipe: I have known when he would have walked ten mile a-foot to
see a good armour; and now will he lie ten nights awake, carving
the fashion of a new doublet. He was wont to speak plain and to   15
the purpose, like an honest man and a soldier; and now is he turned
orthography;[39] his words are a very fantastical banquet,—just so
many strange dishes. May I be so converted, and see with these
eyes? I cannot tell; I think not: I will not be sworn but love may
transform me to an oyster; but I'll take my oath on it, till he have   20
made an oyster of me, he shall never make me such a fool. One
woman is fair, yet I am well; another is wise, yet I am well; another
virtuous, yet I am well: but till all graces be in one woman, one
woman shall not come in my grace. Rich she shall be, that's certain;
wise, or I'll none; virtuous, or I'll never cheapen her; fair, or I'll   25
never look on her; mild, or come not near me; noble, or not I for an
angel; of good discourse, an excellent musician, and her hair shall be
of what colour it please God. Ha! the prince and Monsieur Love! I
will hide me in the arbour.   [*Withdraws.*]

Enter DON PEDRO, CLAUDIO, *and* LEONATO.

DON PEDRO: Come, shall we hear this music?   30

CLAUDIO: Yea, my good lord. How still the evening is,
    As hush'd on purpose to grace harmony!

DON PEDRO: See you where Benedick hath hid himself?

CLAUDIO: O, very well, my lord: the music ended,
    We'll fit the kid-fox with a pennyworth.   35

Enter BALTHASAR *with Music.*

DON PEDRO: Come, Balthasar, we'll hear that song again.

BALTHASAR: O, good my lord, tax not so bad a voice
    To slander music any more than once.

DON PEDRO: It is the witness still of excellency
    To put a strange face on his own perfection.   40
    I pray thee, sing, and let me woo no more.

BALTHASAR: Because you talk of wooing, I will sing;
    Since many a wooer doth commence his suit

---

[39] *turned orthography:* Turned fashionable in his language.

To her he thinks not worthy, yet he wooes,
Yet will he swear he loves.

DON PEDRO: Nay, pray thee, come;   45
Or, if thou wilt hold longer argument,
Do it in notes.

BALTHASAR: Note this before my notes;
There's not a note of mine that's worth the noting.

DON PEDRO: Why, these are very crotchets[40] that he speaks;
Note, notes, forsooth, and nothing.   [Air.]   50

BENEDICK: Now, divine air! now is his soul ravished! Is it not strange
that sheeps' guts should hale souls out of men's bodies? Well, a horn
for my money, when all's done.

BALTHASAR: The Song.

Sigh no more, ladies, sigh no more,
        Men were deceivers ever,   55
One foot in sea and one on shore,
        To one thing constant never:

Then sigh not so, but let them go,
        And be you blithe and bonny,
Converting all your sounds of woe   60
        Into Hey nonny, nonny.

Sing no more ditties, sing no moe,
        Of dumps so dull and heavy;
The fraud of men was ever so,
        Since summer first was leavy: 65
        Then sigh not so, &c.

DON PEDRO: By my troth, a good song.

BALTHASAR: And an ill singer, my lord.

DON PEDRO: Ha, no, no, faith; thou singest well enough for a shift.

BENEDICK: An he had been a dog that should have howled thus, they   70
would have hanged him: and I pray God his bad voice bode no
mischief. I had as lief have heard the night-raven, come what
plague could have come after it.

DON PEDRO: Yea, marry, dost thou hear, Balthasar? I pray thee, get us
some excellent music; for to-morrow night we would have it at the   75
Lady Hero's chamber-window.

BALTHASAR: The best I can, my lord.

---

[40] *crotchets:* Whims or peculiar fancies; also, a quarter note in music.

DON PEDRO: Do so: farewell. [*Exit* BALTHASAR.] Come hither, Leonato. What was it you told me of to-day, that your niece Beatrice was in love with Signior Benedick? 80

CLAUDIO: O, ay: stalk on, stalk on; the fowl sits. I did never think that lady would have loved any man.

LEONATO: No, nor I neither; but most wonderful that she should so dote on Signior Benedick, whom she hath in all outward behaviours seemed ever to abhor. 85

BENEDICK: Is't possible? Sits the wind in that corner?

LEONATO: By my troth, my lord, I cannot tell what to think of it, but that she loves him with an enraged affection; it is past the infinite of thought.

DON PEDRO: May be she doth but counterfeit. 90

CLAUDIO: Faith, like enough.

LEONATO: O God, counterfeit! There was never counterfeit of passion came so near the life of passion as she discovers it.

DON PEDRO: Why, what effects of passion shows she?

CLAUDIO: Bait the hook well; this fish will bite. 95

LEONATO: What effects, my lord? She will sit you, you heard my daughter tell you how.

CLAUDIO: She did, indeed.

DON PEDRO: How, how, I pray you? You amaze me: I would have thought her spirit had been invincible against all assaults of affection. 100

LEONATO: I would have sworn it had, my lord; especially against Benedick.

BENEDICK: I should think this a gull,[41] but that the white-bearded fellow speaks it: knavery cannot, sure, hide himself in such reverence.

CLAUDIO: He 'hath ta'en the infection: hold it up. 105

DON PEDRO: Hath she made her affection known to Benedick?

LEONATO: No; and swears she never will: that's her torment.

CLAUDIO: 'Tis true, indeed; so your daughter says: "Shall I," says she, "that have so oft encountered him with scorn, write to him that I love him?" 110

LEONATO: This says she now when she is beginning to write to him; for she'll be up twenty times a night; and there will she sit in her smock till she have writ a sheet of paper: my daughter tells us all.

---

[41] *gull:* Trick

CLAUDIO: Now you talk of a sheet of paper, I remember a pretty jest
your daughter told us of. 115

LEONATO: O, when she had writ it, and was reading it over, she found
Benedick and Beatrice between the sheet?

CLAUDIO: That.

LEONATO: O, she tore the letter into a thousand halfpence; railed at
herself, that she should be so immodest to write to one that she knew 120
would flout her; "I measure him," says she, "by my own spirit; for I
should flout him; if he writ to me; yea, though I love him, I should."

CLAUDIO: Then down upon her knees she falls, weeps, sobs, beats her
heart, tears her hair, prays, curses; "O sweet Benedick! God give me
patience!" 125

LEONATO: She doth indeed; my daughter says so: and the ecstasy hath
so much overborne her, that my daughter is sometime afeard she
will do a desperate outrage to herself: it is very true.

DON PEDRO: It were good that Benedick knew of it by some other, if
she will not discover it. 130

CLAUDIO: To what end? He would make but a sport of it, and torment
the poor lady worse.

DON PEDRO: An he should, it were an alms to hang him. She's an
excellent sweet lady; and, out of all suspicion, she is virtuous.

CLAUDIO: And she is exceeding wise. 135

DON PEDRO: In every thing but in loving Benedick.

LEONATO: O, my lord, wisdom and blood combating in so tender a
body, we have ten proofs to one that blood hath the victory. I am
sorry for her, as I have just cause, being her uncle and guardian.

DON PEDRO: I would she had bestowed this dotage on me: I would have 140
daffed[42] all other respects, and made her half myself. I pray you, tell
Benedick of it, and hear what a' will say.

LEONATO: Were it good, think you?

CLAUDIO: Hero thinks surely she will die; for she says she will die, if he
love her not; and she will die, ere she make her love known; and 145
she will die, if he woo her, rather than she will bate one breath of
her accustomed crossness.

DON PEDRO: She doth well: if she should make tender[43] of her love, 'tis
very possible he'll scorn it; for the man, as you know all, hath a
contemptible spirit. 150

---

[42] *daffed:* Doffed, put aside.
[43] *make tender:* Make an offer.

CLAUDIO: He is a very proper man.

DON PEDRO: He hath indeed a good outward happiness.

CLAUDIO: Before God! and in my mind, very wise.

DON PEDRO: He doth indeed show some sparks that are like wit.

CLAUDIO: And I take him to be valiant. 155

DON PEDRO: As Hector, I assure you: and in the managing of quarrels you may say he is wise; for either he avoids them with great discretion, or undertakes them with a most Christian-like fear.

LEONATO: If he do fear God, a' must necessarily keep peace: if he break the peace, he ought to enter into a quarrel with fear and trembling. 160

DON PEDRO: And so will he do; for the man doth fear God, howsoever it seems not in him by some large jests he will make. Well, I am sorry for your niece. Shall we go seek Benedick, and tell him of her love?

CLAUDIO: Never tell him, my lord: let her wear it out with good counsel.

LEONATO: Nay, that's impossible: she may wear her heart out first. 165

DON PEDRO: Well, we will hear further of it by your daughter: let it cool the while. I love Benedick well; and I could wish he would modestly examine himself, to see how much he is unworthy so good a lady.

LEONATO: My lord, will you walk? dinner is ready.

CLAUDIO: If he do not dote on her upon this, I will never trust my 170 expectation.

DON PEDRO: Let there be the same net spread for her; and that must your daughter and her gentlewomen carry. The sport will be, when they hold one an opinion of another's dotage, and no such matter: that's the scene that I would see, which will be merely a dumbshow. 175 Let us send her to call him in to dinner.

[*Exeunt* DON PEDRO, CLAUDIO, *and* LEONATO.]

BENEDICK: [*Coming forward*] This can be no trick: the conference was sadly borne. They have the truth of this from Hero. They seem to pity the lady: it seems her affections have their full bent. Love me! why, it must be requited. I hear how I am censured: they say I will 180 bear myself proudly, if I perceive the love come from her; they say too that she will rather die than give any sign of affection. I did never think to marry: I must not seem proud: happy are they that hear their detractions, and can put them to mending. They say the lady is fair,— 'tis a truth, I can bear them witness; and virtuous,—'tis so, I cannot 185 reprove it; and wise, but for loving me,—by my troth, it is no addition to her wit, nor no great argument of her folly, for I will be horribly in love with her. I may chance have some odd quirks and remnants of wit broken on me, because I have railed so long against marriage: but doth not the appetite alter? a man loves the meat in his youth that he cannot endure in his age. Shall quips and sentences and these paper bullets[44] of the brain awe a man from the career of his humour? No, the world must be peopled. When I said I would die a bachelor, I did not think I should live till I were married. Here comes Beatrice. By this day! she's a fair lady: I do spy some marks of love in her. 195

Enter BEATRICE.

BEATRICE: Against my will I am sent to bid you come in to dinner.

BENEDICK: Fair Beatrice, I thank you for your pains.

BEATRICE: I took no more pains for those thanks than you take pains to thank me: if it had been painful, I would not have come.

BENEDICK: You take pleasure, then, in the message? 200

BEATRICE: Yea, just so much as you may take upon a knife's point, and choke a daw[45] withal. You have no stomach, signior: fare you well.
[*Exit.*]

BENEDICK: Ha! "Against my will I am sent to bid you come in to dinner"; there's a double meaning in that. "I took no more pains for those thanks than you took pains to thank me"; that's as much as to say, 205 Any pains that I take for you is as easy as thanks. If I do not take pity of her, I am a villain; if I do not love her, I am a Jew. I will go get her picture. [*Exit.*]

ACT III.

SCENE I. LEONATO's *orchard.*

Enter HERO, MARGARET, *and* URSULA.

HERO: Good Margaret, run thee to the parlour;
There shalt thou find my cousin Beatrice
Proposing[46] with the prince and Claudio:
Whisper her ear, and tell her, I and Ursula
Walk in the orchard, and our whole discourse 5
Is all of her; say that thou overheard'st us;
And bid her steal into the pleached bower,
Where honeysuckles, ripen'd by the sun,
Forbid the sun to enter; like favourites,

---

[44] *paper bullets:* Verbal ammunition.
[45] *daw:* Jackdaw, a bird.
[46] *proposing:* Conversing.

Made proud by princes, that advance their pride   10
    Against that power that bred it: there will she hide her,
    To listen our propose. This is thy office;
    Bear thee well in it, and leave us alone.

MARGARET: I'll make her come, I warrant you, presently.   [*Exit.*]

HERO: Now, Ursula, when Beatrice doth come,   15
    As we do trace this alley up and down,
    Our talk must only be of Benedick.
    When I do name him, let it be thy part
    To praise him more than ever man did merit:
    My talk to thee must be, how Benedick   20
    Is sick in love with Beatrice. Of this matter
    Is little Cupid's crafty arrow made,
    That only wounds by hearsay.

Enter BEATRICE, *behind.*

                        Now begin;
    For look where Beatrice, like a lapwing, runs
    Close by the ground, to hear our conference.   25

URSULA: The pleasant'st angling is to see the fish
    Cut with her golden oars the silver stream
    And greedily devour the treacherous bait:
    So angle we for Beatrice; who even now
    Is couched in the woodbine coverture.   30
    Fear you not my part of the dialogue.

HERO: Then go we near her, that her ear lose nothing
    Of the false sweet bait that we lay for it.
                        [*Approaching the bower.*]
    No, truly, Ursula, she is too disdainful;
    I know her spirits are as coy and wild   35
    As haggerds[47] of the rock.

URSULA: But are you sure
    That Benedick loves Beatrice so entirely?

HERO: So says the prince and my new-trothed lord.

URSULA: And did they bid you tell her of it, madam?

HERO: They did entreat me to acquaint her of it;   40
    But I persuaded them, if they loved Benedick,
    To wish him wrestle with affection
    And never to let Beatrice know of it.

---

[47] *haggerds:* Untamed female hawks.

URSULA: Why did you so? Doth not the gentleman
Deserve as full as fortunate a bed   45
As ever Beatrice shall couch upon?

HERO: O god of love! I know he doth deserve
As much as may be yielded to a man:
But Nature never framed a woman's heart
Of prouder stuff than that of Beatrice;   50
Disdain and scorn ride sparkling in her eyes,
Misprising what they look on; and her wit
Values itself so highly, that to her
All matter else seems weak: she cannot love,
Nor take no shape nor project of affection,   55
She is so self-endeared.

URSULA: Sure, I think so;
And therefore certainly it were not good
She knew his love, lest she make sport at it.

HERO: Why, you speak truth. I never yet saw man,
How wise, how noble, young, how rarely featured,   60
But she would spell him backward: if fair-faced,
She would swear the gentleman should be her sister;
If black, why, Nature, drawing of an antique,
Made a foul blot; if tall, a lance ill-headed;
If low, an agate very vilely cut;   65
If speaking, why, a vane blown with all winds;
If silent, why, a block moved with none.
So turns she every man the wrong side out;
And never gives to truth and virtue that
Which simpleness and merit purchaseth.   70

URSULA: Sure, sure, such carping is not commendable.

HERO: No, not to be so odd, and from all fashions,
As Beatrice is, cannot be commendable:
But who dare tell her so? If I should speak,
She would mock into air; O, she would laugh me   75
Out of myself, press me to death with wit!
Therefore let Benedick, like cover'd fire,
Consume away in sighs, waste inwardly:
It were a better death than die with mocks,
Which is as bad as die with tickling.   80

URSULA: Yet tell her of it: hear what she will say.

HERO: No; rather I will go to Benedick,
And counsel him to fight against his passion.
And, truly, I'll devise some honest slanders

To stain my cousin with: one doth not know 85
How much an ill word may empoison liking.

URSULA: O, do not do your cousin such a wrong!
She cannot be so much without true judgement,—
Having so swift and excellent a wit
As she is prized to have,—as to refuse 90
So rare a gentleman as Signior Benedick.

HERO: He is the only man of Italy,
Always excepted my dear Claudio.

URSULA: I pray you, be not angry with me, madam,
Speaking my fancy: Signior Benedick, 95
For shape, for bearing, argument and valour,
Goes foremost in report through Italy.

HERO: Indeed, he hath an excellent good name.

URSULA: His excellence did earn it, ere he had it.
When are you married, madam? 100

HERO: Why, every day, to-morrow. Come, go in:
I'll show thee some attires; and have thy counsel
Which is the best to furnish me to-morrow.

URSULA: She's limed,48 I warrant you: we have caught her, madam.

HERO: If it prove so, then loving goes by haps: 105
Some Cupid kills with arrows, some with traps.
[Exeunt HERO and URSULA.]

BEATRICE: [Coming forward] What fire is in mine ears? Can this be true?
Stand I condemn'd for pride and scorn so much?
Contempt, farewell! and maiden pride, adieu!
No glory lives behind the back of such. 110
And, Benedick, love on; I will requite thee,
Taming my wild heart to thy loving hand:
If thou dost love, my kindness shall incite thee
To bind our loves up in a holy band;
For others say thou dost deserve, and I 115
Believe it better than reportingly. [Exit.]

SCENE II. *A room in* LEONATO's *house.*

Enter DON PEDRO, CLAUDIO, BENEDICK, *and* LEONATO.

DON PEDRO: I do but stay till your marriage be consummate, and then
go I toward Arragon.

CLAUDIO: I'll bring you thither, my lord, if you'll vouchsafe me.

---

48 *limed:* Birds were ensnared with birdlime, a sticky substance.

DON PEDRO: Nay, that would be as great a soil in the new gloss of your marriage, as to show a child his new coat and forbid him to wear it. I will only be bold with Benedick for his company; for, from the crown of his head to the sole of his foot, he is all mirth: he hath twice or thrice cut Cupid's bow-string, and the little hangman dare not shoot at him; he hath a heart as sound as a bell, and his tongue is the clapper, for what his heart thinks his tongue speaks.

BENEDICK: Gallants, I am not as I have been.

LEONATO: So say I: methinks you are sadder.

CLAUDIO: I hope he be in love.

DON PEDRO: Hang him, truant! there's no true drop of blood in him, to be truly touched with love; if he be sad, he wants money.

BENEDICK: I have the toothache.

DON PEDRO: Draw it.

BENEDICK: Hang it!

CLAUDIO: You must hang it first, and draw it afterwards.[49]

DON PEDRO: What! sigh for the toothache?

LEONATO: Where is but a humour or a worm.

BENEDICK: Well, every one can master a grief but he that has it.

CLAUDIO: Yet say I, he is in love.

DON PEDRO: There is no appearance of fancy in him, unless it be a fancy that he hath to strange disguises; as, to be a Dutchman to-day, a Frenchman to-morrow; or in the shape of two countries at once, as, a German from the waist downward, all slops,[50] and a Spaniard from the hip upward, no doublet. Unless he have a fancy to this foolery, as it appears he hath, he is no fool for fancy, as you would have it appear he is.

CLAUDIO: If he be not in love with some woman, there is no believing old signs: a' brushes his hat o' mornings; what should that bode?

DON PEDRO: Hath any man seen him at the barber's?

CLAUDIO: No, but the barber's man hath been seen with him; and the old ornament of his cheek hath already stuffed tennis-balls.

LEONATO: Indeed, he looks younger than he did, by the loss of a beard.

DON PEDRO: Nay, a' rubs himself with civet:[51] can you smell him out by that?

---

[49] *hang it first, and draw it afterward:* Claudio puns on drawing (extracting), alluding to the practice of executing traitors by hanging, drawing, and quartering them.

[50] *slops:* Loose breeches.

[51] *civet:* Perfume from the civet cat.

CLAUDIO: That's as much as to say, the sweet youth's in love.

DON PEDRO: The greatest note of it is his melancholy.   40

CLAUDIO: And when was he wont to wash his face?

DON PEDRO: Yea, or to paint himself? for the which, I hear what they say of him.

CLAUDIO: Nay, but his jesting spirit; which is now crept into a lute-string, and now governed by stops.[52]   45

DON PEDRO: Indeed, that tells a heavy tale for him: conclude, conclude he is in love.

CLAUDIO: Nay, but I know who loves him.

DON PEDRO: That would I know too: I warrant, one that knows him not.

CLAUDIO: Yes, and his ill conditions; and, in despite of all, dies for him.   50

DON PEDRO: She shall be buried with her face upwards.

BENEDICK: Yet is this no charm for the toothache. Old signior, walk aside with me: I have studied eight or nine wise words to speak to you, which these hobby-horses must not hear.

[Exeunt BENEDICK *and* LEONATO.]

DON PEDRO: For my life, to break with him about Beatrice.   55

CLAUDIO: 'Tis even so. Hero and Margaret have by this played their parts with Beatrice; and then the two bears will not bite one another when they meet.

Enter DON JOHN.

DON JOHN: My lord and brother, God save you!

DON PEDRO: Good den,[53] brother.   60

DON JOHN: If your leisure served, I would speak with you.

DON PEDRO: In private?

DON JOHN: If it please you: yet Count Claudio may hear; for what I would speak of concerns him.

DON PEDRO: What's the matter?   65

DON JOHN: [*To* CLAUDIO] Means your lordship to be married to-morrow?

DON PEDRO: You know he does.

DON JOHN: I know not that, when he knows what I know.

CLAUDIO: If there be any impediment, I pray you discover it.

---

[52] *stops:* Frets on the lute's fingerboard.
[53] *Good den:* Good evening.

DON JOHN: You may think I love you not: let that appear hereafter, and   70
aim better at me by that I now will manifest. For my brother, I think
he holds you well, and in dearness of heart hath holp to effect your
ensuing marriage,—surely suit ill spent and labour ill bestowed.

DON PEDRO: Why, what's the matter?

DON JOHN: I came hither to tell you; and, circumstances shortened, for   75
she has been too long a talking of, the lady is disloyal.

CLAUDIO: Who, Hero?

DON JOHN: Even she; Leonato's Hero, your Hero, every man's Hero.

CLAUDIO: Disloyal?

DON JOHN: The word is too good to paint out her wickedness; I could   80
say she were worse: think you of a worse title, and I will fit her to
it. Wonder not till further warrant: go but with me to-night, you
shall see her chamber-window entered, even the night before her
wedding-day: if you love her then, to-morrow wed her; but it would
better fit your honour to change your mind.   85

CLAUDIO: May this be so?

DON PEDRO: I will not think it.

DON JOHN: If you dare not trust that you see, confess not that you know:
if you will follow me, I will show you enough; and when you have
seen more, and heard more, proceed accordingly.   90

CLAUDIO: If I see any thing to-night why I should not marry her
to-morrow, in the congregation, where I should wed, there will I
shame her.

DON PEDRO: And, as I wooed for thee to obtain her, I will join with
thee to disgrace her.   95

DON JOHN: I will disparage her no farther till you are my witnesses:
bear it coldly but till midnight, and let the issue show itself.

DON PEDRO: O day untowardly turned!

CLAUDIO: O mischief strangely thwarting!

DON JOHN: O plague right well prevented! so will you say when you   100
have seen the sequel.   [*Exeunt.*]

SCENE III. *A street.*

Enter DOGBERRY *and* VERGES *with the* Watch.

DOGBERRY: Are you good men and true?

VERGES: Yea, or else it were pity but they should suffer salvation, body
and soul.

DOGBERRY: Nay, that were a punishment too good for them, if they should have any allegiance in them, being chosen for the prince's watch. 5

VERGES: Well, give them their charge, neighbor Dogberry.

DOGBERRY: First, who think you the most desartless man to be constable?

FIRST WATCH: Hugh Otecake, sir, or George Seacole; for they can write and read.

DOGBERRY: Come hither, neighbour Seacole. God hath blessed you with 10 a good name: to be a well-favoured man is the gift of fortune; but to write and read comes by nature.

SECOND WATCH: Both which, master constable,—

DOGBERRY: You have: I knew it would be your answer. Well, for your favour, sir, why, give God thanks, and make no boast of it; and for 15 your writing and reading, let that appear when there is no need of such vanity. You are thought here to be the most senseless and fit man for the constable of the watch; therefore bear you the lantern. This is your charge: you shall comprehend all vagrom men; you are to bid any man stand, in the prince's name. 20

SECOND WATCH: How if a' will not stand?

DOGBERRY: Why, then, take no note of him, but let him go; and presently call the rest of the watch together, and thank God you are rid of a knave.

VERGES: If he will not stand when he is bidden, he is none of the prince's 25 subjects.

DOGBERRY: True, and they are to meddle with none but the prince's subjects. You shall also make no noise in the streets; for for the watch to babble and to talk is most tolerable and not to be endured.

WATCH: We will rather sleep than talk: we know what belongs to a watch. 30

DOGBERRY: Why, you speak like an ancient and most quiet watchman; for I cannot see how sleeping should offend: only, have a care that your bills[54] be not stolen. Well, you are to call at all the ale-houses, and bid those that are drunk get them to bed.

WATCH: How if they will not? 35

DOGBERRY: Why, then, let them alone till they are sober: if they make you not then the better answer, you may say they are not the men you took them for.

WATCH: Well, sir.

---

[54] *bills:* Axes or blades attached to long poles.

DOGBERRY: If you meet a thief, you may suspect him, by virtue of your   40
    office, to be no true man; and, for such kind of men, the less you
    meddle or make with them, why, the more is for your honesty.

WATCH: If we know him to be a thief, shall we not lay hands on him?

DOGBERRY: Truly, by your office, you may; but I think they that touch
    pitch will be defiled: the most peaceable way for you, if you do take   45
    a thief, is to let him show himself what he is, and steal out of your
    company.

VERGES: You have been always called a merciful man, partner.

DOGBERRY: Truly, I would not hang a dog by my will, much more a man
    who hath any honesty in him.   50

VERGES: If you hear a child cry in the night, you must call to the nurse
    and bid her still it.

WATCH: How if the nurse be asleep and will not hear us?

DOGBERRY: Why, then, depart in peace, and let the child wake her with
    crying; for the ewe that will not hear her lamb when it baes will   55
    never answer a calf when he bleats.

VERGES: 'Tis very true.

DOGBERRY: This is the end of the charge:—you, constable, are to
    present the prince's own person: if you meet the prince in the night,
    you may stay him.   60

VERGES: Nay, by'r lady, that I think a' cannot.

DOGBERRY: Five shillings to one on't, with any man that knows the
    statues, he may stay him: marry, not without the prince be willing;
    for, indeed, the watch ought to offend no man; and it is an offence
    to stay a man against his will.   65

VERGES: By'r lady, I think it be so.

DOGBERRY: Ha, ah, ha! Well, masters, good night: an there be any
    matter of weight chances, call up me: keep your fellows' counsels
    and your own; and good night. Come, neighbour.

WATCH: Well, masters, we hear our charge: let us go sit here upon the   70
    church-bench till two, and then all to bed.

DOGBERRY: One word more, honest neighbours. I pray you, watch about
    Signior Leonato's door; for the wedding being there to-morrow, there
    is a great coil[55] to-night. Adieu: be vigitant, I beseech you.
                            [*Exeunt* DOGBERRY *and* VERGES.]

---

[55] *coil:* To-do, a lot of activity or fuss.

Enter BORACHIO *and* CONRADE.

BORACHIO: What, Conrade! 75

WATCH: [*Aside*] Peace! stir not.

BORACHIO: Conrade, I say!

CONRADE: Here, man; I am at thy elbow.

BORACHIO: Mass, and my elbow itched; I thought there would a scab
follow. 80

CONRADE: I will owe thee an answer for that: and now forward with
thy tale.

BORACHIO: Stand thee close, then, under this pent-house, for it drizzles
rain; and I will, like a true drunkard, utter all to thee.

WATCH: [*Aside*] Some treason, masters: yet stand close. 85

BORACHIO: Therefore know I have earned of Don John a thousand
ducats.

CONRADE: Is it possible that any villany should be so dear?

BORACHIO: Thou shouldst rather ask, if it were possible any villany
should be so rich; for when rich villains have need of poor ones, 90
poor ones may make what price they will.

CONRADE: I wonder at it.

BORACHIO: That shows thou art unconfirmed. Thou knowest that the
fashion of a doublet, or a hat, or a cloak, is nothing to a man.

CONRADE: Yes, it is apparel. 95

BORACHIO: I mean, the fashion.

CONRADE: Yes, the fashion is the fashion.

BORACHIO: Tush! I may as well say the fool's the fool. But seest thou
not what a deformed thief this fashion is?

WATCH: [*Aside*] I know that Deformed; a' has been a vile thief this seven 100
year; a' goes up and down like a gentleman: I remember his name.

BORACHIO: Didst thou not hear somebody?

CONRADE: No; 'twas the vane on the house.

BORACHIO: Seest thou not, I say, what a deformed thief this fashion is?
how giddily a' turns about all the hot bloods between fourteen and 105
five-and-thirty? sometimes fashioning them like Pharaoh's soldiers
in the reechy[56] painting, sometime like god Bel's priests[57] in the old

---

[56] *reechy:* Smoky; dirty.
[57] *god Bel's priests:* Referring to the story of Bel (Baal) and the Dragon, from the Apocrypha.

church-window, sometime like the shaven Hercules in the smirched worm-eaten tapestry, where his codpiece seems as massy as his club?

CONRADE: All this I see; and I see that the fashion wears out more apparel 110 than the man. But art not thou thyself giddy with the fashion too, that thou hast shifted out of thy tale into telling me of the fashion?

BORACHIO: Not so, neither: but know that I have to-night wooed Margaret, the Lady Hero's gentlewoman, by the name of Hero: she leans me out at her mistress' chamber-window, bids me a thousand 115 times good night,—I tell this tale vilely:—I should first tell thee how the prince, Claudio and my master, planted and placed and possessed by my master Don John, saw afar off in the orchard this amiable encounter.

CONRADE: And thought they Margaret was Hero? 120

BORACHIO: Two of them did, the prince and Claudio; but the devil my master knew she was Margaret; and partly by his oaths, which first possessed them, partly by the dark night, which did deceive them, but chiefly by my villany, which did confirm any slander that Don John had made, away went Claudio enraged; swore he would meet 125 her, as he was appointed, next morning at the temple, and there, before the whole congregation, shame her with what he saw o'er night, and send her home again without a husband.

FIRST WATCH: We charge you, in the prince's name, stand!

SECOND WATCH: Call up the right master constable. We have here 130 recovered the most dangerous piece of lechery that ever was known in the commonwealth.

FIRST WATCH: And one Deformed is one of them: I know him; a' wears a lock.[58]

CONRADE: Masters, masters,— 135

SECOND WATCH: You'll be made bring Deformed forth, I warrant you.

CONRADE: Masters,—

FIRST WATCH: Never speak: we charge you let us obey you to go with us.

BORACHIO: We are like to prove a goodly commodity, being taken up of these men's bills. 140

CONRADE: A commodity in question, I warrant you. Come, we'll obey you. [*Exeunt.*]

---

[58] *lock:* Lovelock—a lock of hair worn over the left shoulder by courtiers in Elizabethan times.

SCENE IV. HERO's *apartment.*

Enter HERO, MARGARET, *and* URSULA.

HERO: Good Ursula, wake my cousin Beatrice, and desire her to rise.

URSULA: I will, lady.

HERO: And bid her come hither.

URSULA: Well.   [*Exit.*]

MARGARET: Troth, I think your other rabato[59] were better.   5

HERO: No, pray thee, good Meg, I'll wear this.

MARGARET: By my troth's not so good; and I warrant your cousin will say so.

HERO: My cousin's a fool, and thou are another: I'll wear none but this.

MARGARET: I like the new tire[60] within excellently, if the hair were a   10
thought browner; and your gown's a most rare fashion, i'faith. I saw
the Duchess of Milan's gown that they praise so.

HERO: O, that exceeds, they say.

MARGARET: By my troth's but a night-gown in respect of yours,—cloth
o' gold, and cuts, and laced with silver, set with pearls, down sleeves,   15
side sleeves, and skirts, round underborne with a bluish tinsel: but
for a fine, quaint, graceful and excellent fashion, yours is worth ten
on't.

HERO: God give me joy to wear it! for my heart is exceeding heavy.

MARGARET: 'Twill be heavier soon by the weight of a man.   20

HERO: Fie upon thee! art not ashamed?

MARGARET: Of what, lady? of speaking honourably? Is not marriage
honourable in a beggar? Is not your lord honourable without marriage? I think you would have me say, "saving your reverence, a
husband": an bad thinking do not wrest true speaking, I'll offend   25
nobody: is there any harm in "the heavier for a husband"? None, I
think, an it be the right husband and the right wife; otherwise 'tis
light, and not heavy: ask my Lady Beatrice else; here she comes.

Enter BEATRICE.

HERO: Good morrow, coz.

BEATRICE: Good morrow, sweet Hero.   30

HERO: Why, how now? do you speak in the sick tune?

---

[59] *rabato:* Stiff collar, often supporting a ruff.
[60] *tire:* Headdress.

BEATRICE: I am out of all other tune, methinks.

MARGARET: Clap's into "Light o'love;" that goes without a burden: do you sing it, and I'll dance it.

BEATRICE: Ye light o' love, with your heels! then, if your husband have stables enough, you'll see he shall lack no barns. 35

MARGARET: O illegitimate construction! I scorn that with my heels.

BEATRICE: 'Tis almost five o'clock, cousin; 'tis time you were ready. By my troth, I am exceeding ill: heigh-ho!

MARGARET: For a hawk, a horse, or a husband? 40

BEATRICE: For the letter that begins them all, H.

MARGARET: Well, an you be not turned Turk,[61] there's no more sailing by the star.[62]

BEATRICE: What means the fool, trow?

MARGARET: Nothing I; but God send every one their heart's desire! 45

HERO: These gloves the count sent me; they are an excellent perfume.

BEATRICE: I am stuffed, cousin; I cannot smell.

MARGARET: A maid, and stuffed! there's goodly catching of cold.

BEATRICE: O, God help me! God help me! how long have you professed apprehension? 50

MARGARET: Ever since you left it. Doth not my wit become me rarely?

BEATRICE: It is not seen enough, you should wear it in your cap. By my troth, I am sick.

MARGARET: Get you some of this distilled Carduus Benedictus, and lay it to your heart: it is the only thing for a qualm. 55

HERO: There thou prickest her with a thistle.

BEATRICE: Benedictus! why Benedictus? you have some moral in this Benedictus.

MARGARET: Moral! no, by my troth, I have no moral meaning: I meant, plain holy-thistle. You may think perchance that I think you are in 60
love: nay, by'r lady, I am not such a fool to think what I list; nor I
list not to think what I can; nor, indeed, I cannot think, if I would
think my heart out of thinking, that you are in love, or that you will
be in love, or that you can be in love. Yet Benedick was such another,
and now is he become a man: he swore he would never marry; and 65

---

[61] *turned Turk:* Renounced your faith; i.e., renounced your pledge not to marry.
[62] *star:* The North star.

yet now, in despite of his heart, he eats his meat without grudging:
and how you may be converted, I know not; but methinks you look
with your eyes as other women do.

BEATRICE: What pace is this that thy tongue keeps?

MARGARET: Not a false gallop.   70

Re-enter URSULA.

URSULA: Madam, withdraw: the prince, the count, Signior Benedick,
Don John, and all the gallants of the town, are come to fetch you
to church.

HERO: Help me to dress, good coz, good Meg, good Ursula.   [*Exeunt*]

SCENE V. *Another room in* LEONATO*'s house.*

Enter LEONATO, *with* DOGBERRY *and* VERGES.

LEONATO: What would you with me, honest neighbour?

DOGBERRY: Marry, sir, I would have some confidence with you that
decerns you nearly.

LEONATO: Brief, I pray you; for you see it is a busy time with me.

DOGBERRY: Marry, this it is, sir.   5

VERGES: Yes, in truth it is, sir.

LEONATO: What is it, my good friends?

DOGBERRY: Goodman Verges, sir, speaks a little off the matter: an old
man, sir, and his wits are not so blunt as, God help, I would desire
they were; but, in faith, honest as the skin between his brows.   10

VERGES: Yes, I thank God I am as honest as any man living that is an
old man and no honester than I.

DOGBERRY: Comparisons are odorous: palabras,[63] neighbour Verges.

LEONATO: Neighbours, you are tedious.

DOGBERRY: It pleases your worship to say so, but we are the poor duke's   15
officers; but truly, for mine own part, if I were as tedious as a king, I
could find in my heart to bestow it all of your worship.

LEONATO: All thy tediousness on me, ah?

DOGBERRY: Yea, an 'twere a thousand pound more than 'tis; for I hear
as good exclamation on your worship as of any man in the city; and   20
though I be but a poor man, I am glad to hear it.

---

[63] *palabras:* From the Spanish *pocas palabras,* "few words."

VERGES: And so am I.

LEONATO: I would fain know what you have to say.

VERGES: Marry, sir, our watch to-night, excepting your worship's presence, ha' ta'en a couple of as arrant knaves as any in Messina. 25

DOGBERRY: A good old man, sir; he will be talking: as they say, When the age is in, the wit is out: God help us! it is a world to see. Well said, i' faith, neighbour Verges: well, God's a good man; an two men ride of a horse, one must ride behind. An honest soul, i'faith, sir; by my troth he is, as ever broke bread; but God is to be worshipped; all men 30 are not alike; alas, good neighbour!

LEONATO: Indeed, neighbour, he comes too short of you.

DOGBERRY: Gifts that God gives.

LEONATO: I must leave you.

DOGBERRY: One word, sir: our watch, sir, have indeed comprehended 35 two aspicious persons, and we would have them this morning examined before your worship.

LEONATO: Take their examination yourself, and bring it me: I am now in great haste, as it may appear unto you.

DOGBERRY: It shall be suffigance. 40

LEONATO: Drink some wine ere you go: fare you well.

Enter a MESSENGER.

MESSENGER: My lord, they stay for you to give your daughter to her husband.

LEONATO: I'll wait upon them: I am ready.

[Exeunt LEONATO *and* MESSENGER.]

DOGBERRY: Go, good partner, go, get you to Francis Seacole; bid him 45 bring his pen and inkhorn to the gaol: we are now to examination these men.

VERGES: And we must do it wisely.

DOGBERRY: We will spare for no wit, I warrant you; here's that shall drive some of them to a noncome:[64] only get the learned writer to set down 50 our excommunication, and meet me at the gaol. *[Exeunt.]*

---

[64] *noncome:* Abbreviation of the Latin *non compos mentis,* "not of sound mind," but Dogberry seems to be implying nonplus, "a state of perplexity."

ACT IV.

SCENE I. A *church.*

Enter DON PEDRO, DON JOHN, LEONATO, FRIAR FRANCIS, CLAUDIO, BENEDICK, HERO, BEATRICE, *and* Attendants.

LEONATO: Come, Friar Francis, be brief; only to the plain form of
marriage, and you shall recount their particular duties afterwards.

FRIAR: You come hither, my lord, to marry this lady.

CLAUDIO: No.

LEONATO: To be married to her: friar, you come to marry her.   5

FRIAR: Lady, you come hither to be married to this count.

HERO: I do.

FRIAR: If either of you know any inward impediment why you should
not be conjoined, I charge you, on your souls, to utter it.

CLAUDIO: Know you any, Hero?   10

HERO: None, my lord.

FRIAR: Know you any, count?

LEONATO: I dare make his answer, none.

CLAUDIO: O, what men dare do! what men may do! what men daily do,
not knowing what they do!   15

BENEDICK: How now! interjections? Why, then, some be of laughing,
as, ah, ha, he!

CLAUDIO: Stand thee by, friar. Father, by your leave:
Will you with free and unconstrained soul
Give me this maid, your daughter?   20

LEONATO: As freely, son, as God did give her me.

CLAUDIO: And what have I to give you back, whose worth
May counterpoise this rich and precious gift?

DON PEDRO: Nothing, unless you render her again.

CLAUDIO: Sweet prince, you learn me noble thankfulness.   25
There, Leonato, take her back again:
Give not this rotten orange to your friend;
She's but the sign and semblance of her honour.
Behold how like a maid she blushes here!
O, what authority and show of truth   30
Can cunning sin cover itself withal!
Comes not that blood as modest evidence
To witness simple virtue? Would you not swear,
All that you see her, that she were a maid,

By these exterior shows? But she is none: 35
She knows the heat of a luxurious bed;
Her blush is guiltiness, not modesty.

LEONATO: What do you mean, my lord?

CLAUDIO: Not to be married,
Not to knit my soul to an approved wanton.

LEONATO: Dear my lord, if you, in your own proof,   40
Have vanquish'd the resistance of her youth,
And made defeat of her virginity,—

CLAUDIO: I know what you would say: if I have known her,
You will say she did embrace me as a husband,
And so extenuate the 'forehand sin: 45
No, Leonato,
I never tempted her with word too large;
But, as a brother to his sister, show'd
Bashful sincerity and comely love.

HERO: And seem'd I ever otherwise to you?   50

CLAUDIO: Out on thee! Seeming! I will write against it:
You seem to me as Dian in her orb,[65]
As chaste as is the bud ere it be blown;
But you are more intemperate in your blood
Than Venus, or those pamper'd animals   55
That rage in savage sensuality.

HERO: Is my lord well, that he doth speak so wide?

LEONATO: Sweet prince, why speak not you?

DON PEDRO: What should I speak?
I stand dishonour'd, that have gone about
To link my dear friend to a common stale.   60

LEONATO: Are these things spoken, or do I but dream?

DON JOHN: Sir, they are spoken, and these things are true.

BENEDICK: This looks not like a nuptial.

HERO: True! O God!

CLAUDIO: Leonato, stand I here?
Is this the prince? is this the prince's brother?   65
Is this face Hero's? are our eyes our own?

LEONATO: All this is so: but what of this, my lord?

---

[65] *Dian in her orb:* Diana, the goddess of the moon, was also the goddess of chastity.

CLAUDIO: Let me but move one question to your daughter;
    And, by that fatherly and kindly power
    That you have in her, bid her answer truly.   70

LEONATO: I charge thee do so, as thou art my child.

HERO: O, God defend me! how am I beset!
    What kind of catechising call you this?

CLAUDIO: To make you answer truly to your name.

HERO: Is it not Hero? Who can blot that name   75
    With any just reproach?

CLAUDIO: Marry, that can Hero;
    Hero itself can blot out Hero's virtue.
    What man was he talk'd with you yesternight
    Out at your window betwixt twelve and one?
    Now, if you are a maid, answer to this.   80

HERO: I talk'd with no man at that hour, my lord.

DON PEDRO: Why, then are you no maiden. Leonato,
    I am sorry you must hear: upon mine honour,
    Myself, my brother, and this grieved count
    Did see her, hear her, at that hour last night   85
    Talk with a ruffian at her chamber-window;
    Who hath indeed, most like a liberal villain,
    Confess'd the vile encounters they have had
    A thousand times in secret.

DON JOHN: Fie, fie! they are not to be named, my lord,   90
    Not to be spoke of;
    There is not chastity enough in language,
    Without offence to utter them. Thus, pretty lady,
    I am sorry for thy much misgovernment.

CLAUDIO: O Hero, what a Hero hadst thou been,   95
    If half thy outward graces had been placed
    About thy thoughts and counsels of thy heart!
    But fare thee well, most foul, most fair! farewell,
    Thou pure impiety and impious purity!
    For thee I'll lock up all the gates of love,   100
    And on my eyelids shall conjecture hang,
    To turn all beauty into thoughts of harm,
    And never shall it more be gracious.

LEONATO: Hath no man's dagger here a point for me?   [HERO *swoons.*]

BEATRICE: Why, how now, cousin! wherefore sink you down?   105

DON JOHN: Come, let us go. These things, come thus to light,
    Smother her spirits up.
                [*Exeunt* DON PEDRO, DON JOHN, *and* CLAUDIO.]

BENEDICK: How doth the lady?

BEATRICE: Dead, I think. Help, uncle!
Hero! why, Hero! Uncle! Signior Benedick! Friar!

LEONATO: O Fate! take not away thy heavy hand.   110
Death is the fairest cover for her shame
That may be wish'd for.

BEATRICE: How now, cousin Hero!

FRIAR: Have comfort, lady.

LEONATO: Dost thou look up?

FRIAR: Yea, wherefore should she not?   115

LEONATO: Wherefore! Why, doth not every earthly thing
Cry shame upon her? Could she here deny
The story that is printed in her blood?
Do not live, Hero; do not ope thine eyes:
For, did I think thou wouldst not quickly die,   120
Thought I thy spirits were stronger than thy shames,
Myself would, on the rearward of reproaches,
Strike at thy life. Grieved I, I had but one?
Chid I for that a frugal nature's frame?
O, one too much by thee! Why had I one?   125
Why ever wast thou lovely in my eyes?
Why had I not with charitable hand
Took up a beggar's issue at my gates,
Who smirched thus and mired with infamy,
I might have said, "No part of it is mine;   130
This shame derives itself from unknown loins"?
But mine, and mine I loved, and mine I praised,
And mine that I was proud on, mine so much
That I myself was to myself not mine,
Valuing of her,—why, she, O, she is fallen   135
Into a pit of ink, that the wide sea
Hath drops too few to wash her clean again,
And salt too little which may season give
To her foul-tainted flesh!

BENEDICK: Sir, sir, be patient.
For my part, I am so attired in wonder,   140
I know not what to say.

BEATRICE: O, on my soul, my cousin is belied!

BENEDICK: Lady, were you her bedfellow last night?

BEATRICE: No, truly, not; although, until last night,
I have this twelvemonth been her bedfellow.   145

LEONATO: Confirm'd, confirm'd! O, that is stronger made
    Which was before barr'd up with ribs of iron!
    Would the two princes lie, and Claudio lie,
    Who loved her so, that, speaking of her foulness,
    Wash'd it with tears? Hence from her! let her die.   150

FRIAR: Hear me a little;
    For I have only been silent so long,
    And given way unto this course of fortune,
    By noting of the lady: I have mark'd
    A thousand blushing apparitions   155
    To start into her face; a thousand innocent shames
    In angel whiteness beat away those blushes;
    And in her eye there hath appear'd a fire,
    To burn the errors that these princes hold
    Against her maiden truth. Call me a fool;   160
    Trust not my reading nor my observations,
    Which with experimental seal doth warrant
    The tenour of my book; trust not my age,
    My reverence, calling, nor divinity,
    If this sweet lady lie not guiltless here   165
    Under some biting error.

LEONATO: Friar, it cannot be.
    Thou seest that all the grace that she hath left
    Is that she will not add to her damnation
    A sin of perjury; she not denies it:
    Why seek'st thou, then, to cover with excuse   170
    That which appears in proper nakedness?

FRIAR: Lady, what man is he you are accused of?

HERO: They know that do accuse me; I know none:
    If I know more of any man alive
    Than that which maiden modesty doth warrant,   175
    Let all my sins lack mercy! O my father,
    Prove you that any man with me conversed
    At hours unmeet, or that I yesternight
    Maintain'd the change of words with any creature,
    Refuse me, hate me, torture me to death!   180

FRIAR: There is some strange misprision[66] in the princes.

BENEDICK: Two of them have the very bent of honour;
    And if their wisdoms be misled in this,
    The practice of it lives in John the bastard,
    Whose spirits toil in frame of villanies.   185

---

[66] *misprision:* Misunderstanding or mistake.

LEONATO: I know not. If they speak but truth of her,
  These hands shall tear her; if they wrong her honour,
  The proudest of them shall well hear of it.
  Time hath not yet so dried this blood of mine,
  Nor age so eat up my invention,   190
  Nor fortune made such havoc of my means,
  Nor my bad life reft me so much of friends,
  But they shall find, awaked in such a kind,
  Both strength of limb and policy of mind,
  Ability in means and choice of friends,   195
  To quit me of them thoroughly.

FRIAR: Pause awhile,
  And let my counsel sway you in this case.
  Your daughter here the princes left for dead:
  Let her awhile be secretly kept in,
  And publish it that she is dead indeed;   200
  Maintain a mourning ostentation,
  And on your family's old monument
  Hang mournful epitaphs, and do all rites
  That appertain unto a burial.

LEONATO: What shall become of this? what will this do?   205

FRIAR: Marry, this, well carried, shall on her behalf
  Change slander to remorse; that is some good:
  But not for that dream I on this strange course,
  But on this travail look for greater birth.
  She dying, as it must be so maintain'd,   210
  Upon the instant that she was accused,
  Shall be lamented, pitied, and excused
  Of every hearer: for it so falls out,
  That what we have we prize not to the worth
  Whiles we enjoy it; but being lack'd and lost,   215
  Why, then we rack the value, then we find
  The virtue that possession would not show us
  Whiles it was ours. So will it fare with Claudio:
  When he shall hear she died upon his words,
  The idea of her life shall sweetly creep   220
  Into his study of imagination;
  And every lovely organ of her life
  Shall come apparell'd in more precious habit,
  More moving-delicate and full of life,
  Into the eye and prospect of his soul,   225
  Than when she lived indeed; then shall he mourn,
  If ever love had interest in his liver,
  And wish he had not so accused her,

No, though he thought his accusation true.
Let this be so, and doubt not but success   230
Will fashion the event in better shape
Than I can lay it down in likelihood.
But if all aim but this be levell'd false,
The supposition of the lady's death
Will quench the wonder of her infamy: 235
And if it sort not well, you may conceal her,
As best befits her wounded reputation,
In some reclusive and religious life,
Out of all eyes, tongues, minds, and injuries.

BENEDICK: Signior Leonato, let the friar advise you: 240
And though you know my inwardness and love
Is very much unto the prince and Claudio,
Yet, by mine honour, I will deal in this
As secretly and justly as your soul
Should with your body.

LEONATO: Being that I flow in grief,   245
The smallest twine may lead me.

FRIAR: 'Tis well consented: presently away;
For to strange sores strangely they strain the cure.
Come, lady, die to live: this wedding-day
Perhaps is but prolong'd: have patience and endure.   250
            [*Exeunt all but* BENEDICK *and* BEATRICE.]

BENEDICK: Lady Beatrice, have you wept all this while?

BEATRICE: Yea, and I will weep a while longer.

BENEDICK: I will not desire that.

BEATRICE: You have no reason; I do it freely.

BENEDICK: Surely I do believe your fair cousin is wronged.   255

BEATRICE: Ah, how much might the man deserve of me that would
    right her!

BENEDICK: Is there any way to show such friendship?

BEATRICE: A very even way, but no such friend.

BENEDICK: May a man do it?   260

BEATRICE: It is a man's office, but not yours.

BENEDICK: I do love nothing in the world so well as you: is not that
    strange?

BEATRICE: As strange as the thing I know not. It were as possible for
    me to say I loved nothing so well as you: but believe me not; and   265

yet I lie not; I confess nothing, nor I deny nothing. I am sorry for my cousin.

BENEDICK: By my sword, Beatrice, thou lovest me.

BEATRICE: Do not swear, and eat it.

BENEDICK: I will swear by it that you love me; and I will make him eat   270
it that says I love not you.

BEATRICE: Will you not eat your word?

BENEDICK: With no sauce that can be devised to it. I protest I love thee.

BEATRICE: Why, then, God forgive me!

BENEDICK: What offence, sweet Beatrice?   275

BEATRICE: You have stayed me in a happy hour: I was about to protest I
loved you.

BENEDICK: And do it with all thy heart.

BEATRICE: I love you with so much of my heart, that none is left to
protest.   280

BENEDICK: Come, bid me do any thing for thee.

BEATRICE: Kill Claudio.

BENEDICK: Ha! not for the wide world.

BEATRICE: You kill me to deny it. Farewell.

BENEDICK: Tarry, sweet Beatrice.   285

BEATRICE: I am gone, though I am here: there is no love in you: nay, I
pray you, let me go.

BENEDICK: Beatrice,—

BEATRICE: In faith, I will go.

BENEDICK: We'll be friends first.   290

BEATRICE: You dare easier be friends with me than fight with mine
enemy.

BENEDICK: Is Claudio thine enemy?

BEATRICE: Is he not approved in the height a villain, that hath slandered,
scorned, dishonoured my kinswoman? O that I were a man! What,   295
bear her in hand until they come to take hands; and then, with public
accusation, uncovered slander, unmitigated rancour,—O God, that
I were a man! I would eat his heart in the market-place.

BENEDICK: Hear me, Beatrice,—

BEATRICE: Talk with a man out at a window! A proper saying!   300

BENEDICK: Nay, but, Beatrice,—

BEATRICE: Sweet Hero! She is wronged, she is slandered, she is undone.

BENEDICK: Beat—

BEATRICE: Princes and counties! Sure, a princely testimony, a goodly count, Count Comfect;[67] a sweet gallant, surely! O that I were a man for his sake! or that I had any friend would be a man for my sake! But manhood is melted into courtesies, valour into compliment, and men are only turned into tongue, and trim ones too: he is now as valiant as Hercules that only tells a lie, and swears it. I cannot be a man without wishing, therefore I will die a woman with grieving.

BENEDICK: Tarry, good Beatrice. By this hand, I love thee.

BEATRICE: Use it for my love some other way than swearing by it.

BENEDICK: Think you in your soul the Count Claudio hath wronged Hero?

BEATRICE: Yea, as sure as I have a thought or a soul.

BENEDICK: Enough, I am engaged; I will challenge him. I will kiss your hand, and so I leave you. By this hand, Claudio shall render me a dear account. As you hear of me, so think of me. Go, comfort your cousin: I must say she is dead: and so, farewell. [*Exeunt.*]

SCENE II. *A prison.*

Enter DOGBERRY, VERGES, *and* SEXTON, *in gowns; and the* Watch, *with* CONRADE *and* BORACHIO.

DOGBERRY: Is our whole dissembly appeared?

VERGES: O, a stool and a cushion for the sexton.

SEXTON: Which be the malefactors?

DOGBERRY: Marry, that am I and my partner.

VERGES: Nay, that's certain; we have the exhibition to examine.

SEXTON: But which are the offenders that are to be examined? let them come before master constable.

DOGBERRY: Yea, marry, let them come before me. What is your name, friend?

BORACHIO: Borachio.

DOGBERRY: Pray, write down, Borachio. Yours, sirrah?

CONRADE: I am a gentleman, sir, and my name is Conrade.

DOGBERRY: Write down, master gentleman Conrade. Masters, do you serve God?

---

[67] *Comfect:* Comfect, or comfit, is a candy or sweetmeat.

CONRADE:
BORACHIO: } Yea, sir, we hope.   15

DOGBERRY: Write down, that they hope they serve God: and write God
first; for God defend but God should go before such villains! Masters,
it is proved already that you are little better than false knaves; and it
will go near to be thought so shortly. How answer you for yourselves?

CONRADE: Marry, sir, we say we are none.   20

DOGBERRY: A marvellous witty fellow, I assure you; but I will go about
with him. Come you hither, sirrah; a word in your ear: sir, I say to
you, it is thought you are false knaves.

BORACHIO: Sir, I say to you we are none.

DOGBERRY: Well, stand aside. 'Fore God, they are both in a tale. Have   25
you writ down, that they are none?

SEXTON: Master constable, you go not the way to examine: you must
call forth the watch that are their accusers.

DOGBERRY: Yea, marry, that's the eftest[68] way. Let the watch come forth.
Masters, I charge you, in the prince's name, accuse these men.   30

FIRST WATCH: This man said, sir, that Don John, the prince's brother,
was a villain.

DOGBERRY: Write down, Prince John a villain. Why, this is flat perjury,
to call the prince's brother villain.

BORACHIO: Master constable,—   35

DOGBERRY: Pray thee, fellow, peace: I do not like thy look, I promise thee.

SEXTON: What heard you him say else?

SECOND WATCH: Marry, that he had received a thousand ducats of Don
John for accusing the Lady Hero wrongfully.

DOGBERRY: Flat burglary as ever was committed.   40

VERGES: Yea, by mass, that it is.

SEXTON: What else, fellow?

FIRST WATCH: And that Count Claudio did mean, upon his words, to
disgrace Hero before the whole assembly, and not marry her.

DOGBERRY: O villain! thou wilt be condemned into everlasting redemp-   45
tion for this.

SEXTON: What else?

WATCH: This is all.

---

[68] *eftest*: Dogberry is probably mangling *deftest* or *easiest*.

SEXTON: And this is more, masters, than you can deny. Prince John is
this morning secretly stolen away; Hero was in this manner accused, 50
in this very manner refused, and upon the grief of this suddenly died.
Master constable, let these men be bound, and brought to Leonato's:
I will go before and show him their examination. [*Exit.*]

DOGBERRY: Come, let them be opinioned.

VERGES: Let them be in the hands— 55

CONRADE: Off, coxcomb!

DOGBERRY: God's my life, where's the sexton? let him write down, the
prince's officer, coxcomb. Come, bind them. Thou naughty varlet!

CONRADE: Away! you are an ass, you are an ass.

DOGBERRY: Dost thou not suspect my place? dost thou not suspect my 60
years? O that he were here to write me down an ass! But, masters,
remember that I am an ass; though it be not written down, yet forget not that I am an ass. No, thou villain, thou art full of piety, as
shall be proved upon thee by good witness. I am a wise fellow; and,
which is more, an officer; and, which is more, a householder; and, 65
which is more, as pretty a piece of flesh as any is in Messina; and
one that know the law, go to; and a rich fellow enough, go to; and
a fellow that hath had losses; and one that hath two gowns, and
every thing handsome about him. Bring him away. O that I had
been writ down an ass! [*Exeunt.*] 70

ACT V.

SCENE I. *Before* LEONATO's *house.*

Enter LEONATO *and* ANTONIO.

ANTONIO: If you go on thus, you will kill yourself;
And 'tis not wisdom thus to second grief
Against yourself.

LEONATO: I pray thee, cease thy counsel,
Which falls into mine ears as profitless
As water in a sieve: give me not counsel; 5
Nor let no comforter delight mine ear
But such a one whose wrongs do suit with mine.
Bring me a father that so loved his child,
Whose joy of her is overwhelm'd like mine,
And bid him speak of patience; 10
Measure his woe the length and breadth of mine,
And let it answer every strain for strain,
As thus for thus, and such a grief for such,
In every lineament, branch, shape, and form:

If such a one will smile, and stroke his beard, 15
Bid sorrow wag, cry "hem!" when he should groan,
Patch grief with proverbs, make misfortune drunk
With candle-wasters; bring him yet to me,
And I of him will gather patience.
But there is no such man: for, brother, men 20
Can counsel and speak comfort to that grief
Which they themselves not feel; but, tasting it,
Their counsel turns to passion, which before
Would give preceptial medicine to rage,
Fetter strong madness in a silken thread, 25
Charm ache with air, and agony with words:
No, no; 'tis all men's office to speak patience
To those that wring under the load of sorrow,
But no man's virtue nor sufficiency,
To be so moral when he shall endure 30
The like himself. Therefore give me no counsel:
My griefs cry louder than advertisement.

ANTONIO: Therein do men from children nothing differ.

LEONATO: I pray thee, peace. I will be flesh and blood;
For there was never yet philosopher 35
That could endure the toothache patiently,
However they have writ the style of gods,
And made a push at chance and sufferance.

ANTONIO: Yet bend not all the harm upon yourself;
Make those that do offend you suffer too. 40

LEONATO: There thou speak'st reason: nay, I will do so.
My soul doth tell me Hero is belied;
And that shall Claudio know; so shall the prince,
And all of them that thus dishonour her.

ANTONIO: Here comes the prince and Claudio hastily. 45

Enter DON PEDRO *and* CLAUDIO.

DON PEDRO: Good den, good den.

CLAUDIO: Good day to both of you.

LEONATO: Hear you, my lords,—

DON PEDRO: We have some haste, Leonato.

LEONATO: Some haste, my lord! well, fare you well, my lord:
Are you so hasty now? well, all is one.

DON PEDRO: Nay, do not quarrel with us, good old man. 50

ANTONIO: If he could right himself with quarrelling,
Some of us would lie low.

CLAUDIO: Who wrongs him?

LEONATO: Marry, thou dost wrong me, thou dissembler, thou:—
Nay, never lay thy hand upon thy sword;
I fear thee not.

CLAUDIO: Marry, beshrew my hand,   55
If it should give your age such cause of fear:
In faith, my hand meant nothing to my sword.

LEONATO: Tush, tush, man; never fleer[69] and jest at me:
I speak not like a dotard nor a fool,
As, under privilege of age, to brag   60
What I have done being young, or what would do,
Were I not old. Know, Claudio, to thy head,
Thou hast so wrong'd mine innocent child and me,
That I am forced to lay my reverence by,
And, with grey hairs and bruise of many days,   65
Do challenge thee to trial of a man.
I say thou hast belied mine innocent child;
Thy slander hath gone through and through her heart,
And she lies buried with her ancestors;
O, in a tomb where never scandal slept,   70
Save this of hers, framed by thy villany!

CLAUDIO: My villany?

LEONATO: Thine, Claudio; thine, I say.

DON PEDRO: You say not right, old man.

LEONATO: My lord, my lord,
I'll prove it on his body, if he dare,
Despite his nice fence and his active practice,   75
His May of youth and bloom of lustihood.

CLAUDIO: Away! I will not have to do with you.

LEONATO: Canst thou so daff me? Thou hast kill'd my child:
If thou kill'st me, boy, thou shalt kill a man.

ANTONIO: He shall kill two of us, and men indeed: 80
But that's no matter; let him kill one first;
Win me and wear me; let him answer me.
Come, follow me, boy; come, sir boy, come, follow me:
Sir boy, I'll whip you from your foining[70] fence;
Nay, as I am a gentleman, I will.   85

---

[69] *fleer:* Jeer, ridicule.
[70] *foining:* Thrusting.

LEONATO: Brother,—

ANTONIO: Content yourself. God knows I loved my niece;
    And she is dead, slander'd to death by villains,
    That dare as well answer a man indeed
    As I dare take a serpent by the tongue: 90
    Boys, apes, braggarts, Jacks, milksops!

LEONATO: Brother Antony,—

ANTONIO: Hold you content. What, man! I know them, yea,
    And what they weigh, even to the utmost scruple,—
    Scambling, out-facing, fashion-monging boys,
    That lie, and cog, and flout, deprave, and slander,   95
    Go antiquely,[71] and show outward hideousness,
    And speak off half a dozen dangerous words,
    How they might hurt their enemies, if they durst;
    And this is all.

LEONATO: But, brother Antony,—

ANTONIO: Come, 'tis no matter: 100
    Do not you meddle; let me deal in this.

DON PEDRO: Gentlemen both, we will not wake your patience.
    My heart is sorry for your daughter's death:
    But, on my honour, she was charged with nothing
    But what was true, and very full of proof.   105

LEONATO: My lord, my lord,—

DON PEDRO: I will not hear you.

LEONATO: No? Come, brother; away! I will be heard.

ANTONIO: And shall, or some of us will smart for it.

                        [Exeunt LEONATO *and* ANTONIO.]

DON PEDRO: See, see; here comes the man we went to seek.   110

Enter BENEDICK.

CLAUDIO: Now, signior, what news?

BENEDICK: Good day, my lord.

DON PEDRO: Welcome, signior: you are almost come to part almost a
    fray.

CLAUDIO: We had like to have had our two noses snapped off with two   115
    old men without teeth.

DON PEDRO: Leonato and his brother. What thinkest thou? Had we
    fought, I doubt we should have been too young for them.

---

[71] *antiquely:* Antically, or fantastically dressed.

BENEDICK: In a false quarrel there is no true valour. I came to seek you both. 120

CLAUDIO: We have been up and down to seek thee; for we are high-proof melancholy, and would fain have it beaten away. Wilt thou use thy wit?

BENEDICK: It is in my scabbard: shall I draw it?

DON PEDRO: Dost thou wear thy wit by thy side? 125

CLAUDIO: Never any did so, though very many have been beside their wit. I will bid thee draw, as we do the minstrels; draw, to pleasure us.

DON PEDRO: As I am an honest man, he looks pale. Art thou sick, or angry?

CLAUDIO: What, courage, man! What though care killed a cat, thou 130 hast mettle enough in thee to kill care.

BENEDICK: Sir, I shall meet your wit in the career, an you charge it against me. I pray you choose another subject.

CLAUDIO: Nay, then, give him another staff: this last was broke cross.

DON PEDRO: By this light, he changes more and more: I think he be 135 angry indeed.

CLAUDIO: If he be, he knows how to turn his girdle.[72]

BENEDICK: Shall I speak a word in your ear?

CLAUDIO: God bless me from a challenge!

BENEDICK: [*Aside to* CLAUDIO] You are a villain; I jest not: I will make it 140 good how you dare, with what you dare, and when you dare. Do me right, or I will protest your cowardice. You have killed a sweet lady, and her death shall fall heavy on you. Let me hear from you.

CLAUDIO: Well, I will meet you, so I may have good cheer.

DON PEDRO: What, a feast, a feast? 145

CLAUDIO: I'faith, I thank him; he hath bid me to a calf's-head and a capon; the which if I do not carve most curiously, say my knife's naught. Shall I not find a woodcock too?

BENEDICK: Sir, your wit ambles well; it goes easily.

DON PEDRO: I'll tell thee how Beatrice praised thy wit the other day. I 150 said, thou hadst a fine wit: "True," said she, "a fine little one." "No," said I, "a great wit": "Right," says she, "a great gross one." "Nay," said I, "a good wit": "Just," said she, "it hurts nobody." "Nay," said I, "the gentleman is wise": "Certain," said she, "a wise gentleman." "Nay," said I, "he hath the tongues": "That I believe," said she, "for he swore 155

---

[72] *turn his girdle:* Change his own mood.

a thing to me on Monday night, which he forswore on Tuesday morning; there's a double tongue; there's two tongues." Thus did she, an hour together, trans-shape thy particular virtues: yet at last she concluded with a sigh, thou wast the properest man in Italy.

CLAUDIO: For the which she wept heartily, and said she cared not.   160

DON PEDRO: Yea, that she did; but yet, for all that, an if she did not hate him deadly, she would love him dearly: the old man's daughter told us all.

CLAUDIO: All, all; and, moreover, God saw him when he was hid in the garden.   165

DON PEDRO: But when shall we set the savage bull's horns on the sensible Benedick's head?

CLAUDIO: Yea, and text underneath, "Here dwells Benedick the married man"?

BENEDICK: Fare you well, boy: you know my mind. I will leave you now   170
to your gossip-like humour: you break jests as braggarts do their blades, which, God be thanked, hurt not. My lord, for your many courtesies I thank you: I must discontinue your company: your brother the bastard is fled from Messina: you have among you killed a sweet and innocent lady. For my Lord Lackbeard there, he and I shall meet: 175
and till then peace be with him.   [Exit.]

DON PEDRO: He is in earnest.

CLAUDIO: In most profound earnest; and, I'll warrant you, for the love of Beatrice.

DON PEDRO: And hath challenged thee.   180

CLAUDIO: Most sincerely.

DON PEDRO: What a pretty thing man is when he goes in his doublet and hose, and leaves off his wit!

CLAUDIO: He is then a giant to an ape: but then is an ape a doctor to such a man.   185

DON PEDRO: But, soft you, let me be: pluck up, my heart, and be sad. Did he not say, my brother was fled?

Enter DOGBERRY, VERGES, *and the* Watch, *with* CONRADE *and* BORACHIO.

DOGBERRY: Come, you, sir: if justice cannot tame you, she shall ne'er weigh more reasons in her balance: nay, an you be a cursing hypocrite once, you must be looked to.   190

DON PEDRO: How now? two of my brother's men bound! Borachio one!

CLAUDIO: Hearken after their offence, my lord.

DON PEDRO: Officers, what offence have these men done?

DOGBERRY: Marry, sir, they have committed false report; moreover, they have spoken untruths; secondarily, they are slanders, sixth and lastly, they have belied a lady; thirdly, they have verified unjust things; and, to conclude, they are lying knaves.   195

DON PEDRO: First, I ask thee what they have done; thirdly, I ask thee what's their offence; sixth and lastly, why they are committed; and, to conclude, what you lay to their charge.   200

CLAUDIO: Rightly reasoned, and in his own division; and, by my troth, there's one meaning well suited.

DON PEDRO: Who have you offended, masters, that you are thus bound to your answer? this learned constable is too cunning to be understood: what's your offence?   205

BORACHIO: Sweet prince, let me go no farther to mine answer: do you hear me, and let this count kill me. I have deceived even your very eyes: what your wisdoms could not discover, these shallow fools have brought to light; who, in the night, overheard me confessing to this man, how Don John your brother incensed me to slander the Lady   210
Hero; how you were brought into the orchard, and saw me court Margaret in Hero's garments: how you disgraced her, when you should marry her: my villany they have upon record; which I had rather seal with my death than repeat over to my shame. The lady is dead upon mine and my master's false accusation; and, briefly, I desire   215
nothing but the reward of a villain.

DON PEDRO: Runs not this speech like iron through your blood?

CLAUDIO: I have drunk poison whiles he utter'd it.

DON PEDRO: But did my brother set thee on to this?

BORACHIO: Yea, and paid me richly for the practice of it.   220

DON PEDRO: He is composed and framed of treachery:
And fled he is upon this villany.

CLAUDIO: Sweet Hero! now thy image doth appear
In the rare semblance that I loved it first.

DOGBERRY: Come, bring away the plaintiffs: by this time our sexton hath   225
reformed Signior Leonato of the matter: and, masters, do not forget to specify, when time and place shall serve, that I am an ass.

VERGES: Here, here comes master Signior Leonato, and the sexton too.

Re-enter **LEONATO** *and* **ANTONIO,** *with the* Sexton.

LEONATO: Which is the villain? let me see his eyes,
That, when I note another man like him,   230
I may avoid him: which of these is he?

BORACHIO: If you would know your wronger, look on me.

LEONATO: Art thou the slave that with thy breath hast kill'd
Mine innocent child?

BORACHIO: Yea, even I alone.

LEONATO: No, not so, villain; thou beliest thyself: 235
Here stand a pair of honourable men;
A third is fled, that had a hand in it.
I thank you, princes, for my daughter's death:
Record it with your high and worthy deeds:
'Twas bravely done, if you bethink you of it.   240

CLAUDIO: I know not how to pray your patience;
Yet I must speak. Choose your revenge yourself;
Impose me to what penance your invention
Can lay upon my sin: yet sinn'd I not
But in mistaking.

DON PEDRO: By my soul, nor I: 245
And yet, to satisfy this good old man,
I would bend under any heavy weight
That he'll enjoin me to.

LEONATO: I cannot bid you bid my daughter live;
That were impossible: but, I pray you both,   250
Possess[73] the people in Messina here
How innocent she died; and if your love
Can labour aught in sad invention,
Hang her an epitaph upon her tomb,
And sing it to her bones, sing it to-night: 255
To-morrow morning come you to my house;
And since you could not be my son-in-law,
Be yet my nephew: my brother hath a daughter,
Almost the copy of my child that's dead,
And she alone is heir to both of us: 260
Give her the right you should have given her cousin,
And so dies my revenge.

CLAUDIO: O noble sir,
Your over-kindness doth wring tears from me!
I do embrace your offer; and dispose
For henceforth of poor Claudio.   265

LEONATO: To-morrow, then, I will expect your coming;
To-night I take my leave. This naughty man
Shall face to face be brought to Margaret,
Who I believe was pack'd in all this wrong,
Hired to it by your brother.

---

[73] *possess:* Inform.

BORACHIO: No, by my soul, she was not;   270
Nor knew not what she did when she spoke to me;
But always hath been just and virtuous
In any thing that I do know by her.

DOGBERRY: Moreover, sir, which indeed is not under white and black,
this plaintiff here, the offender, did call me ass: I beseech you, let it   275
be remembered in his punishment. And also, the watch heard them
talk of one Deformed: they say he wears a key in his ear, and a lock
hanging by it; and borrows money in God's name, the which he
hath used so long and never paid, that now men grow hard-hearted,
and will lend nothing for God's sake: pray you, examine him upon   280
that point.

LEONATO: I thank thee for thy care and honest pains.

DOGBERRY: Your worship speaks like a most thankful and reverend youth;
and I praise God for you.

LEONATO: There's for thy pains.   285

DOGBERRY: God save the foundation!

LEONATO: Go, I discharge thee of thy prisoner, and I thank thee.

DOGBERRY: I leave an arrant knave with your worship; which I beseech
your worship to correct yourself, for the example of others. God keep
your worship! I wish your worship well; God restore you to health!   290
I humbly give you leave to depart; and if a merry meeting may be
wished, God prohibit it! Come, neighbour.
                         [*Exeunt* DOGBERRY *and* VERGES.]

LEONATO: Until to-morrow morning, lords, farewell.

ANTONIO: Farewell, my lords: we look for you to-morrow.

DON PEDRO: We will not fail.

CLAUDIO: To-night I'll mourn with Hero.   295

LEONATO: [*To the* WATCH] Bring you these fellows on. We'll talk with
Margaret,
How her acquaintance grew with this lewd fellow.
                                [*Exeunt, severally.*]

SCENE II. LEONATO's *garden.*

Enter BENEDICK *and* MARGARET, *meeting.*

BENEDICK: Pray thee, sweet Mistress Margaret, deserve well at my hands
by helping me to the speech of Beatrice.

MARGARET: Will you, then, write me a sonnet in praise of my beauty?

BENEDICK: In so high a style, Margaret, that no man living shall come over it; for, in most comely truth, thou deservest it.   5

MARGARET: To have no man come over me! why, shall I always keep below stairs?

BENEDICK: Thy wit is as quick as the greyhound's mouth; it catches.

MARGARET: And yours as blunt as the fencer's foils, which hit, but hurt not.   10

BENEDICK: A most manly wit, Margaret; it will not hurt a woman: and so, I pray thee, call Beatrice: I give thee the bucklers.[74]

MARGARET: Give us the swords; we have bucklers of our own.

BENEDICK: If you use them, Margaret, you must put in the pikes with a vice; and they are dangerous weapons for maids.   15

MARGARET: Well, I will call Beatrice to you, who I think hath legs.

BENEDICK: And therefore will come.   [*Exit* MARGARET.]

[*Sings*]   The god of love,
                  That sits above,
                  And knows me, and knows me,   20
                     How pitiful I deserve,—

I mean in singing; but in loving, Leander the good swimmer,[75] Troilus the first employer of pandars,[76] and a whole bookful of these quondam carpet-mongers,[77] whose names yet run smoothly in the even road of a blank verse, why, they were never so truly turned   25 over and over as my poor self in love. Marry, I cannot show it in rhyme; I have tried: I can find out no rhyme to "lady" but "baby," an innocent rhyme; for "scorn," "horn," a hard rhyme; for "school," "fool," a babbling rhyme; very ominous endings: no, I was not born under a rhyming planet, nor I cannot woo in festival terms.   30

Enter BEATRICE.

Sweet Beatrice, wouldst thou come when I called thee?

BEATRICE: Yea, signior, and depart when you bid me.

BENEDICK: O, stay but till then!

BEATRICE: "Then" is spoken; fare you well now: and yet, ere I go, let me go with that I came; which is, with knowing what hath passed   35 between you and Claudio.

---

[74] *give thee the bucklers:* Bucklers are shields; Benedick is admitting defeat in the verbal joust.

[75] *Leander the good swimmer:* Leander swam nightly to see his love, Hero.

[76] *Troilus the first employer of pandars:* Troilus was united to his love, Cressida, through her uncle Pandarus.

[77] *quondam carpet-mongers:* Knights who avoided military service were called carpet knights.

BENEDICK: Only foul words; and thereupon I will kiss thee.

BEATRICE: Foul words is but foul wind, and foul wind is but foul breath, and foul breath is noisome; therefore I will depart unkissed.

BENEDICK: Thou has frighted the word out of his right sense, so forcible is thy wit. But I must tell thee plainly, Claudio undergoes my challenge; and either I must shortly hear from him, or I will subscribe him a coward. And, I pray thee now, tell me for which of my bad parts didst thou first fall in love with me?   40

BEATRICE: For them all together; which maintained so politic a state of evil, that they will not admit any good part to intermingle with them. But for which of my good parts did you first suffer love for me?   45

BENEDICK: Suffer love,—a good epithet! I do suffer love indeed, for I love thee against my will.

BEATRICE: In spite of your heart, I think; alas, poor heart! If you spite it for my sake, I will spite it for yours; for I will never love that which my friend hates.   50

BENEDICK: Thou and I are too wise to woo peaceably.

BEATRICE: It appears not in this confession: there's not one wise man among twenty that will praise himself.   55

BENEDICK: An old, an old instance, Beatrice, that lived in the time of good neighbours. If a man do not erect in this age his own tomb ere he dies, he shall live no longer in monument than the bell rings and the widow weeps.

BEATRICE: And how long is that, think you?   60

BENEDICK: Question: why, an hour in clamour, and a quarter in rheum:[78] therefore is it most expedient for the wise, if Don Worm,[79] his conscience, find no impediment to the contrary, to be the trumpet of his own virtues, as I am to myself. So much praising myself, who, I myself will bear witness, is praiseworthy: and now tell me, how doth   65 your cousin?

BEATRICE: Very ill.

BENEDICK: And how do you?

BEATRICE: Very ill too.

BENEDICK: Serve God, love me, and mend. There will I leave you too,   70 for here comes one in haste.

Enter **URSULA.**

---

[78] *rheum:* Tears (of a widow).

[79] *Don Worm:* A conscience was often described as a gnawing worm.

URSULA: Madam, you must come to your uncle. Yonder's old coil at
    home: it is proved my Lady Hero hath been falsely accused, the
    prince and Claudio are mightily abused; and Don John is the
    author of all, who is fled and gone. Will you come presently?   75

BEATRICE: Will you go hear this news, signior?

BENEDICK: I will live in thy heart, die in thy lap, and be buried in thy
    eyes; and moreover I will go with thee to thy uncle's.   [*Exeunt.*]

SCENE III. *A church.*

Enter DON PEDRO, CLAUDIO, *and three or four with tapers.*

CLAUDIO: Is this the monument of Leonato?

A LORD: It is, my lord.

CLAUDIO: [*Reading out of a scroll*]

> Done to death by slanderous tongues
>   Was the Hero that here lies:
> Death, in guerdon[80] of her wrongs,   5
>   Gives her fame which never dies.
> So the life that died with shame
> Lives in death with glorious fame.

> Hang thou there upon the tomb,
> Praising her when I am dumb.   10
> Now, music, sound, and sing your solemn hymn.

SONG.

> Pardon, goddess of the night,
> Those that slew thy virgin knight;
> For the which, with songs of woe,
> Round about her tomb they go.   15
>   Midnight, assist our moan;
>   Help us to sigh and groan,
>   Heavily, heavily:
>   Graves, yawn, and yield your dead,
>   Till death be uttered,   20
>   Heavily, heavily.

CLAUDIO: Now, unto thy bones good night!
    Yearly will I do this rite.

DON PEDRO: Good morrow, masters; put your torches out:
    The wolves have prey'd: and look, the gentle day,   25

---

[80] *guerdon:* Reward or recompense.

Before the wheels of Phœbus,[81] round about
     Dapples the drowsy east with spots of grey.
Thanks to you all, and leave us: fare you well.

CLAUDIO: Good morrow, masters: each his several way.

DON PEDRO: Come, let us hence, and put on other weeds;[82]   30
    And then to Leonato's we will go.

CLAUDIO: And Hymen now will luckier issue speed's
    Than this for whom we render'd up this woe.   [*Exeunt.*]

SCENE IV. A *room in* LEONATO'*s house.*

Enter LEONATO, ANTONIO, BENEDICK, BEATRICE, MARGARET, URSULA,
FRIAR FRANCIS, *and* HERO.

FRIAR: Did I not tell you she was innocent?

LEONATO: So are the prince and Claudio, who accused her
    Upon the error that you heard debated:
    But Margaret was in some fault for this,
    Although against her will, as it appears   5
    In the true course of all the question.

ANTONIO: Well, I am glad that all things sort so well.

BENEDICK: And so am I, being else by faith enforced
    To call young Claudio to a reckoning for it.

LEONATO: Well, daughter, and you gentlewomen all,   10
    Withdraw into a chamber by yourselves,
    And when I send for you, come hither mask'd.   [*Exeunt* Ladies.]
    The prince and Claudio promised by this hour
    To visit me. You know your office, brother:
    You must be father to your brother's daughter,   15
    And give her to young Claudio.

ANTONIO: Which I will do with confirm'd countenance.

BENEDICK: Friar, I must entreat your pains, I think.

FRIAR: To do what, signior?

BENEDICK: To bind me, or undo me; one of them.   20
    Signior Leonato, truth it is, good signior,
    Your niece regards me with an eye of favour.

LEONATO: That eye my daughter lent her: 'tis most true.

BENEDICK: And I do with an eye of love requite her.

---

[81] *wheels of Phœbus:* Chariot of the sun god.
[82] *weeds:* Clothes.

LEONATO: The sight whereof I think you had from me,   25
    From Claudio, and the prince: but what's your will?

BENEDICK: Your answer, sir, is enigmatical:
    But, for my will, my will is, your good will
    May stand with ours, this day to be conjoin'd
    In the state of honourable marriage: 30
    In which, good friar, I shall desire your help.

LEONATO: My heart is with your liking.

FRIAR: And my help.
    Here comes the prince and Claudio.

Enter DON PEDRO *and* CLAUDIO, *and two or three others.*

DON PEDRO: Good morrow to this fair assembly.

LEONATO: Good morrow, prince; good morrow, Claudio: 35
    We here attend you. Are you yet determined
    To-day to marry with my brother's daughter?

CLAUDIO: I'll hold my mind, were she an Ethiope.

LEONATO: Call her forth, brother; here's the friar ready.
                                 [*Exit* ANTONIO.]

DON PEDRO: Good morrow, Benedick. Why, what's the matter,   40
    That you have such a February face,
    So full of frost, of storm, and cloudiness?

CLAUDIO: I think he thinks upon the savage bull.
    Tush, fear not, man; we'll tip thy horns with gold,
    And all Europa shall rejoice at thee;   45
    As once Europa did at lusty Jove,[83]
    When he would play the noble beast in love.

BENEDICK: Bull Jove, sir, had an amiable low;
    And some such strange bull leap'd your father's cow,
    And got a calf in that same noble feat   50
    Much like to you, for you have just his bleat.

CLAUDIO: For this I owe you: here comes other reckonings.

Enter ANTONIO, *with the* Ladies *masked.*

    Which is the lady I must seize upon?

ANTONIO: This same is she, and I do give you her.

CLAUDIO: Why, then she's mine. Sweet, let me see your face.   55

---

[83] *Europa . . . Jove:* Jove, in the form of a white bull, carried Europa, a Phoenician
princess, to Crete.

LEONATO: No, that you shall not, till you take her hand
Before this friar, and swear to marry her.

CLAUDIO: Give me your hand: before this holy friar,
I am your husband, if you like of me.

HERO: And when I lived, I was your other wife: *[Unmasking.]*   60
And when you loved, you were my other husband.

CLAUDIO: Another Hero!

HERO: Nothing certainer:
One Hero died defiled; but do I live,
And surely as I live, I am a maid.

DON PEDRO: The former Hero! Hero that is dead!   65

LEONATO: She died, my lord, but whiles her slander lived.

FRIAR: All this amazement can I qualify;
When after that the holy rites are ended,
I'll tell you largely of fair Hero's death:
Meantime let wonder seem familiar,   70
And to the chapel let us presently.

BENEDICK: Soft and fair, friar. Which is Beatrice?

BEATRICE: *[Unmasking]* I answer to that name. What is your will?

BENEDICK: Do not you love me?

BEATRICE: Why, no; no more than reason.

BENEDICK: Why, then your uncle, and the prince, and Claudio   75
Have been deceived; they swore you did.

BEATRICE: Do you not love me?

BENEDICK: Troth, no; no more than reason.

BEATRICE: Why, then my cousin, Margaret, and Ursula
Are much deceived; for they did swear you did.

BENEDICK: They swore that you were almost sick for me.   80

BEATRICE: They swore that you were well-nigh dead for me.

BENEDICK: 'Tis no such matter. Then you do not love me?

BEATRICE: No, truly, but in friendly recompence.

LEONATO: Come, cousin, I am sure you love the gentleman.

CLAUDIO: And I'll be sworn upon't that he loves her;   85
For here's a paper, written in his hand,
A halting sonnet of his own pure brain,
Fashion'd to Beatrice.

HERO: And here's another,
Writ in my cousin's hand, stolen from her pocket,
Containing her affection unto Benedick.   90

BENEDICK: A miracle! here's our own hands against our hearts. Come, I will have thee; but, by this light, I take thee for pity.

BEATRICE: I would not deny you; but, by this good day, I yield upon great persuasion; and partly to save your life, for I was told you were in a consumption.   95

BENEDICK: Peace! I will stop your mouth.   [*Kissing her.*]

DON PEDRO: How dost thou, Benedick, the married man?

BENEDICK: I'll tell thee what, prince; a college of wit-crackers cannot flout me out of my humour. Dost thou think I care for a satire or an epigram? No: if a man will be beaten with brains, a' shall wear   100
nothing handsome about him. In brief, since I do purpose to marry, I will think nothing to any purpose that the world can say against it; and therefore never flout at me for what I have said against it; for man is a giddy thing, and this is my conclusion. For thy part, Claudio, I did think to have beaten thee; but in that thou art like to be my   105
kinsman, live unbruised, and love my cousin.

CLAUDIO: I had well hoped thou wouldst have denied Beatrice, that I might have cudgelled thee out of thy single life, to make thee a double-dealer; which, out of question, thou wilt be, if my cousin do not look exceeding narrowly to thee.   110

BENEDICK: Come, come, we are friends: let's have a dance ere we are married, that we may lighten our own hearts, and our wives' heels.

LEONATO: We'll have dancing afterward.

BENEDICK: First, of my word; therefore play, music. Prince, thou art sad; get thee a wife, get thee a wife: there is no staff more reverend than   115
one tipped with horn.

Enter a MESSENGER.

MESSENGER: My lord, your brother John is ta'en in flight,
And brought with armed men back to Messina.

BENEDICK: Think not on him till to-morrow: I'll devise thee brave punishments for him. Strike up, pipers.   120

[*Dance.*]

[*Exeunt.*]

UNDERSTANDING THE PLAY

1. (I.i.) What qualities in a wife lead Claudio to choose Hero? What do these qualities reveal about him?

2. (I.iii.) (a) What motivates Don John to define himself as a villain (lines 8–13; 20–27)? (b) What motivates Don John to impede Claudio's marriage to Hero (lines 48–51)?

3. (II.i.) Consider the conversations about marriage between Beatrice and Leonato (lines 11–60) and between Beatrice and Don Pedro (lines 246–60). What do Beatrice's attitudes reveal about her? How might her attitudes affect those who love her?

4. (II.i.) Leonato tells Claudio, "Count, take of me my daughter, and with her my fortunes: his Grace hath made the match, and all grace say Amen to it" (lines 234–35). What keeps the play from concluding at this point with a happy ending? What is the significance of delaying the marriage ceremony for a week?

5. (II.ii.) Why do Borachio and Don John expect their ruse to succeed?

6. (II.iii.) (a) What are the qualities that Benedick will look for in a wife (lines 21–28)? What do these qualities reveal about him? (b) What does a comparison of Benedick's and Claudio's standards (I.i.) reveal about the difference between these two men?

7. (II.iii.) How do Don Pedro, Leonato, and Claudio contrive to catch Benedick on their hook (lines 78–176)? Why do their arguments appeal to him? What leads Benedick to believe what he overhears (lines 177–79)?

8. (III.i.) (a) How do Hero and Ursula contrive to catch Beatrice on their hook (lines 32–100)? Which of their arguments appeals to her and which disturbs her? What leads Beatrice to believe what she overhears (lines 107–16)? (b) How does this female plot to catch Beatrice differ from the male plot to catch Benedick? What does the difference reveal about women and men in this society?

9. (III.iii.) Why should Claudio and Don Pedro have questioned what they were seeing (lines 116–19)? What factors (lines 121–25) were crucial to the success of Don John's ruse?

10. (IV.i.) (a) What does Claudio expect to gain from his unexpected public denunciation of Hero (lines 25–37)? What is the significance of Claudio's tearful accusation of Hero (lines 98–99 and 149–50)? (b) Explain why Claudio should be blamed or pitied for his behavior.

11. (IV.i.) Why is Leonato so quick to accept Claudio's accusation of his daughter (line 104)? Why does he hope for her death (lines 110–12; 116–39)?

12. (IV.i.) Why does Margaret, who is surely among the wedding guests, remain silent during the accusation? What, if anything, does she have to lose by revealing what she knows?

13. (IV.i.) (a) Why does Beatrice first tell Benedick that he may not avenge Claudio's treatment of Hero (line 261)? Why does she change her mind? (b) What does the conversation between Beatrice and Benedick (lines 251–319) reveal about the man Beatrice would marry? (c) In what ways does Benedick's attitude toward Claudio prove his love for Beatrice (lines 316–19)?

14. (V.i) Why doesn't Claudio express either sorrow or regret about Hero's death (lines 72 and 77)?

15. (V.i.) What changes (lines 115–87) do Don Pedro and Claudio see in Benedick? To what extent, if any, do Benedick's friends take him seriously?

16. (V.i.) Why does Borachio confess to Don Pedro (lines 206–16)?

17. (V.i.) (V.ii.) (V.iv.) To what extent, if any, are Claudio and Don Pedro correct when they tell Leonato, "Yet sinn'd I not / But in mistaking" (V.i.244–45)? Why does Leonato support the idea of Don Pedro's and Claudio's innocence (V.iv.2–3)?

18. (V.i.) (V.iv.) Why does Leonato proceed to have Hero marry Claudio? Why doesn't Leonato solicit Hero's opinion in this matter?

19. (V.iv.) Why does the issue of the love between Benedick and Beatrice need to be resolved?

20. At the end of Act V, what does the audience expect will happen to the marriages of Claudio and Hero and of Benedick and Beatrice? Is all well that ends well? Explain the advantages and disadvantages that each couple will have.

21. In what ways is Dogberry similar to Beatrice and Benedick? What does Shakespeare accomplish by creating Dogberry in their mold?

22. What **themes** do you find in this play?

ANALYZING LITERARY TECHNIQUE

1. Examine the structure of the play:
   a) What does Shakespeare achieve by having characters allude to, but not explain, events that occurred before the play opens? Consider Conrade's **allusion** to Don John's relationship with Don Pedro (I.iii.14–19) as well as Beatrice's allusion to her relationship with Benedick (II.i.215–17).
   b) (III.v.) What does Dogberry's visit to Leonato contribute to the plot?
   c) (IV.i.) What is the dramatic function of Hero's apparent death?
   d) (IV.i.) What is the dramatic function of Beatrice's charge to Benedick about Claudio (line 282)?
   e) How does the Dogberry subplot relate to the plot? Explain two ways the subplot contributes to the play.

f) How does the Beatrice-Benedick subplot relate to the plot? Explain two ways in which it contributes to the play.

g) All three strands of the plot reach their **climax** in Act V. What events mark the climax for Hero and Claudio, for Benedick and Beatrice, and for Dogberry? What is the cumulative effect?

h) (V.iv.) Why does Shakespeare choose the last scene of the play for Benedick to express to Leonato the love that he and Beatrice have for each other and their desire to marry?

2. Examine Shakespeare's use of **tone** in this play.

a) To what extent is *Much Ado* a **comedy? A tragicomedy?**

b) Examine how comedy functions in this play. Give examples of high and low comedy from the play.

c) Give examples of **tragedy** from the play.

3. Find two examples of **foreshadowing** in the play and tell what each example predicts.

4. Examine Shakespeare's use of **verbal** and **situational irony** in *Much Ado*. Give two examples from the play of each type of irony.

5. How does illusion affect reality in the play? Give two examples from the play of characters deceiving themselves or others.

6. Analyze Shakespeare's use of **figurative language.** Find two **metaphors** or **similes** and explain what each contributes to the situation in which it is used.

7. Analyze Shakespeare's use of **oxymorons** in Claudio's speech to Hero. (IV.i.95–103).

WRITING ABOUT LITERATURE

1. Write a character sketch of Benedick. Analyze the qualities that he possesses. Consider Benedick's attitudes toward Beatrice and toward love, both before and after Don Pedro's scheme to make Benedick fall in love with Beatrice. Consider how Benedick handles the conflict between his loyalty to his friend Claudio and his love for Beatrice. Use a quotation to support each of your ideas and explain what each quotation reveals about Benedick. Finally, consider Benedick's reputation with women and anticipate what kind of husband he will be.

2. Write an essay in which you explain how the principal characters in *Much Ado* base their attitudes and actions upon the attitudes, actions, and values of others. Examine the ways in which your explanation applies to Claudio, Don Pedro, and Leonato. Also consider how it applies to Beatrice and Benedick. Support your ideas with quotations from the play. Conclude your essay with a paragraph in which you evaluate whether outer-directed behavior (reliance on others) is better than inner-directed behavior (self-reliance).

3. Write an essay in which you analyze Shakespeare's choice of title. To what extent, if any, is this play "much ado about nothing"? Wherever possible,

support your points with quotations from the play and explain how each quotation is related to your thesis. Consider the following questions:

- Why did Shakespeare add the tragic elements to his principal plot?
- Why did he clothe the tragic elements in comedy?
- If the play is about "something," what is it about?
- What motivates Don Pedro, Claudio, and Leonato to behave as they do, and what do their attitudes and behavior reveal about male attitudes toward women?
- Could such snap judgments and acceptance of slander occur today? Who would be likely accusers? Who would be likely victims?

4. Examine the ways in which the subplots reinforce the principal plot and enrich the play. Consider both the Benedick-Beatrice subplot and the Dogberry subplot. Discuss such factors as humor, emphasis, irony, and unity. Use quotations for your examples and analyze how the words and actions of these characters unify the play.

5. According to the friar,

> That what we have we prize not to the worth
> Whiles we enjoy it; but being lack'd and lost,
> Why, then we rack the value, then we find
> The virtue that possession would not show us
> Whiles it was ours.
> (IV.i.214–18)

To what extent, if any, do you agree with the friar's statement? Apply this idea to weather, wealth, health, and peace.

6. Tell Hero's story from her point of view. Consider the following questions:

- How does Hero feel about her father's reaction to the accusation that she has been having an affair?
- To what extent, if any, does his reaction change her view of him and affect their relationship?
- To what extent, if any, does Hero hold Claudio responsible for what happened? Does she forgive him?
- What is Hero's view of her forthcoming marriage?

7. Tell Claudio's or Hero's story as a modern Claudio or Hero might live it. In telling Claudio's story, give him a relationship like the relationship Claudio has with Don Pedro. In telling Hero's story, mention the relationship Hero has with her father. Use dialogue to reveal personalities, ideas, and values.

My Heart
Leaps Up

WILLIAM WORDSWORTH

ILLIAM WORDSWORTH (1770–1850) is the central figure of English romantic poetry. His *Lyrical Ballads* (published with fellow poet Samuel Taylor Coleridge in 1798) initiated the romantic movement in English literature; it has been called "the most important event in the history of English poetry after Milton." Wordsworth's Preface to the second edition of *Lyrical Ballads* (1800) became the declaration of romantic principles. His innovations in the subject matter and in the style of poetry changed both the artistic and popular conception of English poetry. In addition to *Lyrical Ballads*, he is known for his "Ode: On Intimations of Immortality from Recollections of Early Childhood" (1807) and for *The Prelude* (written 1798–1805; published 1850), an epic poem modeled on John Milton's *Paradise Lost*.

Wordsworth was born in Cockermouth, Cumbria, in the Lake District of England. His mother died when he was eight years old; his father, an attorney, died when he was thirteen. He was already a poet when he entered St. John's College, Cambridge, in 1787. His first major poem was "Lines Written Above Tintern Abbey," published in *Lyrical Ballads*. In 1795 Wordsworth moved to the country to devote himself to "plain living and high thinking." He was accompanied by his sister Dorothy, whose "exquisite regard for common things" taught him to observe the details in nature. Dorothy was also a fine writer, and Wordsworth occasionally used material from her journals in his own work. Wordsworth wrote his greatest poems between 1797 and 1807. By the time he was in his early forties, the poet who had revolutionized English poetry and passionately supported the French Revolution had become conservative in his art and his politics. Wordsworth was named poet laureate of England in 1843, long after he had written his best work.

In the Preface to *Lyrical Ballads*, Wordsworth defines various aspects of poetry. He states: "Poetry is the spontaneous overflow of powerful feelings: it takes its origin from emotion recollected in tranquility."

Poetry should be written about "incidents and situations from common life," without artificiality, "in a selection of language really used by men" and with an emphasis on feeling "the essential passions of the human heart." Wordsworth stressed the idea of experiencing nature directly and of sensing the spiritual bond between human beings and the natural world. "My Heart Leaps Up" expresses a person's ideal relationship to nature.

My heart leaps up when I behold
   A rainbow in the sky:
So was it when my life began;
So is it now I am a man;
So be it when I shall grow old,   5
   Or let me die!
The Child is father of the Man;
And I could wish my days to be
Bound each to each by natural piety.

UNDERSTANDING THE POEM

1. What is most important to the poet in this poem?

2. What does "The Child is father of the Man" (line 7) mean?

3. How does Wordsworth relate "piety" to nature?

4. What **themes** do you find in this poem?

ANALYZING LITERARY TECHNIQUE

1. How does Wordsworth use **paradox** in this poem?

2. Note Wordsworth's goals in writing poetry, as stated in his Preface to *Lyrical Ballads* and quoted in the introductory material. To what extent, if any, is this poem consistent with Wordsworth's goals?

3. Find the one **metaphor** in the poem and explain its appeal and appropriateness.

4. What effect does the capitalization of "Child" and "Man" achieve?

5. What does Wordsworth gain by repeating the word "so"?

WRITING ABOUT LITERATURE

1. Write an essay in which you discuss the paradox of the child's being the parent of the adult. Consider the following questions: In what ways are adults the same people they were as children? What kinds of childhood experiences have important effects on people's later lives? Support your ideas with specific examples.

2. Describe an experience of nature that you have never forgotten. You may express your thoughts in prose or in poetry. Try to choose words that will help others see the sight or feel the experience.

Dover Beach

MATTHEW ARNOLD

MATTHEW ARNOLD (1822–1888) is a major English critic and one of the most important poets of the Victorian Age. He is famous for his poem "Dover Beach," which many consider to be the finest poem of the period, and three volumes of essays: *On Translating Homer* (1861), *Essays in Criticism* (1865), and *On the Study of Celtic Literature* (1867).

Arnold was born near Staines, England. His father was an important educator and headmaster of Rugby, a well-known secondary school. The younger Arnold was an inspector of elementary and secondary schools for thirty-five years. His first collection of poetry was published in 1849. In 1857 he was elected professor of poetry at Oxford and began his career as a critic of English life, contemplating a range of topics that included society, politics, religion, and literature.

In many respects Arnold is the most modern of Victorian writers in that he was sensitive to the emotional implications of the age of transition in which he lived. It was a time when scientific discoveries and Biblical criticism were eroding traditional religious beliefs and the structure of society was changing. People had been accustomed to living their entire lives in small self-contained communities where they felt a close relationship to God, to nature, and to one another. They were entering an era in which many people would move into crowded metropolitan areas, where they would live in impersonal, unsupportive environments. Arnold expresses the feelings of doubt, isolation, and alienation that have become characteristic of the modern age. In his *Essays in Criticism,* Arnold wrote: "More and more, mankind will discover that we have to turn to poetry to interpret life for us, to console us, to sustain us."

"Dover Beach" is one of the world's greatest poems because it expresses a timeless message in striking images. Arnold began the poem in 1851 when he was inspired by the view from a Dover hotel-room window while on his honeymoon; the poem was published in 1867.

The sea is calm tonight,
The tide is full, the moon lies fair
Upon the straits;—on the French coast the light
Gleams and is gone; the cliffs of England stand,
Glimmering and vast, out in the tranquil bay.   5
Come to the window, sweet is the night air!

Only, from the long line of spray
Where the sea meets the moon-blanched land,
Listen! you hear the grating roar
Of pebbles which the waves draw back, and fling,   10
At their return, up the high strand,
Begin, and cease, and then again begin,
With tremulous cadence slow, and bring
The eternal note of sadness in.

Sophocles[1] long ago   15
Heard it on the Aegean,[2] and it brought
Into his mind the turbid ebb and flow
Of human misery; we
Find also in the sound a thought,
Hearing it by this distant northern sea.   20

The Sea of Faith
Was once, too, at the full, and round earth's shore
Lay like the folds of a bright girdle furled.
But now I only hear
Its melancholy, long, withdrawing roar,   25
Retreating, to the breath
Of the night wind, down the vast edges drear
And naked shingles[3] of the world.

Ah, love, let us be true
To one another! for the world, which seems   30
To lie before us like a land of dreams,
So various, so beautiful, so new,
Hath really neither joy, nor love, nor light,
Nor certitude, nor peace, nor help for pain;

---

[1] *Sophocles:* Greek dramatist (c. 496–406 B.C.).
[2] *Aegean:* Sea between Greece and Turkey.
[3] *shingles:* Pebble-covered beaches.

And we are here as on a darkling plain   35
Swept with confused alarms of struggle and flight,
Where ignorant armies clash by night.

UNDERSTANDING THE POEM

1. What leads the speaker to express the thoughts in the poem?
2. What characteristics of the sea lead the speaker to these thoughts?
3. What leads the speaker to think of Sophocles?
4. How has the ebb of "the Sea of Faith" affected the speaker's outlook?
5. What importance does the ebb of "the Sea of Faith" have for human relationships?
6. This poem was written between 1851 and 1867. Could it have been written today?
7. Arnold believed that poetry should be "a criticism of life." To what extent, if any, does "Dover Beach" meet that objective?

ANALYZING LITERARY TECHNIQUE

1. Explain the importance of the **setting** to the poem as a whole.
2. What does Arnold's use of **apostrophe** contribute to the poem?
3. Find examples of **contrast** in the poem and explain their function.
4. Relate the poet's use of contrast to the **tone** of the poem.
5. What is the connection between Arnold's use of contrast and his use of **paradox?**
6. Relate Arnold's use of **metaphor** and **symbol** to his use of contrast.
7. Read the fourth speech of the Chorus in *Antigone* (lines 656–77) by Sophocles, which Arnold refers to in this poem. Why did Arnold choose this passage? What function does his **allusion** serve?
8. Describe the relationship between the **climax** and the **theme** of the poem.
9. Find examples of **connotative language** and explain what each example contributes to the poem.
10. What does Arnold achieve by his repetition of the word "nor" in the last stanza?
11. What is ironic about this poem?

WRITING ABOUT LITERATURE

1. Write an essay in which you analyze how Arnold's use of contrast reinforces the theme of the poem. In the process, consider the relationship of contrast to setting, allusion, metaphor, symbol, paradox, and tone. Use quotations from the poem in your examples and remember that the purpose of your examples is to support your ideas.

2. Write a response to the theme of this poem. You may choose to adopt the point of view of a religious leader, a scientist, a political leader, the poet's companion, or simply a reader.

Sonnet 32

ELIZABETH BARRETT BROWNING

*D*uring her lifetime, Elizabeth Barrett Browning (1806–1861) was considered the greatest female poet since Sappho. Her *Poems* (1844) won such acclaim that she was seriously considered as a successor to William Wordsworth for the position of poet laureate of England. She is best known for her *Sonnets from the Portuguese* (1850), which were considered to be the best sonnets written in any language since William Shakespeare's. Some of her best lyric poems were published posthumously in *Last Poems* (1862).

Barrett was born near Durham, England, into a wealthy family. She was the oldest of twelve children and her father's favorite. She was educated at home, and her first work was privately published by her father in 1820. The first collection of Barrett's poetry to gain critical attention was *The Seraphim, and Other Poems* (1838). She was actively involved in humanitarian causes, deploring the use of child labor in factories and mines (*The Cry of the Children,* 1844) and advocating the education of women (*Aurora Leigh,* 1856, a novel in verse).

In 1845 Robert Browning initiated a correspondence with Barrett. At the time, she was thirty-nine years old (six years older than he), an invalid from an old spinal injury, and a recluse because of her physical condition and her father's domination. Theirs became the courtship of the age and one of the world's famous love stories. Barrett's father prohibited any of his children from marrying, but Browning courted Barrett in secret between 1845 and 1846, during which time Barrett covertly wrote the private love poems to Browning that she called *Sonnets from the Portuguese*. The title had a double meaning: It led anyone who discovered the sonnets to assume that they were translations, and it referred to Browning's private name for Barrett—"my little Portuguese" (because of her olive-toned skin). In 1846 the couple eloped and lived happily together in Florence, Italy, until Barrett Browning died fifteen years later. The following poem, one of the *Sonnets from the Portuguese*, reveals her special qualities: sincerity and an unaffected, eloquent touch.

The first time that the sun rose on thine oath
To love me, I looked forward to the moon
To slacken all those bonds which seemed too soon
And quickly tied to make a lasting troth.
Quick-loving hearts, I thought, may quickly loathe;   5
And, looking on myself, I seemed not one
For such man's love—more like an out-of-tune
Worn viol,[1] a good singer would be wroth
To spoil his song with, and which, snatched in haste,
Is laid down at the first ill-sounding note.   10
I did not wrong myself so, but I placed
A wrong on *thee*. For perfect strains may float
'Neath master-hands, from instruments defaced,—
And great souls, at one stroke, may do and dote.

UNDERSTANDING THE POEM

1. Why does the speaker doubt that she is worthy of being loved?
2. Why is the speaker reluctant to accept her lover's love?
3. How does the speaker's attitude wrong her lover?
4. What does the speaker conclude?
5. What does this poem reveal about the essential aspects of a relationship?

ANALYZING LITERARY TECHNIQUE

1. Analyze the function of **contrast** in the poem.
2. How does the extended **metaphor** function in the poem?
3. How is the **climax** related to the sonnet's structure?
4. How is the **tone** of the sonnet related to its structure?
5. What do **consonance, assonance,** and **rhyme** contribute to the poem?

---

[1] *viol:* A stringed instrument made primarily in the sixteenth and seventeenth centuries.

WRITING ABOUT LITERATURE

1. Write an essay in which you analyze Barrett's use of **figurative language** in the poem. How does she use figurative language to express particular feelings? In your conclusion, evaluate the contribution of figurative language to the poem as a whole.

2. Write a response that a lover might make upon receiving this poem from the woman he loves. You may choose to write the response in the form of a poem or a letter.

The Old Stoic

EMILY BRONTË

MILY BRONTË (1818–1848), one of the three gifted Brontë sisters, is the author of the great English novel *Wuthering Heights* (1847) and of several of the best English poems of the nineteenth century.

Brontë was born in Thornton, in Yorkshire, England, the fifth of six children. In 1820 her family moved to Haworth, Yorkshire, where her mother died in 1821 and her two oldest sisters died in 1825. Her father, a minister, was a stern and sullen man, and the aunt who took over the household was more strict than loving. The four surviving Brontë children—Charlotte, Branwell, Emily, and Anne—became a close-knit group and provided one another with emotional and creative support.

Being isolated in a dreary parsonage in a small remote community, the four siblings paired off and used their unusual literary gifts to write about imaginary lands. Emily and her younger sister, Anne, created the imaginary country of Gondal and wrote literature for it that included legends and poetry. Gondal remained a source of Emily's later art, providing the setting, characters, and situations for many of her best dramatic poems and also for *Wuthering Heights*. In addition, she wrote personal poems, including "The Old Stoic."

Brontë published two works during her lifetime. The first book contained the poetry of Emily and her sisters. It was privately published in 1846 under the pseudonyms of Currer, Ellis, and Acton Bell. The book was a dismal failure. Her novel *Wuthering Heights* was published the following year. The visionary quality of her writing was still not appreciated, and the story itself was considered too morbid and violent.

After Brontë caught cold at her brother's grave in the fall of 1848, she developed tuberculosis and died in mid-December. Her stoicism had long been recognized by her family. Her sister Charlotte described her last months as follows:

Stronger than a man . . . her nature stood alone . . . on herself she had no pity; the spirit was inexorable to the flesh; from the trembling hand, the unnerved limbs, the faded eyes, the same service was exacted as they had rendered in health.

Brontë was passionately attached to the bleak, windy moors that surrounded Haworth, finding them a source of health, happiness, and inspiration. Charlotte wrote, "She found in the bleak solitude many and dear delights, and the best loved was—liberty." In Emily Brontë's personal poem "The Old Stoic," she reveals the values that made her unique as an individual and as an artist.

Riches I hold in light esteem,
And love I laugh to scorn;
And lust of fame was but a dream
That vanished with the morn:

And if I pray, the only prayer   5
That moves my lips for me
Is, "Leave the heart that now I bear,
And give me liberty!"

Yes, as my swift days near their goal,
'Tis all that I implore—   10
Through life and death a chainless soul,
With courage to endure.

UNDERSTANDING THE POEM

1. What value is most important to the speaker of the poem?

2. What else does this poem reveal about the speaker?

ANALYZING LITERARY TECHNIQUE

1. What is the function of **contrast** in the poem?

2. How does the **metaphor** "chainless soul" (line 11) relate to the rest of the poem?

3. What does Brontë's choice of ballad, or hymn, meter (alternating lines of four and three stressed syllables) and a very regular **rhyme** scheme (*abab*) contribute to the poem?

4. What does Brontë achieve by her use of **connotative language?**

5. To what extent, if any, could this be called a **lyric** poem?

WRITING ABOUT LITERATURE

1. Write an essay in which you analyze what Brontë's use of contrast contributes to the poem. Use quotations to support your ideas.

2. Imagine how the speaker became a stoic. What caused her to eschew riches, love, and fame? You may write your response in either prose or poetry.

Goblin Market

CHRISTINA ROSSETTI

C HRISTINA GEORGINA ROSSETTI (1830–1894) is among the greatest English poets of the nineteenth century. Known for a poetic technique that combines clarity of ideas, simplicity of language, and vitality of rhythm, her best-known poems are "Uphill" and "A Birthday" (both published in 1861); "Goblin Market" (1862), her masterpiece; and *Sing-Song* (1872), a collection of children's poetry.

Rossetti, the youngest of four children, was born in London to an artistic family. Her father was a well-known opera librettist and poet from the Kingdom of Naples in Italy. He was living in political exile in London, where he was a professor of Italian at King's College. Rossetti was educated at home by her mother; like her sister (who became a nun) and her mother, Rossetti was a devout Anglican. Incompatible religious convictions caused her to reject the love of two men. According to her brother William Michael Rossetti, who became the editor of her poetry, her inability to marry her first love was "a staggering blow . . . from which she did not fully recover for years." She eloquently expressed her attitude toward life when she stated, "I cannot possibly use the word 'happy' without meaning something beyond this present life." Her poetry expresses her emotional experiences, including her need for love, her resignation about life, and her religious attitudes. Weakened by lifelong heart disease, she spent the last fifteen years of her life at home with her mother. She died while at prayer.

Rossetti began writing English lyrics at the age of twelve. In 1848 her brother Dante Gabriel Rossetti became a founder of the Pre-Raphaelite Brotherhood, a group of poets, artists, and critics whose goals included an artistic style that was simple, direct, and vivid and a moral seriousness. When *Goblin Market and Other Poems* was published in 1862, "Goblin Market" became the first Pre-Raphaelite written work to capture the attention of the public. The poem's simplicity, rhythm, and aural quality appeal to adults and children alike.

Morning and evening
Maids heard the goblins cry:
"Come buy our orchard fruits,
Come buy, come buy:
Apples and quinces,   5
Lemons and oranges,
Plump unpecked cherries,
Melons and raspberries,
Bloom-down-cheeked peaches,
Swart-headed mulberries,   10
Wild free-born cranberries,
Crabapples, dewberries,
Pineapples, blackberries,
Apricots, strawberries;—
All ripe together   15
In summer weather,—
Morns that pass by,
Fair eyes that fly;
Come buy, come buy:
Our grapes fresh from the vine,   20
Pomegranates full and fine,
Dates and sharp bullaces,
Rare pears and greengages
Damsons and bilberries,
Taste them and try: 25
Currants and gooseberries,
Bright-fire-like barberries,
Figs to fill your mouth,
Citrons from the South,
Sweet to tongue and sound to eye;   30
Come buy, come buy."

Evening by evening
Among the brookside rushes,
Laura bowed her head to hear,
Lizzie veiled her blushes: 35
Crouching close together
In the cooling weather,
With clasping arm and cautioning lips,
With tingling cheeks and finger tips.
"Lie close," Laura said,   40
Pricking up her golden head:

"We must not look at goblin men,
We must not buy their fruits:
Who knows upon what soil they fed
Their hungry thirsty roots?"   45
"Come buy," call the goblins
Hobbling down the glen.

"Oh," cried Lizzie, "Laura, Laura,
You should not peep at goblin men."
Lizzie covered up her eyes,   50
Covered close lest they should look;
Laura reared her glossy head,
And whispered like the restless brook:
"Look, Lizzie, look, Lizzie,
Down the glen tramp little men.   55
One hauls a basket,
One bears a plate,
One lugs a golden dish
Of many pounds' weight.
How fair the vine must grow   60
Whose grapes are so luscious;
How warm the wind must blow
Through those fruit bushes."
"No," said Lizzie. "No, no, no;
Their offers should not charm us,   65
Their evil gifts would harm us."
She thrust a dimpled finger
In each ear, shut eyes and ran:
Curious Laura chose to linger
Wondering at each merchant man.   70
One had a cat's face,
One whisked a tail,
One tramped at a rat's pace,
One crawled like a snail,
One like a wombat prowled obtuse and furry,   75
One like a ratel tumbled hurry skurry.
She heard a voice like voice of doves
Cooing all together:
They sounded kind and full of loves
In the pleasant weather.   80

Laura stretched her gleaming neck
Like a rush-imbedded swan,
Like a lily from the beck,
Like a moonlit poplar branch,

Like a vessel at the launch   85
When its last restraint is gone.

Backwards up the mossy glen
Turned and trooped the goblin men,
With their shrill repeated cry,
"Come buy, come buy."   90
When they reached where Laura was
They stood stock still upon the moss,
Leering at each other,
Brother with queer brother;
Signaling each other,   95
Brother with sly brother.
One set his basket down,
One reared his plate;
One began to weave a crown
Of tendrils, leaves, and rough nuts brown   100
(Men sell not such in any town);
One heaved the golden weight
Of dish and fruit to offer her:
"Come buy, come buy," was still their cry.
Laura stared but did not stir,   105
Longed but had no money.
The whisk-tailed merchant bade her taste
In tones as smooth as honey,
The cat-faced purr'd,
The rat-paced spoke a word   110
Of welcome, and the snail-paced even was heard;
One parrot-voiced and jolly
Cried "Pretty Goblin" still for "Pretty Polly";
One whistled like a bird.

But sweet-tooth Laura spoke in haste: 115
"Good Folk, I have no coin;
To take were to purloin:
I have no copper in my purse,
I have no silver either,
And all my gold is on the furze   120
That shakes in windy weather
Above the rusty heather."
"You have much gold upon your head,"
They answered all together:
"Buy from us with a golden curl."   125
She clipped a precious golden lock,
She dropped a tear more rare than pearl,

Then sucked their fruit globes fair or red.
Sweeter than honey from the rock,
Stronger than man-rejoicing wine, 130
Clearer than water flowed that juice;
She never tasted such before,
How should it cloy with length of use?
She sucked and sucked and sucked the more
Fruits which that unknown orchard bore; 135
She sucked until her lips were sore;
Then flung the emptied rinds away
But gathered up one kernel stone,
And knew not was it night or day
As she turned home alone. 140

Lizzie met her at the gate
Full of wise upbraidings:
"Dear, you should not stay so late,
Twilight is not good for maidens;
Should not loiter in the glen 145
In the haunts of goblin men.
Do you not remember Jeanie,
How she met them in the moonlight,
Took their gifts both choice and many,
Ate their fruits and wore their flowers 150
Plucked from bowers
Where summer ripens at all hours?
But ever in the moonlight
She pined and pined away;
Sought them by night and day, 155
Found them no more, but dwindled and grew gray;
Then fell with the first snow,
While to this day no grass will grow
Where she lies low:
I planted daisies there a year ago 160
That never blow.
You should not loiter so."
"Nay, hush," said Laura:
"Nay, hush, my sister:
I ate and ate my fill, 165
Yet my mouth waters still:
Tomorrow night I will
Buy more"; and kissed her.
"Have done with sorrow;
I'll bring you plums tomorrow 170
Fresh on their mother twigs,

Cherries worth getting;
You cannot think what figs
My teeth have met in,
What melons icy-cold   175
Piled on a dish of gold
Too huge for me to hold,
What peaches with a velvet nap,
Pellucid grapes without one seed:
Odorous indeed must be the mead   180
Whereon they grow, and pure the wave they drink
With lilies at the brink,
And sugar-sweet their sap."

Golden head by golden head,
Like two pigeons in one nest   185
Folded in each other's wings,
They lay down in their curtained bed:
Like two blossoms on one stem,
Like two flakes of new-fallen snow,
Like two wands of ivory   190
Tipped with gold for awful kings.
Moon and stars gazed in at them,
Wind sang to them lullaby,
Lumbering owls forebore to fly,
Not a bat flapped to and fro   195
Round their nest:
Cheek to cheek and breast to breast
Locked together in one nest.

Early in the morning
When the first cock crowed his warning,   200
Neat like bees, and sweet and busy,
Laura rose with Lizzie:
Fetched in honey, milked the cows,
Aired and set to rights the house,
Kneaded cakes of whitest wheat,   205
Cakes for dainty mouths to eat,
Next churned butter, whipped up cream,
Fed their poultry, sat and sewed;
Talked as modest maidens should:
Lizzie with an open heart,   210
Laura in an absent dream,
One content, one sick in part;
One warbling for the mere bright day's delight,
One longing for the night.

At length slow evening came: 215
They went with pitchers to the reedy brook;
Lizzie most placid in her look,
Laura most like a leaping flame,
They drew the gurgling water from its deep.
Lizzie plucked purple and rich golden flags, 220
Then turning homeward said: "The sunset flushes
Those furthest loftiest crags;
Come, Laura, not another maiden lags.
No willful squirrel wags,
The beasts and birds are fast asleep." 225
But Laura loitered still among the rushes,
And said the bank was steep.

And said the hour was early still,
The dew not fallen, the wind not chill;
Listening ever, but not catching 230
The customary cry,
"Come buy, come buy,"
With its iterated jingle
Of sugar-baited words:
Not for all her watching 235
Once discerning even one goblin
Racing, whisking, tumbling, hobbling—
Let alone the herds
That used to tramp along the glen
In groups or single, 240
Of brisk fruit-merchant men.

Till Lizzie urged, "O Laura, come;
I hear the fruit-call, but I dare not look;
You should not loiter longer at this brook:
Come with me home. 245
The stars rise, the moon bends her arc,
Each glow-worm winks her spark,
Let us get home before the night grows dark:
For clouds may gather
Though this is summer weather, 250
Put out the lights and drench us through;
Then if we lost our way what should we do?"

Laura turned cold as stone
To find her sister heard that cry alone,
That goblin cry, 255
"Come buy our fruits, come buy."

Must she then buy no more such dainty fruit?
Must she no more such succous pasture find,
Gone deaf and blind?
Her tree of life dropped from the root: 260
She said not one word in her heart's sore ache:
But peering through the dimness, nought discerning,
Trudged home, her pitcher dripping all the way;
So crept to bed, and lay
Silent till Lizzie slept;   265
Then sat up in a passionate yearning.
And gnashed her teeth for balked desire, and wept
As if her heart would break.

Day after day, night after night,
Laura kept watch in vain   270
In sullen silence of exceeding pain.
She never caught again the goblin cry,
"Come buy, come buy";—
She never spied the goblin men
Hawking their fruits along the glen: 275
But when the moon waxed bright
Her hair grew thin and gray;
She dwindled, as the fair full moon doth turn
To swift decay and burn
Her fire away.   280

One day remembering her kernelstone
She set it by a wall that faced the south;
Dewed it with tears, hoped for a root,
Watching for a waxing shoot,
But there came none.   285
It never saw the sun,
It never felt the trickling moisture run:
While with sunk eyes and faded mouth
She dreamed of melons, as a traveler sees
False waves in desert drouth   290
With shade of leaf-crowned trees,
And burns the thirstier in the sandful breeze.

She no more swept the house,
Tended the fowls or cows,
Fetched honey, kneaded cakes of wheat,   295
Brought water from the brook:
But sat down listless in the chimneynook
And would not eat.

Tender Lizzie could not bear
To watch her sister's cankerous care, 300
Yet not to share.
She night and morning
Caught the goblins' cry:
"Come buy our orchard fruits,
Come buy, come buy":— 305
Beside the brook, along the glen,
She heard the tramp of goblin men,
The voice and stir
Poor Laura could not hear;
Longed to buy fruit to comfort her, 310
But feared to pay too dear.
She thought of Jeanie in her grave,
Who should have been a bride;
But who for joys brides hope to have
Fell sick and died 315
In her gay prime,
In earliest winter time,
With the first glazing rime,
With the first snow-fall of crisp winter time.

Till Laura dwindling 320
Seemed knocking at Death's door.
Then Lizzie weighed no more
Better and worse;
But put a silver penny in her purse,
Kissed Laura, crossed the heath with clumps of furze 325
At twilight, halted by the brook:
And for the first time in her life
Began to listen and look.

Laughed every goblin
When they spied her peeping: 330
Came towards her hobbling,
Flying, running, leaping,
Puffing and blowing,
Chuckling, clapping, crowing,
Cluckling and gobbling, 335
Mopping and mowing,
Full of airs and graces,
Pulling wry faces,
Demure grimaces,
Cat-like and rat-like, 340
Ratel- and wombat-like,

Snail-paced in a hurry,
Parrot-voiced and whistler,
Helter skelter, hurry skurry,
Chattering like magpies,   345
Fluttering like pigeons,
Gliding like fishes,—
Hugged her and kissed her:
Squeezed and caressed her:
Stretched up their dishes,   350
Panniers, and plates:
"Look at our apples
Russet and dun,
Bob at our cherries,
Bite at our peaches,   355
Citrons and dates,
Grapes for the asking,
Pears red with basking
Out in the sun,
Plums on their twigs;   360
Pluck them and suck them,—
Pomegranates, figs."

"Good folk," said Lizzie,
Mindful of Jeanie:
"Give me much and many":   365
Held out her apron,
Tossed them her penny.
"Nay, take a seat with us,
Honor and eat with us,"
They answered grinning: 370
"Our feast is but beginning.
Night yet is early,
Warm and dew-pearly,
Wakeful and starry:
Such fruits as these   375
No man can carry;
Half their bloom would fly,
Half their dew would dry,
Half their flavor would pass by.
Sit down and feast with us,   380
Be welcome guest with us,
Cheer you and rest with us."—
"Thank you," said Lizzie: "But one waits
At home alone for me:
So without further parleying,   385

If you will not sell me any
Of your fruits though much and many,
Give me back my silver penny
I tossed you for a fee."—
They began to scratch their pates,   390
No longer wagging, purring,
But visibly demurring,
Grunting and snarling.
One called her proud,
Cross-grained, uncivil;   395
Their tones waxed loud,
Their looks were evil.
Lashing their tails
They trod and hustled her,
Elbowed and jostled her,   400
Clawed with their nails,
Barking, mewing, hissing, mocking,
Tore her gown and soiled her stocking,
Twitched her hair out by the roots,
Stamped upon her tender feet,   405
Held her hands and squeezed their fruits
Against her mouth to make her eat.

White and golden Lizzie stood,
Like a lily in a flood,—
Like a rock of blue-veined stone   410
Lashed by tides obstreperously,—
Like a beacon left alone
In a hoary roaring sea,
Sending up a golden fire,—
Like a fruit-crowned orange-tree   415
White with blossoms honey-sweet
Sore beset by wasp and bee,—
Like a royal virgin town
Topped with gilded dome and spire
Close beleagured by a fleet   420
Mad to tug her standard down.

One may lead a horse to water,
Twenty cannot make him drink.
Though the goblins cuffed and caught her,
Coaxed and fought her,   425
Bullied and besought her,
Scratched her, pinched her black as ink,
Kicked and knocked her,

Mauled and mocked her,
Lizzie uttered not a word;   430
Would not open lip from lip
Lest they should cram a mouthful in:
But laughed in heart to feel the drip
Of juice that syruped all her face,
And lodged in dimples of her chin,   435
And streaked her neck which quaked like curd.
At last the evil people,
Worn out by her resistance,
Flung back her penny, kicked their fruit
Along whichever road they took,·   440
Not leaving root or stone or shoot;
Some writhed into the ground,
Some dived into the brook
With ring and ripple,
Some scudded on the gale without a sound,   445
Some vanished in the distance.

In a smart, ache, tingle,
Lizzie went her way;
Knew not was it night or day;
Sprang up the bank, tore through the furze,   450
Threaded copse and dingle,
And heard her penny jingle
Bouncing in her purse,—
Its bounce was music to her ear.
She ran and ran   455
As if she feared some goblin man
Dogged her with gibe or curse
Or something worse:
But not one goblin skurried after,
Nor was she pricked by fear;   460
The kind heart made her windy-paced
That urged her home quite out of breath with haste
And inward laughter.

She cried, "Laura," up the garden,
"Did you miss me?   465
Come and kiss me.
Never mind my bruises,
Hug me, kiss me, suck my juices
Squeezed from goblin fruits for you,
Goblin pulp and goblin dew.   470
Eat me, drink me, love me;

Laura, make much of me;
For your sake I have braved the glen
And had to do with goblin merchant men."

Laura started from her chair,   475
Flung her arms up in the air,
Clutched her hair:
"Lizzie, Lizzie have you tasted
For my sake the fruit forbidden?
Must your light like mine be hidden,   480
Your young life like mine be wasted,
Undone in mine undoing,
And ruined in my ruin,
Thirsty, cankered, goblin-ridden?"—
She clung about her sister,   485
Kissed and kissed and kissed her:
Tears once again
Refreshed her shrunken eyes,
Dropping like rain
After long sultry drouth;   490
Shaking with anguish, fear, and pain,
She kissed and kissed her with a hungry mouth.

Her lips began to scorch,
That juice was wormwood to her tongue,
She loathed the feast: 495
Writhing as one possessed she leaped and sung,
Rent all her robe, and wrung
Her hands in lamentable haste,
And beat her breast,
Her locks streamed like the torch   500
Borne by a racer at full speed,
Or like the mane of horses in their flight,
Or like an eagle when she stems the light
Straight toward the sun,
Or like a caged thing freed,   505
Or like a flying flag when armies run.

Swift fire spread through her veins, knocked at her heart,
Met the fire smoldering there
And overbore its lesser flame;
She gorged on bitterness without a name: 510
Ah fool, to choose such part
Of soul-consuming care!
Sense failed in the mortal strife:

Like the watch-tower of a town
Which an earthquake shatters down, 515
Like a lightning-stricken mast,
Like a wind-uprooted tree
Spun about,
Like a foam-topped waterspout
Cast down headlong in the sea, 520
She fell at last;
Pleasure past and anguish past,
Is it death or is it life?

Life out of death.
That night long Lizzie watched by her, 525
Counted her pulse's flagging stir,
Felt for her breath,
Held water to her lips, and cooled her face
With tears and fanning leaves.
But when the first birds chirped about their eaves, 530
And early reapers plodded to the place
Of golden sheaves,
And dew-wet grass
Bowed in the morning winds so brisk to pass,
And new buds with new day 535
Opened of cup-like lilies on the stream,
Laura awoke as from a dream,
Laughed in the innocent old way,
Hugged Lizzie but not twice or thrice;
Her gleaming locks showed not one thread of gray, 540
Her breath was sweet as May,
And light danced in her eyes.

Days, weeks, months, years
Afterwards, when both were wives
With children of their own; 545
Their mother-hearts beset with fears,
Their lives bound up in tender lives;
Laura would call the little ones
And tell them of her early prime,
Those pleasant days long gone 550
Of not-returning time:
Would talk about the haunted glen,
The wicked quaint fruit-merchant men,
Their fruits like honey to the throat
But poison in the blood 555
(Men sell not such in any town):

Would tell them how her sister stood
In deadly peril to do her good,
And win the fiery antidote:
Then joining hands to little hands   560
Would bid them cling together,—
"For there is no friend like a sister
In calm or stormy weather;
To cheer one on the tedious way,
To fetch one if one goes astray,   565
To lift one if one totters down,
To strengthen whilst one stands."

UNDERSTANDING THE POEM

1. Why do the goblin men call only to girls and young women? Why don't they appear to Laura after she purchased their fruit?

2. What kind of payment do the goblin men accept for their wares?

3. To what extent, if any, would Laura have been helped if she had been reminded sooner of Jeanie's fate?

4. What inner conflict does Laura's condition create in Lizzie? How does she resolve it?

5. What gives Lizzie the courage to confront the goblin men? In what ways is she a heroic figure?

6. What makes the goblin fruit poisonous? Why does the juice of goblin fruit become an antidote to its own poison?

7. What does Rossetti imply in this poem about the nature of evil? Support your ideas with examples.

8. What **themes** do you find in this poem?

ANALYZING LITERARY TECHNIQUE

1. What do the goblin men and their fruit symbolize in this poem?

2. According to Rossetti's brother, Rossetti considered "Goblin Market" to be a **fairy tale.** To what extent is it a fairy tale, and to what extent can it be read as something more?

3. In psychology, a **night journey** is a series of events experienced by an individual alone that cause a profound spiritual or emotional change in the individual. How does the concept of the night journey relate to this poem?

4. How does Rossetti use **foreshadowing** in this poem?

5. How does Rossetti use sound devices (**assonance, alliteration, consonance, onomatopoeia, repetition, rhyme, rhythm**) in this poem? Choose two or three specific examples and explain their contribution to the poem.

6. Examine Rossetti's use of **figurative language,** especially the chains of **similes** and **metaphors.** What do the chains of images contribute to the poem?

WRITING ABOUT LITERATURE

1. Develop a character sketch of Lizzie as a hero. Consider lines from the poem that reveal heroic behavior. What adjectives best describe that behavior? How does the poem reveal Lizzie's motivations and concerns?

2. Choose a theme from the poem and explain how Rossetti treats it. Use quotations from the poem to support your ideas.

3. Write a fairy-tale-like narrative of your own, in poetry or in prose. Choose an incident and characters that will enable you to convey a moral or a lesson. As an alternative, revise a fairy tale, either to give it a different moral or to give it a definite moral (if it doesn't seem to have a moral). You might try writing a verse version of a fairy tale that you know in prose.

An Outpost of Progress

JOSEPH CONRAD

*J*OSEPH CONRAD (1857–1924), the English short-story writer and novelist, is recognized as one of the leading modernists. He is respected for his eloquent use of English, a language he learned as an adult. Conrad's interest in psychology and anthropology and his focus on human reaction to stress coincide with the early psychological studies of Sigmund Freud, who was Conrad's contemporary, and of the young Carl Jung. Conrad rejected the popular view that progress in societies was inevitable. Instead, he believed that when so-called civilized people are under stress, they can commit acts of great cruelty, a belief that anticipated the horrors of the twentieth century. Conrad is best known for *Lord Jim* (1900), *Heart of Darkness* (1902), and *The Secret Sharer* (1909).

Conrad was born Józef Teodor Konrad Korzeniowski into an educated Polish family in the Ukraine, an area controlled by Russia. His father was a poet, dramatist, and translator of English and French literature. His nationalist political activities caused the family to be exiled to northern Russia. As a Russian subject and the son of a political convict, Conrad faced the possibility of twenty-five years in the Russian army. To escape this grim future and to seek romantic adventure, he went to France at the age of sixteen to become a sailor.

Conrad was twenty-one when he first heard English spoken. Within two years he knew enough English to join the British merchant marine. In 1894, at the age of thirty-seven, poor health and the lack of sailing ships caused him to begin a new career as a writer. In 1895 he published his first novel, *Almayer's Folly*, and by 1897 his literary reputation was established. However, it was not until the publication of *Chance* (1913) that he became a popular and financially successful author.

Conrad's arduous journey up the Congo River into central Africa from 1890 to 1892 changed the course of his life. There he witnessed "the vilest scramble for loot that ever disfigured the history of human conscience and geographical exploration." His experiences in the

Congo taught him that the community, with its values and traditions, is necessary for the psychological well-being of the individual. When people leave family, friends, and customary pursuits for a new environment in which basic survival is an issue, the sense of isolation and the absence of customary human ties can leave people stripped of their civilized veneer and leave them vulnerable to their basest instincts. Conrad describes this process in his masterpiece, *Heart of Darkness*.

"An Outpost of Progress," one of Conrad's earliest stories, was first published in 1897. It is both a fine story in its own right and the forerunner of *Heart of Darkness*. Like many of his later stories, it is based on his journey up the Congo, and it reveals the same psychological focus and thematic material that characterize his greatest works.

I

There were two white men in charge of the trading station. Kayerts, the chief, was short and fat; Carlier, the assistant, was tall, with a large head and a very broad trunk perched upon a long pair of thin legs. The third man on the staff was a Sierra Leone[1] native, who maintained that his name was Henry Price. However, for some reason or other, the natives down the river had given him the name of Makola, and it stuck to him through all his wanderings about the country. He spoke English and French with a warbling accent, wrote a beautiful hand, understood bookkeeping, and cherished in his innermost heart the worship of evil spirits. His wife was a negress from Loanda,[2] very large and very noisy. Three children rolled about in sunshine before the door of his low, shed-like dwelling. Makola, taciturn and impenetrable, despised the two white men. He had charge of a small clay storehouse with a dried-grass roof, and pretended to keep a correct account of beads, cotton cloth, red kerchiefs, brass wire, and other trade goods it contained. Besides the storehouse and Makola's hut, there was only one large building in the cleared ground of the station. It was built neatly of reeds, with a veranda on all the four sides. There were three rooms in it. The one in the middle was the living room, and had two rough tables and a few stools in it. The other two were the bedrooms for the white men. Each had a bedstead and a mosquito net for all furniture. The plank floor was littered with the belongings of the white men; open half-empty boxes, torn wearing apparel, old boots; all the things dirty, and all the things broken, that accumulate mysteriously round untidy men. There was also another dwelling place some distance away from the buildings. In it, under a tall cross much out of the perpendicular, slept the man who had seen the beginning of all this; who had planned and had watched the construction of this

---

[1] *Sierra Leone:* Country in western Africa.
[2] *Loanda:* Luanda, the capital of Angola, in southwestern Africa.

outpost of progress. He had been, at home, an unsuccessful painter who, weary of pursuing fame on an empty stomach, had gone out there through high protections. He had been the first chief of that station. Makola had watched the energetic artist die of fever in the just-finished house with his usual kind of "I told you so" indifference. Then, for a time, he dwelt alone with his family, his account books, and the Evil Spirit that rules the lands under the equator. He got on very well with his god. Perhaps he had propitiated him by a promise of more white men to play with, by and by. At any rate the director of the Great Trading Company, coming up in a steamer that resembled an enormous sardine box with a flat-roofed shed erected on it, found the station in good order, and Makola as usual quietly diligent. The director had the cross put up over the first agent's grave, and appointed Kayerts to the post. Carlier was told off as second in charge. The director was a man ruthless and efficient, who at times, but very imperceptibly, indulged in grim humor. He made a speech to Kayerts and Carlier, pointing out to them the promising aspect of their station. The nearest trading post was about three hundred miles away. It was an exceptional opportunity for them to distinguish themselves and to earn percentages on the trade. This appointment was a favor done to beginners. Kayerts was moved almost to tears by his director's kindness. He would, he said, by doing his best, try to justify the flattering confidence, etc., etc. Kayerts had been in the Administration of the Telegraphs, and knew how to express himself correctly. Carlier, an ex-noncommissioned officer of cavalry in an army guaranteed from harm by several European powers, was less impressed. If there were commissions to get, so much the better; and, trailing a sulky glance over the river, the forests, the impenetrable bush that seemed to cut off the station from the rest of the world, he muttered between his teeth, "We shall see, very soon."

Next day, some bales of cotton goods and a few cases of provisions having been thrown on shore, the sardine-box steamer went off, not to return for another six months. On the deck the director touched his cap to the two agents, who stood on the bank waving their hats, and turning to an old servant of the Company on his passage to headquarters, said, "Look at those two imbeciles. They must be mad at home to send me such specimens. I told those fellows to plant a vegetable garden, build new storehouses and fences, and construct a landing stage. I bet nothing will be done! They won't know how to begin. I always thought the station on this river useless, and they just fit the station!"

"They will form themselves there," said the old stager[3] with a quiet smile.

"At any rate, I am rid of them for six months," retorted the director.

The two men watched the steamer round the bend, then ascending arm in arm the slope of the bank, returned to the station. They had been in this vast and dark country only a very short time, and as yet always in the midst of other white men, under the eye and guidance of their superiors. And now, dull as they were to the subtle influences of surrounding, they felt themselves very much alone, when suddenly left unassisted to face the wilderness; a wilderness rendered more

---

[3] *stager:* Experienced hand.

strange, more incomprehensible by the mysterious glimpses of the vigorous life it contained. They were two perfectly insignificant and incapable individuals, whose existence is only rendered possible through the high organization of civilized crowds. Few men realize that their life, the very essence of their character, their capabilities and their audacities, are only the expression of their belief in the safety of their surroundings. The courage, the composure, the confidence; the emotions and principles; every great and every insignificant thought belongs not to the individual but to the crowd: to the crowd that believes blindly in the irresistible force of its institutions and of its morals, in the power of its police and of its opinion. But the contact with pure unmitigated savagery, with primitive nature and primitive man, brings sudden and profound trouble into the heart. To the sentiment of being alone of one's kind, to the clear perception of the loneliness of one's thoughts, of one's sensations—to the negation of the habitual, which is safe, there is added the affirmation of the unusual, which is dangerous; a suggestion of things vague, uncontrollable, and repulsive, whose discomposing intrusion excites the imagination and tries the civilized nerves of the foolish and the wise alike.

Kayerts and Carlier walked arm in arm, drawing close to one another as children do in the dark, and they had the same, not altogether unpleasant, sense of danger which one half suspects to be imaginary. They chatted persistently in familiar tones. "Our station is prettily situated," said one. The other assented with enthusiasm, enlarging volubly on the beauties of the situation. Then they passed near the grave. "Poor devil!" said Kayerts. "He died of fever, didn't he?" muttered Carlier, stopping short. "Why," retorted Kayerts, with indignation, "I've been told that the fellow exposed himself recklessly to the sun. The climate here, everybody says, is not at all worse than at home as long as you keep out of the sun. Do you hear that, Carlier? I am chief here, and my orders are that you should not expose yourself to the sun!" He assumed his superiority jocularly, but his meaning was serious. The idea that he would, perhaps, have to bury Carlier and remain alone, gave him an inward shiver. He felt suddenly that this Carlier was more precious to him here, in the center of Africa, than a brother could be anywhere else. Carlier, entering into the spirit of the thing, made a military salute and answered in a brisk tone, "Your orders shall be attended to, chief!" Then he burst out laughing, slapped Kayerts on the back and shouted, "We shall let life run easily here! Just sit still and gather in the ivory those savages will bring. This country has its good points, after all!" They both laughed loudly while Carlier thought: "That poor Kayerts; he is so fat and unhealthy. It would be awful if I had to bury him here. He is a man I respect." . . . Before they reached the veranda of their house they called one another "my dear fellow."

The first day they were very active, pottering about with hammers and nails and red calico, to put up curtains, make their house habitable and pretty; resolved to settle down comfortably to their new life. For them an impossible task. To grapple effectually with even purely material problems requires more serenity of mind and more lofty courage than people generally imagine. No two beings could have been more unfitted for such a struggle. Society, not from any tenderness, but because of its strange needs, had taken care of those two men, forbidding them all independent thought, all initiative, all departure from routine; and forbidding it under pain of death. They could only live on condition of being machines. And now, released from the fostering care of men with pens behind the ears, or of men with gold lace on the sleeves, they were like those life-long prisoners who, liberated after many years, do not know what use to make of their freedom. They did not know what use to make of their faculties, being both, through want of practice, incapable of independent thought.

At the end of two months Kayerts often would say, "If it was not for my Melie, you wouldn't catch me here." Melie was his daughter. He had thrown up his post in the Administration of the Telegraphs, though he had been for seventeen years perfectly happy there, to earn a dowry for his girl. His wife was dead, and the child was being brought up by his sisters. He regretted the streets, the pavements, the cafés, his friends of many years; all the things he used to see day after day; all the thoughts suggested by familiar things—the thoughts effortless, monotonous, and soothing of a Government clerk; he regretted all the gossip, the small enmities, the mild venom, and the little jokes of Government offices. "If I had had a decent brother-in-law," Carlier would remark, "a fellow with a heart, I would not be here." He had left the army and had made himself so obnoxious to his family by his laziness and impudence, that an exasperated brother-in-law had made superhuman efforts to procure him an appointment in the Company as a second-class agent. Having not a penny in the world he was compelled to accept this means of livelihood as soon as it became quite clear to him that there was nothing more to squeeze out of his relations. He, like Kayerts, regretted his old life. He regretted the clink of saber and spurs on a fine afternoon, the barrack-room witticisms, the girls of garrison towns; but, besides, he had also a sense of grievance. He was evidently a much ill-used man. This made him moody, at times. But the two men got on well together in the fellowship of their stupidity and laziness. Together they did nothing, absolutely nothing, and enjoyed the sense of the idleness for which they were paid. And in time came to feel something resembling affection for one another.

They lived like blind men in a large room, aware only of what came in contact with them (and of that only imperfectly), but unable to see the general aspect of things. The river, the forest, all the great land throbbing with life, were like a great emptiness. Even the brilliant sunshine disclosed nothing intelligible. Things appeared and disappeared before their eyes in an unconnected and aimless kind of way. The river seemed to come from nowhere and flow nowhither. It flowed through a void. Out of that void, at times, came canoes, and men with spears in their hands would suddenly crowd the yard of the station. They were naked, glossy black, ornamented with snowy shells and glistening brass wire, perfect of limb. They made an uncouth babbling noise when they spoke, moved in a stately manner, and sent quick, wild glances out of their startled, never-resting eyes. Those warriors would squat in long rows, four or more deep, before the veranda, while their chiefs bargained for hours with Makola over an elephant tusk. Kayerts sat on his chair and looked down on the proceedings, understanding nothing. He stared at them with his round blue eyes, called out to Carlier, "Here, look! look at that fellow there—and that other one, to the left. Did you ever see such a face? Oh, the funny brute!"

Carlier, smoking native tabacco in a short wooden pipe, would swagger up twirling his mustaches, and surveying the warriors with haughty indulgence, would say:

"Fine animals. Brought any bone? Yes? It's not any too soon. Look at the muscles of that fellow—third from the end. I wouldn't care to get a punch on the nose from him. Fine arms, but legs no good below the knee. Couldn't make cavalry men of them." And after glancing down complacently at his own shanks, he always concluded, "Pah! Don't they stink! You, Makola! Take that herd over to the fetish" (the storehouse was in every station called the fetish, perhaps because of the spirit of civilization it contained) "and give them up some of the rubbish you keep there. I'd rather see it full of bone than full of rags."

Kayerts approved.

"Yes, yes! Go and finish that palaver over there, Mr. Makola. I will come round when you are ready, to weigh the tusk. We must be careful." Then turning to his companion: "This is the tribe that lives down the river; they are rather aromatic. I remember, they had been once before here. D'ye hear that now? What a fellow has got to put up with in this dog of a country! My head is split."

Such profitable visits were rare. For days the two pioneers of trade and progress would look on their empty courtyard in the vibrating brilliance of vertical sunshine. Below the high bank, the silent river flowed on glittering and steady. On the sands in the middle of the stream, hippos and alligators sunned themselves side by side. And stretching away in all directions, surrounding the insignificant cleared spot of the trading post, immense forests, hiding fateful complications of fantastic life, lay in the eloquent silence of mute greatness. The two men understood nothing, cared for nothing but for the passage of days that separated them from the steamer's return. Their predecessor had left some torn books. They took up these wrecks of novels, and, as they had never read anything of the kind before, they were surprised and amused. Then during the long days there were interminable and silly discussions about plots and personages. In the center of Africa they made acquaintance of Richelieu and of d'Artagnan, of Hawk's Eye and of Father Goriot,[4] and of many other people. All these imaginary personages became subjects for gossip as if they had been living friends. They discounted their virtues, suspected their motives, decried their successes; were scandalized at their duplicity or were doubtful about their courage. The accounts of crimes filled them with indignation, while tender or pathetic passages moved them deeply. Carlier cleared his throat and said in a soldierly voice, "What nonsense!" Kayerts, his round eyes suffused with tears, his fat cheeks quivering, rubbed his

---

[4] *Richelieu . . . Father Goriot:* Characters in adventure and romantic novels. Richelieu and d'Artagnan appear in Alexandre Dumas's *The Three Musketeers.* Hawk's Eye or Hawkeye is in *The Last of the Mohicans* by James Fenimore Cooper. Father Goriot appears in the novels of Honoré de Balzac.

bald head, and declared, "This is a splendid book. I had no idea there were such clever fellows in the world." They also found some old copies of a home paper. That print discussed what it was pleased to call "Our Colonial Expansion" in high-flown language. It spoke much of the rights and duties of civilization, of the sacredness of the civilizing work, and extolled the merits of those who went about bringing light, and faith, and commerce to the dark places of the earth. Carlier and Kayerts read, wondered, and began to think better of themselves. Carlier said one evening, waving his hand about, "In a hundred years, there will be perhaps a town here. Quays, and warehouses, and barracks, and—and—billiard rooms. Civilization, my boy, and virtue—and all. And then, chaps will read that two good fellows, Kayerts and Carlier, were the first civilized men to live in this very spot!" Kayerts nodded, "Yes, it is a consolation to think of that." They seemed to forget their dead predecessor; but, early one day, Carlier went out and replanted the cross firmly. "It used to make me squint whenever I walked that way," he explained to Kayerts over the morning coffee. "It made me squint, leaning over so much. So I just planted it upright. And solid, I promise you! I suspended myself with both hands to the cross-piece. Not a move. Oh, I did that properly."

At times Gobila came to see them. Gobila was the chief of the neighboring villages. He was a gray-headed savage, thin and black, with a white cloth round his loins and a mangy panther skin hanging over his back. He came up with long strides of his skeleton legs, swinging a staff as tall as himself, and, entering the common room of the station, would squat on his heels to the left of the door. There he sat, watching Kayerts, and now and then making a speech which the other did not understand. Kayerts, without interrupting his occupation, would from time to time say in a friendly manner: "How goes it, you old image?" and they would smile at one another. The two whites had a liking for that old and incomprehensible creature, and called him Father Gobila. Gobila's manner was paternal, and he seemed really to love all white men. They all appeared to him very young, indistinguishably alike (except for stature), and he knew that they were all brothers, and also immortal. The death of the artist, who was the first white man whom he knew intimately, did not disturb this belief, because he was firmly convinced that the white stranger had pretended to die and got himself buried for some mysterious purpose of his own, into which it was useless to inquire. Perhaps it was his way of going home to his own country? At any rate, these were his brothers, and he transferred his absurd affection to them. They returned it in a way. Carlier slapped him on the back, and recklessly struck off matches for his amusement. Kayerts was always ready to let him have a sniff at the ammonia bottle. In short, they behaved just like that other white creature that had hidden itself in a hole in the ground. Gobila considered them attentively. Perhaps they were the same being with the other—or one of them was. He couldn't decide—clear up that mystery; but he remained always very friendly. In consequence of that friendship the women of Gobila's village walked in single file through the reedy grass, bringing every morning to the station fowls, and sweet potatoes, and palm wine, and sometimes a goat. The Company never provisions the stations fully, and the agents required those local supplies to live. They had them through the good will of

Gobila, and lived well. Now and then one of them had a bout of fever, and the other nursed him with gentle devotion. They did not think much of it. It left them weaker, and their appearance changed for the worse. Carlier was hollow-eyed and irritable. Kayerts showed a drawn, flabby face above the rotundity of his stomach, which gave him a weird aspect. But being constantly together, they did not notice the change that took place gradually in their appearance, and also in their dispositions.

Five months passed in that way.

Then, one morning, as Kayerts and Carlier, lounging in their chairs under the veranda, talked about the approaching visit of the steamer, a knot of armed men came out of the forest and advanced towards the station. They were strangers to that part of the country. They were tall, slight, draped classically from neck to heel in blue fringed cloths, and carried percussion muskets over their bare right shoulders. Makola showed signs of excitement, and ran out of the storehouse (where he spent all his days) to meet these visitors. They came into the courtyard and looked about them with steady, scornful glances. Their leader, a powerful and determined-looking Negro with bloodshot eyes, stood in front of the veranda and made a long speech. He gesticulated much, and ceased very suddenly.

There was something in his intonation, in the sounds of the long sentences he used, that startled the two whites. It was like a reminiscence of something not exactly familiar, and yet resembling the speech of civilized men. It sounded like one of those impossible languages which sometimes we hear in our dreams.

"What lingo is that?" said the amazed Carlier. "In the first moment I fancied the fellow was going to speak French. Anyway, it is a different kind of gibberish to what we ever heard."

"Yes," replied Kayerts. "Hey, Makola, what does he say? Where do they come from? Who are they?"

But Makola, who seemed to be standing on hot bricks, answered hurriedly, "I don't know. They come from very far. Perhaps Mrs. Price will understand. They are perhaps bad men."

The leader, after waiting for a while, said something sharply to Makola, who shook his head. Then the man, after looking round, noticed Makola's hut and walked over there. The next moment Mrs. Makola was heard speaking with great volubility. The other strangers—they were six in all—strolled about with an air of ease, put their heads through the door of the storeroom, congregated round the grave, pointed understandingly at the cross, and generally made themselves at home.

"I don't like those chaps—and I say, Kayerts, they must be from the coast; they've got firearms," observed the sagacious Carlier.

Kayerts also did not like those chaps. They both, for the first time, became aware that they lived in conditions where the unusual may be dangerous, and that there was no power on earth outside of themselves to stand between them and the unusual. They became uneasy, went in and loaded their revolvers. Kayerts said, "We must order Makola to tell them to go away before dark."

The strangers left in the afternoon, after eating a meal prepared for them by Mrs. Makola. The immense woman was excited, and talked much with the visitors. She rattled away shrilly, pointing here and there at the forests and at the river. Makola sat apart and watched. At times he got up and whispered to his wife. He accompanied the strangers across the ravine at the back of the station-ground, and returned slowly looking very thoughtful. When questioned by the white men he was very strange, seemed not to understand, seemed to have forgotten French— seemed to have forgotten how to speak altogether. Kayerts and Carlier agreed that the native had had too much palm wine.

There was some talk about keeping a watch in turn, but in the evening everything seemed so quiet and peaceful that they retired as usual. All night they were disturbed by a lot of drumming in the villages. A deep, rapid roll nearby would be followed by another far off—then all ceased. Some short appeals would rattle out here and there, then all mingle together, increase, become vigorous and sustained, would spread out over the forest, roll through the night, unbroken and ceaseless, near and far, as if the whole land had been one immense drum booming out steadily an appeal to heaven. And through the deep and tremendous noise sudden yells that resembled snatches of songs from a madhouse darted shrill and high in discordant jets of sound which seemed to rush far above the earth and drive all peace from under the stars.

Carlier and Kayerts slept badly. They both thought they had heard shots fired during the night—but they could not agree as to the direction. In the morning Makola was gone somewhere. He returned about noon with one of yesterday's strangers, and eluded all Kayerts' attempts to close with him: had become deaf apparently. Kayerts wondered. Carlier, who had been fishing off the bank, came back and remarked while he showed his catch, "The natives seem to be in a deuce of a stir; I wonder what's up. I saw about fifteen canoes cross the river during the two hours I was there fishing." Kayerts, worried, said, "Isn't this Makola very queer today?" Carlier advised, "Keep all our men together in case of some trouble."

II

There were ten station men who had been left by the Director. Those fellows, having engaged themselves to the Company for six months (without having any idea of a month in particular and only a very faint notion of time in general), had been serving the cause of progress for upwards of two years. Belonging to a tribe from a very distant part of the land of darkness and sorrow, they did not run away, naturally supposing that as wandering strangers they would be killed by the inhabitants of the country; in which they were right. They lived in straw huts on the slope of a ravine overgrown with reedy grass, just behind the station buildings. They were not happy, regretting the festive incantations, the sorceries, the human sacrifices of their own land; where they also had parents, brothers, sisters, admired chiefs, respected magicians, loved friends, and other ties supposed generally to be human. Besides, the rice rations served out by the Company did not agree with them, being a food unknown to their land, and to which they could not get used. Consequently they were unhealthy and miserable. Had they been of any other tribe they would have made up their minds to die—for nothing is easier to certain savages than suicide—and so have escaped from the puzzling difficulties of existence. But belonging, as they did, to a warlike tribe with filed teeth, they had more grit, and went on stupidly living through disease and sorrow. They did very little work, and had lost their splendid physique. Carlier and Kayerts doctored them assiduously without being able to bring them back into condition again. They were mustered every morning and told off to different tasks—grass-cutting, fence-building, tree-felling, etc., etc., which no power on earth could induce them to execute efficiently. The two whites had practically very little control over them.

In the afternoon Makola came over to the big house and found Kayerts watching three heavy columns of smoke rising above the forests. "What is that?" asked Kayerts. "Some villages burn," answered Makola, who seemed to have regained his wits. Then he said abruptly: "We have got very little ivory; bad six months' trading. Do you like get a little more ivory?"

"Yes," said Kayerts, eagerly. He thought of percentages which were low.

"Those men who came yesterday are traders from Loanda who have got more ivory than they can carry home. Shall I buy? I know their camp."

"Certainly," said Kayerts. "What are those traders?"

"Bad fellows," said Makola, indifferently. "They fight with people, and catch women and children. They are bad men, and got guns. There is a great disturbance in the country. Do you want ivory?"

"Yes," said Kayerts. Makola said nothing for a while. Then: "Those workmen of ours are no good at all," he muttered, looking round. "Station in very bad order, sir. Director will growl. Better get a fine lot of ivory, then he say nothing."

"I can't help it; the men won't work," said Kayerts. "When will you get that ivory?"

"Very soon," said Makola. "Perhaps tonight. You leave it to me, and keep indoors, sir. I think you had better give some palm wine to our men to make a dance this evening. Enjoy themselves. Work better tomorrow. There's plenty palm wine—gone a little sour."

Kayerts said "yes," and Makola, with his own hands, carried big calabashes[5] to the door of his hut. They stood there till the evening, and Mrs. Makola looked into every one. The men got them at sunset. When Kayerts and Carlier retired, a big bonfire was flaring before the men's huts. They could hear their shouts and drumming. Some men from Gobila's village had joined the station hands, and the entertainment was a great success.

In the middle of the night, Carlier, waking suddenly, heard a man shout loudly; then a shot was fired. Only one. Carlier ran out and met Kayerts on the veranda. They were both startled. As they went across the yard to call Makola, they saw shadows moving in the night. One of them cried, "Don't shoot! It's me,

---

[5] *calabashes:* Containers made from gourds.

Price." Then Makola appeared close to them. "Go back, go back, please," he urged, "you spoil all." "There are strange men about," said Carlier. "Never mind; I know," said Makola. Then he whispered, "All right. Bring ivory. Say nothing! I know my business." The two white men reluctantly went back to the house, but did not sleep. They heard footsteps, whispers, some groans. It seemed as if a lot of men came in, dumped heavy things on the ground, squabbled a long time, then went away. They lay on their hard beds and thought: "This Makola is invaluable." In the morning Carlier came out, very sleepy, and pulled at the cord of the big bell. The station hands mustered every morning to the sound of the bell. That morning nobody came. Kayerts turned out also, yawning. Across the yard they saw Makola come out of his hut, a tin basin of soapy water in his hand. Makola, a civilized native, was very neat in his person. He threw the soapsuds skillfully over a wretched little yellow cur he had, then turning his face to the agent's house, he shouted from the distance, "All the men gone last night!"

They heard him plainly, but in their surprise they both yelled out together: "What!" Then they stared at one another. "We are in a proper fix now," growled Carlier. "It's incredible!" muttered Kayerts. "I will go to the huts and see," said Carlier, striding off. Makola coming up found Kayerts standing alone.

"I can hardly believe it," said Kayerts tearfully. "We took care of them as if they had been our children."

"They went with the coast people," said Makola after a moment of hesitation.

"What do I care with whom they went—the ungrateful brutes!" exclaimed the other. Then with sudden suspicion, and looking hard at Makola, he added: "What do you know about it?"

Makola moved his shoulders, looking down on the ground. "What do I know? I think only. Will you come and look at the ivory I've got there? It is a fine lot. You never saw such."

He moved towards the store. Kayerts followed him mechanically, thinking about the incredible desertion of the men. On the ground before the door of the fetish lay six splendid tusks.

"What did you give for it?" asked Kayerts, after surveying the lot with satisfaction.

"No regular trade," said Makola. "They brought the ivory and gave it to me. I told them to take what they most wanted in the station. It is a beautiful lot. No station can show such tusks. Those traders wanted carriers badly, and our men were no good here. No trade, no entry in books; all correct."

Kayerts nearly burst with indignation. "Why!" he shouted, "I believe you have sold our men for these tusks!" Makola stood impassive and silent. "I—I—will— I," stuttered Kayerts. "You fiend!" he yelled out.

"I did the best for you and the Company," said Makola, imperturbably. "Why you shout so much? Look at this tusk."

"I dismiss you! I will report you—I won't look at the tusk. I forbid you to touch them. I order you to throw them into the river. You—you!"

"You very red, Mr. Kayerts. If you are so irritable in the sun, you will get fever and die—like the first chief!" pronounced Makola impressively.

They stood still, contemplating one another with intense eyes, as if they had been looking with effort across immense distances. Kayerts shivered. Makola had meant no more than he said, but his words seemed to Kayerts full of ominous menace! He turned sharply and went away to the house. Makola retired into the bosom of his family; and the tusks, left lying before the store, looked very large and valuable in the sunshine.

Carlier came back on the veranda. "They're all gone, hey?" asked Kayerts from the far end of the common room in a muffled voice. "You did not find anybody?"

"Oh yes," said Carlier, "I found one of Gobila's people lying dead before the huts—shot through the body. We heard that shot last night."

Kayerts came out quickly. He found his companion staring grimly over the yard at the tusks, away by the store. They both sat in silence for a while. Then Kayerts related his conversation with Makola. Carlier said nothing.

At the midday meal they ate very little. They hardly exchanged a word that day. A great silence seemed to lie heavily over the station and press on their lips. Makola did not open the store; he spent the day playing with his children. He lay full-length on a mat outside his door, and the youngsters sat on his chest and clambered all over him. It was a touching picture. Mrs. Makola was busy cooking all day as usual. The white men made a somewhat better meal in the evening. Afterwards, Carlier smoking his pipe strolled over to the store; he stood for a long time over the tusks, touched one or two with his foot, even tried to lift the largest one by its small end. He came back to his chief, who had not stirred from the veranda, threw himself in the chair and said:

"I can see it! They were pounced upon while they slept heavily after drinking all that palm wine you've allowed Makola to give them. A put-up job! See? The worst is, some of Gobila's people were there, and got carried off too, no doubt. The least drunk woke up, and got shot for his sobriety. This is a funny country. What will you do now?"

"We can't touch it, of course," said Kayerts.

"Of course not," assented Carlier.

"Slavery is an awful thing," stammered out Kayerts in an unsteady voice.

"Frightful—the sufferings," grunted Carlier with conviction.

They believed their words. Everybody shows a respectful deference to certain sounds that he and his fellows can make. But about feelings people really know nothing. We talk with indignation or enthusiasm; we talk about oppression, cruelty, crime, devotion, self-sacrifice, virtue, and we know nothing real beyond the words. Nobody knows what suffering or sacrifice mean—except, perhaps the victims of the mysterious purpose of these illusions.

Next morning they saw Makola very busy setting up in the yard the big scales used for weighing ivory. By and by Carlier said: "What's that filthy scoundrel up to?" and lounged out into the yard. Kayerts followed. They stood watching. Makola took no notice. When the balance was swung true, he tried to lift a tusk into the scale. It was too heavy. He looked up helplessly without a word, and for a minute they stood round that balance as mute and still as three statues. Suddenly Carlier said: "Catch hold of the other end, Makola—you beast!" and together they swung the tusk up. Kayerts trembled in every limb. He muttered, "I say! O! I say!" and putting his hand in his pocket found there a dirty bit of paper and the stump of a pencil. He turned his back on the others, as if about to do something tricky, and noted stealthily the weights which Carlier shouted out to him with unnecessary loudness. When all was over Makola whispered to himself: "The sun's very strong here for the tusks." Carlier said to Kayerts in a careless tone: "I say, chief, I might just as well give him a lift with this into the store."

As they were going back to the house Kayerts observed with a sigh: "It had to be done." And Carlier said: "It's deplorable, but, the men being Company's men the ivory is Company's ivory. We must look after it." "I will report to the Director, of course," said Kayerts. "Of course; let him decide," approved Carlier.

At midday they made a hearty meal. Kayerts sighed from time to time. Whenever they mentioned Makola's name they always added to it an opprobrious epithet. It eased their conscience. Makola gave himself a half-holiday, and bathed his children in the river. No one from Gobila's villages came near the station that day. No one came the next day, and the next, nor for a whole week. Gobila's people might have been dead and buried for any sign of life they gave. But they were only mourning for those they had lost by the witchcraft of white men, who had brought wicked people into their country. The wicked people were gone, but fear remained. Fear always remains. A man may destroy everything within himself, love and hate and belief, and even doubt; but as long as he clings to life he cannot destroy fear: the fear, subtle, indestructible, and terrible, that pervades his being; that tinges his thoughts; that lurks in his heart; that watches on his lips the struggle of his last breath. In his fear, the mild old Gobila offered extra human sacrifices to all the Evil Spirits that had taken possession of his white friends. His heart was heavy. Some warriors spoke about burning and killing, but the cautious old savage dissuaded them. Who could foresee the woe those mysterious creatures, if irritated, might bring? They should be left alone. Perhaps in time they would disappear into the earth as the first one had disappeared. His people must keep away from them, and hope for the best.

Kayerts and Carlier did not disappear, but remained above on this earth, that, somehow, they fancied had become bigger and very empty. It was not the absolute and dumb solitude of the post that impressed them so much as an inarticulate feeling that something from within them was gone, something that worked for their safety, and had kept the wilderness from interfering with their hearts. The images of home; the memory of people like them, of men that thought and felt as they used to think and feel, receded into distances made indistinct by the glare of unclouded sunshine. And out of the great silence of the surrounding wilderness, its very hopelessness and savagery seemed to approach them nearer, to draw them gently, to look upon them, to envelop them with a solicitude irresistible, familiar, and disgusting.

Days lengthened into weeks, then into months. Gobila's people drummed and yelled to every new moon, as of yore, but kept away from the station. Makola and Carlier tried once in a canoe to open communications, but were received with a shower of arrows, and had to fly back to the station for dear life. That attempt set the country up and down the river into an uproar that could be very distinctly heard for days. The steamer was late. At first they spoke of delay jauntily, then anxiously, then gloomily. The matter was becoming serious. Stores were running short. Carlier cast his lines off the bank, but the river was low, and the fish kept out in the stream. They dared not stroll far away from the station to shoot. Moreover, there was no game in the impenetrable forest. Once Carlier shot a hippo in the river. They had no boat to secure it, and it sank. When it floated up it drifted away, and Gobila's people secured the carcass. It was the occasion for a national holiday, but Carlier had a fit of rage over it and talked about the necessity of exterminating all the natives before the country could be made habitable. Kayerts mooned about silently; spent hours looking at the portrait of his Melie. It represented a little girl with long bleached tresses and a rather sour face. His legs were much swollen, and he could hardly walk. Carlier, undermined by fever, could not swagger any more, but kept tottering about, still with a devil-may-care air, as became a man who remembered his crack regiment. He had become hoarse, sarcastic, and inclined to say unpleasant things. He called it "being frank with you." They had long ago reckoned their percentages on trade, including in them that last deal of "this infamous Makola." They had also concluded not to say anything about it. Kayerts hesitated at first—was afraid of the Director.

"He has seen worse things done on the quiet," maintained Carlier, with a hoarse laugh. "Trust him! He won't thank you if you blab. He is no better than you or me. Who will talk if we hold our tongues? There is nobody here."

That was the root of the trouble! There was nobody there; and being left here alone with their weakness, they became daily more like a pair of accomplices than like a couple of devoted friends. They had heard nothing from home for eight months. Every evening they said, "Tomorrow we shall see the steamer." But one of the Company's steamers had been wrecked, and the Director was busy with the other, relieving very distant and important stations on the main river. He thought that the useless station, and the useless men, could wait. Meantime Kayerts and Carlier lived on rice boiled without salt, and cursed the Company, all Africa, and the day they were born. One must have lived on such diet to discover what ghastly trouble the necessity of swallowing one's food may become. There was literally nothing else in the station but rice and coffee; they drank the coffee without sugar. The last fifteen lumps Kayerts had solemnly locked away in his box, together with a half-bottle of cognac, "in case of sickness," he explained. Carlier approved. "When one is sick," he said, "any little extra like that is cheering."

They waited. Rank grass began to sprout over the courtyard. The bell never rang now. Days passed, silent, exasperating, and slow. When the two men spoke, they snarled; and their silences were bitter, as if tinged by the bitterness of their thoughts.

One day after a lunch of boiled rice, Carlier put down his cup untasted, and said: "Hang it all! Let's have a decent cup of coffee for once. Bring out that sugar, Kayerts!"

"For the sick," muttered Kayerts, without looking up.

"For the sick," mocked Carlier. "Bosh! . . . Well! I am sick."

"You are no more sick than I am, and I go without," said Kayerts in a peaceful tone.

"Come! Out with that sugar, you stingy old slave dealer."

Kayerts looked up quickly. Carlier was smiling with marked insolence. And suddenly it seemed to Kayerts that he had never seen that man before. Who was he? He knew nothing about him. What was he capable of? There was a surprising flash of violent emotion within him, as if in the presence of something undreamt-of, dangerous, and final. But he managed to pronounce with composure:

"That joke is in very bad taste. Don't repeat it."

"Joke!" said Carlier, hitching himself forward on his seat. "I am hungry—I am sick—I don't joke! I hate hypocrites. You are a hypocrite. You are a slave dealer. I am a slave dealer. There's nothing but slave dealers in this cursed country. I mean to have sugar in my coffee today anyhow!"

"I forbid you to speak to me in that way," said Kayerts with a fair show of resolution.

"You!—What?" shouted Carlier, jumping up.

Kayerts stood up also. "I am your chief," he began, trying to master the shakiness of his voice.

"What?" yelled the other. "Who's chief? There's no chief here. There's nothing here: there's nothing but you and I. Fetch the sugar—you pot-bellied ass."

"Hold your tongue. Go out of this room," screamed Kayerts. "I dismiss you— you scoundrel!"

Carlier swung a stool. All at once he looked dangerously in earnest. "You flabby, good-for-nothing civilian—take that!" he howled.

Kayerts dropped under the table, and the stool struck the grass inner wall of the room. Then, as Carlier was trying to upset the table, Kayerts in desperation made a blind rush, head low, like a cornered pig would do, and over-turning his friend, bolted along the veranda, and into his room. He locked the door, snatched his revolver, and stood panting. In less than a minute Carlier was kicking at the door furiously, howling, "If you don't bring out that sugar, I will shoot you at sight, like a dog. Now then—one—two—three. You won't? I will show you who's the master."

Kayerts thought the door would fall in, and scrambled through the square hole that served for a window in his room. There was then the whole breadth of the house between them. But the other was apparently not strong enough to break in the door, and Kayerts heard him running round. Then he also began to run laboriously on his swollen legs. He ran as quickly as he could, grasping the revolver, and unable yet to understand what was happening to him. He saw in succession Makola's house, the store, the river, the ravine, and the low bushes; and he saw all those things again as he ran for the second time round the house. Then again they flashed past him. That morning he could not have walked a yard without a groan.

And now he ran. He ran fast enough to keep out of sight of the other man.

Then as, weak and desperate, he thought, "Before I finish the next round I shall die," he heard the other man stumble heavily, then stop. He stopped also.

He had the back and Carlier the front of the house, as before. He heard him drop into a chair cursing, and suddenly his own legs gave way, and he slid down into a sitting posture with his back to the wall. His mouth was as dry as a cinder, and his face was wet with perspiration—and tears. What was it all about? He thought it must be a horrible illusion; he thought he was dreaming; he thought he was going mad! After a while he collected his senses. What did they quarrel about? That sugar! How absurd! He would give it to him—didn't want it himself. And he began scrambling to his feet with a sudden feeling of security. But before he had fairly stood upright, a common-sense reflection occurred to him and drove him back into despair. He thought: "If I give way now to that brute of a soldier, he will begin this horror again tomorrow—and the day after—every day—raise other pretensions, trample on me, torture me, make me his slave—and I will be lost! Lost! The steamer may not come for days—may never come." He shook so that he had to sit down on the floor again. He shivered forlornly. He felt he could not, would not move any more. He was completely distracted by the sudden per-ception that the position was without issue—that death and life had in a moment become equally difficult and terrible.

All at once he heard the other push his chair back; and he leaped to his feet with extreme facility. He listened and got confused. Must run again! Right or left? He heard footsteps. He darted to the left, grasping his revolver, and at the very same instant, as it seemed to him, they came into violent collision. Both shouted with surprise. A loud explosion took place between them; a roar of red fire, thick smoke; and Kayerts, deafened and blinded, rushed back thinking: "I am hit—it's over." He expected the other to come round—to gloat over his agony. He caught hold of an upright of the roof—"All over!" Then he heard a crashing fall on the other side of the house, as if somebody had tumbled headlong over a chair—then silence. Nothing more happened. He did not die. Only his shoulder felt as if it had been badly wrenched, and he had lost his revolver. He was disarmed and helpless! He waited for his fate. The other man made no sound. It was a strata-gem. He was stalking him now! Along what side? Perhaps he was taking aim this very minute!

After a few moments of an agony frightful and absurd, he decided to go and meet his doom. He was prepared for every surrender. He turned the corner, steady-ing himself with one hand on the wall; made a few paces, and nearly swooned. He had seen on the floor, protruding past the other corner, a pair of turned-up feet. A pair of white naked feet in red slippers. He felt deadly sick, and stood for a time in profound darkness. Then Makola appeared before him, saying quietly: "Come along, Mr. Kayerts. He is dead." He burst into tears of gratitude; a loud, sobbing fit of crying. After a time he found himself sitting in a chair and looking at Carlier, who lay stretched on his back. Makola was kneeling over the body.

"Is this your revolver?" asked Makola, getting up.

"Yes," said Kayerts; then he added very quickly, "He ran after me to shoot me—you saw!"

"Yes, I saw," said Makola. "There is only one revolver; where's his?"

"Don't know," whispered Kayerts in a voice that had become suddenly very faint.

"I will go and look for it," said the other, gently. He made the round along the veranda, while Kayerts sat still and looked at the corpse. Makola came back empty-handed, stood in deep thought, then stepped quietly into the dead man's room, and came out directly with a revolver, which he held up before Kayerts. Kayerts shut his eyes. Everything was going round. He found life more terrible and difficult than death. He had shot an unarmed man.

After meditating for a while, Makola said softly, pointing at the dead man who lay there with his right eye blown out:

"He died of fever." Kayerts looked at him with a stony stare. "Yes," repeated Makola, thoughtfully, stepping over the corpse, "I think he died of fever. Bury him tomorrow."

And he went away slowly to his expectant wife, leaving the two white men alone on the veranda.

Night came, and Kayerts sat unmoving on his chair. He sat quiet as if he had taken a dose of opium. The violence of the emotions he had passed through produced a feeling of exhausted serenity. He had plumbed in one short afternoon the depths of horror and despair, and now found repose in the conviction that life had no more secrets for him: neither had death! He sat by the corpse thinking; thinking very actively, thinking very new thoughts. He seemed to have broken loose from himself altogether. His old thoughts, convictions, likes and dislikes, things he respected and things he abhorred, appeared in their true light at last! Appeared contemptible and childish, false and ridiculous. He reveled in his new wisdom while he sat by the man he had killed. He argued with himself about all things under heaven with that kind of wrong-headed lucidity which may be observed in some lunatics. Incidentally he reflected that the fellow dead there had been a noxious beast anyway; that men died every day in thousands; perhaps in hundreds of thousands—who could tell?—and that in the number, that one death could not possibly make any difference; couldn't have any importance, at least to a thinking creature. He, Kayerts, was a thinking creature. He had been all his life, till that moment, a believer in a lot of nonsense like the rest of mankind—who are fools; but now he thought! He knew! He was at peace; he was familiar with the highest wisdom! Then he tried to imagine himself dead, and Carlier sitting in his chair watching him; and his attempt met with such unexpected success, that in a very few moments he became not at all sure who was dead and who was alive. This extraordinary achievement of his fancy startled him, however, and by a clever and timely effort of mind he saved himself just in time from becoming Carlier. His heart thumped, and he felt hot all over at the thought of that danger. Carlier! What a beastly thing! To compose his now disturbed nerves—and no wonder!—he tried to whistle a little. Then, suddenly, he fell asleep, or thought he had slept; but at any rate there was a fog, and somebody had whistled in the fog.

He stood up. The day had come, and a heavy mist had descended upon the land: the mist penetrating, enveloping, and silent; the morning mist of tropical lands; the mist that clings and kills; the mist white and deadly, immaculate and poisonous. He stood up, saw the body, and threw his arms above his head with a cry like that of a man who, waking from a trance, finds himself immured forever in a tomb. *"Help! . . . My God!"*

A shriek inhuman, vibrating, and sudden, pierced like a sharp dart the white shroud of that land of sorrow. Three short, impatient screeches followed, and then, for a time, the fog-wreaths rolled on, undisturbed, through a formidable silence. Then many more shrieks, rapid and piercing, like the yells of some exasperated and ruthless creature, rent the air. Progress was calling to Kayerts from the river. Progress and civilization and all the virtues. Society was calling to its accomplished child to come, to be taken care of, to be instructed, to be judged, to be condemned; it called him to return to that rubbish heap from which he had wandered away, so that justice could be done.

Kayerts heard and understood. He stumbled out of the veranda, leaving the other man quite alone for the first time since they had been thrown there together. He groped his way through the fog, calling in his ignorance upon the invisible heaven to undo his work. Makola flitted by in the mist, shouting as he ran:

"Steamer! Steamer! They can't see. They whistle for the station. I go ring the bell. Go down to the landing, sir. I ring."

He disappeared, Kayerts stood still. He looked upwards; the fog rolled low over his head. He looked round like a man who has lost his way; and he saw a dark smudge, a cross-shaped stain, upon the shifting purity of the mist. As he began to stumble towards it, the station bell rang in a tumultuous peal its answer to the impatient clamor of the steamer.

The Managing Director of the Great Civilizing Company (since we know that civilization follows trade) landed first, and incontinently lost sight of the steamer. The fog down by the river was exceedingly dense; above at the station, the bell rang unceasing and brazen.

The Director shouted loudly to the steamer:

"There is nobody down to meet us; there may be something wrong, though they are ringing. You had better come, too!"

And he began to toil up the steep bank. The captain and the engine-driver of the boat followed behind. As they scrambled up the fog thinned, and they could see their Director a good way ahead. Suddenly they saw him start forward, calling to them over his shoulder: "Run! Run to the house! I've found one of them. Run, look for the other!"

He had found one of them! And even he, the man of varied and startling experience, was somewhat discomposed by the manner of this finding. He stood and fumbled in his pockets (for a knife) while he faced Kayerts, who was hanging by a leather strap from the cross. He had evidently climbed the grave, which was high and narrow, and after tying the end of the strap to the arm, had swung himself off. His toes were only a couple of inches above the ground; his arms hung stiffly down; he seemed to be standing rigidly at attention; but with one purple cheek playfully posed on the shoulder. And, irreverently, he was putting out a swollen tongue at his Managing Director.

UNDERSTANDING THE STORY

1. What makes Kayerts and Carlier "two perfectly insignificant and incapable individuals"? Why don't they make the improvements they were told to make in the trading station? What are the consequences?

2. What does Conrad mean when he states that courage, principles, and every thought belong "not to the individual but to the crowd"? How does "contact with pure unmitigated savagery, with primitive nature and primitive man [bring] sudden and profound trouble into the heart"?

3. What do Conrad's depictions of Gobila's ideas and attitudes reveal?

4. What difference does it make that Makola calls himself Henry Price, speaks English and French, writes beautifully, and understands bookkeeping?

5. Why is Makola uncomfortable and uncommunicative with Kayerts and Carlier once the armed men arrive?

6. To what extent, if any, are Kayerts and Carlier responsible for the sale of their station workers into slavery? What is the result of their action?

7. Why do Kayerts and Carlier fight? What does the following line mean: "And suddenly it seemed to Kayerts that he had never seen that man [Carlier] before"?

8. Conrad states, "A man may destroy everything within himself, love and hate and belief, and even doubt; but as long as he clings to life he cannot destroy fear." What role does fear play in this story?

9. What makes death and life "equally difficult and terrible" for Kayerts? Why doesn't he realize what he has done to Carlier?

10. When Makola tells Kayerts that Carlier died of fever, what effect does this have on Kayerts?

11. Why does Kayerts commit suicide?

12. What **themes** do you find in this story?

ANALYZING LITERARY TECHNIQUE

1. What is the relationship between the **setting** and the **plot** of this story?

2. Why did Conrad title this story "An Outpost of Progress"?

3. Analyze Makola's role in the story.

4. Find two or three examples of **foreshadowing** and explain their function.

5. Where are the **crisis** and the **climax** in the story?

6. In what way does Carlier change the **narrative perspective** once Carlier threatens to shoot Kayerts? What does the change in narrative perspective achieve?

7. In what ways does Kayerts experience a **night journey?**

WRITING ABOUT LITERATURE

1. In this story, Conrad writes, "A man may destroy everything within himself, love and hate and belief, and even doubt; but as long as he clings to life he cannot destroy fear." Apply this quotation to the story by examining the role that fear plays in the plot. Use quotations to support your ideas.

2. When the Director complains about his two new agents (Kayerts and Carlier), the old stager replies, "They will form themselves there." Trace Kayerts's psychological disintegration from his arrival to his suicide. Consider the factors that affected Kayerts and then choose two or three key factors to help focus your essay. Use quotations from the story to support your ideas.

3. Write this story from Makola's point of view. Given his character and values, how does he view Kayerts and Carlier? How does he wish to present himself to them, to Gobila, to the armed visitors, and to the Director? You may wish to choose one of these characters as the imagined audience for Makola's narrative.

The Lake Isle of Innisfree

WILLIAM BUTLER YEATS

ILLIAM BUTLER YEATS (1865–1939) is Ireland's greatest lyric poet. He is regarded by many as the greatest poet of the twentieth century. Yeats won the Nobel Prize in 1923 "for his always inspired poetry, which in a highly artistic form gives expression to the spirit of a whole nation." Although he is known primarily as a poet, he also wrote plays, fiction, and literary essays, and he led the Irish Cultural Revival by reviving Celtic mythology and Irish folktales. From 1922 to 1928 he served as a senator of the Irish Free State. Yeats is particularly known for three collections of poems—*The Wanderings of Oisin and Other Poems* (1889), *The Wind Among the Reeds* (1899), and *The Tower* (1928).

Yeats was born in Sandymount, near Dublin, Ireland. His father was a portrait painter, and Yeats studied art for three years before he decided to become a poet. He spent his childhood and later school holidays with his mother's family in the country near Sligo, in western Ireland. Although he lived in London from 1888 to 1896, he always thought of himself as an Irish writer, and Ireland remained the source of his inspiration and imagery.

The Wind Among the Reeds became the seminal work in the development of twentieth-century poetry. Yeats's involvement in the Irish Cultural Revival led him to believe that the world could not be viewed as a totally objective reality. Instead, he believed that imagination shaped every experience. *The Wind Among the Reeds* thus marks the beginning of modern poetry.

"The Lake Isle of Innisfree" (1892) is the best-known lyric of Yeats's early period. Innisfree, from the Irish words for "Heather Island," is a small island in Lough (Lake) Gill in western Ireland, the area in which Yeats grew up. In his autobiography, Yeats writes about the experience in London that inspired this poem:

> When walking through Fleet Street very homesick I heard a
> little tinkle of water and saw a fountain in a shopwindow

which balanced a little ball upon its jet, and began to remember lake water.

The poem typifies Yeats's desire to transform life experience into art and demonstrates his ability to use words to create the intangible qualities of atmosphere and mood.

I will arise and go now, and go to Innisfree,
And a small cabin build there, of clay and wattles[1] made;
Nine bean rows will I have there, a hive for the honey bee,
And live alone in the bee-loud glade.

And I shall have some peace there, for peace comes dropping slow,   5
Dropping from the veils of the morning to where the cricket sings;
There midnight's all a glimmer, and noon a purple glow,
And evening full of the linnet's[2] wings.

I will arise and go now, for always night and day
I hear lake water lapping with low sounds by the shore;   10
While I stand on the roadway, or on the pavements gray,
I hear it in the deep heart's core.

UNDERSTANDING THE POEM

1. What provokes the speaker to think of Innisfree?
2. What do the speaker's thoughts about Innisfree reveal about his current life?

ANALYZING LITERARY TECHNIQUE

1. What is the role of **contrast** in the poem?
2. What is the **tone** of the poem? How does Yeats achieve it?
3. What does Yeats's use of **figurative language** achieve in the poem?
4. What does Yeats's use of sound devices (**rhythm, repetition, alliteration, and rhyme**) contribute to the poem?

---

[1] *wattles:* A framework of a building, made of interwoven poles and branches.
[2] *linnet:* A songbird.

WRITING ABOUT LITERATURE

1. Although Yeats was a modernist, his early poetry is often compared to early nineteenth-century romantic poetry. Romanticism stressed a love of nature, the importance of the individual, the solitary life rather than life in society, and freedom from rules and traditions. Write a brief essay in which you analyze "The Lake Isle of Innisfree" as a romantic poem. Use quotations to support your ideas.

2. Describe the place you would like to live. If you have never been there, imagine it. Close your eyes and visualize the place in your mind. Then paint a verbal picture by using details.

Araby

JAMES JOYCE

$\mathcal{J}$AMES JOYCE (1882–1941) is Ireland's greatest novelist and one of the most important writers of the twentieth century. He is best known for *A Portrait of the Artist as a Young Man* (1916), which is largely autobiographical, and his masterpieces *Ulysses* (1922) and *Finnegans Wake* (1939). His innovative use of language and structure in the latter two novels inspired the development of modern fiction, which presents psychological realism as interior monologue or stream of consciousness.

Joyce was born into a Catholic family in Dublin, Ireland. His father tried to earn a living in a variety of ways but had little financial success. Joyce attended Jesuit schools in Dublin, graduating from University College in 1902. He then left Ireland, returning only for brief visits, the last of which was in 1912. Joyce lived mostly in Trieste, Italy (1904–1915), and Paris, France (1920–1939). Throughout most of his adult life, he was plagued by poverty; in his later life, he had problems with his eyesight. He earned a meager living teaching languages, but the important part of his life was always his writing. *Chamber Music* (1907), a volume of poetry, was his first published work.

Joyce rebelled against the constraints of the religious, social, and political environment in Ireland. He left Ireland to gain artistic freedom; however, he continued to write about life in Dublin. He viewed himself as a high priest of art, with his mission in life being to elevate literature to the stature of religious experience. In 1904, shortly after he had begun the collection of stories that would become *Dubliners* (1914), his first published work of fiction, he told his brother Stanislaus:

> I am trying . . . to give people some kind of intellectual pleasure or spiritual enjoyment by converting the bread of everyday life into something that has a permanent artistic life of its own . . . for their mental, moral, and spiritual uplift.

Joyce's gift with words is already evident in *Dubliners*. "Araby" (1905), one of three stories that involve reminiscences of childhood, refers to the bazaar by that name that was held in Dublin from May 14–19, 1894. One of Joyce's goals in all of his fiction is to emphasize "the significance of trivial things" through his use of the Christian term *epiphany* to describe an event that evokes sudden insight into the significance of a situation. In Joyce's early novel *Stephen Hero* (published belatedly in 1944), Stephen explains an epiphany as "a sudden spiritual manifestation" in which the essential nature of an object or an action becomes apparent. "Araby," from *Dubliners*, artistically captures the importance of a poignant moment in the process of growing up.

North Richmond Street, being blind,[1] was a quiet street except at the hour when the Christian Brothers' School set the boys free. An uninhabited house of two storeys stood at the blind end, detached from its neighbours in a square ground. The other houses of the street, conscious of decent lives within them, gazed at one another with brown imperturbable faces.

The former tenant of our house, a priest, had died in the back drawing-room. Air, musty from having been long enclosed, hung in all the rooms, and the waste room behind the kitchen was littered with old useless papers. Among these I found a few paper-covered books, the pages of which were curled and damp: *The Abbot,* by Walter Scott, *The Devout Communicant* and *The Memoirs of Vidocq*.[2] I liked the last best because its leaves were yellow. The wild garden behind the house contained a central apple-tree and a few straggling bushes under one of which I found the late tenant's rusty bicycle pump. He had been a very charitable priest; in his will he had left all his money to institutions and the furniture of his house to his sister.

When the short days of winter came dusk fell before we had well eaten our dinners. When we met in the street the houses had grown sombre. The space of sky above us was the colour of ever-changing violet and towards it the lamps of the street lifted their feeble lanterns. The cold air stung us and we played till our bodies glowed. Our shouts echoed in the silent street. The career of our play brought us through the dark muddy lanes behind the houses where we ran the gauntlet of the rough tribes from the cottages, to the back doors of the dark dripping gardens where odours arose from the ash-pits, to the dark odorous stables where a coachman smoothed and combed the horse or shook music from the buckled harness. When we returned to the street light from the kitchen windows had filled the areas. If my uncle was seen turning the corner we hid in the shadow until we had seen him safely housed. Or if Mangan's sister came out on the doorstep to call her brother in to his tea we watched her from our shadow peer

---

[1] *North Richmond . . . blind:* A dead-end street in Dublin.

[2] The Abbot . . . Memoirs of Vidocq: A historical novel, a Roman Catholic religious manual, and the autobiography of a French detective.

up and down the street. We waited to see whether she would remain or go in and, if she remained, we left our shadow and walked up to Mangan's steps resignedly. She was waiting for us, her figure defined by the light from the half-opened door. Her brother always teased her before he obeyed and I stood by the railings looking at her. Her dress swung as she moved her body and the soft rope of her hair tossed from side to side.

Every morning I lay on the floor in the front parlour watching her door. The blind was pulled down to within an inch of the sash so that I could not be seen. When she came out on the doorstep my heart leaped. I ran to the hall, seized my books and followed her. I kept her brown figure always in my eye and, when we came near the point at which our ways diverged, I quickened my pace and passed her. This happened morning after morning. I had never spoken to her, except for a few casual words, and yet her name was like a summons to all my foolish blood.

Her image accompanied me even in places the most hostile to romance. On Saturday evenings when my aunt went marketing I had to go to carry some of the parcels. We walked through the flaring streets, jostled by drunken men and bargaining women, amid the curses of labourers, the shrill litanies of shop-boys who stood on guard by the barrels of pigs' cheeks, the nasal chanting of street singers, who sang a *come-all-you* about O'Donovan Rossa,[3] or a ballad about the troubles in our native land. These noises converged in a single sensation of life for me: I imagined that I bore my chalice safely through a throng of foes. Her name sprang to my lips at moments in strange prayers and praises which I myself did not understand. My eyes were often full of tears (I could not tell why) and at times a flood from my heart seemed to pour itself out into my bosom. I thought little of the future. I did not know whether I would ever speak to her or not or, if I spoke to her, how I could tell her of my confused adoration. But my body was like a harp and her words and gestures were like fingers running upon the wires.

One evening I went into the back drawing-room in which the priest had died. It was a dark rainy evening and there was no sound in the house. Through one of the broken panes I heard the rain impinge upon the earth, the fine incessant needles of water playing in the sodden beds. Some distant lamp or lighted window gleamed below me. I was thankful that I could see so little. All my senses seemed to desire to veil themselves and, feeling that I was about to slip from them, I pressed the palms of my hands together until they trembled, murmuring: "O love! O love!" many times.

At last she spoke to me. When she addressed the first words to me I was so confused that I did not know what to answer. She asked me was I going to *Araby*. I forgot whether I answered yes or no. It would be a splendid bazaar, she said; she would love to go.

"And why can't you?" I asked.

While she spoke she turned a silver bracelet round and round her wrist. She could not go, she said, because there would be a retreat that week in her

---

[3] come-all-you . . . *O'Donovan Rossa:* A street ballad about Irish nationalist Jeremiah O'Donovan Rossa.

convent.[4] Her brother and two other boys were fighting for their caps and I was alone at the railings. She held one of the spikes, bowing her head towards me. The light from the lamp opposite our door caught the white curve of her neck, lit up her hair that rested there and, falling, lit up the hand upon the railing. It fell over one side of her dress and caught the white border of a petticoat, just visible as she stood at ease.

"It's well for you," she said.

"If I go," I said, "I will bring you something."

What innumerable follies laid waste my waking and sleeping thoughts after that evening! I wished to annihilate the tedious intervening days. I chafed against the work of school. At night in my bedroom and by day in the classroom her image came between me and the page I strove to read. The syllables of the word *Araby* were called to me through the silence in which my soul luxuriated and cast an Eastern enchantment over me. I asked for leave to go to the bazaar on Saturday night. My aunt was surprised and hoped it was not some Freemason[5] affair. I answered few questions in class. I watched my master's face pass from amiability to sternness; he hoped I was not beginning to idle. I could not call my wandering thoughts together. I had hardly any patience with the serious work of life which, now that it stood between me and my desire, seemed to me child's play, ugly monotonous child's play.

On Saturday morning I reminded my uncle that I wished to go to the bazaar in the evening. He was fussing at the hallstand, looking for the hat-brush, and answered me curtly:

"Yes, boy, I know."

As he was in the hall I could not go into the front parlour and lie at the window. I left the house in bad humour and walked slowly towards the school. The air was pitilessly raw and already my heart misgave me.

When I came home to dinner my uncle had not yet been home. Still it was early. I sat staring at the clock for some time and, when its ticking began to irritate me, I left the room. I mounted the staircase and gained the upper part of the house. The high cold empty gloomy rooms liberated me and I went from room to room singing. From the front window I saw my companions playing below in the street. Their cries reached me weakened and indistinct and, leaning my forehead against the cool glass, I looked over at the dark house where she lived. I may have stood there for an hour, seeing nothing but the brown-clad figure cast by my imagination, touched discreetly by the lamplight at the curved neck, at the hand upon the railings and at the border below the dress.

When I came downstairs again I found Mrs. Mercer sitting at the fire. She was an old garrulous woman, a pawnbroker's widow, who collected used stamps for some pious purpose. I had to endure the gossip of the tea-table. The meal was prolonged beyond an hour and still my uncle did not come. Mrs. Mercer stood

---

[4] *retreat . . . convent:* A retreat is a period of religious study. The convent is a convent school run by nuns.

[5] *Freemason:* A member of a secret society, thought to be anti-Catholic.

up to go: she was sorry she couldn't wait any longer, but it was after eight o'clock and she did not like to be out late, as the night air was bad for her. When she had gone I began to walk up and down the room, clenching my fists. My aunt said:

"I'm afraid you may put off your bazaar for this night of Our Lord."

At nine o'clock I heard my uncle's latchkey in the halldoor. I heard him talking to himself and heard the hallstand rocking when it had received the weight of his overcoat. I could interpret these signs. When he was midway through his dinner I asked him to give me the money to go to the bazaar. He had forgotten.

"The people are in bed and after their first sleep now," he said.

I did not smile. My aunt said to him energetically:

"Can't you give him the money and let him go? You've kept him late enough as it is."

My uncle said he was very sorry he had forgotten. He said he believed in the old saying: "All work and no play makes Jack a dull boy." He asked me where I was going and, when I had told him a second time he asked me did I know *The Arab's Farewell to his Steed.*[6] When I left the kitchen he was about to recite the opening lines of the piece to my aunt.

I held a florin[7] tightly in my hand as I strode down Buckingham Street towards the station. The sight of the streets thronged with buyers and glaring with gas recalled to me the purpose of my journey. I took my seat in a third-class carriage of a deserted train. After an intolerable delay the train moved out of the station slowly. It crept onward among ruinous houses and over the twinkling river. At Westland Row Station a crowd of people pressed to the carriage doors; but the porters moved them back, saying that it was a special train for the bazaar. I remained alone in the bare carriage. In a few minutes the train drew up beside an improvised wooden platform. I passed out on to the road and saw by the lighted dial of a clock that it was ten minutes to ten. In front of me was a large building which displayed the magical name.

I could not find any sixpenny entrance and, fearing that the bazaar would be closed, I passed in quickly through a turnstile, handing a shilling to a weary-looking man. I found myself in a big hall girdled at half its height by a gallery. Nearly all the stalls were closed and the greater part of the hall was in darkness. I recognised a silence like that which pervades a church after a service. I walked into the centre of the bazaar timidly. A few people were gathered about the stalls which were still open. Before a curtain, over which the words *Café Chantant*[8] were written in coloured lamps, two men were counting money on a salver. I listened to the fall of the coins.

Remembering with difficulty why I had come I went over to one of the stalls and examined porcelain vases and flowered tea-sets. At the door of the stall a

---

[6] The Arab's Farewell to his Steed: Sentimental poem by Caroline Norton (1808–1877).

[7] *florin:* A former British coin worth two shillings or ¹/₁₀ of the old British pound. A shilling was worth 12 pence.

[8] Café Chantant: Café providing musical entertainment.

young lady was talking and laughing with two young gentlemen. I remarked their English accents and listened vaguely to their conversation.

"O, I never said such a thing!"

"O, but you did!"

"O, but I didn't!"

"Didn't she say that?"

"Yes. I heard her."

"O, there's a . . . fib!"

Observing me the young lady came over and asked me did I wish to buy anything. The tone of her voice was not encouraging; she seemed to have spoken to me out of a sense of duty. I looked humbly at the great jars that stood like eastern guards at either side of the dark entrance to the stall and murmured:

"No, thank you."

The young lady changed the position of one of the vases and went back to the two young men. They began to talk of the same subject. Once or twice the young lady glanced at me over her shoulder.

I lingered before her stall, though I knew my stay was useless, to make my interest in her wares seem the more real. Then I turned away slowly and walked down the middle of the bazaar. I allowed the two pennies to fall against the sixpence in my pocket. I heard a voice call from one end of the gallery that the light was out. The upper part of the hall was now completely dark.

Gazing up into the darkness I saw myself as a creature driven and derided by vanity; and my eyes burned with anguish and anger.

UNDERSTANDING THE STORY

1. How does the conversation between the young lady and the two young men affect the boy?

2. Why does the narrator conclude by saying "my eyes burned with anguish and anger"? What has happened to cause him anguish? At whom or what is he angry? Why does he remember this experience?

3. To what extent, if any, does the boy experience an initiation, a rite of passage, or a loss of innocence?

ANALYZING LITERARY TECHNIQUE

1. What **narrative perspective** does Joyce use in "Araby"? What advantages does this perspective possess?

2. What religious **allusions** appear in the story? What do these images symbolize?

3. Find examples of **foreshadowing** and explain the contribution of each example to the story.

4. Why does Joyce have the boy arrive at Araby so late? In what ways, if any, would the story have been different if he had arrived much earlier?

5. Find examples of the contrast between illusion and reality and explain what each example contributes to the story.

6. Joyce liked to convey the significance of an experience through an **epiphany.** Where do you find an epiphany in "Araby"? Explain your response.

WRITING ABOUT LITERATURE

1. In the May 17, 1894, issue of the *Irish Times,* a reporter discussed the effect that rainy weather might have on Araby's success. In the process, the writer quoted the following lines of poetry:

> I knew, I knew, it could not last,
> 'Twas bright, 'twas heavenly, but 'tis past,
> Oh ever thus from childhood's hour
> I've seen my fondest hopes decay.

Write an essay in which you relate the idea expressed in these lines to the boy's experience in "Araby." Use quotations from the story and explain how each quotation supports your ideas.

2. Write an essay in which you analyze Joyce's use of **contrast** in "Araby." Choose two or three examples that contrast the boy's illusions with reality. Use quotations and explain the significance of each quotation. In your conclusion, evaluate what contrast contributes to "Araby."

3. Relating a story years after it happened is quite different from telling it at the time. Write about one incident from the story as the boy might have retold the incident just after it occurred. Possibilities include the boy's conversation with Mangan's sister, his wait for his uncle, his ride on the deserted train, and his experience at Araby.

APPENDIX:
Thematic Table of Contents

Note: Some selections appear in more than one theme.

JUSTICE AND DIGNITY

LOVE AND ROMANCE

THE NATURAL WORLD

VALUES AND BELIEFS

GLOSSARY
OF LITERARY TERMS

Note: Each definition concludes with a sampling of selections in this book that illustrate the use of the term. Terms that appear in bold print within a definition are defined in this Glossary.

action.   The process by which **characterization** and **plot** develop. The action includes physical and psychological events, external words and deeds, silent expressions and actions, and characters' expressed inner thoughts. (See *Casely-Hayford, O'Neill, Rossetti.*)

allegory.   A literary work in which a symbolic meaning exists beneath the literal surface meaning. An allegory expresses truths about the human condition by using the actions and attitudes of fictional characters to symbolize virtues, vices, or other abstract ideas and issues. See also **symbolism.** (See *Chaucer, Rossetti, Tagore, Tolstoy.*)

alliteration.   Repetition of the same initial consonant sound, usually in accented syllables of closely positioned words, to achieve an aural effect. (See *Browning, Rossetti, Yeats, "A Woman's Message."*)

allusion.   A reference to a well-known real or fictional person, place, or event. The allusion enriches the meaning of the literary work. (See *Akhmatova, Arnold, Catullus, Cortázar, García Márquez, Sappho.*)

alter ego.   A character's second self and a type of double, usually a character who is the **protagonist**'s close friend or relative and who is similar to the protagonist in age, gender, appearance, and interests. (See *Rossetti, Sophocles.*)

ambiguity.   Double or multiple meaning. (See *Akutagawa, Kafka, Rosa.*)

antagonist.   The major character who opposes the **protagonist** in a work of literature. The antagonist may be either a villain who opposes the hero or a virtuous person who opposes an evil protagonist. (See *Andersen, Desai, Head, Sophocles.*)

antihero.   A **protagonist** who is the opposite of the traditional hero in character, values, and stature. The antihero does not embody the traditional heroic qualities of courage, determination, skill, and creative intelligence. Often he or she is a failure. (See *Borges, Camus, Rosa.*)

antithesis.   The **contrast** of opposites, used for emphasis. (See *Andersen, Pirandello, Sartre.*)

apostrophe.   A **figure of speech** in which the speaker in a poem or play addresses an absent or imaginary person (or a personified place, quality, or abstract idea) as if the person were present and listening. See also **personification.** (See *Dante, Catullus, de la Cruz, Hikmet, Rilke, Rumi, Sappho.*)

appositive.   A descriptive phrase that functions as an adjective. (See *Hikmet.*)

aretē.   See **hubris.**

assonance.   The repetition of similar vowel sounds, usually in accented syllables in closely positioned words, to achieve an aural effect. (See *Eliot, Rossetti, Yeats.*)

atē.   See **hubris.**

avant-garde.   A term used to describe a literary work that is creative, innovative, and experimental rather than traditional in content and form. (See *Eliot, Ibsen, Solórzano, Whitman.*)

black humor.   A humorous response to a serious or even tragic situation. Also called "gallows humor." (See *Desai.*)

catastrophe.   The final disastrous event in a **tragedy.** (See *O'Neill, Sophocles.*)

catharsis.   According to Aristotle, a release from the emotions of pity and fear that have been aroused in an audience watching a **tragedy.** (See *Jiang Fang, O'Neill, Sophocles.*)

characterization.   Presenting a character to reveal his or her personal qualities, such as traits, attitudes, and values. (See *Grace, Jiang Fang, Shen Congwen.*)

chorus.   In early Greek **tragedy,** the chorus acts in the play, comments as an objective observer on the morality of the characters' actions, and recites odes concerning the nature of gods and mortals. (See *Sophocles.*)

classicism.   A literary movement, popular in France and England in the seventeenth and eighteenth centuries, that reflected the following values of ancient Greece and Rome: balance and proportion in artistic form; reason and rationality rather than emotion and irrationality; dignity and restraint; objectivity; and unity of structure. (See *Schiller, Sophocles.*)

climax.   The high point of emotional intensity in a work of literature. The climax may or may not be identical with the **crisis** or turning point. (See *Head, Hemingway, Jiang Fang, Pirandello, Shakespeare, Shen Congwen, Sophocles.*)

comedy.   A work of literature that is designed to be entertaining and humorous. Often its **humor** is achieved by reversing what is expected and normal. In comedy, misfortune ends in happiness. See also **tragicomedy.**

> **low comedy:**   Nonintellectual comedy that relies on jokes, slapstick behavior, ridicule, and humiliation as sources of humor. (See *Shakespeare, Soyinka.*)

> **high comedy:**   Intellectual comedy that relies on the clever use of language, such as **irony,** sarcasm, and **satire,** as the source of humor. (See *Shakespeare, Soyinka.*)

comparison.   The bringing together of similar characters, ideas, or images to emphasize attributes or attitudes. See also **figure of speech, imagery.** (See *Akhmatova.*)

conflict.   Opposition in a work of literature. Common conflicts include (a) the **protagonist** in conflict with the **antagonist** (see *Akutagawa, Andersen, O'Neill, Soyinka*); (b) the protagonist in conflict with emotions and desires within himself or herself (see *Hayashi, Kafka, Munro, Narayan*); (c) the protagonist in conflict with society (see *Head, Hemingway, Ogot, Ting Ling*); and (d) the protagonist in conflict with the natural world (see *Lessing*).

connotative language.   Words that suggest or evoke in the reader's mind—through their context and through the reader's associations—emotions, attitudes, and ideas that are beyond the literal meaning of the words. (See *Arnold, Bombal, Kawabata, Lessing.*)

consonance.   The repetition of identical consonant sounds before and after different vowels in closely positioned words. A number of familiar words, such as *tiptop* and *fulfill,* are consonant. (See *Brontë, Eliot, Whitman, Yeats.*)

context.   The relationships that affect a literary work, both within the work and between the work and external factors.

> (a) Internal relationships include the placement of words, phrases, and ideas; the relationship between acts of a play; and the relationship between the words and actions of one character and those of another. (See *Ibsen, Sophocles, Soyinka.*)

> (b) External relationships include the relationship between aspects of the writer's life and the work (see *García Lorca, Ting Ling*) and the relationship between the work and the social, economic, and political conditions at the time the work was written. (See *Conrad, Dostoyevsky, Lu Hsün, Paton, Walker.*)

contrast. The bringing together of different or opposite characters, ideas, or images to emphasize attributes or attitudes. See also **figure of speech, imagery.** (See *Achebe, Arnold, Akhenaton, Colette, Hikmet, Li Qingzhao, Nguyen Binh Khiem.*)

courtly love. A social code of behavior from the late medieval period. Courtly love often involved the idealization of the loved one, the offer of pure love from the safety of distance, and the passionate expression of emotion on the part of the lover. The lover would despair if his loved one were unattainable, and he would be angry if she rejected his offer of love. (See *Dante.*)

crisis. The turning point of a story, play, or narrative poem; the point at which the **protagonist** makes a significant choice that leads to his or her fate. The crisis either precedes or is the same as the **climax.** (See *Andersen, Hemingway, Ibsen, O'Neill, Pardo Bazán, Sophocles.*)

description. Providing details about **setting** or characters for the purpose of making the experience depicted in the work come alive for the reader. Writers use **figurative language** to heighten their descriptions. (See *Joyce, Kawabata, Lessing, Sartre.*)

dialect. The distinctive use of language—vocabulary, syntax, and pronunciation—to reflect a particular person, social group, or region. (See *Casely-Hayford, Hughes, Soyinka, Welty.*)

discovery. The point—either at or following the **climax** of a story, play, or narrative poem—at which a character suddenly realizes the truth in a situation. The character moves from innocence or ignorance to experience or knowledge. Discovery often involves **dramatic irony.** (See *Colette, Joyce, Lessing, Pirandello, Sartre, Soyinka.*)

doppelgänger. A German term meaning "double-goer," used by G. H. Schubert in *The Symbolism of Dreams* (1814) to describe the passionate subconscious self that continually interjects itself into the life of the rational conscious self. (See *Borges, Rosa, Rossetti.*)

drama. A literary work written to be acted on a stage. It may be in pantomime or dialogue, in poetry or prose, and with or without musical accompaniment; it may be comic or serious. Often, a major goal is to create the illusion of reality. Drama includes **comedy, farce, theater of the absurd,** and **tragedy.** (See *Ibsen, O'Neill, Shakespeare, Solórzano, Soyinka.*)

dramatic irony. See **irony.**

dramatic monologue or **dramatic lyric.** The speaker's words addressed to an absent listener—whether an actual or imagined person—at a critical moment in the speaker's life. A dramatic monologue reveals something significant about the speaker's past or present circumstances, the speaker's attitudes and values, or the speaker's true character. (See *Hikmet.*)

elegy. A formal **lyric** about the death of a person or a tragic incident. Although the lyric is a lament, it expresses praise as well as sorrow, and it often ends with a consoling thought. (See *Catullus, García Lorca, "A Woman's Message."*)

epigraph. A quotation that is set at the beginning of a work of literature or of a chapter to suggest the **theme** of the work. (See *Eliot.*)

epiphany. An event or incident that evokes a sudden significant insight into the deeper meaning of a situation. James Joyce borrowed the term *epiphany* from Christianity, where it refers to the moment when the infant Jesus reveals his divinity to the Magi. Joyce explains his use of the term in *Stephen Hero.* (See *Joyce, Lessing, Mansfield, Pardo Bazán.*)

eulogy. A formal composition of praise, usually about a person who has died. (See *García Lorca.*)

euphony.   The melodious quality of sound and rhythm that is created by the writer's choice and arrangement of words. (See *Eliot, Rossetti, Yeats*.)

existentialism.   A philosophy prominent in France following World War II. According to Jean-Paul Sartre, human beings live in a universe that is irrational and meaningless. Human nature, custom, and religion are outmoded concepts. People are free to create who they are, and their actions give meaning to their lives and to the world in which they live. Such an awesome responsibility creates anxiety and anguish. (See *Camus, Paz, Sartre*.)

exposition.   The presentation of background material about the characters or the situation in a story, play, or narrative poem. It may be presented at the beginning of the work or gradually throughout it. (See *Borges, Ibsen, O'Neill, Paton*.)

expressionism.   An early twentieth-century artistic and literary movement that reacted against **realism** and **naturalism.** The movement originated in Germany in 1905 and became important in Scandinavia. Writers rejected the objective point of view and used a subjective focus that emphasized the subconscious. They looked within themselves to find images from their dreams, and they often used the technique of **stream of consciousness.** The resulting literature presents a distorted view of reality and often has the characteristics of a nightmare. **Surrealism** is related to expressionism. (See *Eliot, García Lorca, Kafka*.)

fairy tale.   A story from the oral tradition that symbolizes the process of psychological maturation. Fairy tales involve difficult trials and the hindrance or help of magical persons such as elves, fairies, goblins, trolls, and witches. (See *Andersen, Lagerlöf, Rossetti*.)

farce.   A comic drama involving the techniques of **low comedy,** such as exaggeration of character, slapstick, ridiculous behavior, and situations that involve the surprises and coincidences that result from a contrived and improbable **plot.** A farce is often satiric in **tone,** and it usually has a happy ending. See also **comedy, satire.** (See *Shakespeare, Soyinka*.)

figurative language or **figure of speech.**   The use of language that is meant to be taken imaginatively rather than literally. Figures of speech make connections between related and unrelated things. **Allusions** connect related things; **metaphor, personification,** and **simile** connect things that are somewhat similar; **oxymorons** connect opposite things. **Imagery** is usually sensory or pictorial language; it may be literal or figurative. (See *Akhmatova, Cortázar, Dadié, David, Desai, HaNagid, Hébert*.)

first-person narrator.   See **narrative perspective.**

flashback.   A break in the chronology of a story, play, or narrative poem during which past events are related. The vehicle for a flashback may be a dream or the telling of a story by one of the characters. (See *Borges, Lagerlöf, Lu Hsün*.)

foil.   A character, often the **antagonist,** whose qualities or actions function to highlight the qualities and actions of the **protagonist** by contrasting the two characters. (See *Gordimer, Sartre*.)

folktale.   A traditional story about common people from a culture's oral tradition. Folktales emphasize **plot** rather than character. Many folktales involve giants, husbands and wives, and masters and servants. The **genre** include fables, **fairy tales,** ghost stories, legends, and tall tales. (See *Andersen, Lagerlöf, Ogot, Rossetti*.)

foreshadowing.   A technique in which an incident, behavior, conversation, or atmosphere prepares the reader for what will happen later. The early information adds credibility to the later situation and helps to unify the work. (See *Colette, Jiang Fang, Narayan, Shen Congwen, Ogot*.)

form. The internal organization or structure of a literary work. Form is related to style. In traditional literature, form is distinguished from content even though form and content are always related.

free verse. Poetry that disregards the traditional use of patterns in **rhythm,** sound, and organization. In free verse, content determines **form,** and natural speech creates **rhythm.** Poets emphasize **repetition** and often do not use **rhyme.** Walt Whitman and the French **Symbolists** originated this type of poetry in the nineteenth century. The Imagists also chose to write free verse. See also **Imagism.** (See *Hughes, Mistral, Rilke, Whitman.*)

genre. A literary class or type. Each genre has its own characteristics. Examples include **drama,** epic poetry, essay, **lyric,** narrative poetry, novel, novella, and **short story.**

Gothic. A literary style that emphasizes the supernatural, mystery, suspense, horror, and terror. (See *Kafka, Lagerlöf.*)

Homeric simile. An elaborate comparison that uses a story to convey an emotion or to describe an action. (See *Catullus.*)

hubris. A feeling of excessive pride in oneself. In the literature and myths of ancient Greece, major characters, including the great heroes, often have a personality in which their greatest strength becomes their greatest weakness.

    The psychological process begins with a person who possesses *aretē* ("excellence" or "striving for excellence") in some area, such as beauty or courage. Great *aretē* leads to *hubris,* which in turn leads to *atē* ("blind recklessness"), when an individual loses his or her sense of human limitations and indulges in behavior that is rash or imprudent. *Atē,* in turn, leads to *nemesis* ("retributive justice") because the person who acted imprudently is punished by other mortals or by the gods.

    In classical **tragedy,** this personality configuration provides the basis for the tragic hero's situation. Although the original literary focus is Greek, this psychological pattern is found in many other cultures' literature. (See *O'Neill, Sophocles.*)

humor. Expression of amusement, incongruity, or absurdity. (See *Desai, García Márquez, Welty.*)

hyperbole. Obvious exaggeration. (See *Cortázar.*)

imagery. Sensory or pictorial language that is used to enrich meaning. It may appeal to the sense of sight, hearing, taste, smell, touch, or movement, and it may be used symbolically. It is often conveyed through **simile, metaphor,** or **personification.** (See *Dadié, García Lorca, Joyce, Lessing, Neruda, Schiller, Zuñi.*)

Imagism. A movement in American and English poetry in the early twentieth century (1912–1917) that was similar to the French **Symbolist** movement. According to the poet Amy Lowell, the Imagists had the following goals: (a) to regard any subject as acceptable for poetry; (b) to suggest rather than to state ideas, expressing them concisely; (c) to emphasize images, choosing those that are specific rather than abstract; (d) to use exact words from common speech, avoiding those that are overused; and (e) to create new **rhythms** to express new moods **(free verse).** See also **imagery.** (See *Desai, Dickinson, Eliot, García Lorca.*)

impressionism. A nineteenth-century artistic and literary movement that emphasized the subjective impression a writer or character had of reality, rather than attempting to re-create objective reality. See also **realism, Symbolist.**

interior monologue. See **monologue.**

irony. Hidden meaning, usually the contrast between appearance and reality (with regard to words and situations) and the contrast between expectations and actuality (with regard to actions).

dramatic or situational irony: A character, seeing only appearances, speaks or acts in ignorance of the reality of which the audience is aware. Dramatic irony is an important technique in **comedy, tragedy,** and in stories of any length. (See *García Márquez, Hayashi, Li Po, Tagore, Tolstoy*.)

verbal irony: A character makes a comment that means something different to a listening character or to the audience. The character may intentionally say the opposite of what he or she means. The listener may be either aware or unaware of the discrepancy. Verbal irony can be dramatic or situational in function. (See *Casely-Hayford, Colette, Ibsen, Ogot, Solórzano*.)

legend. A **folktale** accepted as being based on a historical occurrence. (See *Head*.)

leitmotif. A German term from music criticism, meaning "leading motif." In literature a leitmotif is a word phrase, image, **symbol,** or **theme** that is frequently repeated for the purposes of emphasis and unity. A leitmotif may be associated with a particular character, emotion, or situation. See also **motif.** (See *Bombal, Chekhov, García Lorca, Rossetti*.)

limited omniscience. See **narrative perspective.**

literal meaning. The meaning of words or a work of literature on the surface level, without considering what they suggest. Literal meaning ignores both the figurative and the symbolic use of language. See also **figurative language, symbol.**

lyric. A short, personal poem. The most common form of poetry, lyrics express the thoughts, emotions, or mood of a single speaker, who may or may not be the poet, and emphasize pictorial **imagery** rather than dramatic **action.** (See *Akhenaton, Dante, Rilke, Sappho, Yeats*.)

magic realism. A concept applied specifically to fiction by Latin American authors. Magic realism is defined in two principal ways: (a) an unexpected or improbable (but not impossible) element inserted into a predominantly realistic work in a matter-of-fact way, in order to delight or puzzle the reader; (b) magical elements incorporated into a realistic tale in a matter-of-fact manner. (See *García Márquez*.)

malapropism. Misused word that often sounds something like the appropriate word but, often being the opposite in meaning, is outrageously inappropriate in the context in which it is used. These misused words are called malapropisms after a character, Mrs. Malaprop, who uses such words in Richard Sheridan's comedy *The Rivals* (1775). (See *Shakespeare*.)

masque. A spectacular form of entertainment popular in England in the sixteenth and early seventeenth centuries. Masques were poetic dramas that included music, dancing, singing, lavish costumes, and the use of masks. Spectacle, rather than **plot** or character, was the focus. (See *Shakespeare*.)

melodrama. A type of drama that depends greatly on complex **plot** and sensationalism. It possesses the following characteristics: (a) one-dimensional, stock characters who are extremely good or bad; (b) a focus on the conflict between good and evil that ends happily; (c) violent and bloody action; and (d) an array of supernatural characters, such as ghosts, vampires, and witches. Its focus on plot and its theatrical emphasis have led to the use of *melodramatic* to describe any highly emotional or sensational literary work. (See *Jiang Fang, O'Neill*.)

metaphor. An implied **comparison** of two different objects, ideas, or actions in order to enrich the meaning of the original. A metaphor reveals that the two different things being compared, in fact, share a quality that gives them a surprising resemblance. Unlike a **simile,** a metaphor does not involve the use of *like* or *as.* (See *Eliot, García Lorca, Hughes, Neruda, Nguyen Binh Khiem, Paz, Walker.*)

modernism.   A literary movement that began with the French **Symbolists** in the 1850s, ended in the 1950s, and includes **impressionism, expressionism,** and **existentialism.** Modernists rejected the objective point of view of the realists and naturalists and, instead, emphasized subjective perceptions that often involved a sense of alienation. They expressed their ideas in new and experimental techniques that included **stream of consciousness.** (See *Conrad, Eliot.*)

monologue.   In a literary work, a long speech by one character.

> **soliloquy:**   A long speech to the audience by one character, in which he or she shares private thoughts and feelings, gives underlying reasons, and often states intended behavior. (See *Shakespeare.*)

> **interior monologue:**   The vehicle for the continuous process by which a character reveals his or her thoughts to the reader or audience as if he or she were actually thinking them aloud. (See *Conrad, Desai, Walker.*)

> **stream of consciousness:**   Originally used by William James, in *Principles of Psychology* (1890), the term refers both to the content of an interior monologue and to the organization of that content. Stream of consciousness provides **characterization** both by the nature of the character's thoughts and by the nature of the particular thought process. Thoughts are organized according to the principle of association, so that one thought leads to another based on what the character is taking in from the external world and the associations from the present and the past that result from these perceptions. Consequently, stream of consciousness is frag-mented, disjointed, illogical, and, often, unpunctuated. (See *Conrad, Walker.*)

mood.   Emotional atmosphere of a work of literature, created through descriptions of the character(s) and the **setting.** See also **tone.** (See *Rilke.*)

moral.   The stated or implied lesson about right and wrong that a literary work teaches. The **theme** of a work may be a moral. (See *Jiang Fang, Lu Hsün, Tolstoy.*)

motif.   A word, phrase, idea, image, action, character, or **symbol** that is repeated throughout part or all of a literary work for emphasis and for unity. See also **leitmotif.** (See *García Lorca, Joyce, Rossetti.*)

mythology.   Stories from the oral tradition of a culture that explain that culture's origins, reflect its legendary history, and teach its social, moral, and religious values. Mythology includes stories about (a) the origin of the universe; (b) the creation of gods and mortals; (c) the deeds of the great heroes; and (d) interpersonal relationships. (See *García Márquez, Ogot, Sophocles, Zuñi.*)

narrative perspective.   The point of view from which a story is told. It includes both who is telling the story and at what time the story is taking place.

> **first-person narrator:**   A narrator who is part of the story and refers to himself or herself as "I." This narrator may be the **protagonist,** a participant, or an observer. Even if the reader never enters the narrator's mind, the first-person point of view limits the reader's knowledge to what the narrator experiences and chooses to reveal. This point of view is subjective, in that it reflects the narrator's personal ideas, emotional reactions, and experiences. It may or may not reflect the point of view of the author. Such a narrator may be reliable (see *Kawabata, Paton, Sartre*), unreliable (see *Akutagawa, Gordimer*), or open to question (see *Borges, Rosa*).

limited omniscience: The technique of having the narrator possess limited knowledge, knowing only what he or she experiences directly or hears from other characters. (See *Joyce, Lu Hsün, Paton, Sartre*.)

omniscient narrator: A narrator who knows everything that is important to the story, including the characters' inner thoughts and feelings. The third-person omniscient narrator is most common in literature and often speaks for the author. He or she may tell the story objectively (see *Tolstoy*) or subjectively, by interspersing personal comments into the narrative (see *Dostoyevsky*).

reliable narrator: A narrator who is objective and whose version of the story the reader can trust. (See *Colette, Jiang Fang, Mansfield*.)

third-person narrator: A narrator who is usually an anonymous, objective, and omniscient observer, such as the author, and who refers to the characters as "he," "she," or "they." (See *Andersen, García Márquez, Narayan*.) If a third-person narrator is one of the characters, he or she has **limited omniscience.** (See *Lu Hsün*.)

unreliable narrator: A narrator who is not objective and whose version of the story reflects personal attitudes and judgments that the reader cannot trust. The narrator's distorted point of view can reflect emotional instability, arrogance, lack of sophistication, or prejudice. Usually, the bias is inadvertent, creating **dramatic irony.** (See *Gordimer, Ting Ling*.)

narrator. See **narrative perspective.**

naturalism. A late nineteenth-century branch of **realism** that reflected the new age of science and industry. Naturalist writing emphasizes an objective point of view, historical background, urban settings, characters from the lower classes, and characters who, as passive victims of heredity and their social and economic environment, are often destitute and ill. **Regionalism** is a branch of naturalism. (See *Ibsen, Lagerlöf, O'Neill*.)

Négritude. A literary and cultural movement that originated in Paris in the early 1930s among a group of African students from the French colonies. Its goal was to combat assimilation by instilling pride in African heritage and culture. (See *Dadié, Senghor*.)

nemesis. See *hubris.*

night journey. A particular description of the psychological process that Carl Jung discusses in terms of his concept of the **Shadow.** Albert Guerard, in *Conrad the Novelist* (1958), describes the night journey as "an essentially solitary journey involving profound spiritual change in the voyager." He then explains that the nature of the vision and the nature of the change in the voyager vary with each individual. In literature, the experience may be either a dream or a real journey. (See *Conrad, García Lorca, Kafka, Rossetti*.)

ode. In ancient Greece, a "lyric" or song to be sung. In the Greek **tragedies** of the fifth century B.C., odes divide the plays into acts. They are formal **lyrics** that are chanted by the **chorus** and that are serious in subject and dignified in **tone.** An adapted ode form was popular in later centuries with poets in Italy, France, Germany, and England. (See *Sophocles*.)

omniscient narrator. See **narrative perspective.**

one-act play. A type of **drama** that has a limited and highly controlled focus and few characters, but a wide range of subjects and **moods.** It may be a **comedy,** a **farce,** or a **tragedy.** Originating as a **genre** at the end of the nineteenth century, it has been a popular dramatic form in the twentieth century. (See *O'Neill, Solórzano, Soyinka*.)

onomatopoeia. A **figure of speech** in which a word sounds like what it means in order to capture and describe that particular sound. Examples include: *buzz, bang, clap,* and *pop.* (See *Rossetti.*)

oxymoron. A combination of contradictory words. (See *Shakespeare, "A Woman's Message."*)

parable. A short, simple story that is designed to teach a **moral.** The moral is either implied or stated. See also **allegory, symbol.** (See *Chaucer, Tolstoy.*)

paradox. A statement or situation that appears to be false or self-contradictory, but that proves to be true upon reflection. (See *Camus, Dickinson, Kafka, Schiller.*)

parallelism. In literature, the juxtaposition of words, phrases, or sentences that are similar in structure in order to emphasize particular ideas or to achieve the aural effect of a repetitive form. See also **repetition.** (See *David, Eliot, Rossetti.*)

pastoral. A literary work that is set in a rural or natural landscape. (See *David, Lessing, Mistral, Yeats.*)

personification. A **figure of speech** in which an aspect of nature, an inanimate object, or an abstract idea is treated as if it possessed human qualities. (See *Akhmatova, García Lorca, Rilke, Senghor, Zuñi.*)

plot. The events of a narrative, such as a **short story** or **drama,** arranged so as to create an artistic effect. The most common organization has a beginning, a middle, and a conclusion, with unity created by cause-and-effect relationships among the events. Usually, the **protagonist** is involved in a **conflict** that gets resolved at the end of the story. In modern literature, plots contain a variety of structures. See also **resolution.** (See *Head, Mahfouz, Pardo Bazán.*)

poem. A literary form that emphasizes **rhythm** and **figurative language.** A poem may tell a story (narrative poetry) or express emotions (**lyric** poetry) and does not necessarily **rhyme.** (See *Akhenaton, Brontë, Castellanos, Dante, Li Po, Senghor, Whitman.*)

point of view. See **narrative perspective.**

Pre-Raphaelite Brotherhood. A mid-nineteenth-century English group of artists and writers. The Pre-Raphaelites revolted against prevailing literary values and aimed to return to the artistic values that existed before the time of the Italian Renaissance painter Raphael (1483–1520). Their poetry emphasizes imagination, strong sensory appeal, **symbolism,** and spirituality. (See *Rossetti.*)

protagonist. The principal character in a story or play. (See *Desai, Head, Sophocles, Tagore.*)

psychological realism. See **realism.**

realism. A nineteenth-century literary movement that rejected the values of **romanticism** and had as its goal the depiction of life as it really is, without subjectivity, artificiality, or exaggeration. Realistic writing employs ordinary language, and it focuses on ordinary people, events, and settings, all of which are described in great detail. The narrator, who is usually the author, possesses an objective point of view and takes an unobtrusive role in the narrative. Some realistic writers considered it more realistic to begin and end a story in the middle, and to limit their focus to one complete incident from the protagonist's total life. **Naturalism** is a branch of realism. (See *Ibsen, Lessing, O'Neill.*)

> **psychological realism:** Achieving realism by emphasizing the psychological aspects of character. Psychological realism focuses on a character's thoughts and feelings by depicting his or her thought processes. The story is set in the character's observing and experiencing mind, instead of in the external world. **Stream of**

consciousness provides both the content and the internal structure; **interior monologue** provides the external structure. (See *Bombal, Conrad, Kafka.*)

social or socialist realism: The creation of works of literature as political propaganda designed to promote communism. Social realism requires a literary artist to obey the dictates of the national government. (See *Ting Ling.*)

regionalism. A branch of **naturalism** that reacts to industrialism by rejecting an urban focus and by emphasizing the personality and psychological motivation of characters who live in rural settings, abide by local customs, and speak the language of rural folk. (See *Lagerlöf, Welty.*)

reliable narrator. See **narrative perspective.**

repetition. In literature, a device that creates structural unity and that is considered to be **figurative language.** Structural unity of sound is created by repeated sounds, words, phrases, or lines. Structural unity of meaning is created by repeating ideas, **allusions,** images, or **symbols.** (See *Dahomey, García Lorca, Hafiz, Hemingway, Senghor.*)

resolution. The concluding events of the **plot** that follow from the **climax** and bring the story or play to a conclusion. (See *Hemingway, Jiang Fang, Pirandello, Rossetti, Sophocles.*)

reversal. A sudden change in the **protagonist'**s situation, which causes a reversal of fortune. It usually occurs at the end of a literary work and is the result of **discovery.** In **tragedy,** reversal involves a sudden fall from prosperity to destruction; in **comedy,** it involves the sudden restoration of prosperity. (See *Pirandello, Shakespeare, Sophocles, Soyinka.*)

rhyme. **Repetition** at regular intervals of words that end with the same sound, usually at the end of lines of poetry. Rhyme may be exact or close in sound and is a technique for enhancing sound quality and for organizing and unifying the poem. (See *Browning, Rossetti, Yeats.*)

rhythm. Sound patterns that are regular or irregular, depending on the goals of the poet and the content of the work. Some rhythms form strict metrical patterns, while others, such as in **free verse,** reflect the cadences of spoken language. (See *Brontë, Eliot, Rossetti, Whitman, Yeats.*)

romance. An imaginative story, in prose or in poetry, in which (a) **plot** is the most important element; (b) adventure, love, and heroism are the most common subjects; and (c) entertainment is the most important function. Although a romance can reflect ordinary life, it usually emphasizes the extraordinary. (See *Head, Shakespeare.*)

romanticism. In literature, a late eighteenth- and early nineteenth-century movement that rejected neoclassicism's emphasis on the rational and instead valued the subjective qualities of instinct and spontaneity, originality, imagination, and fantasy, and the expression of powerful emotions. Romantic writers valued individualism, believing the human being to be basically good and society to be potentially perfectible. They valued nature and felt a common bond existed between the natural world and human beings. (See *Andersen, Schiller, Wordsworth.*)

satire. Both a literary **genre** and a particular technique that ridicules or condemns individuals or society for having a lower standard of values, attitudes, and behavior. The satirist exposes popular vices in order to bring about intellectual or social reform. Greed, arrogance, and hypocrisy are common targets. The **tone** of a satire may be comic or bitter; **irony** is always a major component. (See *Dostoyevsky, García Márquez, Gordimer, Ibsen, Lu Hsün, Soyinka.*)

setting. The location and time in which the action of a literary work takes place. (See *Desai, Grace, Ting Ling, Mahfouz, Tagore.*)

Shadow. A term used by Carl Jung in his writings to describe the inherent part of each person's personality that is subconscious. In "Conscious, Unconscious, and Individuation" (1939), Jung states that "the Shadow personifies everything that the subject refuses to acknowledge about himself and yet is always thrusting itself upon him directly or indirectly." The character who functions as the **protagonist's** Shadow and who lacks self-imposed restraints may possess more courage than the protagonist. (See *Andersen, Conrad, Sartre.*)

short story. First defined by Edgar Allan Poe, in a review of Nathaniel Hawthorne's *Twice-Told Tales* (1842), as a story that can be read at one sitting, and in which the incidents and details establish a single, preconceived effect. Short stories actually vary in length from very short to long. However, the limitation of length usually restricts the author's focus to one incident in the life of one character. (See *Colette, García Márquez, Head, Kawabata, Mansfield.*)

simile. A **figure of speech** that is an explicit **comparison,** using *like* or *as,* of two different objects, ideas, or actions in order to enrich the meaning of the original. A simile reveals that the two different things being compared share a quality that gives them a surprising resemblance. *See also* **Homeric simile.** (See *García Lorca, Lessing, Rossetti, Sophocles, Welty.*)

situational irony. See **irony.**

social or socialist realism. See **realism.**

soliloquy. See **monologue.**

sonnet. A poem that contains fourteen lines of equal length and that, in English, is usually written in iambic pentameter (lines with five regular stresses). The types of sonnet include the Italian or Petrarchan and the English or Shakespearean.

> **Italian** or **Petrarchan sonnet:** The most common form of the sonnet, originating in Italy in the thirteenth century and perfected by the Italian poet Petrarch (1304–1374); it is composed of fourteen lines that are divided with a pause into two sections, the octave (usually rhyming *abba abba*) and the sestet (usually rhyming *cdecde* or *cdcdcd*). The Italian sonnet contains two ideas, with a change in attitude (the volta) between the octave and the sestet. (See *Browning, de la Cruz.*)

> **English** or **Shakespearean sonnet:** Named for William Shakespeare (1564–1616), it is composed of fourteen lines that are divided into three quatrains (rhyming *abab cdcd efef*) and a closing couplet (rhyming *gg*). The couplet often is an epigram, summing up the problem or concern raised in the quatrains.

stanza. A line or block of lines, often with a specific **rhyme** and meter, into which a poem is divided. (See *Dante, Hafiz.*)

stream of consciousness. See **monologue.**

subplot. A subordinate **plot,** involving characters of minor importance that parallels the main plot in a story or play. It may amplify or emphasize the main plot, or provide an ironic commentary or comic relief. (See *Shakespeare.*)

surrealism. In literature, a movement originating in France in the early 1920s that was influenced by the writings of Sigmund Freud and the French **Symbolists.** Surrealist writers reviewed reality as including more than what is visible and rational. Therefore, they rejected the objectivity and rationality of **realism** and, instead, emphasized the primitive and the unconscious, in the form of dreams and fantasies. Their artistic techniques included the use of striking images and **monologues** of **stream of consciousness,** with an emphasis on the illogical content and structure of free association. (See *Bombal, García Márquez, Kafka, Paz, Rosa.*)

symbol. A word or phrase that functions on two levels. On the surface, it literally expresses a concrete image. Below the surface, it also represents an abstract idea or an emotion. See also **imagery.** (See *Kafka, Lu Hsün, Mansfield, Welty.*)

symbolism. In literature, the organized use of **symbols** for the purpose of providing the enrichment of a second level of meaning beyond the literal, surface meaning. (See *Bombal, Castellanos, Hughes, Joyce, Lessing, Solórzano.*)

Symbolist. A literary movement begun by French poets in the 1870s. The Symbolists, influenced by Edgar Allan Poe, rejected the values of **realism.** Substituting subjectivism for objectivity, Symbolist writers used **symbols** to suggest personal emotions and attitudes. They also aimed to convey, through suggestion, a level of reality that exists beneath the perceived reality. They wrote in **free verse** and influenced the Imagists. (See *Eliot, García Lorca, Kawabata.*)

theater of the absurd. A post-World War II (1950s) movement in drama that emphasized the lack of meaning in human life. In the content and staging of their plays, these dramatists combine the content of **existentialism** with the techniques of **expressionism** and **surrealism.** Characters feel isolated, confused, and alienated by the irrationality of their situation. Dialogue is often *absurd*, in that it is ambiguous and open-ended in its meaning. (See *Solórzano.*)

theme. The main idea, expressed or implied, of a work of literature. (See *Akutagawa, Andersen, Dahomey, Casely-Hayford, Castellanos, Hughes, Rilke, Mansfield, Walker.*)

third-person narrator. See **narrative perspective.**

tone. The specific atmosphere or **mood** of a work, determined by the writer's attitude toward the subject and created by literary techniques such as use of **setting** and language. (See *Akhenaton, Dostoyevsky, Li Qingzhao, O'Neill, Rumi, Tagore, Yeats.*)

tragedy. A serious story or **drama** in which the **protagonist** begins happily and ends in misery. The process of coping with adversity and accepting misfortune elevates the stature of the human being who is the tragic hero.

> **classical tragedy:** The tragedies of ancient Greece and Rome, and the later tragedies that were modeled on them. Tragedy results when the **protagonist** or tragic hero casts aside prudent human behavior, creates a state of disorder, and reaps the consequences that then bring a return to order. In dramatic terms, the **crisis** leads to **catastrophe,** and then to the **resolution.** In the process, the audience is drawn into the tragic situation, feels pity and fear, and experiences a **catharsis** as these emotions are released with the resolution of the tragedy. See also **hubris.** (See *O'Neill, Sophocles.*)

> **modern tragedy:** A serious story or play in which the **protagonist** or tragic hero is an ordinary person who is a member of the middle or lower class, rather than an aristocrat. Consistent with his or her social status, the events in the drama are also ordinary. Depending on the dramatist, either the protagonist's personality creates his or her tragedy, or tragedy arises from circumstances beyond the protagonist's control. (See *Camus, Gordimer, Ibsen, Lu Hsün, Narayan, Paton, Solórzano.*)

tragicomedy. A form of drama in which a **reversal** turns a potentially tragic situation into one that ends happily. Such plays usually involve **melodrama,** disguises, and an emphasis on **plot** and **discovery** rather than on **characterization.** See also **comedy, tragedy.** (See *Shakespeare.*)

turning point. See **crisis.**

unreliable narrator. See **narrative perspective.**

vaudeville. In the late nineteenth and early twentieth centuries, a popular type of variety show that included acts performed by singers, dancers, comedians, acrobats, and animals. The term is still used in England and France to describe light-hearted, robust entertainment that is performed in a theater. See also **satire.** (See *Solórzano.*)

verbal irony. See **irony.**

voice. The persona who is speaking through the medium of a literary work, usually a poem. The persona may be that of the poet him- or herself or a personality adopted for the poem. (See *David.*)

ACKNOWLEDGMENTS

The publisher has made every effort to contact copyright holders. Errors and omissions will be corrected upon written notification.

Achebe, Chinua. "Marriage Is a Private Affair" from *Girls at War and Other Stories* by Chinua Achebe, copyright © 1972, 1973 by Chinua Achebe. Used by permission of Doubleday, a division of Random House, Inc., and Harold Ober Associates Incorporated.

Akhenaton. "The Hymn to the Aton" from *Ancient Near Eastern Texts Relating to the Old Testament,* edited by James B. Pritchard, copyright © 1950, 1955, 1969 by Princeton University Press. Reprinted by permission of Princeton University Press.

Akhmatova, Anna. "Voronezh" from *Poems* by Anna Akhmatova, translated by Lyn Coffin. Copyright © 1983 by Lyn Coffin. Used by permission of W.W. Norton & Company, Inc.

Akutagawa, Ryūnosuke. "In a Grove" from *Rashomon and Other Stories* by Ryūnosuke Akutagawa, translated by Takashi Kojima. Copyright © 1952 by Liveright Publishing Company. Used by permission of Liveright Publishing Corporation.

Andersen, Hans Christian. "The Shadow" from *Eighty Fairy Tales* by Hans Christian Andersen, translated by R.P. Keigwin, translation copyright © 1976 by Skandinavisk Bogforlag, Flensteds Forlag. Used by permission of Pantheon Books, a division of Random House, Inc.

Anonymous. "A Woman's Message" from *Poems and Prose from the Old English,* translated by Burton Raffel. Reprinted by permission of Yale University Press.

Bombal, María Luisa. "The Tree" by María Luisa Bombal. Translated by Rosalie Torres Rioseco. Published in *Short Stories of Latin America,* New York, Las Américas Publishing Company, 1963.

Borges, Jorge Luis. "The Story from Rosendo Juarez" from *Collected Fictions* by Jorge Luis Borges, translated by Andrew Hurley, copyright © 1998 by Maria Kodama; translation copyright © 1998 by Penguin Putnam Inc. Used by permission of Viking Penguin, a division of Penguin Putnam Inc.

Camus, Albert. "The Guest" from *Exile and the Kingdom* by Albert Camus, translated by Justin O'Brien, copyright © 1957, 1958 by Alfred A. Knopf, a division of Random House, Inc. Used by permission of Alfred A. Knopf, a division of Random House, Inc.

Castellanos, Rosario. "Chess" by Rosario Castellanos, translated by Maureen Ahern. Reprinted by permission of Fondo de Cultura Economica.

Chaucer, Geoffrey. "The Pardoner's Tale" from *The Portable Chaucer,* edited by Theodore Morrison, copyright 1949, © 1975, renewed © 1977 by Theodore Morrison. Used by permission of Viking Penguin, a division of Penguin Putnam Inc.

Colette. "The Other Wife" from *The Collected Stories of Colette,* edited by Robert Phelps and translated by Matthew Ward. Translation copyright © 1983 by Farrar, Straus & Giroux, Inc. Reprinted by permission of Farrar, Straus & Giroux, LLC.

Cortázar, Julio. "End of the Game" from *End of the Game and Other Stories* by Julio Cortázar, translated by Paul Blackburn, copyright © 1963, 1967 by Random House, Inc. Used by permission of Pantheon Books, a division of Random House, Inc.

Dadié, Bernard. "Dry Your Tears, Africa!" by Bernard Dadié, published by Nouvelles Editions Ivoiriennes.

Dahomey. "Song for the Dead" translated by Frances S. Herskovits. Reprinted in *3000 Years of Black Poetry,* edited by Alan Lomax and Raoul Abdul, © 1970, published by Fawcett Publications, Inc.

Dante. "Because you know you're young in beauty in yet" from *Dante's Comedy,* translated by Patrick S. Diehl, copyright © 1979 by Princeton University Press. Reprinted by permission of Princeton University Press.

David. Psalm 8 taken from *Holy Bible: New International Version*® NIV®. Copyright © 1973, 1978, 1984 by International Bible Society. Used by permission of Zondervan. The "NIV" and "New International Version" trademarks are registered in the United States Patent and Trademark Office by International Bible Society.

de la Cruz, Sor Juana Inés. Poem 15, reprinted by permission of the publisher from *A Sor Juana Anthology,* translated by Alan S. Trueblood, p. 67, Cambridge, Mass: Harvard University Press, copyright © 1988 by the President and Fellows of Harvard College.

Desai, Anita. "Pineapple Cake" from *Games at Twilight,* by Anita Desai. Copyright © Anita Desai 1978. Reproduced by permission of Rogers, Coleridge & White Ltd., 20 Powis Mews, London W11 1JN.

Dostoyevsky, Fyodor. "The Heavenly Christmas Tree" by Fyodor Dostoyevsky, trans. by C. Garnett, from *Great Short Stories from the World's Literature,* edited by Charles Neider.

Eliot, T. S. "The Hollow Men" from *Collected Poems 1909–1962* by T. S. Eliot, copyright 1936 by Harcourt, Inc., copyright © 1964, 1963 by T. S. Eliot, reprinted by permission of the publisher.

García Lorca, Federico. "Lament for Ignacio Sánchez Mejías" by Federico García Lorca, translated by Stephen Spender & J. L. Gili, from *The Selected Poems of Federico García Lorca,* copyright © 1955 by New Directions Publishing Corp. Reprinted by permission of New Directions Publishing Corp.

García Márquez, Gabriel. "A Very Old Man with Enormous Wings" from *Leaf Storm and Other Stories* by Gabriel García Márquez. Translated by Gregory Rabassa. Copyright © 1971 by Gabriel García Márquez. Reprinted by permission of HarperCollins Publishers, Inc.

Gordimer, Nadine. "Good Climate, Friendly Inhabitants," copyright © 1964 by Nadine Gordimer, renewed, from *Selected Stories* by Nadine Gordimer. Used by permission of Viking Penguin, a division of Penguin Putnam Inc.

Grace, Patricia. "A Way of Talking" from *Selected Stories,* by Patricia Grace. Copyright © 1975, 1980, 1987 by Patricia Grace. Reprinted by permission of Pearson Education New Zealand.

HaNagid, Shmuel. "Two Eclipses" from *Selected Poems of Shmuel HaNagid,* translated by Peter Cole, copyright © 1996 by Princeton University Press. Reprinted by permission of Princeton University Press.

Hayashi, Fumiko. "Tokyo" ("Downtown") by Fumiko Hayashi, from *Modern Japanese Literature,* edited by Donald Keene. Copyright © 1956 by Grove Press, Inc. Used by permission of Grove/Atlantic, Inc.

Head, Bessie. "The Lovers" from *Tales of Tenderness and Power* by Bessie Head. Copyright © 1989 by The Estate of Bessie Head. Reprinted by permission of John Johnson Ltd.

Hébert, Anne. "Hands" by Anne Hébert, from *Anne Hébert: Selected Poems,* translated by A. Poulin, Jr. Copyright © 1980, 1987, 1988 by A. Poulin, Jr. Published by BOA Editions, Ltd.

Hemingway, Ernest. "Soldier's Home" reprinted with permission of Scribner, an imprint of Simon & Schuster Adult Publishing Group, from *The Short Stories of Ernest Hemingway.* Copyright 1925 by Charles Scribner's Sons. Copyright renewed 1953 by Ernest Hemingway.

Hikmet, Nazim. "Letter to My Wife" from *Poems of Nazim Hikmet,* translated by Randy Blassing and Mutlu Konuk. Copyright © 1994, 2002 by Randy Blassing and Mutlu Konuk. Reprinted by permission of Persea Books, Inc. (New York).

Hughes, Langston. "Mother to Son" from *The Collected Poems of Langston Hughes* by Langston Hughes, copyright © 1994 by The Estate of Langston Hughes. Used by permission of Alfred A. Knopf, a division of Random House, Inc.

Ibsen, Henrik. *A Doll's House,* by Henrik Ibsen, translated by William Archer. Reprinted by permission of Baker's Plays.

Jiang Fang. "Prince Huo's Daughter" by Jiang Fang. Trans. by Yang Xiangi and Gladys Yang, in *Tang Dynasty Stories,* © 1986.

Joyce, James. "Araby" from *Dubliners* by James Joyce, copyright 1916 by B. W. Heubsch. Definitive text copyright © 1967 by the Estate of James Joyce. Used by permission of Viking Penguin, a division of Penguin Putnam Inc.

Kafka, Franz. "A Country Doctor," translated by Willa and Edwin Muir, from *Franz Kafka: The Complete Stories* by Franz Kafka, edited by Nahum Glatzer, copyright 1946, 1947, 1948, 1949, 1954, 1958, 1971 by Schocken Books. Used by permission of Schocken Books, a division of Random House, Inc.

Kawabata, Yasunari. "The Grasshopper and the Bell Cricket," from *Palm-of-the-Hand Stories* by Yasunari Kawabata, translated by Lane Dunlop and J. Martin Holman. Translation copyright © 1988 by Lane Dunlop and J. Martin Holman. Reprinted by permission of North Point Press, a division of Farrar, Straus & Giroux, LLC.

Lagerlöf, Selma. "The Outlaws" from *Invisible Links* by Selma Lagerlöf. Translated by Pauline Bancroft Flach and published by Doubleday.

Lessing, Doris. "A Sunrise on the Veld" reprinted with permission of Simon & Schuster Adult Publishing Group from *African Stories* by Doris Lessing. Copyright © 1951, 1953, 1954, 1957, 1958, 1962, 1963, 1964, 1965, 1972 by Doris Lessing.

Li Po. "Fighting South of the Ramparts," by Li Po, translated by Arthur Whaley, from *Anthology of Chinese Literature,* edited by Cyril Birch. Copyright © 1965 by Grove Press, Inc. Used by permission of Grove/Atlantic, Inc.

Li Qingzhao. "Wuling chun" by Li Qingzhao, from *Women Writers of Traditional China: An Anthology of Poetry and Criticism,* edited by King-i Sun Chang and Huan Saussy. Copyright © 1999 by the Board of Trustees of the Leland Stanford Junior University. Reprinted with the permission of Stanford University Press, <www.sup.org>.

Lu Hsün. "The New Year's Sacrifice" from *Selected Stories of Lu Hsün,* reprinted by permission of Foreign Languages Press.

Mahfouz, Naguib. "The Conjurer Made Off with the Dish" from *The Time and The Place and Other Stories* by Naguib Mahfouz, translation © 1978 by Denys Johnson-Davies. Reprinted by permission of Denys Johnson-Davies.

Mansfield, Katherine. "The Fly" from *The Short Stories of Katherine Mansfield* by Katherine Mansfield, copyright 1923 by Alfred A. Knopf, a division of Random House, Inc., and renewed 1951 by John Middleton Murray. Used by permission of Alfred A. Knopf, a division of Random House, Inc.

Mistral, Gabriela. "Serene Words" by Gabriela Mistral, from *Selected Poems of Gabriela Mistral*, translation copyright © 1971 by Doris Dana. Reprinted by permission of Writers House Inc.

Munro, Alice. "Day of the Butterfly" from *Dance of the Happy Shades* by Alice Munro. Copyright © 1986 by Alice Munro. Reprinted by permission of William Morris Agency, Inc. on behalf of the Author.

Narayan, R. K. "Forty-Five a Month" from *Malgudi Days* by R. K. Narayan, copyright © 1972, 1975, 1978, 1980, 1981, 1982 by R. K. Narayan. Used by permission of Viking Penguin, a division of Penguin Putnam Inc.

Neruda, Pablo. "The Word" translated by Alastair Reid, from *Selected Poems* by Pablo Neruda, edited by Nathaniel Tarn and published by Jonathan Cape. Used by permission of The Random House Group Limited.

Nguyen Binh Khiem. "The Rich Eat Three Full Meals" by Nguyen Binh Khiem, from *A Thousand Years of Vietnamese Poetry*, translated by Nguyen Ngoc Bich with Burton Raffel and W. S. Merwin, copyright © 1962, 1967, 1968, 1969, 1970, 1971, 1972, 1974 by Asia Society Inc. Reprinted by permission of Asia Society Inc.

Ogot, Grace. "The Rain Came" by Grace Ogot, from *Land Without Thunder*, reprinted by permission of East African Educational Publishers Ltd.

Paton, Alan. "A Drink in the Passage," reprinted with the permission of Scribner, an imprint of Simon & Schuster Adult Publishing Group, from *Tales from a Troubled Land* by Alan Paton. Copyright © 1961 by Alan Paton; copyright renewed © 1989 by Anne Paton.

Paz, Octavio. "Two Bodies" by Octavio Paz, translated by Muriel Rukeyser, from *Selected Poems*, copyright © 1973 by Octavio Paz and Muriel Rukeyser. Reprinted by permission of New Directions Publishing Corp.

Pirandello, Luigi. "War" by Luigi Pirandello, reprinted by permission of the Pirandello Estate and Toby Cole, Agent.

Rilke, Rainer Maria. "At Sundown" from *Rainer Maria Rilke: Translations from His Poetry*, by Albert Ernest Fleming, copyright © 1983.

Rumi. "Say Who I Am" by Rumi, from *The Hand of Poetry: Five Mystic Poets of Persia*, translations copyright © 1993 by Coleman Barks. Reprinted by permission of Omega Publications.

Sappho. "Fragment # 41: To an Army Wife, in Sardis" by Sappho, from *Sappho: A New Translation*, copyright © 1958 The Regents of the University of California; © renewed 1986 by Mary Barnard.

Sartre, Jean-Paul. "The Wall" by Jean-Paul Sartre and Maria Jolas, copyright 1945 by Random House, Inc. and renewed 1973, from *Bedside Book of Famous French Stories* by Belle Becker and Robert N. Linscott. Used by permission of Random House, Inc.

Senghor, Léopold Sédar. "Prayer to Masks" by Léopold Sédar Senghor, from *Selected Poems of Léopold Sédar Senghor*, translated by John Reed and Clive Wake.

Shen Congwen. "Life" from *Imperfect Paradise* by Shen Congwen, translation copyright © 1995 by University of Hawaii Press. Reprinted by permission.

Solórzano, Carlos. "Crossroads" by Carlos Solórzano is from *Selected Latin American One-Act Plays*, Frencesca Colecchia and Julio Matas, ed. and trans. Published in 1973 by the University of Pittsburgh Press. Reprinted by permission of the publisher.

Sophocles. *Antigone* by Sophocles, from *Three Theban Plays* by Sophocles, translated by Robert Fagles, copyright © 1982 by Robert Fagles. Used by permission of Viking Penguin, a division of Penguin Putnam Inc.

Soyinka, Wole. "The Trials of Brother Jero" by Wole Soyinka, copyright © 1964, 1992 by Wole Soyinka. Reprinted by permission of Melanie Jackson Agency, L.L.C.

Tagore, Rabindranath. *The Post Office* from *Rabindranath Tagore: An Anthology*, edited by Krishna Dutta and Andrew Robinson. Copyright © 1977 by Krishna Dutta and Andrew Robinson. Reprinted by permission of St. Martin's Press, LLC.

Ting Ling. "A Certain Night" by Ting Ling, translated by W. J. F. Jenner. Reprinted from *Miss Sophie's Diary and Other Stories*, published by Chinese Literature Press, 1985.

Walker, Alice. "Roselily" from *In Love & Trouble: Stories of Black Women*, copyright © 1972 and renewed 2000 by Alice Walker, reprinted by permission of Harcourt, Inc.

Welty, Eudora. "A Worn Path" from *A Curtain of Green and Other Stories*, copyright 1941 and renewed 1969 by Eudora Welty, reprinted by permission of Harcourt, Inc.

Zuñi. "Special Request for the Children of Mother Corn" from *The Sacred Path*, by John Bierhorst. Used by permission of HarperCollins Publishers.

INDEX
OF AUTHORS AND TITLES